The Encyclopaedia of

FLAT RACING

By the same Author

The Jockey Club
History of the Derby Stakes
Twenty Great Horses
Great Racehorses of the World
(in collaboration with Peter Willett)
The History of Steeplechasing (in collaboration with Peter Willett, Michael Seth and John Lawrence)

Other Encyclopaedias published by Robert Hale and Company

BY A. N. GAULTON

Rugby League Football

BY MAURICE GOLESWORTHY

Cricket
Boxing
Association Football

BY J. R. JONES

Rugby Football
(Second Edition edited by Maurice Golesworthy)

BY ANTHONY PRITCHARD AND KEITH DAVEY

Motor Racing

BY ANNE SUNNUCKS

Chess

BY MELVYN WATMAN

Athletics

The Encyclopaedia of

FLAT RACING

compiled by
ROGER MORTIMER

ROBERT HALE · LONDON

First published in Great Britain 1971

ISBN 0 7091 1531 8

Robert Hale & Company
63 Old Brompton Road
London, S.W.7.

PRINTED IN GREAT BRITAIN BY
BRISTOL TYPESETTING CO. LTD.
BARTON MANOR - ST. PHILIPS
BRISTOL

Preface

The racing world is for ever on the move, and inevitably, due to the interval between the completion of writing and the date of publication, records of certain individuals, horses and races are incomplete as from mid-June 1970. This is regrettable but unavoidable. The selection of entries was mine alone and if certain things have been omitted that ought to have been included, the fault is solely mine. I wish to express my gratitude to Mr. Geoffrey Hamlyn of the *Sporting Life*, who has forgotten more about betting than I shall ever know, for his contribution on "Bookmakers"; and to Miss Celia Knight, who gallantly undertook the typing and luckily spotted some of my grosser errors.

R.M.

Illustrations

PICTURE CREDITS

Central Press Photos Ltd.: 1, 5, 6, 14, 16, 19, 20, 31, 33; Radio Times Hulton Picture Library: 2, 3, 7, 8, 9, 11, 12, 13, 18, 23, 25, 26, 29, 30; Topix: 4, 10, 15, 17, 21, 22; Fox Photos: 24, *The British Racehorse*: 27, 28, 32.

A

ABERGAVENNY, Marquess of

Guards from 1936 to 1946. In his youth he rode under National Hunt rules. He has many business interests and is member both of the National Hunt Committee and of the Jockey Club. He is Vice-Chairman of the Turf Board, Trustee of the Ascot Authority, and a director of Cheltenham and Fontwell. His trainer is Peter Cazalet and his colours are scarlet, white cross belts.

ABERMAID

Mr R. More O'Ferrall's grey filly Abermaid, by Abernant, trained by Harry Wragg, won the One Thousand Guineas in 1962.

ABERNANT

One of the fastest horses of this century, Abernant was bred in 1946 by his owner, the Hon Lady Macdonald-Buchanan and is a grey by Owen Tudor out of Rustom Mahal, by Rustom Pasha. His grandam is the famous Mumtaz Mahal and it is no doubt from her that he inherited much of his speed. Trained by Noel Murless, he was beaten first time out at Lingfield, but then won successively the Chesham Stakes, National Breeders Produce Stakes, Champagne Stakes and Middle Park Stakes.

As a three-year-old he was beaten by inches by Nimbus in the Two Thousand Guineas but won the Somerset Stakes at Bath, the King's Stand Stakes, the July Cup, the King George Stakes and the Nunthorpe Stakes. In his final season he failed by half a length to give Tangle 23lb in the King's Stand Stakes, but won the Lubbock Stakes at Sandown, the July Cup, the King George Stakes and the Nunthorpe Stakes. All told he won fourteen of his sixteen races and over £26,000. Until his retirement in 1970 he stood at the Egerton Stud, Newmarket, and his offspring include Abermaid (One Thousand Guineas and £25,446), Aberdeen (£12,712), Abelia (£11,381), Gwen (£10,866), Favorita (£10,474) and Welsh Rake (£10,361).

ABOVE SUSPICION

Above Suspicion was bred in 1956 by the Queen, for whom he won the St James's Palace Stakes and the Gordon Stakes. A bay by Court Martial out of the Cesarewitch winner Above Board, he was syndicated for the stud and stands at the Cloghran Stud, Co Dublin. He is sire of that admirable handicapper Super Sam, winner of over £20,000 in stakes.

ABOYEUR

Mr A. P. Cunliffe's Aboyeur, ridden by E. Piper and trained by T. Lewis at Druids Lodge, near Salisbury, was awarded the 1913 Derby on the disqualification of the favourite, Craganour, who was first past the post but disqualified by the Stewards. Aboyeur, who started at 100-1, never won again. He was sold for £13,000 to the Imperial Racing Club in Russia and disappeared during the Revolution.

ABSURDITY

Mr J. B. Joel's Absurdity was one of the few mares to have bred classic winners in consecutive years. In her case the winners were Jest (One Thousand Guineas) and Black Jester (St Leger). Other mares to have accomplished this rare feat were Galicia, dam of Bayardo (St Leger) and Lemberg (Derby); and Devotion, dam of Thebais (One Thousand Guineas and Oaks) and St Marguerite (One Thousand Guineas).

ACCEPTOR

When the weights for a handicap are published in the *Racing Calendar*, owners, or their officially authorised agents, who reckon that their horses have been given too much weight may withdraw them before a specified date. Horses left in the race are known as 'acceptors' because the handicapper's assessment of their chances has been accepted.

ACCUMULATOR

This is a bet in which a number of horses are backed collectively. They all have to win, or to be placed if the bet is an each way accumulator. If the first horse wins, all the money won, plus the stake, goes on the next horse and so on.

ACROPOLIS

Bred by Lady Halifax in 1952, Acropolis is a chestnut by Donatello II out of Aurora, by Hyperion, and is thus a full brother to Alycidon. He won twice as a two-year-old and at three he won the Thirsk Classic Trial, Newmarket Stakes, Commonwealth Stakes and the Voltigeur Stakes. He was third to Phil Drake and Panaslipper in the Derby after a slightly interrupted preparation, while in the King George VI and Queen Elizabeth Stakes he was beaten a head by Vimy. As a four-year-old he won the John Porter Stakes. Syndicated for the stud, he stands at the Egerton Stud, Newmarket, and is the sire of Espresso (£21,000 in England and 200,000 D.M. in Germany), Mariner (£10,135) and Acrophel (£8,249).

ADAM'S APPLE

Adam's Apple, by Pommern, won the 1927 Two Thousand Guineas for Mr C. W. S. Whitburn at 20-1. He was exported to the Argentine but proved a moderate sire.

ADDED MONEY

'Added money' is money contributed towards the stakes by the race-fund or from other sources, as distinct from money contributed by the owners of the horses engaged in the race.

ADDED TO THE LIST

To say that a horse has been 'added to the list' is an old-fashioned way of saying he has been gelded.

ADMINISTRATION OF RACING

See
JOCKEY CLUB,
TURF BOARD,
LEVY BOARD

ADMIRATION

Foaled in 1892, Admiration, by Saraband, was a moderate performer on the racecourse, perhaps not entirely surprisingly in view of the fact that her dam was sold on one occasion for 7 gn and on another for 15. Admiration herself won a couple of minor events on the flat in Ireland and was placed in a military steeplechase at Punchestown. However, mated with Gallinule, who broke blood-vessels and was unsound in his wind, she produced the famous Pretty Polly, one of the greatest fillies of all time. Moreover she bred eight other winners as well.

ADVERTISED VALUE

The 'advertised value' of a plate is the amount advertised to be given to the winner, and which he would receive (before deducting his entrance money) in the event of a walk-over or if no other horse was placed.

AGA KHAN, H.H. The (1877-1957)

The Aga Khan was the outstanding figure in European racing from 1922, the first year he raced in England, until his death.

He declined to take up racing until he reckoned he had both the time and the money to operate on a big scale, and although he had been inspired with a love of the Turf by Lord Wavertree as far back as 1904, it was not until 1921 that he felt that the time was ripe. He then asked George Lambton to buy him some yearlings with the object of forming a stud. Lambton agreed to do so and as his own stable was full, recommended that the yearlings should be sent to R. C. Dawson.

Lambton did his work well. Of the colts he bought, Diophon and Salmon Trout both won classics, while the fillies Mumtaz Mahal, Cos and Teresina were not only successful on the racecourse, but proved admirable foundation mares for the stud. Eventually the Aga Khan established a chain of studs in Ireland and France that enabled him to breed bloodstock on a scale unapproached by any other British owner-breeder and by only M. M. Boussac in France. In 1931 he fell out with Dawson and sent his horses to be trained by Frank Butters. When Butters retired in 1949, he was succeeded by Marcus Marsh and Noel Murless. In 1954, owing to the lower costs and higher level of prize money, the Aga Khan transferred his racing interests to France. From then on most of his horses were trained by Alec Head at Chantilly.

The Aga Khan enjoyed tremendous success on the English Turf and shares with Lord Egremont the distinction of having won the Derby five times. His winners were Blenheim (1930), trained by Dawson ; Bahram (1935) and Mahmoud (1936), trained by Butters ; My Love (1948) trained by R. Carver in France ; and Tulyar (1952), trained by Marsh, Blenheim he bought as a yearling ; Bahram, Mahmoud and Tulyar he bred himself ; My Love he owned in partnership with the horse's breeder, M. L. Volterra.

He won the Two Thousand Guineas with Diophon and Bahram ; the One Thousand Guineas with Rose Royale II ; the Oaks with Udaipur and Masaka ; and the St Leger with Salmon Trout, Firdaussi, Bahram, Turkhan, Tehran and Tulyar. When Firdaussi won the St Leger, the Aga Khan owned four of the first five horses to finish. He won the Gold Cup with Felicitation and Umiddad and the King George VI and Queen Elizabeth Stakes with Tulyar. He also won twelve Irish Classics.

He was acutely conscious of the commercial aspect of racing and never permitted sentiment to interfere with business. He was the shrewdest of dealers and dealing may even have been the side of his racing activities that appealed to him most. He sold all his Derby winners, and the export of Blenheim, Bahram and Mahmoud hit the British Bloodstock industry hard. He also sold Nasrullah, who became a leading sire in America. By and large the Aga Khan's princely patronage conferred considerable benefits on English racing, but those benefits would have been even greater, and he himself would have been regarded with more respect, had he been a little less commercially-minded.

AGE

No matter when a thoroughbred foal is born, its subsequent birthdays are always on 1st January. Even if a foal were born in December it would automatically become a yearling on the 1st of the following month.

AGED

A horse described as 'aged' is one more than six years old.

AGGRESSOR

Bred in 1955 by the Someries Stud, Aggressor is a bay horse by Combat out of Phaetonia, by Nearco. Trained by Gosden for Sir Harold Wernher, he won eleven races and over £36,000, his successes including the Two Thousand Guineas Trial at Kempton, the Doonside Stakes at Ayr, the Coronation Stakes at Sandown, the Chesterfield Cup, the John Porter Stakes, the Hard wicke Stakes, and the King George VI and Queen Elizabeth Stakes in which he defeated Petite-Etoile. He was syndicated for the stud and stands at the Someries Stud.

AIRBORNE

Mr J. E. Ferguson's Airborne, a grey colt by Precipitation, won the Derby and the St Leger in 1946. It was the first Derby run at Epsom since 1939. As a sire Airborne proved very disappointing.

AKEHURST, R. P. J.

A former National Hunt jockey, he now trains at Epsom. He won the 1970 Greenham Stakes with Gold Rod.

ALCIDE

Owned and bred by Sir Humphrey de Trafford and trained by Capt (later Sir) Cecil Boyd-Rochfort, Alcide is a medium-sized bay by Alycidon out of Chenille, by King Salmon. Chenille also bred Lightning, dam of the 1959 Derby winner Parthia.

Powerful, high-mettled and with a very strong will of his own, Alcide ran twice as a two-year-old in 1957, on the second occasion winning the 7f Horris Hill Stakes at Newbury. It was quite an impressive performance and a number of people who saw him that day marked him down as a likely winner of the Derby.

In his first race in 1958 he was undeservedly beaten by the Queen's Snow Cat, trained by Noel Murless, in what looked a deplorably rough race for the Royal Stakes at Sandown. He then won the Chester Vase, but it was hardly an inspiring performance as Harry Carr was hard at work on him for most of the way. However he showed his true merit in the Lingfield Derby Trial which he won in storming style by a dozen lengths. Money then poured on him for the Derby and it must have been a relief to the bookmakers when he met with an injury (the true cause of which remains a mystery to this day) a week before Epsom, and was consequently unable to run. He was in all probability a far better horse than Hard Ridden who won.

Alcide had fully recovered by August and won the Great Voltigeur Stakes at York by a dozen lengths, following this up by winning the St Leger in equally devastating style by 8 lengths.

As a four-year-old he was narrowly beaten in the Jockey Club Cup and then won the Victor Wild Stakes at Kempton and the Winston Churchill Stakes at Hurst Park. At that point ill-fortune dogged him once more and he had a set-back in training, so that he was not really at his best for the Gold Cup; nor was Harry Carr, who had recently undergone a kidney operation. Under the circumstances Alcide ran a great race but he went under by inches to Wallaby II. However he finished his racing career a month later in a blaze of glory by winning the King George VI and Queen Elizabeth Stakes. It was a particularly fine effort to win this $\frac{1}{2}$m race after being trained for the $2\frac{1}{2}$m Gold Cup. All told he won eight races worth £56,038.

Alcide has done reasonably well as a sire but he has not got a classic winner yet.

ALEXANDRA PARK

Alexandra Park, commonly known as 'Ally Pally' is the only racecourse within the boundaries of London, being six miles from Charing Cross. Miraculously it has survived not only the insatiable appetite of the builder, but also determined assaults on its existence by the late Frederick Temple, Archbishop of Canterbury, when he was holding sway as Bishop of London. The amenities have hardly kept pace with the general rise in the standard of living, and the track itself is somewhat cramped; but 'Ally Pally' has a unique atmosphere of its own and is regarded with affection by many metropolitan racegoers.

Races of 1m 160yd and of 1m 5f start in front of the stands. The horses race down the straight, complete one or two circuits of the round track and then come back up the straight, a manoeuvre known as "round the frying pan and then up the handle". The only other starting gate is for 5f races and is out of sight from the stands. As there is a right-hand bend on the 5f track, high numbers enjoy a considerable advantage.

Clerk of the Course: Mr H. C. Clifton MC, 214-218 Shepherds Bush Road, London W.6. Tel: 603-7211.

Best Times:

Distance	*Horse-Age-Weight*	*Date*	*Time*
5f	Cash'n Carry 3-9-3	18-7-61	58.6
5f	Favoured 2-8-9	9-8-66	58.6
8f 160yd	Scots Fusilier 8-7-3	8-8-67	1min 47
13f	John Cameron 7-7-9	13-6-67	2min 44

Note: All 5f times are taken from the flag.

ALICE HAWTHORN

Foaled in 1838, Alice Hawthorn, by Muley Moloch, is one of the most celebrated of English mares. Possessing a wonderful constitution, she raced for seven seasons, running 71 times and winning 52 races including the Goodwood and Doncaster Cups. At the stud her winners included Thormanby, winner of the Derby and Ascot Gold Cup.

ALLENDALE, Lord (b 1922)

Lord Allendale, who served in the RAF during the war, is a leading personality in northern racing and acts as steward at York, Thirsk, Ripon, Newcastle and Carlisle. He has also served as Steward and Senior Steward of the Jockey Club. His horses are trained by Bill Elsey and his best winner so far is Tenterhooks, winner of the Queen's Vase and Goodwood Cup.

Colours: pink, purple sleeves and cap.

ALLOWANCES

All lads qualified to ride as apprentices are permitted during their apprenticeship to claim the following allowances:

7lb until they have won 10 races;
5lb until they have won 50 races;
3lb until they have won 75 races.

For further details with regard to allowances, see the Rules of Racing, Part XVI, Section 124.

ALOE FAMILY

Aloe was foaled in 1926 and was by that great stayer Son-in-Law. She never won a race herself but proved extremely influential at the stud. From her daughter Feola are descended many of the best performers bred at the Royal Stud at Sandringham such as Hypericum, Angelola, Kingstone, Above Board, Doutelle, and Above Suspicion. Another descendant is the important American winner, Round Table. From another daughter of Aloe, Sweet Aloe, are descended the St Leger winner Alcide and the Derby winner Parthia.

ALSO RAN

Any horse in a race that is not placed, first, second or third by the judge.

ALYCIDON

Alycidon was the last of the many great horses to carry the colours of the seventeenth Earl of Derby, who died in 1948. Foaled in 1945, Alycidon was a long, low chestnut by Donatello II out of Aurora, by Hyperion. Trained at Newmarket by Walter Earl, he was backward as a two-year-old and was unplaced on the two occasions he ran in the autumn. As a three-year-old he made immense improvement; he might even have done better than he did but unfortunately Walter Earl was in failing health—he died in 1950—and Doug Smith had been ill and was not available to ride in the early part of the season. However, after a disastrous first appearance at Hurst Park when he failed to start—he always wore blinkers afterwards—he won the 1m Classic Trial Stakes at Thirsk, thereby showing that he was not devoid of speed; the Royal Standard Stakes at Manchester; the Princess of Wales's Stakes at Newmarket; the St George Stakes at Liverpool; the Jockey Club Stakes at Newmarket; and the 2m King George VI Stakes at Ascot. He was second to Black Tarquin in the St Leger and third in both the Chester Vase and the King Edward VII Stakes.

As a four-year-old he stamped himself as a stayer of the highest class, winning the Ormonde Stakes at Chester; the Corporation Stakes at Doncaster; the Ascot Gold Cup; the Goodwood Cup; and the Doncaster Cup. In the Gold Cup he fairly turned the tables on Black Tarquin; in fact he was never beaten again after the St Leger. In all he won eleven races worth £37,201.

When his racing career was over, Alycidon was syndicated for £140,000. Like his sire Donatello II and other stallions of the Blandford line, he was inclined to be a shy breeder. By 1962 his fertility had dropped below 30 per cent and the following year he was withdrawn from stud duties and painlessly destroyed in the autumn. Fortunately his stock showed no lack of quality; he was champion sire in 1955, second in 1958 and 1959, third in 1957 and fourth in 1964. The best of his colts was Alcide, winner of the St Leger and the King George VI and Queen Elizabeth Stakes; of his fillies the pick were Meld, unbeaten as a three-year-old and winner of the One Thousand Guineas, the Oaks and the St Leger; and Homeward Bound, winner of the Oaks.

ALY KHAN, Prince (1911-1960)

In 1959 the racing career of Prince Aly Khan was on the crest of the wave. That year he was the first owner in the history of the British Turf to win over £100,000 in stakes, and as all his winners were bred by himself, in conjunction with his late father, the Aga Khan, he reached a six-figure total as a breeder, too. In France as well he set up a new record for an owner, winning 212,314,631 francs. Horses carrying his colours in that memorable year won the Two Thousand Guineas, the One Thousand Guineas, the Oaks, the Champion Stakes and the Middle Park Stakes in England, while in France they won the Prix de l'Arc de Triomphe and the French One Thousand Guineas. In addition a filly of the Prince's won the Irish One Thousand Guineas.

On 8th May 1960 two horses of Prince Aly Khan's were shortheaded in successive races at Longchamp. Surveying the photographs of the two finishes displayed outside the weighing room, he observed with a rueful smile that his luck was beginning to run out. Four days later he was killed in a car crash. As far as his horses were concerned, the break in the run of good fortune was brief; later that year Charlottesville won the French Derby and the Grand Prix, Sheshoon the Ascot Gold Cup and the Grand Prix de St Cloud, Petite Etoile the Coronation Cup, and Venture VII the St James's Palace Stakes and the Sussex Stakes.

Possessed of immense charm and unquenchable zest for enjoyment of the good things that life had to offer, Prince Aly Khan was sometimes harshly criticised as regards certain aspects of his life by people who had never met him, but those who actually knew him were almost invariably captivated by his perfect manners, his gaiety and his sense of fun. He was extremely popular with the racing public too, because of his lack of pomposity and the fact that his horses were invariably doing their best to win.

Prince Aly Khan was the second son—the first died in infancy—of the Aga Khan and his second wife, Teresa Maglioni. Educated privately, he took a keen interest in racing and bloodstock breeding from an early age and in addition became an extremely competent amateur rider on the flat. After World War II, in which he served in the Wiltshire Yeomanry and rose to the rank of Lieut-Colonel, he bought a half-share in his father's racing interests and the partnership proved extremely successful. On his father's death he bought out the inherited interests of the Begum Aga Khan and of his step-brother Sadruddin, assuming sole responsibility for an immense racing empire. When he died, he owned six studs in Ireland, four in France and roughly a hundred brood mares. He was also part owner of a dozen mares in America. Most of his horses were trained by Alec Head at Chantilly but he usually had a few with Noel Murless at Newmarket. During the time of his partnership with his father he bought the entire bloodstock interests of Mr Wilfred Harvey and most of the thoroughbreds owned by the American, Mr L. L. Lawrence. Both these package deals paid handsome dividends. Like his father, the Prince was a shrewd dealer and moreover a sound judge of a horse and a pedigree.

He was married twice, the second time to Rita Hayworth the film star.

After his father's death his main winners were as follows:

1957 Ommeyad (Irish St Leger); Rose Royale II (Champion Stakes)

1958 Yla (French One Thousand Guineas); Butiaba (Irish One Thousand Guineas); Amante (Irish Oaks); Taboun (Prix Robert Papin); Saint Crespin III (Imperial Produce Stakes)

1959 Chief III (Prix Ganay); Taboun (Two Thousand Guineas); Petite Etoile (One Thousand Guineas, the Oaks, and Champion Stakes); Saint Crespin III (Eclipse Stakes and Prix de l'Arc de Triomphe); Florentina (Irish One Thousand Guineas); Venture VII (Imperial Produce Stakes and Middle Park Stakes).

AMATEUR RIDER

A person who has never ridden for hire or who has never held a licence to train under any recognised Rules in any country and who is not otherwise disqualified under the Rules of Racing, may ride without a jockey's licence in races the conditions of which permit him to ride:

(*a*) *As the holder of a permit from the Stewards of the Jockey Club, that permit being applied for annually.*

(*b*) *As an Officer on full pay serving in the Regular Forces.*

Persons thus qualified must ride without remuneration.

AMATO

Foaled in 1835, Amato was the first Epsom-trained winner of the Derby; the next one was April the Fifth in 1932. Amato was bred and owned by Sir Gilbert Heathcote who lived at The Durdans, adjoining Epsom racecourse, and was trained by Ralph Sherwood. He had never run before the Derby and never ran again afterwards.

AMBIGUITY

Bred by the Astor Studs in 1950, Ambiguity, by Big Game, won the Oaks and Jockey Club Cup. She proved a disappointing brood mare.

AMERICAN INVASION

The so-called 'American Invasion' at the turn of the century was caused by legislation hostile to racing in the United States. Horses, trainers, jockeys, gamblers and a fair sprinkling of notorious racecourse crooks arrived in England from the United States. Some of the trainers were men of complete integrity and high professional skill, but others were masters at doping and introduced the practice on a scale never before experienced in Britain. In certain respects American training methods were well in advance of English ones, not least with regard to stable hygiene and the plating of horses.

American jockeys certainly brought about a revolution in English jockeyship. Up till then English jockeys had used the traditional English style with long leathers and great length of rein, there being little difference between a racing seat and the seat a man might employ out hunting or on his hack. Races for the most part were run far more slowly than they are today and many events were a mere dawdle ending up with a two furlong sprint. Some of the jockeys, though, were very hard on their horses, wearing sharp spurs and carrying long whips that could really hurt.

Tod Sloan arrived from America in 1897 and introduced the American style. Crouching low with short stirrups and short reins, he had no compunction in setting off in front and winning his races from pillar to post. At first he was ridiculed and disparaged, but his remarkable run of successes soon proved that even if his style was not aesthetically satisfying, it was a great deal more effective than the old one. Other American jockeys such as J. H. Martin and the Reiff brothers were very successful too, and before long the American seat and tactics, with slight modifications, were generally adopted by English riders.

As for the influx of American horses, this caused the regulation known as 'The Jersey Act' which caused deep resentment in American racing circles. (See Jersey Act).

AMERICUS GIRL FAMILY

This family's outstanding characteristic is speed and it has produced brilliant performers such as Mumtaz Mahal, Tudor Minstrel, Abernant, Royal Charger, Fair Trial and Mirza II. It has also produced some top-class middle-distance horses such as Mahmoud, Migoli, Nasrullah and Commotion.

AMISS

If a mare or filly in a race is said to be 'amiss', it means that she is 'in season'. This condition arises about every three weeks in spring and summer and lasts for roughly three days. The performance of the animal in question can be adversely affected.

AMOUR DRAKE

Foaled in 1946, M. L. Volterra's Amour Drake, by Admiral Drake, won the French Two Thousand Guineas and in the first photo-finish for the Derby was narrowly and rather unluckily beaten by Nimbus. The following year he won the Coronation Cup. He went to the stud in Ireland but was not an unqualified success and was subsequently exported to Peru.

ANGUS, Nigel (b 1944)

Educated at Eton, Nigel Angus was two years assistant to Harry Whiteman at Ayr in 1969. Patrons of the stable include Mr C. Carlow, Mr R. W. Cutler, Hon W. Fraser, Mr L. Grant, Sir T. Moore, Mrs M. MacDonald, Col W. Stirling, Mr A. P. Innes and Mrs O. Fletcher.

ANIMAL HEALTH TRUST

The Animal Health Trust was founded in 1942 by Dr W. R. Wooldridge and is a charitable organisation supported by voluntary contributions. Its function is to carry out research into the causes, prevention and treatment of disease in all types of domesticated animals. There are four separate and independent research stations. The Equine Research Station is at Balaton Lodge, Newmarket, and has the co-operation of a committee designated the Bloodstock Industry Committee and presided over by Lord Willoughby de Broke.

Address: 14 Ashley Place, London, S.W.1.
Tel: 01-834 3207.
President: The Duke of Norfolk.
Chairman of Executive Committee: Viscount Leverhulme.
Chairman of Council and Hon Scientific Adviser: Dr R. E. Glover.
Chief Executive Officer: Brigadier J. Clabby.

ANMER

Anmer, owned by King George V,

was brought down in the 1913 Derby by a militant suffragette, Miss Emily Davison, who sustained fatal injuries in so doing. The horse and his jockey, Herbert Jones, escaped serious injury.

ANNE, QUEEN

Queen Anne, second daughter of James II, was largely responsible for starting racing at Ascot. Traditionally the Royal Ascot meeting opens with the Queen Anne Stakes.

ANTHONY, Ivor (1884-1960)

Ivor Anthony is chiefly remembered as a successful rider and trainer under National Hunt rules but he earned his place in flat-racing history as trainer of the famous and popular stayer Brown Jack, who won the Queen Alexandra Stakes at Ascot six years running.

ANY TO COME

A form of bet in which a succession of horses are backed with the stipulation that if the first selection wins, part of the winnings go on the next runner, and so on.

APOLOGY

Apology, by Adventurer, was owned and bred by a parson, Rev Launde, for whom she won the One Thousand Guineas, the Oaks and the St Leger in 1874, and subsequently the Ascot Gold Cup.

APPRENTICE

An apprentice jockey must be over 15 years of age but under 23. His master is a licensed trainer who must apply annually to Weatherbys for the apprentice's licence. An apprentice must bind himself for a period of not less than three years to a trainer and the agreement must be made of his free will and with the consent of his parents or guardians.

APPROVAL

Owned and bred by Sir Humphrey de Trafford and trained by Henry

Cecil, Approval is a handsome chestnut colt by Alcide out of Success by Arctic Prince. He showed high promise when beaten first time out at Ascot and on his next appearance won the £19,000 Observer Gold Cup at Doncaster. In 1970 he won the Dante Stakes at York but failed completely in the Derby.

APRIL THE FIFTH

April the Fifth was foaled on 5th April 1929, which happened to be the birthday of his breeder Mr Sidney McGregor. Actually Mr McGregor owned him in partnership with Mr G. S. L. Whitelaw and when the colt came up for sale at Newmarket 'to dissolve a partnership', Mr McGregor bid 200 gn and retained April the Fifth for himself. He then formed a new partnership, this time with the actor-trainer Mr Tom Walls, Walls training the horse in lieu of payment.

By Craig-an-Eran out of the unfashionably bred mare Sold Again, April the Fifth failed to win as a two-year-old but the following season, ridden by Fred Lane, he won the Lingfield Derby Trial and then the Derby. His preparation for the St Leger was twice interrupted by mishaps and he finished unplaced in that race. He never ran again afterwards. He was a failure as a sire and died in 1954.

AQUINO II

Foaled in France, Aquino II, by Tornado, won the Prix Daru in the land of his birth and the Gold Cup and Doncaster Cup in 1952 when trained in England. A very bad-tempered individual, he went to the stud in Poland.

ARBAR

Foaled in 1944 M. M. Boussac's Arbar, by Djebel, brought off the rare double of the Ascot Gold Cup and its French equivalent, the Prix du Cadran. He was beaten by inches by Sayajirao in the St Leger.

ARCHER, Fred (1857-1886)

Fred Archer was born in Cheltenham, the son of a steeplechase jockey, and became the greatest jockey of the nineteenth century, possibly the greatest of all time. In 1868 he was apprenticed to Matt Dawson at Newmarket and was closely indentified with that stable for the rest of his life. He rode his first winner in 1870 and won the Cesarewitch in 1872 but the turning point of his career came in 1874 when Lord Falmouth selected him to succeed Tom French on French's death. The first season he rode for Lord Falmouth he won the Two Thousand Guineas, the One Thousand Guineas and the Oaks. From then on his career was one of unbroken success. He won the Derby five times, the St Leger six times, the Oaks four times, the Two Thousand Guineas four times and the One Thousand Guineas twice. He rode in 8,084 races and won 2,471 of them. Only Sir Gordon Richards rode more winners and Sir Gordon had a very much longer career. Punters have never had better friends than Archer and Sir Gordon.

Archer was tall for a jockey, 5ft 10in, good-looking but with a hint of melancholy in his expression, quiet in dress and manner and possessed of much charm. He weighed well over 10st in the winter and only kept his weight down during the season by the most drastic methods that were undoubtedly detrimental to his health.

He had a wonderful nerve and like Donoghue was at his best at Epsom. He had immense determination coupled with an uncanny appreciation of the ability of the horses that he rode. In a race he was wonderfully cool and very observant, too. He rode a strong finish although his style of sitting forward with a loose rein was rated more effective than elegant. There was no draw in his day and he used to leave the paddock early to get the best position. He was sometimes unduly hard on a horse he had backed—jockeys were permitted to bet in his day—and sometimes his tactics against a fancied opponent were the reverse of scrupulous.

He enjoyed tremendous popularity and prestige—he could have married a duchess had he wanted to—but success and adulation never turned his head. He owed not a little to the influence of Matt Dawson who kept him well clear of the riff-raff unfortunately inseparable from the Turf.

In 1883 Archer married a daughter of John Dawson, but she died a year later after giving birth to a daughter. It was a blow from which he never really recovered. In 1886 his health was deteriorating fast from the fearful demands he made on it, and a chill after the Cambridgeshire was followed by typhoid. In the course of the illness and in a moment of dire depression he took a revolver and shot himself. The whole of sporting England went into mourning.

ARCTIC PRINCE

Arctic Prince, by Prince Chevalier, was bred and owned by Mr Joseph McGrath and trained by W. Stephenson at Royston. Ridden by C. Spares, better known as a rider over hurdles, he won the 1951 Derby by six lengths. In his next race, the King George VI and Queen Elizabeth Stakes, he broke down badly and he never ran again. He was exported to America in 1956 before he really had a chance to establish his reputation as a sire.

ARD PATRICK

Owned and bred by Mr John Gubbins and trained at Beckhampton by Sam Darling, Ard Patrick won the Derby in 1902. In 1903 he won a famous race for the Eclipse Stakes in which he beat Sceptre, winner of every classic bar the Derby in 1902, and Rock Sand, winner of the Triple Crown in 1903. Ard Patrick was exported to Germany at the end of his racing career but was not a great success as a sire.

ARK ROYAL

Bred in 1952 by Mr R. D. Hollingsworth and trained by George Colling, Ark Royal was a very good staying filly whose misfortune it was to be born in the same year as Meld, an even better one. Nevertheless she won six races, including the Ribblesdale Stakes, Yorkshire Oaks and Park Hill Stakes, besides finishing second to Meld in the Oaks. She bred some useful winners including Eagle, now a leading sire in Japan ; Ocean, winner of the Coronation Stakes ; and Hermes, who won the Dante Stakes, Great Voltigeur Stakes and Jockey Club Cup. She is by Straight Deal out of Felucca, by Nearco.

AMSTRONG, Frederick (b 1904)

'Sam' Armstrong, one of the most consistently successful trainers of modern times is the son of the north-country trainer R. W. Armstrong. After leaving Rossall School, he was a pupil of the Lambourn trainer H. L. Cottrill before taking out a licence himself in 1923. For a time he rode under National Hunt rules, having some fifty successes to his credit between 1921 and 1924. At first he conducted a 'mixed' stable in the North but he has been established now for many years at St Gatien, Newmarket, and restricts his activities to the flat. He is assisted by his son, Robert, and his daughter Susan married Lester Piggott.

The best horses he has trained so far are My Babu who won 10½ races including the Two Thousand Guineas ; Sayajirao, winner of the Irish Derby, St Leger and Hardwicke Stakes ; and Petingo, who won the Gimcrack Stakes, Middle Park Stakes, St James's Palace Stakes and Sussex Stakes. He also trained a high-class filly in Bebe Grande who won the National Breeders Produce Stakes, Gimcrack Stakes and Champagne Stakes and was placed in both the Two Thousand and One Thousand Guineas.

He has won at least one race on every flat-race course in this country and has been particularly successful in handicaps, winning the Cesarewitch three times, the Northumberland Plate three times, the Stewards Cup three times, the November Handicap twice, the Lincolnshire Handicap twice, the Cambridgeshire, the Ebor Handicap, the Royal Hunt Cup, the Wokingham Stakes, the Victoria Cup, the Ayr Gold Cup, the Zetland Gold Cup, the Portland Handicap and the Chester Cup.

His owners include Capt M. Lemos. Mr E. Cooper Bland, Mr Raymond Guest, Mrs J. F. C. Bryce, Mr T. H. Farr, Mr Clifford Nicholdson, Mr J. R. Mullion and Mr R. F. Scully.

ARNULL, John

John Arnull, brother of Sam Arnull, rode five Derby winners—Sergeant (1784), Rhadamanthus (1790), Didelot (1796), Archduke (1799) and Election (1807).

ARNULL, Sam

Sam Arnull won the first Derby on Diomed. He also won on Assassin (1782), Sir Peter Teazle (1787) and Sir Harry (1798). He died in 1800.

ARNULL, William

William Arnull rode three Derby winners—Hannibal (1804), Octavius (1812) and Blucher (1814). He was reputed to be an indifferent judge of pace but absolutely honest. A contemporary writer described him as "a merry little fellow up to all sorts of queer games". In later life Arnull suffered much from gout and became correspondingly less merry.

ARREARS

'Arrears' are any sums unpaid in respect of fines, compensation, fees, entrance money, stakes, subscriptions, forfeits, and purchase money in respect of races with selling conditions.

ASCOT

Ascot was founded at the request of Queen Anne, and the Queen Anne Stakes is the first race on the opening day of the Royal Meeting. It is the only racecourse in England that be-

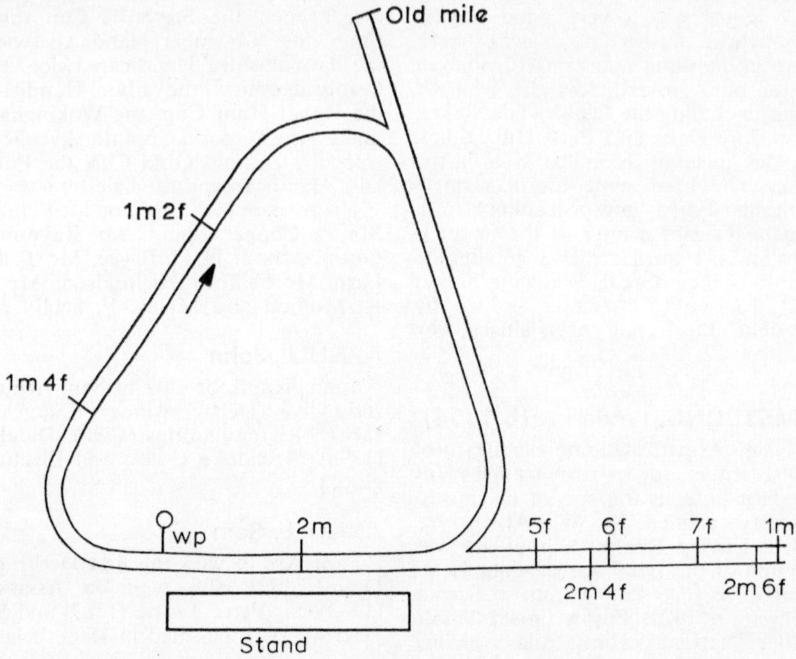

ASCOT

longs to the Crown, the Queen's Ascot representative being the Duke of Norfolk, who is responsible for the general management of the course and for the planning and organisation of the meetings there.

Extremely accessible for Londoners via the M4 motorway, Ascot stands in pleasant surroundings on the edge of Windsor Forest. A lot of money has been spent on improvements in recent years and two big up-to-date stands have been erected. At all meetings the standard of the racing is good and it is unsurpassed during the four-day Royal Meeting in June, when a touch of pageantry in the form of the Royal Procession up the course is added to sport of the highest class. On the Wednesday at this meeting the crowd is usually somewhere around 80,000 and the number of people employed at Ascot that week is roughly equivalent to the strength of an infantry division.

Up till 1939 there were only four days' racing a year on this superb course, but now better use is made of it, and there are 21 days' racing, including 'mixed' and jumping meetings.

The main event at Royal Ascot is the 2½m Gold Cup. In 1844 Czar Nicholas I of Russia visited England and went to Ascot on Gold Cup day. The Cup was won by Lord Albemarle's Defence, and to please the Czar, Lord Albemarle renamed his colt 'Emperor'. The Czar, in return, asked to be allowed to present each year a piece of plate worth £500 to be called the Emperor's Plate and to take the place of the Gold Cup. Accordingly the Gold Cup became the Emperor's Plate until the Crimean war in 1854 when the race reverted to its original title.

In 1859 Queen Victoria visited Ascot for the last time. She never went on a

Best Times: (owing to reconstruction of the course, all are from 1955 onwards)
Royal Enclosure Lodge, Ascot, Berkshire. Tel.: Ascot 83

Distance	*Horse-Age-Weight*	*Date*	*Time*
5f	Chris 3-8-10	19-6-59	60.82
5f	Pall Mall 2-9-0	20-6-57	61.46
6f	Dionisio 4-8-10	21-6-57	1min 13.78
6f	Amerigo 2-9-0	18-6-57	1min 15.22
7f	Fluke 3-8-12	17-6-70	1min 28.36
7f	Mabel 2-8-8	25-9-64	1min 31.06
8f (round)	Meldon 3-7-12	21-6-57	1min 40.97
8f (round)	Royal Palace 2-9-0	23-9-66	1min 43.97
8f (straight)	Welsh Pageant 4-9-5	16-6-70	1min 39.86
10f	Connaught 5-9-4	16-6-70	2min 7.27
12f	Fric 5-9-1	21-6-57	2min 30.17
16f	Bally Russe 4-9-4	14-6-66	3min 24.76
20f	Tubulcain 5-8-0	14-6-66	4min 21.36
22f 34 yd	Gurkha 5-7-3	17-7-64	4min 53.69

racecourse again after the death of the Prince Consort.

The most valuable race at Ascot is the 1½m King George VI and Queen Elizabeth Stakes, run in July. It was largely the creation of the late Sir John Crocker Bulteel, at that time Clerk of the Course. Designed to attract good horses from overseas to take on the best over here, it was staged originally to mark the 1951 Festival of Britain and was in fact that year called the King George VI and Queen Elizabeth Festival of Britain Stakes.

The Ascot course was reconstructed after the last war and the present course dates from 1955. It is a circular track of 1m 6f 34yd, the first 3 furlongs downhill and the last half (including the Old Mile which starts on a chute) uphill with a straight run-in of 2½ furlongs. The Hunt Cup course is one mile straight and is undulating with an uphill finish. All races of under a mile are run on the Hunt Cup course. As on other courses equipped with an artificial watering system, the effect of the draw on the straight course is unpredictable.

Clerk of the Course: Hon N. Beaumont, Royal Enclosure Lodge, Ascot, Berkshire. Tel: Ascot 83.

Ascot Abandoned

In 1964, because of torrential rain, the last two days of the Royal Meeting had to be abandoned. In 1930 a tremendous thunderstorm caused racing to be abandoned for the afternoon after the Royal Hunt Cup, the second of the seven races on the card, had been run. The races that could not be run on the Wednesday took place on the Thursday and Friday.

Queen's Vase, 2m

First run 1838. *Run as Gold Vase until* 1959. *No race* 1940 *to* 1945.

	OWNER	TRAINER	JOCKEY	SP
1930 Trimdon, 4–8–4	Brig-Gen C. Lambton	J. Lawson	R. Jones	6–4
1931 Pomme d'Api, 3–7–12	Aga Khan	Fk. Butters	M. Beary	4–1
1932 Silvermere, 3–7–12	Mrs C. Rich	W. Nightingall	F. Lane	100–6
1933 Gainslaw, 4–8–4	H. Simms	F. Leader	T. Weston	5–4
1934 Duplicate, 3–7–5	Sir C. Hyde	N. Scobie	F. Sharpe	100–6
1935 Flash Bye, 3–7–5	Lord Astor	J. Lawson	J. Sirett	8–1
1936 Rondo, 3–7–5	J. de Rothschild	F. Pratt	P. Maher	20–1
1937 Fearless Fox, 4–8–8	A. Smith	J. Jarvis	E. Smith	11–8
1938 Foxglove II, 3–7–12	P. Beatty	F. Darling	G. Richards	4–1
1939 Atout Maitre, 3–7–9	H. Blagrave	H. Blagrave	W. Sibbritt	11–2
1946 Look Ahead, 3–7–7	Sir H. de Trafford	C. B-Rochfort	D. Smith	20–1
1947 Auralia, 4–9–4	Mrs A. Johnston	R. Day	D. Smith	100–8

Queen's Vase (contd.)	OWNER	TRAINER	JOCKEY	SP
1948 Estoc, 3–7–12	M. Boussac	C. Semblat	R. Bertiglia	7–2
1949 Lone Eagle, 3–7–12	W. Woodward	C. B-Rochfort	D. Smith	100–30
1950 Fastlad, 4–9–4	Baron de Waldner	P. Carter	F. Palmer	100–6
1951 Faux Pas, 3–7–9	Mrs R. Foster	J. Lawson	E. Smith	6–1
1952 Souepi, 4–8–8	G. Digby	G. Digby	C. Elliott	100–7
1953 Absolve, 5–9–6	Sir M. McAlpine	V. Smyth	L. Piggott	20–1
1954 Prescription, 3–7–12	Lord Rosebery	J. Jarvis	E. Smith	6–1
1955 Prince Barle, 3–7–13	J. Barker	J. Lawson	E. Mercer	11–2
1956 French Beige, 3–7–12	R. Dennis	H. Peacock	G. Littlewood	100–8
1957 Tenterhooks, 3–7–12	Lord Allendale	C. Elsey	E. Britt	6–1
1958 Even Money, 3–7–13	C. Palmer	V. O'Brien	A. Breasley	9–4
1959 Vivi Tarquin, 3–7–8	J. McGrath	S. McGrath	D. Greening	100–8
1960 Prolific, 3–7–12	Mrs C. Evans	W. Nightingall	D. Keith	5–2
1961 Black King, 3–7–12	H. Joel	W. Elsey	E. Hide	100–8
1962 Pavot, 3–7–9	E. More O'Ferrall	P. Prendergast	J. Sime	10–1
1963 Hereford, 3–7–12	Mrs W. Macauley	H. Murless	J. Hunter	20–1
1964 I Titan, 3–7–8	Mrs V. H-Williams	N. Murless	M. Giovannelli	10–1
1965 Beddard, 3–7–12	R. Reynolds	H. Murless	J. Sime	9–1
1966 Bally Russe, 4–9–4	F. H.-Williams	N. Murless	A. Breasley	5–1
1967 The Accuser, 3–7–12	Lord Rotherwick	W. Hern	F. Durr	15–2
1968 Zorba II, 3–7–8	C. Clore	P.J. Prendergast	R. Hutchinson	10–1
1969 Tantivy, 3–7–12	N. Hetherton	W. Elsey	A. Barclay	15–8
1970 Yellow River, 3–7–12	D. Sung	A. Breasley	T. Carter	20–1

Ascot Stakes, 2m 4f

Handicap. First run 1839. *No race* 1940 *to* 1945.

	OWNER	TRAINER	JOCKEY	SP
1930 Bonny Boy II, 6–8–5	E. de St. Alary	V. Gilpin	P. Beasley	100–8
1931 Noble Star, 4–7–10	F. Cundell	L. Cundell	F. Fox	10–1
1932 { Son of Mint, 5–8–2	J. Brown	A. D.-Pennant	H. Wragg	100–6
1932 { Sandy Lashes, 4–6–9	Mrs L. Long	L. Cundell	W. Elliott	100–8
1933 Roi de Paris, 5–7–9	J. Cooper	A. D.-Pennant	C. Buckham	100–7
1934 Hands Off, 4–7–1	F. Dennis	G. Digby	A. Richardson	25–1
1935 Doreen Jane, 5–6–11	Sir A. Bailey	H. Cottrill	D. Smith	100–7
1936 Bouldnor, 4–7–6	Maj. J. Walker	H. Leader	K. Robertson	20–1
1937 Valerian, 4–8–13	Sir A. Bailey	J. Lawson	T. Weston	5–1
1938 Frawn, 4–7–12	J. Westoll	G. Barling	E. Smith	5–1
1939 Frawn, 5–8–10	J. Westoll	G. Barling	E. Smith	100–8
1946 Reynard Volant, 4–7–12	Sir J. Jarvis	J. Jarvis	E. Smith	8–1
1947 Reynard Volant, 5–9–4	Sir J. Jarvis	J. Jarvis	E. Smith	8–1
1948 No Orchids, 5–8–11	Mrs V. Dyson	M. Everitt	H. Blackshaw	9–1
1949 Hilali, 5–7–4	Mohamed Bey Sultan	G. Digby	F. Durr	40–1
1950 Honorable II, 6–8–4	H. Blagrave	H. Blagrave	W. Johnstone	100–7
1951 Guerrier, 6–6–12	M. Kingsley	W. Stephenson	T. Mahon	20–1
1952 Flighty Frances, 4–7–9	Mrs F. Jackson	J. Dines	D. Smith	20–1
1953 Pluchino, 4–7–12	J. de Rothschild	D. Watson	E. Fordyce	100–7
1954 Corydalis, 5–7–2	Maj C. Raphael	F. Sneyd	J. Forte	15–2
1955 Wildnor, 4–6–5	J. Williams	S. C. Clark	C. Gaston	25–1
1956 Zarathustra, 5–9–0	T. Gray	C. B-Rochfort	W. Carr	100–8
1957 Bonhomie, 8–6–8	J. Wood	E. Cousins	M. Hayes	25–1
1958 Sandiacre, 6–8–13	M. Cowley	W. Dutton	W. Carr	100–7
1959 Rugosa, 4–7–12	H. Joel	T. Leader	E. Smith	100–7
1960 Shatter, 4–7–9	Maj P. Magor	T. Masson	R. Elliott	100–8
1961 Angazi, 4–7–7	I. Kerman	W. Nightingall	D. Keith	6–1
1962 Trelawny, 6–9–8	Mrs L. Carver	G. Todd	A. Breasley	11–2
1963 Trelawny, 7–10–0	Mrs L. Carver	G. Todd	A. Breasley	9–1
1964 Delmere, 4–7–2	Lady Delamere	W. Stephenson	D. Cullen	8–1
1965 Harvest Gold, 6–8–12	T. Marshall	T. Robson	F. Durr	9–1
1966 Tubulcain, 5–8–0	H. Fellowes	E. Goddard	G. Lewis	100–6
1967 Shira, 7–7–9	Miss I. Bennett	G. Todd	J. Hayward	6–1
1968 King of Peace, 5–7–12	J. Hardy	J. Hardy	A. Murray	8–1
1969 Lexicon, 5–8–11	G. P. Eliot	H. Price	L. Piggott	10–1
1970 Magna Carta, 4–8–4	The Queen	I. Balding	G. Lewis	9–2

Coventry Stakes, 6f

at Newmarket from 1941 *till* 1944. *No race* 1940.

		OWNER	TRAINER	JOCKEY	SP
1930	Lemnarchus	Lord Ellesmere	F. Darling	F. Fox	9–2
1931	Cockpen	Lord Woolavington	F. Darling	F. Fox	13–8
1932	Manitoba	Lord Woolavington	F. Darling	G. Richards	13–8
1933	Medieval Knight	J. Dewar	F. Darling	G. Richards	8–13
1934	Hairan	Aga Khan	F. Butters	G. Richards	4–9
1935	Black Speck	J. Rank	H. Cottrill	T. Burns	7–1
1936	Early School	Lord Astor	J. Lawson	R. Dick	11–4
1937	Mirza II	Aga Khan	F. Butters	C. Smirke	4–11
1938	Panorama	Mrs J. Corrigan	C. B-Rochfort	P. Beasley	2–9
1939	Turkhan	Aly Khan	F. Butters	C. Smirke	100–8
1941	Big Game	King George VI	F. Darling	H. Wragg	2–9
1942	Nasrullah	Aga Khan	F. Butters	G. Richards	7–4
1943	Orestes	Miss D. Paget	W. Nightingall	T. Carey	13–8
1944	Dante	Sir E. Ohlson	M. Peacock	W. Nevett	11–8
1945	Khaled	Aga Khan	F. Butters	G. Richards	9–1
1946	Tudor Minstrel	J. Dewar	F. Darling	G. Richards	2–13
1947	The Cobbler	Lieut-Col G. Loder	F. Darling	G. Richards	4–5
1948	Royal Forest	Major R. M-Buchanan	N. Murless	C. Richards	5–1
1949	Palestine	Aga Khan	F. Butters	G. Richards	1–2
1950	Big Dipper	Mrs J. Bryce	C. B-Rochfort	W. Carr	2–1
1951	Kings Bench	A. Tompsett	M. Feakes	G. Richards	4–6
1952	Whistler	Maharanee of Baroda	P. Nelson	E. Britt	2–5
1953	The Pie King	R. Bell	P. Prendergast	T. Gosling	11–2
1954	Noble Chieftain	Maj L. Holliday	H. Cottrill	F. Barlow	11–8
1955	Ratification	Sir M. McAlpine	V. Smyth	W. Carr	100–30
1956	Messmate	Lord Milford	J. Jarvis	E. Mercer	20–1
1957	Amerigo	Lord Howard de Walden	J. A. Waugh	E. Smith	7–4
1958	Hieroglyph	Mrs J. Hanes	C. B-Rochfort	W. Carr	10–1
1959	Martial	R. Webster	P. Prendergast	W. Swinburn	11–10
1960	Typhoon	N. McCarthy	P. Prendergast	R. Hutchinson	Evens
1961	Xerxes	Mrs D. McCalmont	G. Brooke	D. Smith	9–2
1962	Crocket	D. van Clief	G. Brooke	D. Smith	9–4
1963	Showdown	Mrs D. Prenn	F. Winter	D. Smith	6–1
1964	Silly Season	P. Mellon	I. Balding	G. Lewis	13–2
1965	Young Emperor	Mrs P. Poe	P. Prendergast	L. Piggott	9–4
1966	Bold Lad	Lady Granard	P. Prendergast	D. Lake	4–6
1967	Mark Royal	B. Schmidt-Bodner	P. Norris	A. Breasley	13–2
1968	Murrayfield	Mrs P. Hastings	I. Balding	G. Lewis	15–2
1969	Prince Tenderfoot	Mrs P. Poe	P. Prendergast	W. Williamson	15–8
1970	Mill Reef	P. Mellon	I. Balding	G. Lewis	4–11

St James's Palace Stakes, 1m

Three-year-olds. First run at Newmarket 1941. *No race* 1940 *and* 1942 *to* 1945.

		OWNER	TRAINER	JOCKEY	SP
1930	Christopher Robin, 9–0	Lieut-Col G. Loder	V. Gilpin	P. Beasley	100–7
1931	Cameronian, 9–0	J. Dewar	F. Darling	F. Fox	8–15
1932	Andrea, 9–0	Duke of Marlborough	P. Whitaker	T. Weston	100–8
1933	Canon Law, 9–0	Lord Astor	J. Lawson	R. Dick	9–2
1934	Flamenco, 9–0	Lord Rosebery	J. Jarvis	H. Wragg	100–9
1935	Bahram, 9–0	Aga Khan	Fk. Butters	F. Fox	1–8
1936	Rhodes Scholar, 8–7	Lord Astor	J. Lawson	R. Dick	2–1
1937	Goya II, 9–0	M. Boussac	G. Lambton	C. Elliott	9–4
1938	Scottish Union, 9–0	J. Rank	N. Cannon	B. Carslake	4–7
1939	Admiral's Walk, 8–7	Sir J. Jarvis	J. Jarvis	E. Smith	6–5
1941	Orthodox, 9–0	J. Rank	N. Cannon	D. Smith	6–1
1946	Khaled, 9–0	Aga Khan	Fk. Butters	G. Richards	2–1
1947	Tudor Minstrel, 9–0	J. Dewer	F. Darling	G. Richards	6–100
1948	Black Tarquin, 9–0	W. Woodward	C. B-Rochfort	E. Britt	5–1
1949	Faux Tirage, 9–0	J. Dewer	N. Murless	G. Richards	11–10
1950	Palestine, 9–0	Aga Khan	M. Marsh	C. Smirke	4–7

St James's Palace Stakes (contd)	OWNER	TRAINER	JOCKEY	SP
1951 Turco II, 9–0	W. Woodward	C. B-Rochfort	W. Carr	7–1
1952 King's Bench, 9–0	A. Tompsett	M. Feakes	G. Richards	3–1
1953 Nearula, 9–0	W. Humble	C. Elsey	E. Britt	4–6
1954 Darius, 9–0	Sir P. Loraine	H. Wragg	E. Mercer	evens
1955 Tamerlane, 9–0	Lord Porchester	N. Bertie	A. Breasley	8–11
1956 Pirate King, 9–0	Maj L. Holliday	H. Cottrill	D. Smith	6–1
1957 Chevastrid, 8–7	J. McGrath	S. McGrath	J. Eddery	8–1
1958 Major Portion, 9–0	H. Joel	T. Leader	E. Smith	evens
1959 Above Suspicion, 8–7	The Queen	C. B-Rochfort	W. Carr	9–4
1960 Venture VII, 9–0	Aly Khan	A. Head	G. Moore	1–33
1961 Tudor Treasure, 8–7	Lord Derby	J. Watts	D. Smith	11–4
1962 Court Sentence, 8–7	H. Joel	T. Leader	E. Smith	100–8
1963 Crocket, 9–0	D. van Clief	G. Brooke	D. Smith	9–2
1964 Roan Rocket, 9–0	T. Frost	G. Todd	L. Piggott	5–4
1965 Silly Season, 9–0	P. Mellon	I. Balding	G. Lewis	5–1
1966 Track Spare, 9–0	R. Mason	R. Mason	J. Lindley	100–9
1967 Reform, 9–0	M. Sobell	Sir G. Richards	A. Breasley	4–6
1968 Petingo, 9–0	Capt M. Lemos	F. Armstrong	L. Piggott	10–11
1969 Right Tack, 9–0	J. R. Brown	J. Sutcliffe, Jun.	G. Lewis	4–6
1970 Saintly Song, 9–0	S. Joel	N. Murless	A. Barclay	11–10

Queen Mary Stakes, 5f

Two-year-old fillies carrying 8*st* 12*lb. First run* 1921. *No race* 1940. *Run at Newmarket* 1941 *to* 1944.

	OWNER	TRAINER	JOCKEY	SP
1930 Atbara	Lieut-Col G. Loder	V. Gilpin	P. Beasley	20–1
1931 Diamalt	Mrs V. Sainsbury	A. Holland	H. Wragg	100–9
1932 Supervisor	F. Darling	F. Darling	G. Richards	3–1
1933 Maureen	Lord Woolavington	F. Darling	G. Richards	5–2
1934 Caretta	Lord Lonsdale	F. Darling	G. Richards	6–4
1935 Fair Ranee	Vicomte de Fontarce	R. Dawson	S. Donoghue	100–8
1936 Night Song	J. Whitney	C. B-Rochfort	P. Beasley	4–1
1937 Queen of Simba	Aga Khan	F. Butters	C. Smirke	20–1
1938 Belle Travers	T. Lant	F. Butters	D. Smith	3–1
1939 Snowberry	Lord Lonsdale	F. Darling	G. Richards	4–1
1941 Sun Chariot	King George VI	F. Darling	H. Wragg	11–8
1942 Samovar	Lord Wyfold	H. Persse	M. Beary	100–6
1943 Fair Fame	Mrs B. Lavington	H. Leader	F. Lane	15-2
1944 Sun Stream	Lord Derby	W. Earl	H. Wragg	100–30
1945 Rivaz	Aga Khan	F. Butters	C. Elliott	4–7
1946 Apparition	Mrs R. M-Buchanan	F. Darling	G. Richards	11–8
1947 Masaka	Aga Khan	F. Butters	C. Smirke	4–1
1948 Coronation V	M. Boussac	C. Semblat	C. Elliott	0–0
1949 Diableretta	Aga Khan	F. Butters	W. Johnstone	7–4
1950 Rose Linnet	Mrs A. Johnston	R. Day	D. Smith	10–1
1951 Primavera	Lord Milford	J. Jarvis	E. Mercer	100–6
1952 Devon Vintage	Lady Wyfold	R. J. Colling	E. Mercer	100–8
1953 Sybil's Niece	Lord Milford	J. Jarvis	E. Mercer	100–6
1954 Bride Elect	Maj L. Holliday	H. Cottrill	F. Barlow	6–1
1955 Weeber	J. Olding	P. Nelson	A. Breasley	10–1
1956 Pharsalia	Maj L. Holliday	H. Cottrill	L. Piggott	100–7
1957 Abelia	Col B. Hornung	N. Murless	L. Piggott	11–2
1958 A.20	H. Clifton	F. Sutherland	W. Rickaby	5–1
1959 Paddy's Sister	Mrs J. Mullion	P. Prendergast	G. Moore	15–8
1960 Cynara	G. Oldham	H. Wragg	W. Carr	evens
1961 My Dream	D. Robinson	G. Brooke	D. Smith	2–1
1962 Shot Silk	Lieut-Col D. Cripps	G. Brooke	D. Smith	100–8
1963 Lerida	Mrs R. M-Buchanan	J. A. Waugh	J. Lindley	9–2
1964 Brassia	A. Plesch	V. O'Brien	J. Purtell	7–2
1965 Visp	E. Benjamin	J. Watts	J. Lindley	6–4
1966 Petite Path	R. Mason	R. Mason	J. Lindley	33–1
1967 Sovereign	R. Moller	H. Wragg	R. Hutchinson	10–11
1968 Grizel	Col W. Stirling	P. J. Prendergast	W. Williamson	5–2
1969 Farfalla	D. van Clief	D. Smith	A. Murray	13–2
1970 Cawston's Pride	L. B. Hall	F. Maxwell	B. Taylor	2–1

Royal Hunt Cup, 1m

Handicap. First run 1843. *7f 166yd before* 1930 *and over 7f 155yd from* 1930 *until* 1955. *No race* 1940 *to* 1944.

	OWNER	TRAINER	JOCKEY	SP
1930 The McNab, 4–7–8	J. Dewar	F. Darling	F. Fox	100–7
1931 Grand Salute, 4–7–5	Lord Glanely	T. Hogg	G. Richards	5–1
1932 Totaig, 3–7–3	V. Emanuel	G. Duller	B. Rosen	33–1
1933 Colorado Kid, 4–8–5	Lieut-Col G. Loder	V. Gilpin	C. Buckham	100–8
1934 Caymanas, 4–8–4	C. Ewing	C. Easterbee	C. Ray	50–1
1935 Priok, 4–7–4	H. B-Hankey	P. Whitaker	S. Middleton	66–1
1936 Guinea Gap, 5–8–5	Lady Nuttall	H. Cottrill	R. Jones	28–1
1937 Fairplay, 4–8–3	R. Middlemas	P. Allden	P. Maher	18–1
1938 Couvert, 5–7–12	H. Blagrave	H. Blagrave	C. Richards	100–8
1939 Caerloptic, 4–8–12	Sir A. Bailey	H. Cottrill	M. Beary	100–8
1945 Battle Hymn, 3–7–11	J. Whitney	C. B-Rochfort	P. Maher	20–1
1946 Friar's Fancy, 5–7–12	O. Watney	T. Leader	E. Smith	15–2
1947 Master Vote, 4–7–6	H. Blagrave	H. Blagrave	T. Sidebotham	25–1
1948 Master Vote, 5–8–10	H. Blagrave	H. Blagrave	W. Johnstone	100–7
1949 Sterope, 4–8–12	J. Townley	P. Beasley	J. Caldwell	100–6
1950 Hyperbole, 5–8–8	J. Rank	N. Cannon	A. Breasley	10–1
1951 Val d'Assa, 4–8–8	Maj D. McCalmont	H. Persse	N. Sellwood	100–6
1952 Queen of Sheba, 4–8–4	Maj D. McCalmont	H. Persse	F. Barlow	100–7
1953 Choir Boy, 4–7–8	The Queen	C. B-Rochfort	D. Smith	100–6
1954 Chivalry, 5–8–3	P. Hatvany	T. Rimell	D. Forte	33–1
1955 Nicholas Nickleby, 4–7–9	J. Gerber	F. Armstrong	W. Snaith	50–1
1956 Alexander, 4–8–11	The Queen	C. B-Rochfort	W. Carr	13–2
1957 Retrial, 5–8–2	Lady Z. Wernher	C. B-Rochfort	P. Robinson	100–7
1958 Amos, 4–7–1	L. Carver	S. Mercer	P. Boothman	20–1
1959 Faultless Speech, 4–8–1	H. Wallington	H. Wallington	G. Lewis	8–1
1960 Small Slam, 5–8–2	P. King	G. Barling	R. Elliott	28–1
1961 King's Troop, 4–8–4	Mrs P. Hastings	P. H-Bass	G. Lewis	100–7
1962 Smartie, 4–7–9	R. Mason	R. Mason	J. Sime	22–1
1963 Spaniard's Close, 6–8–6	Mrs B. Davis	F. Winter	L. Piggott	25–1
1964 Zaleucus, 4–8–2	Maj D. McCalmont	G. Brooke	D. Smith	100–7
1965 Casabianca, 4–8–7	Lieut-Col J. Hornung	N. Murless	L. Piggott	100–9
1966 Continuation, 4–7–9	S. McGrath	S. McGrath	J. Roe	25–1
1967 Regal Light, 4–7–6	Mrs L. Lazarus	S. Hall	G. Sexton	100–9
1968 Golden Mean, 5–8–4	S. H. Lee	D. Smith	F. Durr	28–1
1969 Kamundu, 7–8–6	J. Banks	F. Carr	L. Piggott	7–1
1970 Calpurnius, 4–7–13	C. Engelhard	S. W. Watts	G. Duffield	33–1

Ribblesdale Stakes, 1m 4f

Three-year-old and four-year-old colts and fillies until 1939. *First run* 1919. *No race* 1940 *to* 1949. *Three-year-old fillies only from* 1950.

	OWNER	TRAINER	JOCKEY	SP
1930 Flying Argosy, 3–8–0	W. Vincent	H. Powney	T. Weston	7–4
1931 Doctor Dolittle, 3–8–12	A. Basset	H. Persse	H. Beasley	6–4
1932 Rose en Soleil, 4–9–7	Lord H. de Walden	D. Waugh	J. Childs	9–2
1933 Versicle, 3–8–4	Lord Stanley	G. Lambton	T. Weston	100–8
1934 The Blue Boy, 4–9–4	Sir W. Portal	M. Hartigan	J. Childs	11–10
1935 Easton, 4–9–12	Lord Woolavington	F. Darling	G. Richards	1–4
1936 Can-Can, 3–7–11	T. Blackwell	G. Barling	P. Evans	100–8
1937 Rhodes Scholar, 4–9–12	Lord Astor	J. Lawson	R. Jones	11–10
1938 River Prince, 3–8–5	Duke of Marlborough	C. B-Rochfort	P. Beasley	6–1
1939 Ombro, 3–8–4	Lord Portal	C. B-Rochfort	T. Burns	5–1
1950 La Baille, 8–10	Mohamed Bey Sultan	M. Marsh	C. Smirke	15–2
1951 Chinese Cracker, 8–10	Mrs G. Blagrave	H. Blagrave	A. Breasley	7–4
1952 Esquilla, 8–10	M. Boussac	C. Semblat	W. Johnstone	9–2
1953 Skye, 8–6	Lord Rosebery	J. Jarvis	W. Rickaby	4–1

Ribblesdale Stakes (contd.)	OWNER	TRAINER	JOCKEY	SP
1954 Sweet One, 8–10	Lord Milford	J. Jarvis	W. Rickaby	100–8
1955 Ark Royal, 8–10	R. Hollingsworth	G. Colling	D. Smith	2–1
1956 Milady, 8–10	Maj H. Holt	M. Marsh	C. Smirke	100–8
1957 Almeria, 8–6	The Queen	C. B-Rochfort	W. Carr	13–8
1958 None Nicer, 9–0	Maj L. Holliday	W. Hern	S. Clayton	11–2
1959 Cantelo, 9–0	W. Hill	C. Elsey	E. Hide	5–4
1960 French Fern, 8–6	Maj H. Broughton	J. A. Waugh	G. Lewis	8–1
1961 Futurama, 8–6	G. Oldham	H. Wragg	A. Breasley	9–2
1962 Tender Annie, 8–6	Mrs J. Bryce	P. Prendergast	G. Bougoure	5–4
1963 Ostrya, 8–6	Lord H. de Walden	J. A. Waugh	J. Lindley	100–9
1964 Windmill Girl, 8–10	Lieut-Col Sir J. Darell	A. Budgett	A. Breasley	9–4
1965 Bracey Bridge, 8–6	M. W-Boynton	N. Murless	L. Piggott	5–1
1966 Parthian Glance, 8–6	Mrs W. R-Smith	G. Todd	R. Hutchinson	11–2
1967 Park Top, 8–10	Duke of Devonshire	B. van Cutsem	R. Maddock	9–2
1968 Pandora Bay, 8–10	Maj C. Nathan	G. Barling	M. Thomas	11–4
1969 Sleeping Partner, 9–4	Lord Rosebery	D. Smith	J. Gorton	7–4
1970 Permelia, 3–8–6	Lord H. de Walden	N. Murless	A. Barclay	9–1

Ascot Gold Cup, 2m 4f

First run 1807. *Run at Newmarket* 1941 *to* 1944. *No race* 1940 *and* 1964.

	OWNER	TRAINER	JOCKEY	SP
1930 Bosworth, 4–9–0	Lord Derby	Fk. Butters	T. Weston	3–1
1931 Trimdon, 5–9–4	Brig-Gen C. Lambton	J. Lawson	J. Childs	3–1
1932 Trimdon, 6–9–4	Brig-Gen C. Lambton	J. Lawson	J. Childs	15–2
1933 Foxhunter, 4–9–0	E. Esmond	J. Jarvis	H. Wragg	25–1
1934 Felicitation, 4–9–0	Aga Khan	Fk. Butters	G. Richards	9–2
1935 Tiberius, 4–9–0	Sir A. Bailey	J. Lawson	T. Weston	100–30
1936 Quashed, 4–8–11	Lord Stanley	C. Leader	R. Perryman	3–1
1937 Precipitation, 4–9–0	Lady Z. Wernher	C. B-Rochfort	P. Beasley	2–1
1938 Flares, 5–9–0	W. Woodward	C. B-Rochfort	R. Jones	100–7
1939 Flyon, 4–9–0	Lord Milford	J. Jarvis	E. Smith	100–6
1941 Finis, 6–9–0	Sir H. C-Owen	O. Bell	H. Wragg	4–1
1942 Owen Tudor, 4–9–0	Mrs R. M-Buchanan	F. Darling	G. Richards	5–2
1943 Ujiji, 4–9–0	A. Allnatt	J. Lawson	G. Richards	8–1
1944 Umidadd, 4–9–0	Aga Khan	Fk. Butters	G. Richards	5–4
1945 Ocean Swell, 4–9–0	Lord Rosebery	J. Jarvis	E. Smith	6–1
1946 Caracalla II, 4–9–0	M. Boussac	C. Semblat	C. Elliott	4–9
1947 Souvereign, 4–9–0	F. Schmitt	H. Delavaud	M. Lollierou	6–4
1948 Arbar, 4–9–0	M. Boussac	C. Semblat	C. Elliott	4–6
1949 Alycidon, 4–9–0	Lord Derby	W. Earl	D. Smith	5–4
1950 Supertello, 4–9–0	W. Harvey	J. C. Waugh	D. Smith	10–1
1951 Pan II, 4–9–0	E. Constant	E. Pollet	R. Poincelet	100–8
1952 Aquino II, 4–9–0	Maharanee of Baroda	F. Armstrong	G. Richards	4–1
1953 Souepi, 5–9–0	G. Digby	G. Digby	C. Elliott	11–2
1954 Elpenor, 4–9–0	M. Boussac	C. Elliott	J. Doyasbere	100–8
1955 Botticelli, 4–9–0	Marchese della Rocchetta	Marchese della Rocchetta	E. Camici	9–4
1956 Macip, 4–9–0	M. Boussac	C. Elliott	S. Boullenger	6–1
1957 Zarathustra, 6–9–0	T. Gray	C. B-Rochfort	L. Piggott	6–1
1958 Gladness, 5–8–11	J. McShain	V. O'Brien	L. Piggott	3–1
1959 Wallaby II, 4–9–0	Baron de Waldner	P. Carter	F. Palmer	9–4
1960 Sheshoon, 4–9–0	Aly Khan	A. Head	G. Moore	7–4
1961 Pandofell, 4–9–0	H. W. Daw	F. Maxwell	L. Piggott	100–8
1962 Balto, 4–9–0	A. Reuff	M. Bonaventure	F. Palmer	7–4
1963 Twilight Alley, 4–9–0	Lady Sassoon	N. Murless	L. Piggott	100–30
1965 Fighting Charlie, 4–9–0	Lady M. Bury	F. Maxwell	L. Piggott	6–1
1966 Fighting Charlie, 5–9–0	Lady M. Bury	F. Maxwell	G. Starkey	15–8
1967 Parbury, 4–9–0	Maj H. Holt	D. Candy	J. Mercer	7–1
1968 Pardallo II, 5–9–0	Mme L. Volterra	C. Bartholomew	W. Pyers	13–2
1969 Levmoss, 4–9–0	S. McGrath	S. McGrath	W. Williamson	15–8

Queen Alexandra Stakes, 2m 6f and 34yd

Four-year-olds and upwards. First run 1865. *Run over* 2*m* 6*f and* 75*yd until* 1954. *No race* 1940 *to* 1945 *and in* 1964.

	OWNER	TRAINER	JOCKEY	SP
1930 Brown Jack, 6–9–8 .	Sir H. Wernher ..	I. Anthony ..	S. Donoghue ..	11–8
1931 Brown Jack, 7–9–8 .	Sir H. Wernher ..	I. Anthony ..	S. Donoghue ..	8–11
1932 Brown Jack, 8–9–8 .	Sir H. Wernher ..	I. Anthony ..	S. Donoghue ..	8–15
1933 Brown Jack, 9–9–8 .	Sir H. Wernher ..	I. Anthony ..	S. Donoghue ..	1–5
1934 Brown Jack, 10–9–8	Sir H. Wernher ..	I. Anthony ..	S. Donoghue ..	6–4
1935 Enfield, 4–9–5 . ..	M. Field	C. B-Rochfort .	M. Beary . ..	6–4
1936 Cecil, 5–9–6	Sir A. Bailey . ..	J. Lawson ..	T. Weston ..	3–1
1937 Valerian, 4–9–5 ..	Sir A. Bailey . ..	J. Lawson ..	T. Weston ..	3–1
1938 Epigram, 5–9–0 ..	J. Rank	N. Cannon ..	B. Carslake ..	4–1
1939 Pretender II, 5–8–10	J. Bouter	J. Widener ..	G. Delaurie ..	13–8
1946 Marsyas II, 6–9–5 ..	M. Boussac	C. Semblat ..	C. Elliott . ..	1–2
1947 Monsieur l'Admiral, 6–9–5	H. B-Hankey ..	H. Charlier ..	C. Smirke ..	7–2
1948 Vulgan, 5–9–0 . ..	H. Coriat	J. de Moraville	W. Johnstone..	9–4
1949 Alindrake, 4–9–0 ..	E. Toulemonde ..	E. Boullenger .	P. Blanc	7–1
1950 Aldborough, 5–9–0 .	Miss D. Paget ..	F. Walwyn ..	G. Richards ..	2–1
1951 Strathspey, 6–9–5 ..	J. Rank	N. Cannon ..	A. Breasley ..	4–6
1952 Medway, 4–9–0 ..	P. Bartholomew ..	F. Winter . ..	D. Smith.. ..	9–4
1953 Lord Fox, 4–9–0 ..	Aga Khan	M. Marsh ..	C. Smirke ..	9–2
1954 Bitter Sweet, 5–9–0 .	H. Barlow	F. Hudson ..	W. Carr	10–1
1955 Bitter Sweet, 6–9–5 .	H. Barlow	F. Hudson ..	W. Carr	5–2
1956 Borghetto, 5–9–0 ..	A. Weisweiller ..	D. Watson ..	W. Johnstone..	13–8
1957 Flying Flag II, 4–9–0	H. Baranez	J. Laumain ..	L. Flavien ..	evens
1958 Rally, 6–9–0	J. Astor..	R. J. Colling ..	J. Mercer	6–5
1959 Bali Ha'i III, 6–9–5 .	Queen Elizabeth ..	C. B-Rochfort .	W. Carr	15–8
1960 Predominate, 8–9–0 .	H. Joel	T. Leader . ..	E. Smith	8–15
1961 Moss Bank, 5–9–0 ..	T. O'Brien	T. O'Brien ..	W. Williamson.	9–4
1962 Trelawny, 6–9–5 ..	Mrs L. Carver ..	G. Todd	A. Breasley ..	6–5
1963 Trelawny, 7–9–5 ..	Mrs L. Carver ..	G. Todd	A. Breasley ..	11–8
1965 Grey of Falloden, 6–9–5	Lord Astor	W. Hern . ..	J. Mercer . ..	4–5
1966 Panic, 5–9–0	Mrs M. Philippi ..	J. Oxx	J. Roe	5–1
1967 Alciglide, 4–9–0 ..	S. McGrath	S. McGrath ..	W. Williamson.	6–1
1968 Tubalcain, 7–9–5 ..	H. Fellowes	E. Goddard ..	G. Lewis . ..	9–4
1969 Laurence O, 4–9–0 .	S. McGrath	S. McGrath ..	W. Williamson.	7–2

King's Stand Stakes, 5f

First run 1902. *No race* 1940 *to* 1945 *and* 1964.

	OWNER	TRAINER	JOCKEY	SP
1930 Oak Ridge, 7–10–0..	F. Cundell	L. Cundell ..	H. Beasley ..	11–8
1931 Stingo, 4–10–7 . ..	D. Gant	W. Lowe.. ..	H. Wragg ..	2–1
1932 Lemnarchus, 4–10–3	Lord Ellesmere ..	F. Darling ..	G. Richards ..	7–2
1933 Gold Bridge, 4–10–3	A. Macomber ..	W. Beatty ..	H. Beasley ..	11–10
1934 Gold Bridge, 5–10–3	Lord Beatty	W. Beatty ..	C. Elliott . ..	11–2
1935 Shalfleet, 4–9–7 ..	H. Leader	H. Leader ..	H. Jelliss . ..	5–4
1936 Sweet Polly, 4–9–4 .	L. Long	L. Cundell ..	G. Richards ..	7–1
1937 Ticca Gari, 3–7–11 .	Aly Khan	Fk. Butters ..	A. Dupuit. ..	5–1
1938 Foray, 4–9–1	M. Field	C. B-Rochfort .	P. Beasley ..	3–1
1939 Mickey The Greek, 5–9–9	N. Frieze	H. Leach . ..	H. Wragg ..	20–1
1946 Vilmorin, 3–8–0 ..	J. Read	J. Lawson ..	C. Richards ..	10–1
1947 Greek Justice, 3–8–6	J. Dewar	F. Darling ..	G. Richards ..	100–30
1948 Squander Bug, 5–9–1	Mrs E. Moss . ..	M. Collins ..	W. Rickaby ..	33–1
1949 Abernant, 3–8–6 ..	Maj R. M-Buchanan ..	N. Murless ..	G. Richards ..	4–6
1950 Tangle, 3–8–0	Lady Baron	W. Payne . ..	E. Smith . ..	3–1
1951 Stephen Paul, 3–8–6.	J. Olding.	H. Persse . ..	N. Sellwood ..	7–2
1952 Easter Bride, 3–7–11	W. Rimell	T. Rimell . ..	E. Fordyce ..	7–1
1953 Fairy Flax, 4–9–2 ..	R. Clark	J. Lawson ..	A. Breasley ..	20–1
1954 Golden Lion, 3–8–4	W. Barrett	C. Mitchell ..	B. Swift	10–1

King's Stand Stakes (contd)	OWNER	TRAINER	JOCKEY	SP
1955 Pappa Fourway, 3–9–0	Mrs E. Goldson	W. Dutton	W. Carr	4–7
1956 Palariva, 3–8–3	Aga Khan	A. Head	R. Poincelet	6–1
1957 Right Boy, 3–8–6	G. Gilbert	W. Dutton	L. Piggott	4–1
1958 Drum Beat, 5–8–9	J. Gerber	W. O'Gorman	A. Breasley	2–1
1959 Chris, 3–8–10	H. Hartley	W. Nevett	J. Sime	9–4
1960 Sound Track, 3–8–6	Lady Hemphill	A. O'Brien	A. Breasley	8–1
1961 Silver Tor, 3–8–0	S. Joel	R. Fetherstonhaugh	G. Lewis	7–4
1962 Cassarate, 3–7–11	Countess M. Batthyany	V. O'Brien	N. Sellwood	5–1
1963 Majority Blue, 3–8–6	J. Muldoon	W. O'Gorman	L. Piggott	100–8
1965 Goldhill, 4–9–1	R. Johnson	M. H. Easterby	J. Etherington	10–1
1966 Roughlyn, 5–9–9	J. Pickering	W. Francis	G. Cadwaladr	20–1
1967 Be Friendly, 3–8–3	P. O'Sullevan	C. Mitchell	A. Breasley	3–1
1968 D'Urberville, 3–8–3	J. H. Whitney	J. Tree	J. Mercer	4–1
1969 Song, 3–8–8	B. P. Jenks	D. Candy	J. Mercer	evens

King George VI and Queen Elizabeth Stakes, 1m 4f

First run 1951.

	OWNER	TRAINER	JOCKEY	SP
1951 Supreme Court, 3–8–4	Mrs T. Lilley	E. Williams	C. Elliott	100–9
1952 Tulyar, 3–8–6	Aga Khan	M. Marsh	C. Smirke	3–1
1953 Pinza, 3–8–4	Sir V. Sassoon	N. Bertie	G. Richards	2–1
1954 Aureole, 4–9–4	The Queen	C. B-Rochfort	E. Smith	9–2
1955 Vimy, 3–8–4	P. Wertheimer	A. Head	R. Poincelet	10–1
1956 Ribot, 4–9–4	Marchese della Rochetta	U. Penco	E. Camici	2–5
1957 Montaval, 4–9–7	R. Strassburger	G. Bridgland	F. Palmer	20–1
1958 Ballymoss, 4–9–7	J. McShain	V. O'Brien	A. Breasley	7–4
1959 Alcide, 4–9–7	Sir H. de Trafford	C. B-Rochfort	W. Carr	2–1
1960 Aggressor, 5–9–7	Sir H. Wernher	J. Gosden	J. Lindley	100–8
1961 Right Royal V, 3–8–7	Mme. J. Couturié	E. Pollet	R. Poincelet	6–4
1962 Match III, 4–9–7	F. Dupré	F. Mathet	Y. Saint-Martin	9–2
1963 Ragusa, 3–8–7	J. Mullion	P. Prendergast	G. Bougoure	4–1
1964 Nasram II, 4–9–7	Mrs H. Jackson	E. Fellows	W. Pyers	100–7
1965 Meadow Court, 3–8–7	G. Bell	P. Prendergast	L. Piggott	6–5
1966 Aunt Edith, 4–9–4	Lieut-Col J. Hornung	N. Murless	L. Piggott	7–2
1967 Busted, 4–9–7	S. Joel	N. Murless	G. Moore	4–1
1968 Royal Palace, 4–9–7	H. J. Joel	N. Murless	A. Barclay	4–7
1969 Park Top, 5–9–4	Duke of Devonshire	B. van Cutsem	L. Piggott	9–4

Royal Lodge Stakes, 1m

Two-year-olds. First run 1946. *Run over 5f in* 1946 and 1947. *Run at Newbury* 1960 and 1963

	OWNER	TRAINER	JOCKEY	SP
1946 Royal Barge, 9–4	A. Allnatt	J. Lawson	C. Richards	8–15
1947 Black Tarquin, 8–2	W. Woodward	C. B-Rochfort	W. Carr	100–30
1948 Swallow Tail, 9–0	Lord Derby	W. Earl	D. Smith	11–4
1949 Tabriz, 9–0	Aga Khan	Fk. Butters	G. Richards	5–2
1950 Fraise du Bois II, 9–0	Aga Khan	H. Wragg	C. Smirke	7–2
1951 Khor-Mousa, 9–0	S. Tate	P. Thrale	K. Gethin	100–7
1952 Neemah, 8–11	Aga Khan	M. Marsh	C. Smirke	5–2
1953 Infatuation 9–0	Sir M. McAlpine	V. Smyth	G. Richards	100–30
1954 Solarium, 9–0	J. O-Patino	F. Armstrong	W. Snaith	6–1
1955 Royal Splendour, 9–0	Mrs G. Kohn	W. Nightingall	A. Breasley	5–2
1956 Noble Venture, 9–0	Begum Aga Khan	H. Wragg	E. Mercer	3–1
1957 Pinched, 9–0	Sir V. Sassoon	N. Murless	L. Piggott	evens
1958 Cantelo, 8–11	W. Hill	C. Elsey	E. Hide	5–4
1959 St. Paddy, 9–0	Sir V. Sassoon	N. Murless	L. Piggott	11–4
1960 Beta, 8–11	Lord Rosebery	J. Jarvis	E. Larkin	9–4

	OWNER	TRAINER	JOCKEY	SP
1961 Escort, 9–0	J. Astor	J. Colling	J. Mercer	9–2
1962 Star Moss, 9–0	Maj H. Broughton	J. A. Waugh	E. Smith	5–1
1963 Casabianca, 9–0	Col B. Hornung	N. Murless	L. Piggott	4–1
1964 Prominer, 9–0	J. Mullion	P. Prendergast	G. Bougoure	3–1
1965 Soft Angels, 8–11	Lady Sassoon	N. Murless	L. Piggott	5–2
1966 Royal Palace, 9–0	H. Joel	N. Murless	L. Piggott	6–4
1967 Remand, 9–0	J. Astor	W. Hern	L. Piggott	13–8
1968 Dutch Bells, 9–0	G. van der Ploeg	H. Price	A. Murray	100–7
1969 Domineering, 9–0	G. A. Pope	N. Murless	A. Barclay	13–2

Queen Elizabeth II Stakes, 1m

First run 1955. *Run at Newbury* 1960 *and* 1963.

	OWNER	TRAINER	JOCKEY	SP
1955 Hafiz II, 3–8–4	Aga Khan	A. Head	R. Poincelet	9–4
1956 Cigalon, 3–8–1	Comte de Kerouara	M. d'Okhuysen	S. Boullenger	8–1
1957 Midget II, 4–8–8	P. Wertheimer	A. Head	A. Breasley	5–6
1958 Major Portion, 3–8–4	H. Joel	T. Leader	E. Smith	1–3
1959 Rosalba, 3–8–2	J. Astor	J. Colling	J. Mercer	5–2
1960 Sovereign Path, 4–8–11	R. Mason	R. Mason	W. Carr	13–8
1961 Le Levanstell, 4–8–11	J. McGrath	S. McGrath	W. Williamson	20–1
1962 Romulus, 3–8–4	C. Engelhard	R. J. Houghton	W. Swinburn	7–4
1963 The Creditor, 3–8–4	Lady Sassoon	N. Murless	L. Piggott	5–4
1964 Linacre, 4–8–11	F. M. O'Ferrall	P. Prendergast	L. Piggott	11–10
1965 Derring-Do, 4–8–11	Mrs H. Renshaw	A. Budgett	A. Breasley	9–4
1966 Hill Rise, 5–9–1	G. A. Pope, Jn.	N. Murless	L. Piggott	7–2
1967 Reform, 3–8–8	M. Sobell	Sir G. Richards	A. Breasley	6–5
1968 World Cup, 3–8–4	J. R. Mullion	P. Prendergast	W. Williamson	7–2
1969 Jimmy Reppin, 4–9–1	Mrs S. Bates	J. Sutcliffe, Jn.		13–8

ASCOT GOLD CUP

See under Ascot

ASCOT STAKES

See under Ascot

ASHWORTH, Peter (b 1924)

Peter Ashworth trains at Treadwell Stables, Epsom. He is married to a daughter of the former jockey, H. Packham. He was apprenticed to Stanley Wootton and H. Wallington and rode on the flat from 1936 to 1955 when he took out a trainer's licence. The best winner he has had so far is Lady Senator who won the Irish One Thousand Guineas.

ASMENA

Asmena, by Goya II out of that great mare Astronomie, won the 1950 Oaks for M. M. Boussac, who two days previously had won the Derby with Galcador.

ASSUMED NAME

No owner is allowed to use an assumed name for the purpose of entering or running horses. Any horse entered under an assumed name is liable to disqualification.

ASTERUS

Bred in France by Baron E. de Rothschild in 1923, Asterus, by Teddy, won five races including the French Two Thousand Guineas in France, while in England he won the Royal Hunt Cup and Champion Stakes. He proved a most successful sire, having a great influence on bloodstock breeding throughout the world.

ASTOR, second Viscount (1879-1952)

Lord Astor, who died at the age of 73, had been a breeder of thoroughbreds for exactly 50 years when in 1950 he divided his famous stud between two of his sons, Mr W. W.

Astor, who eventually succeeded to the title, and Mr J. J. Astor.

Lord Astor never won the Derby but was second in that race with Blink, Buchan, Craig an Eran, Tamar and St Germans. However he won the Two Thousand Guineas with Craig an Eran (1921), Pay Up (1936) and Court Martial (1945) ; the One Thousand Guineas with Winkipop (1910) and Saucy Sue (1925) ; the Oaks with Sunny Jane (1917), Pogrom (1922), Saucy Sue (1925), Short Story (1926) and Pennycomequick (1929) ; the St Leger with Book Law (1927). He also won the Eclipse Stakes five times, the Champion Stakes twice and the Coronation Cup. His horses were trained at Manton, first by Alec Taylor and later by Joe Lawson.

The foundation mare of his stud was Conjure, whom he bought for £100 when still at Oxford. Two other famous mares he owned were Popinjay and Maid of the Mist. He bred all his great winners himself. He never went racing unless he had a runner and never had a bet. For many years he was a member of the Jockey Club.

ASTOR, third Viscount (1908-1966)

The third Viscount Astor succeeded his father in 1952 and was fifty-eight when he died in 1966. He did not enjoy his father's success on the Turf, but he won the 1953 Oaks with Ambiguity trained by R. J. Colling. Other good horses to carry his colours were Hornbeam, Counsel and that great stayer Grey of Falloden whose finest feat was to win the Cesarewitch carrying 9st 6lb.

ASTOR, Hon John Jacob, MBE (b 1919)

Fourth son of the second Viscount Astor, Mr J. J. Astor served during the war in the Household Cavalry and the SAS. In his younger days he rode under both Rules. An owner-breeder on a big scale, he has the majority of his horses with Major W. Hern at West Ilsley, the remainder being with H. E. Smyth at Epsom. His only classic winner so far is Provoke who won the 1965 St Leger. He has the reputation of being one of the most progressive members of the Jockey Club and acts as steward at Ascot and Kempton. He was a member of the Horserace Totalisator Board and has always adopted a realistic attitude to racing's financial problems. Colours: light blue, pink sash.

ATHASI

Bred by Mr Peter Murphy in Co Wicklow, Athasi was by Farasi, who was sold for 35 gn as a yearling. Athasi herself was sold as a yearling for 270 gn and at one time was competing over hurdles without success. Bought by Mr D. W. Barnett and on his death acquired by his brother, Mr W. Barnett, Athasi proved a wonderfully successful brood mare, being the dam of 10 winners of 29 races worth over £50,000. Her offspring included Trigo, winner of the Derby, St Leger, and Irish St Leger ; Athford, winner of the Coronation Cup ; Harinero, winner of the Irish Derby and Irish St Leger ; Primero, who dead-heated for the Irish Derby and won the Irish St Leger ; and Harina, who won £4,128 in stakes and was the grandam both of the Derby winner Tulyar and of St Crespin III, winner of the Prix de l'Arc de Triomphe. Athasi was 27 years old when she died in 1944.

AUNT EDITH

Aunt Edith was bred in 1962 by the West Grinstead Stud and is by Primera out of Fair Edith, by Hyperion. Owned by Lieut-Col John Hornung and trained by Noel Murless, she won the Nassau Stakes, Prix Vermeille, Yorkshire Cup and King George VI and Queen Elizabeth Stakes. When her racing career was over she was sold for export to America.

AURELIUS

Foaled in 1958, Aurelius, by Aureole, belonged to Mrs V. Lilley (later Mrs Hue-Williams) and was trained by

Noel Murless. He won six races including the St Leger, King Edward VII Stakes and Hardwicke Stakes but unfortunately he proved useless as a stallion and was eventually brought back into training, running with mixed fortune over hurdles and fences.

AUREOLE

Aureole was bred by King George VI and is the best horse to have carried the Queen's colours so far. A high mettled chestnut by Hyperion out of Angelola, he needed a great trainer like Sir Cecil Boyd-Rochfort to get the best out of him. After winning the Lingfield Derby Trial in 1953, the year of the Queen's coronation, he was second to Pinza both in the Derby and in the King George VI and Queen Elizabeth Stakes. In the St Leger he failed to stay the distance. As a four-year-old he was a very good horse indeed, winning the Coronation Cup, Hardwicke Stakes and King George VI and Queen Elizabeth Stakes. He has done extremely well as a sire, being champion in 1960 and again in 1961. He has so far sired one Derby winner, St Paddy, and three St Leger winners, St Paddy, Aurelius, and Provoke.

AUTHORITIES, TURF

The recognised Turf Authorities of Great Britain, Ireland and the Channel Islands are:

The Jockey Club
The National Hunt Committee
The Turf Club of Ireland
The Irish National Hunt Steeplechase Committee
The Channel Islands Racing and Hunt Club.

AUTHORITY TO ACT

Nearly all owners give their trainers an 'Authority to Act'. This is a form drawn up by Messrs Weatherby which permits the trainers to make entries, forfeits, declarations and so forth in the name of the owner. An Authority to Act is only valid for a single season.

AUTUMN DOUBLE

The two big handicaps run at Newmarket in October, the Cesarewitch and the Cambridgeshire, are often called the Autumn Double as a lot of punters like to try to couple in bets the winners of these two races.

AYR

Ayr is one of the best racecourses in Great Britain and certainly provides the best racing in Scotland. Sport at the four-day Western Meeting in September is of a very high order indeed with that famous 6f sprint, the Ayr Gold Cup, as the main attraction.

The course itself is left-handed, just over 1½m round and with a straight run-in of 4f. It has easy bends and is almost flat throughout. High numbers are favoured on the 5f and 6f courses, low numbers in races of 7f and a mile.

Joint Clerks of the Course: Mr W. W. McHarg and Mr C. D. Patterson, 24 Sandgate, Ayr. Tel: Ayr 65033-4.

Best Times:

Distance	*Horse-Age-Weight*	*Date*	*Time*
5f	Salan 5-8-2	17-8-69	57.76
5f	Monte Cristo 2-8-0	17-5-46	57.8
6f	The Country Lass 3-6-9	18-9-69	1min 10.2
6f	Sir Bert 2-7-10	17-9-69	1min 9.73
7f	Bilborrow 5-7-1	28-9-69	1min 23.9
7f	Ludham 2-8-6	19-7-66	1min 26.5
8f	Sufi 4-7-13	16-9-59	1min 36
8f	Calypso 2-8-6	18-9-59	1min 39.92
10f	Alcestre 3-8-3	20-9-69	2min 6.86
11f	Empire Way 6-8-9	17-9-59	2min 15.94

Distance	Horse-Age-Weight	Date	Time
13f	Kingfisher Blue 5-8-5	20-9-69	2min 47.88
15f	Cagirama 7-8-11	18-7-66	3min 12.76
17f 90yd	Curry 4-6-13	16-9-55	3min 45
18f	Danger 4-7-3	18-7-49	3min 48.4

Electric times introduced in 1957.

Ayr Gold Cup, 6f

Handicap. First run 1804. *No race* 1939 *to* 1945.

		OWNER	TRAINER	JOCKEY	SP
1930	Heronslea, 3–8–6	W. Smith	M. Peacock	J. Taylor	5–1
1931	Heronslea, 4–9–11	W. Smith	M. Peacock	J. Taylor	8–1
1932	Solenoid, 3–8–9	Mrs C. Mackean	G. Poole	J. Marshall	7–1
1933	Ken Hill, 9–7–8	Sir L. Green	T. Green	E. Fox	10–1
1934	Figaro, 4–9–1	J. Leach	J. Leach	H. Jelliss	7–2
1935	Greenore, 6–9–3	Lady Ludlow	O. Bell	S. Wragg	5–1
1936	Marmaduke Jinks, 4–6–13	Mrs C. Robinson	H. Peacock	A. Richardson	20–1
1937	Daytona, 4–9–0	Sir G. Bullough	J. Jarvis	M. Beary	100–8
1938	Old Reliance, 3–9–2	Sir J. Jarvis	J. Jarvis	E. Smith	8–1
1946	Royal Charger, 4–9–7	Sir J. Jarvis	J. Jarvis	E. Smith	2–1
1947	Kilbelin, 4–7–13	C. Blyth	B. Bullock	W. Carr	6–1
1948	Como, 6–8–9	Capt J. Fielden	G. Armstrong	J. Marshall	10–1
1949	Irish Dance, 6–9–1	H. Stockdale	H. Whiteman	E. Britt	4–1
1950	First Consul, 4–9–7	Maharaja of Rajpipla	F. Armstrong	C. Smirke	2–1
1951	Fair Seller, 5–9–4	E. Davey	E. Davey	R. Sheather	10–1
1952	Vatellus, 4–8–7	A. Bird	J. Pearce	H. Jones	10–1
1953	Blue Butterfly, 4–8–9	F. M. O'Ferrall	H. Wragg	E. Mercer	11–2
1954	Orthopaedic, 3–8–1	Mrs M. Moss	J. Gosden	J. Lindley	11–2
1955	Hook Money, 4–7–11	R. Clark	A. Budgett	W. Elliott	4–1
1956	Precious Heather 4–7–7	A. Bird	J. Gosden	E. Hide	5–1
1957	Jacintha, 6–7–7	G. Munro	W. Lyde	E. Larkin	100–7
1958	Rythmic, 3–8–5	Maj A. Straker	W. Dutton	F. Durr	20–1
1959	Whistling Victor, 3–7–8	R. Galloway	G. Laurence	J. Sime	7–1
1960	Dawn Watch, 5–7–2	W. Kendrick	E. Cousins	L. C. Parkes	100–9
1961	Klondyke Bill, 3–8–7	A. Comerford	C. Benstead	E. Smith	100–8
1962	Janeat, 3–7–11	G. Turnbull	A. Vasey	B. Henry	25–1
1963	Egualita, 3–8–0	R. Sigtia	S. Hall	F. Durr	10–1
1964	Compensation, 5–8–10	Mrs G. Lambton	E. Lambton	P. Robinson	10–1
1965	Kamundu, 3–8–1	M. Higgins	E. Cousins	G. Cadwaladr	100–8
1966	Milesius, 4–7–12	G. Boyd	G. Boyd	N. McIntosh	25–1
1967	Be Friendly, 3–8–9	P. J. O'Sullevan	C. Mitchell	G. Lewis	100–8
1968	Petite Path, 4–7–6	Mrs R. Mason	R. Mason	J. Higgins	100–7
1969	Brief Star, 3–7–0	R. E. Sangster	E. Cousins	L. C. Parkes	10–1

B

BACHELOR'S DOUBLE

Bachelor's Double, a good racehorse and a most influential sire, was an extremely rare type: he was by a non-winning sire, Tredennis, out of a non-winning dam, by a non-winning maternal grandsire, out of a non-winning grandam.

BAHRAM

Bahram, the last horse to win the 'Triple Crown', died in the Argentine in 1956 at the age of 24. Bred and owned by the Aga Khan, he was by Blandford out of Friar's Daughter, a mare the Aga Khan had bought for less than £300. Trained by Frank Butters, Bahram proved himself one of the outstanding horses of the century, winning all his nine races and over £43,000 in stakes. His five successes as a two-year-old included the National Breeders Produce Stakes, the Gimcrack Stakes and the Middle Park Stakes. the following year (1935) he won the Two Thousand Guineas, the Derby, the St James's Palace Stakes and the St Leger.

Placid and indolent by nature, Bahram's victories were seldom spectacular but he was never really in danger of defeat and certainly no opponent ever succeeded in getting to the bottom of him. He might well have made a superb four-year-old, but his owner hustled him off to the stud with almost indecent haste after the St Leger.

The Aga Khan once declared he would never part with Bahram, but to the undisguised resentment of many English breeders, he sold him in 1940 for £40,000 to an American syndicate. Bahram was not in the best of health when he landed in America and breeders there never really took to him. In 1946 he was exported to the Argentine. For so great a horse his stud record was rather disappointing, but his career as a sire was hardly helped by the changes in climate and environment. The best horses he sired in England were Big Game (Two Thousand Guineas), Turkhan (St Leger) and Persian Gulf (Coronation Cup).

BAILEY, Sir Abe (1865-1940)

For more than fifty years one of the leading personalities in public life in South Africa, Sir Abe Bailey bred and raced on a lavish scale in England, among his trainers being H. L. Cottrill, R. Day, Hon. G. Lambton, H. S. Persse and J. Lawson. He made many attempts to win the Derby but the nearest he came to success was when Robin Goodfellow finished second to Bahram in 1935. The following year Sir Abe gained his only classic success when his 33-1 outsider Lovely Rosa won the Oaks. He owned that fine stayer and very successful sire Son-in-Law and he won the Ascot Gold Cup with Foxlaw and Tiberius. He was made a member of the Jockey Club in 1929. Towards the end of his life he had to have both his legs amputated but this misfortune was not permitted to interfere with his many interests or his pleasure in the society of his friends.

BAILLIE, John Ursel (b 1905)

Mr Baillie, before becoming a member of the London Stock Exchange, was a regular soldier in the Coldstream Guards. Before the war he was a well-known point-to-point rider and also rode winners under Jockey Club and National Hunt rules. His first trainer was the late Dawson Waugh, and he now has horses with J. A. J. Waugh,

H. R. Price, Hon T. A. Corbett and Capt P. R. Lowis. He is the owner of the successful Crimbourne Stud, where those two fine sprinters Lucasland and So Blessed were bred. He has recently assumed office as President of the Racehorse Owners' Association. Colours: black, straw sleeves, light blue cap.

BAIRD, Brig, E. W. D. (1866-1956)

Brig Baird was a member of the Jockey Club for no fewer than 62 years. He won the Grand National in 1887 with his half-bred hunter Playfair and the St Leger in 1907 with Wool Winder. When in the 10th Hussars he was a very useful amateur rider and a high class polo player.

BALDING, Arthur (b 1906)

Arthur Balding served his apprenticeship with Bert Lines and Peter Gilpin. He won the One Thousand Guineas in 1927 on Cresta Run, and other races of which he rode the winner were the Chester Cup, Kempton Jubilee, City and Suburban and Queen's Prize. He began training in 1930 and his stables are at Bawtry, near Doncaster.

BALDING, Gerald (b 1936)

Elder brother of Ian Balding, Gerald ('Toby') Balding first took out a licence in 1957. His stable at Fyfield House, Weyhill, near Andover, is a 'mixed' one and the emphasis is on jumpers rather than on flat-race horses. Balding's big triumph was to win the 1969 Grand National with Highland Wedding, but on the flat he has won the Portland Handicap and the Buckingham Palace Stakes.

BALDING, Ian (b 1938)

Ian Balding is a son of the late Gerald Balding, an outstanding polo player and also a successful trainer, and younger brother of Gerald.

A good all-round athlete—he played rugby for Cambridge—Ian Balding was a successful amateur rider and still takes an occasional ride in hunter-chases. He assisted the late Capt Peter Hastings-Bass at Kingsclere after a period with Herbert Blagrave and on the former's death in 1964 he took over the Kingsclere stable. The best horse he has so far trained is Silly Season who won over £60,000 in stakes, including the Coventry Stakes, Dewhurst Stakes, St James's Palace Stakes, Champion Stakes and Lockinge Stakes. He also trained Berkeley Springs who won the Cheveley Park Stakes and was second in the One Thousand Guineas and the Oaks.

The Queen is a patron of the Kingsclere stable and other owners include Lord Sefton, Mr Paul Mellon, Mrs Peter Hastings, Lord Cadogan, Hon Julian Berry, Mrs J. A. MacDougal, Mrs John Rogerson and Mr H. G. Blagrave.

In 1969 Ian Balding married the late Capt Hastings-Bass's daughter.

BALLYMOSS

One of the greatest of Irish horses, Ballymoss is a chestnut by Mossborough out of Indian Call. He was bred by Mr Richard Ball and bought as a yearling by the American owner Mr J. McShain for 4,500 gn. Trained by Vincent O'Brien, he was second to Crepello in the 1957 Derby and then won the Irish Derby and the St Leger. As a four-year-old he was the best horse in Europe, his victories including the Coronation Cup, the Eclipse Stakes, the King George VI and Queen Elizabeth Stakes and the Prix de l'Arc de Triomphe. He failed in the Laurel Park International Stakes. Altogether he won £107,165 in stakes for his owner. The best horse he has so far sired is Royal Palace, winner of the Two Thousand Guineas, Derby, Coronation Cup, Eclipse Stakes and King George VI Stakes.

BALTO

The French stayer Balto, by Wild Risk, won the Ascot Gold Cup in 1962.

BANKS, John

John Banks, a native of Glasgow, is an owner of racehorses and a brash, bold and cheerful bookmaker who has introduced some much-needed life and enterprise into the betting-ring in recent seasons. In 1969 he won the Royal Hunt Cup at Ascot with Kamundu. In June 1970 he announced his intention of giving up ownership and concentrating on bookmaking.

BARCALDINE

Foaled in 1878, Barcaldine was a great racehorse, never meeting with defeat, and a very successful sire. The interesting point about him is that he was almost incestuously bred, his sire Solon being out of Darling's Dam, while his grandam was out of Darling's Dam, too, He himself was largely responsible for the continuation of the Matchem male line.

BARCLAY, Alexander (b 1948)

'Sandy' Barclay is the son of the Scottish trainer John Barclay. He joined Harry Whiteman's stable in 1964, rode his first winner in 1965 and in 1968 was appointed first jockey to Noel Murless's stable, the most powerful in the country. In that season he rode 116 winners and only Lester Piggott rode more. He won the One Thousand Guineas on Caergwrle; the Coronation Cup, Eclipse Stakes and King George VI and Queen Elizabeth Stakes on Royal Palace; The Oaks in 1970 on Lupe, the Coronation Cup in 1970 on Caliban and the Grand Prix de St Cloud on Hopeful Venture. He is already a great favourite with French racegoers, while in England he is regarded as the best young rider since Lester Piggott. He was top apprentice in 1966.

BARCLAY, Andrew Tannock (b 1923)

Andrew Barclay trains at Annan, Dumfriesshire. He himself rode as a professional under National Hunt rules and started training in 1951. His successes include the Northumberland Plate, Cumberland Plate, Lanark Silver Bell (twice), and the Caledonian Hunt Cup.

BARLING, Frank (d 1935)

Originally a veterinary surgeon in Wales, Frank Barling became trainer to Lord Glanely at the end of World War I but his health was poor and he did not retain the appointment for long. His big year was 1919 when he won the Derby with Lord Glanely's Grand Parade and trained seven winners for the same owner at Royal Ascot. He was the father of Geoffrey Barling, a much-respected Newmarket trainer.

BARLING, Geoffrey (b 1902)

Geoffery Barling is son of the late Frank Barling. He himself has held a trainer's licence since 1932 but his career was interrupted during World War II by service overseas with the Royal Artillery. His best winners include Pandora Bay (Ribblesdale Stakes and third in the Oaks), Tower Walk (National Stakes, Greenham Stakes, Nunthorpe Stakes and Prix de l'Abbaye), Frawn (Ascot Stakes, twice), Le Tellier (Chester Cup), Small Slam (Royal Hunt Cup), Piaco (Doncaster Cup and Northumberland Plate), Granados (City and Suburban) and Outcrop (Yorkshire Oaks and Park Hill Stakes). His stables are at Primrose Cottage, Newmarket, and his owners include the Duke of Sutherland, Mrs J. L. Priestman, Mr J. Westall, Lady Jessel, Lady Fisher, Mr V. Hardy, Major C. Nathan, Mr E. Benjamin, Commander and Lady Doris Vyner, Mrs C. Philipson, Mrs E. H. Vestey and Lady Beaverbrook.

BASTARD, THE

The Bastard, by Spion Kop, belonged to the late Lord Rosebery and his most important success was the Yorkshire Cup. He won a race at Newmarket at 100-1 when the Tote was just beginning to operate and bookmakers were offering extravagant prices. He was exported to Australia where, with surprising refinement, he was re-named The Buzzard. He proved an outstanding success as a sire there.

BATH

Bath provides opportunities in congenial surroundings for horses that for the most part are of modest ability. It is an oval track of just over 1½m with a straight run-in of 4f. The course is laid on old downland turf and the going is usually good. Low numbers are favoured in races from 5f to 1m.

Clerk of the Course and Secretary: Capt C. B. Toller, Greenfields, Little Rissington, nr Cheltenham, Glos. Tel: Bourton-on-the-Water 517.

BATTHYANY, Countess Margit (b 1911)

Countess Margit Batthyany lives in Switzerland and is a well-known figure in European racing. She has horses in England with W. Elsey, in Ireland with J. Oxx, in France with A. Klimscha, and in Germany with Count Pejacsevics. She won the 1967 Oaks with Pia whom she had bred herself. Pia had been sent up for sale as a yearling but failed to reach a modest reserve. Colours: blue, orange sleeves, check cap.

BATTHYANY, Prince

A Hungarian who loved the British way of life, or at any rate the way of

Best Times:

Distance	*Horse-Age-Weight*	*Date*	*Time*
5f	Dayspring 3-9-0	27-8-66	62.5
5f	Port Margaret 2-8-0	13-5-53	62.2
5f 167yd	Shipwreck 5-7-10	26-8-66	1min 10.7
5f 167yd	Greek Skittle 2-8-12	27-8-66	1min 11.9
7f 8yd	Diplomatic Cloak 4-8-3	2-9-61	1min 27.8
7f 8yd	Spry 2-8-10	23-8-62	1min 31.8
8f 8yd	Danella 6-8-7	5-7-68	1min 40.2
8f 8yd	Sweet Sour 2-8-5	1-9-62	1min 45.4
10f 50yd	Ribomar 3-9-4	14-6-69	2min 10.1
13f 12yd	Vendage 4-7-9	11-6-65	2min 49.4
17f 27yd	Cuillins 7-8-2	15-6-68	3min 48.4
17f 194yd	Baytree 3-7-11	30-8-69	4min 0.5

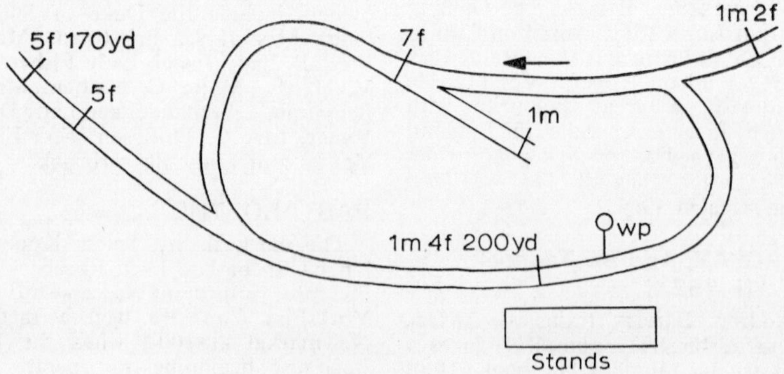

BATH

life of the British aristocracy, Prince Batthyany won the 1875 Derby with Galopin and was the breeder of the great St Simon. The Prince died on Two Thousand Guineas day 1884 on the steps of the Jockey Club Luncheon Room at Newmarket.

BAXTER, Geoffrey (b 1946)

Geoffrey Baxter was five years with A. Budgett and then transferred to I. Lewis's stable. He rode his first winner in 1962 and his best total so far for one season is 17. In 1970 he became attached to Budgett's stable again.

BAYARDO

Bayardo, owned and bred by Mr A. W. Cox who raced under the name of 'Mr Fairie', was probably the best of the many great horses trained by Alec Taylor at Manton. Foaled in 1906, he was by Bay Ronald, who was no more than a fair sort of handicapper, out of Galicia, by Galopin. Galicia also bred the Derby winner Lemberg and Kwang-Su who was second in the Derby. In appearance Bayardo was a long, lop-eared bay who stood noticeably over at the knee. His weak point was his sensitive, fleshy feet that gave him trouble throughout his career.

He came to hand early and was a brilliant two-year-old, winning in succession the New Stakes, the National Breeders Produce Stakes, the Richmond Stakes, the Buckenham Stakes, the Rous Memorial Stakes, the Middle Park Plate and the Dewhurst Plate.

It was a very cold, dry spring in 1909. Even the best Manton gallops were hard and Bayardo had to be treated with care on account of his feet. He was nothing like at his best when he finished unplaced in the Two Thousand Guineas and he was still backward when he was down the course behind Minoru in the Derby. Soon afterwards, though, Taylor had him to his liking and Bayardo won in succession the Prince of Wales's Stakes at Ascot, the Sandringham Foal Stakes at Sandown, the Eclipse Stakes, the Duchess of York Plate at Hurst Park, the St Leger, the Doncaster Stakes, the Champion Stakes, the Lowther Stakes, the Sandown Foal Stakes, the Limekiln Stakes and the Liverpool St Leger.

As a four-year-old he was better than ever and started off by winning the Newmarket Biennial Stakes, the Chester Vase, the Ascot Gold Cup and the Dullingham Plate. In the Goodwood Cup he started at 20-1 on and the race was regarded as a mere formality. Unfortunately Danny Maher rode a foolish, over-confident race on him and the great horse, in what was his final appearance on a racecourse was beaten a neck by a three-year-old, White Magic. In all Bayardo had won 22 races worth over £44,000.

He was a great success as a sire, and it was a severe loss to breeders when he died of a thrombosis aged 11. He sired two 'Triple Crown' winners, Gay Crusader and Gainsborough.

BAYTOWN

Baytown was a somewhat unfashionably bred grey, by Achtoi out of Princess Herodias, by Poor Boy. He was a pretty good horse, though, and won 10 races, including the Irish Two Thousand Guineas and Derby. He is remembered today chiefly as the sire of Kong, dam of the Two Thousand Guineas and Derby winner Nimbus, and of that highly successful sire Grey Sovereign.

BAYUDA

Bayuda, by Bayardo, won the Oaks in 1919 for Lady James Douglas. At the stud she bred one moderate winner.

BEAM

Lord Durham's Beam, by Galloper Light, won the Oaks in 1927. She was not a success as a brood mare.

BEARY, Michael (d 1956)

Michael Beary was a voluble and engaging Irishman from Tipperary. He spent part of his apprenticeship in H. S. Persse's stable and it was on Steve Donoghue's recommendation that he obtained his first ride in public. At his best—consistency was hardly one of his virtues—he was a top-class jockey, a stylist and often brilliant with difficult horses. He won the 1937 Derby on Midday Sun, the St Leger on Trigo and Ridge Wood, and the Oaks on Udaipur. He started training in 1951 and won the Two Thousand Guineas that year with Ki Ming, but he never had any head for business and was soon in financial difficulties. He was a poor man when he died. His great trouble throughout his life was his own unequable temperament and an over-abundant self-confidence that at times could be extremely irritating.

BEASLEY, Harry (d 1959)

Harry Beasley was the brother of Pat Beasley and the son of Harry Beasley senior who won the 1891 Grand National on Come Away. His uncle, Tom Beasley, rode three Grand National winners, while his own son Bobby won the 1961 National on Nicolaus Silver.

Soon after the conclusion of World War I Harry Beasley came to England and rapidly established himself as a highly competent rider. For several seasons he rode for 'Atty' Persse's stable and in 1929 he won the Two Thousand Guineas on Mr Jinks. His best season was in 1930 when he rode 56 winners.

BEASLEY, Patrick Thomas (b 1906)

A member of a famous Irish racing family, 'Rufus' Beasley was born in 1906. He had a long and successful career as a jockey and for many years was associated with Sir Cecil Boyd-Rochfort's stable. He won the St Leger on Boswell and the Ascot Gold Cup on Precipitation. Since 1946 he has trained at Malton in Yorkshire. He has won the Cambridgeshire three times (twice with Sterope), the Royal Hunt Cup, the Wokingham Stakes, the Middle Park Stakes, the Zetland Gold Cup and the Manchester November Handicap. His patrons include Mr W. G. Barker, Mrs A. J. R. Collins, Mrs John Galbraith, Mr W. H. Harrison, Lord Lambton, Sir Kenneth Parkinson and Major J. Shaw.

BEATTY, Hon Peter (1910-1949)

Younger son of Admiral of the Fleet Lord Beatty, Mr Peter Beatty was 28 years of age when he bought the French colt Bois Roussel for 8,000 gn in April 1938. Two months later Bois Roussel, trained by Fred Darling, won him the Derby by four lengths. Mr Beatty, who bred the 1948 Two Thousand Guineas winner My Babu, suffered throughout his life from defective eyesight. He knew he was faced with total blindness when he fell to his death from a window of the Ritz Hotel in 1949.

BEAVERBROOK, Lady

Lady Beaverbrook took up racing following the death of her husband, the newspaper proprietor, on the advice, it is said, of Lord Rosebery. In recent years she has become one of the boldest bidders at the sale ring, both here and on occasion also in America. Her horses were trained originally by Walter Nightingall; on his death they went to Sir Gordon Richards and A. Breasley. In October 1969 she also became a patron of G. Barling's stable. Colours: beaver brown, maple green cross-belts and cap.

BEBE GRANDE

Owned and bred by Mr J. S. Gerber and trained by 'Sam' Armstrong, Bebe Grande, by Niccolo dell'Arca, won eight races and over £18,000 in stakes. As a two-year-old in 1952 her victories included the National Breeders Produce Stakes and the Champagne Stakes. The following season she was second in the Two Thousand Guineas and third two days later in the One Thousand Guineas. She has failed so far to come up to expectations as a brood mare.

BECKWITH-SMITH, Major Peter (b 1919)

Major Peter Beckwith-Smith was educated at Eton and the RMC and served in the Welsh Guards from 1938-46. He is a Justice of the Peace and a Deputy Lieutenant in the County of Surrey. He has been Clerk of the Course at Lingfield since 1947; at Epsom since 1964; and at Sandown since 1966. He held that office at Aintree from 1950 to 1956 and at Hurst Park from 1956 to 1962.

BEDFORD, fifth Duke of (1765-1802)

The Duke of Bedford was only 25 years of age when he won the 1789 Derby with Skyscraper. The Duke also won the Derby in 1791 and 1797. He was 37 years old when he died as the result of an old injury received when playing cricket as a boy at Westminster.

BEEBY, George (b 1904)

The son of a well-known horse-dealer in the Midlands, George Beeby took out a trainer's licence in 1924. At first he was associated with jumpers and trained many good chasers for the first Lord Bicester, including Silver Fame, Roimond and Finnure. In due course his stable became a 'mixed' one but now he confines his attention to the flat. He trained that good but temperamental sprinter Grey Sovereign, subsequently a highly successful sire, and among the races he has won are the Stewards Cup, the Cambridgeshire, the Wokingham Stakes and the City and Surburban. His stables are at Compton in Berkshire and his owners include Mrs G. Janson, Mr G. C. Todd, Mrs R. Lamb and Mr A. E. S. Nuttall.

BEESWING

Foaled in 1833, Beeswing, by Dr Syntax, was a very tough mare that raced for eight seasons. She won 51 races including the Ascot Gold Cup and the Doncaster Cup (four times). She was then used as a pack hack for a year before starting her stud career. She was dam of Newminster, who won the St Leger and became champion sire, and of Nunnykirk, winner of the Two Thousand Guineas.

BELL, Capt O. M. D. (1871-1949)

Capt 'Ossie' Bell was a charming, modest Australian who, after service in World War I, started training at Lambourn. He met with considerable success, winning the Derby in 1928 with Felstead and the One Thousand Guineas and the Oaks in 1938 with that very fine filly Rockfel. He died aged 78.

BELLACOSE

Foaled in 1932, Bellacose, by Sir Cosmo, was a fine sprinter of superb physique who shouldered big weights without apparent difficulty. Owned by Capt P. Dunne and trained by R. J. Colling, he won 12 races worth over £8,000, including the July Cup twice, the Cork and Orrery Stakes and the Granville Stakes. He carried 9st 10lb when he won the July Cup as a two-year-old, 10st 8lb when he won the following season.

BELLA PAOLA

Bella Paola, owned and bred by M. F. Dupré and trained in France by F. Mathet, was foaled in 1955 and is by Ticino out of a mare by Gundomar; thus she is essentially German in pedigree. A filly of quite outstanding ability, she won the One Thousand Guineas, the Oaks and the Champion Stakes in England; the Grand Criterium and the Prix Vermeille in France.

BELLE OF ALL

Bred by the Earl of Dunraven in

1948, Belle of All, by Nasrullah, won four races and over £25,000 for Lord Hothfield, including the One Thousand Guineas, Coronation Stakes and Cheveley Park Stakes. The best of her offspring has been Principal Boy, winner of the News of the World Stakes and the Peter Hastings Stakes.

BENSTEAD, Christopher John (b 1928)

John Benstead began training under National Hunt rules in 1955 and in 1960 he took out a licence for the flat. His stables are at Epsom and his owners include Mr B. G. Bearman, Lieut-Col J. D. C. Brownlow, Mr R. C. Boucher, Mr E. R. Hill, Col J. D. Clague, Lady Hyndley, Miss M. J. Hindley, Mr J. de Las Casas and Mr C. F. Sparrowhawk. He trained Orchardist, who was first past the post in the 1929 Cesarewitch but was subsequently relegated to second place by the Stewards for 'boring'. However, the most notable performer with which he has so far been associated is Operatic Society who won 30 races and well over £20,000 in stakes.

BENTINCK, Lord George (1802-1848)

The outstanding personality in English racing from 1836 to 1846 was unquestionably Lord George Bentinck, son of the fifth Duke of Portland. "He feared no one", wrote the diarist Charles Greville, who knew him as well as any man, "and did nothing by halves".

Lord George was an owner on a big scale and a fearless gambler. In 1846 he quite suddenly sold his horses and decided to devote himself to politics as assiduously as he had devoted himself to the Turf. In the House of Commons he became the leader of the newly formed Protectionist Party with Disraeli as his lieutenant. Two years later he died of a heart attack.

He was the dominating member of the Jockey Club and introduced order and regularity into race-meetings, up till then very rough and ready affairs, with a view to improving the sport from the spectators' point of view. He declared unrelenting war on the crooks and defaulters that infested the Turf and it was largely through his efforts that the Running Rein fraud was unmasked, Running Rein, first past the post in the 1844 Derby, being in reality a four-year-old called Maccabaeus. In appreciation, grateful followers of racing presented him with a sum of money which at his suggestion was used to start a fund (Bentinck Benevolent Fund) to help trainers, jockeys and dependants who had fallen on hard times. Lord George devised the system of different priced enclosures and insisted on punctuality, fining clerks of the course ten shillings for every minute that a race was started late. He also insisted on a comprehensive number board and every horse being numbered on the racecard. He ordered horses to be saddled in one special place and to parade in front of the stands. He banned the pernicious custom of winning owners giving a present to the judge after a big race. He greatly improved the system of starting and he was largely responsible for the development of Goodwood. To sum up, he did much to banish the corruption that was bringing the Turf into utter disrepute, while his administrative reforms were a stepping-stone between the haphazard, rough-and-ready race-meetings of the early nineteenth century and the organised, disciplined sport that exists today.

Lord George was not a wholly likeable character although by and large he served racing so well. Aloof to the point of arrogance, he himself sometimes did things in the sphere of racing that in a more enlightened and less privileged age might well have got him 'warned off'. Those who knew him intimately could detect a strain of hypocrisy, or at the very least of remarkable self deception, that enabled him to pursue unblushingly a course of conduct that he would have been the first to condemn in others.

BENTLEY, Walter (b 1936)

Walter Bentley was apprenticed to A. Vasey and rode his first winner in 1953. He can go to scale at 7st 3lb and in his best season so far rode 23 winners.

BERTIE, Norman

Norman Bertie was for many years employed in Fred Darling's stable and rose to the position of head lad there. After Darling's retirement, he trained for some years at Newmarket, but although he held the actual licence much of the control of the stable was in the hands of Jack Clayton, at that time the late Sir Victor Sasson's racing manager. The stable's main triumphs were to win the Derby and the King George VI and Queen Elizabeth Stakes with Pinza; the National Breeders Produce Stakes, Cheveley Park Stakes, One Thousand Guineas and Coronation Stakes with Belle of All.

BETTING SHOPS

Betting shops opened under the new Betting and Gaming Act on 1st May 1961.

BEVERLEY

Beverley can hardly be rated one of the leading North-country courses but it is run in enterprising go-ahead fashion and provides a friendly atmosphere and good entertainment. It is a wide, flat, oval course of just over 1½m with a straight run-in of 4f. High numbers are favoured in races over 5 and 6f. The Charles Elsey Challenge Trophy run at the Spring Meeting honours the memory of one of the most famous and popular of Yorkshire trainers.

Clerk of the Course: Major D. W. A. Swannell, MBE, 9 North Bar Without, Beverley, Yorkshire. Tel: Office—Beverley 882587; Racecourse—882645.

Best Times:

Distance	*Horse-Age-Weight*	*Date*	*Time*
5f	Raffingora 4-9-7	18-10-69	61.8
5f	Folle Rousse 2-8-4	5-7-68	62.6
7f	Bilsborrow 9-7-6	28-8-69	1min 25.2
7f	Fair Winter 2-8-7	28-9-66	1min 29.4
8f	Candid Picture 6-8-9	9-6-66	1min 38.2
8f	Laroyso 2-7-11	18-10-69	1min 40.2
10f	Bestofive 4-7-13	18-10-69	2min 2.4
12f	Chicago 3-7-5	15-6-67	2min 33.2
16f	Farur 4-7-4	15-6-67	3min 34.8

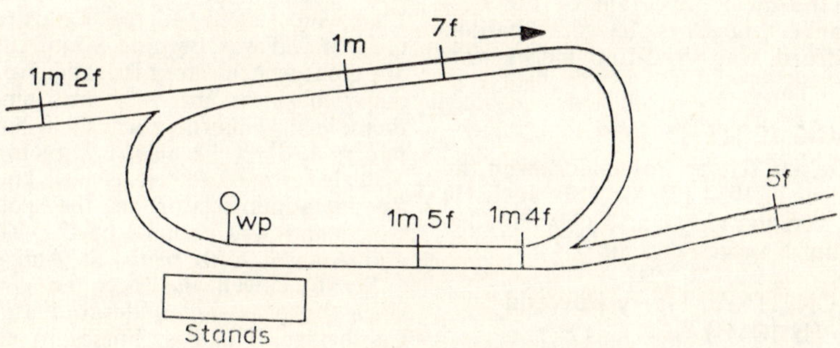

BEVERLEY

BIDWELL-TOPHAM, James

Mr Bidwell-Topham has been connected with Aintree since he was a small boy and was appointed Clerk of the Course there in 1956.

BIG GAME

Bred at the National Stud in 1939, Big Game was a massive heavy-topped colt by Bahram out of the brilliant Myrobella, by Tetratema. Leased to King George VI for racing and trained by Fred Darling, he was a really good horse up to 1¼m; in fact his only defeat was in the Derby, in which his stamina gave out. His eight victories included the Two Thousand Guineas, the Champion Stakes, the Coventry Stakes and the Champagne Stakes.

He never quite fulfilled expectations as a sire and his fillies were noticeably more successful than his colts. He got two classic winners, Queenpot (One Thousand Guineas) and Ambiguity (Oaks). The best of his colts was Combat, the unbeaten winner of nine races worth over £7,000. He died in 1963.

BIGGEST FIELD

The biggest field for a race under Jockey Club rules was 58 in the Lincolnshire Handicap in 1948.

BLACK CHERRY FAMILY

Foaled in 1892, Black Cherry is the ancestress of classic winners such as Sun Chariot, Carrozza, Santa Claus, Night Hawk and Cherry Lass. Perhaps the most important of her descendants, though, is the great stallion Blandford, who sired four Derby winners.

BLACK JESTER

Black Jester, by Polymelus, won the St Leger in 1914 for Mr J. B. Joel. He also won the City and Suburban. He was not a succes as a sire.

BLACKSHAW, Harry Fawcus (b 1919)

Harry Blackshaw was apprenticed to the late Dawson Waugh at Newmarket. He rode with considerable success and had lost his right to claim the allowance before he was 17. He joined the Army in 1939 and served for six years in the Royal Army Veterinary Corps. On demobilisation he rode for a time under both Rules before taking out a licence to train in 1951. His stables are at Middleham, Yorkshire, and his owners include Mrs June Fattorini, Mr D. Ward, Mr W. Gibson, Mr R. W. Dods and Mr E. A. Brown.

BLACK TARQUIN

Bred in America in 1945, Mr W. Woodward's Black Tarquin, by Rhodes Scholar, was trained by Sir Cecil Boyd-Rochfort. He won eight races including the Gimcrack Stakes, St James's Palace Stakes and the St Leger. In a famous race for the Ascot Gold Cup he was vanquished by Alycidon. He was not a very successful sire but got that very game stayer Trelawny.

BLACKWELL, George

He is one of the few trainers to have won both the Derby and the Grand National. He won the Derby in 1903 with Rock Sand and the Grand National in 1923 with Sergeant Murphy.

BLACKWELL, Thomas Francis, M.B.E. (b 1912)

During World War II Mr Tom Blackwell served in the Coldstream Guards and was Brigade Major to the 5th Guards Armoured Brigade. He has many business interests and among them he is Chairman of Turf Newspapers Ltd. He is also a Director of Tote Investors Ltd. He is well known as an administrator in the golfing world and was captain of the Royal and Ancient Golf Club, St Andrews.

Mr Blackwell has been an owner since he was an undergraduate at Cambridge. The best horses to carry his colours so far are Rich and Rare, whose victories included the Windsor Castle Stakes and Cheveley Park Stakes; Silver Cloud, winner of the Chester Vase and Princess of Wales's Stakes; and Potier, winner of the Stewards Cup. All these three were trained by Sir Jack Jarvis, and both Silver Cloud and Potier were bred at Mr Blackwell's Langham Hall Stud, Bury St Edmunds. His energy, drive and business experience have made Mr Blackwell an invaluable member of the Jockey Club and his term of office as Senior Steward in 1966 was rated an eminently successful one. He was largely responsible for the introduction of starting stalls.

On the death of Sir Jack Jarvis in 1968, his horses were transferred to Bruce Hobbs. When the Jockey Club and the National Hunt Committee were amalgamated, he was appointed a Deputy Senior Steward.

BLAGRAVE, Herbert Gratwicke (b 1899)

Herbert Blagrave was a goodish cricketer in his younger days. He took out a licence to train in 1928 and since then has conducted an extremely successful private stable at Beckhampton, Wiltshire, the horses belonging either to himself or, until her death, to his wife. Ascot has always been his lucky course and his victories there include the Royal Hunt Cup (three times), the Gold Vase, the King Edward VII Stakes, the Coronation Stakes, the Ribblesdale Stakes, the Ascot Stakes and the Granville Stakes. He has also won the Manchester Cup and the Kempton Jubileee (three times). He is Governing Director of the Harwood Stud, Newbury, and of the Mount Prospect Stud, Co Kildare. Colours: maroon and light blue hoops, maroon cap.

BLAIR ATHOL

Blair Athol was bred, owned and trained by Mr William I'Anson at Malton, Yorkshire. He was a superbly bred colt being by the great sire Stockwell out of Blink Bonny, winner of the Derby and the Oaks. He had never run before the Derby but he won that race comfortably and he won the St Leger as well. The year of Blair Athol's triumphs was 1864 and that was the last year that the owner of the Derby winner had to contribute towards the cost of the police at Epsom and to the judge's fee as well.

BLAKENEY

Blakeney was bred by Arthur Budgett in 1966 and is a handsome bay colt by Hethersett out of Windmill Girl, by Hornbeam. Windmill Girl ran second in the Oaks. As a yearling Blakeney went up for sale at Newmarket but failed to reach a reserve of 5,000 gn. Budgett therefore retained him to train himself, disposing of shares to Mrs H. H. Renshaw and Mrs J. M. Carnegie.

As a two-year-old Blakeney ran twice, winning the Houghton Stakes at Newmarket on the second occasion. As a three-year-old he was a distinctly unlucky second to The Elk in the Lingfield Derby Trial and then, ridden by E. Johnson, he won the Derby by a length from Shoemaker with the unlucky Prince Regent a length away third.

Subsequently Blakeney was unplaced in the Irish Sweeps Derby, the St Leger and the Prix de l'Arc de Triomphe. Excuses were advanced for him on each occasion but inevitably his stock slumped and it began to be thought that he was a below-average winner of the Derby, which indeed is probably the case. In 1970 he failed in the Jockey Club Stakes but managed to win the Ormonde Stakes at Chester.

BLANDFORD

Blandford was one of the greatest sires of this century. Bred at the National Stud, he was by Swynford out of Blanche. He was a delicate foal and as a yearling he was bought by Mr R. C. Dawson, the Whatcombe trainer, and his brother, Mr S. C. Dawson, for 720 gn. He was by no means easy to train, being heavy-topped and not possessing the best of joints. In fact he only ran four times, winning on three occasions. When he died at the comparatively early age of 16 in 1935 his stock had won over 300 races worth over £327,000. He sired four Derby winners—Trigo (1929), Blenheim (1930), Windsor Lad (1934) and Bahram (1935). He was champion sire three times and in the year of his death he was champion both in England and France. In France he sired Brantôme, one of the most brilliant horses in France in the inter-war era.

BLENHEIM

Bred by Lord Carnarvon and bought as a yearling on behalf of the Aga Khan for 4,100 gn, Blenheim was by Blandford out of Malva. He won the 1930 Derby, trained by R. C. Dawson and ridden by Harry Wragg. Owing to a strained tendon he never ran again afterwards. As a sire he was an outstanding success. In his first crop of runners he got Mumtaz Begum, dam of Nasrullah ; in his second crop the Derby winner Mahmoud. He also sired Donatello II, who was bred in Italy and after a distinguished racing career became an influential sire in England. Exported to America in his prime, Blenheim did equally well over there, his best winners being Whirlaway and Jet Pilot.

BLINK BONNY

Blink Bonny, by Melbourne, was owned by Mr William I'Anson and trained by him at Malton in Yorkshire. She won eight of her eleven races as a two-year-old and the following season won both the Derby and the Oaks. Charlton, the jockey who partnered her in her Epsom triumphs, pulled her in the St Leger at the instigation of John Jackson, a bookmaker who specialised in the corruption of jockeys. Blink Bonny was the dam of the 1864 Derby winner Blair Athol.

BLOODSTOCK

See THOROUGHBRED, ORIGINS OF THE.

BLOWER, THE

'The Blower' is a special office-to-course telephone service for the benefit of bookmakers. It is operated by the Exchange Telegraph Co. ('Extel') which has direct telephonic communication with most racecourses, paying rental for special telephones.

BLUE PETER

Bred and owned by Lord Rosebery, Blue Peter was an exceptionally handsome chestnut colt by Fairway out of Fancy Free. Jack Jarvis gave him every chance to develop his strength and as a two-year-old he did not appear till the autumn when he was fifth in the Imperial Produce Stakes at Kempton and second in the Middle Park Stakes at Newmarket.

This policy of patience paid a rich dividend. Blue Peter was a magnificent three-year-old and was undefeated in 1939, winning the Blue Riband Trial Stakes at Epsom, the Two Thousand Guineas, the Derby and the Eclipse Stakes, in all of which races he was ridden by Eph Smith. He did a marvellous trial before the St Leger, in which he would have met the unbeaten French colt Pharis, but the outbreak of war prevented the St Leger from being run. As such uncertainty existed over the future of racing, Lord Rosebery retired Blue Peter to stud forthwith. Blue Peter, who died aged 21 in 1957, was hardly the success anticipated as a sire. The best horses he got were Ocean Swell (Derby and Gold Cup), Botticelli (Gold Cup) and Peter Flower (Hardwicke Stakes and Kempton Jubilee).

BOIARD

The French colt Boiard won the Ascot Gold Cup in 1874, beating the strongest field there has ever been for that race. He defeated the first and second in the Two Thousand Guineas ; the first, second and third in the

Derby; the winner of the Oaks; the first, second and third in the St Leger; and the first, second and third in the Grand Prix de Paris.

BOIS ROUSSEL

Bois Roussel was bred in France by M. L. Volterra and was by Vatout out of that famous mare Plucky Liège, who was 23 years old when she foaled him. He never ran as a two-year-old and after winning the Prix Juigné the following April, the 28-year-old Mr Peter Beatty bought him for 8,000 gn and sent him to be trained in England by Fred Darling. Starting at 20-1 and ridden by Charles Elliott, Bois Roussel won the 1938 Derby by four lengths after being at the tail end of the field at Tattenham Corner. In his only other race he was third in the Grand Prix de Paris. Although a good many of his stock were unreliable, he was champion sire in 1949. He sired two St Leger winners in Tehran and Ridge Wood; and Migoli, winner of the Eclipse Stakes and the Prix de l'Arc de Triomphe.

BONGRACE

Bred by the late Lord Rosebery in 1923, Bongrace, by Spion Kop, was a very game filly that won eight races including the Doncaster Cup and the Coronation Cup. She bred four winners, among them that game but desperately unlucky filly Ribbon.

BOOK LAW

She was probably the best filly ever bred at Lord Astor's Cliveden Stud. She won the Coronation Stakes at Ascot and the St Leger and was second in both the One Thousand Guineas and the Oaks. By Buchan out of Popingaol, she bred five winners including Rhodes Scholar, who won the Eclipse Stakes. She was also the dam of Archive, sire of the great steeplechaser Arkle.

BOOKMAKERS AND BOOKMAKING

Although there has been more or less organised racing in England since the days of Charles II, the bookmaker is a comparatively recent phenomenon.

In his book *Come Racing with Me* Major Eric Rickman, a leading authority on betting for the past forty years, states that it was about 1790 that a man named Ogden began laying bets against more than one runner in a race after the style of the present day bookmaker. Prior to then, owners and their stable connections had only betted with each other.

In the late eighteenth century two famous names appear, both of whom made a considerable impact on racing and betting generally. They were Richard Tattersall and William Crockford.

Richard Tattersall, born in 1724, came from West Yorkshire to London, where he was much engaged in the sale of horses. He was a constant visitor to Beevor's Horse Repository in St Martin's Lane, and he eventually obtained an interest in this concern. Later he was put in charge of the Duke of Kingston's stud.

There was at this time no place where sales could be held at fixed periods, so he offered his services as auctioneer, and the project was taken up by Lord Grosvenor, and the first Tattersalls premises were built on his estate at Hyde Park Corner.

The present day reference to the main racecourse ring as Tattersalls stems from the days when it was an enclosure used principally by bookmakers and backers who were members of Tattersalls Subscription Rooms, set aside for them in the London premises of Richard Tattersall's firm of auctioneers. The Subscription Rooms as such ceased many years ago, but Tattersalls Committee, authorised by, and responsible to the Jockey Club was formed in 1886 to settle betting disputes, and to report or have 'posted' all defaulters, whether backers or layers. This Committee still gets through an immense amount of work in the course of a year, sitting approximately 20 times.

William Crockford, the founder of Crockford's gambling saloon in Newmarket, had originally been a fishmonger. At this trade he had prospered exceedingly, and bought a gaming table in King Street, St James's. A lucky wager on a Derby outsider caused his table to thrive, and in company with a man called Gye, proceeded to fleece various members of the nobility to the tune of £100,000 odd. Following this success he acquired his famous premises on the site of 50-53 St James's Street, and to this gaming club went all the leading personalities of the day including Disraeli, Bulwer Lytton and the Duke of Wellington. The cuisine, which was free to all members, had a nation-wide reputation. By 1809, Crockford had become a bookmaker, and bought a house in Newmarket High Street, and also a farm in the district. Subsequently he bought a large house in New Station Road with gaming premises just across the street, on the site of which is now Rothsay House.

By 1859, *The Sporting Life* had been founded, and shortly afterwards the present starting price system began to be evolved. What happened was this. On race days, bookmakers used to congregate in Hyde Park on what is now the site of Speaker's Corner, and chalk up their own lists of runners and prices, usually on blackboards or affixed to trees. This was obviously illegal, and the police moved them on until eventually they came to congregate in clubs and dens, mainly in the Fleet Street area. Most of their clients were gentry, who preferred to settle their accounts weekly, so the bookmakers stated in their rules that they would settle weekly, on the prices published in the sporting press. The first national newspaper to publish the starting prices was the *Evening News* in 1883, whose editor at that time was the notorious Frank Harris. It is significant that the circulation of the paper trebled within three months. For the next 40 years or so, until after World War I, each sporting paper published its own set of starting prices, until *The Sporting Life* (in modern parlance) 'took over' Bell's *Life in London, The Sportsman* and *The Sporting Telegraph*. Then in 1926, the *Sporting Chronicle*, by then the only other sporting paper interested, agreed with *The Sporting Life* to publish a combined return of prices compiled by a representative of each paper. This in turn, is sent out to all newspapers and bookmakers (and now disseminated by radio and television) by the two agencies, the Press Association and the Exchange Telegraph. Although now very much more streamlined, this system still obtains today, and has withstood the test of time, a second world war, and the introduction of 15,000 betting shops.

Prior to 1939, the volume of Starting Price business was not enormous. The bookmakers who advertised in the sporting press could be numbered on two hands, though it included such well-known names as Duggie Stuart, David Cope, James Maclean and McLauchlans.

William Hill was a meteor who had not yet appeared in the sky, and Coral's and Ladbrokes were relatively small (though exclusive) family concerns. Hill appeared at Northolt Park pony racing track in the early 1930s, and he also bet in the cheaper rings at Harringay and White City.

When the war broke out he was 36, but medically unfit for military service. At that time, somewhat naturally, the advertising bookmakers began to draw in their horns, and in any case the sporting papers were only coming out two or three times a week. Hill, always a dissenter, took exactly the opposite course. He embarked on a programme of expansion, sinking every penny of his capital into his Park Lane premises, advertised widely, and made a book on the rails at every principal meeting throughout the war. This policy paid off handsomely, and by the time the boom period of betting began in 1945, he was well on the way to being the biggest bookmaker in the land. Within five years he had achieved that object, and moved his offices to Piccadilly Circus. About that time he began to concentrate on Fixed Odds football betting, up till then a relatively untapped source, and within a year or so his firm was taking nearly £500,000 a week. The death knell to this remarkable enterprise was sounded in 1964 by the then Chancellor of the Exchequer, Mr Reginald Maudling. He slapped on a 25 per cent tax on this type of betting, and within eighteen months it was virtually wiped out. In 1965, by reason of this tax, the Hill organisation showed a loss for the first time.

Hill has ploughed an enormous amount of money back into racing, and is the owner of two of the leading studs in the country, at Whitsbury and Sezincote. Up to date he has bred the winner of the Derby and the Two Thousand Guineas (Nimbus), the St Leger (Cantelo) and the Gimcrack Stakes and Champagne Stakes (Be Careful). He also bred Grey Sovereign, one of the most prolific sires of sprinters since the war.

The other big names in bookmaking today are of course Corals and Ladbrokes. Joe Coral, the presiding genius of the firm that bears his name, has been a bookmaker since 1926. He has built up his business enormously over the past fifteen years, and by his promotion of what is now come to be known as 'Coral's Day' at Folkestone, has done much to save that attractive little racecourse from extinction. In addition, he now promotes the Newbury Autumn Cup, which had the misfortune to be abandoned in its first year, owing to a torrential thunderstorm.

Ladbroke's is now run by Cyril Stein, nephew of Max Stein (better known to racing people as Maxie Parker) who died three years ago. The four brothers Stein, Harry, Jack, Max and Isaac, were the sons of European immigrants before World War I. Harry (or 'Dick' or 'Snouty' as he was variously called) traded under the name of Parker, and was probably the biggest bookmaker on the rails by 1939. He died in 1945, and his business was taken over by Max, who also traded under the name of Parker. In 1957, he obtained control of the old established firm of Ladbroke's, and installed his nephew Cyril as managing director. An immediate policy of expansion was embarked upon, and various firms have been taken over, and innumerable betting shops purchased over a wide area. The empire now controlled by Cyril Stein almost certainly surpasses all other firms with the exception of Hill's. In addition, the company has launched out into the hotel business in Malta. All this is a very far cry from the illegal bookmakers in Hyde Park. Nowadays, bookmakers are just ordinary businessmen.

The bookmaking organisations, which, like the trades unions, have such difficulty in controlling their members, date back no further than 1921. In that year, the late 'Hoppy' Beresford, a lame bookmaker who used to bet sitting on a stool, together with a few South-country colleagues, formed what was then called The Bookmakers and Backers Protection Association, and a year later a northern branch was formed by George Picken and George Yates. The latter, a highly respected member of his profession, became the first chairman of the famous Victoria Club, in Wellington Street, Strand. The Bookmakers and Backers Association later became the National Bookmakers Protection Association, together with Southern and Northern Associations plus more than a dozen affiliated bodies. Now called the National Association of Bookmakers, its chairman is George Lodge, who has more than 6,000 members to control and administer.

What does the future hold in store for the bookmaking profession? Precious little if the signs are interpreted correctly, and the present political course is not put violently into reverse by a different administration. It is impossible to take £30 or £40 million a year out of any industry and expect it to survive. And that is precisely what is happening at the moment.

As Sir Henry Benson said in the course of his wholly admirable Report on the Racing Industry, racing and betting is the only industry in the country, which is subject to an additional 5 per cent tax added to the usual crippling range of taxes, Corporation Tax, SET, and the like. The only conceivable solution is that proposed by Sir Henry, namely that the Government return to racing, 1 per cent of the 5 per cent at present inflicted, or raise it to 6 per cent (and no further) if the Government are unwilling to make do with a mere 4 per cent of the amount at present wagered on betting throughout the country.

Geoffrey Hamlyn
(of *The Sporting Life*)

BOOTS

Some horses wear boots of felt, leather or elastic or of a combination of those materials. They are close fitting and kept in position by straps. They protect a horse that is liable to strike into itself with its own feet or alternatively they provide a support in the case of some leg weakness.

BOSWELL

Mr W. Woodward's Boswell, foaled in 1933, a son of the Gold Cup winner Bosworth, won the St Leger and the Eclipse Stakes. He failed as a sire in America and Canada.

BOSWORTH

Bred in 1926 by the late Lord Derby, Bosworth, by Son-in-Law, won four races, one of them being the Ascot Gold Cup. He was not a great success as a sire, but got Boswell (see above) and Plassy, winner of the Coronation Cup and Jockey Club Stakes.

BOTTICELLI

Bred in Italy by the famous Razza Dormello, Botticelli, by Blue Peter, won many races including the Italian Derby, Italian St Leger and Ascot Gold Cup. He was not a success as a sire in England and is now in Germany.

BOTTOMLEY, Horatio (1860-1933)

Born in the East End of London, the son of a tailor's cutter, Horatio Bottomley, a squat dumpy man with a huge head, was one of the most remarkable public figures of this century. Journalist, promoter of scores of dubious financial schemes, a formidable lay lawyer and a Member of Parliament, he was perhaps the greatest 'con' man of his time. It is a tribute to his knowledge of the law and to the uncanny influence he exercised over a considerable section of the public that he managed to escape gaol until 1922 when he received a seven-year sentence.

On the Turf he was a heavy, but rash and unskilful gambler. At first his horses were trained at Alfriston by Batho, but later he ran his own private stable at his Sussex home, The Dicker, and installed James Hare as trainer. Most of his horses were very bad, but their mediocrity did not diminish his affection for them and he spent a fortune buying-in bad selling platers when they happened to win. However, he won a lot of money when Wargrave won the Cesarewitch for him and Northern Farmer the Stewards' Cup. He also cleared £15,000 when his sprinter, Le Blizon, beat Mr Jack Joel's Sundridge in a match at Hurst Park.

It is interesting to recall that in parliament over 60 years ago Bottomley was demanding the annual licensing of bookmakers and the introduction of a betting tax. During World War I he was Chairman of the Racing Emergency Committee, designed to ensure the continuance of the sport, and for his work in this capacity he was presented at a luncheon in his honour with an antique silvergilt rosewater dish weighing 179 ounces by the Hon George Lambton.

Bottomley died penniless in the public ward of a London hospital.

BOUSSAC, M. Marcel

M. M. Boussac, the great French

industrialist, gained an appreciable number of successes in English racing before World War II when he had horses with Basil Jarvis and George Lambton. In addition he won the Two Thousand Guineas in 1940 with that good horse Djebel, later a most distinguished sire.

It was immediately after the war, though, that the powerful Boussac stable reached its peak and looked likely to dominate European racing for an appreciable period. M. Boussac's main successes in England at this time were the Derby with Galcador (1950); the Oaks with Asmena (1950); the St Leger with Scratch II (1950) and Talma II (1951); the Gold Cup with Caracalla II (1946), Arbar (1948), Elpenor (1954) and Macip (1956); the Eclipse Stakes with Djeddah (1949) and Argur (1953); the Champion Stakes with Djeddah (1949) and Dynamiter (1951-52).

In the early 1950s, though, the tide of success started to ebb away and over the past fifteen years or so Boussac successes, not only in this country but also in France, have been meagre considering the scope of his racing empire.

Probably the best horse ever to carry the famous orange jacket and grey cap was the unbeaten Pharis II, winner of the Prix du Jockey Club and the Grand Prix in 1939.

BOWES, John (1814-1885)

Mr John Bowes of Streatlam Castle, Co Durham, won the Derby four times—with Mündig (1835), Cotherstone (1843), Daniel O'Rourke (1852) and West Australian (1853). A member of the Jockey Club, he owned horses for more than fifty years and until John Scott's death in 1871, he was a patron of Scott's powerful stable at Malton.

Bowes was a son of Lord Strathmore and would have succeeded to the title but for the fact that he was born nine years before his parents married. Shy and reserved, he lived for the most part quietly in Paris and in later life tended to become a complete recluse. In fact for 30 years before his death in 1885, he never set foot on a racecourse. He was only 21 and still at Cambridge when he won the Derby with Mündig (*Mündig* is the German for 'of age').

BOYD, George Henderson (b 1907)

George Boyd, one of the most consistently successful of Scottish trainers, learnt the trainer's art from his father, the late J. N. Boyd. He rode under both rules as an amateur from 1929 to 1939, and apart from a spell of service in the RAF, assisted his brother Alec from 1936 till he set up on his own ten years later. He retired in 1969.

His main triumph was to win the Two Thousand Guineas with Rockavon, but his imposing list of successes in handicaps includes the Northumberland Plate three times, the Lincoln, the Cambridgeshire, the Zetland Gold Cup, the Lanark Silver Bell, the Manchester Cup and the Ayr Gold Cup. His stables were at Westbarns, Dunbar, East Lothian, and his owners included Mr and Mrs C. W. Tosh, Mr J. N. Adam, Mr R. Chalmers-Watson, Mr M. A. Blyth, Mr T. C. Yuill, Mrs F. Bullock-Marsham, Mr H. C. Hutchinson and Mrs J. F. Bell.

BOYD-ROCHFORT, Capt Sir Cecil Charles, CVO (b 1887)

Capt Sir Cecil Boyd-Rochfort was educated at Eton and served in the Scots Guards in World War I when he was awarded the Croix de Guerre. He learnt the art of training from 'Atty' Persse and was for a time assistant to Capt R. H. Dewhurst. He set up on his own in 1921.

He soon proved extremely successful and within a few years was firmly established in the front rank of trainers. There he remained until he retired in 1968, although admittedly there was a falling off in the prize money he won during his last three or four seasons.

He won almost every important race in the Calendar and was particularly successful with stayers. He certainly did not scorn handicaps, and his stable landed some notable gambles in races like the Cesarewitch, the Cambridgeshire and the Royal Hunt Cup.

A perfectionist, he demanded the highest standards, and had as little use for clock-watching employees as for indifferent horses. No doubt he was fortunate in that he trained for wealthy patrons, many of them American, who sent him high-class horses and could afford to be patient. However, they would not have remained his patrons for long had they not been justifiably confident of his high professional ability.

His greatest honour was to be appointed trainer to King George VI on the death of W. R. Jarvis, and he continued to hold this appointment after the accession of Queen Elizabeth. During the early years of the Queen's reign, the Sandringham stud was enjoying a phase of brilliant success and among the good horses that carried the royal colours in that period were Aureole, Doutelle, Almeria, Pall Mall and Above Suspicion.

Probably the two best horses he ever trained were the triple classic winner Meld, and the St Leger and King George VI and Queen Elizabeth Stakes winner Alcide.

His chief successes were as follows:

Two Thousand Guineas: Pall Mall (1958).

One Thousand Guineas: Brown Betty (1933), Hypericum (1946) and Meld (1955).

Derby: Parthia (1959).

Oaks: Hycilla (1944) and Meld (1955).

St Leger: Boswell (1936), Sun Castle (1941), Black Tarquin (1948), Premonition (1953), Meld (1955) and Alcide (1958).

Coronation Cup: Persian Gulf (1944) and Aureole (1954).

Gold Cup: Precipitation (1937), Flares (1938) and Zarathustra (1957).

Eclipse Stakes: Royal Minstrel (1929), Loaningdale (1933), Boswell (1937) and Canisbay (1965).

King George VI and Queen Elizabeth Stakes: Aureole (1954) and Alcide (1959).

Goodwood Cup: Zarathustra (1956), Dickens (1959), Sagacity (1962), Raise You Ten (1964), Apprentice (1965) and Gaulois (1966).

Champion Stakes: Flares (1937) and Hycilla (1944).

He also won the Kempton Jubilee four times, the Lingfield Derby Trial 10 times, the St James's Palace Stakes three times, the Coronation Stakes three times, the Royal Hunt Cup four times, the Champagne Stakes five times, the Park Hill Stakes five times, the Middle Park Stakes three times, the Cesarewitch three times and the Cambridgeshire twice.

Tall, erect and impeccably dressed, a figure of considerable dignity, Sir Cecil has always been an easily recognised figure on English racecourses. He has clear-cut likes and dislikes in the racing world and is inclined to express himself freely. With members of the racing press he has always been invariably courteous and helpful. He was awarded his knighthood in 1968.

BREASLEY, Arthur (b 1914)

'Scobie' Breasley ranks with the best Australian jockeys who have ridden in Britain such as Frank Wootton, Frank Bullock and Bernard Carslake. Born in Australia, he was apprenticed there to P. B. Quinlan and rode his first winner in August 1928. In 1950 he came to England to ride for Noel Cannon's stable and swiftly established his reputation. His first classic success came in 1951 when he rode Ki Ming to victory in the Two Thousand Guineas. He subsequently won the One Thousand Guineas on Festoon, the Derby on Santa Claus and Charlottown. He also won the King George VI and Queen Elizabeth Stakes, the Prix de l'Arc de Triomphe, the Grand Prix de Saint Cloud and the Irish One Thousand Guineas. He was particularly effective at Newmarket and three times rode the winner of the Cambridgeshire. He was champion jockey four times, his best season being in 1962 when he had 179 winners. He retired in 1967, and in 1968 began training at Epsom, where his son-in-law Brian Swift also has a stable.

Level-headed, businesslike, unemotional, a dedicated professional in fact, Breasley, like the best Australian riders, was a superb judge of pace and excelled in split-second timing. He was a master, too, at winning on two-year-olds or highly strung fillies without subjecting them to a hard race. Throughout his career, though never as popular with the racegoing public as Lester Piggott, he gave connoisseurs of the art of race-riding continual pleasure. If he had a weakness it was perhaps a tendency to stick to the rails at all costs, a habit that sometimes resulted in his getting boxed-in, while his marked preference for waiting tactics made him seem at times inflexible in his methods compared to the best English riders. He lacked nothing in toughness and courage and some bad falls towards the close of his riding career never affected his nerve. He trains for Mr J. Astaire, Lady Beaverbrook, Mr P. Hamlyn, Mr A. J. A. Kennedy, Mr D. Sung, Mr M. Sobell and Mr A. Weinstock.

BREEDER

According to the Rules of Racing, the breeder is the person who owns the dam when the foal is dropped.

BREEDERS, LEADING

1919	Lord Derby	£22,419
1920	Lord Derby	£17,048
1921	Mr S. B. Joel	£32,004
1922	Lord Derby	£32,277
1923	Lord Derby	£39,275
1924	Lady Sykes	£36,409
1925	Lord Astor	£36,323
1926	Lord Woolavington	£39,869
1927	Lord Derby	£41,039
1928	Lord Derby	£64,944
1929	Lord Derby	£30,644
1930	Lord Derby	£35,681
1931	Lord Dewar	£40,837
1932	HH Aga Khan	£59,087
1933	Sir Alec Black	£35,229
1934	HH Aga Khan	£57,733
1935	HH Aga Khan	£49,285
1936	Lord Astor	£38,290
1937	HH Aga Khan	£46,252
1938	Lord Derby	£31,847
1939	Lord Rosebery	£37,377
1940	Mr H. E. Morris	£7,647
1941	Lord Glanely	£8,288
1942	National Stud	£11,990
1943	Miss D. Paget	£20,001
1944	Lord Rosebery	£9,549
1945	Lord Derby	£27,763
1946	Lieut-Col H. Boyd-Rochfort	£23,059
1947	HH Aga Khan	£41,165
1948	HH Aga Khan	£38,509
1949	HH Aga Khan	£69,976
1950	M. M. Boussac	£59,859
1951	M. M. Boussac	£44,444
1952	HH Aga Khan	£93,058
1953	Mr F. Darling	£48.099
1954	Major L. B. Holliday	£45,651
1955	Someries Stud	£50,125
1956	Major L. B. Holliday	£37,333
1957	Eve Stud	£53,823
1958	Mr R. Ball	£46,653
1959	Prince Aly Khan and the late HH Aga Khan	£100,668
1960	Eve Stud	£90,124
1961	Eve Stud	£41,354
1962	Major L. B. Holliday	£72,629
1963	Mr H. F. Guggenheim	£66,012
1964	Mrs H. E. Jackson	£98,270
1965	Mr J. Ternynck	£65,301
1966	Someries Stud	£80,154
1967	Mr H. J. Joel	£109,882
1968	Mrs R. W. Bell	£97,176
1969	Lord Rosebery	£65,491

BRIENZ

Third in the Derby in 1929, Brienz became one of the best staying chasers in the country, racing till he was 13 and winning innumerable races over fences.

BRIGHTON

Brighton racecourse occupies a nice breezy position on a hill above the town with a view of the sea. A lot of money has been spent in recent years on improving the standard of comfort and the meetings are now equally popular with regular racegoers and with South-coast holidaymakers. Sport is nearly always brisk even if top-class performers are somewhat scarce. Few meetings there pass without at least one winner from the not far-distant Arundel stable, of which the Duke of Norfolk is the principal patron.

The track is left-hand, U-shaped and 1½m long. In fact no race longer than 1½m is run there. The first 3f of the 1½m course are slightly uphill. Then there is a slight descent, followed by a rise to about 4f from home. The ground then falls quite steeply until 2f from the finish when there is a rise with the final 100yd level.

It is rather a sharp course and a horse needs good conformation and a good action as well to cope with the various gradients. A low draw is an advantage in sprint races. In olden times they used to have hurdle races here with one hurdle sited half way down that steep hill. They must have been brave men in those days.

Clerk of the Course: Mr D. Hubbard, 214-218 Shepherds Bush Road, London, W.6. Tel: 603 7211.

Best Times:

Distance	*Horse-Age-Weight*	*Date*	*Time*
5f 66yd	St Alphage 5-10-3	28-8-68	60.1
5f 66yd	King's Mate 2-8-7	12-7-67	61.4
6f	Coldyke 3-8-7	28-8-68	1min 8.1
6f	Pierina 2-8-3	20-9-62	1min 10
7f	Last Case 3-8-12	9-6-66	1min 19.8
7f	Totland 2-8-12	20-9-55	1min 23
8f	Loose Cover 3-7-12	9-6-66	1min 31.8
8f	Arbutus 2-8-10	19-9-63	1min 33.8
10f	Fion Buidhe 4-8-7	29-6-53	1min 58.6
12f	Fraxinus 4-8-1	5-8-64	2min 27.5

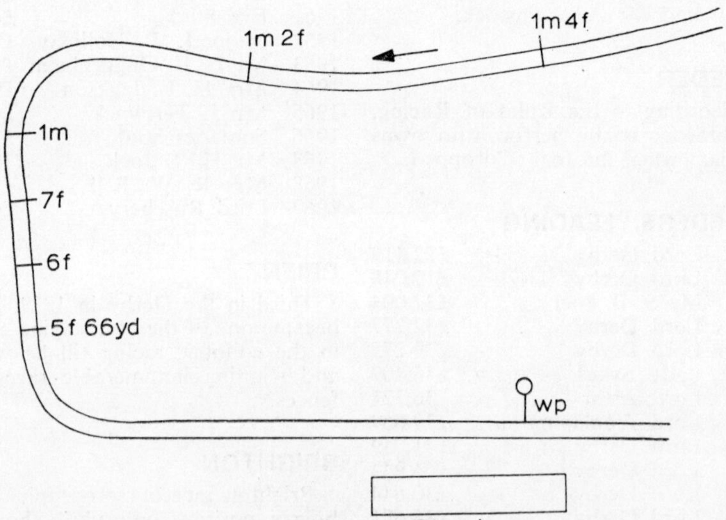

BRIGHTON

BRITT, Edgar

Edgar Britt is an Australian who rode with much success in Britain after World War II, retiring in 1959. He won the Two Thousand Guineas on Nearula, the One Thousand Guineas on Musidora, the Oaks on Musidora and Frieze, and the St Leger on Sayajirao and Black Tarquin. He had a particularly successful association with the late Capt Charles Elsey's stable.

BROADCASTING

The first successful broadcast of a race was the Grand National won by Sprig in 1927. An attempt to broadcast the 1926 Derby had proved a failure.

BROOD MARE

A brood mare is a mare kept at a stud for breeding purposes.

BROOKE, Geoffrey (b 1896)

Geoffrey Brooke for twenty years assisted the late 'Atty' Persse before taking out a licence himself in 1949. For a brief spell he acted as private trainer to the late Major Lionel Holliday and when that arrangement came to an end, he set up as a public trainer at Newmarket and enjoyed consistent success until his retirement in 1967. A delightful personality with a lively wit, he is undoubtedly one of racing's most popular characters. Like 'Atty' Persse, he preferred speed to stamina and most of his successes were with fast two-year-olds, sprinters and milers rather than with stayers. However, he won the 1951 Oaks with Neasham Belle. Unfortunately, owing to a car accident, he was not at Epsom to see her win. He won the Two Thousand Guineas with Our Babu and among other good horses he trained were Durante, Masham, Rustam, Crocket and Sammy Davis. He now lives in Ireland.

BROOKE, Major Peter

Major Brooke assisted the late 'Atty' Persse at Stockbridge from 1928-34. From 1936-40 he served the Royal Calcutta Turf Club as handicapper and stewards' secretary. From 1940-46 he was in the 19th KGVO Lancers (Indian Army). He returned to the Royal Calcutta Turf Club till 1948 when he came to England and was appointed a stewards' secretary under the Rules of Racing.

BROWN BETTY

An exceptionally good-looking filly by Friar Marcus, Brown Betty, foaled in 1930, won six races including the One Thousand Guineas. She went to the stud in America.

BROWNHYLDA

Brownhylda, by Stedfast, was foaled in 1920 and won five races, including the Oaks. Her one winner at the stud was Firdaussi, who won the St Leger and Jockey Club Stakes.

BROWN JACK

Brown Jack, a stayer famous for his courage and toughness, was one of the most popular horses ever to run on the English Turf.

Foaled in 1924, he was bred in Ireland and was by Jackdaw out of Querquidella, by Kroonstad. After a brief and unsuccessful racing career in Ireland, he was bought as a three-year-old for 750 gn by Aubrey Hastings, who trained at Wroughton and was acting for Col Sir Harold Wernher, at that time a jumping enthusiast and particularly keen to win the Champion Hurdle.

Brown Jack's first outing in England was at Bournemouth in the autumn of 1927 when he finished third in a novices' hurdle. He soon proved himself a formidable hurdler, though, and won seven times that season, his big triumph being his victory in the Champion Hurdle, a fine achievement for a four-year-old. Among those who saw him win at Cheltenham was Steve Donoghue, who advised that Brown Jack's attention should be turned to the flat. Brown Jack in fact never ran again under National Hunt rules and in races under Jockey Club rules he and Donoghue proved a most popular and successful combination.

As a four-year-old Brown Jack won the Ascot Stakes and the following six years he won the Queen Alexandra Stakes, thereby achieving the unequalled feat of winning a race at Royal Ascot seven years running. His final Ascot victory was the occasion of a memorable scene of enthusiasm and affection, the old gelding being given a reception that a Derby winner in the royal colours might have envied.

Brown Jack's other wins included the Goodwood Cup, the Ebor Handicap and the Rosebery Memorial Plate. In all he ran 65 times, winning 25 races worth over £23,000. He lived in happy retirement after his racing career was over till his death in 1948.

It only remains to add that Aubrey Hastings died suddenly in 1929 and that his successor at Wroughton was Ivor Anthony who trained Brown Jack for the rest of his career.

BROWN, L. G. (b 1933)

L. G. Brown was apprenticed to G. Colling and E. Davey. He rides successfully in the North and in his best season so far he rode 59 winners.

BRULETTE

Bred in France by Lieut-Col C. W. Birkin, Brulette, by Brûleur, was foaled in 1928. A fine stayer, she won the Oaks, Goodwood Cup and Prix du Cadran. She bred seven winners, but not one of any account.

BUCHAN

Buchan, foaled in 1916, was a good but unlucky horse belonging to the second Lord Astor. He was narrowly beaten in the Derby, a race he ought to have won, and was disqualified after winning the 1920 Gold Cup. He did, however, win the Eclipse Stakes twice. He did well at the stud and was champion sire in 1927, the year his daughter Book Law won the St Leger.

BUCKLE, Dennis (b 1929)

Apprenticed to E. Davey he rode his first winner in 1946. He was top apprentice in 1947 and 1948. He can go to scale at 7st 13lb and in his best season so far rode 29 winners.

BUCKLE, Frank (1766-1832)

Frank Buckle was a great jockey and in his heyday enjoyed a popularity equal to that of Fred Archer, Steve Donoghue and Sir Gordon Richards. He won the Derby five times, the Oaks nine times and the St Leger twice.

Son of a Newmarket saddler, he had a long career as a jockey, his final ride being 50 years after joining Mr Vernon's stable as a small boy. For much of his life he lived at Peterborough, where he farmed successfully, being famous for his butter. He also bred greyhounds, bulldogs and fighting cocks and at one period was a Master of Hounds. He was a tough little man who thought nothing of hacking over to Newmarket to ride work and then riding home to Peterborough in time for tea, a total distance of 90 miles. His whip, covered in silver, and bearing the record of his classic successes, was for many years a coveted racing trophy in Germany.

BUDGETT, Arthur Maitland (b 1915)

Arthur Budgett comes from a family well-known in hunting and polo circles. He was educated at Eton and Oxford and took out a licence to train in 1939. Army service interrupted his career and Commissar, whom he owned in partnership with his elder brother, was trained by Eric Stedall when he won the 1946 Stewards Cup. However, Budgett trained Commissar when he won the 1948 Lincoln as an eight-year-old.

In 1969 he won the Derby with Blakeney, of whom he is part owner and who carried his colours, while later that season he won the Middle Park Stakes with Huntercombe. He also trained Huntercombe's sire Derring-Do, who won over £20,000 in stakes, his victories including the Imperial Stakes, Cornwallis Stakes and Queen Elizabeth II Stakes. The best filly he has so far had is Windmill Girl, who was second in the Oaks, won the Ribblesdale Stakes and is the dam of Blakeney. Other successes to Budgett's credit are the Park Hill Stakes, Manchester November Handicap (twice), Ayr Gold Cup, Queen's Prize, Jockey Club Stakes and July Cup.

His stables are at Whatcombe, Berkshire, and among his owners are Mrs J. Benskin, Brig Sir Jeffrey Darell, Mrs J. M. Carnegie, Mr J. S. Pearson-Gregory, Mr and Mrs H. H. Renshaw, Mr R. N. Richmond-Watson, Miss E. Rigden, Col Percy Wright and Mrs G. Trimmer-Thompson.

He is married to a sister of Major Peter Towers-Clark, editor of *Stud and Stable*.

BUG, THE

Owned by Mr N. H. Wachman and trained by Marcus Marsh, The Bug, a son of Signal Light, was one of the most brilliant sprinters of the post-war era. At one stage of his career he won ten races in succession. He won the Wokingham Stakes at Ascot as a three-year-old in a canter carrying 8st 7lb. He did not prove a success as a sire.

BUISSON ARDENT

Bred in France in 1953 by Mr L. L. Lawrence, Buisson Ardent, by Relic out of Rose o' Lynn, won the Middle Park Stakes and the French Two Thousand Guineas. Before he died comparatively young, he sired that good miler and promising sire Roan Rocket. He was a full brother to Venture VII, who won the Middle Park Stakes and Imperial Produce Stakes.

BULL, Phil (b 1910)

Mr Phil Bull was born in 1910 and has been an easily recognisable figure in the racing world for more than a quarter of a century. He has strong views on the conduct of the sport and is not averse to expressing them in public. As Governing Director of the Portway Press, he has conferred services of great value to many followers of racing by the publication of *Timeform, Timeform Race Cards,* and of that highly informative annual *Racehorses of 19—*.

Mr Bull has also had many successes as breeder and owner. Among the good winners to carry his colours are Orgoglio (Champagne Stakes and Victoria Cup); Orinthia (Kempton Jubilee and Manchester Cup); Pheidippides (Gimcrack Stakes); and Sostenuto (Ebor Handicap). He also bred Eudaemon (Gimcrack Stakes and Champagne Stakes), and Romulus (Sussex Stakes and Queen Elizabeth II Stakes). His current trainer is S. Ingham. Colours: cerise, white hoop.

BULTEEL, Sir John Crocker, KCVO, DSO, MC (1890-1956)

Sir John Crocker Bulteel was Clerk of the Course at Ascot and at Hurst Park when he died. By common consent he was the outstanding racing official of his time, bringing to racecourse management and programme planning an imaginative and enlightened conception of modern needs in an era when the general standard was out-dated and deplorably unprogressive. One of his more important contributions to racing was to institute the King George VI and Queen Elizabeth Stakes at Ascot. Invariably courteous and with a charming personality, he was extremely well-liked in the racing world.

BUMPER

'Bumper' is a slang term for an amateur rider on the flat.

BUNBURY, Sir Charles (1740-1821)

Sir Charles Bunbury, whose name is still remembered at Newmarket through the 'Bunbury Mile', represented Mildenhall in Parliament for many years and was at one time Chief Secretary for Ireland. He played a very important part not only in the development of English racing, but in the extension of the authority of the Jockey Club, of which he was regarded as 'the Perpetual President'. On the Turf his word was law and it was his action after the inconsistent running of the Prince of Wales's horse Escape that led to the Prince (afterwards George IV) shaking the dust of Newmarket off his heels for good (see Chifney, Sam, senior).

Sir Charles won the first Derby with Diomed. He also won that race with Eleanor and Smolensko, but the best horse he ever bred was Highflyer, whom he sold to Lord Bolingbroke.

BURNS, Major-Gen. Sir George, KCVO, DSO, OBE, MC (b 1911)

Major-Gen Sir George Burns served in the Coldstream Guards. He inherited the racing interests of the late Mrs Arthur James and also her well-known colours, lilac. He is a member of the Jockey Club and has served a term of office as Senior Steward. The best horse he has so far bred is Firestreak and his trainer is John Oxley.

BURNS, Thomas P. (b 1924)

Apprenticed in England to Steve Donoghue, he returned to Ireland, the land of his birth, on the outbreak of war. He rode his first winner at the tender age of 14. For many years he has been one of the leading Irish riders, equally good on the flat or over hurdles. His main triumph in England was to win the St Leger on Ballymoss.

BURTON, Captain Van Duzer (b 1921)

Captain Burton served for fifteen years in the 12th Lancers. From 1959-67 he was secretary of the Grand Military Race Committee. He is an official Judge both under the Rules of Racing and National Hunt rules.

BURY, Lady Mairi

Lady Mairi Bury owned and bred the dual Ascot Gold Cup winner Fighting Charlie. Her trainers are F. Maxwell and H. Cecil. Colours: rose pink.

BUSHBY, D. W.

Clerk of the Course at Yarmouth and Windsor and also at the National Hunt courses of Cheltenham and Towcester.

BUTLER, Frank (1818-1856)

Frank Butler was a nephew of Sam Chifney junior and inherited a touch of his genius. He rode two winners of the Derby, Daniel O'Rourke and West Australian, and six winners of the Oaks, four of them in succession. He was only 38 when he died.

BUTTERS, Frank (1878-1957)

Frank Butters was one of the most successful and most respected trainers of his time. He was born in Vienna, the eldest son of Joseph Butters who was training there at the time. After being educated in England, he returned to Austria where he helped his father for some years before becoming private trainer to Mautrer de Markham. During World War I he was interned in Austria, and after the Armistice he trained with success for a number of years in Italy.

In 1926 he succeeded George Lambton as Lord Derby's trainer, being given a four-year contract. He won the St Leger and Eclipse Stakes with Fairway, the Eclipse Stakes with Colorado, the One Thousand Guineas with Fair Isle, the Oaks with Toboggan and the Gold Cup with Bosworth. All these belonged to Lord Derby and he won the Oaks for Lord Durham with Beam. However, in August 1930 Lord Derby informed him that owing to the world economic crisis he was reducing his racing commitments and that the contract with Butters would not be renewed. Thus at the age of 52 and at a time of acute financial depression,

Butters found himself out of a job.

However, he was not unemployed for long, and after the Aga Khan's break with Dick Dawson he was asked to take the Aga Khan's horses. He agreed to do so and trained them with immense success until he retired in 1949, that retirement being caused by a serious accident when riding his bicycle. He trained the following classic winners for the Aga Khan:

Two Thousand Guineas: Bahram.
Derby: Bahram and Mahmoud.
Oaks: Udaipur and Masaka.
St Leger: Firdaussi, Bahram, Turkhan, and Tehran.

He also won the Oaks for Sir Alfred Butt with Steady Aim. Altogether he won in England 1,019 races worth over £930,000. At Royal Ascot in 1934 he trained the winners of nine of the 28 races.

Butters combined a high degree of professional skill with intense devotion to the interests of his patrons. He seldom betted and his one big bet was on Fairway in the Derby, in which the horse ran unplaced. He believed in giving his horses plenty of work and those who stood up to his methods came on to the racecourse fit to run for their lives. The tragedy of his life was when his son Victor, his valued assistant, died suddenly during a holiday in Switzerland. His brother Fred was also a trainer (see below).

BUTTERS, Fred (1888-1967)

Fred Butters' racing career was overshadowed by that of his brother Frank. Before World War I he trained in Austria. After four years' internment in Austria, he returned to England where for some years he assisted his father before setting up on his own. His big success was to win the 1937 Derby with Mid-day Sun.

C

CADOGAN, sixth Earl of, MC (b 1914)

Lord Cadogan is a member of the Jockey Club. His trainer is Harvey Leader. Colours: Eton blue.

CADWALADR, George (b 1945)

George Cadwaladr served his apprenticeship with Eric Cousins. In 1966 he rode 31 winners. His successes include the Ayr Gold Cup, Wokingham Stakes and the King's Stand Stakes.

CAERGWRLE

Caergwrle, by Crepello, was a very fast filly up to a mile and won the 1968 One Thousand Guineas for Mrs Noel Murless.

CAERLEON

Foaled in 1927, Caerleon was a full brother to the Two Thousand Guineas winner Colorado, and won the Eclipse Stakes for his owner-breeder, Lord Derby.

CALIGULA

Owned by Mr M. Goculdas and trained by H. Leader, Caligula won the St Leger in 1920. He was one of the three sons of The Tetrarch to win that race. He was exported to Germany but proved very infertile as a sire.

CALL BOY

Call Boy, owned by Mr Frank Curzon and trained by J. Watts, won the Derby in 1927. Mr Curzon was a dying man at the time and knew it but he bravely mustered his last reserves of strength and led his colt in at Epsom. A few weeks later he was dead. Call Boy, who died in 1940, proved virtually sterile at the stud.

CALVERT, John Boyd (b 1917)

J. B. Calvert first took out a licence to train on the flat in 1950. His stables are at Hambleton, Yorkshire. So far he has trained close on 400 winners, among them the notable sprinters Dondeen and Highland Melody.

CAMAREE

The grey French filly Camaree, by Maurepas, won the One Thousand Guineas in 1950.

CAMBREMER

Mr R. B. Strassburger's Cambremer, by the English sire Chamossaire, won the St Leger in 1956. The following season he won the Prix du Cadran and was second in the Ascot Gold Cup.

CAMBRIDGESHIRE STAKES

See under NEWMARKET.

CAMERA PATROL

The camera patrol films a race to provide a lateral and head-on view of it. The film is available to the Stewards within minutes of the race being over and is an invaluable witness in cases of alleged rough-riding, crossing, swerving, excessive use of the whip and so forth. It also exposes the cruder examples of lack of effort on the part of a jockey. The cost of operating the camera patrol is borne by the Levy Board.

CAMERON, Major Ewen Murdoch (b 1908)

Major Cameron, particularly well-known in Scottish racing circles, rode 80 winners under National Hunt rules. He is a member of the Jockey Club and is a steward at Ayr, Hamilton Park and Lanark. His trainers are R. Fairbairn and W. A. Stephenson. Colours: silver, bronze cross belts, hoop on cap.

CAMERONIAN

Cameronian was foaled in 1928. He was bred by Lord Dewar and on Lord Dewar's death in 1930 he passed into the possession of Mr J. A. Dewar, Lord Dewar's nephew. By Pharos out of Una Cameron, Cameronian was trained by Fred Darling and in 1931 won the Two Thousand Guineas and the Derby. He then started a hot favourite for the St Leger. Normally a placid individual, he behaved like a mad horse both before the St Leger, when he kicked Orpen savagely, and also during it when he fought for his head, ran himself out and was stone cold over half a mile from home.

Darling calmly refuted any suggestion that Cameronian had been 'got at' and, incredible as it may now seem, the Stewards took no action. Cameronian had a temperature after the race and ran a slight put persistent temperature for a year afterwards. It was not until October 1932 when he really recovered his form and won the Champion Stakes in splendid style. As a sire he enjoyed only modest success both in this country and in the Argentine where he was exported at the age of 13. He died in 1955.

CAMPANULA

Bred by her owner Sir George Bullough in 1931, Campanula was a beautiful little Blandford filly that won the One Thousand Guineas and three other races. She bred four moderate winners.

CANDY, Derrick (b 1908)

Derrick Candy was for a few years a regular soldier in the Sherwood Foresters. He then served for three years as assistant to Miss Norah Wilmot and set up on his own in 1937. His stables are at Kingston Warren, near Wantage, and he is assisted there by his son, Henry. Among his patrons are Major H. P. Holt, Mr H. J. Joel, J. A. P. Martin, Mr A. R. B. Owen, Hon. R. F. Watson, Mr W. Barnett, and Major M. G. Wyatt. His most important success has been to win the 1967 Ascot Gold Cup with Parbury. In 1968 and 1969 he won good races with that fine sprinter Song.

CANISBAY

Foaled in 1961, Canisbay was bred by the Queen and is by Doutelle out of Stroma. He won two races worth over £30,000, one of them being the Eclipse Stakes. He now stands at the Sandringham Stud at a fee of 300 gn.

CANNON, Kempton (d 1951)

Kempton Cannon, a great-uncle of Lester Piggott, was the son of Tom Cannon, a great rider in his day, and brother of a fine rider in Mornington Cannon, who won the Derby on Flying Fox. He rode his first winner at the age of 14 and continued riding till shortly before World War I in which he served in the RFC. He had a long association with Mr Leopold de Rothschild for whom he won the St Leger on Doricles in 1901 and the Two Thousand Guineas and the Derby on St Amant in 1904. He married the widow of the famous jockey Jack Watts and for some years conducted a garage at Newmarket, finally retiring to Hove where he lived in placid retirement till his death.

CANNON, Mornington (b 1873)

Mornington Cannon was the son of that fine rider Tom Cannon. He was named after a horse that won at Bath for his father the day he was born. 'Morny' himself was a beautiful horseman and excelled in waiting tactics. He was at his best before the 'American Invasion', which caused races to be run at a faster pace and jockeys to pull up their leathers. He won the Derby in 1899 on Flying Fox and was champion jockey on six occasions. He lived in retirement for many years in Brighton.

CANNON, Noel (1898-1959)

Born near Newmarket in 1897, Noel Cannon was the son of Joe Cannon who had won the Grand National on Regal and had a distinguished record as a trainer. Noel Cannon, who had been wounded in World War I when serving in the 3rd Hussars, trained at the famous Druids Lodge establishment for its successive owners, Mr J. V. Rank, Mr J. A. Dewar and Mr Jack Olding. He won the St Leger with Scottish Union, the Oaks with Why Hurry and the One Thousand Guineas with Festoon. He was runner-up in the Derby with Scottish Union and Gay Time. Other notable winners he trained were Knight's Armour, Black Speck, Strathspey and Highland Division. A forthright, friendly man, he was genuinely devoted to his horses, particularly to some of the old geldings that served him well season after season. He died after a long illness at the age of 61.

CANNON, Tom (b 1846)

Born at Eton, Tom Cannon was one of the best riders of his day and won the Derby in 1882 on Shotover. Imperturbable, a shrewd tactician and a wonderful judge of pace, he was gifted with the lightest of hands and was unequalled as a rider of two-year-olds. Delicate in appearance, he was tougher than he looked, both on and off a horse, and seldom came off second best in a matter of business. When he gave up riding he trained a lot of winners at Danebury and he was a very good trainer of jockeys too. His sons Mornington and Kempton both won the Derby in their day, and as a boy Jack Watts, who rode four Derby winners, was under his care.

CANTELO

Cantelo, owned and bred by Mr W. Hill and trained by Capt Charles Elsey, won the St Leger in 1959. As she had been beaten in the Park Hill Stakes two days previously, her victory was not well received by certain sections of the crowd. By Chanteur II out of Rustic Bridge, Cantelo also won the Royal Lodge Stakes, Cheshire Oaks and Ribblesdale Stakes, while she was second in the Oaks.

CANTERBURY PILGRIM

Canterbury Pilgrim was one of the many famous mares owned by the seventeenth Earl of Derby. She was by Tristan, a bad-tempered but game horse whose 25 victories included the Ascot Gold Cup, out of Pilgrimage, who won the Two Thousand and One Thousand Guineas and who bred the 100-1 Derby winner Jeddah, and also Loved One, sire of the dams of the Derby winners Sunstar and Sansovino. Canterbury Pilgrim herself won the Oaks and the Jockey Club Cup and bred Swynford, who won the St Leger and the Eclipse Stakes. She also bred Chaucer, who was outstandingly successful as a sire of brood mares.

CANYON

Canyon, by Chaucer, was one of the many good mares owned by the seventeenth Earl of Derby. She won the 1916 One Thousand Guineas herself and bred seven winners including Colorado (£30,358) and Caerleon (£11,210).

CAPTAIN CUTTLE

Bred in 1919 by Lord Woolavington, Captain Cuttle was by Hurry On out of Bellavista, by Cyllene. A fine, big chestnut, he was trained by Fred Darling and won four races, including the Derby and St James's Palace Stakes. Owing to leg trouble he could not compete in the St Leger. As a four-year-old he ran only once and failed to stand further training. Retired to the stud, he got Scuttle in his first crop of runners, a good filly that won the One Thousand Guineas for King George V. He was exported to Italy in 1927. He did well there, but died following an accident in 1932.

CARACALLA II

M. Boussac's Caracalla II, by Tourbillon, won the Ascot Gold Cup in

1946 and was one of the best winners of that race this century. He also won the Grand Prix, the French St Leger and the Prix de l'Arc de Triomphe. He was not a success as a sire.

CARBINE

Bred in New Zealand in 1885, Carbine was by Musket out of Mersey. He had a fine racing record there and also in Australia, winning 33 races in four seasons. After four years at the stud in Australia, he was bought by the Duke of Portland and brought to England. He was not an unqualified success in this country, but sired Spearmint, winner of the Derby and the Grand Prix in 1906.

CARD

See RACE CARD.

CAREY, Thomas

Tommy Carey was born in London and apprenticed to Walter Nightingall senior at Epsom at the age of fourteen. He rode a winner over hurdles when he was only sixteen but he established his reputation before the war as the outstanding rider under Pony Turf Club rules. He won the Northolt Derby on several occasions. One of his principal Northolt patrons was Miss Dorothy Paget and having been granted a licence to ride under the Rules of Racing in 1941, he won the 1943 Derby for her on Straight Deal. After the war he set up as a trainer at Epsom and for a time was very successful but unfortunately heavy gambling brought about his eventual downfall.

CARLISLE

Carlisle provides unpretentious racing in a most attractive setting, the Lakeland hills forming the background. It is a right-handed, pear-shaped course just over $1\frac{1}{2}$m round. The run-in of $3\frac{1}{2}$f is uphill to the distance post from which point it is level. The 6f course bears right for the first $1\frac{1}{2}$f and there is a further bend just before the run-in. In races up to a mile, high numbers have the advantage. The main meeting is a three-day one in July when the Cumberland Plate ($1\frac{1}{2}$m) and the Carlisle Bell (1m) are run.

Clerk of the Course: Mr C. D. Patterson, 4 Gilesgate Bank, Hexham, Northumberland. Tel.: Hexham 2342.

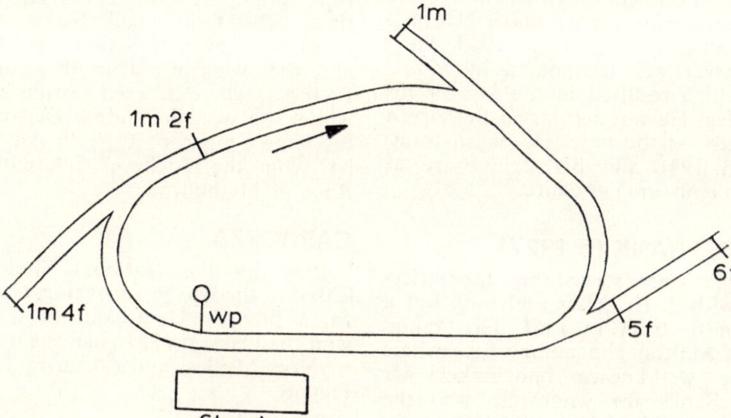

CARLISLE

Best Times:

Distance	Horse-Age-Weight	Date	Time
5f	Rock Sail 5-7-11	22-7-59	60.6
5f	Erudite 2-9-5	29-6-60	60.8
6f	Merry Tune 3-7-13	29-6-60	1min 13.5
6f	Connemara Kid 2-8-10	28-7-62	1min 15.6
8f	Aberdeen 4-9-8	2-7-65	1min 39
10f	War Eagle 3-8-1	5-7-62	2min 8
12f	Master Barry 4-8-8	1-7-65	2min 29.2

CARNARVON, sixth Earl of (b 1898)

Lord Carnarvon served in the 7th Hussars from 1915 to 1923. He rode on the flat as an amateur for 14 years and won seven races on Patmos. He has bred many good horses at the Highclere Stud, including Blenheim, winner of the Derby, and King Salmon, second in the Derby and winner of the Eclipse Stakes. The best horse to carry his colours in recent years was Queens Hussar who won seven races, including the Sussex Stakes, worth over £21,000. Lord Carnarvon's trainer is Major P. M. Nelson. Colours: scarlet, blue collar, white cap.

CARR, Ernest Joseph (b 1915)

E. J. Carr was born in 1915 and was apprenticed from 1930 to 1935 to Capt (later Sir) Cecil Boyd-Rochfort. He rode with some success under National Hunt rules from 1936 to 1940, when his career was terminated by a bad fall which resulted in the loss of his right leg. He was serving in the Green Howards at the time. He began training in 1941 and his stables are at Hambleton in Yorkshire.

CARR, FRANK (b 1927)

Frank Carr served his apprenticeship with J. E. Davis and took out a licence to train in 1961. His stables are at Malton and among his owners is the well-known bookmaker Mr John Banks for whom he won the 1969 Royal Hunt Cup with Kamundu. That season he won 24 races worth over £22,000.

CARR, William Henry (b 1916)

Harry Carr was born in Cumberland and as a boy was apprenticed to R. W. Armstrong, to whom his father acted as head lad. He rode his first winner in 1930. He was a sound, reliable, sensible rider and an extremely loyal servant. For many years he was associated with Sir Cecil Boyd-Rochfort's stable and was retained by the Queen. His daughter is married to Joe Mercer. He retired in 1964.

His big winners were as follows:

One Thousand Guineas: Meld (1955).
Derby: Parthia (1959).
Oaks: Meld (1955).
St Leger: Meld (1955), Alcide (1958) and Hethersett (1962).
King George VI and Queen Elizabeth Stakes: Alcide (1959).

He also won the Lingfield Derby Trial five times, the Lingfield Oaks Trial five times, the Chesterfield Cup four times, the Doncaster Cup three times, the Goodwood Stakes three times, the Coventry Stakes three times and the Yorkshire Cup three times. In India, where he used to ride in the winter, he won the Indian Derby and the King Emperor's Cup. In Australia he won the Jockeys' International Race at Melbourne.

CARROZZA

Bred by the National Stud and leased to the Queen for racing, Carrozza, a filly by Dante out of Calash, won the Oaks in 1957. She was trained by Noel Murless and ridden by Lester Piggott.

CARSLAKE, Bernard (1886-1941)

Dark and somewhat saturnine, Bernard Carslake was popularly known as 'Brownie' and was one of the best and most stylish of the many good Australian jockeys that have ridden in England. Before World War I he rode with success in Austria-Hungary, moving on the outbreak of war to Rumania and from there to Russia, whence he escaped with difficulty during the Revolution, arriving in England penniless in 1917. A particularly powerful finisher, he soon established himself and though he never won the Derby, he had six victories in classic events. His win in the 1924 St Leger on Salmon Trout was a truly remarkable one and gave rise to some sinister rumours. One leading bookmaker, who had laid Salmon Trout as if he knew that the horse could not possibly win, was placed in grave financial difficulties.

Throughout his career Carslake had trouble in keeping his weight down and constant wasting ultimately undermined his health. He was only 55 when he died. His ashes were scattered over Newmarket Heath.

CARSON, Alexander (b 1926)

Jock Carson has been a well-known light-weight for many years. While still apprenticed to the late M. Peacock, he rode 38 winners in 1946, 20 of them trained by Noel Murless. His victories include the Chester Cup, Manchester Cup and Prince Edward Handicap.

CARSON, William Hunter (b 1942)

'Willie' Carson was apprenticed firstly to Gerald Armstrong and later to 'Sam' Armstrong. He rode his first winner in 1962. His best season was in 1969 when he rode 66 winners. He is attached to B. van Cutsem's stable.

CARTER, Tommy (b 1930)

Tommy Carter served his apprenticeship with George Todd and has been known for a good many years as a reliable light-weight rider. Big races he has won include the Nunthorpe Stakes, the City and Suburban and the William Hill Gold Cup.

CAST IN HIS BOX

A horse is said to be cast in his box when he has got down in a stable or vehicle and has difficulty in getting up again.

CATHERINA

Catherina raced from 1833 to 1841 and established a record that has never been broken by winning 79 races. She ran 174 times.

CATTERICK

Catterick is not one of Yorkshire's major racecourses, but under the enterprising direction of Major Leslie Petch, a lot of improvements have been carried through in recent years. It is a sharp, undulating, left-handed course that is only just over a mile round with a run-in of 3f. It is an ideal track for quick starters and front-runners; the reverse for big, long-striding horses that take time to settle down.

Clerk of the Course: Major L. Petch, Liverton Lodge, Loftus, Saltburn, Yorkshire. Tel: Loftus 318. (For National Hunt racing the Clerk of the Course is: Mr C. D. Patterson, 5 Cattle Market, Hexham, Northumberland. Tel: Hexham 2342.)

Best Times:

Distance	*Horse-Age-Weight*	*Date*	*Time*
5f	Fox Covert 3-7-13	22-7-59	58.6
5f	Granville Greta 2-8-6	22-7-59	59
7f	Ringmaster 4-7-10	1-10-55	1min 24
7f	Fair Saying 2-7-10	26-9-64	1min 26
11f 40yd	Grosgrain 3-7-13	26-6-57	2min 23.6
12f 40yd	Crescent Moon 4-7-13	6-6-62	2min 36.4
13f 180yd	Rarti 4-8-2	5-7-66	2min 59
15f 180yd	Pass of Killiecrankie	2-10-59	3min 24.2

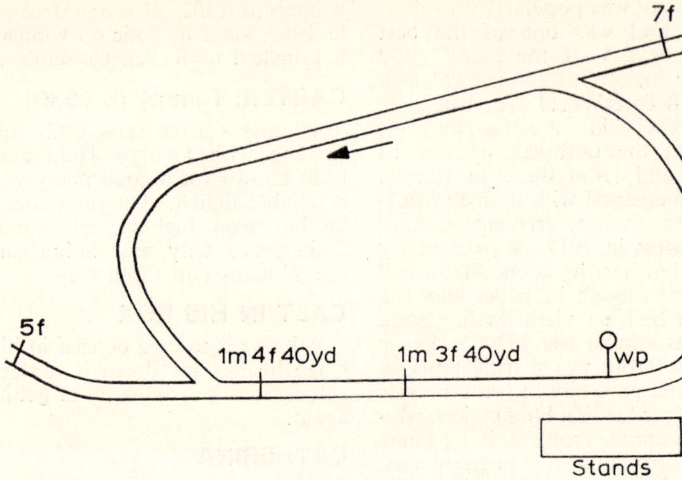

CATTERICK

CECIL, David

Twin-brother of Henry Cecil and step-son of Sir Cecil Boyd-Rochfort, David Cecil began training at Stork House, Lambourn, in 1969. Among his patrons are Lady Boyd-Rochfort, Col I. G. Collins, Lady Rowallan, Mr C. F. Fischer and Mr John F. Taylor.

CECIL, Henry

Step-son of Sir Cecil Boyd-Rochfort, Henry Cecil is married to Noel Murless's daughter. He began training at Newmarket after Sir Cecil's retirement in 1968 and had a very successful first season, his main achievement being to win the Eclipse Stakes with Wolver Hollow and the *Observer* Gold Cup with Approval. His owners include Lady Mairi Bury, Earl of Dunraven, Sir Humphrey de Trafford, Mr H. J. Joel, Mr and Mrs Stanhope Joel, Mrs J. W. Hanes, Mr R. J. Kleberg, Mr H. F. Guggenheim, Mr J. H. Whitney, Mr P. A. B. Widener and Mrs J. R. Mullion.

CESAREWITCH STAKES

See under NEWMARKET.

CHALEUREUX

Chaleureux was an unfashionably-bred horse that began his career as a selling plater but later won some good handicaps, including the Cesarewitch. With few opportunities at the stud, he sired Signorinetta, winner of the Derby and the Oaks in 1908.

CHALK JOCKEY

At most courses there are boards with the names of established jockeys on them ready for use in the number boards. Little known riders have their names inscribed on blank boards in white chalk.

CHALONER, Tom

Tom Chaloner rode Macaroni to victory in the 1863 Derby. It was his only success in that race but he rode five winners of the St Leger and three of the Two Thousand Guineas. He had the reputation of being an honest, reliable and unassuming man.

CHAMOSSAIRE

Bred by the National Stud in 1942, Chamossaire, by Precipitation out of

(*above left*) AGA KHAN, H. H. THE. The Aga Khan leads in his 1936 Derby winner Mahmoud (C. Smirke up). (*above right*) ARCHER, FRED. One of the greatest of English jockeys

ASCOT. Pre-war Royal Ascot and the finish of the famous Gold Cup battle between Quashed and Omaha

(*left*) ASTOR, SECOND VISCOUNT. A great owner-breeder, the late Lord Astor, with Joe Lawson (in bowler hat) and Bobby Dick. (*below*) BAHRAM. The last horse to win the Triple Crown. Fred Fox is the jockey in this picture

Snowberry, was owned by Mr Stanhope Joel and trained by R. Perryman. He won four races worth over £11,000 including the St Leger which in that year was run at York. His record as a sire was inconsistent, but he was champion in 1964 when his son Santa Claus won the Derby and the Irish Derby. He also sired the St Leger winner Cambremer. He died in 1964.

CHAMPION

Champion, winner of the Derby in 1800, was the first Derby winner to win the St Leger as well. He was owned by Mr Christopher Wilson, of Tadcaster, Yorkshire.

CHAMPION JOCKEYS

See Leading Jockeys.

CHAMPION STAKES

See under Newmarket.

CHANTEUR II

Bred in France, Chanteur II was by Chateau Bouscaut out of La Diva. He won seven races in France and three in England, including the Coronation Cup. He was twice second in the Gold Cup. He did well as a sire and was champion in 1953, the year his son Pinza won the Derby. He also sired the St Leger winner Cantelo and Only For Life, winner of the Two Thousand Guineas.

CHAMPAGNE STAKES

See under Doncaster.

CHARLEBELLE

Owned and bred by Mr A. P. Cunliffe, Charlebelle, by Charles O'Malley, won the Oaks in 1920. She bred one moderate winner.

CHARLOTTESVILLE

Charlottesville, foaled in 1957, is by Prince Chevalier out of Noorani, by Nearco. Owned by the Aga Khan and bred in Ireland by the late Aga

E

Khan and Prince Aly Khan, he was trained in France by Alec Head. He won 1,020,748 NF in stakes, and his victories include the Prix du Jockey Club and the Grand Prix. He is now at the Ballymany Stud, Co Kildare, and his offspring include Charlottown, winner of the Derby, and Carlemont, winner of the Sussex Stakes.

CHARLOTTOWN

Charlottown is a bay by Charlottesville out of the famous Meld, winner of the One Thousand Guineas, Oaks and St Leger. Bred and owned by Lady Zia Wernher and trained by Gordon Smyth at Lewes, Charlottown was unbeaten as a two-year-old in 1965. The following year he won the Derby and ridden by A. Breasley was runner-up in the Irish Derby and the St Leger. As a four-year-old he won the Coronation Cup. Game and consistent, the only poor race he ran was when he finished down the course in the Grand Prix de St Cloud as a four-year-old. He never ran again afterwards. He stands at the Someries Stud, Newmarket.

CHATELAINE

Bred at the famous Sledmere Stud, Chatelaine, by Phalaris, won the Oaks in 1933 for Mr E. Thornton-Smith. She made no mark at the stud.

CHELANDRY

The late Lord Rosebery's Chelandry, a half-sister to the Derby winner Ladas by Goldfinch, won the One Thousand Guineas and over £13,000 in stakes. At the stud she bred six winners of over £42,000 in stakes including Neil Gow, winner of the Two Thousand Guineas. Chelandry is one of the great tap roots of modern bloodstock and her descendants include the English classic winners (apart from Neil Gow) Pogrom, Saucy Sue, Pay Up, Book Law, Galatea II, Ocean Swell and Never Say Die; the Italian Derby winners Traghetto and Barba Toni; and the Kentucky Derby winner Tomy Lee.

CHEPSTOW

Chepstow is the newest flat-race course in England, having first come into operation in the 1920s. The setting is most attractive but the standard of the sport there, despite the somewhat grandiose ideas that existed to start with, has always been of a modest character. In the past attendances have been restricted by a certain inaccessibility, but the opening of the new Severn Bridge and the South Wales motorway has brought about a notable improvement in that respect. It was at Chepstow in 1933 that Sir Gordon Richards rode all six winners on the first day of the meeting and the first five winners on the second day.

It is a left-handed track about 2m round with a run-in of 5f. The mile course is straight and undulating. The various gradients call for an adaptable, well-balanced horse. High numbers are reckoned to hold a slight advantage on the straight course.

Clerk of the Course: Mr John Hughes, Windrush, Black Bourton, Oxon. Tel: Carterton 397.

Best Times:

Distance	*Horse-Age-Weight*	*Date*	*Time*
5f	Thoroughwort 4-7-13	28-6-49	58.2
5f	Chalkey 2-9-4	22-5-61	58.2
6f	Nerium 5-9-11	6-8-62	1min 9.2
6f	Scot's Beam 2-8-8	1-8-55	1min 10.6
7f	Cintrist 3-7-3	3-7-54	1min 21.2
7f	Empetrum 2-9-0	7-8-62	1min 24.4
8f	Alizarene 4-8-8	28-6-49	1min 32.6
10f	Sculptor 4-9-5	10-6-57	2min 6.4
12f	Alistair 4-8-6	11-7-38	2min 32.6

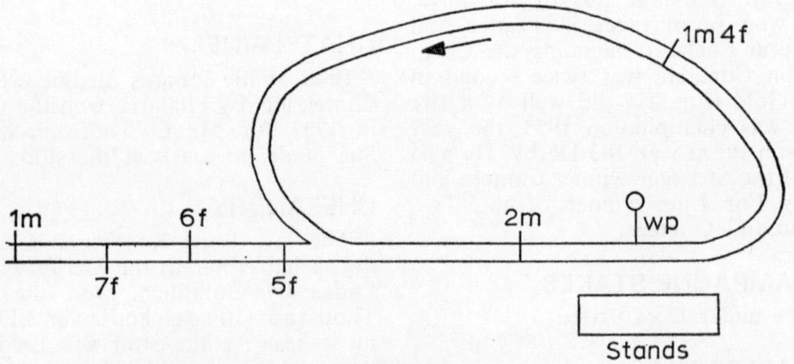

CHEPSTOW

CHERIMOYA

Ridden by Fred Winter, father of the famous National Hunt rider, Cherimoya won the Oaks in 1911 at 25-1. A daughter of Cherry Tree, she bred three winners of no particular significance.

CHERRY LASS

Col W. Hall Walker's Cherry Lass won the One Thousand Guineas and the Oaks in 1905. She unfortunately died young after breeding a couple of winners.

CHESTER

Chester's Roodee is one of the most famous and unique courses in the country. It is also one of the most ancient and records of racing there exist from 1540. It is shaped like a plate, just over a mile in circumference, and the run-in is only 230yd, the shortest on any English track. Low numbers are favoured in the draw over all distances. Horses are racing on the bend the whole way and not surprising a fair number fail to adapt themselves to the conditions. Nevertheless the Chester Vase is regarded as a significant Derby trial and numbers among the winners Derby victors such as Papyrus, Hyperion and Windsor Lad, Tulyar and Parthia, too, scored at Chester before going on to triumph at Epsom.

The big meeting at Chester is early in May and the most famous race, the Chester Cup, is a 2¼m handicap in which the runners pass the stands three times. Particularly on Cup day, spectators throng the city walls in thousands to watch the sport. In the last century the Cup was second only to the Derby in volume of ante-post betting it inspired.

Clerk of the Course: Capt R. C. G. Vivian, Charlton House, Tetbury, Glos. Tel: Tetbury 310.

Best Times:

Distance	*Horse-Age-Weight*	*Date*	*Time*
5f	Althrey Don 3-10-0	10-7-64	59.29
5f	Cynara 2-8-11	3-5-60	60.4
6f	Welsh Warrior 4-7-5	27-7-68	1min 12.8
6f	Stung 2-9-3	27-7-68	1min 13.4
7f 118yd	Cock of the North 4-8-13	7-5-53	1min 33.2
7f 118yd	Contemptuous 2-8-0	4-9-64	1min 35
10f 10yd	Colonel Blimp 6-9-7	27-7-68	2min 6.2
10f 10yd	Hard and Soft 5-8-7	3-5-60	2min 6.8
12f 53yd	Courtesan 3-9-0	3-5-60	2min 38.2
13f 75yd	Empire Honey 3-8-0	5-5-53	2min 51.8
16f 77yd	Curry 6-8-0	8-5-57	3min 59.2

Chester Cup, 2m 2f 77yd

Handicap. First run 1824. *No race* 1940 *to* 1945.

	OWNER	TRAINER	JOCKEY	SP
1930 Mountain Lad, 5–7–11	H. Sutton	R. Gooch	F. Lane	20–1
1931 Brown Jack, 7–9–6	Sir H. Wernher	I. Anthony	M. Beary	100–8
1932 Bonny Brighteyes, 4–7–3	Mrs C. Robinson	M. Peacock	J. Dines	20–1
1933 Dick Turpin, 4–7–10	R. F. Watson	M. Hartigan	G. Richards	9–1
1934 Blue Vision, 7–7–11	M. Evans	I. Anthony	F. Fox	100–6
1935 Damascus, 4–7–1	G. Lambton	G. Lambton	H. Foster	10–1
1936 Cho-sen, 4–7–2	Mr W. Ahern	W. Higgs	J. Dines	100–7
1937 Faites vos Jeux, 6–7–4	Lady Nuttall	H. L. Cottrill	P. Maher	8–1
1938 Mr Grundy, 4–7–5	Sir A. Bailey	J. Lawson	G. Richards	10–1
1939 Winnebar, 5–7–12	Sir F. Eley	F. Templeman	G. Richards	100–8
1946 Retsel, 4–7–9	H. Lester	G. Todd	G. Richards	4–1
1947 Asmodee II, 4–9–1	P. Duboscq	W. Halsey	T. Burns	10–1
1948 Billet, 4–8–3	B. Hilliard	H. Wragg	W. Nevett	5–1
1949 John Moore, 5–6–10	W. Chapman	H. Weatherill	A. Carson	25–1
1950 Heron Bridge, 6–9–7	J. Davies	D. Rogers.	T. Burns	11–2
1951 Wood Leopard, 4–7–5	Lord Durham	R. J. Colling	J. Egan	20–1
1952 Le Tellier, 7–8–11	J. Westoll	G. Barling	G. Littlewood	6–1
1953 Eastern Emperor, 5–9–2	Lord Milford	J. Jarvis	W. Rickaby	2–1
1954 Peperium, 4–8–6	C. Elsey	C. Elsey	E. Britt	13–2
1955 Prescription, 4–8–9	Lord Rosebery	J. Jarvis	W. Rickaby	8–1

Chester Cup (contd)

	OWNER	TRAINER	JOCKEY	SP
1956 Golovine, 6–8–2 ..	Begum Aga Khan	H. Wragg ..	P. Robinson ..	9–2
1957 Curry, 6–8–0	F. Honour	F. Armstrong..	J. Gifford ..	11–4
1958 Sandiacre, 6–8–5 ..	M. Cowley	W. Dutton ..	L. Piggott ..	15–2
1959 Agreement, 5–9–4 ..	The Queen	C. B-Rochfort .	W. Carr	3–1
1960 Trelawny, 4–7–11 ..	Mrs L. Carver ..	S. Mercer . ..	F. Durr	100–6
1961 Hoy, 5–8–0	C. Spencer	L. Dale	G. Lewis ..	15–2
1962 Golden Fire, 4–7–9 .	Mrs G. Ridley ..	D. Marks . ..	D. Yates . ..	7–1
1963 Narratus, 5–7–5 ..	D. Symonds . ..	D. Thom . ..	D. Yates . ..	8–1
1964 Credo, 4–8–3	L. Gelb	P. Prendergast .	P. Cook	4–1
1965 Harvest Gold, 6–7–11	T. Marshall	T. Robson ..	F. Durr	11–2
1966 Aegean Blue, 4–8–7 .	Lieut-Cmdr P. Emmet	R. Houghton .	L. Piggott ..	22–1
1967 Mahbub Aly, 6–8–1	Lord Rotherwick .	W. Hern . ..	P. Cook	7–1
1968 Major Rose, 6–8–7..	R. Heaton	H. R. Price ..	L. Piggott ..	11–4
1969—Abandoned—Course Waterlogged				
1970 Altogether, 4–7–0 ..	W. Bolton	W. Murray ..	W. Bentley ..	33–1

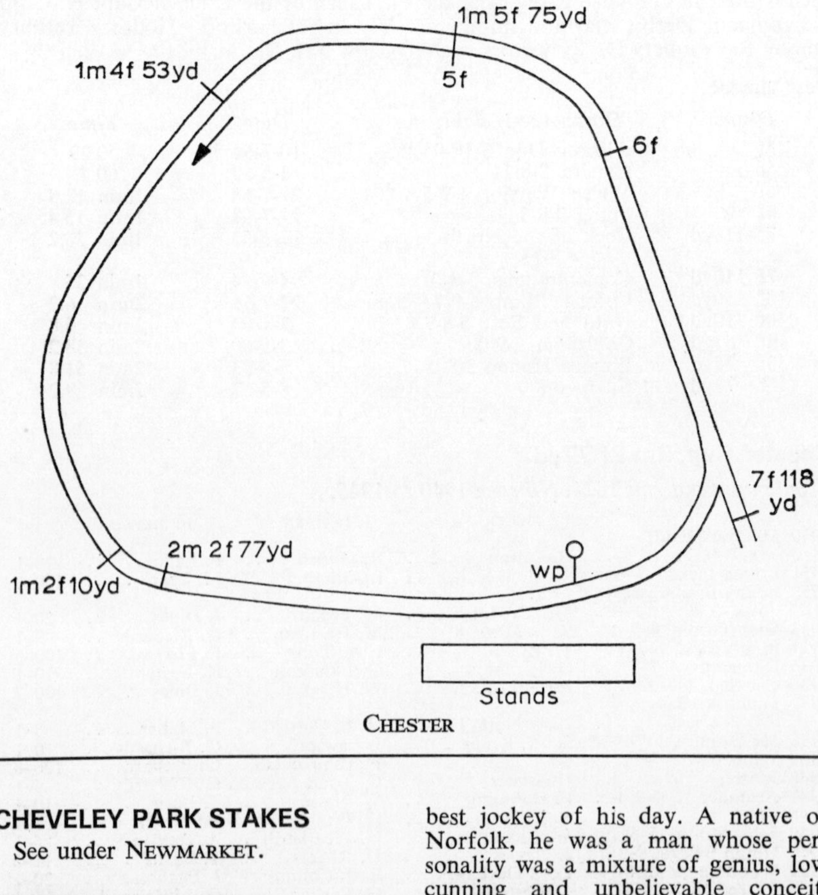

CHESTER

CHEVELEY PARK STAKES

See under NEWMARKET.

CHIFNEY, Sam, senior

Sam Chifney senior, who won the 1789 Derby on Skyscraper, was the best jockey of his day. A native of Norfolk, he was a man whose personality was a mixture of genius, low cunning and unbelievable conceit. However, his reiterated claim—"I could ride horses in a better manner in a race than any other person known in my time"—was doubtless justified. Moreover, he was responsible for the training of his son, also Sam Chifney, who became an even better rider than his father.

The Escape affair was Chifney's downfall. On 20th October 1791, he rode the Prince of Wales's Escape at Newmarket and finished last of four. Escape was favourite and there was a widely held suspicion that Chifney had not done his best to win. Chifney, however, said the horse was short of a gallop. Escape ran again the following day and won. There was an inquiry by the Stewards and Sir Charles Bunbury, the leading figure on the Turf at that period, told the Prince that no gentleman would run his horse against him if he continued to employ Chifney. The Prince stood up for his servant, shook the dust of Newmarket off his heels and never raced there again. The Prince promised to continue paying Chifney his retaining fee of 200 gn, but the promise was not fulfilled and Chifney died in the Fleet Prison, to which he had been committed for debt.

In modern times Chifney's explanation might well have been accepted. Escape had never been a consistent horse and in any case he may well have needed a race. Furthermore the two races were over different distances. Probably the Stewards were determined to drop on Chifney, who had for long been under suspicion, but selected an unsuitable occasion for so doing.

CHIFNEY, Sam, junior

Sam Chifney junior was, like his father, a brilliant rider, and like his father, too, he was rated unscrupulous. He was 32 when he won the Derby in 1818 on Sam and he won the race again two years later on Sailor. He was 57 when he won his last classic race, the One Thousand Guineas, on Extempore in 1843. Phlegmatic and indolent by nature, he became downright slothful as he grew older and in consequence missed many winning rides, a deprivation that did not perturb him in the least. He died at Hove aged 70.

CHIFNEY, Will

Son of Sam Chifney senior, Will Chifney became a very successful trainer. His three Derby winners were Sam (1818), Sailor (1820) and Priam (1830). Priam, generally rated an outstanding Derby winner, was owned by Chifney who bought him as a yearling for 1,000 gn.

CHILDS, Joe (1885-1958)

Joe Childs, a great jockey, rode fifteen English classic winners and two winners of the Grand Prix. For the last ten years of his career he was jockey to King George V, a post that afforded him immense satisfaction.

He was born in France at Chantilly, one of five brothers who all became jockeys. He went to England to be apprenticed to Tom Jennings junior and rode his first winner in 1900. He soon proved his ability, but receiving scant patronage once he had lost his allowance, he returned to France in 1903. At that stage of his life he could never control his explosive temper in face of criticism, and jobs with M. Caillault, the Duc de Gramont and with an Italian stable were of brief duration. His luck turned in 1908 when he won the Grand Prix on North East, and the following year he rode with success for Prince Murat. Constant wasting, though, was affecting his health and he agreed to ride for two years for the Weinberg brothers in Germany, the contract containing no stipulation with regard to a minimum weight. Fred Darling was then training for the Weinberg brothers and with two such peppery individuals in one stable, the sparks flew with no little frequency.

In 1912 Childs returned to France and that year he won the Oaks on Mirska. In 1914 he got out of Chantilly by the last train before the Germans arrived, leaving all his possessions behind him. He joined the

RFC but even the fairly liberal concept of discipline in that organisation was too much for him and he transferred to the 4th Hussars, a friendly regiment that gave him plenty of riding leave. In 1918, when he won the 'Triple Crown' on Gainsborough, he gave all his riding fees to regimental funds. In 1916 he had ridden his first Derby winner on Fifinella.

In 1919 he was beaten in the St Leger on the odds-on favourite, Lord Astor's Buchan. Major Gerald Deane, Lord Astor's racing manager, made some sarcastic comments; Childs never rode for Lord Astor again.

He had his third Derby winner in 1926 on Coronach, who also won the St Leger. In 1928 he won the One Thousand Guineas for the King on Scuttle. Probably the best race he ever rode was to win the Hardwicke Stakes for the King on Limelight.

Strong and exceptionally patient, Childs excelled at the waiting game. Tall for a jockey, lithe and beetle-browed, he could be formidable and young jockeys stood in fearful awe of him, but he mellowed considerably with age. On retirement he controlled a greyhound racing track at Portsmouth and occasionally owned a horse in partnership with his friend George Digby.

Here is a list of his classic winners:

Two Thousand Guineas: Gainsborough (1918), Cameronian (1931).

One Thousand Guineas: Scuttle (1928), Brown Betty (1933).

Derby: Fifinella (1916), Gainsborough (1918), Coronach (1928).

Oaks: Mirska (1912), Fifinella (1916), Bayuda (1919), Love-in-Idleness (1921).

St Leger: Gainsborough (1918), Polemarch (1921), Solario (1925), Coronach (1926).

CHULMLEIGH

Bred and owned by Lord Glanely, Chulmleigh was by the St Leger winner Singapore out of Rose of England, winner of the Oaks. He won the 1937 St Leger, trained by Capt T. Hogg and ridden by Gordon Richards. He was exported to the Argentine after seven stud seasons in England.

CHURCHILL, Sir Winston

Lord Randolph Churchill, Winston's father, had been a keen racing man and won the Oaks with L'Abbesse de Jouarre. Sir Winston himself liked horses and hunting and was an enthusiastic polo-player during his service in India with the 4th Hussars, but he was 75 years of age when he first registered his colours and appointed Walter Nightingall his trainer. His first horse was the stouthearted French-bred grey, Colonist II, who won thirteen races, including the Jockey Club Cup and the Winston Churchill Stakes, and became a great favourite with the public. High Hat won for Sir Winston over £15,000 in stakes and has become a successful sire, while Vienna won £14,900 in stakes in England, 103,350 NF in France, and sired Vaguely Noble, who won the *Observer* Gold Cup at Doncaster, was sold at Newmarket for 136,000 gn, a record price for a horse in training, and as a three-year-old won the Prix de l'Arc de Triomphe. Sir Winston also owned Welsh Abbot, who won the Portland Handicap at Doncaster as a three-year-old with 9st 2lb, and Tudor Monarch, who won the Stewards Cup at Goodwood. Sir Winston was a member of the Jockey Club.

CICERO

Cicero, by Cyllene, won the 1905 Derby for the late Lord Rosebery. At stud the best horse he got was the speedy Friar Marcus.

CIECHANOWSKI, John (b 1921)

Educated at Ampleforth, John Ciechanowski is a well-known and much-liked personality in English and French racing circles. He served in the 1st Polish Armoured Division in the war and was engaged from 1945-47 in the reclamation of Polish bloodstock in Germany. He was a learner with Tom Masson at Lewes from 1948-50, and from 1950-51 he worked at the French National Stud. From 1954-56 he managed a stud and a racing stable in Brazil. A prolific journalist, he has contributed to many publications in this country, including the *Daily Telegraph* and *Sunday Telegraph*. A competent amateur rider both on the flat and under National Hunt rules, he has taken part more than once in the Grand National. He has a small stud in France and boards yearlings for sale.

CINNA

Cinna, by Polymelus, won the One Thousand Guineas in 1920. She was also second in the Oaks. She bred eight winners, including Beau Pere, a moderate racehorse that became an outstanding sire in New Zealand, Australia and finally in America.

CITY AND SUBURBAN HANDICAP

See under Epsom.

CLAIMING

If it is said of an apprentice that 'he claims the five', it means he is still entitled to the 5lb allowance. For fuller information see Allowance.

CLARISSIMUS

Clarissimus, foaled in 1913, was by Radium and won the Two Thousand Guineas and Champion Stakes. He was exported to France and did well as a sire there, his mares being particularly successful.

CLARK, Robert Sterling (1877-1956)

Mr R. S. Clark, a great American sportsman with no interest in the betting side of racing, became a patron of the English Turf in 1930, and after a dispute with the New York Jockey Club in 1946 he transferred all his racing interests, bar his stud, to Britain. At one time he owned a stud in France, but all the buildings there were destroyed in the Normandy battle in 1944. He won the One Thousand Guineas and the Oaks in 1939 with Galatea II, and the Derby and the St Leger in 1954 with Never Say Die. Both were trained for him by Joe Lawson. As a token of his regard for the English Turf, he presented Never Say Die to the National Stud. In appreciation of this gesture he was elected a member of the Jockey Club.

CLASSIC RACE

There are five classics. They are the Two Thousand Guineas and the One Thousand Guineas, both run over 1m at Newmarket; the Derby and the Oaks, both run over 1½m at Epsom; and the St Leger run over 1m 6f 132yd at Doncaster. No horse has won all five classics but Sceptre won all bar the Derby in which she was fourth.

CLAYTON, John Maurice

Jack Clayton, a very well-liked member of the racing community, has been a familiar figure on the Turf for over forty years. In his younger days he had the reputation of being a bold punter. Later he was racing manager to the late Mr and the late Mrs J. V. Rank and subsequently to the late Sir Victor Sassoon. He was a powerful influence in the Newmarket stable for which Norman Bertie held the licence and which won the Derby with Pinza and the One Thousand Guineas with Belle of All. When at length Bertie retired, Clayton took out a licence himself. His stables are at Bedford House, Newmarket, and his patrons include Lady Hothfield, M Maurice Hennessy, Marchese Incisa della Rochetta, Lord and Lady Porchester, Mrs J. A. De Rothschild, Count Charles Seilern and Mr Jack Thursby. In 1969 he won the *News of the World Stakes* and the Peter Hastings Stakes with Principal Boy.

CLAYTON, Stanley (b 1926)

Stan Clayton, born in 1926, was apprenticed from 1940 to 1949 to W. Smallwood and rode his first winner in 1943 at Pontefract. His two most important successes have been to win the Oaks for Major Holliday on Neasham Belle and the Eclipse for the Queen on Canisbay. He also won the Portland Handicap on Sir Winston Churchill's Black Abbot on Sir Winston's golden wedding anniversary. His other notable successes include the Goodwood Cup (twice), the City and Suburban (three times), the Ribblesdale Stakes, Yorkshire Oaks and Yorkshire Cup. A sound rider who has never been bothered by his weight, he is a cheerful character and a noted fancier of budgerigars. In 1969 he accepted a post as trainer in Sweden.

CLIFT, William

William Clift rode the first of his five Derby winners in 1793, the last in 1819. A rough, hardy Yorkshireman who began life as a shepherd, he was notoriously uncouth and a contemporary described him as a "rough, uncultivated Indian". His manners towards his employers were brusque in the extreme, no matter how exalted their status. He was honest but unpolished in his methods and inclined to be hard on his horses. When he was nearly 80 years old he used to walk to Newmarket from Bury St Edmunds and back again "just to give my legs a stretch".

CLIFTON, H. C., MC

Clerk of the Course, Alexandra Park.

COATES, David

Apprenticed to D. H. Williams who trains at Ferryhill, Co. Durham. In 1968 he dead-heated with R. Dicey for the position of top apprentice, both riding 40 winners. He rode 18 winners in 1969.

COBBLER, THE

Bred in 1945 by Lieut-Col Giles Loder, The Cobbler, by Windsor Slipper, was a very fast horse that won nine races, including the Coventry Stakes, Middle Park Stakes, Victoria Cup and Wokingham Stakes. He was second in the Two Thousand Guineas. He was exported as a sire to New Zealand where he did well.

COHEN, Sir Rex KBE (b 1906)

Few members of the Jockey Club possess wider business experience than Sir Rex Cohen. He was a member of the Benson Committee of Inquiry into the Racing Industry, and subsequently headed an inquiry into the question of racehorse management. His trainer is Gordon Smyth. Colours: black and gold stripes, hooped cap.

COLLING, George Scott (1904-1959)

George Colling came of sound racing stock. His father was the Newmarket trainer R. W. Colling, who had married a daughter of the steeplechase jockey Robert l'Anson. Jack Colling, George's brother, was for years a successful trainer. George himself married a sister of the Newmarket trainer Geoffrey Barling.

George Colling was a fine rider in his youth and as an apprentice rode over 70 winners in 1919. Increasing weight, though, caused him to relinquish his licence in 1922. For many years he assisted his brother and it was not until 1935 that he set up as a trainer on his own. He was just beginning to establish himself when war broke out. He at once joined the Royal Artillery in which he served till invalided out in 1942.

After the war his stable as Hurworth House, Newmarket, rapidly filled. In 1947 he paid 5,000 gn at the Newmarket Yearling Sales for a Nearco colt on behalf of Mr A. Glenister, an official of the Midland Bank. The yearling was named Nimbus and in 1949 won the Two Thousand Guineas and the Derby. Colling was ill on Derby Day and never saw the race.

In 1950 he was asked by Lord Derby to train for him at Stanley House and agreed to do so, but he never settled down really happily there and in 1956 he was back at Hurworth House. Among the notable horses he trained were Wilwyn, the only English horse so far to win the Laurel Park International; Ark Royal, a great staying filly whose misfortune it was to be born the same year as Meld; Acropolis, third in the Derby, and Mossborough, who became an outstanding sire.

Quiet, courteous and extremely shrewd, Colling possessed a high degree of professional ability. For much of his life, though, he was dogged by indifferent health which was doubtless the cause of his somewhat pessimistic views on many aspects of life.

COLLINGWOOD, Lieut-Gen Sir George, KBE CB DSO (b 1903)

Lieut-Gen Sir George Collingwood had a distinguished military career. An owner on a modest scale, his trainer is R. D. Peacock. He is a member of the Jockey Club and has served as Steward and Senior Steward. His home is in Northumberland and he is a steward at Ayr, Newcastle, and Thirsk. Colours: light blue, black hooped sleeves, black cap.

COLOMBO

Bred by Sir Alec Black and owned by Lord Glanely, who bought him as a yearling in 1932 for 510 gn, Colombo was by Manna out of Lady Nairne. As a two-year-old Colombo swept all opposition aside and was hailed as "the horse of the century". The following season he maintained his unbeaten record in the spring by winning the Craven Stakes and the Two Thousand Guineas. He was favourite for the Derby at 11-8 but in a sensational race he could only finish third to Windsor Lad and Easton. Possibly he was not a true stayer, but the fact remains that his rider, W. R. Johnstone, rode a very indifferent race. After the Derby Colombo, still feeling the effects of his Epsom exertions, was beaten by Flamenco in the St James's Palace Stakes at Ascot. He never ran again. As a sire he was not altogether a success although he got the Two Thousand Guineas winner Happy Knight and Dancing Time, winner of the One Thousand Guineas.

COLONIST II

A French-bred grey by Rienzo, Colonist II was the first horse to carry Sir Winston Churchill's colours. Trained by Walter Nightingall, he proved a tough, game stayer and won 13 races worth over £11,000, including the Jockey Club Cup, Ribblesdale Stakes, Winston Churchill Stakes and White Rose Stakes. He was second in the Gold Cup at Ascot.

COLORADO

Bred and owned by the seventeenth Earl of Derby, Colorado, foaled in 1923, was a brilliant horse by Phalaris out of the One Thousand Guineas winner Canyon. Trained by George Lambton, he won nine races worth over £30,000 including the Two Thousand Guineas and the Eclipse Stakes. He made a wonderful start as a sire and his death after only two years at the stud represented an extremely serious loss to British breeders.

COLORADO KID

Bred in 1929 by his owner Lieut-Col Giles Loder, Colorado Kid, by Colorado, was a most versatile performer, his victories including the Royal Hunt Cup (then 7f), the 10f Kempton Jubilee and the 2¼m Doncaster Cup.

COLOURS

Racing colours have to be registered

annually at a fee of £2. Colours thus registered cannot be taken by any other person. Disputes as to the right to particular colours must be settled by the Stewards of the Jockey Club. Any person running a horse in colours other than those registered in his own name without a special declaration to the Overnight Declarations Office is liable to a fine of not less than £1 and not more than £10.

COLT

An ungelded male horse under five years of age.

COMMON

Owned in partnership by Lord Alington and Sir Frederick Johnstone and bred at Crichel by the former, Common, a son of Isonomy, won the 'Triple Crown' in 1891. He was trained by John Porter at Kingsclere. As a sire he was a failure.

COMMOTION

Owned and bred by Mr J. A. Dewar, Commotion was by Mieuxcé out of Riot. She won three races including the 1941 Oaks. She bred seven winners, among them Combat, the unbeaten winner of nine races and a successful sire; Faux Tirage, winner of over £8,000 and a successful sire in New Zealand; and Aristophanes, who won over £4,000 and did well as a sire in the Argentine.

COMPENSATION

Foaled in 1959, Compensation is a chestnut horse by Gratitude. Trained by Teddy Lambton, he won eight races and over £17,000, his victories including the Imperial Stakes, Cork and Orrery Stakes and Ayr Gold Cup. Syndicated for the stud, he stands at the Offchurch Bury Stud, near Leamington Spa.

COMRADE

Comrade, bred in Ireland by Mr L. Neumann, was by Bachelors Double out of a mare by Spearmint. Sold for 25 gn as a yearling, he won some £25,000 in stakes, including the 1920 Grand Prix de Paris. He was trained at Newmarket by Peter Gilpin.

CONJURE

Conjure was a foundation mare of the second Lord Astor's stud. A daughter of Juggler, she was foaled in 1895 and her descendants include Winkipop (One Thousand Guineas), Blink (second in the Derby), Short Story (Oaks), Pennycomequick (Oaks), Sunny Devon (Coronation Stakes).

CONNORTON, Brian (b 1935)

Brian Connorton was successively apprenticed to N. Bertie, P. Ward and W. Gray and rode his first winner in 1953 at Yarmouth. He rides chiefly in the North where he has had a fruitful association with W. Gray's stable.

COOK, Paul Allen (b 1946)

Paul Cook was apprenticed to H. Nicholson and before long was displaying outstanding promise. In 1963 he rode his first winner; in 1966 he was riding for Jack Jarvis's stable and very nearly won the Derby on Pretendre. That season he rode 93 winners and won the One Thousand Guineas on Glad Rags. Perhaps he had gone to the top rather more swiftly than was really good for him and he was markedly less successful in 1967. However, there were hopeful signs of revival of his fortunes in 1968 and 1969. He is attached to I. Balding's stable.

CORBETT, Hon Thomas Anthony, MC (b 1921)

A son of Lord Rowallan, at one time the Chief Scout, 'Atty' Corbett was educated at Eton and served with distinction in the Grenadier Guards. For a time he was attached to Fred

Rimell's stable and rode with success under National Hunt rules, first as an amateur and later as a professional, winning the National Hunt Chase on Ellesmere and the Mildmay Memorial Chase on Domata.

He started off his training career in 1958 with a few jumpers, but gradually he switched to the flat and he now controls a powerful stable at Lagrange, Newmarket. His owners include Mr J. U. Baillie, Mr M. Bonsor, Major J. Eyre, Mr H. Loebstein, Sir William Dugdale, Mr W. A. Gillilan, Lieut-Col I. G. Collins, Mr C. Pollock and Mr R. Longrigg. Among his many good winners have been Talahasse (Gimcrack and Champagne Stakes) and Queen's Hussar (Lockinge and Sussex Stakes). He is a bachelor, with a considerable sense of humour and is one of the few 'characters' in the game today.

CORONACH

Coronach was bred and owned by Lord Woolavington and trained by Fred Darling. A big, light-coloured chestnut with a flaxen mane and tail, he was high-mettled, wilful and hated restraint. As a three-year-old he was trounced by Colorado in the Two Thousand Guineas but won the Column Produce Stakes, the Derby, the St James's Palace Stakes, the Eclipse Stakes and the St Leger. He won the Derby by five lengths, the St James's Palace Stakes by twenty lengths, the Eclipse Stakes by six lengths and the St Leger in record time. There had always been rumours, though, that he was not quite sound in his wind and as a four-year-old he was undoubtedly hampered by respiratory trouble. He won the Coronation Cup and the Hardwicke Stakes, but Colorado slammed him in the Princess of Wales's Stakes and the Eclipse Stakes. Coronach was not a stud success in England but he sired a top-class filly in M. Boussac's Corrida (see below). In 1940 Mrs (now the Hon Lady) Macdonald-Buchanan, Lord Woolavington's daughter, made a gift of Coronach to New Zealand, and it was there that he spent the last nine years of his life. His stud record there was good.

CORONATION CUP

See under EPSOM.

CORRIDA

Corrida, by Coronach, was bred and owned by M. M. Boussac and was foaled in 1932. One of the best fillies to race in Europe between the wars, she twice won the Prix de l'Arc de Triomphe and won good races in England, Belgium and Germany as well. She was stolen by the Germans during the war and was never recovered. Her son Coaraze won the French Derby.

COTTRILL, Harry Lawson (d 1955)

Harry Cottrill had a happy, sanguine disposition and never lacked friends. Before World War I he was well known in hunting and point-to-pointing circles in Cheshire. He paid for his fun by making hunters and selling them. He began his training career with a few jumpers at Tarporley, but he was granted a licence to train on the flat in 1915 and at the end of the war he went to Seven Barrows, Lambourn, to train for the uncouth, ill-fated Lancashire financier, Mr James White. White, vain and self-opinionated, was a difficult man to get on with, but fortunately the debonair Cottrill had a buoyant temperament. Perhaps the best horse he trained for White, who eventually committed suicide, was Irish Elegance, who put up a memorable performance to win the Royal Hunt Cup with 9st 11lb.

Cottrill was very successful in big handicaps. He won the Cesarewitch with Ivanhoe; the Portland Handicap with Irish Elegance, who carried 10st 3lb; The Royal Hunt Cup, apart from Irish Elegance, with Guinea Gap and Caerloptic; the Stewards Cup with Western Wave and Solerina; the Chester Cup with Chivalrous (twice) and Faites vos Jeux; the Cambridgeshire with Dan Bulger; the Lincoln with Granely; and the Ascot Stakes with Miss Sport and Doreen Jane. His two classic successes were the Two Thousand Guineas in 1927 with Col S. Whitburn's Adams Apple and the Oaks in 1936 with Sir A. Bailey's Lovely Rosa.

Harry Cottrill had two sons, Humphrey (see below) and Alec. Alec, a fine amateur rider was assistant to George Lambton at Stanley House when he died in 1933 as the result of a fall at Lewes.

COTTRILL, Humphrey Lawson (b 1906)

Humphrey Cottrill was born in 1906 and is a son of the late Harry Cottrill (see above). He assisted his father from 1928 to 1937. He served in India and Burma during the war, and for four years after it was a Stipendiary Steward in South Africa. Returning to England in 1950, he assisted Willie Pratt and then Marcus Marsh. He took out a licence in 1952 and had a spell as private trainer for the late Major Lionel Holliday, for whom he trained such good horses as Narrator, Chatsworth, Pirate King and Gratitude. With the termination of that arrangement, he became a public trainer at Beverley House, Newmarket, where his owners include Mr and Mrs S. Joel, and Mr and Mrs P. Oppenheimer. Among the big races he has won are the Irish Derby, the Champion Stakes, the Manchester Cup (twice), the Kempton Jubilee, the Coventry Stakes, the St James's Palace Stakes, the Queen Mary Stakes, the National Breeders Produce Stakes, the Coronation Cup and the Nunthorpe Stakes.

One of Newmarket's most cheerful and hospitable characters, he is noted for his extremely forthright views, which he is seldom backward in expressing, and for a lively and sometimes sardonic sense of humour.

COUNSEL

Bred at the Astor Studs, Counsel is a bay by Court Martial (see below) out of Wheedler. In Lord Astor's colours he won ten races worth over £9,000. After his racing career was over, he was bought cheaply by Mr E. H. Covell for 2,700 gn and swiftly established his reputation by siring Privy Councillor, winner of the Two Thousand Guineas in 1962. He stands at the Southdown Stud, Sussex, where he is now owned by a syndicate, the National Stud having a controlling interest.

COURT MARTIAL

Court Martial, foaled in 1942, was bred and raced by the second Viscount Astor. A chestnut colt by Fair Trial, he won the Two Thousand Guineas and the Champion Stakes and was third in the Derby. He was an outstanding success as a sire, being twice champion before being exported to America in 1958.

COUSINS, Eric (b 1921)

Eric Cousins served as a pilot in the RAF. Keen on hunting, he rode with some success as an amateur under National Hunt rules and took out a licence to train in 1954. He has enjoyed a remarkable record of success in important handicaps and he won the Jubilee at Kempton four years running. He has also won the Ascot Stakes, Ayr Gold Cup (three times), Lincolnshire Handicap (twice), Victoria Cup, Cambridgeshire, Wokingham Stakes and the Portland Handicap. His stables are at Tarporley, Cheshire, and his owners include Mr W. L. Armitage, Mr R. Bell, Mr P. Brown, Mr B. P. Jenks, Mr J. Kennedy, Mrs D. Rosenfeld, Mr and Mrs R. E. Sangster, Mr R. West and Mr T. West.

COVENTRY STAKES

See under Ascot.

CRACKNELL, Edwin James (b 1926)

Eddie Cracknell's early days were spent in Australia where he rode his first winner in 1944 at Newcastle, New South Wales. Since then he has become well known as a jockey in England and also in India. In England he has won the Victoria Cup, the New Stakes and the White Rose Stakes; in India he has won the Derby on six occasions.

CRAGANOUR

Mr C. Bower Ismay's Craganour, ridden by Johnny Reiff, was first past the post in the 1913 Derby but was disqualified by the Stewards for not keeping a straight course, interfering with other horses, and boring Aboyeur who was awarded the race. Craganour was subsequently sold to Senor Marinez de Hoz for £30,000 and proved a great success as a sire in the Argentine. W. T. (Jack) Robinson, who trained Craganour, was never the same man after Craganour's disqualification and died two years later.

CRAIG AN ERAN

Bred and owned by Lord Astor, Craig An Eran was foaled in 1918 and was by Sunstar out of Maid of the Mist. He won the Two Thousand Guineas, St James's Palace Stakes and the Eclipse Stakes. In the Derby he was beaten a neck, perhaps a shade unluckily, by Humorist. He sired April the Fifth, winner of the Derby; Admiral Drake, winner of the French Derby; and Mon Talisman, winner of the Prix du Jockey Club.

CRATHORNE, Lord (b 1897)

Lord Crathorne was, as Sir Thomas Dugdale, for thirty years Conservative M.P. for the North Riding of Yorkshire (Richmond). From 1951 to 1954 he was Minister of Agriculture. He is a member of the Jockey Club and was Senior Steward in 1962. His trainer is R. D. Peacock. Colours: scarlet and yellow hoops, yellow cap.

CREMORNE

Mr H. Savile's Cremorne won the Derby and the Grand Prix in 1872 and in the following year the Ascot Gold Cup. His Grand Prix victory was ill-received in France as the English were thought to have been unhelpful in the recent Franco-Prussian war. In fact Cremorne had to be hustled out of France without a moment's delay as it was feared that hotheaded anglophobes might do him an injury.

CREPELLO

Crepello owned and bred by the late Sir Victor Sassoon is by Donatello II out of Crepuscule (see below). Trained by Noel Murless he was a very good horse indeed if not an entirely sound one. Ridden by Lester Piggott he won the Two Thousand Guineas and the Derby in 1957. In the Derby he showed himself clearly superior to another great horse in Ballymoss. He never ran again after Epsom. The best horse he has so far sired is Busted, winner of the Eclipse Stakes and King George VI Stakes in 1967. He also sired Caergwrle, winner of the 1968 One Thousand Guineas, Crepellana, winner of the French Oaks, and Lucyrowe, winner of the Coronation Stakes, Nassau Stakes and Sun Chariot Stakes. He was top sire in 1969.

CREPUSCULE

Lady Sassoon's Crepuscule, by Mieuxcé out of Red Sunset, by Solario, is one of the most successful of modern brood mares, her offspring including Crepello (Two Thousand Guineas and Derby), Honeylight (Free Handicap and One Thousand Guineas) and Twilight Alley (Ascot Gold Cup).

CRESTA RUN

Bred in 1924 by Lieut-Col Giles Loder, Cresta Run was by Hurry On out of Bridgemount. She won three races, including the One Thousand Guineas. She made no mark as a brood mare.

CROCKET

Bred in 1960 by Lord Harrington. Crocket is a chestnut horse by King of the Tudors out of Chandelier, by Goyama. Trained by Geoffrey Brooke for Mr D. Van Clief, he was unbeaten as a two-year-old, winning the Coventry, Gimcrack and Middle Park Stakes. The following season he was not entirely dependable but won the Craven Stakes and St James's Palace Stakes. He won over £9,000 in stakes. Syndicated for the stud, he stands at the Greenmount Stud, Co Limerick, and is doing well.

CROSS, Vernon

Vernon Cross was employed for 20 years by the late Lord Stalbridge and the late Lady Stalbridge, for the last five years of these (1947-52) acting as private trainer. He was associated with such notable jumpers as the 1940 Grand National winner Bogskar and Red April. He is now a public trainer and has a stable of nearly 40 horses at Chattis Hill, Stockbridge, where the late 'Atty' Persse used to train.

CULLEN, Desmond

A very useful light-weight rider who can go to scale at 7st 3lb, Des Cullen rode 40 winners in 1968. In 1967 he won the Stewards Cup on Sky Diver. He served his apprenticeship with W. Stephenson.

CUNDELL, Francis Lawrence (b 1909)

Frank Cundell is a qualified veterinary surgeon as was his father, who owned that fine stayer Noble Star, before him. He joined the Royal Army Veterinary Corps in 1931 and became a highly competent amateur rider under National Hunt rules. During his Army service in India, he rode the winner of the Indian Grand National. On leaving the Army, he was for three years Veterinary Officer and Stipendiary Steward to the Royal West India Turf Club before returning to England to assist his uncle, the late L. A. Cundell, who was training at Chilton. He himself took out a licence to train in 1939, but shortly afterwards was called up for military service.

After the war he had to start again from scratch but gradually built up a powerful 'mixed' stable at Aston Tirrold near Didcot. The majority of his most important successes have been gained with jumpers.

CUNDELL, Kenneth Stratton (b 1914)

Ken Cundell began training in 1947, having assisted the late L. A. Cundell for some years before the war. His stable at Compton, Berkshire, is a 'mixed' one and his notable successes on the flat include the Wokingham Stakes, Cork and Orrery Stakes, Queen Anne Stakes, Blue Riband Trial Stakes and the Imperial Produce Stakes. March Past and Zucchero are two good horses he has trained. His owners include the Viscountess Clifden, Mrs D. M. Thompson, Sir Leslie Doubleday, Mr D. W. Molins, Mr P. B. Raymond, Mr R. N. Richmond-Watson, Mrs G. Trimmer-Thompson, Mr J. Ismay and Mr D. Sieff.

CUP

A 'cup' is any prize not given in money.

CURANT, John

A very smart apprentice attached to D. Whelan's stable. In 1969 he could go to scale at 6st 7lb and rode winners.

CUSTANCE, Harry (b 1841)

Harry Custance was born at Peterborough in 1841. He was better educated than most of the jockeys of his era, better conducted and more reliable. He kept the money he made and on retirement for some time acted as a starter. He is the only man to have ridden in the Derby and to have started it as well; he despatched the 1885 Derby field in faultless fashion.

He rode three Derby winners—Thormanby (1860), Lord Lyon (1866) and George Frederick (1874).

CYLLENE

Cyllene was so small as a yearling that he was never entered for any classic event. A chestnut by Bona Vista, he later grew to full size and won the Ascot Gold Cup. He sired four Derby winners (Cicero, Minoru, Lemberg and Tagalie) before being exported to Argentina for £25,000 at the age of 13. He did well there, too, until his death at the age of 30.

D

D'ABERNON, Viscount (1858-1941)

A noted diplomat, he served as British Ambassador in Berlin. He bred a number of good horses including Diadem, who won the One Thousand Guineas and 23 other races, and Diophon who won the Two Thousand Guineas. He was the first President of the Thoroughbred Breeders Association. A man of wide interests, he was a subaltern in the Coldstream Guards when in 1879 he published a grammar of Modern Greek that became the standard work in Greece.

DALE, L. S. (b 1915)

Sid Dale was originally apprenticed to David Dale senior. After serving Ryan Price at Head Lad for eleven years, he took out a licence to train in 1956. His stables are at Epsom, and the most important flat race he has won is the Chester Cup. Among his owners are Mr G. J. Van Der Ploeg, Mr R. J. Cohen, Mrs F. J. Parsons, Mrs E. Nolan, Mr J. Bunn, Mr E. G. Loveridge and Mr C. A. Spencer. In 1969 he trained the winners of 57 races worth over £49,000.

DANCING TIME

Foaled in 1938, Dancing Time was bred and owned by Lord Glanely and was by Colombo out of Show Girl, by Son-in-Law. She won the One Thousand Guineas and was third in the Oaks and St Leger. She bred six winners, but not one of any particular distinction.

DANTE

Dante, by Nearco out of Rosy Legend, was bred by Sir Eric Ohlson. He was offered for sale as a yearling in 1943 but failed to reach his reserve and remained in Sir Eric's ownership. Trained at Middleham by Matt Peacock, he ran six times as a two-year-old and was undefeated. The following season he was beaten a neck by Court Martial in the Two Thousand Guineas, but was handicapped by an eye affliction that had only become apparent a few days earlier. He had probably become used to this eye weakness by the time he ran in the Derby, which he won in great style by two lengths. It was the last war-time Derby to be run at Newmarket.

Before the St Leger there were persistent rumours about Dante's well-being. On 22nd August there was an encouraging statement from Middleham, but only three days later he was scratched from the final classic on the grounds that "he could not be got ready in time". He never ran again and was retired to the stud where in due course he became totally blind. As a sire he was a qualified success. He got a fair number of winners, but a good many of his offspring were distinctly temperamental. The best horse he sired was Darius, winner of the Two Thousand Guineas and the Eclipse Stakes. He himself died in 1956.

DARIUS

Bred and owned by Sir Percy Loraine and trained by Harry Wragg, Darius was a bay colt by Dante out of Yasna, by Dastur. He won nine races worth over £38,000 including the Two Thousand Guineas, Eclipse Stakes and St James's Palace Stakes. His most notable winners at the stud were Pia (Oaks), Dart Board (third in the Derby, Dewhurst Stakes), Derring-Do, Darling Boy and Cyrus. He died of cancer in 1968 aged 17.

(*left*) BREASLEY, ARTHUR. A great Australian rider, 'Scobie' Breasley

(*right*) DARLING, FRED. Fred Darling with the brilliant but temperamental Sun Chariot

(*above left*) DAWSON, DANIEL. Daniel Dawson, hanged for poisoning racehorses at Newmarket. (*above right*) DAWSON, MATTHEW. A great Victorian trainer, Matthew Dawson

DERBY, THE. At the 1913 Derby Amner, belonging to George V, is brought down by the suffragette, Emily Davison, who was killed. The horse and his jockey, H. Jones, escaped serious injury

DARLEY ARABIAN

The Darley Arabian is a significant name in tracing the origins and development of the thoroughbred. Foaled in 1700, he was a bay with a white blaze and three white feet and was stated to belong "to the most esteemed race among the Arabs both by sire and dam". He was sent to England as a four-year-old by Thomas Darley, the British Consul in Aleppo. He lived to the age of 30, and standing in Yorkshire he founded a dynasty that has persisted to the present day.

Of the potent male lines of the present day, the Blandford, the Phalaris, the Teddy, the The Boss, the Son-in-Law, the Gainsborough and the St Simon are all derived from the Darley Arabian.

DARLING BOY

Bred at the Astor Studs, Darling Boy was foaled in 1958 and is by Darius out of Sugar Bun, by Mahmoud. He won ten races worth over £7,000, including the Jockey Club Cup, in England and La Coupe at Longchamp. He stands at the Hamilton Stud, Newmarket.

DARLING, Fred (1884-1953)

Son of Sam Darling, who trained two Derby winners, Fred Darling is widely held to be the outstanding English trainer of this century.

Darling served as an apprentice for a brief period but never held a jockey's licence. He began his training career at Kentford near Newmarket with a few jumpers, owned by Lady de Bathe (the famous Lily Langtry). He next trained for the Weinberg brothers in Germany returning to England just before the start of World War I to take over the famous Beckhampton stable from his father.

Though often handicapped by ill-health, his record was one of remarkable success up to his retirement in 1947. Taciturn, secretive and quick-tempered, he had no time for fools, bores or importunate members of the racing press. A perfectionist, he was a ruthless martinet in the stable, insisting at all times on the highest standards and the closest attention to detail. In a clash of wills with a difficult horse he rarely came off second best. His training methods were based on the conservation of vital energy for the racecourse rather than expending it on the gallops, and his horses could be relied on to be at their peak on the day that really mattered. Moreover they invariably carried an air of well-being and distinction that set them apart from their rivals in the paddock. To an unusual degree Darling possessed the art of getting a horse fit and building up its constitution simultaneously.

F

He had 19 successes in classic races. He won the Derby with Captain Cuttle (1922), Manna (1925), Coronach (1926), Cameronian (1931), Bois Roussel (1938), Pont l'Eveque (1940) and Owen Tudor (1941). Only R. Robson and John Porter have trained as many Derby winners. The best horse he ever trained was Hurry On, who was never beaten; the best filly, the brilliant but temperamental Sun Chariot, who won the One Thousand Guineas, the Oaks and the St Leger in 1942.

Darling died in 1953, just after Pinza, whom he had bred, had won the Derby.

DARLING, Samuel Henry (1881-1967)

Sam Darling's racing career was overshadowed by that of his brother Fred. His main achievement on the Turf was to land the Autumn Double in 1925, Forseti winning the Cesarewitch and Masked Marvel the Cambridgeshire. Both horses were owned by Mr A. K. Macomber.

DASTUR

The Aga Khan's Dastur was second in the Two Thousand Guineas, Derby and St Leger in 1932. He won the Irish Derby and the following year the Coronation Cup. He was not a success as a sire.

DAVEY, Ernest (b 1890)

Ernest Davey served his apprenticeship with Bert Gordon at Wroughton and rode winners under National Hunt rules. He has been a trainer since 1922 and his stables are at Malton. He usually has some sharp two-year-olds for the start of the season and has won the Brocklesby Plate four times. He has also won the Buckingham Palace Stakes four times, the Harewood Handicap four times, the Epsom Sprint three times and the Ayr Gold Cup. His patrons include Mr J. Batty, Mr M. Hyman, Mr C. T. Whiting, Mr G. Mitchell, Mr G. Newsome, Mr M. Babbage, Mrs M. Hipple and Mr T. W. Newton. His only son is Paul Davey (see below).

DAVEY, Robert Paul

Paul Davey is the only son of the veteran Yorkshire trainer Ernest Davey. In 1968 he became one of Mr Robinson's private trainers at Newmarket.

DAVID JACK

Foaled in 1963, David Jack is by Pampered King out of Judy Owens, by Owenstown. He was bred by Mr A. L. Lowry and sold as a yearling to the Newmarket trainer E. Lambton for only 690 gn. He won four races worth over £14,000 and was third in the St Leger. He stands at the Rossenarra Stud, Thomastown, Co Kilkenny.

d'AVIGDOR-GOLDSMID, Major-Gen James Arthur, CB OBE MC (b 1909)

Major-Gen d'Avigdor-Goldsmid served in the 4th/7th Dragoon Guards and had a distinguished military career. He is a member of the Jockey Club and a steward at Ascot, Lingfield and Windsor. His trainer is S. Ingham. Colours: black and red halved, old gold sash and cap.

DAWNAY, Major-Gen Sir David, CB. DSO (b 1903)

Major-Gen Sir David Dawnay, a 10th Hussar, had a distinguished military career. A top-class polo player, he was little known in the racing world when he became Clerk of the Course at Ascot in 1957 following the death of Sir John Crocker Bulteel. He held the appointment until his retirement in 1969.

DAWSON, Daniel

Daniel Dawson was hanged before 15,000 spectators at Cambridge in 1811 for poisoning a number of horses at Newmarket. Daniel, a tout by trade, was hired to do the dirty work by two unscrupulous bookmakers called Bland.

DAWSON, Matthew (d 1897)

One of the greatest of trainers, Matthew Dawson won the Derby with Thormanby (1860), Kingcraft (1870), Silvio (1877), Melton (1885) Ladas (1894) and Sir Visto (1895). He also trained St Simon who was never beaten and was possibly the greatest horse ever seen on the English Turf. A Scotsman, Dawson cared nothing for petty economies and ran his stable in a lavish manner. He was a strong, fearless character who was never reluctant to speak his mind but was invariably courteous not only to his owners, but to those whom he employed. He had no patience with weak men and bad horses and he loathed heavy betting. In fact he fundamentally despised money, unlike Fred Archer with whom he was closely associated and whom he once summarised as "that damned, long-legged, tin-scraping young devil". He was as good a gardener as he was a trainer and liked to appear on the gallops in a top hat and varnished boots and with a wonderful flower in his button-hole. He spoke with a pronounced Scottish accent which made his strongest comments sound like a benediction.

DAWSON, Peter Thomas (b 1935)

Peter Dawson served his apprenticeship with Peter Cazelet. He took out a trainer's licence in 1960 and his stables are at Kingswood, Surrey. His patrons include Mrs B. P. Gourdeau, Mr E. W. Gourdeau and Mr J. F. Wickins.

DAWSON, Richard C. (1866-1955)

Richard Dawson, one of the most successful trainers in the first 30 years or so of this century, died in 1955 at the age of 89. Born in Ireland, he trained there for some years after leaving Dublin University. In 1897 he moved to Whatcombe in Berkshire and the following year he won the Grand National with Drogheda, a horse he had bought at the Dublin Show. During World War I he moved to Newmarket and trained Fifinella to win the Derby for Mr E. Hulton. He returned to Whatcombe in 1919, and in 1921 was appointed trainer to the Aga Khan, George Lambton having previously declined that position. The association was a fruitful one for both parties during its 10-year duration, among the notable winners being Diophon (Two Thousand Guineas), Blenheim (Derby), Salmon Trout (St Leger) and Mumtaz Mahal, a brilliant grey filly with phenomenal speed. During the same period Dawson won the Derby and the St Leger for Mr W. Barnett with Trigo, and the Oaks for Vicomte de Fontarce with Brownhylda. In 1931 there was a serious disagreement between the Aga Khan and Dawson and the Aga Khan's horses left the stable.

In appearance Dawson was hardly the typical trainer, and in manner he was not the Englishman's notion of an Irishman. With his drooping moustache, pince-nez and sombre style of dress, he looked more like an old-fashioned schoolmaster. He had little sense of humour to help him through the ups and downs of fortune that are inevitable in racing.

DAY, John

John Day trained at Danebury and won the Derby with Pyrrhus the First (1846), Cossack (1847) and Andover (1854).

DAY, Reginald (b 1883)

Reg Day was the son of Mr F. W. Day, MRCVS. His own son, Frederick Day, FRCVS, is the highly esteemed Newmarket veterinary surgeon. Reg Day had an exceptionally long career as a trainer, taking out a licence in 1900 and retiring in 1968. At one period he trained in Germany and he won the German Derby three times. He also won the Grand Prix d'Ostende. In his younger days he rode under National Hunt rules and it is said that he is the last man living to have ridden the winner of a steeplechase at Newmarket.

He was particularly renowned as a trainer of stayers; he won the Ascot Gold Cup twice, the Goodwood Cup twice, the Doncaster Cup twice, the Jockey Club Cup four times, the Yorkshire Cup, the Gold Vase, the Jockey Club Stakes and the Goodwood Stakes. He also did well with fast two-year-olds, winning the Middle Park Stakes twice, the Gimcrack Stakes twice, the Queen Mary Stakes and the Imperial Produce Stakes. For Sir Abe Bailey he trained two fine stayers in Son-in-Law (Goodwood Cup, Jockey Club Cup and Cesarewitch) and Foxlaw (Northumberland Plate, Jockey Club Stakes and Ascot Gold Cup). The best horse, though, to pass through his hands was Solario (St Leger and Gold Cup). Towards the close of his career he trained Sweet Solera, winner of the One Thousand Guineas and the Oaks.

DAY, Sam (1802-1864)

Sam Day was a member of a famous nineteenth-century racing family, the Days of Danebury. Cheerful, hardy and a good deal more honest than certain members of the Day family of that era, Sam was a fine rider and won the Derby on Gustavus (1821), Priam (1830) and Pyrrhus the First (1846).

DEAD-HEAT, RUN-OFF OF

The last dead-heat to be run-off was

at Newbury in 1930. There are several recorded instances of horses dead-heating and then dead-heating again in the run-off.

Triple Dead Heat

The triple dead-heat in this country was between Breezy Heather, Golden Book and Rocos in the Stayers Handicap at Folkestone in 1925. Rocos was in fact subsequently disqualified. There was a triple dead-heat at Newmarket in 1924 and at Windsor in 1923.

DEAN SWIFT

Mr J. B. Joel's popular handicapper Dean Swift ran eight times in the City and Suburban. He won in 1906 and in 1908, was second twice, third twice and twice unplaced.

DECLARATIONS

See ENTRIES, FORFEITS AND DECLARATIONS.

DERBY, twelfth Earl of (d 1834)

The Derby was named in honour of the twelfth Earl of Derby, a popular, easy-going, hospitable and self-indulgent man. He himself won the Derby in 1787 with Sir Peter Teazle, by Highflyer. Despite long and liberal support of the Turf, the Stanley family failed to win the Derby again till Sansovino triumphed in 1924.

DERBY, seventeenth Earl of (1865-1948)

A great Englishman, whose long life was devoted to the service of his country, the seventeenth Earl of Derby inherited from his father a love of racing and bloodstock breeding. As an owner he proved wonderfully successful and there were no more popular colours in his day than the familiar black jacket, white cap. As a breeder, his stock exerted immense influence on the breeding of thoroughbreds all over the world.

His classic successes were as follows:

Two Thousand Guineas: Colorado (1926); Garden Path (1944)

One Thousand Guineas: Canyon (1916); Ferry (1918); Tranquil (1923); Fair Isle (1930); Tideway (1936); Herringbone (1943); Sun Stream (1945)

Derby: Sansovino (1924); Hyperion (1933); Watling Street (1942)

Oaks: Toboggan (1928); Sun Stream (1945)

St Leger: Swynford (1910); Keysoe (1919); Tranquil (1923); Fairway (1928); Hyperion (1933); Herringbone (1943)

A multitude of other important victories included the Gold Cup with Bosworth and the Eclipse Stakes with Colorado, Fairway and Caerleon. The last really good horse to carry his colours was Alycidon who won the Ascot, Goodwood and Doncaster Cups in 1948.

Among the great stallions he owned were Chaucer, Swynford, Phalaris, Pharos, Colorado, Fairway and Hyperion, while there are few more famous mares in the Stud Book than Canterbury Pilgrim, Gondolette, Serenissima, Selene, Scapa Flow and Aurora.

Lord Derby's eldest son, Lord Stanley, died in 1938 and the famous Stanley House Stud passed to Lord Stanley's eldest son, the present Lord Derby (see below).

DERBY, eighteenth Earl of, MC (b 1918)

Lord Derby was born in 1918 and served with distinction throughout the war in the Grenadier Guards. He inherited the racing interests of his grandfather, but neither as owner or breeder has he enjoyed success in anyway comparable to that of the seventeenth Earl. He is a member of the Jockey Club and a steward at Ascot, Epsom, Haydock Park and Liverpool. His colours are the once famous black jacket, white cap, and his trainer is Bernard van Cutsem.

DERBY, THE

See under EPSOM.

DERBY AND OAKS, WINNERS OF

The following fillies won both the Derby and the Oaks: Eleanor (1801), Blink Bonny (1857), Signorinetta (1908) and Fifinella (1916). Fifinella's victories were in war-substitute races at Newmarket.

DERRING-DO

Derring-Do was bred by the Burton Agnes Stud and is by Darius out of Sipsey Bridge, by Abernant. Bought for 1,200 gn as a yearling by Mrs H. H. Renshaw and trained by Arthur Budgett, Derring-Do won six races worth over £20,000, including the Imperial Stakes, Cornwallis Stakes and Queen Elizabeth II Stakes. He stands at the Aston Park Stud, Oxfordshire, and is the sire of Huntercombe, winner of the Middle Park Stakes in 1969.

de TRAFFORD, Sir Humphrey, MC (b 1891)

Sir Humphrey de Trafford served with the Coldstream Guards and rode with some success under National Hunt rules. He has been a noted racing administrator and has served more than one term of office as Senior Steward of the Jockey Club. As an owner his two great years were in 1958 and 1959. In 1958 he won the St Leger with Alcide; in 1959 he won the Derby with Parthia and the King George VI and Queen Elizabeth Stakes with Alcide. Both were trained by Sir Cecil Boyd-Rochfort. Colours: scarlet and white halved, quartered cap.

DEVONSHIRE, eleventh Duke of, PC, MC (b 1920)

The Duke of Devonshire served with distinction throughout World War II in the Coldstream Guards. He was Minister of State, Commonwealth Relations Office 1962-64 and is Chancellor of Manchester University. He is a member of the Jockey Club and at present holds office as one of the Stewards. He is a steward at Ascot and Leicester. By far the best performer to carry his colours so far is Park Top, whom he bought for 500 gn. Her many successes include the Ribblesdale Stakes, Coronation Cup, Hardwicke Stakes and King George VI and Queen Elizabeth Stakes. The Duke's colours are straw and his trainer is Bernard van Cutsem.

DEWAR, John Arthur (d 1954)

When just over forty years of age, Mr John Dewar inherited from his uncle, Lord Dewar, a vast fortune, a stud, and a string of racehorses that included Cameronian, destined to win the Two Thousand Guineas and the Derby in 1931. Mr Dewar had had little interest in the Turf before this stroke of good fortune, but he soon developed one, and maintained it until his death. His other classic winners were Tudor Minstrel, a superb miler that won the Two Thousand Guineas by eight lengths in 1947; Commotion, winner of the Oaks in 1947; and Festoon, who won the One Thousand Guineas in 1954. He also owned Fair Trial, a good racehorse and a highly successful sire. He bought the Beckhampton gallops and establishment on Fred Darling's retirement for £60,000, but sold the property in 1952 when Noel Murless, Darling's successor there, announced his intention of moving to Newmarket. Mr Dewar's last trainer was Noel Cannon, who trained at Druid's Lodge. Mr Dewar left an estate valued at over £3,000,000 and when his horses in training, mares, yearlings and foals were sold, they realised the gigantic total of £398,595.

DEWHURST STAKES

See under NEWMARKET.

DIADEM

Bred and owned by Lord D'Abernon and trained by George Lambton, Diadem, who was foaled in 1914, was by Orby out of Donetta, by Donovan. She was noted for her speed, toughness and courage, and racing up to the age of seven, she won 24 races including the One Thousand Guineas. She was a half-sister to Diophon (Two Thousand Guineas) and a full sister to Diadumenos (Kempton Jubilee and Liverpool Autumn Cup). She herself bred three winners, including Dian who won over £4,000 in stakes.

DIAMOND JUBILEE

Bred and owned by the Prince of Wales, later King Edward VII, and trained by Richard Marsh, Diamond Jubilee was foaled in 1897 and was a full brother of the 1896 Derby winner Persimmon. His ability was of the highest but he was temperamental and at times savage. Marsh found it no easy task to train and control him without taking measures that might have broken the colt's spirit.

Diamond Jubilee and the stable jockey Jack Watts regarded each other with mutual dislike so Mornington Cannon was engaged to ride Diamond Jubilee in the Two Thousand Guineas. However, after a gallop not long before the race, Diamond Jubilee tried to kill Cannon and the ride was then given to Herbert Jones, a lad of Marsh's who rode Diamond Jubilee in most of his work. Jones not only won the Guineas on the royal colt, but the Derby, St Leger and Eclipse Stakes as well.

Diamond Jubilee never found his form as a four-year-old. He was sold for 31,500 gn to a South American breeder and did well at the stud in the Argentine where he died aged 26.

DICEY, RICHARD

Richard Dicey, attached to H. E. Smyth's Epsom stable, rode 40 winners in 1968 and shared the position of top apprentice with D. Coates. Very surprisingly, he announced his retirement from racing in the spring of 1970.

DICTA DRAKE

Dicta Drake was foaled in 1958 and is a bay by the Derby and Grand Prix winner Phil Drake out of Dictature, by Transtevere. Bred and raced by Madame L. Volterra, in France he won the Prix du Printemps at St Cloud and the Grand Prix de St Cloud. In England he won the Coronation Cup, was second in the Derby and third in the St Leger. He stands at the Aston Park Stud, Oxfordshire.

DILLON, Bernard (1887-1941)

Bernard Dillon was born in Ireland and brought to England as a boy by Capt W. B. Purefoy. He was apprenticed to Jack Fallon at Druids Lodge and later rode as first jockey for Peter Gilpin's powerful Clarehaven stable. His career as a rider began in 1901 and ended in 1911. Brilliant at his best, he became notorious for his addiction to the bottle and towards the close of his career he was liable to be alarmingly erratic. He died penniless.

Dillon won the Derby in 1910 on Lemberg and rode a brilliant race on Spearmint to win the Grand Prix in 1906. He was also associated with Pretty Polly in some of her victories. He was the third husband of the famous Music Hall artiste Marie Lloyd, but the marriage proved anything but a success.

DINGWALL, Mrs L. E.

Now in her mid-eighties, Mrs Dingwall conducts a small stable at Poole, Dorset. She has trained some winners.

DIOLITE

Diolite was foaled in 1927 and was a bay by Diophon out of Needle Rock, by Rock Sand. Owned by Sir H. Hirst and trained by F. Templeman, he won six races worth over £17,000 including the Two Thousand Guineas and the Coventry Stakes. He was not a success as a sire and was exported to Japan.

DIOMED

Diomed was owned by Sir Charles

Bunbury and won the first Derby on 4th May 1780. As a sire in England he was not a success and his fee sank to two guineas. At the advanced age of 20 he was exported to America. He survived the voyage, lived for another 10 years and founded a dynasty. From him are descended many of the greatest horses, such as Lexington, in American racing history. When he died there was as much grief among horse-loving Virginians as there had been at the passing of George Washington, and his death was regarded as a national catastrophe.

DIOMEDES

Diomedes, by Argos out of Capdane, was foaled in 1922 and proved himself one of the greatest sprinters of this century, winning 16½ races worth over £11,000. He proved a disappointing sire.

DISTANCE

The expression 'leading at the distance' is commonly used. 'The distance' is in fact a point 240yd from the winning post. One or two courses have 'distance posts' to mark the point. On the other hand if a judge rules that a horse has 'won by a distance', he means by a margin greater than 20 lengths.

DJEBEL

Bred and owned by M. M. Boussac, Djebel was foaled in 1937 and was a smallish horse of great quality, very tough and game. In England he won the Middle Park Stakes and the following year the Two Thousand Guineas. He would very likely have won the Derby, too, but owing to the war situation his owner sent him to the south of France out of harm's way. Djebel resumed racing in the autumn and won the long-postponed French Two Thousand Guineas. The older he got, the better he got and as a five-year-old he ran seven times and was undefeated.

By Tourbillon out of Loika, by Gay Crusader, Djebel proved a highly successful sire. Among his offspring were Galcador (Derby), My Babu (Two Thousand Guineas and Victoria Cup), Hugh Lupus (Irish Two Thousand Guineas and Champion Stakes), Djelfa (French One Thousand Guineas), Coronation V (French One Thousand Guineas and Prix de l'Arc de Triomphe), Arbar (Ascot Gold Cup and second in the St Leger), and Djeddah (Eclipse Stakes, Champion Stakes and six races in France). Djebel died in 1958.

DJEDDAH

Foaled in 1945, Djeddah was bred and owned by M. M. Boussac and was a chestnut by Djebel out of Djezima, by Asterus. He won six good races in France and the Eclipse Stakes and Champion Stakes in England. He was exported as a stallion to the United States.

DR SYNTAX

Dr Syntax won the Preston Gold Cup seven years running (1815-21).

DOG

A 'dog' is a term commonly given to a horse that clearly dislikes racing.

DONATELLO II

Donatello II, foaled in 1934, was bred in Italy by the famous Italian breeder Signor Federico Tesio. He was a chestnut horse by the Derby winner Blenheim out of Delleana by Clarissimus. Delleana won the Italian Two Thousand Guineas and One Thousand Guineas and the Gran Premio d'Italia. Donatello II was unbeaten in Italy; his one defeat came when he was most unluckily defeated in the Grand Prix de Paris. Shortly afterwards Mr E. Esmond bought him for £47,500 and sent him to the stud in England.

Donatello II was not a prolific sire

of winners, but he got some very good horses and exerted immense influence on bloodstock breeding in this country. His most notable winners were the great stayer Alycidon, who won the Ascot Gold Cup and over £37,000 in stakes; and Crepello, winner of the Two Thousand Guineas and the Derby. Alycidon was champion sire in 1955 and Crepello in 1969. Donatello II also sired the One Thousand Guineas winner Picture Play, from whom the 1967 Two Thousand Guineas and Derby winner Royal Palace is descended.

Donatello mares did well at the stud. The 1953 Derby winner, Pinza, is out of a Donatello mare, and so are Aureole, winner of the King George VI and Queen Elizabeth Stakes and twice champion sire; and Wilwyn, who won the Washington International at Laurel Park. Donatello II died in 1955.

DONCASTER

Doncaster is a great racecourse and now that the re-building scheme has been completed the amenities are of the same high standard as the course itself. The course, which has a sandy subsoil and only becomes heavy after very prolonged rain, stands on the historic Town Moor, one of the old commons of England, now vested in the Doncaster Corporation by virtue of a charter granted by Henry VIII.

The big race at Doncaster is of course the St Leger, the last of the five classic races, run over 1m 6f 132 yd in September. It is in fact the oldest of the classics, having been founded in 1776, four years before the Derby. It is named after a highly esteemed Yorkshire sportsman of that period, Lieut-Gen Anthony St Leger, who lived at Park Hill, near Doncaster. The Park Hill Stakes is also run in September and is for three-year-old fillies competing over the full St Leger course.

The track is left-handed and pear-shaped. It is nearly 2m round with a sweeping turn into the straight about $4\frac{1}{2}$f from the winning post. The straight mile is wide and flat. Mile races are also run on the round course. High numbers are favoured in the draw on the straight course.

Since 1965 the Lincoln Handicap has been run at Doncaster. The *Observer* Gold Cup is run in October, the season's richest prize for two-year-olds.

Clerk of the Course: Mr M. Hancock, Yew Tree House, Broom, nr Alcester, Warwickshire. Tel: Bidford-on-Avon 2322.

Best Times:

Distance	*Horse-Age-Weight*	*Date*	*Time*
5f	Sir Gatric 3-8-8	10- 9-59	58.2
5f	D'Urberville 2-9-0	13- 9-67	58.4
5f 152yd	Welsh Abbot 3-9-2	12- 9-58	1min 6.2
5f 152yd	Crown Flatts 2-8-10	25-10-47	1min 8
6f	Ryecroft 4-7-9	16- 5-59	1min 10.2
6f	Paddy's Sister 2-8-11	9- 9-59	1min 11.2
7f	Pinolli 3-9-4	3- 6-63	1min 22.6
7f	Chebs Lad 2-9-0	12- 9-67	1min 24.4
8f (straight)	Lovestone 3-8-0	12- 9-58	1min 37
8f (straight)	Corinthian 2-7-8	21-10-55	1min 39.6
8f (round)	Old Tom 4-8-1	3- 6-63	1min 35.6
8f (round)	Doon 2-9-7	13- 9-67	1min 38.6
10f 56yd	Silver Cloud 4-8-7	12- 9-63	2min 6.4
11f	Nadir Shah 3-8-6	10- 9-63	2min 18.2
12f	Tudor Gay 3-9-0	3- 6-63	2min 31.8
14f 132yd	Cantelo 3-8-11	12- 9-59	3min 4.4
18f	Alycidon 4-9-5	21- 5-49	3min 53

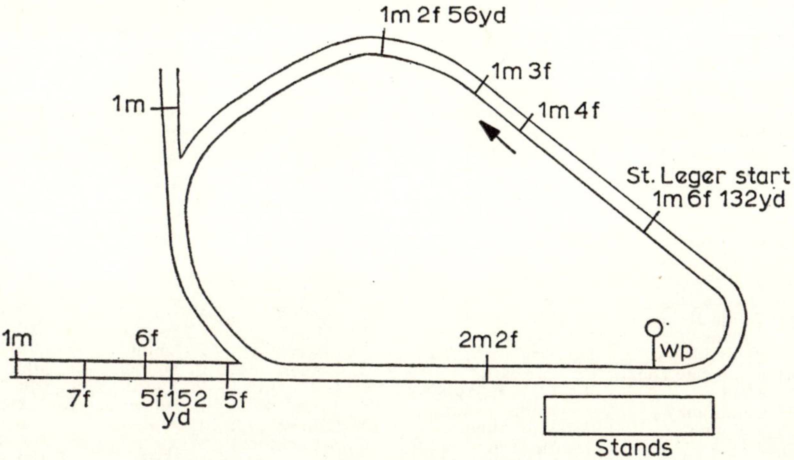

DONCASTER

The St Leger, 1m 6f 132yd

First run in 1776. *No race* 1939. *Run at Newmarket* 1915 *to* 1918 *and from* 1942 *to* 1944. *Run at Thirsk* 1940. *At Manchester* 1941 *and at York in* 1945.

		OWNER	TRAINER	JOCKEY	SP
1900	Diamond Jubilee	Prince of Wales	R. Marsh	H. Jones	2–7
1901	Doricles	L. de Rothschild	A. Hayhoe	K. Cannon	40–1
1902	Sceptre	R. Sievier	R. Sievier	F. Hardy	100–30
1903	Rock Sand	Sir J. Miller	G. Blackwell	D. Maher	2–5
1904	Pretty Polly	Maj E. Loder	P. Gilpin	W. Lane	2–5
1905	Challacombe	W. Singer	A. Taylor	O. Madden	100–7
1906	Troutbeck	Duke of Westminster	W. Waugh	G. Stern	5–1
1907	Wool Winder	Col E. Baird	H. Enoch	W. Halsey	11–10
1908	Your Majesty	J. Joel	C. Morton	Wal Griggs	11–8
1909	Bayardo	'Mr Fairie'	A. Taylor	D. Maher	10–11
1910	Swynford	Lord Derby	G. Lambton	F. Wootton	9–2
1911	Prince Palatine	T. Pilkington	H. Beardsley	F. O'Neill	100–30
1912	Tracery	A. Belmont	J. Watson	G. Bellhouse	8–1
1913	Night Hawk	Col H-Walker	W. Robinson	E. Wheatley	50–1
1914	Black Jester	J. Joel	C. Morton	Wal Griggs	10–1
1915	Pommern	S. Joel	C. Peck	S. Donoghue	1–3
1916	Hurry On	J. Buchanan	F. Darling	C. Childs	11–10
1917	Gay Crusader	'Mr Fairie'	A. Taylor	S. Donoghue	2–11
1918	Gainsborough	Lady Douglas	A. Taylor	J. Childs	4–11
1919	Keysoe	Lord Derby	G. Lambton	B. Carslake	100–8
1920	Caligula	M. Goculdas	H. Leader	A. Smith	100–6
1921	Polemarch	Lord Londonderry	T. Green	J. Childs	50–1
1922	Royal Lancer	Lord Lonsdale	A. Sadler	R. Jones	33–1
1923	Tranquil	Lord Derby	C. Morton	T. Weston	100–9
1924	Salmon-Trout	Aga Khan	R. Dawson	B. Carslake	6–1
1925	Solario	Sir J. Rutherford	R. Day	J. Childs	7–2
1926	Coronach	Lord Woolavington	F. Darling	J. Childs	8–15
1927	Book Law	Lord Astor	A. Taylor	H. Jelliss	7–4
1928	Fairway	Lord Derby	Fk. Butters	T. Weston	7–4
1929	Trigo	W. Barnett	R. Dawson	M. Beary	5–1
1930	Singapore	Lord Glanely	T. Hogg	G. Richards	4–1
1931	Sandwich	Lord Rosebery	J. Jarvis	H. Wragg	9–1
1932	Firdaussi	Aga Khan	Fk. Butters	F. Fox	20–1
1933	Hyperion	Lord Derby	G. Lambton	T. Weston	6–4
1934	Windsor Lad	M. Benson	M. Marsh	C. Smirke	4–9

The St Leger (contd)

Year	Horse	Owner	Trainer	Jockey	SP
1935	Bahram	Aga Khan	Fk. Butters	C. Smirke	4–11
1936	Boswell	W. Woodward	C. B-Rochfort	P. Beasley	20–1
1937	Chulmleigh	Lord Glanely	T. Hogg	G. Richards	18–1
1938	Scottish Union	J. Rank	N. Cannon	B. Carslake	7–1
1940	Turkhan	Aga Khan	Fk. Butters	G. Richards	4–1
1941	Sun Castle	Lord Portal	C. B-Rochfort	G. Bridgland	10–1
1942	Sun Chariot	King George VI	F. Darling	G. Richards	9–4
1943	Herringbone	Lord Derby	W. Earl	H. Wragg	100–6
1944	Tehran	Aga Khan	Fk. Butters	G. Richards	9–2
1945	Chamossaire	S. Joel	R. Perryman	T. Lowrey	11–2
1946	Airborne	J. Ferguson	R. Perryman	T. Lowrey	3–1
1947	Sayajirao	Maharaja of Baroda	F. Armstrong	E. Britt	9–2
1948	Black Tarquin	W. Woodward	C. B-Rochfort	E. Britt	15–2
1949	Ridge Wood	G. Smith	N. Murless	M. Beary	100–7
1950	Scratch II	M. Boussac	C. Semblat	W. Johnstone	9–2
1951	Talma II	M. Boussac	C. Semblat	W. Johnstone	7–1
1952	Tulyar	Aga Khan	M. Marsh	C. Smirke	10–11
1953	Premonition	Brig W. Wyatt	C. B-Rochfort	E. Smith	10–1
1954	Never Say Die	R. Clark	J. Lawson	C. Smirke	100–30
1955	Meld	Lady Z. Wernher	C. B-Rochfort	W. Carr	10–11
1956	Cambremer	R. Strassburger	G. Bridgland	F. Palmer	8–1
1957	Ballymoss	J. McShain	V. O'Brien	T. P. Burns	8–1
1958	Alcide	Sir H. de Trafford	C. B-Rochfort	W. Carr	4–9
1959	Cantelo	W. Hill	C. Elsey	E. Hide	100–7
1960	St. Paddy	Sir V. Sassoon	N. Murless	L. Piggott	4–6
1961	Aurelius	Mrs V. Lilley	N. Murless	L. Piggott	9–2
1962	Hethersett	Maj L. Holliday	W. Hern	W. Carr	100–8
1963	Ragusa	Mrs J. Mullion	P. Prendergast	G. Bougoure	2–5
1964	Indiana	C. Engelhard	J. Watts	J. Lindley	100–7
1965	Provoke	J. Astor	W. Hern	J. Mercer	28–1
1966	Sodium	R. J. Sigtia	G. Todd	F. Durr	7–1
1967	Ribocco	C. Engelhard	R. Houghton	L. Piggott	7–2
1968	Ribero	C. Engelhard	R. Houghton	L. Piggott	100–30
1969	Intermezzo	G. Oldham	H. Wragg	R. Hutchinson	7–1

Champagne Stakes, 7f

Two-year-olds. First run 1823. *Run over 6f until* 1961. *Run at Newbury in* 1941. *No race* 1939, 1940 *and* 1942 *to* 1945.

Year	Horse	Owner	Trainer	Jockey	SP
1930	Portlaw, 9–0	Sir A. Bailey	H. Persse	H. Beasley	5–4
1931	Orwell, 9–0	W. Singer	J. Lawson	R. A. Jones	1–4
1932	Myrobella, 8–11	Lord Lonsdale	F. Darling	G. Richards	11–8
1933	Blazonry, 9–0	Lord H. de Walden	D. Waugh	R. Perryman	11–2
1934	Kingsem, 9–0	Sir C. Hyde	N. Scobie	S. Donoghue	8–1
1935	Mahmoud, 9–0	Aga Khan	Fk. Butters	F. Fox	13–8
1936	Foray, 9–0	M. Field	C. B-Rochfort	P. Beasley	7–4
1937	Portmarnock, 9–0	Sir H. de Trafford	C. B-Rochfort	P. Beasley	11–2
1938	Panorama, 9–0	Mrs J. Corrigan	C. B-Rochfort	P. Beasley	8–13
1941	Big Game, 9–0	King George VI	F. Darling	H. Wragg	1–2
1946	Petition, 9–0	Sir A. Butt	Fk. Butters	H. Wragg	2–7
1947	Lerins (re-named My Babu), 9–0	Maharaja of Baroda	F. Armstrong	E. Britt	21–20
1948	Abernant, 9–0	Maj R. M-Buchanan	N. Murless	G. Richards	2–5
1949	Palestine, 9–0	Aga Khan	Fk. Butters	G. Richards	1–9
1950	Big Dipper, 9–0	Mrs J. Bryce	C. B-Rochfort	W. Carr	4–7
1951	Orgoglio, 9–0	P. Bull	C. Elsey	E. Britt	100–8
1952	Bebe Grande, 8–11	J. Gerber	F. Armstrong	W. Snaith	4–9
1953	Darius, 9–0	Sir P. Loraine	H. Wragg	E. Mercer	7–4
1954	Our Babu, 9–0	D. Robinson	G. Brooke	D. Smith	100–8
1955	Rustam, 9–0	Lady Wyfold	G. Brooke	D. Smith	8–15
1956	Eudaemon, 9–0	Mrs E. Foster	C. Elsey	E. Britt	5–2
1957	Kelly, 9–0	J. Olding	N. Cannon	J. Purtell	10–1
1958	Be Careful, 8–11	W. Hill	C. Elsey	E. Hide	4–7

		OWNER	TRAINER	JOCKEY	SP
1959	Paddy's Sister, 8–11	Mrs J. Mullion ..	P. Prendergast .	G. Moore ..	8–15
1960	Ambergris, 8–11 ..	Sir P. Loraine ..	H. Wragg ..	J. Lindley ..	7–2
1961	Clear Sound, 9–0 ..	Mrs M. Sheehan .	P. Prendergast .	R. Hutchinson	3–1
1962	King of Babylon, 9–0	R. Dennis	W. Elsey . ..	E. Hide	100–7
1963	Talahasse, 9–0.. ..	H. Loebstein ..	.. T. Corbett ..	A. Breasley ..	4–7
1964	Hardicanute, 9–0 ..	J. Mullion	P. Prendergast .	G. Bougoure ..	7–1
1965	Celtic Song, 9–0 ..	M. Rayne	P. Prendergast .	L. Piggott ..	2–1
1966	Bold Lad, 9–0 . ..	Lady Granard ..	P. Prendergast .	D. Lake	8–11
1967	Chebs Lad, 9–0 ..	H. Brown	P. Prendergast .	B. Connorton .	7–1
1968	Ribofilio, 9–0	C. Engelhard . ..	R. Houghton .	L. Piggott ..	7–2
1969	Saintly Song, 9–0 ..	S. Joel	N. Murless ..	A. Barclay ..	11–4

Manchester Handicap, 1m 4f

First run 1876. *Run at Manchester as Manchester November Handicap until* 1963, *except for* 1942 *to* 1945, *when run at Pontefract, and* 1954 *when race was abandoned. Run at Doncaster since* 1964.

		OWNER	TRAINER	JOCKEY	SP
1930	Glorious Devon, 3–7–5	Lord Glanely ..	T. Hogg	G. Richards ..	25–1
1931	North Drift, 4–7–6..	J. Downing	M. Vasey	C. Dowdall ..	8–1
1932	Hypostyle, 3–7–5 ..	Mrs C. Beatty ..	H. Fergusson .	A. Richardson	20–1
1933	Jean's Dream, 3–7–5	A. Boazman . ..	M. Peacock ..	J. Dines	20–1
1934	Pip Emma, 3–7–9 ..	Lord Rosebery ..	J. Jarvis	E. Smith	100–7
1935	Free Fare, 7–8–4 ..	B. Warner	E. Gwilt	S. Wragg . ..	22–1
1936	Newton Ford, 4–8–4	A. Boazman . ..	M. Peacock ..	W. Nevett ..	100–8
1937	Solitaire, 6–8–1 ..	Sir E. Hoyle . ..	H. Peacock ..	J. Taylor . ..	25–1
1938	Pappageno, 3–8–6 ..	G. Hartigan . ..	M. Hartigan ..	G. Richards ..	100–7
1939	Tutor, 3–8–3	Lord Rosebery ..	J. Jarvis	E. Smith . ..	9–2
1940	Beinn Dearg, 5–8–2 .	Lord Zetland ..	H. Peacock ..	W. Nevett ..	9–1
1941	Crown Colony, 5–7–9	Lord Glanely ..	J. Lawson ..	C. Richards ..	100–6
1942	Golden Boy, 4–8–11	W. Carr	W. Carr	D. Smith.. ..	10–1
1943	Mad Carew, 4–7–6..	Mrs W. Robottom	P. Vasey	J. Sime	33–1
1944	Kerry Piper, 3–8–0..	Sir H. Bruce.. ..	F. Armstrong..	C. Spares ..	25–1
1945	Oatflake, 3–7–13 ..	W. Barnett	F. Armstrong..	E. Britt	100–8
1946	Las Vegas, 4–8–8 ..	Sir W. Chaytor ..	A. Boyd	H. Wragg ..	20–1
1947	Regret, 4–6–3	Mrs F. Senior ..	P. Vasey	J. Walker . ..	66–1
1948	Sports Master, 3–6–13	D. Morris	J. Beary	D. Greening ..	20–1
1949	Fidonia, 5–9–2 . ..	A. Halford	E. Parker . ..	W. Carr	40–1
1950	Coltbridge, 4–7–6 ..	D. Thomson . ..	S. Hall	J. Sime	100–6
1951	Good Taste, 7–7–13	J. Bullock	S. Hall	W. Nevett ..	28–1
1952	Summer Rain,3–7–13	Lord Milford ..	J. Jarvis	P. Evans . ..	100–6
1953	Torch Singer, 4–6–5	J. Hanson	S. Hall	D. Ward . ..	40–1
1955	Tearaway, 5–6–11 ..	J. Hanson	S. Hall	W. Bentley ..	40–1
1956	Trentham Boy, 5–7–6	T. Degg	J. Gosden ..	J. Gifford . ..	100–6
1957	Chief Barker, 4–6–5	N. Cohen	H. Price	D. Walker ..	33–1
1958	Paul Jones, 3–8–2 ..	Col P. Wright ..	A. Budgett ..	J. Mercer . ..	100–7
1959	Operatic Society, 3–8–9	R. A-Walker . ..	C. Benstead ..	K. Gethin ..	18–1
1960	Dalnamein, 5–7–10 .	J. Phang.	S. Hall	H. Greenaway	28–1
1961	Henry's Choice, 4–8–2	W. Harrison.. ..	P. Beasley ..	E. Hide	100–8
1962	Damredub, 5–8–1 ..	T. Degg	J. Gosden ..	M. Germon ..	20–1
1963	Best Song, 4–9–6 ..	H. Allen	J. Gosden ..	J. Lindley ..	100–7
1964	Osier, 4–7–10	D. Montagu ..	B. van Cutsem	D. Smith.. ..	20–1
1965	Concealdem, 6–8–10	G. Taylor	J. Gosden ..	R. Hutchinson	100–8
1966	Polish Warrior,3–7–3	Col P. Wright ..	A. Budgett ..	A. Barclay ..	100–6
1967	Bugle Boy, 4–7–8 ..	Miss E. Rigden ..	A. Budgett ..	A. Barclay ..	22–1
1968	Zardia, 4–7–8	S. Gillatt	A. Vasey . ..	R. Still	25–1
1969	Tintagel II, 4–9–0 ..	Mrs. R. Sturdy ..	R. Sturdy ..	L. Piggott ..	15–2

Portland Handicap, 5f 152yd

First run 1855. *Run as Coronation Handicap* 1937. *Run at Newmarket* 1941. *No race* 1939, 1940 *and* 1942 *to* 1945.

		OWNER	TRAINER	JOCKEY	SP
1930	Polar Bear, 3–7–2	Mrs J. Joel	H. Cottrill	J. Dines	10–1
1931	Xandover, 4–9–7	J. Schwob	B. Jarvis	C. Elliott	11–4
1932	Polar Bear, 5–8–8	Mrs J. Joel	C. Peck	B. Carslake	100–6
1933	Valkyrie, 4–7–5	O. Watney	C. Leader	T. Barber	100–7
1934	Rosemary's Pet, 5–8–12	J. Joel	C. Peck	B. Carslake	6–1
1935	Shalfleet, 4–9–7	Maj J. Walker	H. Leader	H. Jelliss	8–1
1936	Shalfleet, 5–9–2	Maj J. Walker	H. Leader	H. Jelliss	10–1
1937	Carissa, 3–8–3	Sir V. Sassoon	H. Peacock	S. Donoghue	100–8
1938	The Drummer, 6–7–3	W. Carr	W. Carr	D. Smith	7–1
1941	Comatas, 4–8–11	Miss K. Farrar	O. Bell	W. Nevett	100–7
1946	The Shah, 4–7–5	D. Scott	B. Bullock	J. Sime	7–1
1947	Good View, 5–8–0	A. Halford	E. Parker	M. Beary	100–7
1948	Gold Mist, 3–7–12	Capt. A. Wills	N. Murless	C. Richards	20–1
1949	Le Lavandou, 5–7–7	Lieut-Col J. Innes	G. Houghton	P. Evans	25–1
1950	Paramount, 4–8–9	Sir H. de Trafford	M. Marsh	C. Smirke	100–7
1951	Reminiscence, 4–8–10	Mrs J. Rank	W. Nightingall	C. Smirke	100–6
1952	Stephen Paul, 4–9–3	J. Olding	H. Persse	G. Richards	100–30
1953	Reminiscence, 6–8–8	L. Bland	J. Ormston	E. Britt	100–7
1954	Vilmoray, 4–9–0	A. Green	B. Bullock	A. Shrive	100–7
1955	Princely Gift, 4–9–4	Sir V. Sassoon	N. Murless	L. Piggott	5–2
1956	Epaulette, 5–8–2	J. Gerber	F. Armstrong	W. Snaith	8–1
1957	Refined, 3–8–10	Lady M. van Cutsem	P. Prendergast	D. Smith	9–1
1958	Welsh Abbot, 3–9–2	Sir W. Churchill	W. Nightingall	S. Clayton	100–9
1959	New World, 6–7–3	R. Shaw	G. Balding	D. Greening	25–1
1960	Accompanist, 5–7–6	Mrs A. Palmer	F. Maxwell	D. W. Morris	7–1
1961	Winna, 4–7–2	Lieut-Col N. Frieze	H. Wragg	C. Parkes	100–8
1962	Harmon, 3–8–2	Mrs J. Aspinall	P. Beasley	A. Breasley	9–1
1963	Marcher, 3–8–9	R. Zelker	D. Hanley	R. Hutchinson	100–6
1964	Comefast, 5–7–13	H. Walton	J. Vickers	E. Hide	9–1
1965	Go Shell, 3–8–7	Lord Derby	B. van Cutsem	D. Smith	100–7
1966	Audrey Joan, 3–7–3	Mrs D. Rosenfeld	E. Cousins	A. Barclay	20–1
1967	Florescence, 3–8–13	J. R. Mullion	F. Armstrong	W. Williamson	100–9
1968	Gold Pollen, 3–7–7	W. Gaskin	R. Jarvis	E. Johnson	11–4
1969	Mountain Call, 4-8-11	I. E. Kornberg	B. van Cutsem	L. Piggott	11–4

Park Hill Stakes, 1m 6f 132yd

Three-year-old fillies. First run 1839. *Run at Newmarket* 1941. *No race* 1939, 1940 *and* 1942 *to* 1945.

		OWNER	TRAINER	JOCKEY	SP
1930	Glorious Devon, 8–13	Lord Glanely	T. Hogg	G. Richards	7–2
1931	Volume, 8–0	Lord Astor	J. Lawson	F. Lane	8–1
1932	Fury, 7–11	Sir E. Hanmer	M. Peacock	W. Nevett	9–2
1933	Typhonic, 9–3	Maj J. Courtauld	B. Jarvis	G. Richards	7–2
1934	Poker, 8–3	J. de Rothschild	F. Pratt	G. Bezant	7–2
1935	Foxlair, 8–0	Mrs C. Glorney	L. Cundell	S. Donoghue	3–1
1936	Traffic Light, 8–3	Lord Astor	J. Lawson	J. Sirett	11–10
1937	Nadushka, 8–10	G. Fairhurst	V. Gilpin	H. Wragg	10–1
1938	Gainly, 8–0	W. Woodward	C. B-Rochfort	M. Beary	9–2
1941	Bright Lady, 7–7	T. Venn	V. Hobbs	J. Hine	11–2
1946	Procne, 8–4	Miss J. Clayton	C. Elsey	E. Britt	2–1
1947	Mitrailleuse, 8–8	Lord Astor	R. J. Colling	G. Richards	9–4
1948	Vertencia, 8–8	W. Hill	A. Smyth	M. Beary	100–8
1949	Sea Idol, 8–4	A. Hedley	J. Lawson	E. Smith	100–7
1950	La Baille, 9–0	Mohamed Bey Sultan	M. Marsh	C. Smirke	100–6
1951	Verse, 8–8	J. Rank	N. Cannon	A. Breasley	10–1
1952	Moon Star, 8–8	W. Woodward	C. B-Rochfort	W. Carr	5–2
1953	Kerkeb, 9–0	Aga Khan	M. Marsh	C. Smirke	9–2
1954	Bara Bibi, 9–0	Aga Khan	N. Murless	C. Smirke	100–9
1955	Ark Royal, 9–0	R. Hollingsworth	G. Colling	E. Mercer	4–1

	OWNER	TRAINER	JOCKEY	SP
1956 Kyak, 8–4	R. Hollingsworth	G. Colling	E. Mercer	100–6
1957 Almeria, 9–0	The Queen	C. B-Rochfort	W. Carr	2–7
1958 Cutter, 9–0	R. Hollingsworth	G. Colling	E. Mercer	100–8
1959 Collyria, 9–0	Sir V. Sassoon	N. Murless	E. Smith	33–1
1960 Sunny Cove, 9–0	M. Sobell	Sir G. Richards	A. Breasley	5–1
1961 Never Say, 9–0	J. Astor	J. Colling	J. Mercer	7–2
1962 Almiranta, 9–0	Lord H. de Walden	J. A. Waugh	W. Carr	7–2
1963 Outcrop, 9–0	Maj J. Priestman	G. Barling	E. Smith	4–1
1964 Cursorial, 9–0	Maj L. Holliday	W. Wharton	J. Mercer	100–6
1965 Bracey Bridge, 9–0	M. W-Boynton	N. Murless	L. Piggott	7–2
1966 Parthian Glance, 9–0	Mrs W. R-Smith	G. Todd	L. Piggott	4–5
1967 { Pia, 9–0	Countess M. Batthyany	W. Elsey	E. Hide	7–2
1967 { Pink Gem, 9–0	H. Joel	N. Murless	G. Moore	2–1
1968 Bringley, 9–0	R. Midwood	H. Leader	B. Taylor	3–1
1969 Aggravate, 9–0	L. van Moppes	A. Budgett	E. Johnson	8–1

Doncaster Cup, 2m 2f

First run 1801. *No race* 1939 *to* 1945.

	OWNER	TRAINER	JOCKEY	SP
1930 Brown Jack, 6–9–11	Sir H. Wernher	I. Anthony	J. Childs	11–10
1931 Singapore, 4–9–12	Lord Glanely	T. Hogg	G. Richards	13–8
1932 Foxhunter, 3–7–8	E. Esmond	J. Jarvis	G. Richards	13–8
1933 Colorado Kid, 4–8–6	Lieut-Col G. Loder	V. Gilpin	G. Richards	4–9
1934 Alcazar, 3–8–8	W. Woodward	C. B-Rochfort	J. Childs	30–100
1935 Black Devil, 4–9–9	W. Woodward	C. B-Rochfort	J. Childs	4–6
1936 Buckleigh, 4–9–2	Lord Glanely	T. Hogg	G. Richards	7–2
1937 Haulfryn, 4–9–2	F. Minoprio	R. Metcalfe	G. Richards	8–1
1938 Epigram, 5–10–0	J. Rank	N. Cannon	B. Carslake	7–4
1946 Marsyas II, 6–9–9	M. Boussac	C. Semblat	C. Elliott	1–7
1947 Trimbush, 7–9–6	Mrs F. Senior	P. Vasey	D. Smith	10–1
1948 Auralia, 5–9–7	Mrs A. Johnston	R. Day	D. Smith	6–1
1949 Alycidon, 4–9–7	Lord Derby	W. Earl	D. Smith	2–7
1950 Aldborough, 5–9–9	Miss D. Paget	F. Walwyn	D. Smith	6–1
1951 Fast Fox, 4–9–4	Baron de Waldner	P. Carter	F. Palmer	3–1
1952 Aquino II, 4–9–7	Maharanee of Baroda	F. Armstrong	G. Richards	2–1
1953 { Souepi, 5–9–9	G. Digby	G. Digby	C. Elliott	5–1
1953 { Nick la Rocca, 4–9–4	F. Williams	R. J. Colling	J. Mercer	100–7
1954 Osborne, 7–9–6	Brig W. Wyatt	C. B-Rochfort	W. Carr	5–1
1955 Entente Cordiale, 4–9–4	Lord Derby	G. Colling	D. Smith	5–2
1956 Atlas, 3–8–3	The Queen	C. B-Rochfort	W. Carr	11–4
1957 French Beige, 4–9–4	R. Dennis	H. Peacock	G. Littlewood	5–1
1958 Agreement, 4–9–4	The Queen	C. B-Rochfort	D. Smith	25–1
1959 Agreement, 5–9–9	The Queen	C. B-Rochfort	W. Carr	11–4
1960 Exar, 4–9–7	Dr C. Vittadini	N. Murless	L. Piggott	6–100
1961 Pandofell, 4–9–7	H. W. Daw	F. Maxwell	L. Piggott	9–4
1962 Bonnard, 4–8–12	Marchese della Rocchetta	J. Clayton	R. Hutchinson	6–1
1963 Raise You Ten, 3–7–11	P. Widener	C. B-Rochfort	D. Smith	5–1
1964 Grey of Falloden, 5–9–0	Lord Astor	W. Hern	J. Mercer	8–1
1965 Prince Hansel, 4–8–12	J. Barker	D. Thom	D. Yates	2–1
1966 Piaco, 3–7–11	Mrs O. Watney	G. Barling	M. Thomas	11–8
1967 Crozier, 4–8–12	A. D. Oldrey	P. Walwyn	F. Durr	20–1
1968 The Accuser, 4–8–12	Lord Rotherwick	W. Hern	J. Mercer	2–1
1969 Canterbury, 4–8–12	J. M. Olin	P. Prendergast	W. Williamson	100–30

Observer Gold Cup, 1m

Two-year-olds. First run 1961. *Run as Timeform Gold Cup until* 1964.

		OWNER	TRAINER	JOCKEY	SP
1961	Miralgo, 8–12	G. Oldham	H. Wragg ..	W. Williamson	10–1
1962	Noblesse, 8–12 ..	Mrs J. Olin	P. Prendergast .	G. Bougoure ..	11–10
1963	Pushful, 8–12	Maj L. Holliday ..	S. Meaney ..	W. Carr	100–6
1964	Hardicanute, 8–12 ..	J. Mullion	P. Prendergast .	W. Williamson.	13–8
1965	Pretendre, 8–12 ..	J. Lilley..	J. Jarvis	R. Hutchinson	6–1
1966	Ribocco, 8–12 . ..	C. Engelhard . ..	R. Houghton .	L. Piggott ..	4–9
1967	Vaguely Noble, 8–12	L. B. Holliday ..	W. Wharton ..	W. Williamson.	8–1
1968	The Elk, 8–12	Miss M. Sheriffe ..	J. Tree	W. Pyers . ..	10–1
1969	Approval, 8–12 ..	Sir H. de Trafford	H. Cecil	D. Keith . ..	5–1

Lincoln Handicap, 1m

First run 1853. *Run at Lincoln as Lincolnshire Handicap until* 1964, *except for* 1942 *to* 1945, *when it was run at Pontefract. Run at Doncaster since* 1965.

		OWNER	TRAINER	JOCKEY	SP
1930	Leonidas II, 5–8–0 .	M. Boussac	S. Darling ..	H. Southey ..	66–1
1931	Knight Error, 5–7–7	Capt A. Wilson ..	P. Whitaker ..	F. Fox	100–9
1932	Jerome Fandor, 4–6–13	A. McKinlay . ..	H. Peacock ..	W. Christie ..	40–1
1933	Dorigen, 4–9–1 ..	G. Lambton . ..	G. Lambton ..	T. Weston ..	25–1
1934	Play On, 4–7–8 ..	M. Simon	J. Russell . ..	J. Dines	100–9
1935	Flamenco, 4–9–0 ..	Lord Rosebery ..	J. Jarvis	E. Smith . ..	8–1
1936	Over Coat, 5–7–12 .	H. Selby	J. Russell . ..	T. Weston ..	10–1
1937	Marmaduke Jinks, 5–8–0	Mrs C. Robinson .	H. Peacock ..	D. Smith.. ..	33–1
1938	Phakos, 4–8–3 . ..	E. Esmond	J. Jarvis	E. Smith . ..	8–1
1939	Squadron Castle, 6–7–7	S. Oxenham . ..	H. Smallwood .	V. Mitchell ..	40–1
1940	Quartier Maitre, 5–8–1	Mrs A. Bendir ..	I. Anthony ..	G. Richards ..	7–2
1941	Gloaming, 4–7–4 ..	S. Raphael	G. Lambton ..	D. Dick	100–7
1942	Cuerdley, 4–9–4 ..	E. Pilcher	R. Renton ..	J. Taylor . ..	3–1
1943	Lady Electra, 4–8–10	W. Richardson ..	C. Ray	R. Colven ..	9–2
1944	Backbite, 5–7–8 ..	A. Tully	A. Boyd	M. Pearson ..	33–1
1945	Double Harness, 4–6–10	J. Hetherton.. ..	C. Elsey	D. Stansfield ..	33–1
1946	Langton Abbot, 4–8–2	T. Best	E. Lambton ..	T. Weston ..	7–1
1947	Jockey Treble, 5–6–0	S. Oxenham . ..	W. Smallwood	E. Mercer ..	100–1
1948	Commissar, 8–8–9 ..	R. Budgett	A. Budgett ..	W. Rickaby ..	33–1
1949	Fair Judgment, 4–7–10..	C. Gordon	J. Jarvis	E. Smith . ..	6–1
1950	Dramatic, 5–8–13 ..	A. Saunders . ..	G. Todd	G. Richards ..	7–1
1951	Barnes Park, 5–8–0 .	H. Lane	G. Boyd	J. Sime	33–1
1952	Phariza, 5–6–12 ..	C. O-Lee	J. Powell . ..	D. Forte . ..	33–1
1953	Sailing Light, 4–7–11	Mrs M. Farr . ..	G. Armstrong .	A. Roberts ..	100–8
1954	Nahar, 7–8–0	Aly Khan	A. Head	J. Massard ..	100–7
1955	Military Court, 5–8–2	Begum Aga Khan	H. Wragg ..	E. Mercer ..	8–1
1956	Three Star II, 8–6–13	G. Graham	H. Davison ..	D. W. Morris .	40–1
1957	Babur, 4–7–13 . ..	Capt S. Lord . ..	C. Elsey	E. Hide	25–1
1958	Babur, 5–9–0	Capt S. Lord . ..	C. Elsey	E. Britt	25–1
1959	Marshal Pil, 5–7–13	Dr S. Lip	S. Hall	P. Robinson ..	15–2
1960	Mustavon, 5–6–13 ..	Mrs L. McVey ..	S. Hall	N. McIntosh ..	8–1
1961	Johns Court, 6–7–7 .	K. Wheldon . ..	E. Cousins ..	B. Lee	25–1
1962	Hill Royal, 4–7–9 ..	D. Murray	E. Cousins ..	J. Sime	50–1
1963	Monawin, 8–7–9 ..	R. Mason	R. Mason ..	J. Sime	25–1
1964	Mighty Gurkha, 5–7–8	Mrs G. Lambton .	E. Lambton ..	P. Robinson ..	33–1
1965	Old Tom, 6–8–7 ..	J. Ellis	M. H. Easterby	A. Breasley ..	22–1
1966	Riot Act, 4–8–3 ..	Mrs J. Bryce . ..	F. Armstrong..	A. Breasley ..	8–1
1967	Ben Novus, 5–7–10 .	I. N. Peatt	W. Hide	P. Robinson ..	22–1
1968	Frankincense, 4–9–5	Lady Halifax . ..	J. Oxley	G. Starkey ..	100–8
1969	Foggy Bell, 4–7–11..	J. Forrester	Denys Smith ..	A. Barclay ..	20–1
1970	New Chapter, 4–8–1	C. Goulandris ..	F. Armstrong..	A. Barclay ..	100–9

DONCASTER CUP

See under DONCASTER.

DONOGHUE, Stephen (1884-1945)

Steve Donoghue, destined to become the most famous and popular jockey of his day, was the son of an iron-worker and was born in that very unattractive town, Warrington. His early life was hard, even by the standards of those days, and fame and fortune did not come to him swiftly or easily. He ran away from home more than once and had experience of a number of well-known English stables, among them those of Dobson Peacock and Alfred Sadler, before, at the age of 18, he accepted a post in France with the American trainer, Edward Johnson. It was in France that he rode his first winner in 1904. He gained useful experience, if not much else, in riding second-rate horses at trappy little French courses in the provinces. After some of those tracks, Epsom seemed easy. In 1906 he left France and rode in Ireland for several seasons. His first English retainer was with 'Atty' Persse's stable in 1911. Thus he was associated in 1913 with The Tetrarch, probably the fastest horse ever seen on the English Turf.

Once established in England, Donoghue made rapid headway and he won war-substitute Derbys on Pommern (1915) and Gay Crusader (1917). The heyday of his career was the 1920s, particularly the first six years of that decade, and it was then that the famous cry of "Come on, Steve!" became incorporated into the English language. He won the Derby on Humorist (1921), Captain Cuttle (1922), Papyrus (1923) and Manna (1925). Altogether he had 14 victories in English classic races. He also won the Irish Derby four times and the Grand Prix de Paris twice. He partnered the great stayer Brown Jack, who won the Queen Alexandra Stakes at Royal Ascot six years running. His last important success was to win the 1937 Oaks on Exhibitionnist. He was then 52 years of age. His last mount was in the Final Plate at Manchester that year. Not once in his 33 years as a jockey was he up before the stewards for an infringement of the rules.

He was above all a superb horseman with beautiful hands and it was a pleasure to see him cantering down to the start on a highly-strung two-year-old. He genuinely loved horses and they went kindly for him. His iron nerve remained unimpaired to the end. He had some dreadful falls and after a shattering crash in the 1920 Derby on very hard ground when he lay prone in the path of the oncoming field, he walked back to the weighing room and rode two more winners that afternoon. He was at his brilliant best at Epsom and that downhill gallop to Tattenham Corner never gave him a second's anxiety.

A little short-legged man with a husky voice and a charming smile, he had a most attractive personality. He was kind and generous—too generous for his own good, in fact—and even at the zenith of his popularity, he never became swollen-headed or overbearing. Sometimes he was deplorably casual towards those who employed him, but his charm usually extricated him from unpromising situations. Both as a breeder of bloodstock and as a trainer he was notably less successful than he had been as a rider. All who followed racing felt they had lost a friend when he died quite suddenly in 1945.

DOPING

Doping falls into two categories: doping to win and doping to stop a horse from winning.

Doping to win was introduced into Britain by the American trainers who came to this country at the turn of the century. Some of them were very good at it indeed. In general it is reasonable to assume that doping to win is done by the trainer or by someone closely connected with the horse who knows its physical condition, disposition and the plans that have been made for it. Horses do not all react in the same manner to a stimulant administered to affect their speed; a dose that may produce highly satisfactory results in one horse may send another almost mad.

A few years ago there was probably a fair amount of doping to win taking place but this evil has now been firmly tackled by the authorities and it is doubtful if much of it now goes on. The Levy Board spends a lot of money yearly on anti-doping precautions. The danger, of course, is that chemists, for ever discovering new drugs, may always be a step or two in front of the analysts.

Doping to stop a horse from winning is certainly never done by the trainer, who has simpler methods at his disposal if he does not wish a horse of his to win.

If the object is to prevent a horse from running, crude methods can be used once access has been obtained, and it does not matter to the perpetrators if the horse is seriously injured. In ante-post betting, punters lose their money if a horse does not run. Not many years ago a heavily-backed Derby favourite was successfully 'got at'. Cruel methods were used and the horse never ran again.

A higher degree of skill is needed if a horse is to be well enough to go to the post but at the same time sure to run badly. The ideal situation is a small field with only two horses fancied. Those in the know, not necessarily only the perpetrators, can then lay the doped horse and back the other.

DOUBLE JUMP

Foaled in 1962, Double Jump is a chestnut by Rustam out of Fair Bid, by My Babu. He was bred by Mr A. P. Harris, bought by Mr Charles Englehard for 7,800 gn and trained by Jeremy Tree. As a two-year-old he won four races worth over £14,000 in England, including the National Stakes and the Gimcrack Stakes. In France he won the Prix Robert Papin. In the Middle Park Stakes he broke a blood vessel and he never ran again. He stands at the Bolton Stud, Harewood, Yorkshire.

DOUBLE LIFE

Double Life was the famous foundation mare of Lady Zia Wernher's Someries Stud, Newmarket, where there is a well-deserved memorial stone in her honour. A chestnut by Bachelor's Double out of St Joan, she was bought as a yearling by Capt (later Sir) Cecil Boyd-Rochfort for 600 gn on behalf of Lady Zia Wernher. She proved a wonderful bargain. She herself won the Cambridgeshire, Duke of York Handicap and the Chesterfield Cup. Among her offspring were Precipitation, who won seven races worth over £17,000, including the Ascot Gold Cup, and who sired the Derby winner Airborne; and Persian Gulf, who won the Coronation Cup and sired the Derby winner Parthia. Double Life's other two winners were Casanova, who won the Dewhurst Stakes; and Fairly, dam of the Irish St Leger winner Judicate. Among Double Life's most distinguished descendants are that great filly Meld, winner of the One Thousand Guineas, Oaks, and St Leger; the 1966 Derby winner Charlottown; and Double Eclipse, winner of the Princess of Wales's Stakes and third in the Derby.

DOUBLES

A common form of betting is 'a double', in which a bet is made on two horses in separate races. In a win double, both horses must win; in an each way double, both horses must be placed. In a successful win double, the odds of the two horses are multiplied together and then added. Thus a 4-1 winner doubled with a 3-1 winner means 4 x 3=12; to this is added 4 + 3 = 7. The double, therefore, represents odds of 19-1. In antepost bets, that is to say bets made before the day of the race, the odds for doubles are multiplied but not added.

In 'mixed doubles' a punter selects a number of horses and each horse selected is doubled with all the others.

DOUGLAS, Lady James (1854-1941)

Lady James Douglas was born in France, the daughter of Mr F. Hennessy, a member of the famous Anglo-French brandy-distilling family. She first married a relation, Mr R. Hennessy, and after Mr Hennessy's death in 1888 Lord James Douglas who died in 1891. She bought the Harwood property near Newbury in 1910 and there she bred Gainsborough, winner of the 'Triple Crown' in 1918. Lady James Douglas became, therefore, the first woman to win a classic race in her own colours and the first woman to own a winner of the Derby.

DRUID'S LODGE CONFEDERACY

In the early years of this century, the Druid's Lodge stable near Salisbury was famous, even notorious, for bringing off successful coups in big handicaps. 'The Confederacy' consisted of Capt W. B. Purefoy, Capt F. Forester, Mr A. P. Cunliffe and Mr E. A. Wigan. They knew the racing game from A to Z and their skill in weighing up form and a horse's capabilities was remarkable. They betted heavily and won very large sums when Hacklers Pride won the Cambridgeshire in 1903 and again in 1904. Jack Fallon was the trainer at Druid's Lodge during its heyday, but his job there was merely to carry out the instructions he was given by 'The Confederacy', the shrewdest of whom was Capt Purefoy. Jack Fallon died 'broke'; the members of 'The Confederacy' all left big fortunes behind them.

DUFFIELD, George

He can do 7st 4lb and rides for Jack Waugh and John Oxley. He rode

39 winners in 1968 and 34 in 1969. He was originally apprenticed to Jack Waugh.

DUGDALE, Sir William, MC (b 1922)

Sir William Dugdale served in the Grenadier Guards. He is a member of the Jockey Club and a steward at Ascot, Nottingham, Warwick and Wolverhampton. His trainer is 'Atty' Corbett. Colours: black, white sleeves.

DUNLOP, John Leeper (b 1939)

John Dunlop did his National Service in the Royal Ulster Rifles. He was an assistant for two years with N. J. Dent and for a further two years with Gordon Smyth. He succeeded the latter as trainer at the Duke of Norfolk's Arundel stable in 1966. The Duke and Duchess of Norfolk are of course the main patrons of the stable; other owners include Lady Mary FitzAlan-Howard, Lady Sarah FitzAlan-Howard; Miss G. Grant-Lawson, Mrs A. J. Scratchley, Col and Mrs W. Stirling, the Countess of Rosebery and Mr A. J. Struthers. The best horse he has so far trained is Mount Athos, winner of the Scottish and Newcastle Breweries Handicap, the Princess of Wales's Stakes and the Gordon Stakes. Mount Athos was also third to Sir Ivor in the Derby. In 1970 he won the Irish One Thousand Guineas with Black Satin.

DURBAR II

Bred and trained in France and owned by Mr H. B. Duryea, an American, Durbar II won the Derby in 1914. He was the first French horse to win since Gladiateur in 1865. In fact he had no French blood in his veins, being by the English-bred Rabelais, who had won the Goodwood Cup for Mrs Arthur James, out of a mare called Armenia who was by the English-bred Meddler out of the American-bred Urania. Under the rules then existing, Durbar II was not classified as a thoroughbred since

Urania's family, one of the best known in America at that time, was ineligible for inclusion in the English Stud Book. As a sire Durbar II is best remembered through Durban who was a very fast two-year-old and later bred Tourbillon, winner of the French Derby and four times champion sire in France. Durbar II was eventually exported to America where he died aged 21.

DURHAM, third Earl of (1855-1928)

Lord Durham, brother of the famous trainer George Lambton, was a member of the Jockey Club from 1882 till his death. Sagacious, fearless, impulsive at times but never vindictive, he served five terms of office as Steward and his energy as a Turf administrator stood out in contrast to the complacent inertia of most of his contemporaries.

In 1887 he made a hard-hitting speech at the Annual Dinner of the Gimcrack Club, making biting allusions to the in-and-out running of horses in Sherrards's stable which in fact was controlled by Sir George Chetwynd, a former Senior Steward of the Jockey Club who was in reality little more than a professional backer; and by the stable jockey, Charles Wood. Sir George at once sued Lord Durham for libel, having been dissauded from challenging him to a duel. A protracted case ended with the downfall of Sir George, who was compelled to retire from the Turf, and also of Wood, who forfeited his licence for a number of years.

Lord Durham was a powerful advocate for the introduction of the starting gate to supplant starting by flag. Careless of unpopularity, he banned smoking in the weighing room and the jockeys' room. During World War I he never set foot on a racecourse himself, but did all he could to maintain the continuance of the sport in a much-reduced form. As an owner he was never very lucky but he won the Oaks with Beam in 1927.

DURR, Frank (b 1927)

Frankie Durr, who can go to scale at 7st 12lb, was born in Liverpool and apprenticed to Jack Payne and then to Willie Pratt. He had his first ride in 1942. In 1945 he shared the position of top apprentice with Tommy Gosling. After completing his apprenticeship, it took him some little time to establish his reputation but in the early 1950s he began a six-year association with the Duke and Duchess of Norfolk. Subsequently he rode for Joe Lawson and more recently he has ridden many winners for Mr David Robinson. His most important victories were in the Irish Sweeps Derby and the St Leger on Sodium. At one time or another he has won most of the important handicaps. In 1968 he rode 78 winners and in 1969 87. He is now riding for G. Barling's stable.

E

EARL, Walter (1890-1950)

Walter Earl, an extremely good trainer and a very popular personality, was born in Bohemia of British parents, his father being a trainer for over 40 years in Austria-Hungary. At the age of 14 Walter Earl came to England and was apprenticed to Willie Waugh, riding his first winner in 1906. He soon became too heavy for the flat and rode quite successfully for a time under National Hunt rules.

In 1920 he took out a licence to train and in 1924 became private trainer to Mr 'Solly' Joel, for whom he won the Eclipse Stakes, the Goodwood Cup, the Manchester Cup, the Doncaster Cup, the Ebor Handicap, the Irish Derby and many other good races. When Mr Joel died in 1931 he became a public trainer, but in 1939, following College Leader's death, he was appointed private trainer to Lord Derby at Stanley House. For Lord Derby he won five classic races within four seasons, including the 1942 Derby with Watling Street. He also had active charge of the great stayer Alycidon from Alycidon's arrival at Stanley House till his triumph in the Gold Cup at Ascot. Unfortunately Earl had a serious illness in 1949 and he died the following year.

EAST, David (b 1937)

David East was apprenticed to W. Payne and F. L. Armstrong. An experienced and competent light-weight who can go to scale at 7st 2lb, he rode his first winner in 1958. Good handicaps he has won include the Wokingham Stakes and Kempton Jubilee, while he has also ridden with success in India.

EASTERBY, Michael W.

'Mick' Easterby is the younger brother of 'Peter' Easterby (see below). He took out a trainer's licence in 1961 and his stables are at Flaxton, Yorkshire. His owners include Mr A. Barnett, Mr P. Bell, Mr C. Gledhill, Mrs M. Oates, Mr John Henderson, Dr W. Roy Heylings, Mr T. L. Batty, Mrs Elizabeth Smith, Mr J. Rowbottom, Dr W. J. Heffernan, Mr W. H. Lockwood, Hon Mrs S. Taylor, Mr S. Holmes and Mr W. Newton.

EASTERBY, Miles Henry (b 1929)

Born in 1929, 'Peter' Easterby has one of the biggest stables in the North at Habton Grange, Malton. After working for the late Frank Hartigan and for his uncle Walter Easterby, he took out a trainer's licence in 1967 and successfully combines flat-racing with jumping. He won the Lincolnshire Handicap with Old Tom and two races at Royal Ascot with the sprinter Goldhill. His patrons include Mrs W. G. Blow, Mr Stanhope Joel, Mr M. K. Callender, Mrs E. E. Dawson, Mrs M. Ingram, Mr T. K. Kindon, Mr J. W. Roylance, Mr Fred Smith, Mr W. Steele, Mr A. Snipe, Mrs C. Straker and Mr C. E. Rudkin.

EASTON

Easton was bred in France by Mr R. B. Strassburger and was by Dark Legend out of Phaona. Bought by Lord Woolavington and trained by Fred Darling, he ran second in the Two Thousand Guineas and the Derby in 1934; in the following year he was second in the Coronation Cup.

He won the Select Stakes and March Stakes in England while in Belgium he won the Grand International at Ostend. He failed as a sire and died in the United States.

EBOR HANDICAP

See under YORK.

ECCLESTON, Clive

Top apprentice in 1969 with 41 winners. He rides for F. Carr.

ECLIPSE

Eclipse, foaled in 1764, was one of the greatest horses in English racing history. Bred by William, Duke of Cumberland, he was sold after his breeder's death for 75 gn to Mr Wildman, a meat salesman of Leadenhall Market. In 1770 Major O'Kelly bought a half share in him for 650 gn and later paid 1,750 gn to buy him outright. O'Kelly was an Irish adventurer who had been a billiards marker; it was said that the nearest he ever got to religion was to own a parrot that could whistle one of the psalms.

Eclipse was never beaten; furthermore he was never even extended. In the famous words of O'Kelly, it was always a case of "Eclipse first, the rest nowhere". He won £25,000 in stakes, a huge sum for those days and at the stud he sired 335 winners of £160,000. When he died aged 25 he was still covering 50 mares a season. He sired three winners of the Derby.

The element of pure chance is inseparable from racing. Squirt, grandsire of Eclipse, was being led off to a dog-kennel for execution when a groom persuaded his owner, Sir Harry Harpur, to spare his life and he was reprieved at the very last moment.

ECLIPSE STAKES

See under SANDOWN PARK.

EDDERY, Pat

Attached to H. Nicholson's stable, he is one of the most promising riders in the game today and rode 23 winners in 1969. He is a son of J. Eddery who rode with much success in Ireland and was second in the 1955 Derby on Panaslipper.

EDINBURGH

A few years ago it looked very much as if Edinburgh was going to disappear from the fixture list but the Betting Levy Board found a doughty opponent in Lord Rosebery and thanks largely to his efforts Edinburgh was saved. The racing there is of modest quality but it provides bright entertainment for the citizens of Edinburgh and opportunities for moderate horses trained in Scotland and the North of England. The course is a seaside one, being situated at Musselburgh, about five miles outside Edinburgh and consists of an oval track about 1¼m round and with a run-in of approximately 4f. The straight 5f course is generally reckoned a fast one and to favour the quick starter. The turns at the top end of the course and into the straight are rather sharp and need a handy horse to negotiate them to the best advantage. High numbers are favoured in races of 7f and 1m.

Clerk of the Course: Col W. W. McHarg, Racecourse Office, 2 Whitletts Road, Ayr. Tel: Ayr 64179, Musselburgh 2859 on race days only.

Best Times:

Distance	*Horse-Age-Weight*	*Date*	*Time*
5f	Le Garcon d'Or 4-8-12	18-9-62	58.8
5f	Baroda 2-8-10	20-9-49	58.6
7f	Wheel of Fortune 6-7-4	20-4-53	1min 26.8
7f	Arethusa 2-8-11	16-9-63	1min 30
8f	Ditched 6-7-12	22-7-63	1min 39.4

Distance	*Horse-Age-Weight*	*Date*	*Time*
8f	Pipeclay 2-8-9	20-9-49	1min 41.6
11f	Sunnyray 4-8-7	19-9-49	2min 19.8
12f	Glengrigor 5-7-9	15-4-46	2min 32.2
15f	Cunningham 3-8-0	21-9-53	3min 10.4

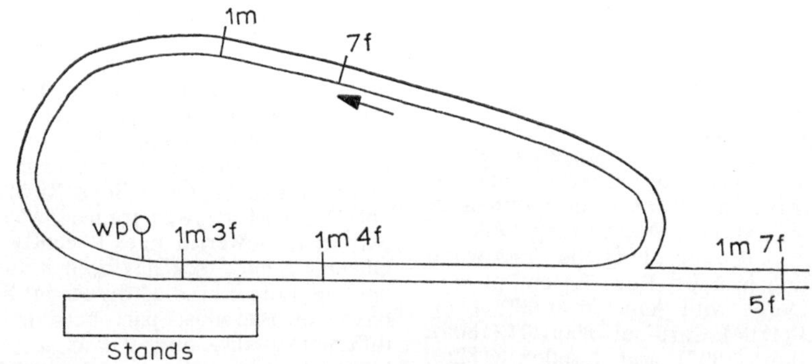

EDINBURGH

EDWARD VII, KING (1841-1910)

King Edward VII, as Prince of Wales, registered his colours in 1875. At first he contented himself with a few jumpers trained by John Jones at Epsom but in 1885 he went to the Newmarket Sales to buy some fillies with a view to founding a stud at Sandringham. He first trained with John Porter at Kingsclere but in 1893 his horses were transferred to Richard Marsh at Newmarket. There had been a frequent clash of wills between honest, stubborn John Porter and the Prince's racing manager, that witty and sometimes impetuous Irishman Lord Marcus Beresford.

Porter had scant success with the Prince's horses but he supplied the Sandringham Stud with a great foundation mare when he bought Perdita II for the Prince for £900. She bred two Derby winners, Persimmon and Diamond Jubilee, and altogether the winners of over £72,000 in stakes.

In 1896 Persimmon won the Derby amid scenes of unforgettable enthusiasm ; he also won the St Leger and as a four-year-old the Eclipse Stakes and Gold Cup at Ascot. He is the last Epsom Derby winner to have carried off the Cup. Diamond Jubilee, also by St Simon, won the 'Triple Crown' in 1900, the year the Prince won the Grand National with Ambush II. A brilliant but ill-tempered horse, Diamond Jubilee was exported to South America where he did well as a sire. The King's third and final Derby winner was in 1909 when he won with Minoru, leased from Col W. Hall-Walker, later Lord Wavertree. Minoru was exported to Russia and disappeared there during the Revolution.

The King was keener on racing and the so smart racing set than his son, King George V, but he was not as good a judge of a horse.

EGERTON, Thomas Edward Sydney (b 1918)

Mr Egerton served in the Coldstream Guards. He is a member of the Jockey Club and a steward at Bath, Lingfield and Windsor. His trainers are W. Hern and H. E. Smyth and his colours are drab, scarlet hoop, quartered cap.

EGREMONT, third Earl of (1751-1837)

The third Earl of Egremont was a man of immense wealth and remarkable generosity. He gave away £20,000 every year and it was said that he delighted in giving as other rich men delighted in accumulating. He never married and on his death his estates passed to his illegitimate son Col Wyndham, later Lord Leconfield.

For many years Lord Egremont ran a great race meeting in his park at Petworth and it was the discontinuance of this fixture that led to the Duke of Richmond establishing the Goodwood meeting in 1801. Lord Egremont won the Derby with Assassin (1782), Hannibal (1804), Cardinal Beaufort (1805), Election (1807) and Lapdog (1826). Some of these Derby winners were probably four-year-olds. Bird, who trained for Lord Egremont, admitted on his death-bed that he had twice won the Derby with four-year-olds by the simple expedient of slipping two-year-olds into the yearling paddock. There were usually three hundred horses at Petworth, and as the management was casual to a degree, discovery was highly unlikely. Lord Egremont himself knew nothing of the deception practised.

ELDIN, Eric (b 1932)

Eric Eldin, a thoroughly sound and reliable rider, was apprenticed to Ryan Jarvis. In 1966 he rode 60 winners and among the good horses with which he has been associated were Lomond, whose many victories included the Ebor Handicap; and that fine sprinter Lucasland, winner of the Diadem Stakes and July Cup. He rode regularly in India from 1952-58. He can go to scale at 8st and is attached to J. A. J. Waugh's stable.

ELEANOR

Sir Charles Bunbury's filly Eleanor won the Derby and the Oaks in 1801. She was the first of the four fillies that have accomplished that feat. She continued to race till she was seven and is probably the only Derby winner to have won a race at Huntingdon as well.

ELIZABETH II, HM QUEEN

The Queen is as great a racing enthusiast as was her great grand-father, King Edward VII, and on all Turf matters she is very knowledgeable indeed. In the years immediately following her accession to the Throne, she was extremely successful both as owner and breeder, and the combination of Capt Charles Moore as racing manager and Sir Cecil Boyd-Rochfort and Noel Murless as trainers was an extremely powerful one. Recently the Queen's racing luck has been indifferent: the horses bred at the Royal Stud have for the most part been of indifferent quality and it was a great blow when Doutelle, who looked like making a really good sire, met with a fatal accident. Nowadays, too, there are no superbly bred colts and fillies leased to the Queen for their racing career by the National Stud. It was these National Stud products, among which were Hopeful Venture and Carrozza, that were trained by Noel Murless. Now Capt Charles Moore is dead and Sir Cecil Boyd-Rochfort has retired. The Queen's horses in training are divided between Dick Hern and Ian Balding. In 1968 the number of mares at the Royal Stud was sharply reduced and it is now hoped to introduce a bit of speed, the essential quality that seems to have been lacking of late. In 1969 Lord Porchester was appointed the Queen's racing manager.

Good winners to have carried the Queen's colours include Aureole (King George VI and Queen Elizabeth Stakes, Coronation Cup, Hardwicke Stakes); Pall Mall (Two Thousand Guineas, Lockinge Stakes twice); Canisbay (Eclipse Stakes); Carrozza (Princess Elizabeth Stakes, Oaks); Doutelle (John Porter Stakes, Ormonde Stakes, Lingfield Derby Trial); Above Suspicion (St James's Palace Stakes, Gordon Stakes); Choir Boy (Royal Hunt Cup); Miner's Lamp (Blue Riband Trial Stakes, Princess of

Wales's Stakes); Mulberry Harbour (Cheshire Oaks); Hopeful Venture (Grand Prix de St Cloud, Princess of Wales's Stakes, Hardwicke Stakes, Ormonde Stakes); Angel Bright (Lingfield Oaks Trial); Aiming High (Coronation Stakes); Almeria (Ribblesdale Stakes, Yorkshire Oaks, Park Hill Stakes); Restoration (King Edward VII Stakes); Pindari (King Edward VII Stakes, Great Voltigeur Stakes); Landau (Sussex Stakes); Gaulois (Goodwood Cup); Apprentice (Goodwood Cup, Yorkshire Cup); Agreement (Doncaster Cup twice, Chester Cup); and Castle Yard (Zetland Gold Cup).

ELLANGOWAN

Ellangowan was foaled in 1920 and was by Lemberg out of Lammermuir. Owned and bred by the late Lord Rosebery, he won the 1923 Two Thousand Guineas ridden by Charles Elliott. He also won the St James's Palace Stakes and the Champion Stakes. He was not a success as a sire.

ELLIOTT, Charles (b 1904)

Charles Elliott was for more than 25 years a leading jockey. He was still apprenticed to Jack Jarvis when he deposed Donoghue from the position of champion jockey in 1924, a position that Donoghue had occupied for the previous ten years. In 1923 he had shared the lead with Donoghue, both of them riding 89 winners. A very polished and resourceful horseman, strong, self-confident and intelligent, Elliott had 14 successes in English classic races. They were as follows:

One Thousand Guineas: Plack (1924); Four Course (1931); Kandy (1932); Picture Play (1944)

Two Thousand Guineas: Ellangowan (1923); Flamingo (1928); Djebel (1940); Lambert Simnel (1941); Nimbus (1949)

Derby: Call Boy (1927); Bois Roussel (1938); Nimbus (1949)

Oaks: Brulette (1931); Why Hurry (1943).

Elliott rode many big winners in France, the best horse he was associated with there being M. Boussac's unbeaten Pharis, winner of the French Derby and Grand Prix in 1939. When he gave up riding he became trainer to M. Boussac in France but unfortunately he assumed that post just as M. Boussac's racing fortunes were beginning to decline. In 1958 he returned to Newmarket and trained a few horses there, but before very long he dropped out of the racing game.

ELLIOTT, Robert Peter (b 1941)

Bobby Elliott was born in Lewes. He was apprenticed to the Lewes trainer Tom Masson and his first winner was at Lewes in 1958. In 1960 he rode 39 winners. Amongst the races he has won are the Wokingham Stakes, Ascot Stakes, Royal Hunt Cup, Vaux Gold Tankard and the Jubilee Handicap. He is now attached to D. Candy's stable.

ELPENOR

Elpenor, by Owen Tudor out of a mare by Bahram, is one of the few horses to have won the Ascot Gold Cup and also its French equivalent, the Prix du Cadran. He was bred and owned by M. M. Boussac, and was foaled in 1950.

ELSEY, Capt Charles, CBE (1881-1966)

One of the most respected and best liked personalities in the racing world, particularly in the North, Capt Charles Elsey year after year sent out a stream of winners from his stable at Malton in Yorkshire, and altogether he won 1,548 races worth nearly £800,000. He was leading trainer in 1956.

He won the Two Thousand Guineas with Nearula; the One Thousand Guineas with Musidora and Honeylight; the Oaks with Musidora and Frieze; and the St Leger with Cantello. Handicap victories included the Lincoln with Double Harness and

Babur (twice); the City and Suburban with Light Sussex; the Chester Cup with Peperium; the Jubilee with Commander III and Orinthia; the Victoria Cup with Orgoglio and Dionisio; the Northumberland Plate with Leonard, Union Jack and Gusty; the Ebor Handicap with Yorkshire Hussar, Procne and Bob; the Cesarewitch with Woodburn; and the Cambridgeshire with Disarmament.

Charles Elsey was a dedicated trainer, intensely loyal to his friends, and devoted to every form of sport. His elder brother took orders and became a bishop.

ELSEY, W. E.

W. E. Elsey trained 124 winners in 1905. This is certainly a record for this century. J. Day is said to have trained 146 in 1867.

ELSEY, William (b 1921)

Bill Elsey is the son of that distinguished Yorkshire trainer the late Capt Elsey (see above), whom he assisted from 1951 to 1960. On his father's retirement he took out a licence himself in 1961 and assumed control of the stables at Highfield House, Malton. Among the good horses he has had under his care are Pia (Oaks); Henry the Seventh (Eclipse Stakes and Zetland Gold Cup); Sostenuto (Ebor Handicap); and Alignment (Ebor Handicap). His patrons include Lord and Lady Allendale, Countess Margot Batthyany, Lady Doris Vyner, Mr H. J. Joel, Mr N. Hetherton, Mr G. B. Turnbull, Col W. E. Behrens, Mr A. J. Massingbird-Mundy, Mr R. F. Dennis and Mr H. C. Hutchinson.

ENCLOSED MEETING

The first enclosed meeting was Sandown Park, where racing began in 1875.

ENGELHARD, Charles William (b 1917)

An American who is a lavish patron of racing in the United States, England, Ireland and South Africa, Mr Engelhard is chairman and president of Engelhard Industries Inc. The best horses to carry his colours in England so far are Indiana (St Leger), Ribocco (*Observer* Gold Cup, Irish Derby and St Leger), Ribero (Irish Derby and St Leger), Ribofilio (Champagne Stakes, Dewhurst Stakes, second in the Irish Derby and the St Leger), Romulus (Sussex Stakes and Queen Elizabeth Stakes) and Habitat (Lockinge Stakes, Wills Mile and Prix du Moulin). Other good winners of his include Double Jump, Green Park, Manacle, Holborn, Piccadilly, Solstice and Tin King. His racing affairs in England and Ireland are managed by Mr David McCall. His English trainers are Jeremy Tree, Fulke Johnson Houghton and Jack Watts, while Vincent O'Brien trains for him in Ireland. Colours: green, yellow sleeves, scarlet cap. He is an honorary member of the Jockey Club. In 1970 he won the two thousand Guineas and the Derby with his Canadian-bred colt Nijinsky, trained by Vincent O'Brien.

ENTRIES, FORFEITS AND DECLARATIONS

Every entry and every acceptance is fixed to be made at 12 noon on Wednesdays only. The entry or acceptance must be lodged at the *Racing Calendar* office and is subject to withdrawal or alteration up to the time of closing. Entries may also close at the Irish Turf Club or to any recognised Turf Authority if special mention is made of this in the advertisement of the race in the *Racing Calendar*. All races, with the exception of sweepstakes with £4,000 or more added, shall close not earlier than 31 days before the first day of the meeting. No race can close earlier than the February in the year in which the horses concerned are two years old, and no race can close after the last Wednesday in November.

Every declaration of forfeit is fixed to be made at 12 noon on Tuesdays only and must be lodged at the *Racing Calendar* office at that time. No declaration of forfeit can be fixed for races closing within 31 days of the first day of the meeting. In all other races a declaration of forfeit shall be fixed for the Tuesday in the week two weeks before the first day of the meeting.

All other declarations of forfeit, except those for handicaps, shall be confined to the following days: the Tuesday after the Newmarket Craven Meeting; the first Tuesday in July; and the third Tuesday in November.

In the case of handicaps, forfeit can be declared on any Tuesday after the publication of the weights.

In races closing before the year of running, the first declaration of forfeit shall not be fixed before the third Tuesday in November in the year of closing.

Every declaration of a runner must be lodged at the Overnight Declarations Office by 12 noon, or at such a place and at such a time as the Stewards of the Jockey Club may from time to time direct, on the day fixed for declarations in the conditions of the race. Such declarations are subject to withdrawal or alteration up to the time fixed for declaration.

All declarations, withdrawals or alterations must state the name of the horse, the name of the meeting, and the name of the race, and have to be in writing, signed by the owner or his authorised agent. They may also be made by telegram, telex or telephone, subject to any restriction that the Stewards of the Jockey Club may from time to time impose.

EPIGRAM

Epigram, owned by Mr J. V. Rank and trained by Noel Cannon, was a fine stayer by Son-in-Law. His victories included the Goodwood Stakes, Goodwood Cup, Queen Alexandra Stakes and Doncaster Cup. He was foaled in 1933. He sired Souepi, winner of the Ascot Gold Cup, Goodwood Cup and Doncaster Cup; and Cornice, dam of the Oaks winner Frieze.

EPINARD

Foaled in 1920, Epinard, by Badajoz, was an extremely fast horse that won 11 races in France. In England he won the Steward's Cup as a three-year-old with 8st 6lb and was a rather unlucky second to Verdict in the Cambridgeshire. He sired Rodosto, who won the Two Thousand Guineas for France in 1933.

EPSOM

Epsom is perhaps the most celebrated of all English racecourses because the Derby, the most famous race in the world, is run there.

Epsom is not by any means an easy meeting to run because the course is on a Metropolitan Common and is therefore subject to all the regulations applicable to London Commons. In the old days no racing could take place there before the consent of the Lord of the Manor had been obtained. The stewards of the meeting had a small stand almost opposite the present grandstand, while on the other side of the course there was the Prince's Stand, which was originally built for the Prince Regent and is now known as the Warwick Stand.

There was no permanent stand for racegoers until in 1828 a rather shady Doncaster speculator called Charles Bluck applied to the Manor Court for permission to erect one. It was completed in 1830. Bluck had in fact obtained from the Lord of the Manor a 90-year lease for an acre of land at £30 a year. Not long afterwards, though, some local notables bought Bluck out for £750, formed the Epsom Grandstand Association and raised £20,000 for building the stand and running it. At first the Association were merely concerned with the running of the stand but eventually they took over the control and management of the racing as well.

In 1890 the Association obtained

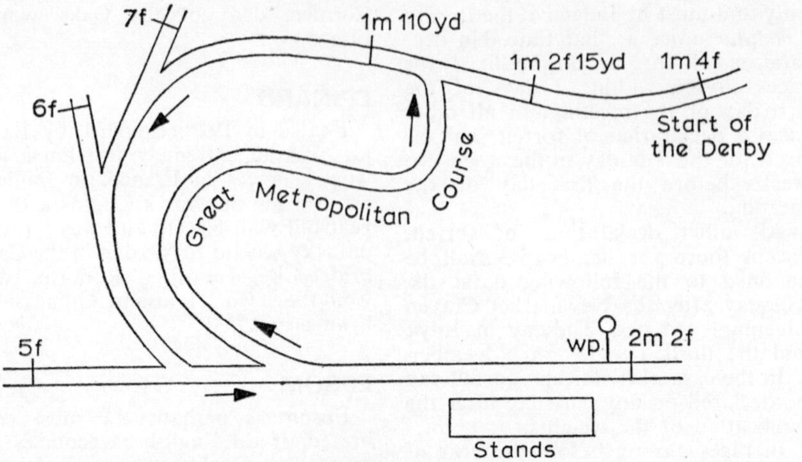

EPSOM

a lease of the whole downs, including the course, from the Lord of the Manor, and in 1903 Mr H. M. Dorling, on behalf of the Association, arranged with the Lord of the Manor to surrender the existing lease and to pay him a premium of £25,000 and a yearly rental of £3,354 for a new lease covering 106 years. In 1888 the Association had purchased from the Lord of the Manor of Walton over two hundred acres of Walton Downs so they now appeared to be comfortably in control of the situation. That appearance was subsequently to prove deceptive.

After World War I it was somewhat tardily admitted that the old 1830 grandstand and the other stands were totally inadequate for Derby Day. The Association, therefore, decided to face the big expenditure involved and to construct a new stand. As the Association only leased the site of the stands, it was decided to purchase the freehold of the Downs and the Lord of the Manor's rights attached to it. This was done in 1925 for £57,000. At the same time, the greater part of Walton Downs was sold to the Epsom trainer, Mr Stanley Wootton, for £35,000. Mr Wootton in 1969 assigned his part of Walton Downs to the Levy Board to ensure the continuance of racing. The new grandstand was completed in 1927 at a cost of nearly £250,000, a trifling sum compared to what it would cost today.

The Association were faced with a new worry in 1925 by the passing of the Law of Property Act which gave members of the public the right of air and exercise over any part of a Metropolitan Common and prohibited the erection of any building, enclosure or fence which might impede the public from enjoying full use of the common. By this Act the Association were deprived of the right to stop people walking on the course even while a race was in progress, while the erection of temporary stands, rails and car-park enclosures became illegal. Luckily for the continuance of Epsom as a racecourse, the Act gave the Association the right to petition the Minister of Agriculture to impose conditions on the public's rights that would enable the Association to continue in business without injury.

As a result of many meetings with the Epsom and Ewell Urban District Council, a scheme was devised by the Association for the running of Epsom Downs and the adjacent Walton Downs, much of which is used as gallops by local trainers. The final outcome was the Epsom and Walton Downs Regulation Act of 1936. This empowered the formation of a body to conserve the downs, and set down in detail the powers of the conservators, the rights of the public, and also the rights of the Association and of Mr Wootton.

This Act, while making Epsom racing safe for the future, still leaves the Association with certain difficulties. Owing to the ban on permanent buildings, rails and so forth, the Association has yearly to erect some seven miles of ropes and stakes for carparks. Every year, too, it has to erect a great deal of temporary fencing to keep the public off the course and to prevent people from surging round the horses at the various starting gates.

No fewer than seven roads cross the racecourse and much labour is involved in making these roads safe to race over. On Derby Day between a quarter and half a million people probably cross the course.

Epsom in fact remains very much a law to itself and most of the discomfort and annoyances that exist are unavoidable. It must be remembered, too, that of the immense crowd that assembles on Derby Day, only those in the stands have to pay anything. Admission to the Downs is free.

It is impossible to say when racing first took place at Epsom but in 1648, during the Civil War, The Earl of Clarendon recorded that a party of Royalists met at Epsom Downs "under pretence of a horse-race, intending to cause a diversion on the King's behalf". After the Restoration, the first recorded race-meeting on the Downs took place on 7th March 1661 and the King himself was present.

At the end of the seventeenth century Epsom enjoyed wide popularity as a spa and regular race meetings took place there. When in the following century the spa became less fashionable, racing was little affected as the Downs were so handily situated for sportsmen from London. Regular spring and summer meetings were established as far back as 1730.

The turning point in Epsom's fortunes can be said to have come in 1773 when the twelfth Earl of Derby, then aged 21, took over the lease of The Oaks, a country house on the outskirts of Epsom, from his uncle by marriage, Gen Burgoyne. The Earl used to act as a steward at Epsom and invariably entertained a large party of friends for the races. The May meeting of 1778 was of the customary type, being composed of races run in heats over two or four miles. Possibly inspired by the example of the St Leger, which had been instituted two years previously, Lord Derby and his friends founded a race for three-year-old fillies, to be called the Oaks, and to be run the following year.

The first race for the Oaks, which attracted a field of 12, was rated a success and another three-year-old race, this time for colts and fillies and to be run over a mile, was proposed for the following year. A toss of the coin is said to have decided whether the new race was named the Derby Stakes or alternatively the Bunbury Stakes in honour of Sir Charles Bunbury, the foremost racing man of the day. As the late Lord Rosebery said a century later: "A roystering party at a country house founded two races, and named them gratefully after their host and his house, the Derby and the Oaks. Seldom has a carouse had a more permanent effect".

The first race for the Derby was in 1780 and was won by Sir Charles Bunbury's Diomed. In 1784 the distance of the race was increased to 1½m and has remained so ever since.

By 1830 the Derby had gradually established itself as the prime event of the racing year. By then racing had ceased to be the pastime of the privileged few; it was becoming the business and pleasure of many, while betting, together with bookmakers, was playing an ever-increasing part. Newspapers, in particular *Bells Life,* were starting to exploit the growing public interest, and the introduction of the railway system was not only to abolish the long and tedious journeys on foot for horses but to enable enthusiasts for the sport to travel from meeting to meeting with comparative speed and in modest comfort. Amenities for the racing public were still primitive, but Lord George Bentinck (q.v.) was to instil some badly needed order and discipline into a sport which was apt to reflect, unpleasantly so at times, the hard, rough standards of the times.

In the mid-Victorian era, Derby Day was essentially a great public holiday. Parliament did not sit on Derby Day and it was Disraeli himself who first described the Derby as "the Blue Riband of the Turf". People went in thousands to Epsom, not really to see the race but to enjoy themselves at the gigantic fairground on the Downs. For years Barnum's Show occupied a site on the rails between Tattenham Corner and the winning post. Whatever aesthetic shortcomings it possesses, Frith's famous picture of Derby Day accurately reflects the carnival atmosphere of Epsom Downs in the heyday of Queen Victoria. By the end of the century something of the festival spirit had disappeared while the race itself assumed a greater significance. The crowd began to be composed of a higher proportion of racing enthusiasts and fewer people just out for a 'beano'. There is still a fairground on the Downs today but it is an anaemic affair compared to the acres of brash, colourful, hilarious entertainment provided for a less sophisticated public a hundred years previously.

For many years there were intermittent hostilities between those who paid to use the stands at Epsom and the 'Dictator of Epsom', Henry M. Dorling, Clerk of the Course from 1873 to 1919. This official possessed abundant energy but neither tact nor manners. He was disliked by everyone and relished the fact. "Everyone hates me", he declared, "and I like it". He was frequently in trouble with the stewards and was several times fined for derelictions of duty, on the last occasion when he was over 80 years of age. In his days scant attention was paid to the subject of public relations, but Dorling's truculent intransigence certainly did Epsom no good.

Curiously enough, with the spread in general use of the motor-car, Derby Day traffic problems have become less intense. In the old days a two-hour block of horse-drawn vehicles at Mitcham Common was not unusual.

The Derby is a great test of a thoroughbred and it is a race rarely won by a horse of poor conformation or of indifferent pedigree. In order to win a horse must possess a combination of speed and stamina. The ability to gallop downhill is essential and this is usually something beyond the power of horses that are back at the knee or straight in the shoulder. Sometimes, of course, luck plays an important part in the Derby but usually the race is won by the best horse on the day. With the passing of the years and in face of the United States, the Derby has retained its prestige and it is not too much to say that the moment the winner passes the post, its value is at least £250,000.

When jockeys adopted the forward seat at the beginning of this century and race-riding became a much more streamlined affair, the pace of the Derby became hotter. In 1856 Ellington took 3min 4sec when he won the Derby; 80 years later the record time of Mahmoud was 2min 33 4/5ths sec. As well as the pace, the value of the race has increased. For example, Diamond Jubilee won £5,450 by his victory in 1900; Royal Palace £61,918 in 1967.

The Oaks, for three-year-old fillies over the Derby course, has never aroused an interest comparable to the Derby. The Coronation Cup, first run in 1902, is a prestige race for four-year-olds and upwards over the Derby course. At the spring meeting there are these popular and old-established handicaps, the Great Metropolitan and the City and Suburban, as well as the classic trials, the Blue Riband Trial

Stakes and the Princess Elizabeth Stakes.

The 1½m Derby course is left-handed and shaped something like a horse-shoe. There is a rise of roughly 150 feet over the first ½m. The next ¼m is virtually level. Then, however, there is a sharp descent to Tattenham Corner, 3½f from the winning post. There is a gradual descent in the straight until the final 50yd which are uphill. The 5f course, a very fast one, joins the Derby course at Tattenham Corner. The 6f and 7f courses are on short spurs leading from the Derby course. The 2¼m Metropolitan Course starts near the winning post and runs the reverse way of the Derby course for ½m before branching right-handed across the Downs to rejoin the Derby course 1m from home. Low numbers are favoured in the draw in races from 5f to 1m inclusive. In races of 1¼m and 1½m middle numbers are thought advantageous when there is a big field.

Clerk of the Course: Major P. Beckwith-Smith, the Racecourse Paddock, Epsom, Surrey. Tel: Epsom 26311.

Best Times:

Distance	*Horse-Age-Weight*	*Date*	*Time*
5f	Indigenous 4-9-5	2-6-60	53.6
5f	Cerise 2-8-9	4-6-54	55.2
6f	Masham 4-9-9	2-6-60	1min 8
6f	My Babu 2-9-0	4-8-47	1min 8.4
7f	Tylers Hill 4-7-13	1-8-60	1min 20.4
7f	Leonardo 2-9-0	5-9-64	1min 22.44
8f 110 yds	Arietta 3-7-9	5-6-56	1min 41.6
10f	Crossbow 3-7-13	7-6-67	2min 3.5
12f	Mahmoud 3-9-0	27-5-36	2min 33.8
18f	Gay Ballad 4-6-8	23-4-57	3min 54

Derby Records

Most Successful Owners

Lord Egremont (5): Assassin 1782
Hannibal 1804
Cardinal Beaufort 1805
Election 1807
Lapdog 1826

H.H. Aga Khan (5): Blenheim 1930
Bahram 1935
Mahmoud 1936
My Love 1948
Tulyar 1952

Mr J. Bowes (4): Mundig 1835
Cotherstone 1843
Daniel O'Rourke 1852
West Australian 1853

Sir J. Hawley (4): Teddington 1851
Beadsman 1858
Musjid 1859
Blue Gown 1868

First Duke of Westminster (4):
Bend Or 1880
Shotover 1882
Ormonde 1886
Flying Fox 1899

Sir V. Sassoon (4): Pinza 1953
Crepello 1957
Hard Ridden 1958
St Paddy 1960

The first woman to own a Derby winner was Lady James Douglas who won a war-substitute race with Gainsborough in 1918.

The first woman to own an Epsom Derby winner was Mrs G. B. Miller, whose Mid-day Sun which she owned in partnership with her mother, Mrs Talbot, won in 1937.

Most Successful Jockeys

J. Robinson (6): Azor 1817
Cedric 1824
Middleton 1825
Mameluke 1827
Cadland 1828
Bay Middleton 1836

S. Donoghue (6): Pommern 1915
Gay Crusader 1917
Humorist 1921
Captain Cuttle 1922
Papyrus 1923
Manna 1925

J. Arnull (5): Sergeant 1784
Rhadamanthus 1790
Didelot 1796
Archduke 1799
Election 1807

W. Clift (5): Waxy 1793
Champion 1800
Ditto 1803
Whalebone 1810
Tiresias 1819

F. Buckle (5): John Bull 1792
Daedalus 1794
Tyrant 1802
Phantom 1811
Emilius 1823

F. Archer (5): Silvio 1877
Bend Or 1880
Iroquois 1881
Melton 1885
Ormonde 1886

L. Piggott (5): Never Say Die 1954
Crepello 1957
St Paddy 1960
Sir Ivor 1968
Nijinsky 1970

Four winners were ridden by S. Arnull, T. Goodison, W. Scott, J. Watts and C. Smirke; three by C. Hindley, W. Arnull, S. Day, S. Templeman, J. Wells, H. Custance, C. Wood, D. Maher, J. Childs, E. C. Elliott, H. Wragg, W. Nevett and W. Johnstone.

The oldest winning rider is J. Forth, who was over 60 when he won on Frederick in 1829. The youngest, at any rate this century, is Lester Piggott who was 18 when he won on Never Say Die in 1954. The age of the boy Parsons, who won on Caractacus in 1862, is unknown.

Most Successful Trainers

R. Robson (7): Waxy 1793
Tyrant 1802
Pope 1809
Whalebone 1810
Whisker 1815
Azor 1817
Emilius 1823

J. Porter (7): Blue Gown 1868
Shotover 1882
St Blaise 1883
Ormonde 1886
Sainfoin 1890
Common 1891
Flying Fox 1899

F. Darling (7): Captain Cuttle 1922
Manna 1925
Coronach 1926
Cameronian 1931
Bois Roussel 1938
Pont l'Eveque 1940
Owen Tudor 1941

M. Dawson (6): Thormanby 1860
Kingcraft 1870
Silvio 1877
Melton 1885
Ladas 1894
Sir Visto 1895

J. Scott trained five Derby winners and R. Marsh four.

Most Successful Sires

Sir Peter Teazle, Waxy, Cyllene and Blandford all sired four Derby winners.

Sir Peter Teazle sired the first three to finish in the Derby in 1803; Stockwell accomplished the same feat in 1866.

The following owners won the Derby and the Oaks the same year: Lord Clermont (1785), Duke of Bedford (1791), Sir F. Standish (1796), Mr J. Gully (1846), Mr J. Merry (1873) and M. M. Boussac (1950).

The following fillies have won the Derby and the Oaks: Eleanor (1801), Blink Bonny (1857), Signorinetta (1908) and Fifinella (1916). Other fillies to win the Derby are Shotover (1882) and Tagalie (1912).

The only horse to have won the Two Thousand Guineas, the Derby, the St Leger, the Grand Prix de Paris and the Ascot Gold Cup is the French horse Gladiateur (1865-66).

Thirty-four Derby winners have been sired by Derby winners.

Fifty-four Derby winners have been exported.

The longest-priced winners: Jeddah (100-1) and Signorinetta (100-1).

Fastest time: Mahmoud, 2min 33 4/5ths sec in 1936.

Dead-heats: Cadland and The Colonel, 1828. Cadland won the run-off. St Gatien and Harvester, 1884. Stakes divided.

The Prince of Wales won the Derby and the Grand National in 1900.

G. Blackwell, R. C. Dawson, J. Jewitt, M. V. O'Brien and W. Stephenson have trained winners of the Derby and the Grand National.

In 1893 H. Barker rode the second in both the Derby and the Grand National.

The smallest field was four in 1794; the largest 34 in 1862.

The Derby, 1m 4f

Three-year-olds, colts 9st, fillies 8st 9lb. First run 1780. *Run at Newmarket* 1915 *to* 1918 *and* 1940 *to* 1945.

		OWNER	TRAINER	JOCKEY	SP
1780	Diomed	Sir C. Bunbury	—	S. Arnull	6–4
1781	Young Eclipse	Maj D. O'Kelly	—	Hindley	10–1
1782	Assassin	Lord Egremont	—	S. Arnull	5–1
1783	Saltram	Mr Parker	—	Hindley	5–2
1784	Sergeant	Col D. O'Kelly	—	J. Arnull	3–1
1785	Aimwell	Lord Clermont	—	Hindley	7–1
1786	Noble	Mr Panton	—	J. White	30–1
1787	Sir Peter Teazle	Lord Derby	—	S. Arnull	2–1
1788	Sir Thomas	Prince of Wales	—	W. South	5–6
1789	Skyscraper	Duke of Bedford	—	S. Chifney, Sn.	4–7
1790	Rhadamanthus	Lord Grosvenor	—	J. Arnull	5–4
1791	Eager	Duke of Bedford	—	Stephenson	5–2
1792	John Bull	Lord Grosvenor	—	F. Buckle	6–4
1793	Waxy	Sir F. Poole	Robson	W. Clift	12–1
1794	Daedalus	Lord Grosvenor	—	F. Buckle	6–1
1795	Spread Eagle	Sir F. Standish	—	A. Wheatley	3–1
1796	Didelot	Sir F. Standish	—	J. Arnull	—
1797	Colt by Fidget	Duke of Bedford	—	J. Singleton	10–1
1798	Sir Harry	J. Cookson	—	S. Arnull	7–4
1799	Archduke	Sir F. Standish	—	J. Arnull	12–1
1800	Champion	Mr Wilson	—	W. Clift	7–4
1801	Eleanor	Sir C. Bunbury	—	Saunders	5–4
1802	Tyrant	Duke of Grafton	Robson	F. Buckle	7–1
1803	Ditto	Sir H. Williamson	—	W. Clift	7–2
1804	Hannibal	Lord Egremont	—	W. Arnull	3–1
1805	Cardinal Beaufort	Lord Egremont	—	D. Fitzpatrick	20–1
1806	Paris	Lord Foley	—	J. Shepherd	5–1
1807	Election	Lord Egremont	—	J. Arnull	3–1
1808	Pan	Sir H. Williamson	—	F. Collinson	25–1
1809	Pope	Duke of Grafton	Robson	T. Goodison	20–1
1810	Whalebone	Duke of Grafton	Robson	W. Clift	2–1
1811	Phantom	Sir J. Shelley	—	F. Buckle	5–1
1812	Octavius	R. Ladbroke	—	W. Arnull	7–1
1813	Smolensko	Sir C. Bunbury	—	T. Goodison	evens
1814	Blücher	Lord Stawell	—	W. Arnull	5–2
1815	Whisker	Duke of Grafton	Robson	T. Goodison	8–1
1816	Prince Leopold	W. Lake	—	W. Wheatley	20–1
1817	Azor	J. Payne	Robson	J. Robinson	50–1
1818	Sam	T. Thornhill	W. W. Chifney	S. Chifney, Jn.	7–2
1819	Tiresias	Duke of Portland	—	W. Clift	5–2
1820	Sailor	T. Thornhill	W. Chifney	S. Chifney, Jn'	4–1
1821	Gustavus	J. Hunter	—	S. Day	2–1
1822	Moses	Duke of York	—	T. Goodison	6–1
1823	Emilius	J. Udny	Robson	F. Buckle	11–8
1824	Cedric	Sir J. Shelley	—	J. Robinson	9–2
1825	Middleton	Lord Jersey	Edwards	J. Robinson	7–4
1826	Lapdog	Lord Egremont	Bird	G. Dockeray	50–1
1827	Mameluke	Lord Jersey	Edwards	J. Robinson	9–1
1828	Cadland	Duke of Rutland	—	J. Robinson	4–1
1829	Frederick	W. Gratwicke	J. Forth	J. Forth	40–1
1830	Priam	W. Chifney	W. Chifney	S. Day	4–1
1831	Spaniel	Lord Lowther	—	W. Wheatley	50–1
1832	St. Giles	R. Ridsdale	—	W. Scott	3–1

The Derby (contd)	OWNER	TRAINER	JOCKEY	SP
1833 Dangerous	I. Sadler	—	J. Chapple	30–1
1834 Plenipotentiary	S. Batson	—	P. Conolly	9–4
1835 Mündig	J. Bowes	J. Scott	W. Scott	6–1
1836 Bay Middleton	Lord Jersey	—	J. Robinson	7–4
1837 Phosphorus	Lord Berners	—	G. Edwards	40–1
1838 Amato	Sir G. Heathcote	R. Sherwood	J. Chapple	30–1
1839 Bloomsbury	W. Ridsdale	W. Ridsdale	S. Templeman	25–1
1840 Little Wonder	D. Robertson	W. Forth	W. Macdonald	50–1
1841 Coronation	A. Rawlinson	—	P. Conolly	5–2
1842 Attila	Col Anson	J. Scott	W. Scott	5–1
1843 Cotherstone	J. Bowes	J. Scott	W. Scott	13–8
1844 Orlando	Col Peel	Cooper	E. Flatman	20–1
1845 The Merry Monarch	W. Gratwicke	J. Forth	F. Bell	15–1
1846 Pyrrhus the First	J. Gully	J. Day	S. Day	8–1
1847 Cossack	T. Pedley	J. Day	S. Templeman	5–1
1848 Surplice	Lord Clifden	J. Kent	S. Templeman	evens
1849 The Flying Dutchman	Lord Eglinton	Fobert	Marlow	2–1
1850 Voltigeur	Lord Zetland	R. Hill	J. Marson	16–1
1851 Teddington	Sir J. Hawley	A. Taylor	J. Marson	3–1
1852 Daniel O'Rourke	J. Bowes	J. Scott	F. Butler	25–1
1853 West Australian	J. Bowes	J. Scott	F. Butler	6–4
1854 Andover	J. Gully	J. Day	A. Day	7–2
1855 Wild Dayrell	F. Popham	Rickaby	R. Sherwood	evens
1856 Ellington	Admiral Harcourt	T. Dawson	T. Aldcroft	20–1
1857 Blink Bonny	W. I'Anson	W. I'Anson	Charlton	20–1
1858 Beadsman	Sir J. Hawley	G. Manning	J. Wells	10–1
1859 Musjid	Sir J. Hawley	G. Manning	J. Wells	9–4
1860 Thormanby	J. Merry	M. Dawson	H. Custance	4–1
1861 Kettledrum	Col Towneley	Oates	Bullock	16–1
1862 Caractacus	C. Snewing	Zachary	J. Parsons	40–1
1863 Macaroni	R. Naylor	Godding	T. Challoner	10–1
1864 Blair Athol	W. I'Anson	W. I'Anson	J. Snowden	14–1
1865 Gladiateur	Count de Lagrange	T. Jennings	H. Grimshaw	5–2
1866 Lord Lyon	R. Sutton	J. Dover	H. Custance	5–6
1867 Hermit	H. Chaplin	Bloss	J. Daley	66–1
1868 Blue Gown	Sir J. Hawley	J. Porter	J. Wells	7–2
1869 Pretender	J. Johnstone	T. Dawson	J. Osborne	11–8
1870 Kingcraft	Lord Falmouth	M. Dawson	T. French	20–1
1871 Favonius	Baron de Rothschild	J. Hayhoe	T. French	9–1
1872 Cremorne	H. Savile	W. Gilbert	C. Maidment	3–1
1873 Doncaster	J. Merry	P. Peck	F. Webb	45–1
1874 George Frederick	W. Cartwright	T. Leader	H. Custance	9–1
1875 Galopin	Prince Batthyany	J. Dawson	Morris	2–1
1876 Kisber	A. Baltazzi	J. Hayhoe	C. Maidment	4–1
1877 Silvio	Lord Falmouth	M. Dawson	F. Archer	100–9
1878 Sefton	W. Crawfurd	A. Taylor	H. Constable	100–12
1879 Sir Bevys	Mr Acton	J. Hayhoe	G. Fordham	20–1
1880 Bend Or	Duke of Westminster	R. Peck	F. Archer	2–1
1881 Iroquois	P. Lorillard	J. Pincus	F. Archer	11–2
1882 Shotover	Duke of Westminster	J. Porter	T. Cannon	11–2
1883 St. Blaise	Sir F. Johnstone	J. Porter	C. Wood	5–1
1884 { St. Gatien	J. Hammond	R. Sherwood	C. Wood	100–8
1884 { Harvester	Sir J. Willoughby	J. Jewitt	S. Loates	100–7
1885 Melton	Lord Hastings	M. Dawson	F. Archer	75–40
1886 Ormonde	Duke of Westminster	J. Porter	F. Archer	4–9
1887 Merry Hampton	'Mr Abington'	M. Gurry	J. Watts	100–9
1888 Ayrshire	Duke of Portland	G. Dawson	F. Barrett	5–6
1889 Donovan	Duke of Portland	G. Dawson	T. Loates	8–11
1890 Sainfoin	Sir J. Miller	J. Porter	J. Watts	100–15
1891 Common	Sir F. Johnstone	J. Porter	G. Barrett	10–11
1892 Sir Hugo	Lord Bradford	T. Wadlow	F. Allsopp	40–1
1893 Isinglass	H. McCalmont	J. Jewitt	T. Loates	4–9
1894 Ladas	Lord Rosebery	M. Dawson	J. Watts	2–9
1895 Sir Visto	Lord Rosebery	M. Dawson	S. Loates	9–1
1896 Persimmon	Prince of Wales	R. Marsh	J. Watts	5–1
1897 Galtee More	J. Gubbins	S. Darling	C. Wood	1–4
1898 Jeddah	J. Larnach	R. Marsh	O. Madden	100–1

Year	Horse	OWNER	TRAINER	JOCKEY	SP
1899	Flying Fox	Duke of Westminster	J. Porter	M. Cannon	2–5
1900	Diamond Jubilee	Prince of Wales	R. Marsh	H. Jones	6–4
1901	Volodyovski	W. Whitney	J. Huggins	L. Reiff	5–2
1902	Ard Patrick	J. Gubbins	S. Darling	J. Martin	100–14
1903	Rock Sand	Sir J. Miller	G. Blackwell	D. Maher	4–6
1904	St. Amant	L. de Rothschild	A. Hayhoe	K. Cannon	5–1
1905	Cicero	Lord Rosebery	P. Peck	D. Maher	4–11
1906	Spearmint	Maj E. Loder	P. Gilpin	D. Maher	6–1
1907	Orby	R. Croker	Col. McCabe	J. Reiff	100–9
1908	Signorinetta	E. Ginistrelli	E. Ginistrelli	W. Bullock	100–1
1909	Minoru	King Edward VII	R. Marsh	H. Jones	7–2
1910	Lemberg	'Mr Fairie'	A. Taylor	B. Dillon	7–4
1911	Sunstar	J. Joel	C. Morton	G. Stern	13–8
1912	Tagalie	W. Raphael	D. Waugh	J. Rieff	100–8
1913	Aboyeur	A. Cunliffe	T. Lewis	E. Piper	100–1
1914	Durbar II	H. Duryea	T. Murphy	M. MacGee	20–1
1915	Pommern	S. Joel	C. Peck	S. Donoghue	11–10
1916	Fifinella	E. Hulton	R. Dawson	J. Childs	11–2
1917	Gay Crusader	'Mr Fairie'	A. Taylor	S. Donoghue	7–4
1918	Gainsborough	Lady J. Douglas	A. Taylor	J. Childs	8–13
1919	Grand Parade	Lord Glanely	F. Barling	F. Templeman	33–1
1920	Spion Kop	Maj G. Loder	P. Gilpin	F. O'Neill	100–6
1921	Humorist	J. Joel	C. Morton	S. Donoghue	6–1
1922	Captain Cuttle	Lord Woolavington	F. Darling	S. Donoghue	10–1
1923	Papyrus	B. Irish	B. Jarvis	S. Donoghue	100–15
1924	Sansovino	Lord Derby	G. Lambton	T. Weston	9–2
1925	Manna	H. Morriss	F. Darling	S. Donoghue	9–1
1926	Coronach	Lord Woolavington	F. Darling	J. Childs	11–2
1927	Call Boy	F. Curzon	J. Watts	C. Elliott	4–1
1928	Felstead	Sir H. C-Owen	O. Bell	H. Wragg	33–1
1929	Trigo	W. Barnett	R. Dawson	J. Marshall	33–1
1930	Blenheim	Aga Khan	R. Dawson	H. Wragg	18–1
1931	Cameronian	J. Dewar	F. Darling	F. Fox	7–2
1932	April the Fifth	T. Walls	T. Walls	F. Lane	100–6
1933	Hyperion	Lord Derby	G. Lambton	T. Weston	6–1
1934	Windsor Lad	Maharaja of Rajpipla	M. Marsh	C. Smirke	15–2
1935	Bahram	Aga Khan	Fk. Butters	F. Fox	5–4
1936	Mahmoud	Aga Khan	Fk. Butters	C. Smirke	100–8
1937	Mid-day Sun	Mrs G. Miller	Fred Butters	M. Beary	100–7
1938	Bois Roussel	P. Beatty	F. Darling	C. Elliott	20–1
1939	Blue Peter	Lord Rosebery	J. Jarvis	E. Smith	7–2
1940	Pont L'Eveque	F. Darling	F. Darling	S. Wragg	10–1
1941	Owen Tudor	Mrs R. M-Buchanan	F. Darling	W. Nevett	25–1
1942	Watling Street	Lord Derby	W. Earl	H. Wragg	6–1
1943	Straight Deal	Miss D. Paget	W. Nightingall	T. Carey	100–6
1944	Ocean Swell	Lord Rosebery	J. Jarvis	W. Nevett	28–1
1945	Dante	Sir E. Ohlson	M. Peacock	W. Nevett	100–30
1946	Airborne	J. Ferguson	R. Perryman	T. Lowry	50–1
1947	Pearl Diver	Baron de Waldner	C. Halsey	G. Bridgland	40–1
1948	My Love	Aga Khan	R. Carver	W. Johnstone	100–9
1949	Nimbus	Mrs M. Glenister	G. Colling	C. Elliott	7–1
1950	Galcador	M. Boussac	C. Semblat	W. Johnstone	100–9
1951	Arctic Prince	J. McGrath	W. Stephenson	C. Spares	28–1
1952	Tulyar	Aga Khan	M. Marsh	C. Smirke	11–2
1953	Pinza	Sir V. Sassoon	N. Bertie	G. Richards	5–1
1954	Never Say Die	R. Clark	J. Lawson	L. Piggott	33–1
1955	Phil Drake	Mme L. Volterra	F. Mathet	F. Palmer	100–8
1956	Lavandin	P. Wertheimer	A. Head	W. Johnstone	7–1
1957	Crepello	Sir V. Sassoon	N. Murless	L. Piggott	6–4
1958	Hard Ridden	Sir V. Sassoon	J. Rogers	C. Smirke	18–1
1959	Parthia	Sir H. de Trafford	C. B-Rochfort	W. Carr	10–1
1960	St Paddy	Sir V. Sassoon	N. Murless	L. Piggott	7–1
1961	Psidium	Mrs A. Plesch	H. Wragg	R. Poincelet	66–1
1962	Larkspur	R. Guest	V. O'Brien	N. Sellwood	22–1
1963	Relko	F. Dupré	F. Mathet	Y. Saint-Martin	5–1
1964	Santa Claus	J. Ismay	J. Rogers	A. Breasley	15–8
1965	Sea Bird II	J. Ternynck	E. Pollet	T. Glennon	7–4

The Derby (*contd.*)

		OWNER	TRAINER	JOCKEY	SP
1966	Charlottown	Lady Z. Wernher	G. Smyth	A. Breasley	5–1
1967	Royal Palace	H. Joel	N. Murless	G. Moore	7–4
1968	Sir Ivor	R. Guest	V. O'Brien	L. Piggott	4–5
1969	Blakeney	A. Budgett	A. Budgett	E. Johnson	15–2
1970	Nijinsky	C. W. Engelhard	V. O'Brien	L. Piggott	11–8

Derby Times

1846	2min55sec
1847	2min52sec
1848	2min48sec
1849	3min
1850	2min50sec
1851	2min51sec
1852	3min2sec
1853	2min55½sec
1854	2min52sec
1855	2min54sec
1856	3min4sec
1857	2min45sec
1858	2min54sec
1859	2min59sec
1860	2min55sec
1861	2min45sec
1862	2min45½sec
1863	2min50½sec
1864	2min43sec
1865	2min46sec
1866	2min50sec
1867	2min52sec
1868	2min43½sec
1869	2min52½sec
1870	2min45sec
1871	2min50sec
1872	2min45½sec
1873	2min50sec
1874	2min46sec
1875	2min48sec
1876	2min44sec
1877	2min50sec
1878	2min56sec
1879	3min2sec
1880	2min46sec
1881	2min50sec
1882	2min45⅗th sec
1883	2min48⅔rd sec
1884	2min46⅕th sec
1885	2min44⅕th sec
1886	2min45⅗th sec
1887	2min43sec
1888	2min43sec
1889	2min44⅔rd sec
1890	2min49⅘th sec
1891	2min56⅘th sec
1892	2min44sec
1893	2min43sec
1894	2min45⅘th sec
1895	2min43⅔rd sec
1896	2min42sec
1897	2min44sec
1898	2min47sec
1899	2min42⅘th sec
1900	2min42sec
1901	2min40⅘th sec
1902	2min42⅕th sec
1903	2min42⅘th sec
1904	2min45⅔rd sec
1905	2min39⅗th sec
1906	2min36⅘th sec
1907	2min44sec
1908	2min39⅘th sec
1909	2min42⅔rd sec
1910	2min35⅕th sec
1911	2min36⅘th sec
1912	2min38⅘th sec
1913	2min37⅗th sec
1914	2min38⅔rd sec
1915	2min32⅗th sec
1916	2min36⅗th sec
1917	2min40⅗th sec
1918	2min33⅕th sec
1919	2min35⅘th sec
1920	2min34⅘th sec
1921	2min36⅕th sec
1922	2min34⅗th sec
1923	2min38sec
1924	2min46⅗th sec
1925	2min40⅗th sec
1926	2min47⅘th sec
1927	2min34⅔rd sec
1928	2min34⅘th sec
1929	2min36⅔rd sec
1930	2min38⅕th sec
1931	2min36⅗th sec
1932	2min43⅕th sec
1933	2min34sec
1934	2min34sec
1935	2min36sec
1936	2min37⅘th sec
1937	2min37⅗th sec
1938	2min39⅕th sec
1939	2min36⅘th sec
1940	2min30⅘th sec
1941	2min32sec
1943	2min29⅖th sec
1944	2min31sec
1945	2min26⅗th sec
1946	2min44⅗th sec
1947	2min38⅔rd sec
1948	2min40sec
1949	2min42sec
1950	2min36⅘th sec
1951	2min39⅔rd sec
1952	2min36⅔rd sec
1953	2min35⅔rd sec
1954	2min35⅘th sec
1955	2min39⅘th sec
1956	2min36⅔rd sec
1957	2min35⅔rd sec
1958	2min41⅕th sec
1959	2min36sec
1960	2min35⅗th sec
1961	2min36½sec
1962	2min37⅗th sec
1963	2min39⅖th sec
1964	2min41.98sec
1965	2min38.41sec
1966	2min37.63sec
1967	2min38.36sec
1968	2min38.73sec
1969	2min40.3sec
1970	2min34.68sec

The Oaks, 1m 4f

Three-year-old fillies carrying 9st. First run in 1779. *Run at Newmarket from* 1915 *to* 1918 *and from* 1940 *to* 1945.

		OWNER	TRAINER	JOCKEY	SP
1900	La Roche	Duke of Portland	J. Porter	M. Cannon	5–1
1901	Cap and Bells II	F. Keen	S. Darling	M. Henry	9–4
1902	Sceptre	R. Sievier	R. Sievier	H. Randall	5–2
1903	Our Lassie	J. Joel	C. Morton	M. Cannon	6–1
1904	Pretty Polly	Maj E. Loder	P. Gilpin	W. Lane	8–100
1905	Cherry Lass	W. H. Walker	W. Robinson	H. Jones	4–5
1906	Keystone II	Lord Derby	G. Lambton	D. Maher	5–2
1907	Glass Doll	J. Joel	C. Morton	H. Randall	25–1
1908	Signorinetta	E. Ginistrelli	E. Ginistrelli	W. Bullock	3–1
1909	Perola	W. Cooper	G. Davies	F. Wootton	5–1
1910	Rosedrop	Sir W. Bass	A. Taylor	C. Trigg	7–1
1911	Cherimoya	W. B. Cloete	C. Marsh	F. Winter	25–1
1912	Mirska	J. Prat	T. Jennings	J. Childs	33–1

	OWNER	TRAINER	JOCKEY	SP
1913 Jest	J. Joel	C. Morton	F. Rickaby	8–1
1914 Princess Dorrie	J. Joel	C. Morton	W. Huxley	11–4
1915 Snow Marten	L. Neumann	P. Gilpin	W. Griggs	20–1
1916 Fifinella	E. Hulton	R. Dawson	J. Childs	8–13
1917 Sunny Jane	Maj W. Astor	A. Taylor	O. Madden	4–1
1918 My Dear	A. Cox	A. Taylor	S. Donoghue	3–1
1919 Bayuda	Lady Douglas	A. Taylor	J. Childs	100–7
1920 Charlebelle	A. Cunliffe	H. Braime	A. Whalley	7–2
1921 Love in Idleness	J. Watson	A. Taylor	J. Childs	5–1
1922 Pogrom	Lord Astor	A. Taylor	E. Gardner	5–4
1923 Brownhylda	Vicomte de Fontarce	R. Dawson	V. Smyth	10–1
1924 Straitlace	Sir E. Hulton	D. Waugh	F. O'Neill	100–30
1925 Saucy Sue	Lord Astor	A. Taylor	F. Bullock	30–100
1926 Short Story	Lord Astor	A. Taylor	R. Jones	5–1
1927 Beam	Lord Durham	Fk. Butters	T. Weston	4–1
1928 Toboggan	Lord Derby	Fk. Butters	T. Weston	100–15
1929 Pennycomequick	Lord Astor	J. Lawson	H. Jelliss	11–10
1930 Rose of England	Lord Glanely	T. Hogg	G. Richards	7–1
1931 Brulette	Lieut-Col C. Birkin	In France	C. Elliott	7–2
1932 Udaipur	Aga Khan	Fk. Butters	M. Beary	10–1
1933 Chatelaine	E. T-Smith	F. Templeman	S. Wragg	25–1
1934 Light Brocade	Lord Durham	Fk. Butters	B. Carslake	7–4
1935 Quashed	Lord Stanley	C. Leader	H. Jelliss	33–1
1936 Lovely Rosa	Sir Abe Bailey	H. Cottrill	T. Weston	33–1
1937 Exhibitionnist	Sir V. Sassoon	J. Lawson	S. Donoghue	3–1
1938 Rockfel	Sir H. C-Owen	O. Bell	H. Wragg	3–1
1939 Galatea II	R. Clark	J. Lawson	R. Jones	10–11
1940 Godiva	Lord Rothermere	W. Jarvis	D. Marks	7–4
1941 Commotion	J. Dewar	F. Darling	H. Wragg	8–1
1942 Sun Chariot	King George VI	F. Darling	G. Richards	1–4
1943 Why Hurry	J. Rank	N. Cannon	C. Elliott	7–1
1944 Hycilla	W. Woodward	C. B-Rochfort	G. Bridgland	8–1
1945 Sun Stream	Lord Derby	W. Earl	H. Wragg	6–4
1946 Steady Aim	Sir A. Butt	Fk. Butters	H. Wragg	7–1
1947 Imprudence	Mme P. Corbiere	J. Lieux	W. Johnstone	7–4
1948 Masaka	Aga Khan	Fk. Butters	W. Nevett	7–1
1949 Musidora	N. Donaldson	C. Elsey	E. Britt	4–1
1950 Asmena	M. Boussac	C. Semblat	W. Johnstone	5–1
1951 Neasham Belle	Maj L. Holliday	G. Brooke	S. Clayton	33–1
1952 Frieze	A. Keith	C. Elsey	E. Britt	100–7
1953 Ambiguity	Lord Astor	J. Colling	J. Mercer	18–1
1954 Sun Cap	Mme R. Forget	R. Carver	W. Johnstone	100–8
1955 Meld	Lady Z. Wernher	C. B-Rochfort	W. Carr	7–4
1956 Sicarelle	Mme L. Volterra	F. Mathet	F. Palmer	3–1
1957 Carrozza	The Queen	N. Murless	L. Piggott	100–8
1958 Bella Paola	F. Dupré	F. Mathet	M. Garcia	6–4
1959 Petite Etoile	Aly Khan	N. Murless	L. Piggott	11–2
1960 Never Too Late II	Mrs H. Jackson	E. Pollet	R. Poincelet	6–5
1961 Sweet Solera	Mrs S. Castello	R. Day	W. Rickaby	11–4
1962 Monade	G. Goulandris	J. Lieux	Y. Saint-Martin	7–1
1963 Noblesse	Mrs J. Olin	P. Prendergast	G. Bougoure	4–11
1964 Homeward Bound	Sir F. Robinson	J. Oxley	G. Starkey	100–7
1965 Long Look	J. C. Brady	V. O'Brien	J. Purtell	100–7
1966 Valoris	C. Clore	V. O'Brien	L. Piggott	11–10
1967 Pia	Countess M. Bathyany	W. Elsey	E. Hide	100–7
1968 La Lagone	M. Berlin	F. Boutin	G. Thibourf	11–8
1969 Sleeping Partner	Lord Rosebery	D. Smith	J. Gorton	100–6
1970 Lupe	Mrs S. Joel.	N. Murless	A. Barclay	100–30

Coronation Cup, 1m 4f

First run 1902. *Run at Newbury* 1941. *Run at Newmarket* 1943 *to* 1945. *No race* 1940, 1942, 1948.

	OWNER	TRAINER	JOCKEY	SP
1930 Plantago, 5–9–6	W. Singer	J. Lawson	C. Ray	7–2
1931 Parenthesis, 4–9–3	Lord Woolavington	F. Darling	F. Fox	9–4

Coronation Cup (contd)

	OWNER	TRAINER	JOCKEY	SP
1932 Salmon Leap, 5–9–6	Mrs A. James ..	G. Lambton ..	T. Weston ..	7–2
1933 Dastur, 4–9–3	Aga Khan	Fk. Butters ..	C. Elliott . ..	7–4
1934 King Salmon, 4–9–3	Sir A. Brooke ..	O. Bell	H. Wragg ..	7–4
1935 Windsor Lad, 4–9–3	M. Benson	M. Marsh ..	C. Smirke ..	evens
1936 Plassy, 4–9–3	Lord Derby	C. Leader ..	R. Perryman ..	11–8
1937 {Cecil, 6–9–6	Sir A. Bailey . ..	J. Lawson ..	T. Weston ..	100–8
1937 {His Grace, 4–9–3 ..	J. Rank	R. Dawson ..	G. Richards ..	100–9
1938 Monument, 5–9–6 ..	Duke of Marlborough ..	C. B-Rochfort .	P. Beasley ..	9–2
1939 Scottish Union,4–9–3	J. Rank	N. Cannon ..	G. Richards ..	85–40
1941 Winterhalter, 4–9–3 .	Aga Khan	Fk. Butters ..	D. Smith.. ..	7–2
1943 Hyperides, 4–9–0 ..	Lord Rosebery ..	J. Jarvis	E. Smith . ..	7–4
1944 Persian Gulf, 4–9–0 .	Lady Z. Wernher .	C. B-Rochfort .	R. Jones	5–2
1945 Borealis, 4–9–0 . ..	Lord Derby	W. Earl	H. Wragg ..	5–2
1946 Ardan, 5–9–3	M. Boussac	C. Semblat ..	C. Elliott . ..	5–6
1947 Chanteur II, 5–9–3 .	P. Magot	H. Count . ..	R. Brethes ..	1–3
1949 Goyama, 5–9–3 ..	M. Boussac	C. Semblat ..	C. Elliott . ..	5–2
1950 Amour Drake, 4–8–7	Mme L. Volterra..	R. Carver ..	R. Poincelet ..	15–8
1951 Tantieme, 4–8–7 ..	F. Dupré	F. Mathet ..	J. Doyasbere ..	2–7
1952 Nuccio, 4–8–7 . ..	Aga Khan	A. Head	R. Poincelet ..	3–1
1953 Zucchero, 5–8–10 ..	G. Rolls	W. Payne . ..	L. Piggott ..	100–7
1954 Aureole, 4–8–7 . ..	The Queen	C. B-Rochfort .	E. Smith . ..	5–2
1955 Narrator, 4–8–7 ..	Maj L. Holliday ..	H. Cottrill ..	F. Barlow ..	100–30
1956 Tropique, 4–8–7 ..	Baron de Rothschild	G. Watson ..	P. Blanc	13–8
1957 Fric, 5–8–10	M. Calmann . ..	P. Lallie	J. Deforge ..	7–2
1958 Ballymoss, 4–8–7 ..	J. McShain	V. O'Brien ..	A. Breasley ..	evens
1959 Nagami, 4–8–7 . ..	Mrs A. Plesch ..	H. Wragg ..	L. Piggott ..	5–4
1960 Petite Etoile, 4–8–4 .	Aly Khan	N. Murless ..	L. Piggott ..	1–3
1961 Petite Etoile, 5–8–7 .	Aga Khan	N. Murless ..	L. Piggott ..	2–5
1962 Dicta Drake, 4–8–7 .	Mme L. Volterra..	F. Mathet ..	Y. Saint-Martin	2–1
1963 Exbury, 4–8–7 . ..	Baron de Rothschild	G. Watson ..	J. Deforge ..	11–8
1964 Relko, 4–8–7	F. Dupré	F. Mathet ..	Y. Saint-Martin	4–6
1965 Oncidium, 4–8–11 ..	Lord H. de Walden	G. Todd	A. Breasley ..	11–2
1966 I Say, 4–8–10	L. Freedman . ..	W. Nightingall.	J. Lindley ..	10–1
1967 Charlottown, 4–8–10	Lady Z. Wernher .	G. Smyth . ..	D. Keith . ..	11–8
1968 Royal Palace, 4–8–10	H. J. Joel	N. Murless ..	A. Barclay ..	4–9
1969 Park Top, 5–9–0 ..	Duke of Devonshire	B. van Cutsem.	L. Piggott ..	11–4
1970 Caliban, 4–9–0 ..	S. Joel	N. Murless ..	A. Barclay ..	8–1

Great Metropolitan Handicap, 2m 2f

First run 1846. *No race* 1940 *to* 1945.

	OWNER	TRAINER	JOCKEY	SP
1930 Servus, 7–7–10 . ..	Lord Derby	Fk. Butters ..	T. Weston ..	4–1
1931 Summer Princess, 5–6–7	C. Gulliver	R. Barclay ..	F. Sharpe . ..	20–1
1932 Roi de Paris, 4–6–8 .	J. Cooper	A. D-Pennant .	E. Smith . ..	100–8
1933 Joyous Greeting, 9–7–12	Maj H. Lyons ..	F. Sneyd . ..	S. Wragg . ..	20–1
1934 Annihilation, 4–8–3 .	J. Rank	H. Cottrill ..	J. Caldwell ..	100–8
1935 Crawley Wood, 5–8–0	J. Cottrell	J. Waugh . ..	F. Lane	20–1
1936 {Quashed, 4–9–4 ..	Lord Stanley . ..	C. Leader ..	R. Perryman ..	7–2
1936 {Jack Tar, 6–7–6 ..	Lady Nuttall . ..	H. Cottrill ..	E. Smith . ..	100–8
1937 Corofin, 5–6–11 ..	M. McDonough ..	J. Parkinson ..	W. Wing . ..	100–8
1938 Irish Stew, 6–7–13 ..	Miss B. Jameson .	G. Beeby . ..	P. Maher . ..	5–1
1939 Lillibullero, 4–6–12 .	J. de Rothschild ..	F. Pratt	B. Lynch.. ..	100–6
1946 Golden Horus,4–8–11	W. Little	G. Duller . ..	G. Richards ..	7–1
1947 Star Song, 7–7–9 ..	Mrs D. C-Marsh..	V. Smyth . ..	D. Smith.. ..	100–7
1948 Now or Never, 4–9–0	F. Harris	V. Smyth . ..	C. Elliott . ..	6–1
1949 Yoyo, 5–7–12	Lord Rosebery ..	J. Jarvis	W. Cook.. ..	7–2
1950 Blue Fox II, 4–7–8 .	Aly Khan	H. Delavaud ..	P. Blanc	8–1
1951 Barnacle, 5–7–10 ..	A. Aman	A. Budgett ..	L. Piggott ..	10–1
1952 French Squadron, 6–8–11	Miss Z. Daniels ..	M. Beary . ..	W. Johnstone..	7–1
1953 Father Thames,7–8–9	R. Deakin	M. Feakes . ..	R. Fawson ..	100–8
1954 Luxury Hotel, 4–8–4	E. McAlpine . ..	M. Pope	G. Richards ..	4–1
1955 Babylonian, 5–8–6 ..	G. Dowty	T. Rimell . ..	J. Mercer . ..	11–2
1956 Curry, 5–8–3	F. Honour	F. Armstrong..	P. Tulk.. ..	4–1

	OWNER	TRAINER	JOCKEY	SP
1957 Gay Ballad, 4–6–8 ..	J. Pearce	G. Brooke ..	J. Lynch	100–8
1958 Hollyhock, 6–8–4 ..	D. H-Hutchinson .	A. Budgett ..	S. Millbanks ..	9–1
1959 Miss McTaffy, 4–9–2	T. H-Martin.. ..	P. Walwyn ..	L. Piggott ..	10–1
1960 Kaffirboom, 4–8–0 .	H. Oppenheimer ..	F. Armstrong..	W. Snaith ..	5–1
1961 Little Buskins, 4–7–11	T. Gray..	C. B-Rochfort .	W. Snaith ..	20–1
1962 Narratus, 4–8–1 ..	R. Stone	D. Thom . ..	E. Smith . ..	100–7
1963 Byng, 6–7–8	D. Griffiths	D. Griffiths ..	D. Cullen . ..	100–7
1964 Gold Aura, 4–7–9 ..	The Queen	C. B-Rochfort .	J. Sime	11–2
1965 Romp Home, 4–8–3.	W. Hill	W. Elsey . ..	Don Morris ..	15–8
1966 Cullen, 5–6–12 . ..	M. Tate	M. Tate	F. Messer ..	100–6
1967 Noon Storm, 4–7–2 .	Mrs S. Robinson..	K. Cundell ..	A. Murray ..	33–1
1968 Pick Me Up, 5–9–4 .	B. P. Jenks	T. F. Rimell ..	L. Piggott ..	6–1
1969 Clever Scot, 4–7–9..	H. S. Alper	C. Davies . ..	R. Dicey . ..	100–6
1970 Hickleton, 4–7–5 ..	R. Dawson	B. Hills	E. Johnson ..	8–1

City And Suburban Handicap, 1m 2f 15yd

First run 1851. *No race* 1940 *to* 1945.

	OWNER	TRAINER	JOCKEY	SP
1930 Lucky Tor, 5–7–6 ..	W. Singer	J. Lawson ..	G. Richards ..	13–2
1931 Anthurium, 4–7–1 ..	J. de Rothschild ..	F. Pratt	B. Lynch.. ..	25–1
1932 Clogheen, 4–7–4 ..	Mrs C. Jones ..	F. Gilbert ..	C. Richards ..	20–1
1933 Great Scot, 7–8 ..	Mrs C. Beatty ..	H. Fergusson .	J. Collins . ..	20–1
1934 Light Sussex, 4–8–6 .	Maj C. Behrens ..	C. Elsey	H. Wragg ..	100–7
1935 Montrose, 5–8–13 ..	Lord Woolavington	F. Darling ..	G. Richards ..	7–2
1936 His Reverence, 5–8–12	G. Annesley . ..	H. Wellesley ..	T. Burns . ..	100–7
1937 William of Valence, 5–9–6	A. Sainsbury . ..	H. Smyth . ..	H. Packham ..	11–4
1938 Pigskin, 6–7–5 . ..	Mrs C. Beatty ..	J. Lawson ..	C. Richards ..	6–1
1939 Bistolfi, 4–8–10 ..	Mrs L. Corbett ..	O. Bell	H. Wragg ..	100–8
1946 Hobo, 4–9–0	Lord Rosebery ..	J. Jarvis	E. Smith . ..	2–1
1947 Banco, 4–7–13.. ..	Duchess of Norfolk	W. Smyth ..	T. Burns . ..	10–1
1948 Fast Soap, 5–9–0 ..	A. Jarvis	G. Houghton .	E. Smith . ..	2–1
1949 Impeccable, 5–9–0 ..	R. McIlhagga ..	J. Powell . ..	G. Richards ..	4–1
1950 Iron Duke, 4–8–7 ..	G. Gibson	M. Marsh ..	E. Britt	5–1
1951 Burnt Brown, 5–9–3.	Mrs S. Jacobson ..	N. Scobie. ..	W. Evans . ..	100–6
1952 Sunny Brae, 4–8–4 .	J. de Rothschild ..	D. Watson ..	E. Fordyce ..	100–6
1953 Damremont, 6–8–11	T. Degg	T. Rimell ..	J. Lindley ..	8–1
1954 Sunny Brae, 6–9–3 .	J. de Rothschild ..	D. Watson ..	W. Elliott ..	100–8
1955 Coronation Year, 4–7–13	A. Thomas	A. Thomas ..	D. Smith.. ..	100–9
1956 Great Pacha, 6–8–1 .	Maharanee of Baroda	J. Rogers . ..	D. Smith.. ..	100–8
1957 Coronation Year, 6–8–11	A. Thomas	A. Thomas ..	D. Smith.. ..	5–1
1958 Setting Star, 6–8–9 .	Maj L. Holliday ..	W. Hern . ..	S. Clayton ..	100–9
1959 Guersillus, 4–9–3 ..	P. Bull	C. Elsey	E. Hide	9–4
1960 Firestreak, 4–9–5 ..	J. Lewis	P. Nelson . ..	L. Piggott ..	11–4
1961 Nerograph, 5–7–3 ..	T. Frost	G. Todd	T. Carter . ..	8–1
1962 Eastern Nip, 4–7–0 .	Maj L. Gardner ..	W. Stephenson	B. Raymond ..	5–1
1963 Tahiri, 4–8–4	Sir H. Wernher ..	J. Gosden ..	S. Clayton ..	10–1
1964 The Bo'sun, 4–9–0 ..	Lord Rosebery ..	J. Jarvis	S. Smith	4–1
1965 Minor Portion, 4–8–6	Sir P. Dunn	J. Tree	J. Lindley ..	2–1
1966—Abandoned. Course	Waterlogged.			
1967 Hotroy, 6–9–11 ..	A. Kennedy	W. Nightingall.	D. Keith . ..	100–7
1968 My Swanee, 5–9–6 –	Mrs L. Napier ..	W. Marshall ..	L. Piggott ..	11–2
1969 Karabas, 4–9–2 ..	Lord Iveagh . ..	B. van Cutsem.	L. Piggott ..	9–1
1970 Granados, 4–8–1 ..	E. Benjamin.. ..	G. Barling ..	F. Durr.. ..	15–2

ESPRESSO

Espresso, a chestnut horse by Acropolis out of Babylon, by Bahram, was bred by Major Pat Dennis and sold as a yearling in 1959 to Mr G. Oldham for 1,000 gn. Trained by H. Wragg, he won eight races worth over £20,000 in England, including the Newbury Summer Cup, Manchester Cup and Vaux Gold Tankard. In

Germany he twice won the Grosser Preis von Baden. He was syndicated for stud purposes and stands at the Barton Stud, Bury St Edmunds.

ETHERINGTON, James (b 1934)

Jimmy Etherington, one of the best known riders in the North, was apprenticed to the Malton trainer, E. Davey. He rode his first winner in 1951. Among the races he has won are the Northumberland Plate, King's Stand Stakes, Windsor Castle Stakes and Yorkshire Cup. The jockeys L. G. Brown and P. J. Willett are his brothers-in-law.

This former north-country jockey is now training at Malton, Yorkshire.

EVELEIGH, Major Michael, MC (b 1914)

Major Eveleigh served in the 17th/21st Lancers and the 3rd Hussars. He was appointed a starter in January 1965.

EXBURY

Foaled in 1959, Exbury was bred and is owned by Baron Guy de Rothschild. A beautifully made little chestnut horse by Le Haar out of a mare by Mossborough, he proved himself a top class performer on the racecourse, winning seven races in France including the Prix Daru, Prix Ganay, Grand Prix de St Cloud and the Prix de l'Arc de Triomphe. In England he won the Coronation Cup. He retired to the stud in 1964 and stands at Haras de Meautry, Calvados, France.

EXHIBITIONNIST

Bred and owned by Sir Victor Sassoon and trained by Joe Lawson, Exhibitionnist was a Solario filly that won the One Thousand Guineas and the Oaks in 1937. At the stud she bred half a dozen winners. She was the last classic winner ridden by Steve Donoghue.

F

FAGGOTTER, Valentine (b 1927)

Val Faggotter was born in Australia and rode his first winner at Moorfield, Sydney, in 1944. He rode with success both in Australia and India. His best season in England so far was 1963 when he rode 38 winners.

FAIR COPY

Owned and bred by the late Lord Derby and foaled in 1934, Fair Copy was by Fairway out of Composure. He won eight races worth more than £10,000, including the Middle Park Stakes. He was second in the St Leger, Coronation Cup and Eclipse Stakes. At the stud he sired the 1952 Grand Prix winner Orfeo and Sayani, who won the Cambridgeshire as a three-year-old with 9st 4lb.

FAIRFAX-BLAKEBOROUGH, Major John Freeman, MC

A very well-known figure in northern racing circles, Major Fairfax-Blakeborough is still an active journalist though nearer 90 than 80. In his time he has acted as judge, starter, stakeholder, clerk of the scales and club secretary. He is the author of over 100 books.

FAIRHURST, T.

He trains at Middleham and won eighteen races in 1969.

FAIR ISLE

Owned and bred by the late Lord Derby, Fair Isle was by Phalaris out of Scapa Flow and thus a sister of the St Leger winner Fairway. She won the One Thousand Guineas in 1930. She bred St Magnus who won over £3,000 in stakes and became a leading sire in Australia.

FAIR TRIAL

Fair Trial, owned and bred by Mr J. A. Dewar and trained by Fred Darling, was by the St Leger winner Fairway out of Lady Juror, a staying mare by the great stayer Son-in-Law. In fact, the most potent influence in his pedigree was that of the speedy Americus Girl. He himself proved a good horse up to a mile, winning seven races worth over £5,000.

As a sire he was an outstanding success and when he died aged 26 in 1958 his stock had won $529\frac{1}{2}$ races worth £302,389. He was leading sire in 1950 and on nine other occasions he finished in the top six. His best winners were Palestine (Two Thousand Guineas), Court Martial (Two Thousand Guineas and Champion Stakes), Festoon (One Thousand Guineas) and Petition (Eclipse Stakes). The triple classic winner Meld was out of a Fair Trial mare and so was the St Leger winner Premonition.

FAIRWAY

Foaled in 1925, Fairway was one of the best of the many great horses owned by the seventeenth Earl of Derby. By Phalaris out of Scapa Flow, he was bred by his owner and was a full-brother to Pharos, second in the Derby, and to Fair Isle, winner of the One Thousand Guineas.

Fairway won twelve races worth over £42,000, including the St Leger and the Eclipse Stakes. He was favourite for the 1928 Derby but the crowd got out of control and mobbed him on his way to the post, pulling hair out of his tail by the handful. By the time he reached the starting gate he looked as if he had been dragged through a pond. Not surprisingly, as he was a highly-strung colt, he failed utterly in the race. He was undoubtedly, though, the best three-year-old of that season.

At the stud he did extremely well and was four times leading sire. The best horse he got was Blue Peter, winner of the Two Thousand Guineas and the Derby in 1939. His other Derby winner was Watling Street, who won in 1942. Altogether he sired the winners of seven classic races. He died in 1948.

FALMOUTH, sixth Viscount (1819-1889)

The son of a parson, the sixth Viscount Falmouth began to own horses in 1857 and won the One Thousand Guineas with Hurricane in 1862 and the Oaks with Queen Bertha in 1863. Those fillies were trained for him by John Scott and after Scott's death his horses were sent to Matthew Dawson at Newmarket. Between 1870 and his retirement from racing in 1883 he enjoyed an era of outstanding success with animals bred by himself at Mereworth in Kent. In that period he won the Two Thousand Guineas three times, the One Thousand Guineas three times, the Derby twice, the Oaks three times and the St Leger three times. He never betted and earned the respect of everyone connected with racing.

FEILDEN, Major-Gen Sir Randle, CB, CBE, KCVO (b 1904)

Major-Gen Sir Randle Feilden served in the Coldstream Guards. He made his military reputation as a highly efficient administrator, and on his retirement in 1949 he was Vice-Quartermaster-General at the War Office. Since then he has had many business interests and has also proved himself the outstanding Turf administrator of the post-war era. He was a Steward of the Jockey Club from 1952-55 and again from 1959-61. He is at present Senior Steward of the Jockey Club and Chairman of the Turf Board. At one time he was a member of the Racecourse Betting Control Board. His trainer is John Oxley. Colours: light blue and dark blue check, light blue sleeves and cap.

FELICITATION

Bred and owned by the late Aga Khan, Felicitation was foaled in 1930 and was by Colorado out of Felicita, by Cantilever. A great stayer, he won eight races worth over £14,000, including the Gold Cup, in which he trounced Hyperion, the Jockey Club Cup, the Yorkshire Cup and the Churchill Stakes. After a brief period at the stud in Britain, he was exported to Brazil.

FELSTEAD

Bred and owned by Sir Hugo Cunliffe-Owen and trained by Capt O. M. Bell, Felstead was by Spion Kop out of Felkington by Lemberg. Ridden by Harry Wragg and starting at 33-1, he won the 1928 Derby. He never ran again afterwards. At stud he sired Rockfel, a great filly that won the One Thousand Guineas and the Oaks; and Steady Aim, who won the Oaks. He died in 1946.

FERGUSON, R. J.

Attached to Tom Jones's stable at Newmarket, he was one of the most successful apprentices in 1969 and rode 20 winners. He can go to scale at 7 stone.

FERRY

Owned and bred by the late Lord Derby, Ferry won the One Thousand Guineas in 1918. A full sister to the Derby winner Sansovino, she was not a success at the stud.

FESTOON

Foaled in 1951, Festoon, by Fair Trial out of Monsoon, was bred and owned by Mr J. A. Dewar and was trained by Noel Cannon. She won the One Thousand Guineas, Coronation Stakes and over £15,000 in stakes. After Mr Dewar's death in 1954 she came up for sale at Newmarket and was bought for 36,000 gn by Mr A. B. Askew. The best of her offspring so far is Atilla, winner of over £16,000 in stakes.

FIDALGO

Bred by Mr D. Stewart and owned when in training by Mr G. Oldham, Fidalgo is by Arctic Star out of Miss France, by Jock II. He won the Chester Vase and the Irish Derby and was second in the Derby and the St Leger. In 1966, when he was ten years of age, he was exported to Japan.

FIELDEN, Lieut-Col Philip Brand, MC (b 1919)

Lieut-Col Fielden served in the Royal Dragoons from 1940-61. He won the Grand Military Gold Cup on Atom Bomb in 1953 and on Skatealong in 1955. He was appointed a Stewards' Secretary in 1963.

FIFINELLA

Owned by Mr (later Sir) Edward Hulton and trained at Newmarket by R. C. Dawson, Fifinella was a chestnut filly by Polymelus out of Silver Fowl. Ridden by Joe Childs, she won a war-substitute Derby and Oaks at Newmarket in 1916. She was a highly-strung, rather wayward filly and at the stud was inclined to transmit similar characteristics to her stock, the best of which was Press Gang, winner of the Middle Park Stakes.

FIGHTING CHARLIE

Owned and bred by Lady Mairi Bury, Fighting Charlie was foaled in 1961 and is by Tenerani out of Flight of the Heron, by Cameronian. A good, game stayer, he won the Ascot Gold Cup in 1965 and again in 1966. He stands at the Hamilton Stud, Newmarket, at a fee of £248.

FIGHTING SHIP

Owned and bred by Lord Rosebery, Fighting Ship was foaled in 1960 and is by Doutelle out of Jane, by Alycidon. He won four races worth £7,896 including the Jockey Club Stakes and stands at his owner's Mentmore Stud at a fee of £300.

FINANCE OF RACING

Racing finance of course has many aspects. Owners breed, buy or lease their horses and pay their training fees which vary slightly according to the trainer. According to the Racehorse Owners Association, it cost £1,431 to keep a horse in training on the flat in 1969. Training fees are paid direct to the trainer. Most trainers own or lease their own training establishment; but some stables are owned by an owner, or by a syndicate of owners, the trainer being paid a salary plus percentages on races won.

Owners maintain an account at Weatherbys through which entrance fees, forfeits, jockeys' fees, registrations fees etc are paid. Into this account prize money won is paid.

As for racecourses, some are run as companies to make profits for shareholders; others operate on a non-profit-making basis—that is to say the profits, if any, are used for improving amenities or augmenting the prize money.

Bookmakers and the Horserace Totalisator Board pay an annual contribution to the Horserace Betting Levy Board, the money received being spent by the board for the general benefit of the sport. For example, the following items appear in the Eighth Report of the Horserace Betting Levy Board, covering the period 1st April 1968-31st March 1969:

Improvements to racecourses	£1,099,143
Prize money	£731,375
Guaranteed fixtures	£13,587
Transport of racehorses	£286,904
Racecourse Technical Services (camera patrol, photo finish, public address and commentary at racecourses, starting stalls)	£328,918
Suppression of Doping (Veterinary Field Force, Forensic Laboratory, Research, Security Guards	£127,755

Publicity for racing £21,589
Apprentice Training Scheme £5,849
Racing Industry Benefit Scheme £90,368
Overnight declarations scheme £25,000

The Horserace Betting Levy Board may also make loans and advances to racecourse proprietors.

FIRDAUSSI

Foaled in 1929, Firdaussi was bred and owned by the late Aga Khan and was by Pharos out of the Oaks winner Brownhylda. He won eight races worth over £21,000 including the St Leger and Jockey Club Stakes. He spent one year at the stud in England, four years in France, and was then sent to Rumania.

FIRESTREAK

Bred by Major-Gen Sir George Burns, Firestreak was foaled in 1956 and is by Pardal out of Hot Spell, by Umidwar. He won nine races worth over £11,000 including the City and Suburban and the Rous Memorial Stakes at Ascot. He is syndicated for stud purposes and stands at the Aislabie Stud, Newmarket.

FIRING

'Firing' is veterinary treatment for weakened tendons and consists of the application of a red-hot iron (the horse, of course, is given an anaesthetic) to the skin over the part to be treated. This toughens the structures underneath and acts as a support. 'Pin-firing' is similar in principle but, the operation being carried out with a pointed instrument, the deeper structure of the horse's leg may be treated.

FIRTH, L. L. (d 1955)

He was appointed starter to the Jockey Club in 1948, having first been licensed as a starter 26 years previously. He fell dead when walking at his home

FIRTH, P. B.

Clerk of the Course, Newmarket, since 1964. He is a son of the former Jockey Club Starter, the late Mr L. L. Frith.

FISHERMAN

Fisherman won 23 races in 1856—a record.

FLAGS

The significance of flags displayed on the number boards after a race on the authority of the Clerk of the Scales is as follows:

Blue Flag: All right.
Red Flag: Objection to winner.
Red and White Flag: Objection to any other placed horse.
Red Flag with White E: Enquiry called for by the stewards.
White Flag: Objection overruled.
Green Flag: Objection sustained.

FLAMINGO

Foaled in 1925, Flamingo was owned by Sir Laurence Philipps (later Lord Milford) and was by Flamboyant, winner of the Goodwood and Doncaster Cups, out of Lady Peregrine, by White Eagle. Trained by Jack Jarvis he won the Two Thousand Guineas and was a somewhat unlucky second in the Derby, in which he was not ridden with the best judgement. He sired the Gold Cup winner Flyon and Flamenco, winner of the St James's Palace Stakes and the Lincoln.

FLARES

An American-bred horse trained by Sir Cecil Boyd-Rochfort, Flares was foaled in 1933 and was by Gallant Fox out of Flambino. He won eight races worth over £17,000 including the Ascot Gold Cup, Champion Stakes, Newmarket Stakes and Princess of Wales's Stakes. He failed as a sire in the United States and ended up in Canada.

FLATMAN, Nat (1810-1860)

Nat Flatman was a leading jockey

during the mid-Victorian era. He rode for 30 years and his services were in great demand as not only was his skill of a high order but he was honest and could keep his mouth shut.

FLAT-RACING SEASON

No flat-race can be run earlier than the week that includes the 25th March (unless that be the one next before Easter Sunday, in which case races may be run in the week preceding) nor later than the week that includes the 22nd November.

FLEET

Bred in Ireland in 1964 by Commander Peter FitzGerald, Fleet is by Immortality, who never ran, out of the famous mare Review, dam of other good winners such as Affair, Pourparler and Democratie. Bought for 11,000 gn as a yearling by Mr R. C. Boucher, who sent her to Noel Murless to be trained, Fleet was a fast filly of the highest class, her wins including the Princess Margaret Stakes, Cheveley Park Stakes, One Thousand Guineas and Coronation Stakes. After a year at her owner's stud, she was exported to America.

FLORIBUNDA

Bred and owned by Mr J. R. Mullion, Floribunda was foaled in 1958 and is by Princely Gift out of Astrentia, by Denturius. He won five races worth over £7,000 including the New Stakes, King George Stakes and Nunthorpe Stakes. He is syndicated for stud purposes and stands at the Littleton Stud, Winchester.

FLYING CHILDERS

The Duke of Devonshire's Flying Childers, foaled in 1715, has been described as "the first great racehorse". Few of his performances were in fact recorded but it is known that he ran against the best horses of his time at Newmarket and was never beaten. He achieved such a reputation for invincibility that eventually he received forfeit in most of his matches.

FLYING DUTCHMAN, THE

Owned by Lord Eglinton, The Flying Dutchman won the 1849 Derby. The following year he was beaten in the Doncaster Cup by Lord Zetland's Voltigeur, winner of the 1850 Derby and St Leger. The sequel was the famous match at York the following spring, when The Flying Dutchman before a huge crowd defeated Voltigeur, who was receiving 8½lb, by a length.

FLYING FOX

The first Duke of Westminster is the only man that has bred and owned two 'Triple Crown' winners—Ormonde in 1886 and Flying Fox, by Orme out of Vampire, in 1899. Both were trained by John Porter at Kingsclere.

Flying Fox won just over £40,000 in stakes for the Duke. Because of his owner's death, Flying Fox came up for sale in 1900 and was bought by M. Edmond Blanc for 37,500 gn, a huge price at that time. Flying Fox proved a stud success and founded sire lines of powerful influence in France, Italy and America.

FLYON

Foaled in 1935, Flyon was bred and owned by Lord Milford and was by Flamingo out of Acquit, by Hurry On. Trained by Jack Jarvis, he won seven races worth over £12,000 including the Ascot Gold Cup. He was a failure as a sire.

FOLKESTONE

This is a very attractive course, particularly in the summer, and the quality of the sport has improved a lot in recent years. It is a right-handed track, about 1m 3f round, with a run-in of 3½f. Both the round course and the straight 6f are undulating but the final 2f are flat. It is generally reckoned a fairly easy course that demands adaptability more than stamina.

Clerk of the Course: Mr Bryan E. Robinson, 214-218 Shepherds Bush Road, London, W.6.

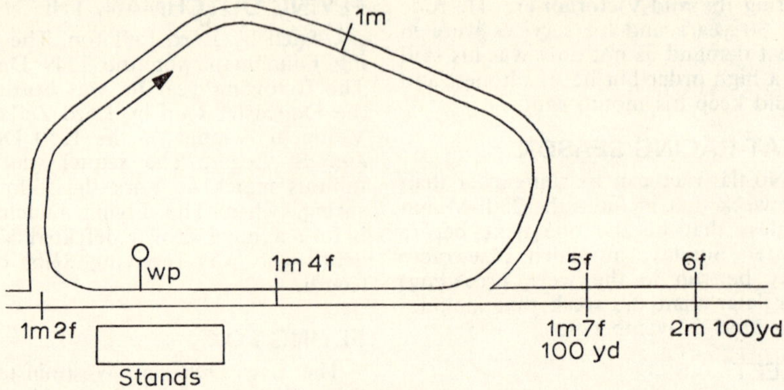

FOLKESTONE

Best Times:

Distance	*Horse-Age-Weight*	*Date*	*Time*
5f	Tammany 3-6-10	12-8-63	58.8
5f	Ragtags 2-9-0	18-7-60	59.6
6f	The Birdman 3-8-8	6-6-66	1min 10.6
6f	Pray Move 2-8-12	21-8-61	1min 11.4
10f	Marlhurst 4-8-1	4-7-66	2min 2.7
12f	Gamecourt 3-8-10	5-8-68	2min 33.3
15f 100 yd	Terrington 5-7-10	26-6-56	3min 21.4

FORDHAM, George (1837-1887)

George Fordham, one of the greatest of nineteenth-century riders, was born at Cambridge. He was very small indeed when he won his first race in 1851 at Brighton and the following year he won the Cambridgeshire at the astonishing weight of 3st 12lb. As he grew older and stronger his skill increased and in his prime he was inferior only to Fred Archer, and very little inferior at that. For years the Derby eluded him and in fact he retired without winning that race. However, unsuccessful business ventures compelled him to return to the saddle and at long last he achieved his great ambition and won the 'Blue Riband' on Sir Bevys in 1879.

His style was unique and by no means graceful but it was undoubtedly effective. His sense of timing was superb and again and again he got up in the last few strides to win by inches. He used the whip far less than most of his contemporaries and had the knack of getting the utmost from a horse while just riding it out with his hands. Much respected for his integrity, he loathed gambling and did all he could to stop his own son from coming into contact with the racing world. He died at Slough.

FOREIGN HORSES

A horse foaled elsewhere than in Great Britain, Ireland or the Channel Islands cannot be declared a runner for any race until certificates of pedigree and identification have been lodged at the Registry Office. A fee of five shillings is payable on each certificate.

FORFEIT LIST

The 'forfeit list' is a record of arrears published under the sanction of the Turf Authorities of Great Britain, Ireland and the Channel Islands. See Arrears and Entries, Forfeits and Declarations.

FORFEIT LIST, UNPAID

An Unpaid Forfeit List is kept at the Registry Office and is published in the *Sheet Calendar* after the Newmarket July Meeting and again at the conclusion of the racing season in every year. It includes all arrears that have been notified to the Stakeholder, or as otherwise provided under the Rules of Racing, and gives the names of the persons from whom, and the horses in respect of which the arrears are due. Arrears which have been so published must be paid directly into the Registry Office and until they have been thus paid they are not removed from the list.

When a person is prevented by the rules from entering or starting a horse for any race without paying arrears, for which he would not otherwise be liable, he may, by paying the same, enter or start the horse and place the arrears on the Forfeit List as due to himself, and in the same way the seller of a horse with engagements may, if compelled to pay them by the purchaser's default, place the amount on the Forfeit List, as due from the purchaser himself.

As long as the name of a person is in the Unpaid Forfeit List, or in the official Forfeit List published by the recognised Turf Authority of any country, he is a disqualified person.

A corrected alphabetical index of the horses and owners in the last Forfeit List and the Irish Forfeit List is published in the first *Calendar* of every month during the racing season. This monthly list commences not less than three years before the time of its publication and is carried down to and includes the latest Forfeit List published in the *Sheet Calendar*.

If a horse which, or the owner of which is in the Forfeit List, is entered for any race in contravention of the rules, the nominator of the horse is liable to a fine of £50.

FORLORN RIVER

Bred by Mr B. J. Fagan, Forlorn River was foaled in 1962. Though somewhat unfashionably bred, being by Fighting Don out of Starflight, by Black Rock, he proved an extremely good sprinter, winning 11 races worth over £14,000 including the July Cup, Nunthorpe Stakes and Challenge Stakes. He stands at the Cheveley Park Stud, Newmarket, at a fee of £350.

FORSTER, Lieut-Col Douglas, DSO (b 1902)

Lieut-Col Forster served in the 11th Hussars. He is a member of the Jockey Club and acts as steward at Ascot, Windsor and Newbury. He is father of the National Hunt trainer Timothy Forster. His horses are trained by J. A. J. Waugh. Colours: crimson, gold sleeves, hooped cap.

FORTH, John

Forth was probably the oldest man ever to ride a Derby winner as he was over 60 years of age when he trained Frederick and rode him to victory in the Derby of 1829.

FORTINO II

Fortino II, bred in France, is a grey by Grey Sovereign out of a mare by Relic. A fine sprinter, he won eight races worth over 173,000 NF. in France. He retired to the stud in 1963. He is syndicated and stood in Ireland till exported to Japan in 1970.

FOUR COURSE

Four Course, foaled in 1928, was bred by Mrs J. P. Arkwright and was by Tetratema out of Dinner, by Dinneford. In the colours of Lord Ellesmere she won the One Thousand Guineas, Gimcrack Stakes, Richmond Stakes and July Stakes. She was second in the Oaks. Unfortunately she died early in her stud career.

FOUR FURLONG RACE

The last four furlong race to be run under Jockey Club Rules was on 27th May 1912

FOX, Fred (1888-1945)

Fred Fox was born in Wiltshire. Apprenticed to Fred Pratt at Lambourn, he rode his first winner in 1907 and the following season won the Cesarewitch on Yentoi. For two years before World War I he rode in Germany and Austria for the von Weinberg stable but he had numerous pre-war successes in England, including the One Thousand Guineas on Atmah and the Gold Cup on Bomba and Aleppo.

From 1914 till he retired in 1936 he rode with much success in England. He won the Two Thousand Guineas on Diolite in 1930, the Derby on Cameronian in 1931, the Two Thousand Guineas and the Derby on Bahram in 1935, and the St Leger on Firdaussi in 1932. He rode five winners in a day at Sandown in 1929 and was Champion Jockey in 1930. A sound horseman—he rode regularly to hounds in the winter—he was never bothered by weight troubles and to the end of his career could go to scale without difficulty at 7st 7lb.

Affectionately known at 'The Mayor of Wantage', he became a Justice of the Peace. A thoroughly kindhearted and generous man, his closing years were saddened by the death of his son Michael who was killed while serving in the RAF. He himself was killed in a car accident.

FOXHUNTER

Foaled in 1929, Foxhunter was a half-brother by Foxlaw to Trimdon, who twice won the Ascot Gold Cup. Trained by Jack Jarvis for Mr E. Esmond, Foxhunter won the Ascot Gold Cup and the Doncaster Cup. He was at the stud firstly in France, secondly in England and finally in the Argentine. He did well in all three locations.

FOXLAW

Owned by Sir Abe Bailey and trained by Reg Day, Foxlaw was a fine stayer by Son-in-Law out of Alope, by Gallinule. He won the Ascot Gold Cup, Prince of Wales's Stakes, Northumberland Plate and Jockey Club Stakes. He died at the age of 13 but had done well in his comparatively brief spell at the stud.

FOY, B.

Attached to K. Cundell's stable. He can go to scale at 7st 12lb and won 19 races in 1969.

FRAMPTON, Tregonwell (1641-1727)

At his death, Tregonwell Frampton was described as 'Father of the Turf'. He trained for William III and held the post of Keeper of the Running Horses at Newmarket to Queen Anne, George I and George II. Born in Oxfordshire, the son of a country gentleman, he was equally devoted to field sports and to money. His appearance was unattractive as he habitually wore an expression in which meanness and guile seemed to battle for supremacy. He was eccentric in his dress and found women detestable.

He was very shrewd in matching his horses, betted heavily, and was rarely hampered by the exercise of moral scruples. He could be very cruel and it was sometimes said "that sin came upon the Turf with the advent of Frampton". However, he had an unrivalled knowledge of horses and he did much to improve the art of training. Bit by bit he succeeded in introducing rules and methodical procedure into racing. Respect for him, if not affection, increased with the years, and despite his many faults he unquestionably played a valuable part in the development of English racing.

FRANCIS, Richard Stanley

Dick Francis was born in 1920 and served in the RAF from 1940 to 1945. For many years a leading jockey under National Hunt rules, he has been a racing correspondent for the *Sunday Express* since 1957. He is the author of a number of highly successful racing thrillers.

FREDERICK, Duke of York

Frederick, Duke of York, one of the unattractive and unsatisfactory sons of George III, won the Derby with Prince Leopold in 1816 and with Moses in 1822. Prince Leopold actually ran in the name of Mr Lake. An inveterate gambler, the Duke left a mountain of debts behind him when he died. To discharge these debts, the Government is said to have ceded Cape Breton to his creditors.

FREE HANDICAP

A 'Free Handicap' is one in which no liability for stakes or forfeit is incurred until acceptance. At the end of each season the Jockey Club handicapper makes a free handicap of the leading three-year-olds and also of the leading two-year-olds, thereby providing an official estimate of the best performers, of both sexes, of those ages. The race for the Two-Year-Old Free Handicap is run over 7f at the Newmarket Craven Meeting the following April and is frequently a useful guide to the classics. There is no longer any actual race for the three-year-old free handicap.

FREER, Geoffrey Hubert (1887-1968)

Mr Geoffrey Freer was an outstanding racing official. From 1945 till 1962 he was the Jockey Club handicapper and was rated even superior to his uncle Mr T. F. Dawkins who had held that position from 1912 till 1931. Mr Freer was also at various times Clerk of the Course at Newmarket, Newbury, Manchester, Salisbury and Warwick. Immensely popular and with a wonderful dry sense of humour, he was rightly regarded as one of the wisest men in racing.

FRENCH BEIGE

Bred by Stenigot Ltd, French Beige was foaled in 1953 and is by Bois Roussel out of Nivea, by Nearco. A good, game stayer he won 12 races worth over £13,000 including the Gold Vase, Doncaster Cup and Jockey Club Cup. He was third in the St Leger. He stands at the Maiden Erleigh Stud, Berkshire, at a fee of £300. He is the sire of Mabel (£11,953) and French Possession (£11,947).

FRIAR MARCUS

Foaled in 1912, Friar Marcus, by Cicero out of Prim Nun, was bred at the Sandringham Stud and was probably the best colt ever owned by King George V. He had great speed and won nine races worth over £9,000 including the Middle Park Plate. He did well as a sire and among his offspring were the One Thousand Guineas winner Brown Betty and Friar's Daughter, dam of the 'Triple Crown' winner Bahram.

FRIAR'S DAUGHTER

Friar's Daughter, by Friar Marcus, was one of the late Aga Khan's cheaper purchases as she cost him only 240 gn as a yearling. Though of small account on the racecourse she proved a wonderful bargain as she bred the 'Triple Crown' winner Bahram as well as Dastur, second in the Two Thousand Guineas, Derby and the St Leger. She also bred Fille de Salut, grandam of Sunny Boy, a leading sire in France; and Fille d'Amour, grandam of The Phoenix, winner of the Irish Two Thousand Guineas and the Irish Derby.

FRIEZE

Frieze, foaled in 1949, was bred and owned by Capt A. M. Keith and was trained by Capt Charles Elsey. By Phideas out of Cornice, by Epigram, she won the Oaks and the Yorkshire Oaks. Her record at the stud has been disappointing.

FRITH, William Geoffrey (b 1903)

After considerable experience as a racing official in India, Mr Frith became Clerk of the Course at Manchester in 1947. He has been Clerk of the Course at Thirsk since 1959 and Managing Director of Thirsk since 1963.

FRIZETTE FAMILY

Frizette was foaled in 1905 and her descendants have achieved success in Great Britain, the United States and France. In England have been Baldric II (Two Thousand Guineas and Champion Stakes) and Black Tarquin (St Leger). In America there was the Kentucky Derby winner Jet Pilot. Good French winners from this family include Golestan, Tourbillon, Djeddah, Auriban, Corejada and Macip.

FULL DRESS II

Bred in 1966 at the White Lodge Stud and owned by Mr R. B. Moller, Full Dress II is a bay filly by Shantung out of Fusil, by Fidalgo. Trained by Harry Wragg, she won once as a two-year-old and the following season won the One Thousand Guineas Trial at Ascot and then the One Thousand Guineas, surviving an objection for boring and crossing in the latter event. After this she seemed to lose her form, failing in both the Oaks and the Coronation Stakes.

G

GAINSBOROUGH

Gainsborough, bred and owned by Lady James Douglas (q.v.), was by the St Leger winner Bayardo out of the Oaks winner Rosedrop. Trained by Alec Taylor and ridden by Joe Childs, he won a war-substitute 'Triple Crown' in 1918. As a sire he was a great success, being champion in 1932 and 1933, second in 1931, third in 1930 and 1935, and fourth in 1925, 1926 and 1927. His best winners were Hyperion (Derby and St Leger), Solario (St Leger and Gold Cup), Orwell (Two Thousand Guineas) and Singapore (St Leger). His fillies were markedly inferior to his colts, but two of his daughters bred Derby winners. Incidentally, Gainsborough was the first Derby winner to be owned by a woman.

GALATEA II

Owned and bred by Mr R. S. Clark and trained by Joe Lawson, Galatea II was by Dark Legend out of Galaday II, by Sir Gallahad III. A filly of the highest class, she won the One Thousand Guineas and the Oaks in 1939.

GALCADOR

Galcador, by Djebel out of Pharyva, by Pharos, won the 1950 Derby for his owner-breeder M. M. Boussac. Ridden by W. Johnstone and trained by C. Semblat in France, he started at 100-9 and beat the favourite Prince Simon by a head. He has proved a failure as a sire.

GALICIA

Mr A. W. Cox's Galicia is one of the most famous mares in the Stud Book. Foaled in 1898, she was by Galopin, who was 26 years old when she was born, out of Isoletta, by Isonomy. She bred Lemberg, who won six good races as a two-year-old, the Derby, the St James's Palace Stakes, the Eclipse Stakes (dead-heat), Jockey Club Stakes, Champion Stakes and Coronation Cup. She also bred an even better horse in Bayardo whose 22 victories included the National Breeders Produce Stakes, Middle Park Plate, Dewhurst Plate, Prince of Wales's Stakes, Eclipse Stakes, St Leger, Champion Stakes, Chester Vase and Ascot Gold Cup. Another of Galicia's sons, Kwang-Su, was second in the Two Thousand Guineas and the Derby. Her daughter Silesia bred the Oaks winner My Dear and was grandam of the brilliant Picaroon who won over £13,000 in stakes and died when in training.

GALIVANTER

Bred and owned by the late Major L. B. Holliday, Galivanter was foaled in 1956 and is by Golden Cloud out of Lycia, by Nearco. He was a high-class sprinter, winning nine races worth over £11,000 including the July Cup. He is syndicated for stud purposes and stands at the Hamilton Stud, Newmarket.

GALLINULE

Foaled in 1884, Gallinule was by Isonomy out of Moorhen, a very tough mare who won on the flat, including selling plates and hunters' flat-races, over hurdles and over fences. Gallinule was a good two-year-old but he went wrong in his wind and developed a tendency to break blood-vessels so it is hardly surprising he failed to win during the next three seasons. However, Capt Greer, later Sir Henry Greer, Director of the National Stud, thought he had possibilities as a sire and bought him for £1,000. Gallinule proved a wonderful investment as he sired four classic winners, including Pretty Polly, one of the greatest fillies of all time. He was on two occasions champion sire.

GALLOPER LIGHT

He is one of the few English horses to have won the Grand Prix de Paris at Longchamp this century, a feat he accomplished in 1919 when French racing had not recovered from the war. He was not on the whole a successful sire, but among his offspring was the Oaks winner Beam.

GALOPIN

Prince Batthyany's Galopin, by Vedette out of Flying Duchess, won the 1875 Derby trained by J. Dawson and ridden by Morris. After a slow start he became a highly successful sire and was champion on three occasions. He exercised a profound influence on bloodstock breeding as he sired the mighty St Simon (q.v.).

GALTEE MORE

Bred in Ireland by his owner Mr John Gubbins and trained at Beckhampton by Sam Darling, Galtee More won the 'Triple Crown' in 1897. At the end of his three-year-old season he was sold to the Russian Government for £21,000. He did well as a sire in Russia until the Russians exported him to Germany for £14,000.

GARDEN PATH

Bred by the late Lord Derby, Garden Path was by Fairway out of Ranai, by Rabelais, and thus a full sister of the Derby winner Watling Street. Trained by Walter Earl, she won the 1944 Two Thousand Guineas. She bred five winners, of which Leading Light, by Hyperion, won over £4,000 in stakes.

GASELEE, Nicholas (b 1939)

Nicholas Gaselee served for six years in the Life Guards. A leading amateur rider under National Hunt rules, in 1965 he joined the *Evening Standard*. In 1968 he was appointed assistant to Hon N. Beaumont, Clerk of the Course at Ascot. He is a brother-in-law of the trainer Peter Walwyn.

GAY CRUSADER

Gay Crusader, bred and owned by Mr Fairie (the *nom-de-course* of Mr A. W. Cox) and trained by Alec Taylor at Manton, won the 'Triple Crown' in 1917. He was not a success as a sire.

GELDING

Geldings tend to maintain their zest for racing longer than do entire horses, but because of the breeding aspect they cannot be entered for certain major events, including the classics.

GEORGE V, KING (1865-1936)

George V was keener on racing than many people imagined although, unlike his father, he was unattracted by the smart racing set. He was fond of horses, a good judge of them, and he possessed a fair knowledge of the Stud Book. In particular he liked Newmarket and staying informally at the Jockey Club Rooms. Best of all he enjoyed going round stables quietly in the evening. He never had much luck as an owner and his best horses were Friar Marcus, who was unbeaten as a two-year-old and was later a successful sire; Scuttle, who won the One Thousand Guineas; Weathervane, winner of the Royal Hunt Cup; and Limelight, winner of the Jersey Stakes, Hardwicke Stakes and Newbury Spring Cup. His trainers were Richard Marsh and William Jarvis.

On his coronation, the lads at Newmarket subscribed sixpence each and gave him a pair of raceglasses. He was greatly touched by this, and of all the thousands of presents he received, this was the one he insisted on giving thanks for in person.

GEORGE VI, KING (1895-1952)

King George VI won four of the five classic races in 1942. Big Game won the Two Thousand Guineas; Sun Chariot won the One Thousand Guineas, Oaks and St Leger. Both were leased from the National Stud and were trained by Fred Darling. He also won the One Thousand Guineas with Hypericum whom he had bred himself and was trained by Sir Cecil Boyd-Rochfort.

GEORGE, Prince of Wales

The first success gained by the royal colours in the Derby was that of the Prince of Wales's Sir Thomas in 1788. The Prince began racing in 1784 at the age of 21. His ownership was conducted in absurdly extravagant fashion and two years later he was heavily in debt. However, he was rescued by Parliament and restored to solvency. In 1790 he ran no fewer than 39 horses. The following year came the scandal over the in-and-out running of his horse Escape at Newmarket. This separated him temporarily from the Turf although it must be emphasised that his own integrity was never called in question. The Prince of Wales later became Prince Regent and subsequently King George IV.

GIBSON, Major W. D. (b 1925)

Major Gibson served in the Welsh Guards from 1944 to 1957. He rode under National Hunt rules winning the Grand Military Gold Cup at Sandown four times. He is a member of the Jockey Club and has been Senior Steward of the National Hunt Committee. His flat-race horses are trained by W. Wightman. On the amalgamation of the Jockey Club with the National Hunt Committee in 1969 he became a Deputy Senior Steward of the Jockey Club. Colours: black; red, white and blue sash and cap.

GILLES DE RETZ

Gilles de Retz was bred by the Eveton Stud and is by Royal Charger out of Ma Soeur Anne, by Majano. Owned by Mr A. G. Samuel, trained by C. Jerdein and ridden by Frank Barlow, he won the 1956 Two Thousand Guineas at 50-1. His subsequent career was disappointing. He failed to make much mark as a sire and was exported to Japan in 1965.

GILPIN, Peter Purcell

Peter Gilpin served for some time in the 5th Lancers and was a successful amateur rider. After marriage, he left the army and began training at the Curragh where he soon established his reputation. On moving to Newmarket he was equally successful; he won the Derby with Spearmint (1906), who also won the Grand Prix, and with Spion Kop (1920). He also trained the immortal Pretty Polly, one of the outstanding fillies of this century and winner of the One Thousand Guineas, Oaks and St Leger. Gilpin had a second Grand Prix success when he won the race with Comrade, bought for 25 gn as a yearling. Comrade also won the Prix de l'Arc de Triomphe. On his retirement in the 1920s, Gilpin's stable, Clarehaven at Newmarket, was taken over by his son Victor who, however, gave up training during World War II.

GIMCRACK

Gimcrack, who stood only just over 14 hands, was a famous racehorse of the eighteenth century. His fame is commemorated in the Gimcrack Stakes at York. At the annual dinner of the Gimcrack Club in December, it is a tradition that the main speech of the evening is made by the guest of honour, the owner of the winner of that year's Gimcrack Stakes.

For details of the Gimcrack Stakes see YORK.

GINISTRELLI, the Chevalier

The Chevalier Ginistrelli came to England from Italy in the 1880s and trained a few horses for himself at Newmarket. He was not taken very seriously by the racing world but he undoubtedly knew his job and he had a wonderful triumph in 1908 when he won the Derby and the Oaks with Signorinetta, whom he had bred himself. In both races Signorinetta was ridden to victory by William Bullock, who certainly did not profit financially, the Chevalier evidently considering that presents for jockeys were unnecessary.

GLADIATEUR

Owned and bred by Comte F. de Lagrange, Gladiateur was foaled in 1862 and was the first French-bred horse to win the Derby, an event that aroused immense enthusiasm in France and inflicted a painful blow to English self-esteem. Gladiateur was indeed a remarkable horse as he suffered from chronic lameness yet besides winning the Derby, he won the Two Thousand Guineas, the St Leger, the Grand Prix and the Ascot Gold Cup, a record that remains unequalled. Not for nothing was he called 'The Avenger of Waterloo' and his statue occupies a prominent place in the paddock at Longchamp. Rumours that he was a four-year-old when he won the Derby had no foundation in fact and stemmed from the chagrin of defeat at the hands of a foreigner.

GLADNESS

Gladness, bred in England by Mr S. McGregor and Mr T. Venn and trained in Ireland by Vincent O'Brien, was a very good staying mare by Sayajurao out of Bright Lady, by April the Fifth. Foaled in 1953, she won eight races worth over £27,000, including the Ascot Gold Cup, Goodwood Cup and the Ebor Handicap. She was also second in the Prix du Cadran and in the King George VI and Queen Elizabeth Stakes. Her daughter Merry Mate, by Ballymoss, won the 1966 Irish Oaks.

GLAD RAGS

Bred in 1963 at the Airlie Stud, Glad Rags, a chestnut filly by High Hat out of Dryad, by Panorama, was bought for 6,800 gn as a yearling on behalf of Mrs J. P. Mills. Trained by Vincent O'Brien and ridden by Paul Cook, she won the 1966 One Thousand Guineas at 100-6, beating Berkeley Springs by a neck.

GLANELY, Lord (1868-1942)

Lord Glanely, who was killed in an air-raid in 1942, was born William Tatem. A Cardiff ship-owner, he was a vigorous, forceful personality and was raised to the peerage in 1918. After World War I he was an owner and breeder on a very lavish scale indeed and spent quite a fortune on bloodstock. On the racecourse he was irreverently but affectionately known as 'Guts and Gaiters'. He won the 1919 Derby with Grand Parade. Other notable winners were Rose of England (Oaks), Colombo (Two Thousand Guineas), Singapore (St Leger), Chulmleigh (St Leger) and Dancing Time (One Thousand Guineas).

GLOVER, Major Gerald (b 1908)

Major Glover is a lawyer and landowner. He has horses with T. A. Waugh and F. L. Cundell and won the Two Thousand Guineas in 1962 with Privy Councillor. He is a steward at Folkestone and is the owner of the Pytchley House Stud. Colours: white, maroon hoops on body, white cap.

GODDARD, E. C. (b 1908)

Ted Goddard served his apprenticeship with Colledge Leader. From 1928 to 1948 he assisted Capt A. B. Holland at West Horsley and for him he rode a number of winners over hurdles. He started training himself at West Horsley in 1949 and among the good horses with which he has been associated are

Robson's Choice (Chesterfield Cup), Q.C. (Bessborough Stakes), and Tubalcain (Ascot Stakes, Queen Alexandra Stakes and the Greenall Whitley Gold Trophy). His owners include Mr S. A. Thorne, Miss P. M. Rogers, Mr P. Lee, Mrs Eileen Robinson, Mr Jabez Barker and Mr S. N. Weston. In his younger days he was a very competent boxer.

GODIVA

Godiva, by Hyperion out of Carpet Slipper, by Phalaris, was foaled in 1937. Owned by Lord Rothermere and trained by W. Jarvis, she won the One Thousand Guineas and the Oaks in 1940. She was a high-mettled, temperamental filly with a strong will of her own and in both her classic successes she was ridden by D. Marks, then a little-known apprentice and now a successful trainer. Godiva unfortunately died before she went to the stud.

GOLD BRIDGE

Foaled in 1929, Gold Bridge was by Swynford or Golden Boss out of Flying Diadem, by Diadumenos. An exceptionally handsome chestnut horse, Gold Bridge was a top-class sprinter and later a highly successful sire. Golden Boss incidentally was a nine guineas sire that met with such scant success that he was sold as a remount sire to the American Government. Among the sons of Gold Bridge, Golden Cloud and Vilmorin were both successful sires.

GOLDEN CORN

Golden Corn was the first of the many good winners trained by Sir Cecil Boyd-Rochfort. By Golden Sun, she was a very fast two-year-old, winning five races including the Middle Park Stakes in 1921. As a four-year-old she won the July Cup. She was not a success as a brood mare.

GOLDEN MYTH

Sir George Bullough's Golden Myth was the horse that established Sir Jack Jarvis's reputation as a trainer. By Tredennis out of Golden Lily, by Persimmon, he was a really good four-year-old and in 1922 won the Queen's Prize, Gold Vase, Gold Cup and Eclipse Stakes. It was a remarkable performance to win the 1¼m Eclipse only a month after the 2½m Gold Cup. He was a sad failure as a sire.

GONDOLETTE

Gondolette, by Loved One out of Dongola, is one of the most famous mares in the Stud Book. She was bought for 75 gn as a yearling by Mr George Edwards of Gaiety Theatre fame and he resold her for 360 gn to Col W. Hall-Walker (later Lord Wavertree) for whom she bred Great Sport and Let Fly, both placed in the Derby, and Dolabella, dam of the very fast Myrobella who bred the Two Thousand Guineas winner Big Game.

In 1912 Lord Derby purchased Gondolette who was then ten years old. She bred six winners for him including Serenissima, Ferry (One Thousand Guineas) and the 1924 Derby winner Sansovino. Serenissima bred eight winners of 40 races worth over £47,000 including Bosworth (Gold Cup), Tranquil (One Thousand Guineas and St Leger), and Selene, who won £14,000 in stakes and bred Hyperion, winner of the Derby and the St Leger, to say nothing of Sickle and Pharamond, both successful sires in the United States, and Hunters Moon, a leading sire in the Argentine.

GOODISON, Tom (1782-1840)

Tom Goodison was the son of Dick Goodison, a blunt, rough-tongued Yorkshireman who for years was trainer and jockey to the Duke of Queensberry, commonly known as 'Old Q'. Tom, a sound rider, was retained for many years by the Duke of York and he also rode frequently for the Duke of Grafton and Sir Charles Bunbury. He rode four Derby winners—Pope (1809), Smolensko (1813), Whisker (1815) and Moses (1822).

GOODWILL, A. W. (b 1911)

'Fiddler' Goodwill is said to have earned the nickname by which he is widely known when he arrived as an apprentice at Harvey Leader's stable with a violin in his luggage. For a short time he rode on the flat and for a much longer period under National Hunt rules. From 1933-39 and from 1945-46 he rode jumpers for T. Leader. He took out a licence to train in 1945 and has earned a reputation for his skill in placing moderate horses to the best possible advantage. On 1st August 1966 he trained four winners with four runners at Wolverhampton. His owners include Lady Cambridge, Miss C. G. French, Mrs J. Gilbert, Mrs D. Carvalho and Mr Stuart May. His stables are at Sackville House, Newmarket.

GOODWOOD

Admittedly Goodwood is not the most easily accessible of courses, but it is beyond question the loveliest in England. Laid out on the Duke of Richmond's estate some five miles from Chichester, it overlooks a superb stretch of the Sussex countryside with hardly a house to be seen, while behind the stands in the valley lies Chichester Cathedral and beyond it the Solent. It is a gay sight on a fine summer afternoon when the crowds throng Trundle Hill as they do the Epsom Downs during Derby week.

The course was laid out by the third Duke of Richmond and the first meeting, organised by members of the Goodwood Hunt and officers of the Sussex Militia, took place in 1801. Goodwood has come a long way since then and its successful development was due largely to the energy and organising ability of Lord George Bentinck (q.v.). The five-day meeting at the end of July provides sport that is not far short of Royal Ascot standard, while at the same time there is a pleasing air of holiday informality. The other meetings are of less significance, but the £13,700 Wills Mile,

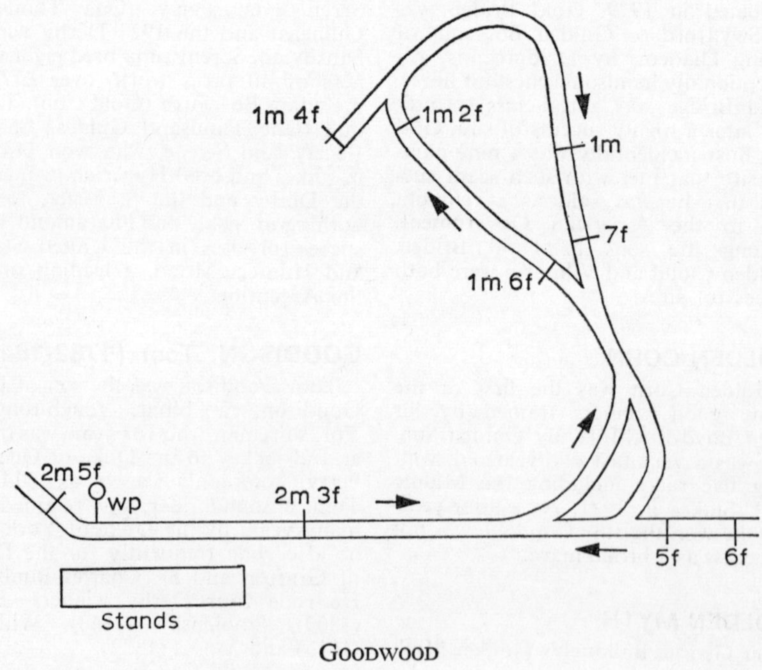

GOODWOOD

sponsored by W. D. and H. O. Wills Ltd, attracts strong competition and has given a big boost to the second August fixture.

At the big meeting perhaps the most popular event is the 6f Stewards Cup, a handicap that always secures a big field and inspires some lively betting. The Goodwood Cup, still started by flag, is a prestige race for stayers, while the Sussex Stakes, with £17,000 added, is one of the most important and keenly contested mile races of the season. The programme was temporarily strengthened by the institution of the £10,000 *News of the World* Stakes, a 10f handicap for three-year-olds, but that event was run for the last time in 1969. However, its place has been taken by another sponsored event, the £10,000 Extel Stakes.

The Cup Course is about 2m 5f. It starts below the winning post and runs the reverse way of the course, turning left after about 4f and returning to the straight 5f run-in by the top bend. The Stakes Course is the last 2m 3f, the Bentinck Course the last 1m 6f, and the Gratwicke Course the last 1m 4f of the Cup Course. The Craven Course is 1¼m, starting in almost the same place as the Gratwicke Course but running in the reverse direction and returning to the straight 5f run-in by the top bend. The Old Mile starts on the Cup Course and joins the 5f course on the lower bend. The 5f and 6f (Stewards Cup) courses are dead straight, the first furlong of the latter being uphill, followed by a descent for 4f. High numbers are favoured over 5f and 6f. Both sprint courses are fast and demand a quick start.

Clerk of the Course: Mr R. A. Hubbard, Estate Office, Goodwood. Tel: Chichester 7107.

Best Times:

Distance	*Horse-Age-Weight*	*Date*	*Time*
5f	Secret Step 4-9-6	31-7-63	57.8
5f	Crimea II 2-8-11	30-7-63	58.4
6f	Sky Diver 5-7-6	30-7-68	1min 11
6f	Welsh Pageant 2-8-4	30-7-68	1min 11.8
8f	Petingo 3-8-4	31-7-68	1min 39
10f	Finalist 5-9-7	30-7-37	2min 7
11f 200yd	Karabas 3-8-3	30-7-68	2min 35.1
14f	Almeria 3-8-5	30-7-57	3min 4.4
19f	Fearless Fox 4-9-2	29-7-37	4min 42
21f	Acharacle 4-8-7	31-7-64	4min 11.1

Stewards Cup, 6f

Handicap. First run 1840. *No race* 1940 *to* 1945.

	OWNER	TRAINER	JOCKEY	SP
1930 Le Phare, 4–8–1	Aga Khan	R. Dawson	M. Beary	100–6
1931 Poor Lad, 4–7–11	Sir H. C-Owen	O. Bell	S. Wragg	9–1
1932 Solenoid, 3–7–10	Mrs C. Mackean	G. Poole	T. Barber	33–1
1933 Pharacre, 4–7–5	Capt A. Wills	Fred Butters	F. Fox	22–1
1934 Figaro, 4–8–5	J. Leach	J. Leach	T. Weston	100–7
1935 Greenore, 6–8–8	Lady Ludlow	O. Bell	S. Wragg	7–1
1936 Solerina, 4–8–11	C. Mackean	H. Cottrill	E. Smith	10–1
1937 Firozepore, 3–8–3	R. Strassburger	F. Darling	G. Richards	100–8
1938 Harmachis, 5–7–6	Mrs G. Farrand	B. Bullock	P. Evans	100–7
1939 Knight's Caprice, 4–8–6	Col T. Clarke	R. Dawson	J. Canty	100–8
1946 Commissar, 6–7–12	A. Budgett	E. Stedall	A. Richardson	10–1
1947 Closeburn, 3–8–10	R. White	N. Murless	G. Richards	100–7
1948 Dramatic, 3–7–7	A. Saunders	G. Todd	E. Smith	9–1
1949 The Bite, 4–7–7	Mrs W. Armstrong	J. Wood	H. Packham	33–1
1950 First Consul, 4–8–13	Maharaja of Rajpipla	F. Armstrong	E. Britt	100–9
1951 Sugar Bowl, 4–7–12	J. Gerber	F. Armstrong	W. Snaith	100–6
1952 Smokey Eyes, 5–8–10	D. Robinson	R. Jarvis	C. Smirke	100–7

Stewards Cup (contd)

	OWNER	TRAINER	JOCKEY	SP
1953 Palpitate, 4–7–13	F. Armstrong	F. Armstrong	W. Snaith	5–1
1954 Ashurst Wonder, 4–6–11	R. Merrick	L. Hall	A. Shrive	50–1
1955 King Bruce, 4–8–11	W. Tarry	P. H-Bass	W. Rickaby	100–6
1956 Matador, 3–9–2	S. Joel	J. A. Waugh	E. Smith	100–8
1957 Arcandy, 4–8–9	Mrs M. Linde	G. Beeby	T. Gosling	100–7
1958 Epaulette, 7–9–0	J. Gerber	W. O'Gorman	F. Durr	33–1
1959 Tudor Monarch, 4–7–13	Sir W. Churchill	W. Nightingall	G. Lewis	25–1
1960 Monet, 3–8–5	Sir P. Dunn	J. Tree	J. Lindley	20–1
1961 Skymaster, 3–8–12	W. Kelly	G. Smyth	A. Breasley	100–7
1962 Victorina, 3–8–9	Sir B. Mountain	P. Nelson	W. Williamson	10–1
1963 Creole, 4–9–1	Lord Rosebery	J. Jarvis	S. Smith	20–1
1964 Dunme, 5–7–12	J. Simmons	R. Read	P. Cook	9–1
1965 Potier, 3–8–5	T. Blackwell	J. Jarvis	R. Hutchinson	100–7
1966 Patient Constable, 3–7–7	I. Allen	R. Smyth	R. Reader	33–1
1967 Sky Diver, 4–7–5	J. Fane	P. P-Gallwey	D. Cullen	20–1
1968 Sky Diver, 5–7–6	J. Fane	P. P-Gallwey	T. Sturrock	100–6
1969 Royal Smoke, 3–7–9	I. Allen	W. A. O'Gorman	M. Thomas	100–7

Sussex Stakes, 1m

Three-year-olds and four-year-olds. Three-year-olds only until 1959. *First run* 1841. *No race* 1940 *to* 1945.

	OWNER	TRAINER	JOCKEY	SP
1930 Paradine, 3–9–1	W. Cazalet	J. Lawson	R. Jones	13–8
1931 Inglesant, 3–8–5	S. Tattersall	J. Lawson	R. Jones	10–11
1932 Dastur, 3–9–3	Aga Khan	Fk. Butters	M. Beary	8–15
1933 The Abbot, 3–8–13	King George V	W. Jarvis	J. Childs	11–2
1934 Badruddin, 3–9–3	Aga Khan	Fk. Butters	F. Fox	2–5
1935 Hairan, 3–8–12	Aga Khan	Fk. Butters	R. Perryman	6–4
1936 Corpach, 3–8–2	Lord Astor	J. Lawson	G. Richards	4–1
1937 Pascal, 3–9–3	H. Morris	F. Darling	G. Richards	5–2
1938 Faroe, 3–9–1	Lord Derby	C. Leader	R. Perryman	20–1
1939 Olein, 3–9–5	Lord Glanely	B. Jarvis	T. Lowrey	7–4
1946 Radiotherapy, 3–9–3	T. Lilley	F. Templeman	G. Richards	7–4
1947 Combat, 3–9–3	J. Dewar	F. Darling	G. Richards	8–13
1948 My Babu, 3–9–8	Maharaja of Baroda	F. Armstrong	C. Smirke	1–3
1949 Krakatao, 3–9–1	Lord Feversham	N. Murless	G. Richards	2–11
1950 Palestine, 3–9–8	Aga Khan	M. Marsh	C. Smirke	1–2
1951 Le Sage, 3–9–3	S. Sanger	T. Carey	G. Richards	6–4
1952 Agitator, 3–9–1	J. Dewar	N. Murless	G. Richards	8–15
1953 King of the Tudors, 3–8–10	F. Dennis	W. Stephenson	C. Spares	11–10
1954 Landau, 3–9–1	The Queen	N. Murless	W. Snaith	6–4
1955 My Kingdom, 3–8–9	J. Armstrong	W. Nightingall	D. Smith	13–2
1956 Lucero, 3–9–1	G. Oldham	H. Wragg	E. Mercer	8–1
1957 Quorum, 3–9–1	T. Farr	W. Lyde	A. Russell	10–11
1958 Major Portion, 3–9–7	H. Joel	T. Leader	E. Smith	–11
1959 Petite Etoile, 3–9–4	Aly Khan	N. Murless	L. Piggott	8–10
1960 Venture VII, 3–8–4	Aga Khan	A. Head	G. Moore	1–13
1961 Le Levanstell, 4–8–10	J. McGrath	S. McGrath	W. Williamson	108–7
1962 Romulus, 3–8–4	C. Engelhard	R. J. Houghton	W. Swinburn	0–1
1963 Queen's Hussar, 3–8–3	Lord Carnarvon	T. Corbett	R. Hutchinson	9 25–1
1964 Roan Rocket, 3–8–5	T. Frost	G. Todd	L. Piggott	4–6
1965 Carlemont, 3–8–3	L. Gelb	P. Prendergast	R. Hutchinson	7–2
1966 Paveh, 3–8–3	P. Widener	T. Ainsworth	R. Hutchinson	5–1
1967 Reform, 3–8–3	M. Sobell	Sir G. Richards	A. Breasley	evens
1968 Petingo, 3–8–4	Capt M. Lemos	.. ..	L. Piggott	6–4
1969 Jimmy Reppin, 4–9–4	Mrs S. Bates	J. Sutcliffe, Jn.	G. Lewis	7–4

Goodwood Stakes, 2m 3f

Handicap. First run 1823. *No race* 1940 *to* 1945.

		OWNER	TRAINER	JOCKEY	SP
1930	Joyous Greetings, 6–7–2	Mrs C. Glorney	F. Sneyd	J. Dines	100–7
1931	Noble Star, 4–8–11	F. Cundell	L. Cundell	F. Fox	4–1
1932	Forum II, 5–6–8	Capt H. Wilson	C. Leader	W. Rickaby	20–1
1933	Prince Oxenden, 5–7–13	C. Jackson	V. Smyth	J. Caldwell	100–6
1934	Claran, 5–7–13	H. Sutton	R. Gooch	F. Fox	6–1
1935	Hoplite, 4–8–11	Capt L. Montagu	H. Cottrill	H. Wragg	100–6
1936	Avondale, 8–7–4	Lady H. McCalmont	G. Lambton	P. Maher	100–8
1937	Epigram, 4–7–8	J. Rank	N. Cannon	P. Maher	5–1
1938	Naval Display, 4–7–12	Lord Glanely	T. Hogg	M. Beary	100–9
1938	Snake Lightning, 4–7–9	Sir H. Gray	V. Gilpin	E. Smith	10–1
1939	Valedictory, 4–7–13	J. Whitney	C. B-Rochfort	W. Nevett	100–9
1946	Reynard Volant, 4–8–10	Sir J. Jarvis	J. Jarvis	E. Smith	7–4
1947	Strathmore, 4–6–10	D. H-Hutchinson	R. Bennett	T. Sidebotham	100–8
1948	Auralia, 5–9–6	Mrs A. Johnstone	R. Day	D. Smith	100–8
1949	Harlech, 4–8–8	Mrs E. Williams	E. Williams	C. Elliott	9–2
1950	Strathspey, 5–9–0	J. Rank	N. Cannon	A. Breasley	3–1
1951	Veuillin, 4–7–13	R. Costain	J. Bisgood	E. Mercer	8–1
1952	French Design, 5–6–12	S. Banks	G. Todd	R. Arnold	100–8
1953	Papillio, 4–8–6	Sir H. de Trafford	C. B-Rochfort	W. Carr	11–2
1954	Osborne, 7–9–7	Brig W. Wyatt	C. B-Rochfort	W. Carr	100–7
1955	French Design, 8–8–7	S. Banks	G. Todd	V. Gardner	9–1
1956	Terrington, 5–6–10	E. Somers	W. Marshall	N. Pearson	100–6
1957	Persian Flag, 4–8–7	Col F. Halse	W. Nightingall	W. Carr	13–2
1958	Predominate, 6–8–8	H. Joel	T. Leader	E. Smith	100–9
1959	Predominate, 7–9–5	H. Joel	T. Leader	E. Smith	3–1
1960	Predominate, 8–9–5	H. Joel	T. Leader	E. Smith	15–8
1961	Alcove, 4–8–5	Lord Derby	J. Watts	D. Smith	11–2
1962	Golden Fire, 4–7–10	G. Ridley	D. Marks	D. Yates	13–2
1963	Golden Fire, 5–8–6	G. Ridley	D. Marks	D. Yates	10–1
1964	Tree Leopard, 4–8–8	Lord Durham	W. Hern	J. Mercer	100–8
1965	Gold Aura, 5–7–12	The Queen	C. B-Rochfort	S. Clayton	5–1
1966	All Found, 4–7–6	H. Blagrave	H. Blagrave	D. Maitland	10–1
1967	Tubulcain, 6–8–13	H. Fellowes	E. Goddard	G. Lewis	8–1
1968	Acharacle, 4–8–7	J. K. Munro	T. Leader	B. Taylor	100–8
1969	Amberwood, 4–8–0	Col J. Clague	C. Benstead	A. Errington	7–1

Goodwood Cup, 2m 5f

First run 1812. *No race* 1940 *to* 1945.

		OWNER	TRAINER	JOCKEY	SP
1930	Brown Jack, 6–9–7	Sir H. Wernher	I. Anthony	S. Donoghue	4–9
1931	Salmon Leap, 4–9–3	Mrs A. James	G. Lambton	T. Weston	5–2
1932	Brulette, 4–9–4	Lord Woolavington	F. Darling	G. Richards	5–2
1933	Sans Peine, 3–7–11	E. Esmond	J. Jarvis	E. Smith	20–1
1934	Loosestrife, 5–9–6	P. Johnson	E. Richards	G. Richards	11–2
1935	Tiberius, 4–9–7	Sir A. Bailey	J. Lawson	T. Weston	2–9
1936	Cecil, 5–9–6	Sir A. Bailey	J. Lawson	T. Weston	13–8
1937	Fearless Fox, 4–9–2	A. Smith	J. Jarvis	E. Smith	6–1
1938	Epigram, 5–9–6	J. Rank	N. Cannon	B. Carslake	6–1
1939	Dubonnet, 4–8–1	J. Hornung	B. Jarvis	T. Lowrey	6–4
1946	Marysas II, 6–9–11	M. Boussac	C. Semblat	C. Elliott	1–3
1947	Monsieur l'Amiral, 6–9–2	Mrs I. Henderson	E. Charlier	C. Smirke	1–2
1948	Tenerani, 4–8–12	F. Tesio	N. Bertie	E. Camici	100–30

Goodwood Cup (contd)	OWNER	TRAINER	JOCKEY	SP
1949 Alycidon, 4–8–12 ..	Lord Derby	W. Earl	D. Smith.. ..	30–100
1950 Val Drake, 4–8–12 .	Mme L. Volterra..	R. Carver ..	R. Poincelet ..	4–1
1951 Pan II, 4–8–12 . ..	E. Constant	E. Pollet	R. Poincelet ..	5–6
1952 Medway, 4–8–12 ..	P. Bartholomew ..	F. Winter . ..	D. Smith.. ..	5–1
1953 Souepi, 5–9–0	G. Digby	G. Digby . ..	C. Elliott . ..	2–1
1954 Blarney Stone, 5–9–0	M. McAlpine ..	V. Smyth . ..	W. Rickaby ..	13–2
1955 Double Bore, 4–9–0	J. Tree	J. Tree	T. Gosling ..	9–1
1956 Zarathustra, 5–9–0 .	T. Gray..	C. B-Rochfort .	W. Carr	10–11
1957 Tenterhooks, 3–7–10	Lord Allendale ..	C. Elsey	E. Britt	2–1
1958 Gladness, 5–8–11 ..	J. McShain	V. O'Brien ..	L. Piggott ..	1–2
1959 Dickens, 3–7–10 ..	Lady Z. Wernher .	C. B-Rochfort .	D. Smith.. ..	9–4
1960 Exar, 4–9–0	Dr C. Vittadini ..	N. Murless ..	L. Piggott ..	4–9
1961 Predominate, 9–9–0 .	H. Joel	T. Leader . ..	E. Smith . ..	11–4
1962 Sagacity, 4–9–0 ..	Lady Cholmondeley	C. B-Rochfort .	W. Carr	5–1
1963 Trelawny, 7–9–0 ..	Mrs L. Carver ..	G. Todd	A. Breasley ..	8–13
1964 Raise You Ten, 4–9–0	P. Widener	C. B-Rochfort .	S. Clayton ..	evens
1965 Apprentice, 5–9–0 ..	The Queen	C. B-Rochfort .	S. Clayton ..	8–1
1966 Gaulois, 3–7–10 ..	The Queen	C. B-Rochfort .	R. Hutchinson	15–2
1967 Wrekin Rambler, 4–9–0	G. C. Murphy ..	Sir G. Richards	A. Breasley ..	2–1
1968 Ovaltine, 4–9–0 ..	G. Cooper	J. F. Watts ..	B. Taylor . ..	5–2
1969 Richmond Fair, 5–9–0	T. Blackwell . ..	B. Hobbs . ..	J. Gorton . ..	5–4

News Of The World Stakes, 1m 2f

Three-year-old Handicap. First run 1962.

	OWNER	TRAINER	JOCKEY	SP
1962 Tamerlo, 9–0	M. Sobell	Sir G. Richards	A. Breasley ..	100–7
1963 Fraxinus, 7–7	Mrs W. Wightman	W. Wightman .	D. Yates . ..	25–1
1964 French Possession, 7–9	R. Dennis	G. Brooke ..	D. Smith.. ..	20–1
1965 Super Sam, 7–9 ..	C. Cooper	J. Watts	P. Robinson ..	5–1
1966 Le Cordonnier, 9–2 .	Mrs S. Jacobson ..	S. Ingham ..	G. Lewis . ..	100–7
1967 Sucaryl, 8–8	Lady Sassoon ..	N. Murless ..	G. Moore ..	5–6
1968 Principal Boy, 8–1 ..	Lady Hothfield ..	J. Clayton ..	E. Eldin	4–1
1969 Irish Mail II, 8–0 ..	A. J. M-Buchanan	J. A. J. Waugh	E. Eldin	7–1

GOODWOOD CUP

See under GOODWOOD.

GOODWOOD STAKES

See under GOODWOOD.

GORTON, Major H. V. H.

Inspector of Courses under the Rules of Racing.

GORTON, John (b 1926)

Born in South Africa, John Gorton had his first full season's riding in England in 1969. He had come over for a few weeks in the autumn some years previously and had made an excellent impression by his competence and his agreeable personality. It was actually Sir Jack Jarvis who persuaded him to ride in England and on Sir Jack's death in December 1968, it was arranged that Gorton should ride Lord Rosebery's horses, which had then been taken over by Douglas Smith. He also received a retainer from Bruce Hobbs.

Gorton certainly made the most of his opportunities. Particularly before the coughing epidemic, he enjoyed a great run of success on Lord Rosebery's horses and he won the Lingfield Oaks Trial, the Oaks and Ribblesdale Stakes on Sleeping Partner. At Goodwood he rode a brilliant race on Mr

Blackwell's Richmond Fair to win the Goodwood Cup.

In South Africa Gorton received much help and advice from the former English jockey Fred Rickaby, who now trains there. He is well educated and extremely intelligent, and as he has no weight troubles, no doubt his services will continue to be in high demand. He rode 56 winners in 1969.

GOSDEN, John Montague (1904-1968)

'Towser' Gosden, as he was always known on the racecourse, made a name for himself in the 1920s as an amateur rider under National Hunt rules and from 1924 to 1927 he assisted the Lewes trainer, G. C. Poole. He himself began training at Lewes in 1928 and up till World War II he conducted an extremely successful jumping stable. After the war his stable became a 'mixed' one but in the end he dropped the jumpers and concentrated on the flat. A dedicated professional, he was an extremely skilful trainer, equally at home with a high-class horse or placing moderate performers to the best advantage in small handicaps. Among the good horses he trained were Aggressor (King George VI and Queen Elizabeth Stakes and Hardwicke Stakes); Impatient (Hardwicke Stakes); Tintinnabulum (Manchester Cup, twice); Orthopaedic (Ayr Gold Cup); Precious Heather (Ayr Gold Cup); Damredub (Manchester November Handicap); Concealdem (Ovaltine Manchester Handicap) and Tahiri (City and Suburban). He trained the 1966 Derby winner Charlottown as a two-year-old, but ill-health compelled him to retire at the end of that season, the stable being taken over by Gordon Smyth.

GOSLING, Capt H. M.

Capt Gosling served for five years in the 11th Hussars and was a competent amateur rider under National Hunt rules. He was elected a member of the National Hunt Committee in 1965 and became a steward of that body in 1966. On the amalgamation of the Jockey Club with the National Hunt Committee in 1969, he became a Steward of the Jockey Club. His trainer is Frank Cundell. Colours: crimson, gold striped sleeves, quartered cap.

GOSLING, Tommy (b 1926)

Tommy Gosling was apprenticed to Capt O. M. D. Bell at Lambourn. He was a strong, competent rider and was for many years associated with Walter Nightingall's stable, scoring many wins on Sir Winston Churchill's stouthearted grey stayer Colonist II. In 1945 he shared the position of top apprentice with F. Durr. In 1964 he set up as a trainer at Priam Lodge, Epsom, and among the good races he has won have been the Greenham Stakes with Excel; the Irish One Thousand Guineas with Ardent Dancer; and the Vaux Gold Tankard and Yorkshire Cup with Quartette. His owners include Mr H. L. Vickery, Mr L. Sainer, Mr A. Sainer, Mr J. Levy, Mr P. Ambrose, Mr K. B. Huber, and Mr and Mrs Threadwell.

GRAFTON, third Duke of (1735-1811)

The third Duke of Grafton, who was Prime Minister at the age of 31, won the Derby with Tyrant (1802), Pope (1809) and Whalebone (1810).

GRAHAM, Capt E. T., RN(Ret.)

Secretary and General Manager of the Horserace Totalisator Board from 1959-69.

GRAND PARADE

Foaled in 1916, Grand Parade was bred by Mr R. Croker and bought by Lord Glanely as a foal for 470 gn. He was a black colt by Orby out of Grand Geraldine, by Desmond, and won five of his six races as a two-year-old. Trained by Frank Barling at Newmarket, he won the first post-war Derby, ridden by Fred Templeman and starting at 33-1. He also won the St James's Palace Stakes at Ascot. He was the first black to win the Derby since Smolensko in 1813. At the stud he sired a large number of moderate winners, but his solitary classic winner was Diophon who won the Two Thousand Guineas for the Aga Khan.

GRAY, William Harrison (b 1902)

This popular and successful North-country trainer served his apprenticeship with Sir John Renwick and from 1925 to 1949 he assisted Capt J. C. Storie at Beverley. In 1950 he took out a licence to train and among his many good winners have been Ballymarais (Dante Stakes), Lucky Brief (Dante Stakes and Champion Trophy, Ripon) and Cheb's Lad (Hyperion Stakes, Champagne Stakes, Champion Trophy, Ripon, and Thirsk Classic Trial Stakes). His stables are at York Road, Beverley, and his owners include Mr Harry Brown, Mr G. R. Barker, Mr G. B. Turnbull, Mr W. H. Hodgson, Mr E. S. Dixon and Mrs A. Perratt.

GREAT JUBILEE HANDICAP

See under KEMPTON PARK.

GREAT METROPOLITAN HANDICAP

See under EPSOM.

GREAT VOLTIGEUR STAKES

See under YORK

GREAT NEPHEW

Foaled in 1963, Great Nephew was bred and owned by Mr J. P. Philipps and is a bay by Honeyway out of Sybil's Niece, by Admirals Walk. Racing in England and France he won five races and over £64,000 in stakes, his victories including le Prix du Moulin de Longchamp, le Prix Dollar and le Prix de Paques; he was beaten a short head in the Two Thousand Guineas and was second to Busted in the Eclipse Stakes. He is syndicated for stud purposes and stands at the Derisley Stud, Newmarket.

GREEN, Brigadier Henry, CBE

Brigadier Green served in the Coldstream Guards from 1932-64. From 1961-64 he was Chief of Staff, London District. He is a former Master of the Crawley and Horsham. He was appointed Director of Security to the Turf Authorities in 1964.

GREENING, D.

An experienced free-lance lightweight that can go to scale at 7st 2. He won the 1958 Wokingham Stakes on Magic Boy.

GREY DERBY WINNERS

The only greys to have won the Derby are Gustavus, Tagalie, Mahmoud and Airborne.

GREY SOVEREIGN

Bred by Mr William Hill, Grey Sovereign was foaled in 1948 and is a three parts brother to the Derby winner Nimbus, being by Nasrullah out of Kong, by Baytown. A good but somewhat temperamental sprinter, he won eight races worth over £8,000. As a sire he has proved an outstanding success and his stud fee eventually rose to £1,750. Among his offspring are Don II (French Two Thousand Guineas), Zeddaan (Prix Robert Papin and French Two Thousand Guineas), Sovereign Lord (Richmond and Gimcrack Stakes); Sovereign Path (Queen Elizabeth II Stakes and a leading sire); Silver King (£14,372); La Tendresse (£10,412); Queensbury (£10,221); Matatina, Young Emperor, Cynara and Gustav. He stands at the Dalham Hall Stud, Newmarket.

GROSVENOR, first Earl (1731-1802)

The first Earl Grosvenor raced on a gigantic scale which cost him a quarter of a million pounds during his lifetime. He won the Derby in 1790, 1792 and 1794.

GUEST, Raymond (b 1907)

Mr Guest was for several years

American Ambassador in Ireland. His horses in Ireland are trained by Vincent O'Brien and he won the Derby in 1962 with Larkspur and in 1968 with Sir Ivor. Colours: chocolate, pale blue hoops and cap.

GULF STREAM

Foaled in 1943, Gulf Stream was bred and owned by the late Lord Derby. He won the Gimcrack Stakes and Eclipse Stakes and was second in the Derby. By Hyperion out of the One Thousand Guineas winner Tideway, he was exported to the Argentine and did well there as a sire.

GULLY, John

John Gully was a former prize-fighter who became Member of Parliament for Pontefract and won the 1846 Derby with Pyrrhus the First, and the 1854 Derby with Andover.

GUSTAVUS

Mr J. Hunter's Gustavus, foaled in 1818, was the first grey horse to win the Derby. See Grey Derby Winners.

H

HABITAT

An American-bred colt by Sir Gaylord, Habitat cost Mr Charles Engelhard $105,000 as a yearling. Sent to Fulke Johnson Houghton, he proved difficult to train and as a two-year-old in 1968 he never ran and in fact hardly ever left his box. Thanks largely to his trainer's patience, he was able to run as a three-year-old and by the autumn had proved himself the best miler in Europe, at any rate provided the ground was not too firm. His victories included the Lockinge Stakes, the £7,000 Prix Quincey at Deauville, the Wills Mile and the Prix du Moulin at Longchamp. He is now standing at the Grange William Stud, Co Kildare.

HALF-BRED

A horse is said to be half-bred if one of its parents is ineligible for inclusion in the Stud Book.

HALIFAX, Countess of (b 1916)

Lady Halifax is well known as a breeder and owner. She is the owner of the Swynford Paddocks Stud, Newmarket, where many good horses, including Acropolis, have been bred. The best horse to carry her colours so far is Frankincense, who won the 1968 Lincolnshire Handicap with 9st 5lb. Her trainer is John Oxley. Colours: light blue, chocolate striped sleeves, hooped cap.

HALIFAX, Earl of (b 1912)

Lord Halifax served in the Royal Horse Guards. He is a member of the Jockey Club and was Senior Steward in 1950-51 and in 1958-59. He acts as steward at Ascot, Beverley, Doncaster, Epsom and Thirsk. The best horse he has so far owned is Banco whose many victories included the City and Suburban. His trainer is John Oxley. Colours: light blue, chocolate sleeves, hooped cap.

HALL, Leslie Alexander (b 1907)

Les Hall was apprenticed to Capt Percy Whitaker and Walter Earl. He trained for a time under Pony Turf Club rules before taking out a licence under Jockey Club rules in 1952. He won the 1954 Stewards Cup with Ashurst Wonder and the 1964 Middle Park Stakes with Spanish Express. His stables are at Littleton, Winchester, and his owners include Mr H. L. Wilks, Mr J. Couzens, Mr W. N. Wilfred, Mr E. E. Wilks, Mrs I. C. Miller, Mrs J. T. Davis and Mr S. Hoddinott.

HALL, Miss Sally

Niece of Sam Hall, Miss Sally Hall, who knows the racing game from A to Z, is the first licensed woman trainer in the North. She has a string of 30 horses at Brecongill, Middleham, and won 13 races in 1968, her first season, and 11 in 1969.

HALL, Sam (b 1918)

This stout and genial Yorkshireman has for a long period been one of the most successful northern trainers. He served in the Royal Navy from 1940-46 and assisted his brother, the late Tom Hall, before taking out a licence himself in 1949. He has been notably successful in big handicaps, winning the Cesarewitch, Ebor Handicap (twice), Manchester November Handicap (four times), Lincolnshire Handicap (twice), Zetland Gold Cup (three times), Vaux Gold Tankard, Liverpool Cup (five times), Wokingham Stakes (twice), Royal Hunt Cup, Ayr Gold

Cup and William Hill Gold Cup. He used to train at Brecongill, Middleham, but in 1967 he moved to Spigot Lodge, near Leyburn. Among his many patrons are Mrs A. W. Carr, Lady Clarissa Collin, Lord and Lady Delamere, Lord Derby, Mrs R. Fell, Mr and Mrs L. G. Lazarus, Mr and Mrs C. A. B. St George, Mr R. J. Sigtia and Mr M. Wickham-Boynton.

HALSEY, William (1865-1961)

William Halsey was a fine all-round rider. In 1900 he was second in the Grand National on Barsac and in 1901 he won the Two Thousand Guineas on Handicapper. On giving up riding, he trained with success at Newmarket, his chief patron being Sir Ernest Cassell. In 1907 he won the St Leger with Wool Winder and he won the Ascot Gold Cup in 1907 and 1908 with that fine stayer The White Knight. He retired in 1924 and died at the age of 94. His son Claud Halsey trained with success in France between the wars and subsequently in England.

HAMBRO, J. O., MC (b 1919)

Mr Hambro served during World War II in the Coldstream Guards and was severely wounded. Head of a famous banking firm, he is one of those valuable members of the Jockey Club who combine a knowledge of racing with profound business experience. He is a member of the Horserace Levy Board and a steward at Epsom, Ascot and Alexandra Park. The best horse to carry his colours so far is the sprinter Sammy Davis. His trainers are Bruce Hobbs and Doug Smith. Colours: emerald green, white hooped sleeves, white cap.

HAMILTON OF DALZELL, Lord, KT, CVO, MC (d 1952)

A member of the Jockey Club for 44 years, he was largely responsible for the introduction of the totalisator on to English racecourses. From 1935 to 1945 he was His Majesty's representative at Ascot and effected many important improvements there.

HAMILTON PARK

This popular Lanarkshire course is a straight six furlong track with a pear-shaped, right-handed loop. The 1m 5f start takes place in front of the stands; the horses then run down the straight, round the loop, and back up the straight to the winning post. The turns are not sharp and the track is mainly undulating. It is laid out at the head of a valley, the hollow of which is responsible for a pronounced dip about 2½f out, from which point there is a stiff climb to the winning post. Middle numbers are favoured in the draw on the straight course.

Clerk of the Course: Mr W. H. Robertson-Aikman, The Ross, Hamilton, Scotland. Tel: Hamilton 22955.

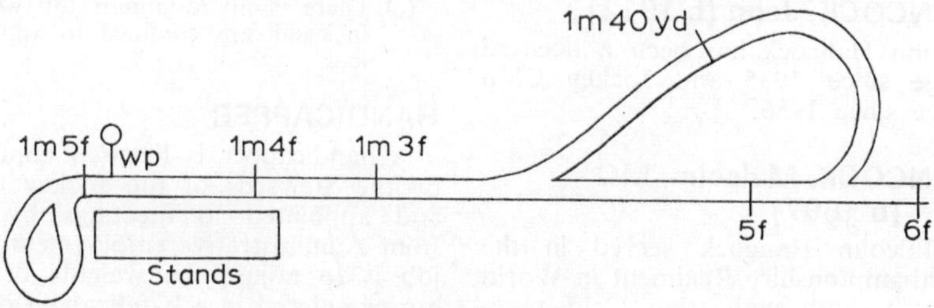

HAMILTON PARK

Best Times:

Distance	Horse-Age-Weight	Date	Time
5f	Crystal Bar 6-8-8	13-7-62	59.4
5f	Broken Past 2-8-5	15-7-49	60.4
6f	Man of Aran 3-9-1	30-8-47	1min 12
6f	Scottish Venture 2-8-6	24-9-55	1min 13.6
8f 40yd	Freddy M. 3-8-9	16-7-49	1min 36.8
8f 40yd	Inyanga 2-8-4	30-9-63	1min 55.4
11f	Trigaro 3-9-0	16-7-49	2min 24.6
12f	Las Vegas 5-9-0	30-8-47	2min 36.2
13f	Lady of Aske 3-7-11	13-7-62	2min 53.2

HAMLYN, Geoffrey (b 1910)

Geoffrey Hamlyn has, except for his war service in the Rifle Brigade, been with the *Sporting Life* since 1932. He has been a starting price reporter since 1933 and senior starting price reporter since 1957. He is noted equally for his punctuality and integrity, and in his responsible position enjoys the trust of both bookmakers and backers. From 1960 to 1967 he was Vice-Chairman of the Racecourse Press Association.

HAMPTON

Foaled in 1871, Hampton, by Lord Clifden, was a small horse standing only 15.2 hands and began his racing career in selling plates. He made immense improvement, though, and became a top class stayer winning the Goodwood and Doncaster Cups and the Northumberland Plate. He proved a highly successful sire, and sired three Derby winners, Merry Hampton, Ayrshire and Ladas. He also established a sire line, to which Hyperion belongs, that holds a leading position today.

HANCOCK, John (b 1912)

John Hancock has been a licensed judge since 1935 and Jockey Club judge since 1956.

HANCOCK, Malcolm, MC (b 1897)

Malcolm Hancock served in the Northamptonshire Regiment in World War I and with the Coldstream Guards in World War II. He was appointed a judge in 1920 and was Jockey Club judge when he retired in 1956. He is now Clerk of the Course at Doncaster and Worcester.

HANCOCK, R. M. S.

A judge under the Rules of Racing and National Hunt rules.

HANDICAP

A 'handicap' is a race in which the weights carried by the horses are adjusted by the handicapper for the purpose of equalising their chances of winning.

As far as is known, the first handicap ever run was at Ascot in 1790.

See also Free Handicap.

Special Rules for Handicaps

No horse is allowed to run in a handicap unless it has run three times or won a race before the Sunday previous to the publication of the weights.

The top weight allotted is:

(a) Not less than 9st 7lb in handicaps confined to three-year-olds taking place before 1 August; and also in nursery handicaps.
(b) Not less than 10st in all other handicaps, except handicaps confined to apprentices.
(c) There is no minimum top weight in handicaps confined to apprentices.

HANDICAPPER

A handicapper is licensed annually by the Stewards of the Jockey Club and appointed to meetings by the Joint Administrative employment. His job is to adjust the weights of the horses entered in a handicap in order to equalise their chances of winning.

Unless otherwise instructed, he must attend in person those meetings to which he is appointed.

HANDS

The unit of horse measurement is the hand, which equals four inches. Measurements are taken from the ground to a horse's withers.

HANLEY, David (b 1928)

David Hanley, who trains at Lambourn, rode as an apprentice on the flat from 1943-46 and he held a licence to ride under National Hunt rules from 1944-58. He was apprenticed to Walter Nightingall and was assistant trainer to his father, S. D. Hanley, from 1956-60. He took out a licence to train in 1960 and among the races he has won are the Portland Handicap, the Wokingham Stakes, the Senior Service Trophy and Ebor Handicap. His owners include Lady Aitken, Mr F. Barber, Mr A. M. C. Hanna, Mrs K. B. Nicoll, Mr A. J. Richards and Mrs D. Tennant.

HANMER, Sir Edward, Bart (b 1893)

Sir Edward Hanmer became a member of the Jockey Club in 1937. The best horses to carry his colours so far are Moneybox (Manchester Cup) and Fury (Park Hill Stakes). His flat-race horses are trained by R. D. Peacock. Colours: primrose, dark blue collar and cuffs, dark blue cap with yellow spots.

HAPPY KNIGHT

Happy Knight, bred and owned by Sir William Cooke and trained by H. Jelliss, won the Two Thousand Guineas in 1946. By Colombo out of Happy Morn, he was not a success as a sire.

HAPPY LAUGHTER

Foaled in 1950, Happy Laughter, by Royal Charger, was bred by the Ballykisteen Stud, owned by Mr David Wills and trained by Sir Jack Jarvis. Although dogged by ill-health throughout her life, she won nine races worth over £26,000, including the One Thousand Guineas, Coronation Stakes and Falmouth Stakes. She was not a success at the stud.

HAPSBURG

Bred by Sir Tatton Sykes and owned by Sir Ernest Cassel, Hapsburg was second in the 1914 Derby and won the Champion Stakes and Eclipse Stakes. By Desmond out of Altesse, he sired that good stayer Noble Star, winner of the Ascot Stakes, Goodwood Stakes, Cesarewitch and Jockey Club Cup.

HARD RIDDEN

Hard Ridden, trained by J. M. Rogers at the Curragh, was Ireland's second Derby winner, the first being Orby in 1907. By the sprinter Hard Sauce out of Toute Belle II, he was bought at the 1956 Dublin Sales as a yearling for only 270 gn by Sir Victor Sassoon. Besides winning the Derby, he also won the Irish Two Thousand Guineas. He failed in the King George VI and Queen Elizabeth Stakes and never ran again. Possibly he was a lucky Derby winner as Alcide, indisputably the best three-year-old that season, met with a mishap just before Epsom and could not run. Hard Ridden was partnered in the Derby by Charlie Smirke who was then in his 51st year. As a stallion he was only fairly successful and was eventually exported to Japan.

HARD SAUCE

Hard Sauce, foaled in 1948, was by Ardan out of Saucy Bella, by Bellacose, and was a high-class sprinter, winning six races worth over £5,000, including the July Cup and Challenge Stakes. He was one of the very few sprinters that have sired a Derby winner as he sired Hard Ridden, who won the Irish Two Thousand Guineas and the Derby in 1958. He died in 1969.

HARD TACK

Foaled in 1955, Hard Tack, by Hard Sauce out of Cowes, by Blue Peter, enjoyed only modest success on the racecourse, winning a couple of races in Ireland worth £404. However, he has done well as a sire, the best of his offspring being Right Tack, winner of the Imperial and Middle Park Stakes in 1968, and the following year the Two Thousand Guineas and St James's Palace Stakes. Hard Tack is syndicated and stands at the Lisieux Stud, Co Kildare.

HARDY, J.

His stables are at Staunton, Nottinghamshire. In 1968 he won the Ascot Stakes with King of Peace and he had 13 successes to his credit in 1969.

HARGREAVES, C. H .

Clerk of the Course at Kempton Park from 1937 to 1970.

HARICOT

Foaled in 1847, Haricot, by Mango or Lanercost, was famous for toughness and vitality. After racing till she was six, she retired to the stud, producing her first foal at eight and her last at 25. She was dam of Caller Out, winner of the St Leger. When 21, she produced Lady Longden, dam of the Derby winner Sir Bevys and of Hampton, a great racehorse and a remarkably influential sire.

HARLEY, William Henry

An official handicapper since 1954.

HARRIES, S. A. B.

A judge under the Rules of Racing and National Hunt rules.

HARTER, John Francis Adair

An official handicapper since 1946.

HARTIGAN, Frank (1880-1952)

The son of an army veterinary officer, Frank Hartigan was a big tall Irishman who rode with success under National Hunt rules, firstly as an amateur and later as a professional. He subsequently trained with success both jumping and on the flat. He won the One Thousand Guineas twice and the Grand National with Shaun Goilin. He was trainer for some years for the late Lord Rosebery before Lord Rosebery transferred his horses to Jack Jarvis. His son Joe Hartigan holds a trainer's licence today.

HARTIGAN, Joseph Henry, MC (b 1919)

Joe Hartigan served in World War II with the 27th Lancers and the 12th Lancers, being awarded the MC. He assisted his father, the late Frank Hartigan from 1936 to 1940 and again from 1945 to 1952. He then assisted Noel Murless for a year before taking out a licence himself. His stables are at Thorngill, Middleham, Yorkshire, and his owners include Mr and Mrs R. L. Heaton, Lord Masham, Mr C. R. Maxsted, Lieut-Col J. Medlicott, Mr N. Millar, Mr G. Bloor, Capt Hon A. G. Lowther and Major T. R. Riley.

HARTIGAN, Captain Martin, MC (d 1942)

Martin Hartigan trained between the wars at Ogbourne in Wiltshire. He was a highly competent member of his profession and won many races, but is chiefly remembered because it was to him that Sir Gordon Richards was apprenticed. He gave Sir Gordon his first chance and till his death he and Sir Gordon remained close friends.

HARVEY, Brig Charles Barnet, DSO (b 1900)

Brig 'Roscoe' Harvey was appointed a Stewards' Secretary in 1946 and was Senior Stewards' Secretary from 1951 till he retired in 1969. He joined the 10th Hussars in 1920 and had a distinguished military career in which he was awarded the DSO and two bars.

In his younger days he was a good amateur rider with experience in England, India and Egypt, during which he gained useful knowledge of many aspects of the racing game. He was also a dashing polo player, a hard man to hounds and won innumerable point-to-points. He is greatly liked in the racing world and it is generally agreed that he performed his duties efficiently, with tact and good humour. On his retirement he was elected a member of the Jockey Club.

HARWOOD, Guy (b 1939)

Guy Harwood rode a number of winners as an amateur under National Hunt rules and for a time assisted Bryan Marshall before taking out a licence himself in 1966. His stables are at Pulborough, Sussex, and his owners include Mr R. Zelker, Mr J. Tilling, Mr and Mrs Dan Abbott, Mr and Mrs T. G. Johnson, Mr John Rogerson and Mrs B. S. L. Trafford.

HASTINGS-BASS, Capt Peter (1921-1964)

Capt Peter Hastings-Bass was only 43 and seemed to have a great future ahead of him when he was stricken with a grave illness and died in 1964. He was in his very first season as one of the Queen's trainers.

A notable athlete, he won the quarter mile for Oxford and played rugby for Oxford and the Army. During the war he served with the Welsh Guards and was wounded. Racing was in his blood, though, as his father, the Hon Aubrey Hastings, had trained four Grand National winners, riding one of them to victory himself. Aubrey Hastings died suddenly in 1929 and the Wroughton stable, then primarily concerned with jumping, was taken over by Ivor Anthony. Peter Hastings, who assumed the additional name of Bass by deed poll in 1954, assisted Anthony at Wroughton from 1946 to 1952. In the meantime he purchased the famous Kingsclere training establishment from Evan Williams, at one time the Wroughton stable jockey, and in 1953 he set out to train flat-racers there. He was immediately successful and among the 340 winners he had sent out before his death were Kings Troop (Royal Hunt Cup), King Bruce (Stewards Cup), and Midsummer Night II (Cambridgeshire). He was succeeded at Kingsclere by Ian Balding, who in 1969 married his daughter.

HAWLEY, Sir Joseph (1814-1875)

An outstanding figure in mid-Victorian racing, Sir Joseph Hawley, after serving for a short time in the 9th Lancers, settled in Italy, and it was there that he developed a taste for racing.

His connection with English racing began in 1844. Alec Taylor trained for him at Fyfield, in Wiltshire, and it was Taylor who trained Teddington to win the 1851 Derby for Sir Joseph. Subsequently, after a brief and unsatisfactory period with the Days at Danebury, Sir Joseph's horses were trained by George Manning at Cannons Heath, and after Manning's death by John Porter at Kingsclere. Sir Joseph won the Derby on four occasions, his winners after Teddington being Beadsman (1858), Musjid (1859) and Blue Gown (1868).

Sir Joseph, as a member of the Jockey Club, interested himself in Turf reform, and there was much to be said for his plans to restrict two-year-old racing and to extend the privilege of Jockey Club membership to a wider circle. He was, though, neither liked nor entirely trusted, and his speeches on the iniquities of gambling, in view of his own record in that respect, laid him open to the charge of hypocrisy. He was never able to enlist the all-important support of Admiral Rous and his proposals for reform were defeated.

HAYDOCK PARK

Though Manchester has vanished

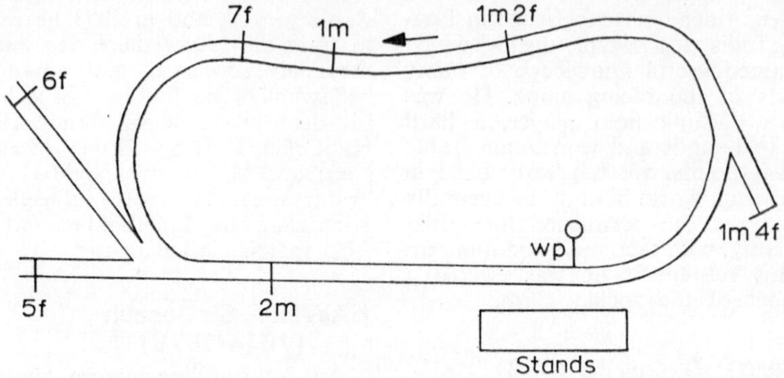

HAYDOCK PARK

from the fixture list and the future of Liverpool is uncertain, this deservedly popular Lancastrian course continues to prosper. Within handy reach of big industrial areas, it is nevertheless attractively set out in parkland surroundings. The track is a left-handed, undulating circuit about 1m 5f round, with one right-handed turn just over a mile from home. The straight 5f, the 6f course and the 1½m course all start on spurs projecting from the round course. The 4f run-in is slightly uphill the whole way. It is a fair track in all essentials but short-runners do not care for the stiff finish. Low numbers are thought to possess a slight advantage in races of 6f, 7f and 1m.

Clerk of the Course: Mr John Hughes, 33 Kings Paddock, Park Close, Hampton, Middlesex. Tel: 01-979-6638.

Best Times:

Distance	*Horse-Age-Weight*	*Date*	*Time*
5f	Fish and Chips 3-7-5	6-6-70	58.6
5f	Lush Park 2-8-12	6-6-70	58.4
6f	Cul-de-Sac 3-9-4	10-10-47	1min 12.4
6f	El Commandante 2-8-11	12- 8-65	1min 12.5
7f	Alimony 3-8-7	11- 8-55	1min 25.2
7f	Royal Flirt 2-8-9	12- 8-65	1min 27.4
8f	Court Dress 3-8-6	13- 8-59	1min 38
8f	Three Wishes 2-8-8	18- 9-59	1min 41
10f 70yd	Delacroix 3-7-5	6- 6-70	2min 10.4
12f	Menelek 4-8-4	1- 7-61	2min 26.5
16f	Atlas 4-9-2	17- 5-57	3min 30.6

HAYNES, Robert (b 1917)

Bob Haynes served in the Coldstream Guards from 1937 to 1941 and in the Essex Regiment from 1941 to 1946. After World War II he worked for some years for *Raceform* and in 1952, following the original experiment at Goodwood, he became the first regular racecourse commentator.

HELIOPOLIS

Bred by the late Lord Derby, Heliopolis was by Hyperion out of Drift by Swynford. He won five races worth over £14,000 and was third in the 1939 Derby. Exported to the United States, he proved a brilliant success there and was twice champion sire.

HENRY THE SEVENTH

Bred by Miss O. Hoole, owned by Mr H. J. Joel and trained by W. Elsey, Henry the Seventh was foaled in 1958 and is by King of the Tudors out of Vestal Girl, by Fairy Prince. He won over £26,000 in stakes, including the Eclipse Stakes and the Zetland Gold Cup. Syndicated for the stud, he stands at the Longholes Stud, Newmarket. Among his offspring is Luciano, winner of the German Derby, German St Leger and the Grosser Preis von Baden.

HERMIT

Mr H. Chaplin's Hermit, despite a tendency to break blood-vessels, won the 1867 Derby on a day when snow fell. He proved an outstanding sire and was champion six years in succession.

HERN, Major William Richard

Dick Hern has one of the most powerful stables in the country at West Ilsley, Berkshire, and the Queen is one of his patrons. From 1952 to 1957 he assisted Major M. B. Pope and he became private trainer to Major L. B. Holliday for whom he won the 1962 St Leger with Hethersett, as well as many other good races. He gave up his appointment with Major Holliday to succeed R. J. Colling at West Ilsley where besides the Queen his patrons are Mr J. J. Astor, Lady Durham, Mr T. E. S. Egerton, Lord Hartington, Mr L. B. Holliday, Major L. S. Marler, Lord Rotherwick Mr R. L. Basset, Lieut-Col J. Chandos-Pole, Lord Irwin and Mrs C. L. Loyd. He won his second St Leger with Provoke in 1965 and other successes include the Acorn Stakes (Gallop On), Chesham Stakes (Narrow Escape), July Stakes (Burning Thoughts), Princess Margaret Stakes (Attitude), Lowther Stakes (Fortune's Darling), Solario Stakes (Happy Omen and Remand) Royal Lodge Stakes (Remand), Blue Seal Stakes (Number One), Horris Hill Stakes (Foothill), Greenham Stakes (Heathen), Fred Darling Stakes and Highest Hopes (Who Can Tell), Jockey Club Stakes (Darling Boy), Cheshire Oaks (Bell Top), Lingfield Oaks Trial (None Nicer, Nortia), Queen Alexandra Stakes (Grey of Falloden), July Cup (Galivanter), Yorkshire Oaks (None Nicer), Great Voltigeur Stakes (Hethersett), Doncaster Cup (Grey of Falloden, The Accuser), Irish St Leger (Craighouse), Queens Prize (Minute Gun, Grey of Falloden), City and Suburban (Setting Star), Chester Cup (Mahbub Aly), Zetland Gold Cup (Red Tears), Rosebery Memorial Handicap (Avons Pride, twice), Magnet Cup (Nortia), Goodwood Stakes (Tree Leopard), Newbury Autumn Cup (Ruantallan), Cesarewitch (Avon's Pride, Grey of Falloden). His record would be even better but in three of the last four seasons his stable has been badly hit by virus infections.

HERRINGBONE

Bred and owned by the late Lord Derby, Herringbone was by King Salmon out of Schiaparelli, by Schiavoni. In 1943 she won the One Thousand Guineas and the St Leger. At the stud she bred eight winners, including Entente Cordiale, who won over £9,000 in stakes.

HETHERINGTON, P.

He can go to scale at 7st 12 and rides for E. Weymes's stable. He rode 18 winners in 1969.

HETHERSETT

Owned and bred by Major Lionel Holliday and trained by Major W. Hern, Hethersett was by Hugh Lupus out of Bride Elect by Big Game. After winning the Brighton Derby Trial, he started favourite for the 1962 Derby but was one of seven horses brought down in a pile-up on the descent to Tattenham Corner. In the autumn he won the St Leger, having little difficulty in defeating the Derby winner Larkspur. He soon began to make his mark as a sire and it was a severe loss to British breeders when he died in 1966, a loss emphasised by the victory of his son Blakeney in the 1969 Derby.

HEYMAN, David Francis

Mr David Heyman is an official handicapper and is also Clerk of the Course at Wolverhampton and Warwick.

HIDE, Edward (b 1937)

Edward Hide, son of the former trainer Bill Hide, was following hounds on his pony at the tender age of six. Apprenticed to his father, he rode his first winner in 1951 at Chepstow. His first major success came in 1956 when he won the 1956 Cesarewitch on Prelone, trained by his father. The following season he rode 131 winners, his best effort to date. He had a long and successful association with the Malton stable of the late Capt Charles Elsey, and subsequently with Capt Elsey's son Bill. For them he rode his classic winners Cantelo (St Leger) and Pia (Oaks). However, at the close of the 1968 season he received an invitation to ride for Sir Gordon Richards's stable and elected to leave the north and come south. Besides those already mentioned, big races he has won include the Lincoln, Ayr Gold Cup, Northumberland Plate, City and Suburban, Victoria Cup, Cambridgeshire, Gimcrack Stakes, Champagne Stakes, Manchester November Handicap, Jockey Club Cup, Zetland Gold Cup, Magnet Cup and Portland Handicap. He has also won the Norwegian and Danish Derbys.

HIGGINS, J.

He was one of the most successful apprentices in 1969 and rode 28 winners.

HIGGS, William (1880-1958)

Billy Higgs rode over 1,000 winners and was champion jockey in 1906. On that fine stayer Willonyx he won the Chester Cup, Ascot Stakes, Ascot Gold Cup, the Cesarewitch (with 9st 5lb) and the Jockey Club Cup. He trained with moderate success at Blewbury from 1923 to 1940.

HIGHEST TOTALS WON IN A SEASON

Horse: Sir Ivor won £97,075 in England in 1968. In 1964 Santa Claus won £72,067 in England and £60,036 in Ireland.

Trainer: Noel Murless won £256,699 in stakes for his owners in 1967.

Owner: Mr H. J. Joel won £120,923 in 1967 and the late Prince Aly Khan £100,668 in 1959.

HIGHFLYER

Highflyer, who sired three Derby winners, was bred by Sir Charles Bunbury and then sold to Lord Bolingbroke, who gave him his name through being foaled in a field where some highflyer walnut trees were growing. In 1779 Lord Bolingbroke re-sold him to Mr Richard Tattersall of the famous firm of auctioneers. Highflyer, by Herod, was never beaten and was the outstanding horse of his day. His pedigree contained the blood of the Byerly Turk, the Godolphin Arabian and the Darley Arabian in almost equal proportions and at the stud he proved the ideal sire for mares by Eclipse. Tattersall always tried to purchase an Eclipse mare if one happened to come on the market and he made a handsome fortune in selling his young stock. When Highflyer died aged 20, his owner had the following words engraved on the memorial stone: "Here lieth the perfect and beautiful symmetry of the much lamented Highflyer, by whom and his wonderful offspring the celebrated Tattersall acquired a noble fortune, but was not ashamed to acknowledge it."

HIGH HAT

High Hat, foaled in 1957, was bred by Sir Winston Churchill and is by Hyperion out of Madonna, by Donatello II. His victories in Sir Winston's colours included the Oxfordshire

Stakes, Paradise Stakes, Aly Khan Memorial Gold Cup and Winston Churchill Stakes. In the Prix de l'Arc de Triomphe, he finished fourth, less than a length behind the winner, Right Royal V, to whom he was giving 10lb. He stands at the Airlie Stud, Lucan, Co Dublin, at a fee of 1,200 gn and his winners include Glad Rags (One Thousand Guineas), White Gloves (Irish St Leger), Hametus (Imperial Stakes and Dewhurst Stakes), and Big Hat (Ebor Handicap).

HIGH PERCH

Foaled in 1956, High Perch is by Alycidon out of Phaetonia, by Nearco, and is thus a half-brother to Aggressor, winner of the King George VI and Queen Elizabeth Stakes. He won 11 races worth over £11,000, including the Gainsborough Stakes, Ormonde Stakes, Liverpool Spring Cup, Winston Churchill Stakes and Cumberland Lodge Stakes. He was syndicated for the stud and stood at the Aislabie Stud, Newmarket, but was eventually exported to Sweden. He is sire of Kassar, winner of over £30,000 in Venezuela.

HIGH STAKES

Foaled in 1942, High Stakes, by Hyperion out of the Oaks winner Pennycomequick, was a tough and consistent gelding that won 32 races (including two dead-heats) worth over £21,000 for his breeder Lord Astor.

HILLS, Barry

He was for many years with the late George Colling and with Colling's successor John Oxley. In 1969 he began training at Lambourn and won 17 races that season. He now has over 40 horses in his stable.

HINDLEY, C.

Very little is known of this jockey bar the fact that he rode three Derby winners—Young Eclipse (1781), Saltram (1783) and Aimwell (1785).

HINDLEY, Sir Clement

Formerly Chief Commissioner of Railways with the Government of India, he was selected in 1928 to be the first Chairman of the Racecourse Betting Control Board on the introduction of the totalisator into English racing.

HIPPIUS

Foaled in 1937, Hippius, by Hyperion, twice won the Champion Stakes for Lord Rosebery. He was sold for export during the war but was unfortunately lost at sea.

HISLOP, John Leslie, MC (b 1911)

John Hislop was educated at Wellington and the RMC, but ill-health prevented him from becoming a regular soldier. Before the war he assisted Victor Gilpin who trained first at Newmarket and later at Findon. He became a highly proficient amateur rider both under National Hunt rules and on the flat. On the flat he was in fact outstanding and was leading amateur from 1946 to 1955. For many years he was racing correspondent of *The Observer* and he then acted in that capacity for the *News of the World*. He is the author of numerous books and managing director of *The British Racecourse*. In the war he served in the Sussex Yeomanry and in 'Phantom', attached to the SAS.

HISTORY OF ENGLISH HORSE-RACING

The development of horse-racing in England can really be said to date from the seventeenth century although it is known to have taken place in many parts of the country for a great many years before then. There are records of it during the Roman occupation. During the reign of Henry II there were races on public holidays at Smithfield, the great London horse-market, while at Chester there are very old records of Shrove Tuesday races for a wooden ball embellished with flowers.

It was during the reign of James I that racing first began to be an organised sport. James took a great liking to Newmarket, then an obscure, wooden-hutted village, and had a royal palace constructed there. James was in fact keener on hawking and hunting than on racing, but racing at this period was very popular in Scotland and members of the court from north of the border lost little time in establishing the sport at Newmarket. James himself realised the importance of testing and improving the breed of horses in England and established public races in many parts of the country. The prize was usually a silver bell and courses where these races were held were known as 'Bell Courses'. An ancient silver bell is still a trophy at one of the Lanark meetings today. James also saw that British blood was judiciously reinforced by the import of suitable horses from abroad.

Charles I maintained the royal association with Newmarket and Charles II was a racing enthusiast. He rode in races himself, founded races known as Royal Plates, while the Rowley Mile course at Newmarket is named after him, as 'Old Rowley' was his nickname, derived from his favourite hack which bore that name.

As the popularity of racing increased under royal patronage, the evolution of the racehorse was taking place with remarkable swiftness, thanks largely to the import of Arabian horses. At the same time the control of the sport gradually fell into the hands of the Jockey Club, which was founded—the precise date is unknown—somewhere around the middle of the eighteenth century. Up to this time racing had been comprised for the most part of matches run over long distances, racing men of that era placing much emphasis on stamina and the quality they described as 'bottom'. Gradually, however, more attention was given to speed; horses began to compete at a younger age than had previously been the case and over shorter distances. The first classic race, the St Leger, was instituted in 1776, and was followed by the Oaks in 1779 and the Derby in 1780.

Racing continued to prosper in the nineteenth century. Improved transport facilities were of great assistance to the sport, which began to receive more attention in the leading newspapers. There was a marked increase, too, in the volume of betting. Originally betting on horse-racing had been largely confined to owners wagering on the result of matches in which one of their own horses was engaged. With the advent of professional betting men and of bookmakers (then known as 'legs', short for 'blacklegs') a new and often undesirable element crept into the sport. Villainy in fact abounded and but for the unrelenting war waged by Lord George Bentinck on crooks and welshers, racing might have become too disreputable to survive. Lord George also established order, discipline and punctuality in the conduct of race-meetings, and improved the quality of officials which till then had been low.

As leading figure of the Jockey Club, Lord George was followed by the forthright, honourable and occasionally impulsive Admiral Rous, who brought the Rules of Racing up to date and set a new high standard in handicapping. The level of integrity throughout racing, and particularly among jockeys, gradually improved and in the 1890s the patronage of the Prince of Wales afforded fresh prestige to the sport.

This century, racing has survived two major wars, but only just. The fact that racing was permitted to continue on a greatly reduced scale in both world wars was largely due to the tact and negotiating skill of the Stewards of the Jockey Club, who had to contend with some bitter, and occasionally prejudiced, opposition.

After the Second World War the status of the British thoroughbred suffered a temporary decline through the many successes of horses from overseas in our main races. The demand for British bloodstock, though, is probably higher now than ever before. On the racecourses, many technical innovations have been introduced and the Betting and Gaming Act, which legalised betting, means that betting now makes a substantial contribution towards the general good of the sport.

At the present time racing is confronted by many problems and in the next decade it is conceivable that the long and mostly beneficial rule of the Jockey Club may come to an end.

See also American Invasion; Ascot; Bentinck, Lord George; Darley Arabian; Durham, Third Earl Of; Epsom; Frampton, Tregonwell; Horserace Betting Levy Board; Jersey Act; Jockey Club; Newmarket; Peppiate Committee; Rous, Admiral Henry John; Tattersalls; Thoroughbred, Origins of the; Tote, The.

HOBBS, Bruce, MC (b 1920)

Bruce Hobbs is the son of the former National Hunt trainer Reg Hobbs. He was a brilliant horseman as a boy and had his first ride over fences as an amateur at the age of 14. He turned professional and was only 17 when he won the Grand National on the American horse Battleship, trained by his father. He also won the Welsh Grand National and the Cedarhurst Grand National, USA.

In the war he served as a captain in the Queens Own Yorkshire Dragoons and was awarded the MC. He took out a licence to train under National Hunt rules in 1945 and had jumpers belonging to Mr and Mrs John Rogerson, but in 1951 he gave up his licence to become assistant to George Beeby. Subsequently he was assistant to Sir Cecil Boyd-Rochfort from 1953-60 and to Jack Clayton from 1961-63. There followed a brief but successful spell as private trainer to Mr and Mrs D. Robinson before setting up as public trainer at Palace House, Newmarket, where his patrons include Mr T. F. Blackwell, Mr J. P. Philipps, Mr and Mrs J. O. Hambro, Mr and Mrs J. Rogerson, Mr W. Hill, Capt M. T. Wills, Mr H. D. H. Wills, Major A. H. G. Broughton, Lord Fairhaven, Mr K. Freeman, Mrs J. Kenny, Lady Pilkington, Marquess of Tavistock, Mr J. H. Weller-Poley and Mr Julian Wilson. Among the good races he has won are the Blue Riband Trial Stakes, the Oxfordshire Stakes and the Goodwood Cup.

HOBDAYING

'Hobdaying' is an operation to relieve a horse's respiratory trouble and in fact frequently affords permanent relief. It was originated by the late Sir Frederick Hobday, principal of the Royal Veterinary College.

HOGG, Capt Thomas (1879-1942)

Capt Hogg served in the Royal Army Veterinary Corps in South Africa, later becoming not only veterinary surgeon to the Johannesburg Turf Club but also one of the most successful trainers in South Africa. He returned to England in 1910 and set up as a vet at Epsom and the following year took out a trainer's licence. After World War I, in which he again served with the RAVC, he resumed training and won the 1923 Ascot Gold Cup with Happy Man, bought for 30 gn as a yearling. From 1928 to 1938 he was private trainer to Lord Glanely for whom he won 259 races worth over £170,000 in stakes.

HOLDEN, William (b 1930)

William Holden was apprenticed to Jack Reardon. He rode on the flat as an apprentice and later under National Hunt rules. He took out a licence to train in 1955 and has a small stable at Newmarket.

HOLLIDAY, L. Brook

Mr. L. Brook Holliday is the son of the famous owner-breeder the late Major Lionel Holliday. He is a member of the Jockey Club and a steward at Newcastle and Teesside Park. His horses are trained by W. R. Hern and

Denys Smith. Colours: white, maroon hoops, armlets and cap.

HOLLIDAY, Major Lionel B., OBE (1881-1966)

Major Lionel Holliday died aged 85 in 1966, his wife having died earlier that week. He was one of racing's 'characters' and no one could ever accuse him of courting popularity; quite the reverse in fact. Self-opinionated and self-assertive, he was never an easy or pleasant man to work for and changed his trainers and jockeys with considerable frequency. He was liked and admired by the racing public, as his horses were always out to win.

He founded a powerful racing empire and could have justly claimed to be the foremost English owner-breeder of his day. Lost Soul, by Solario, was the famous foundation mare of his stud, and she and her daughter Phase were the cornerstones of his racing successes. He never won the Derby but he won the 1951 Oaks with Neasham Belle, trained by Geoffrey Brooke, the 1962 St Leger with Hethersett, trained by Dick Hern; and the 1965 One Thousand Guineas with Night Off, trained by Walter Wharton. He was leading owner in 1956, 1961 and 1962, and leading breeder in 1954, 1956 and 1962. He bred Vaguely Noble who was sold as a two-year-old in 1967 for the record price for a horse in training in England of 136,000 gn and later won the Prix de l'Arc de Triomphe.

A good judge of a horse and a better one of a foxhound, Major Holliday was the head of a dye manufacturing firm in Huddersfield. A few years before his death he was elected to the Jockey Club, an honour that would have come sooner had he been less dictatorial and more willing to compromise.

HOLLINGSWORTH, Richard Dunbavin (b 1918)

Mr R. D. Hollingsworth served in World War II in the Royal Berkshire Regiment. He is a member of the Jockey Club and a steward at Kempton and Alexandra Park. He owns the Arches Hall Stud, Hertfordshire, and among the good horses bred there were Ark Royal (Ribblesdale Stakes, Lingfield Oaks, Yorkshire Oaks, Newmarket Oaks and Park Hill Stakes), Kyak (Park Hill Stakes); Cutter (Park Hill Stakes and Yorkshire Cup); Hermes (Dante Stakes, Great Voltigeur Stakes and Jockey Club Cup); and Mariner (King Edward VII Stakes). His trainer is John Oxley. Colours: crimson, silver braid.

HOLLINSHEAD, Reginald (b 1924)

Reg Hollinshead rode under National Hunt rules, firstly as an amateur and then as a professional. He has a 'mixed' stable at Upper Longdon, near Rugeley, Staffordshire.

HOMEWARD BOUND

Bred and owned by the late Sir Foster Robinson and trained by John Oxley, Homeward Bound won the Princess Elizabeth Stakes, Oaks and Yorkshire Oaks in 1964. She is by Alycidon out of Sabie River, by Signal Light, and after Sir Foster Robinson's death she was sold for export to America.

HONEYLIGHT

By Honeyway out of Crepuscule, and thus a half sister to Crepello and Twilight Alley, Honeylight was bred by Sir Victor Sassoon and trained by Capt Charles Elsey. In 1956 she won the Free Handicap and the One Thousand Guineas. She has not proved a success at the stud.

HONEYWAY

Bred and owned by Lord Milford and trained by Sir Jack Jarvis, Honeyway was foaled in 1941 and died in 1968. By Fairway out of Honey Buzzard, he was a great sprinter, his 16 victories including the Victoria Cup, July Cup, Cork and Orrery Stakes and

King George Stakes. He was certainly not devoid of stamina either, as he proved by winning the 10f Champion Stakes. He did consistently well as a sire and among his many winners were Honeylight (One Thousand Guineas), Dictaway (French One Thousand Guineas) and Donald (Ebor Handicap and Jockey Club Cup).

HORNBEAM

Bred at the Astor Studs, owned by the third Lord Astor and trained by R. J. Colling, Hornbeam was foaled in 1953 and is by Hyperion out of Thicket by Nasrullah. A good, game stayer, he won 11 races worth over £10,000, including the Great Voltigeur Stakes and the Winston Churchill Stakes. He was second nine times, including the St Leger and the Gold Cup. He made rather a slow start as a sire but there have been a number of useful winners by him since he was exported to Sweden in 1966. Among his offspring are Windmill Girl, who was second in the Oaks, won the Ribblesdale Stakes and was dam of Blakeney. He was also sire of Intermezzo.

HORNET'S BEAUTY

Hornet's Beauty, a gelding by Tredennis, won 31 races worth over £12,000. As a three-year-old in 1911, he went through the season unbeaten, winning on 15 occasions.

HORNUNG, Lieut-Col John Derek, OBE, MC (b 1915)

Lieut-Col John Hornung served in the Irish Guards for 13 years. He is a member of the Jockey Club and a steward at Ascot, Brighton, Goodwood and Sandown. The best horses to carry his colours so far are Aunt Edith (Prix Vermeille, Nassau Stakes, Yorkshire Cup and King George VI and Queen Elizabeth Stakes) and Casabianca (Royal Lodge Stakes and Royal Hunt Cup). His trainers are Noel Murless and J. A. J. Waugh. Colours: white, black spots, black sleeves, red cap.

HORSERACE BETTING LEVY BOARD

The Levy Board was established by the Betting Levy Act 1961 with effect from 1st September 1961. The first chairman was Field-Marshal Lord Harding, the first secretary Major-Gen Sir Rupert Brazier-Creagh. Under the Betting, Gaming and Lotteries Act 1963, which consolidated all previous betting legislation, the Levy Board is charged with the task of assessing and collecting monetary contributions from bookmakers and the totalisator, and of applying the monetary contributions for purposes conducive to the following:

(a) the improvement of breeds of horses;

(b) the advancement and encouragement of veterinary science or veterinary education;

(c) the improvement of horse-racing.

The composition of the Levy Board is as follows:

	Appointed by	*Number of Members*
Chairman	Home Secretary	1
Independent Members	Home Secretary	2
Other Members	Jockey Club National Hunt Committee	1
Chairman of the Horserace Totalisator Board	Ex-officio	1
Chairman of the Bookmaker's Committee	Ex-officio	1

The chairman and the two members appointed by the Home Secretary must be persons who have no interests connected with horse-racing which might hinder them from discharging their functions as members of the Board in an impartial manner.

The present chairman is Lord Wigg.

The offices of the Board are at 17-23 Southampton Row, London, WC1.

HORSERACE TOTALISATOR BOARD

The Horesrace Totalisator Board evolved from the Racecourse Betting Control Board which was set up by the Racecourse Betting Act 1928. The Board's constitution and powers are consolidated in the Betting, Gaming and Lotteries Act 1963, under which it is empowered to operate a pool betting business on any recognised horserace. The Board comprises a chairman and three members, all appointed by the Home Secretary. Under the Racecourse Betting Act 1928 the Racecourse Betting Control Board was responsible for the issue of Certificates of Approval to racecourses, these Certificates requiring racecourses to provide a place for bookmakers to carry on their business and to limit the charge that may be made to a bookmaker to stand up and bet. This responsibility passed to the Totalisator Board. The Chairman of the Board is ex-officio a member of the Horserace Betting Levy Board (see above). Sir Alexander Sim resigned as Chairman in 1970 and was succeeded by Mr A. W. Taylor, C.B., formerly of Customs and Excise.

HORSERACE WRITERS AND REPORTERS ASSOCIATION.

This body represents the interests of racing journalists. The Chairman is Clive Graham.

HOT NIGHT

Sir Victor Sassoon's Hot Night, by Gay Crusader, was second in the Derby and the St Leger in 1927. He made little mark as a sire.

HOUGHTON, Richard Johnson Fulke (b 1940)

Fulke Johnson Houghton is certainly bred to be a trainer. His father, Gordon Johnson Houghton, was a successful trainer till killed in the prime of life in an accident out hunting, while his mother is Fulke Walwyn's sister. After her husband's death Mrs Johnson Houghton kept the stable at Blewbury going, assisted successively by Col Dick Poole, Charles Jerdein and Peter Walwyn.

After leaving Eton, Fulke Johnson Houghton was a pupil with Major John Goldsmith and later with Jack Cunnington in France. He also travelled horses abroad for the Epsom bloodstock agent, George Forbes. In 1961 he took over the stable from his mother and backed by her guidance and experience, he has proved extremely successful. He has won the St Leger with Ribocco and Ribero and both those horses carried off the Irish Sweeps Derby as well. He has also won the Sussex Stakes (Romulus), New Stakes (Tin King, Falcon), Queens Prize (Aegean Blue), Champagne Stakes (Ribofilio), Dewhurst Stakes (Ribofilio), Cornwallis Stakes (Tin King), Chester Cup (Aegean Blue), Usher Vaux Gold Tankard (Aegean Blue), Coronation Stakes (Haymaking), National Stakes (Falcon), Nassaut Stakes (Haymaking), Molecomb Stakes (Smooth), *Observer* Gold Cup (Ribocco), Queen Elizabeth II Stakes (Romulus), Prix du Moulin de Longchamp (Romulus and Habitat) and Wills Mile (Habitat).

Among his owners are Mr C. W. Engelhard, Mr E. Cooper Bland, Mr C. L. Lloyd, Mr C. Nicholson, Lord Leverhume, Mr. D. A. Rasbotham, Major H. D. H. Wills and Hon Mrs B. Rootes.

HOWARD de WALDEN, ninth Lord (b 1912)

Lord Howard de Walden served in

World War II in the Westminster Dragoons. He is an industrious and go-ahead racing administrator and was Senior Steward of the Jockey Club in 1957 and 1964. He acts as steward at Ascot, Newbury, Salisbury and Sandown and was at one time a member of the Racecourse Betting Control Board. He owns the Plantation Stud, Newmarket, and the good horses he has bred include Amerigo who won the Coventry Stakes at Ascot and 12 races worth $419,000 in America; Oncidium (Jockey Club Cup, Coronation Cup, Lingfield Derby Trial and Royal Stakes) and Almiranta (Princess Elizabeth Stakes and Park Hill Stakes). His trainers are Noel Murless, J. A. J. Waugh and E. Weymes. Colours: apricot.

HUBBARD, Derek

Clerk of the Course at Brighton.

HUBBARD, Ralph Arthur

Clerk of the Course at Goodwood.

HUE-WILLIAMS, Mrs Vera

Mrs Hue-Williams, vice-chairman of Berger, Jenson and Nicholson Ltd, has enjoyed many successes as breeder and owner. In conjunction with her husband, Col F. R. Hue-Williams, she owns the Woolton Hill Stud, Newbury, and the Rathasker Stud, Co Kildare. The best horses she has so far owned are Supreme Court (Chester Vase, King Edward VII Stakes and King George VI and Queen Elizabeth Festival of Britain Stakes); and Aurelius (King Edward VII Stakes and St Leger). She trains in England with Noel Murless and P. Walwyn, and with G. Bridgland in France. Colours: scarlet, white V and cap.

HUGHES, John Philip Victor

Clerk of the Course at Haydock Park, Nottingham, Leicester and Chepstow.

HUGH LUPUS

Bred by the late Duke of Westminster and raced by his daughter Lady Ursula Vernon, Hugh Lupus was foaled in 1952 and died in 1967. He was born in France and his pedigree was essentially French as he was by Djebel out of a mare by Goya. He was originally trained in Ireland by Hubert Hartigan and on Hartigan's death by J. Lenehan, but he eventually came to Noel Murless's stable at Newmarket. Altogether he won eight races worth over £15,000, including the Irish Two Thousand Guineas, Champion Stakes and Hardwicke Stakes. At the stud his best winners were Hethersett (St Leger) and Pourparler (One Thousand Guineas).

HULA DANCER

Bred in the United States by Mrs P. A. Widener, Hula Dancer is a grey by Native Dancer out of Flash On, by Ambrose Light. Foaled in 1960, she was trained in France by F. Pollet and her victories included the Grand Criterium and the Prix du Moulin de Longchamp in France; the One Thousand Guineas and the Champion Stakes in England. At the dispersal of Mrs Widener's bloodstock in 1968, she was bought by Mr Raymond Guest to be mated with Sir Ivor. The price paid was Fr 1,020,000.

HULTON, Sir Edward

Sir Edward Hulton is the only leading newspaper owner to have gone in for racing in a big way. Lord Beaverbrook admittedly launched out in great style in the 1920s but soon got bored and gave up. Hulton was trained for the priesthood but when his elder brother died he entered the newspaper business to help his father. At first he went in for coursing—he twice won the Waterloo Cup—but eventually racing became his hobby and relaxation. Thus, unlike many rich men, he entered the racing world with an expert knowledge of the sport. When he died at the early age of 53, his horses were sold and realised 288,000 gn. He won the Derby with Fifinella; the One Thousand Guineas with Roseway; and the Oaks with Fifinella and Straitlace.

HUMBLE DUTY

Humble Duty was bred by Mr F. F. Tuthill and is by Sovereign Path out of a mare by Abernant. A handsome, well-grown grey with a lovely temperament, she was bought as a yearling for 17,000 gn by Jean, Lady Ashcombe who sent her to be trained by Peter Walwyn. She proved herself an outstanding two-year filly in 1969, winning three races, including the Lowther Stakes at York and the Cheveley Park Stakes. Her only defeat was in the Queen Mary Stakes at Ascot. She had had sore shins just before that event and was short of a gallop in consequence. In her first outing in 1970 she was beaten by Highest Hopes in the Fred Darling Stakes but she subsequently won the One Thousand Guineas in brilliant style and then carried off the Ebbisham Stakes at Epsom and the Coronation Stakes at Ascot.

HUMORIST

Mr J. B. Joel's Humorist, trained by Charles Morton, won the Derby in 1911. He must have been a very game horse as he was suffering from a tubercular lung condition and within a fortnight of his Epsom triumph he was dead.

HUNTERCOMBE

Bred and owned by Mr H. H. Renshaw and trained by Arthur Budgett, Huntercombe is a good-looking, well-proportioned bay colt by Derring-Do out of Ergina, by Fair Trial. He was one of the best two-year-olds of 1969, winning the July Stakes, Middle Park Stakes and Cornwallis Stakes, and finishing second, when not fully recovered from the cough, in the Gimcrack Stakes. As a three-year-old he began with defeats in the Two Thousand Guineas Trials at Kempton and Ascot. After finishing unplaced in the Two Thousand Guineas he reverted to sprinting, and this may prove to be his game.

HUNTER, Gavin (b. 1941)

He was first of all a pupil with Tom Jones and then assisted 'Atty' Corbett. He began training at East Ilsley, near Newbury, in 1966. In 1969 he won 19 races worth over £10,000. His patrons include Captain T. E. Langton, Lord Masserene, Mr G. S. B. Cooke, Mrs J. D. Seward, Mr J. Gompertz and Mr G. Panton.

HUNTER'S MOON

Bred by the late Lord Derby, Hunter's Moon was a half-brother to Hyperion by Hurry On. In 1929 he won the Newmarket Stakes and was fourth in the Two Thousand Guineas and the Derby. Exported to the Argentine, he became a leading sire there.

HURRY ON

It is conceivable that the best horse to run in England during World War I was Hurry On, described by his trainer, the eminent Fred Darling, as "the best horse I have ever seen, the best I am ever likely to see". By Marcovil, who was not an outstanding racehorse and had very bad legs, out of Toute Suite, a little pony too small to be put into training, Hurry On was a magnificent great chestnut standing 17 hands with a girth of 82½ in and 9½ in of bone below the knee. Bought as a yearling for 500 gn by Mr James Buchanan, later Lord Woolavington, he only ran as a three-year-old, winning all his six races including the September Stakes and the Jockey Club Cup. He was never extended. At the stud he was champion sire in 1926 and got three Derby winners, Captain Cuttle, Coronach and Call Boy. At the age of 20 he sired his most influential son, Precipitation. Above all he revived the Matchem male line which was nearly extinct when he retired to the stud.

HYCILLA

Owned and bred by Mr W. Woodward and trained by Sir Cecil Boyd-Rochfort, Hycilla was by Hyperion out of the American mare Priscilla Carter. In 1944 she won the Oaks and the Champion Stakes.

HYPERICUM

Foaled in 1943, Hypericum was bred by King George VI and was by Hyperion out of Feola. Trained by Sir Cecil Boyd-Rochfort, she won the Dewhurst Stakes in 1945 and the following season the One Thousand Guineas. She bred five winners, including Restoration who won over £5,000 in stakes.

HYPERIDES

Lord Rosebery's Hyperides, by Hyperion, was second in the 1942 Derby and won the Coronation Cup as a four-year-old. He was then sold to Lady Yule as a sire but unfortunately died not long afterwards.

HYPERION

Bred and owned by the seventeenth Earl of Derby, Hyperion won the Derby and the St Leger in 1933 and was the greatest 'little' horse of this century. He also proved an outstanding success as a sire.

He was by Gainsborough out of the Chaucer mare Selene, who won over £14,000 in stakes. Selene also bred Sickle, from whom are descended the great American horse Native Dancer and Dan Cupid, sire of the Derby winner Sea Bird. A chestnut with four white stockings, Hyperion was so small and weedy as a foal that there was talk of putting him down. He gradually improved but he was not sent into training with Lord Derby's other yearlings and would probably have been sold but for the intervention of Lord Derby's trainer George Lambton, who was impressed by the little colt's beautiful action and by his head, so full of character and courage. When fully grown Hyperion stood only 15.1½ hands high. His lack of inches, though, was deceptive as his length and depth were those of a taller horse; it was the shortness of his cannon bones that brought him so near to the ground.

Hyperion never showed much at home and in his first race, a maiden event at Doncaster worth £162 to the winner, he started at 25-1. He displayed encouraging promise, though, to finish fourth and on his next appearance he won the New Stakes at Royal Ascot. At Goodwood he was a hot favourite for the 6f Prince of Wales's Stakes but in heavy ground he only dead-heated with the Nancy Stair filly, who could certainly go when in the mood. He was rested till the autumn when over 5f at Newmarket he was outpaced by the brilliant but erratic Manitoba. However, he finished the season well by winning the 7f Dewhurst Stakes at Newmarket very smoothly. In the Free Handicap he was given 9st, 7lb less than the speedy grey filly Myrobella.

As a three-year-old he was never beaten. He won the Chester Vase, the Derby by four lengths, the Prince of Wales's Stakes at Ascot, and the St Leger in a canter by three lengths. The following year his career was an anti-climax. George Lambton had ceased to train for Lord Derby and was succeeded by Colledge Leader, who did not understand Hyperion as well as Lambton had done. The little chestnut was not an easy horse to get fit as he was habitually indolent at home; moreover he was a distinct individualist with a number of odd little habits, including an inclination to play to the gallery. Lambton understood him thoroughly, realised he was a 'character' and was never disturbed or put out by his moods and quirks. Leader probably failed to realise the amount of work required to get such a lazy horse fit for the Gold Cup and perhaps he was a bit too tender and respectful to a dual classic winner. In the Gold Cup Hyperion finished a very weary third behind the Aga Khan's Felicitation who made all the running and, as had been planned, kept Hyperion at full stretch from the start. In his final outing, the Dullingham Stakes at Newmarket, Hyperion failed to concede 29lb to his solitary opponent Caithness who beat him by a short head. He had won nine races worth £29,509.

As a sire Hyperion was a great success. Not only did he get many winners himself, his sons made good sires and his daughters admirable brood mares. When at length he died in 1960 he had sired the winners in Great Britain of 748 races worth £557,009. It must be remembered, too, that many of the best of his offspring ran during World War II when opportunities were scarce and prize money low. He was leading sire in 1940, 1941, 1942, 1945, 1946 and 1955. He was second four times and third once. He was leading sire of brood mares in 1948 and 1957 and was five times second. His classic winners were Godiva (One Thousand Guineas and Oaks); Owen Tudor (Derby); Sun Castle (St Leger); Sun Chariot (One Thousand Guineas, Oaks and St Leger); Hycilla (Oaks); Sunstream (One Thousand Guineas and Oaks); Hypericum (One Thousand Guineas).

His skeleton is preserved in the Natural History Museum, South Kensington.

DOUGLAS, LADY JAMES. Shown here with Gainsborough (J. Childs up), Lady James Douglas was the first woman to have her colours carried to victory at the Derby.

EDWARD VII, KING. The Prince of Wales leads in Persimmon (J. Watts up) after winning the 1896 Derby

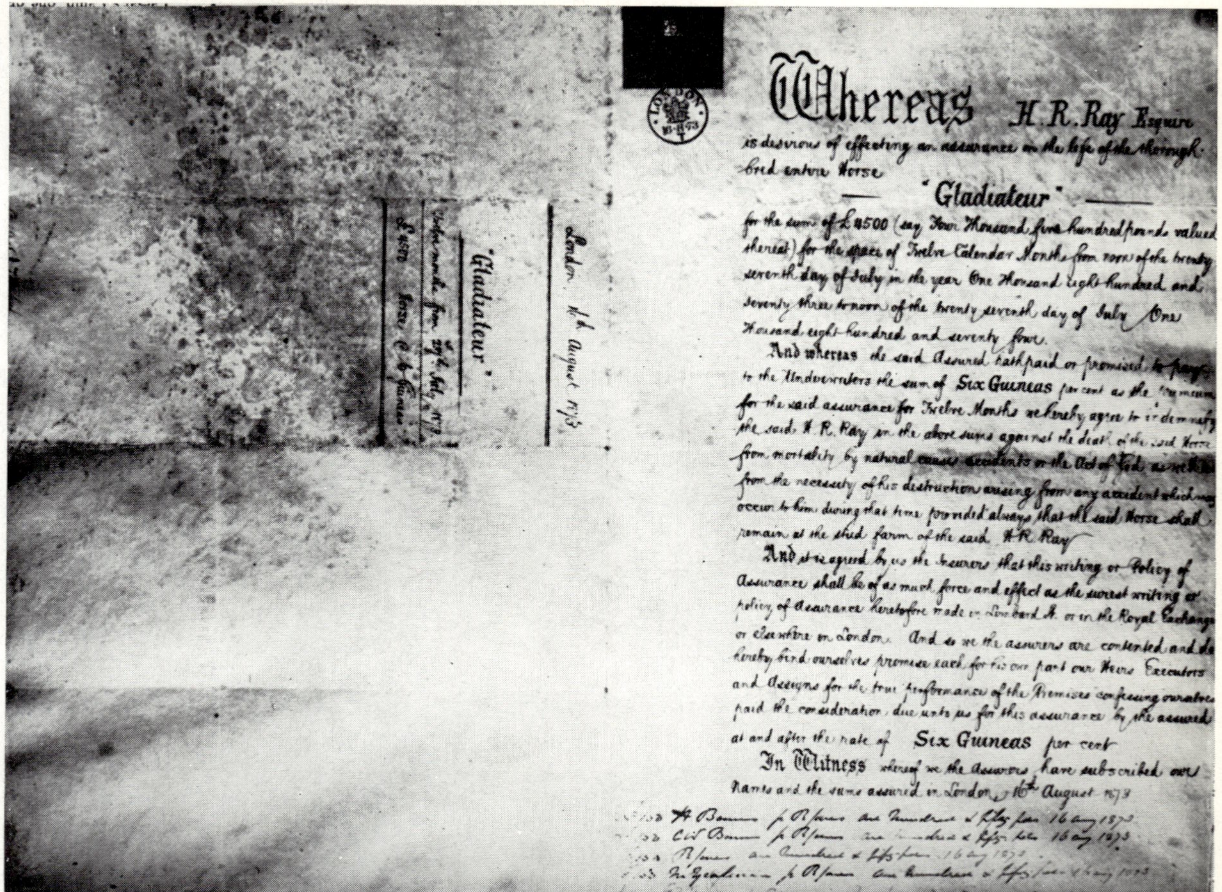

Whereas H. R. Ray Esquire is desirous of effecting an assurance on the life of the thorough-bred entire Horse

"Gladiateur"

for the sum of £4500 (say Four Thousand five hundred pounds valued thereat) for the space of Twelve Calendar Months from noon of the twenty seventh day of July in the year One Thousand eight hundred and seventy three to noon of the twenty seventh day of July One Thousand eight hundred and seventy four.

And whereas the said Assured hath paid or promised to pay to the Underwriters the sum of Six Guineas per cent as the Premium for the said assurance for Twelve Months we hereby agree to indemnify the said H. R. Ray in the above sums against the death of the said Horse from mortality by natural causes accidents or the Act of God as well as from the necessity of his destruction arising from any accident which may occur to him during that time provided always that the said Horse shall remain at the stud farm of the said H. R. Ray

And it is agreed by us the Insurers that this writing or Policy of Assurance shall be of as much force and effect as the surest writing or policy of Assurance heretofore made in Lombard St. or in the Royal Exchange or elsewhere in London. And so we the assurers are contented and do hereby bind ourselves promise each for his own part our Heirs Executors and Assigns for the true performance of the Premises confessing ourselves paid the consideration due unto us for this assurance by the assured at and after the rate of Six Guineas per cent

In Witness whereof we the Assurers have subscribed our Names and the sums assured in London, 16th August 1873

London 16th August 1873

"Gladiateur"

Twelve months from 27th July 1873

£4500 Horse @ 6 Guineas

GLADIATEUR. Lloyds Policy, dated, 16th August 1873, for £4500 at six guineas per cent, insuring against the death of Gladiateur, who in 1865 became the first French horse to win the Derby

I

IDENTIFICATION OF HORSES

Passports are issued annually for named two-year-old horses in the care of licensed trainers and other horses as authorised by the Stewards of the Jockey Club. They are returnable on demand and are issued subject to the instructions laid down by the stewards for their use. The Stewards of the Jockey Club may require such passports to be lodged with the Clerk of the Course for any race before the runners are declared under Rule 129 (a) so that the horse's identification can be verified by a veterinary surgeon before running.

IMPERIAL STAKES

See under KEMPTON PARK.

IMPRUDENCE

Madame P. Corbière's Imprudence, by Canot, won the One Thousand Guineas and the Oaks in 1947. She was trained in France by J. Lieux and ridden by W. R. Johnstone.

INBREEDING

Inbreeding has been defined as the mating of closely related individuals as opposed to outbreeding which means the mating of less related or unrelated individuals. All thoroughbreds are inbred in comparison with the members of most human societies.

INDIANA

Indiana, by Sayajirao out of Willow Ann, won the 1964 St Leger for Mr Charles Engelhard. He was ridden by J. Lindley and trained by J. F. Watts. In the Derby he was second to Santa Claus, beaten a length. After a brief period at the stud he was exported to Japan.

INGHAM, Stafford Walter Henry (b 1908)

'Staff' Ingham was apprenticed to Stanley Wootton. Before he became too big and tall, he rode with success on the flat, winning the Irish Two Thousand Guineas and also the 1923 Royal Hunt Cup on Weathervane, who belonged to King George V. With the swift increase in his weight, he turned his attention to jumping and became a stylish and most accomplished rider over hurdles. He chose not to ride over fences.

He took out a licence to train in 1939 but then came the war in which he rose to be a squadron leader in the RAF. Since 1945 he has trained with consistent success at Epsom. At one time his team included some jumpers, but nowadays he concentrates on the flat. Among his good winners have been Richer (Cambridgeshire), Chantry (Cesarewitch), Just Great (Great Voltigeur Stakes), Le Cordonnier (*News of the World* Stakes) and Soderini (Hardwicke Stakes). His owners include Mr and Mrs L. L. Lawrence, Mrs S. Jacobson, Mr S. Wootton, Mr J. Straus, Mr W. Sherman, Major-Gen J. A. d'Avigdor-Goldsmith, Mr W. J. McEnery, Mr J. L. Swift, Mr P. Bull, Mrs C. A. S. Palmer and Dr D. A. Fermont.

INTERMEZZO

Bred in 1966 by his owner Mr G. A. Oldham and trained by Harry Dragg, Intermezzo is a brown colt by Hornbeam out of Plaza, by Persian Gulf. As a two-year-old he won twice and was second to The Elk in the *Ob-*

server Gold Cup. The following season he was first past the post in the Great Voltigeur Stakes in August but was disqualified. However, most intelligently ridden by Hutchinson, he won the St Leger by 1½ lengths from Ribofilio at 7-1.

INVERSHIN

Invershin, bred and owned by Mr J. Reid Walker, won the Ascot Gold Cup in 1928 and again in 1929. He proved a stud failure.

IONIAN

Foaled in 1960, Ionian is by Milesian out of Persian View, by Persian Gulf. He won the Duke of Edinburgh Stakes and was beaten a short head by Only For Life in the Two Thousand Guineas. He stood at the Palmerstown Stud, Co Kildare, at a fee of £198 before being exported to Japan in 1968.

IRISH ELEGANCE

Foaled in 1915 and trained by Harry Cottrill, Irish Elegance, by Sir Archibald, was a brilliant horse that won the Royal Hunt Cup with 9st 11lb and the Portland Handicap with 10st 2lb. He failed as a sire.

IRONS

This is merely an abbreviation for stirrup irons. If a jockey is said to have 'lost his irons', it means that his feet have come out of the stirrups.

IROQUOIS

Iroquois, owned by Mr P. Lorillard, won the Derby and the St Leger in 1882. He was the first American-bred horse to win the Derby.

I SAY

I Say was foaled in 1962 and is by Sayajirao out of Isetta, by Morland. He won five races, including the Coronation Cup, and over £23,000 in prize money. He stands at the Sandwich Stud, Newmarket, at a fee of 198 gn.

ISINGLASS

Isinglass, who gained the 'Triple Crown' in 1893 was one of the greatest of Derby winners. Only once was he beaten during the four seasons he was in training and all told he won £57,455 in stakes, a sum that stood as a record in England till surpassed by Tulyar in 1952.

He was a big, strong bay by Isonomy and was owned by Mr (later Col) Harry McCalmont. Throughout his career he was trained by James Jewitt, whose stable was managed by the shrewd Capt Machell.

Isinglass resented hard ground and it so happened that he had to contend with firm going for much of his career. In consequence his victories were rarely impressive and usually at some stage of the contest the cry went up "The favourite's beat". In addition he was always ridden by the short-legged Tommy Loates, who could not really get the best out of such a big horse. When he ran in the Eclipse Stakes as a four-year-old, Isinglass at last got the going he really needed and showed the critics just what he could do. As a five-year-old he won the Gold Cup at Ascot, his only race that season. As a sire he was not a failure, but at the same time hardly fulfilled expectations considering his own racing record and the high quality of the mares sent to him.

ISONOMY

Isonomy stood barely 15.2 hands but was a really good horse, winning the Ascot Gold Cup twice, the Goodwood Cup, the Doncaster Cup and the Cambridgeshire. He did not run in the classics as his owner, Mr Gretton, preferred to keep him dark and go for a big win in the Cambridgeshire. When Isonomy won that race, Mr Gretton won over £40,000 in bets and the Derby in those days was seldom worth more than £6,000 to the winner. Isonomy proved a stud success and sired two Derby winners, Isinglass and Common. In fact both Isinglass and Common won the 'Triple Crown'.

J

JAGO, Brian (b 1938)

Brian Jago was apprenticed to Victor Smyth. His best season so far was 1958 when he rode 32 winners. Good races he has won are the Zetland Gold Cup, Liverpool Spring Cup, Newbury Summer Cup and the Brighton Cup.

JARVIS, Basil (1887-1957)

Basil Jarvis was born at Newmarket and was the son of the trainer William A. Jarvis who trained there. He rode for a time on the flat but soon became too heavy. He then rode a few winners under National Hunt rules, including one at Newmarket's last jumping meeting, before taking out a licence to train in 1909.

In 1921 he trained four winners at Royal Ascot, one of them being Mr Ben Irish's Periosteum, who won the Gold Cup. Mr Irish had paid 260 gn for Periosteum; with part of his Gold Cup winnings he paid 3,500 gn for a yearling by Tracery out of Miss Matty. He named this colt Papyrus and in 1923, trained by Basil Jarvis and ridden by Steve Donoghue, Papyrus won the Derby. On the same afternoon at Epsom, Basil's brothers Jack and William both won races.

Basil Jarvis trained a few horses for M. M. Boussac, for whom he won the Hardwicke Stakes and the Champion Stakes in 1932. Other patrons included Mr J. P. Hornung, Major J. S. Courtauld, Lord Glanely and Sir Victor Sassoon. He retired in 1948.

JARVIS, Sir John Layton (1887-1968)

One of the most capable and distinguished trainers of the twentieth century, Jack Jarvis was deservedly knighted for his services to racing in 1967. He was the son of the Newmarket trainer William A. Jarvis, while his brothers, William and Basil (see above) were successful trainers, too. Apprenticed to his father, he was a good light-weight jockey and among his victories were the 1903 Cambridgeshire on Hacklers Pride, the Ayr Gold Cup and the Derby Cup. When he became too heavy for the flat, he rode for a time under National Hunt rules, his chief win being in the Liverpool Hurdle.

He began training in 1914 and enjoyed consistent success throughout his long career. His principal patrons were the fifth Lord Rosebery, the sixth Lord Rosebery, Sir George Bullough, Mr E. Esmond, Mr A. Gordon-Smith, Sir John Jarvis, Lord Milford, Mr J. P. Philipps, Mr T. F. Blackwell, Mr D. H. Wills and Mr J. A. C. Lilley. His success in classic races were as follows:

Two Thousand Guineas: Ellangowan (1923); Flamingo (1928); and Blue Peter (1939)

One Thousand Guineas: Plack (1924); Campanula (1934); and Happy Laughter (1953)

Derby: Blue Peter (1939); and Ocean Swell (1945)

St Leger: Sandwich (1931).

He had four Gold Cup winners—Golden Myth, Foxhunter, Flyon and Ocean Swell—and three Eclipse Stakes winners—Golden Myth, Miracle and Blue Peter. He has also won the Victoria Cup four times, the Ayr Gold Cup three times, the Blue Riband Trial Stakes three times and the Stewards Cup Twice. He excelled in the preparation of stayers, but trained two outstanding sprinters in Honeyway and Royal Charger.

He had the reputation of possessing a somewhat explosive temper, but he never harboured resentment and was well known to be one of the most generous and hospitable characters in the racing world. He was a coursing enthusiast—he won the Waterloo Cup—and a supporter in one way or another of nearly every form of sport He died suddenly in December 1968.

JARVIS, Michael

Michael Jarvis, a son of the former steeplechase jockey Andrew Jarvis, was for many years associated with J. M. Gosden's stable. In 1968 he became one of Mr and Mrs David Robinson's private trainers and won the July Cup, King George Stakes and Nunthorpe Stakes with So Blessed; the Richmond Stakes and Gimcrack Stakes with Tudor Music. In 1969 he won the July Cup with Tudor Music and trained the winners of 46 races, worth over £48,000.

JARVIS, Ryan (b 1913)

Ryan Jarvis is a member of a famous family, his father being William Jarvis (see below), who trained for King George V and King George VI. He himself first of all assisted Fred Butters and then took out a licence to train in 1936, his career being interrupted by service in the Grenadier Guards from 1939 to 1945. Among the good horses he has trained are Constantia (National Breeders Produce Stakes), Lomond (Princess of Wales's Stakes, Ebor Handicap) and Front Row (Irish One Thousand Guineas). His stables are at Phantom House, Newmarket, and his owners include Mr J. N. Adam, Mr J. R. Adam, Mrs F. G. Allen, Maj Hon A. H. G. Broughton, Mr and Mrs R. Green, Hon. Lady Legh, Mr H. M. Knighton, Mr R. Lamb, Mr W. Ruane, Lady Rowlandson, Mr and Mrs W. J. Simms, Earl of Stradbroke, Mr and Mrs S. Terry and Mr T. West. In 1966 he won over £35,000 in stakes for his owners.

JARVIS, William (1885-1943)

The eldest son of William Arthur Jarvis, a respected Newmarket trainer, William, like his brothers Sir Jack Jarvis and Basil Jarvis, also became a trainer. In 1924 he succeeded Richard Marsh as trainer to King George V and in due course he trained for King Edward VIII and King George VI as well. He won the One Thousand Guineas in 1928 for King George V with Scuttle. In 1940 he won the One Thousand Guineas and the Oaks with the brilliant but temperamental Godiva, owned by Mr E. Harmsworth. His son is Ryan Jarvis (see above).

JAVELOT

Bred in France by Baron de Waldner and owned by him, Javelot by Fast Fox, won five races in France and in 1960 the Eclipse Stakes. He is syndicated and stands at the Fort Union Stud, Co Limerick. He is sire of The Accuser, winner of the Queen's Vase and the Doncaster Cup.

JEDDAH

Owned by Mr J. W. Larnach and trained by Richard Marsh, Jeddah won the Derby in 1898 and was the first 100-1 winner of that race. He made no mark as a sire.

JERSEY ACT

At the beginning of the twentieth century the importation of horses from America, many of them extremely moderate, was causing concern to those who were intent on preserving the purity of the English thoroughbred, as in many cases the pedigrees of these imported horses could not be traced back beyond a certain point.

The problem was referred to the Stewards of the Jockey Club who, after consulting most of the leading breeders, concluded that any animal claiming admission to the Stud Book should be able to prove satisfactorily some eight or nine crosses of pure blood, to trace back for at least a century, and to show such performances of its immediate family on the Turf as to warrant belief in the purity of its blood. Therefore all the imported horses and mares included in Volume XIX of the Stud Book, published in 1901, had been submitted to the test.

Among the famous animals who thus secured admission were Rhoda B, Americus Girl and Sibola. Rhoda B was dam of the 1907 Derby winner, Orby. Americus Girl, by the imported American sire Americus, has left an army of high-class descendants, including Mumtaz Mahal, Mahmoud, Nasrullah, Never Say Die, Tudor Minstrel, My Babu and Palestine. Sibola was great-grand-dam of Nearco, one of the greatest stallions of recent times and sire of the Derby winners Dante and Nimbus. But for the relaxation afforded by the ruling of 1901, not one of the descendants of Rhoda B, Americus Girl and Sibola would be eligible for the Stud Book.

In 1909 racing in America faced a dangerous crisis and legislation was in fact introduced that almost brought the sport to a close for a number of years. In England the Turf authorities visualised with horror the prospect of the country being overrun by a horde of American horses of doubtful pedigree. The result was the following notice in Volume XXI of the Stud Book published in September 1909:

> The Editors beg to inform subscribers that, since the last volume of the Stud Book was published, they have had cause to consider the advisability of admitting into the Stud Book horses and mares which cannot be traced to a thoroughbred root, but which have fulfilled the requirements given in the Preface to Volume XIX. They have decided that, in the interests of the English Stud Book, no horse or mare can be admitted unless it can be traced to a strain already accepted in the earlier volumes of the Book. The Editors, must therefore, rescind the Notice published in Volume XIX. The Stewards of the Jockey Club, who kindly consented to consider the question, fully endorse the decision arrived at by the Editors.

The barrier erected in 1909 proved only partially successful in checking the flow of American horses into England and at a Jockey Club meeting in 1913 Lord Jersey, who had held office as Senior Steward the year before, put the following question before the stewards:

> Whether, in view of the fact that a new volume of the Stud Book will be published this year, they will consider the advisability of suggesting to Messrs Weatherby, the Editors, that the last sentence of the first paragraph of the preface be added to, so as to read as follows: 'They have decided, in the interests of the English Stud Book, no horse or mare can, after this date, be considered as eligible for admission, unless it can be traced, without flaw on both sire's and dam's side of its pedigree, to horses and mares already accepted in the earlier volumes of the Book'?

The members of the Jockey Club gave full approval to Lord Jersey's suggestion and thus was born what came to be known as the 'Jersey Act'. The Americans were naturally furious. The English had placed the stamp of 'half-breds' on American horses with dire results to the American export market. Moreover, the Americans declined to accept that the English were really motivated by a burning desire to keep the Stud Book 'pure'; they reckoned the Jersey Act was framed to protect the export trade of English thoroughbreds and that the Jockey Club's action was typical of English selfishness and hypocrisy. Forced into the half-bred category was the 1914 Derby winner Durbar II, who has had great influence on bloodstock breeding in France through his daughter Durban, dam of Tourbillon. Descendants of Tourbillon such as Djebel (Two Thousand Guineas), Caracalla II (Gold Cup) and Arbar (Gold Cup) were all ineligible for the Stud Book at the time of their victories.

The post-war successes of the descendants of Durbar II gave rise to a feeling that the rules for Stud Book inclusion were too rigid. That sentiment was reinforced in 1947 and 1948 when My Babu and Black Tarquin were not only top-class two-year-olds, but the following season won the Two Thousand Guineas and the St Leger respectively. Neither was eligible for the Stud Book but it was thought that if they retired to the stud in this country, breeders would not hesitate to patronise them and a situation might eventually arise in which the Stud Book could be thrown into chaos and ridicule.

A committee was therefore appointed by the Jockey Club to look into the matter and the committee, consisting of the Duke of Norfolk, Lord Rosebery, Lord Allendale, Mr Peter Burrell and Mr Francis Weatherby, reported that some modification was in fact desirable. In Volume XXXI of the Stud Book published in 1949 the Jersey Act was repealed and it was stated that any animal claiming admission from then onwards had to be able to prove satisfactorily some eight or nine crosses of pure blood, to trace back for at least a century, and to show such performance of its immediate family on the Turf as to warrant belief in the purity of its blood.

The Americans, of course, were delighted but regarded the repeal of the Jersey Act not as a belated act of justice and fair play to American breeders, but as a recognition by the English Turf authorities that the high quality of French and American half-breds was in process of making the Stud Book, in its battle for purity, look frankly absurd.

JERSEY, fifth Earl of (1773-1859)

A tall handsome man who was Lord Chamberlain to William IV and Master of the Horse to Queen Victoria, the 5th Earl of Jersey won the Derby with Middleton (1825), Mameluke (1827) and Bay Middleton (1836). Despite 10 successes in classic events, his racing is said to have cost him over £400,000.

JEST

Foaled in 1910, Jest was bred and owned by Mr J. B. Joel and was by Sundridge out of Absurdity, by Melton. Trained by Charles Morton, she won the One Thousand Guineas and the Oaks in 1913. The only winner she bred was Humorist, winner of the 1921 Derby.

JIMMY REPPIN

Jimmy Reppin, foaled in 1965, is not bred in the height of fashion, being by Midsummer Night II out of Sweet Molly, by Chamier. Trained by John Sutcliffe junior, he did not win as a two-year-old. The following season, however, he showed immense improvement and after winning a maiden race at Newmarket, he was third in the Two Thousand Guineas. Later he won the Hungerford Stakes at Newbury and the Wills Mile at Goodwood. As a four-year-old he won six races including the Sussex Stakes, Hungerford Stakes, Queen Elizabeth II Stakes and the £7,900 Prix Perth at Saint-Cloud. At the end of the season he was retired to the stud, having proved himself beyond doubt a high-class miler.

JOCKEY

A 'jockey' is a person who holds a licence from the Stewards of the Jockey Club to ride for hire.

No one is allowed to ride in any race until he has obtained a licence from the Stewards of the Jockey Club, and a jockey must apply for his licence annually, giving his full name and address to the Registry Office. (There are different regulations for apprentices and amateur riders.)

Licences are only granted on the condition that the jockey is not the owner or part-owner of any racehorse, and does not bet on horses racing or receive presents in connection with a race from persons other than the owner of the horse he rides in that race. Any jockey who is proved to the satisfaction of the Stewards of the Jockey Club to have contravened any of the above conditions may have his licence withdrawn.

No person is allowed to ride in any race while under suspension by any recognised Turf authority.

A list of licensed jockeys is published in the *Racing Calendar*.

Every jockey has to pay £1 for his licence, and every apprentice 10s, that money serving as his provision to the Bentinck Benevolent and Provident Fund.

A jockey whose licence has been withdrawn for misconduct is a disqualified person. If a jockey becomes a disqualified person, his licence is revoked.

Once a jockey has ceased to be an apprentice (q.v.), he is free to form engagements for himself irrespective of any made for him during his apprenticeship. Employers retaining the same jockey have precedence according to the priority of their retainers. The terms of all agreements have to be duly registered at Weatherbys and half the fee paid in advance, the rest at the termination of the retainer.

For jockey's fees see Rules of Racing, Rule 70.

Leading Jockeys

Year	Jockey	Wins
1850	E. Flatman	88
1851	,,	78
1852	,,	92
1853	J. Wells	86
1854	,,	82
1855	G. Fordham	70
1856	,,	108
1857	,,	84
1858	,,	91
1859	,,	118
1860	,,	146
1861	,,	106
1862	,,	166
1863	,,	103
1864	J. Grimshaw	164
1865	G. Fordham	142
1866	S. Kenyon	123
1867	G. Fordham	143
1868	,,	110
1869	,,	95
1870	W. Gray & C. Maidment	76
1871	G. Fordham & C. Maidment	86
1872	T. Cannon	87
1873	H. Constable	110
1874	F. Archer	147
1875	,,	172
1876	,,	207
1877	,,	218
1878	,,	229
1879	,,	197
1880	,,	120
1881	,,	220
1882	,,	210
1883	,,	232
1884	,,	241
1885	,,	246
1886	,,	170
1887	C. Wood	151
1888	F. Barrett	108
1889	T. Loates	167
1890	,,	147
1891	M. Cannon	137
1892	,,	181
1893	T. Loates	222
1894	M. Cannon	167
1895	,,	184
1896	,,	164
1897	,,	145
1898	O. Madden	161
1899	S. Loates	160
1900	L. Reiff	143
1901	O. Madden	130
1902	W. Lane	170
1903	O. Madden	154
1904	,,	161
1905	E. Wheatley	124
1906	W. Higgs	149
1907	,,	146
1908	D. Maher	139
1909	F. Wootton	165
1910	,,	137
1911	,,	187
1912	,,	118
1913	D. Maher	115
1914	S. Donoghue	129
1915	,,	62
1916	,,	45
1917	,,	42
1918	,,	66
1919	,,	129
1920	,,	120
1921	,,	141
1922	,,	102
1923	S. Donoghue & E. C. Elliott	89

1924	E. C. Elliott	106
1925	G. Richards	118
1926	T. Weston	95
1927	G. Richards	164
1928	,,	148
1929	,,	135
1930	F. Fox	129
1931	G. Richards	145
1932	,,	190
1933	,,	259
1934	,,	212
1935	,,	210
1936	,,	177
1937	,,	214
1938	,,	206
1939	,,	155
1940	,,	68
1941	H. Wragg	71
1942	G. Richards	67
1943	,,	65
1944	,,	88
1945	,,	104
1946	,,	212
1947	,,	269
1948	,,	224
1949	,,	261
1950	,,	201
1951	,,	227
1952	,,	231
1953	,,	191
1954	D. Smith	129
1955	,,	168
1956	,,	155
1957	A. Breasley	173
1958	D. Smith	165
1959	,,	157
1960	L. Piggott	170
1961	A. Breasley	171
1962	,,	179
1963	,,	176
1964	L. Piggott	140
1965	,,	160
1966	,,	191
1967	,,	117
1968	,,	139
1969	,,	163

JOCKEY CLUB

There is no precise knowledge of how, when and why the Jockey Club was founded. The first intimation of its existence came in 1752. There is no evidence to suggest that the club was founded with any high-minded notion of governing or reforming the Turf. No doubt it was originally just a social club aiming to promote good fellowship among racing and horse-breeding gentlemen from all over the country. As the members included some of the most influential men of the day, the club naturally acquired authority and prestige.

Originally the club used to meet at the Star and Garter in Pall Mall, but meetings also took place at the Thatched House in St James's Street, the Clarendon in Bond Street and at the Corner, Hyde Park, where Mr Tattersall was good enough to provide a room and a cook. When Tattersall's premises moved to Knightsbridge, the club's London headquarters became established with those of their agents, Messrs Weatherby, in Bond Street.

Naturally the club wanted a place to foregather at Newmarket. In 1752 the lease of a plot of land there was obtained and a building, known as the Coffee Room, was constructed. There is reason to believe that the original Coffee Room stood upon the site of the room of that name in the present Jockey Club premises. Before half the lease had expired, it was transferred to Mr R. Vernon, a member of the club, and the other members became Mr Vernon's tenants. When in due course Mr Vernon's lease of the Coffee Room expired, the freehold of the lots comprising the Coffee Room, the New Rooms and adjuncts thereof was bought with money advanced by the Duke of Portland. In 1831 the estate was conveyed in trust to Lord Lowther, the Duke of Richmond and the Earl of Verulam, presumably stewards of the club at that time. It was not until 1835 that an official list of members of the club was published.

Once the Jockey Club was established and began to exercise authority, its most important member was Sir Charles Bunbury (q.v.), born in 1740. When he was only 28 he was Steward of the Jockey Club, there being a single steward at that time. As from 1770, though, it became the custom to have three stewards. That practice held good for nearly two hundred years, a steward holding office for three years, becoming Senior Steward the final year, at the termination of which he nominated his successor. Bunbury is best remembered today as having owned Diomed, the first winner of the Derby, and for the part he played in the sensational case involving Escape, a horse belonging to the Prince of Wales (later George IV) and the Prince's jockey Sam Chifney.

In 1757 a dispute over a race at the Curragh was referred to the Jockey Club, proof of the club's growing influence beyond its own immediate jurisdiction, while the following year, in respect of overweight, it issued for the first time an authoritative order. In 1784, when the Government proposed to increase the tax that already existed on racehorses, a deputation from the Jockey Club went to see Mr Pitt in London and the proposed increase was cancelled. In 1807 the Calendar for the first time published the details of certain cases dealt with by the Jockey Club, this being done to provide a guide for the stewards at other meetings. Nine years later the club, which still in fact possessed no power of jurisdiction outside Newmarket, expressed a willingness to help settle racing disputes if called upon to do so.

The first 'Warning Off' notice appeared in 1821 when William Taylor, a tout commonly known as 'Snipe', was warned by notice from Mr Weatherby to keep off that part of the Heath occupied by tenants of the Jockey Club. 'Snipe' was not in a position to fight back, but Mr S. Hawkins, whose chief offence was to swear horribly at Lord Wharncliffe, was made of sterner material and declined to accept a 'warning off' notice. However, in an action for trespass against him in 1827, the Jockey Club established a legal right to warn an individual off Newmarket Heath.

In 1832 the Jockey Club issued a notice in the Calendar to the effect that as much uncertainty prevailed with regard to the Rules and Orders of the club, they thought it proper to declare that these applied solely to races run at Newmarket. They themselves had no authority whatsoever to extend their rules and orders to any other place, but for the sake of uniformity and certainty, they recommended the adoption of those rules to stewards at other courses. It was furthermore made clear that the Jockey Club were unwilling to settle disputes that arose at meetings at which the Rules and Regulations of Newmarket were not in force.

This announcement clearly had for its object the uniting of all meetings under the single control of the Jockey Club and placing all others outside the pale of recognised authority, a policy bound to exert a most beneficial affect on the organisation and conduct of the sport. This small start towards uniting the various race-meetings in this country under a single authority finally culminated in reciprocal agreements with the Jockey Club and Turf authorities of practically every country in the world where racing takes place today.

From 1836 to 1946 the outstanding member of the club was Lord George Bentinck (q.v.), second son of the fifth Duke of Portland. Aloof, arrogant, dictatorial and at times impulsive, there were undoubtedly aspects of his racing career that were open to criticism and made him seem on occasions hypocritical, but on balance he unquestionably conferred great benefits on the Turf. Before he took matters in hand racing was carried on in a haphazard, disorganised fashion, no attention being paid to the comfort or well-being of spectators. Lord George decreed different priced enclosures, with amenities varying according to the price paid. He insisted on punctuality and ensured it by fining clerks of the course 10s. for every minute a race started late. He installed comprehensive number boards and insisted on proper racecards with the horses numbered. He ordered horses to be saddled in one special place and to parade in front of the stands before a race. He abolished the pernicious practice of the winning owner giving a present to the judge and he raised both the standard of officials, which was lamentably low, and the standard of starting. Above all he waged unrelenting war on the crooks and parasites that had started to infest the Turf when the scale of betting began to increase and but for his efforts, which included the exposure of the Running Rein scandal in the 1844 Derby, racing might, like the prize-ring, have sunk into utter disrepute. He gave up racing quite suddenly to devote himself to politics. He was still in the prime of life when he died from a heart attack.

In 1836 the Jockey Club tried to tackle the ever-present problem of non-triers and published a notice expressing extreme disapprobation of horses that were started with no intention of winning. An important step was taken in 1843 when the club decided to take no further cognisance of matters connected with betting. Up till then much of the stewards' time had been consumed by betting problems and disputes. Such matters are now handled by Tattersalls' Committee (q.v.).

In 1858, in order to cope with the ever-changing conditions of the Turf, the existing rules having been found totally inadequate, the stewards appointed a committee to revise and recast the rules concerning horse-racing in general and also the rules and orders of the Jockey Club. The rules concerning horse-racing governed all meetings subject to the established Rules of Racing, but the orders of the Jockey Club applied to Newmarket only. The old rules, which with slight alteration and addition had sufficed for over a hundred years, were superseded by a new code of 66 rules which were thought to be sufficiently comprehensive to deal with any eventuality. So rapid was the Turf's expansion, though, that they only lasted ten years. Furthermore, there was another thorough revision that came into force in 1871.

Admiral Rous, who died in 1877, dominated racing in the mid-Victorian era. A man of complete integrity, greatly liked and immensely respected, he guided the Jockey Club along the paths of progress and commonsense, his one weakness being a tendency to write letters for publication in *The Times* without first having ascertained all the facts of the case. By shrewd management, he greatly strengthened the Jockey Club's financial position, while he was largely instrumental in ensuring that the Rules of Racing were in line with the requirements of those times. A tireless worker, he laboured unceasingly for the good of the sport and set new standards by the excellence of his handicapping. Of the three so-called 'Dictators of the Turf', Bunbury, Bentinck and himself, he was the greatest benefactor to racing and he never permitted his determination to achieve his objectives to degenerate into conduct that could have been condemned as arrogant. He formed a link between the haphazard sport characteristic of the early days of the Jockey Club and the beginnings of the highly organised racing that we know today.

In 1879 the club decided that jockeys should be licensed and issued a warning that if any jockey was found to be an owner, or part-owner, of racehorses, or in the habit of betting, his licence could be withdrawn at the discretion of the stewards. Four years later it was found necessary to put some check on the great increase in race-meetings throughout the country, there being serious difficulty in allotting days for racing at meetings already in existence.

A major Jockey Club scandal occurred in 1887. At the annual dinner of the Gimcrack Club, Lord Durham, a member of the Jockey Club, in the course of his speech, cast reflections on the conduct of Sir George Chetwynd, another member, who not long before had held office as Senior Steward. The matter became a subject of litigation and eventually it was decided, in view of the technical nature of the matters involved, to submit it to arbitration. Owing to legal delays the case was not heard till 1889 when the stewards, acting as arbitrators, awarded purely nominal damages to Sir George Chetwynd, who at once resigned from the Jockey Club and severed his connection with the Turf.

The starting gate was introduced at the turn of the century, and in 1903, in consequence of certain notorious incidents, the stewards found it necessary to introduce the following rule: "If any person shall administer, or cause to be administered, for the purpose of affecting the speed of a horse, drugs or stimulants internally or by hypodermic or other method, he shall be warned off the Turf".

During World War I there was a strong movement in certain quarters to curtail racing completely for the duration of hostilities. That racing was permitted to continue on a greatly reduced scale was largely due to the tact and commonsense of Lord Jersey, Senior Steward at the time, supported by Lord Rosebery, Lord Derby, Lord Durham and Lord Crewe. Powerful support for these influential noblemen came from that famous demagogue and notorious con-man, Horatio Bottomley, MP.

After the war serious gang warfare broke out on English racecourses, and the Jockey Club wisely appointed their own officials under Major Wymer to protect the public and to supervise security arrangements on individual racecourses.

In 1919 the Jockey Club set up a committee under Lord Hamilton of Dalzell to inquire into the policy to be adopted for racing in the future. The committee suggested that certain courses could with advantage be amalgamated with others, and that steps should be taken to improve transport, lower costs and bring amenities up to date.

The war had to some extent lowered the rigid social barriers existing up to 1914 and the Jockey Club, thanks to the example of Lord Jersey and Lord Hamilton of Dalzell, managed to shed a little of its traditional aloofness. There was a marked improvement, too, in relations between the Jockey Club and members of the racing press. Incidentally it was Lord Hamilton who was largely responsible for the introduction of the totalisator into English racing.

For many years the Jockey Club had been worried by the question of nominations rendered void by the death of an owner. The club, on legal advice, had always acted on the assumption that fees and forfeits incurred for horses entered under Jockey Club rules could not be recovered under process of law, because if they were contracts, they were contracts by way of gaming and wagering and therefore without legal sanction.

The matter was under discussion in 1927 when Edgar Wallace, the well-known journalist and author, suggested a 'friendly' action between the Jockey Club and himself. The final verdict went to the Jockey Club (for details, see Nominations, Void).

The change in the rule made possible by this action came just in time for Cameronian to win the 1931 Derby. Lord Dewar, owner-breeder of Cameronian, died in 1930 and left the colt to his nephew, whose colours Cameronian carried to victory at Epsom.

An incident occurred in 1930 which ultimately involved the Jockey Club in an important law suit. Don Pat, trained by Charles Chapman at Lavant, won a race at Kempton Park. Don Pat was tested for dope and it was found that a fairly large dose of caffeine had been administered.

The matter was the subject of a thorough investigation by the Stewards of the Jockey Club, who, at the conclusion of the case, addressed Chapman in these words: "We have given most careful thought to this case. We have come to the conclusion that Don Pat was doped and he is disqualified for life. We consider you, as trainer, were directly responsible for the care of the horse. Your licence to train is revoked and you are warned off Newmarket Heath".

The findings and decision were fully within the powers conferred on the stewards by the Rules of Racing. Chapman, bound by those rules as a licensed trainer, had no redress. Furthermore the wording seemed to make it clear that the stewards found nothing against him bar the fact that he had failed in his duty as a trainer in so far as a horse under his care had been doped. There was no imputation against his integrity. Unfortunately when the stewards published their decision the wording was altered. The words "you, as trainer, were directly responsible for the care of the horse" were omitted. The statement in the *Racing Calendar* was repeated in *The Times* under a heading: "Racing. Another trainer warned off. The doping of Don Pat".

The press naturally seized with relish on what was considered a first-class racing scandal and from the articles that appeared, it was clear that most people thought that Chapman himself had been guilty of fraud. Thus, besides losing his licence, Chapman found himself branded as a crook. He thereupon brought an action for libel against the stewards for their publication in the *Racing Calendar*, and against *The Times* as well for having repeated the statement.

The case was heard by Mr Justice Horridge. Sir Patrick Hastings, representing Chapman, made a great point of the fact that the stewards had done nothing to remove the false impression created, though it would have been perfectly easy for them to have done so. The jury found for Chapman and awarded him £13,000 against the *Racing Calendar*, and £3,000 against *The Times*.

An appeal was at once lodged. It was argued for four days and eventually the Court decided that the stewards and Messrs Weatherby were protected and the verdict against them could not be maintained. On the other hand there was no privilege in the case of *The Times*, but the view was taken that the damages awarded all defendants were too high and a new trial was ordered in respect of *The Times*. The new trial, however, never came into court, Mr Chapman deciding, quite rightly, that his character had been publicly vindicated.

In 1948 another trainer, James Russell, whose licence had been withdrawn following a case of doping, sued the stewards, alleging that his licence had been wrongfully withdrawn, and claiming damages for alleged breach of contract. He also claimed damages for libel from Messrs Weatherby, publishers of the *Racing Calendar*. Both actions were unsuccessful and that verdict was upheld by the Court of Appeal.

In 1936 the Jockey Club decided to appoint officials designated stewards' secretaries, who were to hold no executive powers, their duty being to bring to the notice of local stewards any matter in connection with the running or riding of any horse at the meeting that might, on investigation, be found to be irregular. Some of the local stewards, a fair number of whom were notoriously incompetent—at one course the stewards were known as the 'Three Blind Mice', at another as 'unburied dead'—resented at first this innovation which on the whole has proved highly successful.

During phases of World War II there was bitter hostility to racing from certain quarters and it required considerable tact on the part of the Jockey Club to keep the sport going at all, even on a greatly reduced scale. Lord Ilchester, who had just retired from being Senior Steward, made an admirable reply to a leading article in *The Times* which had stated that the resumption of racing in the autumn of 1940—there had been no racing at all from June till mid-September—was deeply resented. Lord Sefton was Senior Steward for much of the war period and carried out his duties at a very difficult time with marked success.

In the dark days of 1941 the Jockey Club formed a committee, with Lord

Ilchester as chairman, to consider the whole future of racing. In 1943 an excellent report was produced, progressive and far-reaching. Unfortunately many of the reforms suggested never came into force, possibly for financial reasons. "It is like the Beveridge Report", said one influential Jockey Club member. "It is a very good plan when they have the money". Looking back, it is hard to avoid the impression that a great opportunity was missed, particularly as the spirit of reform, which had temporarily infected the Jockey Club, soon seemed to fade quietly away.

However, there were certain changes. At last the Jockey Club recognised the significance of public relations and appointed Mr J. H. Freeman, late of the *Daily Mail*, as Public Relations Officer. The photo-finish was introduced and so was the racecourse commentary. The programmes at Newmarket were revised, strengthened and in certain cases curtailed, while a number of Saturday programmes were introduced. None too soon an attempt was made to shed the Newmarket meetings of their old-fashioned exclusiveness and to attract the general public. Gradually admission to the members' enclosure was made far more accessible. To alleviate the possible tedium of race after race on the straight course, a round course, named after Lord Sefton, was constructed, but in fact has not proved a notable success. In 1967 a re-building scheme was begun on the Rowley Mile course, and when completed a year later it met with general approval, it being considered that the standard of comfort had been greaty increased and the bleak, rather unfriendly, atmosphere substantially reduced.

A long-standing and ridiculous attitude by the Jockey Club was to permit horses to run un-named. It was not until 1946 that a rule was brought in demanding that all horses were named before they ran.

A disquieting episode took place in 1951 when a private test showed that Lord Rosebery's filly Snap had been doped, Lord Rosebery having initiated the test because Snap had run far below her usual form. At that time a trainer lost his licence when a horse of his was found to have been doped, regardless of whether the animal in question had been doped to win or to lose, although, as Lord Rosebery pointed out, no trainer in his right mind would dope one of his own horses to lose when so many simpler and equally effective methods were available. The racing public was naturally disturbed at the thought that if the test had been official, Lord Rosebery's much respected trainer, Jack Jarvis would have lost his licence. The Jockey Club set up a committee under Major (later Sir) Reginald Macdonald-Buchanan to inquire into the whole problem of doping, but to the indignation of many people closely concerned with the sport, the Jockey Club apparently saw no reason to alter the rules after the presentation of the committee's report.

In 1954 the Jockey Club decided that its own stewards should not function at Newmarket meetings, a pool being created from within the membership of the club from which 'local' stewards would from then on be drawn. This year, too, the stewards let it be known that they were prepared to grant licences to Newmarket trainers whose patrons included bookmakers.

By the mid-fifties it had become apparent that some big changes in the laws affecting betting and gaming in this country were due in the not far distant future. It had also become distressingly obvious that English racing was resting on a dangerously insecure financial basis, largely because such a tiny proportion of the vast profits from betting was ploughed back into the sport. In 1956, therefore, the Jockey Club set up a joint committee, which included various interested organisations, to work out a plan that would embody certain fundamental principles which would be of benefit to the sport as a whole and that could be presented at the opportune moment to the Home Secretary. The following year the Jockey Club greatly disappointed many followers of racing by declining to introduce overnight declarations.

In 1960 public confidence in the conduct of racing was shaken by a series of doping scandals. The Jockey Club felt compelled to set up a three-man committee to review the rules and procedures dealing with the administration of dope to racehorses, and to look into the efficiency of the existing rules on that subject.

There was fortunately a much brighter side to racing that year. The government-appointed committee under Sir Leslie Peppiatt reported that it was both desirable and practicable that persons engaged in betting on horses should make a contribution for purposes conducive to the improvement of the breed and of the sport in general. The committee outlined suggestions for raising £1-£1¼ million, annually although the Jockey Club had in fact requested a sum of £3 million. Despite some disappointment that the Jockey Club's request had been turned down, it was generally recognised that the Peppiatt Committee's report represented a milestone of great significance in English racing history and that financial assistance would be forthcoming just in time to save the racing industry from a possible collapse.

The provisions of the report were incorporated into the Betting Levy Bill which set up a board, under the Home Office, empowered to collect contributions from the bookmakers and the tote and to apply those contributions to the general good of racing.

The new situation meant that all punters, on-course and off-course, were contributing to racing and clearly the Jockey Club had from then on to give far more attention to the demands of the betting public than it had done in the past. Accordingly the existing system of declaring runners was scrapped and a form of overnight declaration instituted in its place.

In 1961 the Duke of Norfolk's committee on doping, which included Sir Laurence Byrne, lately a High Court Judge, and Dr Wooldridge, chairman and scientific director of the Animal Health Trust, published a comprehensive report. The whole subject was put in its proper focus and not the least of its recommendations was to remove 'the sword of Damocles' from over the heads of trainers, through which, under the old rule, they had immediately and irrevocably been disqualified if any of their horses were found to have been doped, whether the doping was done to improve a horse's chance of success or to prevent it from winning.

Another committee, under Lord Rosebery, was established to investigate the effect which the existing Rules of Racing had on the production of middle-distance horses. It made certain recommendations which were incorporated into the rules, the most important being to increase the number of two-year-old races to be run at seven or eight furlongs, and to allow seven-furlong races to be staged from 1st July.

In 1963 a committee, comprising members of both the Jockey Club and the National Hunt Committee, was set up under the chairmanship of Lord Howard de Walden to analyse the various categories of stewards' work, to recommend a method which would enable that work to be more easily handled, and to suggest any necessary reorganisation.

The committee's report was received the following year and was accepted in principle. The main feature was the formation of a new supreme authority, the Turf Board, to operate as from 1st January 1965. The Turf Board was to be formed from the Jockey Club and the National Hunt Committee, and there was to be continuous representation as well of the policy and views of the Levy Board.

It was stated that the main function of the Turf Board was to deal with matters of general policy, the board's decisions being implemented by the

Jockey Club and the National Hunt Committee. The chairman of the Turf Board was to be *ipso facto* the Senior Steward of the Jockey Club, working with one vice-chairman from the Jockey Club and another from the National Hunt Committee. To ensure a certain continuity of office, the chairman was to hold office for five years, the vice-chairman for two.

In addition the Jockey Club and the National Hunt Committee would continue to have the normal three stewards, whose concern would be not policy, but the day-to-day business of racing. The first chairman of the Turf Board was Major-Gen Sir Randle Feilden (q.v.), the outstanding racing administrator of the post-war era.

The year 1965 saw the publication of the Duke of Norfolk's Committee on the pattern of racing, the first serious attempt at long-term planning for the sport; and also the first tentative use of starting stalls in this country, a reform ultimately carried through in the face of much opposition largely through the energy and determination of Mr T. F. Blackwell. The following year the Jockey Club at last gave way to the gallant persistence of Mrs Florence Nagle and women, barred for years by the medieval thinking of the rulers of English racing, became eligible to receive a trainer's licence. In 1967 the Jockey Club suffered a heavy loss when its secretary, Mr Bill Weatherby, died suddenly on his way to see the Irish Derby.

In 1968, in order to streamline racing administration and to render it more efficient, the Jockey Club and the National Hunt Committee amalgamated, the new body, designated the Jockey Club (incorporating the National Hunt Committee), coming into force on 12th December of that year. Major-Gen Sir Randle Feilden became Senior Steward of this new body (for the names of other stewards, see below). Brig S. H. Kent was appointed General Manager, Secretary to the Senior Steward, and Co-Secretary of the Joint Racing Board, his main functions being policy and liaison with Ministries and bodies outside racing. Mr Peter Weatherby was appointed Chief Executive, his duties including all licensing, disciplinary cases and appeals, reports from Inspectors of Courses, and a constant review of the rules. Mr David Weatherby became Secretary to the Jockey Club and Keeper of the Match Book, with responsibility for the day-to-day conduct of racing, administration and finance, fixtures and prize money, and liaison with foreign Turf authorities. The work of the stewards, two of whom retire annually, was divided into four main groups—Licensing, Racecourses and Rules; Discipline; Administration and Finance; Fixtures and Prize Money—certain stewards being made responsible for each group. Discipline is the responsibility of a group under a disciplinary chairman, who acts in this capacity for not less than two of his three years as a steward.

The new Jockey Club no longer has responsibility for the activities at Newmarket, which include the racecourses, the properties and the investments. These have become the responsibility of the Newmarket Estates and Property Company. Newmarket racecourses have now the same relationship to the new Jockey Club as other racecourses.

Undoubtedly the Jockey Club has made in recent years the most strenuous efforts to improve its image and to render the direction and organisation of the sport more modern and more businesslike. Racing, however, tends to become less and less of a sport; more and more an immensely complex business. Moreover, this is an era of professionals, not of amateurs, however dedicated or gifted. It remains to be seen whether in the next decade the power of the Jockey Club, a self-elected, self-perpetuating, essentially upper-class body, will be gradually transferred to the Levy Board, a statutory body, which in its turn may assume the functions of a government-appointed, salaried Racing Board, directing every aspect of the sport and not merely its finances.

JOCKEY CLUB, Members of

The Jockey Club and the National Hunt Committee amalgamated as from 12th December 1968. The new body, which is designated the Jockey Club (incorporating the National Hunt Committee) took over the functions and powers of the old Jockey Club and of the National Hunt Committee as from 1st January 1969. As from that date the stewards were as follows:

Major-Gen Sir Randle Feilden (Senior Steward)
Mr T. F. Blackwell (Deputy Senior Steward)
Major W. D. Gibson (Deputy Senior Steward)
Duke of Devonshire
Capt H. M. Gosling
Lieut-Col J. D. Hornung
Earl of Cadogan
Mr J. J. Astor
Brig F. B. B. Noble

At the time of the amalgamation the Jockey Club consisted as follows:

Patron: H.M. The Queen

H.R.H. The Prince Philip, Duke of Edinburgh (Honorary Member)
H.R.H. The Duke of Gloucester (Honorary Member)
H.R.H. The Duke of Windsor (Honorary Member)
Marquess of Abergavenny
Viscount Allendale
Hon J. J. Astor
Col the Hon Julian Berry
Mr T. F. Blackwell
Major-General Sir George Burns
Earl Cadogan
Major E. M. Cameron
Sir Rex Cohen
Lieut-Gen Sir George Collingwood
Lord Crathorne
Major-Gen J. A. d'A'vigdor Goldsmid
Gen Sir Miles Dempsey (died in 1969)
Earl of Derby
Duke of Devonshire
Sir William Dugdale, Bart
Earl of Durham
Mr T. E. S. Egerton
Major-Gen Sir Randle Feilden
Lieut-Col D. Forster
Major W. D. Gibson
Earl of Halifax
Mr J. O. Hambro
Sir Edward Hanmer, Bart
Mr E. Holland-Martin
Mr L. Brook Holliday
Mr R. D. Hollingsworth
Lieut-Col J. D. Hornung
Lord Howard de Walden
Mr H. J. Joel
Lord Kilmany
Viscount Leverhulme
Mr C. L. Lloyd
Sir R. McAlpine
Capt J. Macdonald-Buchanan
Major S. R. Macdonald-Buchanan
Lord Manton
Lord Margadale
Mr P. Mellon (Honorary Member)
Duke of Norfolk
Hon J. P. Philipps
Lord Porchester
Mr J. Rogerson
Earl of Rosebery
Duke of Roxburghe
Earl of Sefton
Mr R. R. Shelley (Hon. Member)
Rt Hon Christopher Soames
Hon R. Stanley
Duke of Sutherland
Sir Richard Sykes, Bart
Brig Lord Tryon
Sir Francis Weatherby
Major-Gen Sir Harold Wernher, Bart
Mr J. H. Whitney (Hon. Member)
Mr G. D. Widener (Hon. Member)
Lord Willoughby de Broke
Marquis of Zetland

Since that date Mr C. W. Engelhard has been elected an Honorary Member.

This was the composition of the National Hunt Committee at the time of the amalgamation:

Patrons: H.M. The Queen
H.M. Queen Elizabeth the Queen Mother

Members of the Committee:
H.R.H. The Duke of Gloucester (Honorary Member)
Marquess of Abergavenny
Major P. H. G. Bengough
Major-Gen C. H. Blacker
Earl Cadogan
Major E. M. Cameron
Viscount Chelsea
Mr E. R. Courage
Major D. R. Daly
Sir Humphrey de Trafford
Mr H. W. Dufosse
Cmdr H. S. Egerton

(*right*) GORTON, JOHN). A moment of triumph. John Gorton has just won the 1969 Oaks on Sleeping Partner. (*below*) Hyperion Lord Derby leads in Hyperion (T. Weston up) after winning the Derby. Next to Lord Derby (in top hat is the late Alec Cottrill, and on the extreme right Teddy Lambton, later a successful trainer

(*right*) LAMBTON, HON GEORGE. Two great trainers: Hon George Lambton (nearest camera) and Fred Butters

(*left*) MURLESS, CHARLES FRANCIS NOEL

Major-Gen Sir Randle Feilden
Capt P. M. Forsythe Forrest
Major W. D. Gibson
Lieut-Col Sir Martin Gilliatt
Capt H. M. Gosling
Earl of Halifax
Sir Edward Hanmer, Bart
Mr J. R. Henderson
Major R. Hoare
Mr E. Holland-Martin
Mr H. J. Joel
Lord Kilmany
Mr G. Kindersley
Col Sir Peter Grant-Lawson, Bart
Lord Leigh
Viscount Leverhulme
Lieut-Col H. M. Llewellyn
Mr J. A. Marshall
Lieut-Cmdr R. J. B. Mildmay-White
Major J. C. Vernon-Miller
Lieut-Col R. B. Moseley
Brig F. B. B. Noble
Duke of Norfolk
Lieut-Gen Lord Norrie
Major H. M. Peacock
Hon J. P. Philipps
Col Sir John Carew-Pole, Bart
Mr J. Rogerson
Earl of Rosebery
Mr J. S. Schilizzi
Earl Of Sefton
Mr J. J. Straker
Major-Gen V. W. Street
Mr J. R. H. Sumner
Col John Thomson
Wing-Cmdr P. D. O. Vaux
Col G. R. Westmacott
Mr W. H. Whitbread
Mr J. H. Whitney (Hon Member)
Major D. Wigan
Mr R. S. Wilkins
Lord Willoughby de Broke
Col the Hon E. H. Wydnham

Since the amalgamation the Earl of Durham, Sir Francis Weatherby, Cmdr H. S. Egerton, Lt-Cmdr R. J. B. Mildway-White, Maj-Gen V. W. Street have all died. Members elected since then include Maj James Morrison, Mr R. N. Richmond-Watson, Mr R. R. Tweedie, Maj M. G. Wyatt and Mr A. Kidston.

JOCKEYS ASSOCIATION OF GREAT BRITAIN

This is a body that represents the interests of professional riders under both Jockey Club and National Hunt

M

rules. The Flat Race Jockeys Association and the Professional National Hunt Jockeys Association were amalgamated in 1969.

JOEL, H. J. (b 1896)

The son of the late Mr J. B. Joel (see below), Mr Jim Joel served in World War I with the 15th/19th Hussars. He owns the Childwick Bury Stud, St Albans, and the best horse he has so far bred is Royal Palace (Royal Lodge Stakes, Two Thousand Guineas, 1967 Derby, Coronation Cup, Eclipse Stakes and King George VI and Queen Elizabeth Stakes). He also bred Picture Play (One Thousand Guineas); West Side Story (Yorkshire Oaks and beaten by inches in the Oaks); and Major Portion (Middle Park Stakes, St James's Palace Stakes, Sussex Stakes and Queen Elizabeth II Stakes). He purchased Predominate who won the Goodwood Stakes three years running and at 9 years of age the Goodwood Cup.

In 1969 he purchased for a stiff price the brilliant sprinter Song. In 1967 he won the record total for an English owner of £120,923. A bachelor, he is one of the most modest, kind and unassuming of men and enjoys great popularity in the racing world. He is a member of the Jockey Club and a steward at Alexandra Park, Ascot and Goodwood. For many years most of his horses were trained by T. Leader but they are now with N. Murless, T. Waugh, W. Elsey, D. Candy and H. Cecil. Colours: black, scarlet cap. In 1970 Mr Joel's Welsh Pageant won successively the Victoria Cup, the Lockinge Stakes and the Queen Anne Stakes, while the unpredictable Connaught, second in the 1968 Derby, won the Prince of Wales Stakes at Ascot for the second year running.

JOEL, Jack Barnato (1862-1940)

A man of humble origin, Mr Jack Barnato Joel went out to South Africa as a young man and rapidly accumulated an immense fortune. Towards the close of the last century he returned to England and in 1900 he registered his colours, black jacket, red cap. From then on gold, diamonds, breeding and racing were his main interests in life. Because of his successes in business and on the Turf he was generally regarded as a lucky man. Mr Joel himself did not believe in luck; he believed in hard work and plenty of it.

In 1901 he engaged Charles Morton as private trainer and the combination proved highly successful, as between 1903 and 1921 Mr Joel won no fewer than eleven classic events. The Gold Cup was the one big race that always eluded him. He won the Derby with Sunstar in 1911 and with Humorist in 1921. His other classic successes were the Two Thousand Guineas with Sunstar; the One Thousand Guineas with Jest and the Oaks with Our Lassie, Glass Doll, Jest and Princess Dorrie; and the St Leger with Your Majesty and Black Jester.

In the closing stages of his racing career Mr Joel was notably less successful. Since his death the Childwick Bury Stud has been carried on by his son, Mr H. J. Joel (see above).

JOEL, S. B. (1866-1931)

Usually referred to as 'Solly' Joel, Mr S. B. Joel made a fortune in South Africa as a young man as did his brother Mr J. B. Joel. A forceful and rather self-assertive character, he raced on a big scale but was less shrewd and less successful than his brother. Pommern, who won the 'Triple Crown' in 1915, was his sole classic winner. His most successful purchase was to buy Polymelus for 4,000 gn at the Newmarket October Sales. Within a month Polymelus had won the Duke of York Handicap at Kempton and the Cambridgeshire. Over the latter race Mr Joel and his friends won £100,000. Mr Joel himself had a final bet of £6,000 to £5,000 when the horses were at the post. Polymelus was a stud success and five times champion sire.

JOEL, Stanhope, H. (b 1903)

Mr Stanhope Joel is the son of the late Mr S. B. Joel (see above). Mr Stanhope Joel, who rose to the rank of Squadron-Leader in the RAF during the war, now lives in Bermuda and is not often seen in England but he nevertheless maintains considerable racing interest. He is part-owner of the Snailwell Stud, Newmarket, and has horses with N. Murless, H. L. Cottrill, M. H. Easterby and H. Thompson Jones in England, and with R. Fetherstonhaugh in Ireland. The best horses he has owned are Chamossaire (St Leger); Busted (Eclipse Stakes and King George VI and Queen Elizabeth Stakes); Matador (Stewards Cup); Primera (Ebor Handicap, Churchill Stakes and Princess of Wales's Stakes); and Refresher (Manchester Cup and Brighton Cup, twice). Colours: green and pink stripes, pink cap. In 1970 Mr Joel won the Coronation Cup with Caliban and the St James's Palace Stakes with Saintly Song, while Mrs Joel won the Oaks with Lupe.

JOHNSON, Ernest (b 1948)

Ernie Johnson was born at Sunderland. His mother is Greek by birth and her brother rode many winners in Greece. When his parents went to live in Cirencester, Ernie worked at a local riding-school before being apprenticed to Ian Balding at Kingsclere. He had his first ride in 1965 and that season rode a couple of winners.

In 1966 he rode 28 winners, in 1967 39, one of his victories being on Ovaltine in the Ebor Handicap. Balding at this time thought that Johnson would not get sufficient opportunities in his own stable and transferred his indentures to Sam Hall with happy results, Johnson making swift progress in jockeyship and confidence. In 1968 he rode 68 winners, more than any other rider in the north, and again won the Ebor, this time on Alignment.

In 1969 he got his big chance when given the ride on Blakeney in the

Derby, in which he rode a faultless race. He has a great capacity for taking trouble and is still always ready to learn. He rode 79 winners in 1969.

JOHNSTONE, William Raphael (1905-1964)

Nicknamed 'Togo' before the war but more commonly referred to as 'Rae' after it, W. R. Johnstone was born in Australia. In 1931 he was champion jockey in Sydney and the following year he migrated to France at the invitation of M. Pierre Wertheimer. He headed the jockeys' list in France in three of his first six seasons there. In 1934 he accepted a retainer to ride for Lord Glanely in England. He won the Two Thousand Guineas on Colombo, but after Colombo's defeat in the Derby he was sharply criticised for the tactics he had employed. He ceased to ride for Lord Glanely not long afterwards.

The following year Johnstone won the One Thousand Guineas on Mesa and he ought to have won the Oaks on her, too. As it was she finished a desperately unlucky third. After the war, during which he lived an adventurous life in France, he enjoyed a period of resounding success. In 1947 he won the One Thousand Guineas and the Oaks on Imprudence, and the following year the Derby on My Love. He was narrowly beaten in the 1949 Derby on Amour Drake, but won again in 1950 on Galcador. That year he also won the One Thousand Guineas on Camaree, the Oaks on Asmena, and the St Leger on Scratch II. He won the 1951 St Leger on Talma, the 1954 Oaks on Sun Cap, and the 1956 Derby on the unglamorous Lavandin. At one time or another he won all the French classic events and he had two victories in the Prix de l'Arc de Triomphe, as well. At his best he was a brilliant rider and was always liable to be at his best on the big occasion. He was admired in England—at any rate after the war—but the racing public never really took him to their hearts. Perhaps they could not forgive him for Colombo's defeat. He retired in 1957 and took up training.

JOINT ASSOCIATIONS LIAISON COMMITTEE

This body includes representatives of the Racecourse Association, Racehorse Owners Association, Thoroughbred Breeders Association, National Trainers Association, National Hunt Trainers Association and Jockeys Association. Quarterly meetings, attended by the Stewards of the Jockey Club and by Jockey Club members of the Levy Board, are held to discuss policy matters affecting the bodies whose representatives attend the meeting. An opportunity is thus provided for those concerned in the detailed running of racing to put forward their problems.

JOINT RACING BOARD

The Joint Racing Board is designed to be a forum for the joint discussion of problems facing the racing industry and to be a joint policy-making body of the Jockey Club and the Levy Board.

JONES, Harry Thomson (b 1925)

'Tom' Jones is a son-in-law of Mr Stanhope Joel. Educated at Eton, he served in the Royals and was then assistant trainer to Bob Fetherstonhaugh for two years and to Sam Armstrong for four years. He took out a licence himself in 1951 and runs a highly successful 'mixed' stable at Newmarket. On the flat he has won the Imperial Stakes with Saucepan, the Lowther Stakes with Our Betters, and the Churchill Stakes with London Gazette. His owners include Mr and Mrs Stanhope Joel, Mrs C. Brudenell-Bruce, Dr L. Slotover, Lord James Crichton Stuart, Major R. F. Dill, Mrs J. Rogerson, Mrs P. Robeson, Mr J. R. Hindley, Mr Donovan Drewery and Sir W. Pigott-Brown.

JONES, Herbert (1880-1951)

Herbert Jones was a son of King Edward VII's first trainer, Jack Jones, who had a stable of jumpers at Epsom.

Apprenticed to Richard Marsh, the royal trainer, at the tender age of 10, Herbert Jones rode his first winner in 1896. He was very little known to the public, however, when in 1900 he was given the ride in the Two Thousand Guineas on Diamond Jubilee, a brother of the King's first Derby winner Persimmon. Diamond Jubilee (q.v.) was a high-class colt but temperamental and at times savage. The horse and Jones got on well together and the combination won not only the Guineas, but the Derby, Eclipse Stakes and the St Leger. These successes established Jones's reputation and in 1909 he won his second Derby in the royal colours, that time on Minoru, who also won the Two Thousand Guineas. Jones had two other victories in the Two Thousand Guineas and one in the Oaks. His final win was in 1923 on a horse of King George V's called Erne. He was 71 when he was found dead in the kitchen of his home at Girton.

JONES, Herbert (b 1933)

Herbert Jones was apprenticed to Joe Thwaites and later to J. L. Pearce. He rode on the flat from 1949 to 1963 and won races in England, India, Norway, Denmark and Sweden. In England he won the Ayr Gold Cup and the Ebor Handicap. He took out a licence to train in 1964 and owns stables at Norton, near Malton.

JUDGE, THE

The Judge must occupy the judge's box at the time the horses pass the winning post. He must announce his decision immediately, or after consulting the photograph, and such decision shall be final unless an objection to the winner, or any placed horses, is made and sustained. This rule, though, does not prevent a judge from correcting any mistakes, such correction being subject to confirmation by the stewards.

Judges are licensed annually by the Stewards of the Jockey Cub. They are appointed to meetings by the Joint Administrative Authority and are paid by that body according to their terms of employment.

K

KALYDON

Bred by the Northmore Stud, Kalydon was foaled in 1956 and is by Alycidon out of Lackaday, by Bobsleigh. He was a very useful stayer, winning five races worth £4,225. In the St Leger he started second favourite but was unplaced. He now stands at the Side Hill Stud, Newmarket, at a fee of £400 and the best of his stock so far is Park Top, a great mare whose victories so far include the Ribblesdale Stakes, Coronation Cup, Hardwicke Stakes and King George VI and Queen Elizabeth Stakes.

KANDY

Kandy, foaled in 1929, was a bay filly by Alcantara II out of Kiao Tehau, by Alcantara II or Chouberski. Owned by M. E. de Saint-Alary and trained in France by F. Carter, she won the One Thousand Guineas, ridden by E. C. Elliott, in 1932.

KARABAS

Foaled in 1965, Karabas is a bay horse by Worden III out of a Tantième mare. Trained in Ireland as a three-year-old, he was a useful performer and won the Warren Stakes at Goodwood. The following season he joined Bernard van Cutsem's stable and improved out of all knowledge, his victories including the City and Suburban, the Prix du Conseil Municipal at Longchamp, and finally the Washington International at Laurel Bank. He is still in training and in 1970 won the Hardwicke Stakes at Ascot.

KASHMIR II

Kashmir II was bred in Ireland by Mrs A. Levins Moore and was foaled in 1963, being a black or brown by Tudor Melody out of Queen of Speed, by Blue Train. As a yearling he was sold for 8,600 gn to Dr J. Burkhardt who was acting for Mr P. Butler. Trained in France by C. Bartholomew, Kashmir II won three times as a two-year-old, while the following season he won the Prix Djebel at Maisons-Laffitte and the Two Thousand Guineas. In the latter event he won by inches from Great Nephew. He retired to the stud in 1967 and is the property of a syndicate. He stands at the Haras des Vignes, Evron (Mayenne), France.

KEITH, Duncan (b 1938)

Duncan Keith was born in Glasgow and served his apprenticeship with H. E. Smyth. He had a successful association with the late Walter Nightingall's stable but his career was seriously interrupted by two bad falls. In 1964 he fractured his pelvis when riding London Melody, and in 1965 he was very bady hurt in a fall at Lingfield, again when riding London Melody. The biggest number of winners he has ridden in one season is 70 and his most important victories have been the Two Thousand Guineas on Niksar and the Coronation Cup on I Say. He is attached to P. Walwyn's stable but had weight difficultics in the spring of 1970 and because of this he missed riding Humble Duty in the One Thousand Guineas.

KEMPTON PARK

Photographs of Kempton Park taken at the turn of this century show it to be in remarkably pleasant and rural surroundings. The horrid spread of subtopia has inevitably taken its hideous toll, but the course itself is still a pretty one in the summer, bear-

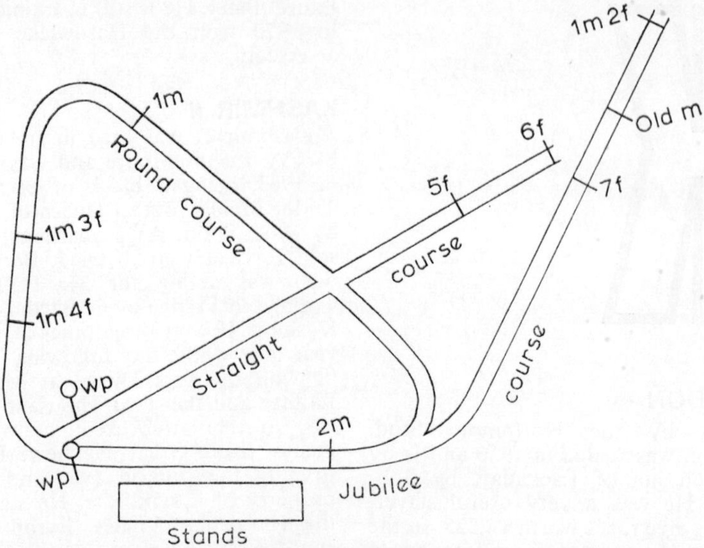

KEMPTON PARK

ing in mind how close it is to London. It is still possible to enjoy a tolerable day's pheasant shooting there, or at least it was possible until the recent decision, dictated presumably by financial needs, to permit gravel digging operations on the far side of the course. A controlling interest in Kempton was recently acquired by David Robinson.

Probably Kempton's most profitable fixture, at least as far as flat-racing is concerned, is the one held on the Saturday and the Monday of Easter. The main events then are the Two Thousand Guineas Trial and the 10f Rosebery Stakes on the Saturday; the One Thousand Guineas Trial and the 2m Queens Prize on the Monday. The Great Jubilee Handicap, run in May, has lost something of its old-time glamour, and the same can be said of the Imperial Stakes for two-year-olds in September, formerly the Imperial Produce Stakes and a race won by many famous horses.

It is a right-handed, triangular track roughly 1m 5f round and with only very gentle undulations. The straight 6f course, which intersects the back straight of the triangular course, is perfectly flat. The 10f Jubilee course, which has a slight downhill slope for the first 2f, joins the triangular course at the home turn.

Clerk of the Course: Mr C. H. Hargreaves, Kempton Park, Sunbury-on-Thames. Tel: Sunbury 8-2292.

Best Times:

Distance	*Horse-Age-Weight*	*Date*	*Time*
5f	Henpecked 3-7-6	2-6-66	58.2
5f	Fair Reward 2-8-11	18-9-59	58.6
6f	Backgammon 3-7-10	21-6-66	1min 11.2
6f	Zabara 2-8-10	22-9-51	1min 10.8
7f Jubilee course	Careless Lad 5-8-9	3-6-47	1min 24.2
7f Jubilee course	Cursorial 2-8-8	20-9-63	1min 26
8f Jubilee course	Wise Ruler 3-8-8	21-9-63	1min 38.4

Distance	*Horse-Age-Weight*	*Date*	*Time*
8f Jubilee course	Batanolius 2-7-4	19-10-62	1min 42.5
8f round	Maestoso 5-8-2	10-6-67	1min 36.9
8f round	Fascinating 2-7-0	3-11-56	1min 43.4
10f	Someo 5-8-3	27-3-48	2min 1.4
11f	Crozier 3-9-0	2-6-66	2min 18.2
12f	Alcide 4-9-3	9-5-59	2min 31.6
16f	Incredule 4-7-6	26-7-56	3min 23.8

Great Jubilee Handicap, 1m 2f

First run 1887. *Run at Hurst Park* 1946. *No race* 1940 *to* 1945.

	OWNER	TRAINER	JOCKEY	SP
1930 Lucky Tor, 5–7–8 ..	W. Singer	J. Lawson ..	F. Fox	8–1
1931 Racedale, 5–8–1 ..	Lady Nunburnholme	C. B-Rochfort .	A. Wragg . ..	9–4
1932 Venturer, 4–7–9 ..	H. Eves	G. Clancy ..	K. Gethin ..	100–9
1933 Colorado Kid, 4–7–12	Lieut-Col G. Loder	V. Gilpin . ..	C. Buckham ..	100–9
1934 Cotoneaster, 4–7–11	E. T-Smith	F. Templeman	G. Nicoll . ..	10–1
1935 Wychwood Abbot, 4–9–2	O. Watney	T. Leader . ..	H. Wragg ..	7–1
1935 British Quota, 4–7–6	A. Saville	J. Beary	T. Weston ..	11–2
1936 Inflation, 4–8–0 ..	C. Winn	C. B-Rochfort .	C. Richards ..	20–1
1937 Commander III, 7–8–9	N. Christie	C. Elsey	H. Wragg ..	100–7
1938 Monument, 5–8–13 .	Duke of Marlborough ..	C. B-Rochfort .	P. Beasley ..	10–1
1939 Antonym, 4–9–2 ..	H. Holdert	H. Count . ..	A. Tucker ..	10–1
1946 Paper Weight, 4–8–9	Sir A. Butt	Fk. Butters ..	H. Wragg ..	4–1
1947 Royal Tara, 4–7–12 .	D. Morris	J. Beary	T. Gosling ..	100–8
1948 Royal Tara, 5–8–11 .	D. Morris	J. Beary	K. Gethin ..	20–1
1949 Fil d'Or II, 5–8–3 ..	Aga Khan	Fk. Butters ..	G. Richards ..	6–1
1950 Peter Flower, 4–8–4	Lord Rosebery ..	J. Jarvis	W. Rickaby ..	10–1
1951 Roman Way, 6–8–1	Mrs J. Bryce . ..	C. B-Rochfort .	D. Savage ..	100–8
1952 Durante, 4–7–7 ..	Maj D. McCalmont	H. Persse . ..	J. Sirett	10–1
1953 Durante, 5–7–11 ..	Maj D. McCalmont	H. Persse . ..	P. Evans . ..	100–9
1954 Chatsworth, 4–8–10	Maj L. Holliday ..	H. Cottrill ..	F. Barlow ..	9–2
1955 Swept, 4–7–0	Maj T. Bardwell ..	W. Stephenson	D. Ryan	100–9
1956 Tudor Jinks, 4–7–7 .	A. Tompsett.. ..	M. Feakes ..	D. Forte . ..	7–1
1957 Orinthia, 4–6–13 ..	P. Bull	C. Elsey	G. Starkey ..	4–1
1958 Alcimedes, 4–8–3 ..	Lord Astor	J. Colling . ..	J. Mercer . ..	100–8
1959 Alcimedes, 5–8–3 ..	Lord Astor	J. Colling . ..	J. Mercer . ..	10–1
1960 Rocky Royale, 4–7–9	J. Norris	D. Whelan ..	D. Smith.. ..	3–1
1961 Chalk Stream, 6–7–5	Mrs R. Sangster ..	E. Cousins ..	B. Lee	8–1
1962 Water Skier, 5–7–10.	D. Murray	E. Cousins ..	P. Robinson ..	100–7
1963 Water Skier, 6–7–11.	D. Murray	E. Cousins ..	D. Yates . ..	8–1
1964 Commander in Chief, 5–8–7 . ..	H. Whitehouse ..	E. Cousins ..	F. Durr	100–7
1965 Antiquarian, 4–7–9 .	H. Blagrave	H. Blagrave ..	J. Sharman ..	10–1
1966 Antiquarian, 5–7–11	H. Blagrave	H. Blagrave ..	P. Cook	6–1
1967 Red Bar, 5–8–2 ..	C. Clore	H. Price	P. Elliott . ..	20–1
1968 Pally's Double, 4–6–11	G. Cooper	J. Watts	J. Lowe	33–1
1969 Sovereign Ruler, 4–7–0	H. Blagrave	H. Blagrave ..	D. East	6–1
1970 Blue Yonder, 4–8–2 .	J. H. Whitney ..	J. Tree.. ..	A. Murray ..	15–2

Imperial Stakes, 6f

Two-year-olds. Formerly Imperial Produce Stakes. First run 1889. *No race* 1939 *to* 1946.

	OWNER	TRAINER	JOCKEY	SP
1930 Doctor Dolittle, 8–9	A. Basset	H. Persse . ..	H. Beasley ..	2–1
1931 Orwell, 9–6	W. Singer	J. Lawson ..	R. Jones	2–11
1932 Gino, 8–3..	Aga Khan	Fk. Butters ..	M. Beary . ..	6–5

Imperial Stakes (contd)

		OWNER	TRAINER	JOCKEY	SP
1933	Colombo, 9–6	Lord Glanely	T. Hogg	S. Donoghue	4–9
1934	Shahali, 9–6	Aga Khan	Fk. Butters	R. Perryman	9–4
1935	Harina, 8–0	W. Barnett	R. Dawson	S. Donoghue	10–1
1936	Lover's Path, 8–5	R. McAlpine	V. Smyth	J. Sirett	5–1
1937	Glen Loan, 7–11	Mrs W. Murray	C. B-Rochfort	S. Donoghue	6–4
1938	Heliopolis, 8–1	Lord Derby	C. Leader	T. Weston	7–2
1947	Ottoman, 9–4	Lord Irwin	W. Earl	D. Smith	6–5
1947	Henley-in-Arden, 9–4	Mrs G. Kohn	W. Nightingall.	C. Smirke	4–1
1948	Gigantic, 8–3	King George VI	N. Murless	G. Richards	2–1
1949	Kisaki, 7–12	Aga Khan	Fk. Butters	D. Smith	100–8
1950	Clutha, 9–1	Sir M. McAlpine	V. Smyth	A. Breasley	4–1
1951	Zabara, 8–10	Sir M. McAlpine	V. Smyth	W. Rickaby	9–4
1952	Bluefin, 8–1	J. Gerber	F. Armstrong	G. Richards	1–3
1953	Fluorescent, 7–12	Mrs C. Woodbridge	R. Day	D. Smith	8–1
1954	Grass Court, 8–1	Mrs C. Evans	K. Cundell	W. Elliott	7–1
1955	Milesian, 8–1	Mrs R. M. O'Ferrall	P. Prendergast	T. M. Burns	30–100
1956	Sarcelle, 8–5	K. Mason	N. Cannon	A. Breasley	100–30
1957	Pin-wheel, 8–4	Sir V. Sassoon	N. Murless	L. Piggott	6–1
1958	Saint Crespin III, 8–4	Aly Khan	A. Head	M. Garcia	5–1
1959	Venture VII, 9–0	Aly Khan	A. Head	G. Moore	7–4
1960	The Axe, 8–4	J. Whitney	C. B-Rochfort	S. Clayton	20–1
1961	Compensation, 9–5	Mrs G. Lambton	E. Lambton	S. Smith	11–2
1962	Saucepan, 8–1	Mrs H. T. Jones	H. T. Jones	G. Starkey	100–8
1963	Derring-Do, 8–4	Mrs H. Renshaw	A. Budgett	L. Piggott	2–1
1964	Gulf Pearl, 8–8	J. Whitney	J. Tree	J. Lindley	50–1
1965	Conjuror, 8–4	Maj L. Holliday	W. Wharton	R. Hutchinson	2–1
1966	Heath Rose, 8–1	Maj L. Holliday	W. Wharton	W. Williamson	20–1
1967	Hametus, 8–9	Lady Beaverbrook	W. Nightingall.	R. Hutchinson	20–1
1968	Right Tack, 8–12	J. R. Brown	J. Sutcliffe, Jn.	G. Lewis	3–1
1969	Yellow God, 9–2	D. Robinson	P. Davey	L. Piggott	4–5

KENNYMORE

Kennymore, by John O'Gaunt, won the Two Thousand Guineas in 1914 and was second in the St Leger. He died after a single season at the stud.

KERR, Alexander Macdonald (b 1904)

Alexander Kerr has been conducting a small 'mixed' stable at Holmwood, Dorking, since 1947. From 1934-40 he assisted his father, the late J. Kerr.

KEYSOE

Keysoe, bred and owned by the late Lord Derby, was a bay filly by Swynford out of Keystone II. She won the St Leger in 1919, trained by Hon G. Lambton and ridden by B. Carslake. She bred Caissot, winner of over £4,000, and Flittemere, grandam of Ballymoss.

KEYSTONE II

The late Lord Derby's Keystone II, by Persimmon, won the Oaks in 1906 and bred six winners that included Keysoe, winner of the 1919 St Leger.

KHALED

Khaled was bred by the Aga Khan and was by Hyperion out of Eclair, by Ethnarch. In 1945 he won the Coventry and Middle Park Stakes, while the following year he was second in the Two Thousand Guineas and won the St James's Palace Stakes. He did well as a stallion in America, where he sired Swaps, winner of the Kentucky Derby.

KHALKIS

Foaled in 1960, Khalkis is a bay by Vimy out of Merry Xmas, by Chamossaire. He was owned by Lord Elveden, and trained by Paddy Prendergast won the Eclipse Stakes at Sandown. Altogether he won three races worth over £22,000. In 1965 he retired to the Irish National Stud, Tully, Co Kildare, at a fee of 250 gn. By 1970 his fee had been lowered to 98 guineas.

KIBENKA

Kibenka was foaled in 1963 and is a bay by King's Bench out of Kathie, by Zuccero. A good, consistent handicapper, he won six races and £15,000 in stakes, his successes including the Free Handicap and the Totalisator Spring Handicap. He was syndicated for the stud and stands at the Tudor Stud, Buntingford, Hertfordshire.

KI MING

Ki Ming, by Ballyogan, won the 1951 Two Thousand Guineas, owned by Mr Ley On and trained by Michael Beary. He also won the Diadem Stakes. He failed as a sire.

KINCSEM

Kincsem, foaled in 1874, was by Cambuscan and was bred in Hungary. One of the greatest fillies in racing history, she ran 54 times and was never defeated, winning the Austrian Derby, Hungarian Oaks and St Leger, and the Goodwood Cup. Her descendants proved very successful in European racing but the family suffered heavy losses in both World Wars and was almost obliterated.

KING GEORGE VI AND QUEEN ELIZABETH STAKES

See under Ascot.

KING OF THE TUDORS

King of the Tudors was foaled in 1950 and is by Tudor Minstrel out of Glen Line, by Blue Peter. Trained by W. Stephenson, he won six races worth over £16,000, including the Sussex, Knights Royal and Eclipse Stakes. A half-brother to Our Babu, winner of the Middle Park Stakes and the Two Thousand Guineas, he was exported to America in 1959.

KING SALMON

Bred by Lord Carnarvon and owned by Sir Richard Brooke, King Salmon was a half-brother to the Derby winner Blenheim by Salmon Trout. In 1933 he was second in the Two Thousand Guineas and the Derby, while the following year he won the Coronation Cup and Eclipse Stakes. Before being exported to Brazil he sired Herringbone, winner of the One Thousand Guineas and the St Leger. He also sired Chenille, dam of the St Leger winner Alcide.

KING'S BENCH

King's Bench, trained by M. Feakes, won four races worth over £11,000, including the Coventry and Middle Park Stakes in 1951 and the St James's Palace Stakes in 1952. He was second in the Two Thousand Guineas. By Court Martial out of King's Cross, by King Salmon, he did quite well as a sire before being exported to Japan in 1968.

KING'S LEAP

Foaled in 1959, King's Leap was bred by the National Stud and is a bay by Princely Gift out of Impala, by Big Game. Sold for 2,400 gn as a yearling, he was a genuine handicap sprinter, racing till he was six and winning eight races and nearly £6,000 in stakes. He stands at the Mitchelstown Stud, Athboy, Co Meath, at a fee of £148 and has made an excellent start as a sire.

KING'S STAND STAKES

See under Ascot.

KING'S TROOP

Foaled in 1957, King's Troop was bred by Mrs P. Hastings and is a bay by Princely Gift out of Equiria, by Atout Maitre. He won five races, including the Royal Hunt Cup, and nearly £7,000 in stakes. He stands at the Ballykisteen Stud, Co Tipperary, at a fee of £250 and is doing well as a sire.

KINGSWAY

Kingsway, by Fairway, won the

Two Thousand Guineas in 1943. He was exported to America in 1955.

KLAIRON

Bred in France, Klairon is by Clarion out of Kalmia, by Kantar. In 1955 he won the French Two Thousand Guineas and was third in the English Two Thousand. While at the stud in France he sired Monade (Oaks and Prix Vermeille), Altissima (French One Thousand Guineas) and Premier Violin (Prix Juigné and Prix Noailles). Imported into England, he is the property of a syndicate and stands at the Kingwood Stud, Lambourn. In England he has sired D'Urberville (Windsor Castle Stakes, King's Stand Stakes) and Lorenzaccio (July Stakes and Prix Jean Prat).

KONG

Kong, a grey, was not bred in the height of fashion being by Baytown out of Clang, by Hainault, but apart from winning the Wokingham Stakes at Ascot, she was dam of Nimbus, winner of the Two Thousand Guineas and the Derby; and also of Grey Sovereign, who won over £8,000 in stakes and became one of the most consistently successful of modern sires.

L

LAD

A common term for stable employees, but covering also responsible individuals such as the head lad and travelling head lad.

LADY JOSEPHINE

Lady Josephine, foaled in 1912, was by Sundridge out of Americus Girl, by Americus. She is one of the most influential mares in the Stud Book, being the dam of Lady Juror (q.v.) and Mumtaz Mahal (q.v.).

LADY JUROR

Lady Juror, foaled in 1919, was bred by Lady Sykes and was by Son-in-Law out of Lady Josephine, by Sundridge. She won three races worth over £8,000, including the Jockey Club Stakes, a race that carried far more prestige then than it does now. At the stud she bred Fair Trial, a high-class miler that was later an outstanding sire; and Jurisdiction, second in the One Thousand Guineas. She is the ancestress of Tudor Minstrel (Two Thousand Guineas), Commotion (Oaks), Combat (unbeaten winner of nine races and a successful sire), Faux Tirage (winner of over £8,000 and a successful sire in New Zealand) and Aristophanes (winner of over £4,000 and sold for 22,000 gn to go to Argentina).

LA FLECHE

Foaled in 1889, Baron de Hirsch's La Fleche was by St Simon out of Quiver and had been bred at the Royal Stud, Hampton Court. Bought as a yearling for 5,500 gn, she proved a filly of the highest class, winning 16 races worth over £34,000. Her victories included the Champagne Stakes, the One Thousand Guineas, the Oaks, the St Leger, the Cambridgeshire, the Champion Stakes and the Gold Cup. In the Derby she was beaten less than a length by Sir Hugo and ought to have won, but her jockey, George Barrett, who was showing signs of insipient insanity, rode a deplorable race. At the stud she bred John O'Gaunt, who was second in the Derby and sired that fine horse Swynford. Up till the end of her three-year-old season she was trained by John Porter, after that by Richard Marsh.

LAMBERT SIMNEL

Lambert Simnel was by Fair Trial out of Simnel, by Blandford. Owned by the Duke of Westminster and trained by Fred Templeman, he won the Two Thousand Guineas in 1941. As a sire he was very undistinguished.

LAMBTON, Hon George (1860-1945)

George Lambton was the fifth son of the second Earl of Durham. After an undistinguished educational career at Eton and Cambridge he became an outstanding amateur rider, winning the Grand Steeplechase de Paris on Parasang in 1888 and on one occasion being desperately unlucky not to win the Grand National. After a crashing fall at Sandown in 1892 he decided to take up training, this at a time when 'gentlemen' trainers were a rarity on the Turf.

In 1893 came the turning point of his life when he was appointed trainer to the sixteenth Earl of Derby who was intent on reviving the fortunes of the Stanley colours and of laying a-new the foundations of the famous Knowsley Stud. Lambton had his first classic success in 1896 when he won the Oaks for Lord Derby with Canterbury Pilgrim, subsequently a most successful and influential brood mare. In 1906, he won the Oaks again, this time with Keystone. In 1908 Lord Derby died suddenly and was succeeded by his eldest son, who was in due course to prove the greatest English owner-breeder of this century (see Derby, seventeenth Earl of).

For the seventeenth Earl, Lambton won the Two Thousand Guineas with Colorado (1926); the One Thousand Guineas with Canyon (1916), Ferry (1918) and Tranquil (1923); the Derby with Sansovino (1924) and Hyperion (1933); and the St Leger with Swynford (1910), Keysoe (1919), Tranquil (1923) and Hyperion (1933). He also won the One Thousand Guineas in 1917 for Lord D'Abernon with Diadem. Other famous horses he trained included Stedfast, Phalaris, Pharos and Corrida. He was three times leading trainer.

In 1926 he was succeeded as Lord Derby's trainer by Frank Butters, he himself remaining as manager. In 1931 he was re-appointed as trainer. It came as a shock to the racing world when in 1933, the year of Hyperion's Derby victory, Lord Derby announced that at the age of 73 Lambton ought to be spared the burden and anxiety of running a big stable and replaced him with Colledge Leader. It is extremely doubtful if Lambton in fact was gratified by Lord Derby's thoughtfulness. He became a public trainer and remained one till his death in 1945, among his patrons being M. M. Boussac.

A man of infinite charm, dandified in his dress to the last, Lambton loved and understood horses. He was a marvellous judge of a thoroughbred, and entrusted with buying yearlings for the Aga Khan, he laid the foundations of the Aga Khan's highly profitable racing empire. His autobiography *Men and Horses I have Known* is deservedly regarded as the best book on racing ever written. His younger son, Edward, trained with varying success till he retired in 1968.

LANARK

Situated 25 miles from Glasgow and just over 30 from Edinburgh, this is a right-handed course 1¼m round with a straight run-in of 4f. The turns are easy, and though perhaps not ideally suited to big, long-striding horses, it can hardly be described as a sharp track. Low numbers in the draw are favoured over the straight 5f, high numbers in races of 7f and 1m. The going is usually good.

Clerk of the Course: Mr C. D. Patterson, 4 Gilesgate Bank, Hexham, Northumberland. Tel: Moffat 131.

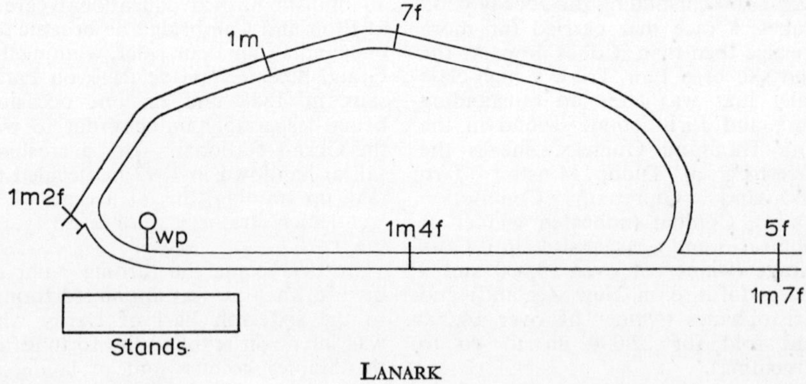

LANARK

Best Times:

Distance	Horse-Age-Weight	Date	Time
5f	Rock Sail 5-8-3	1-9-62	60.0
5f	Rightful 2-8-11	20-7-49	62.4
7f	Mutineer 4-7-4	1-5-54	1min 25.8
7f	Bob Junior	6-9-52	1min 26.8
8f	Sunny Turk 5-7-8	23-7-52	1min 38.8
8f	Stainsley 2-8-1	29-9-62	1min 45.4
10f	Devancer 5-8-5	21-7-49	2min 4.8
12f	Anamnestes 4-8-11	6-9-52	2min 33.2
15f	Tanetta 3-8-8	18-7-63	3min 20

LANARK SILVER BELL

This is the oldest race run annually, it having been instituted by William Lion (1165-1214).

LANE, Fred

A sound if unspectacular rider, Fred Lane rode a faultless race to win the 1933 Derby on April the Fifth. He had a long career in the saddle and was at his best in long distance races. A quiet and unassuming character, he was much in demand to ride work at Newmarket even in late middle age.

LARKIN, Edward

A useful North Country jockey who is attached to L. Shedden's stable and can go to scale at 8st 2. He has twice ridden more than seventy winners in a season.

LARKSPUR

Larkspur was bred by Mr Philip Love and is by Never Say Die out of Skylarking, by Precipitation. Owned by Mr Raymond Guest and trained by Vincent O'Brien, he won the 1962 Derby and was probably very lucky to do so as about a quarter of the field came to grief in a pile-up on the descent to Tattenham Corner. Among the fallers was the favourite Hethersett, who beat Larkspur without difficulty in the St Leger. Larkspur was exported to Japan in 1967.

LAUSO

Lauso was foaled in Italy in 1958 and is a bay by Ocarina out of La Canea, by Vatellor. His four victories included the Italian Derby; his dam and his grandam were both winners of the Italian Oaks. Imported into England, he stands at the Tudor Stud, Aspenden, Hertfordshire, at a fee of 400 gn. He is sire of the 1970 Gold Cup winner Precipice Wood.

LAVANDIN

M. P. Wertheimer's Lavandin, trained by Alec Head and ridden by W. R. Johnstone, won the 1956 Derby. He is judged to have been one of the more moderate winners of that race this century. He failed to make much mark as a sire and was exported to Japan.

LAWSON, Joseph (1881-1964)

Joe Lawson was born in Durham and rode in a few races as a boy but soon became too heavy. In 1898 he joined Alec Taylor's famous stable at Manton and rapidly made his mark, becoming firstly travelling head lad and later Taylor's assistant.

When Taylor retired in 1927, Lawson was appointed to succeed him. Taylor was a difficult man to follow but Lawson followed the same methods and proved an outstanding success. In 1931 he was leading trainer with a then record total of £93,899 gained in prize money, a record that stood until 1957 when Noel Murless won over £116,000 for his owners.

Lawson trained at Manton for 20 years and then moved to Newmarket. It was there he had perhaps his greatest triumphs, winning the 1954 Derby and St Leger with Never Say Die.

Altogether he had a dozen successes in classic races, while he also won the Ascot Gold Cup on two occasions. His classic winners were as follows:

Two Thousand Guineas: Orwell (1932); Pay Up (1936); Kingsway (1933) and Court Martial (1945)

One Thousand Guineas: Exhibitionnist (1937); Galatea II (1939) and Dancing Time (1941)

Derby: Never Say Die (1954)

Oaks: Pennycomequick (1929); Exhibitionnist (1937) and Galatea II (1939)

St Leger: Never Say Die (1954).

Among Lawson's many patrons were the late Lord Astor, Sir Abe Bailey, Sir Victor Sassoon, Mr Washington Singer, Mr Somerville Tattersall and Mr R. S. Clark. No publicity seeker, he was much respected in the racing world for his skill and integrity.

LEAD

Metal weights, carried in weight-cloths, to make up poundage a horse may be set to carry.

LEADER, Colledge (1883-1938)

Colledge Leader was a son of 'old' Tom Leader who trained George Frederick to win the St Leger in 1874. Like his brothers Tom, Harvey and Fred, he became a trainer. He was appointed private trainer to Lord Derby in 1934 but unfortunately died four years later. He won the One Thousand Guineas with Tideway, and the Oaks and the Gold Cup with that great mare Quashed.

LEADER, Harvey (b 1893)

Harvey Leader, more commonly known as 'Jack' Leader, is a son of 'old' Tom Leader, and was born in 1893. He rode his first winner on the flat at the age of 12 and for a short time rode under National Hunt rules. He took out a licence to train in 1918 and gained his first big success in 1920 when he won the St Leger with Mr Goculdas's Caligula. At one period he conducted a 'mixed' stable and he won the 1926 Grand National with Mr A. C. Schwartz's Jack Horner. He trained two brilliant sprinters in Diomedes and Shalfleet, while he won the Lincoln with Elton and the Cambridgeshire with Hidden Meaning and Dites. His owners include Lord Willoughby de Broke, Lady Willoughby de Broke, Hon Mrs W. Eykyn, Dr G. Gray, Sir John Musker, Lady Noble, Mr E. Leigh Windsor, Earl Cadogan, Mrs D. McNab, Mr S. Grey, Mr and Mrs O. H. Hammond, Mr C. B. Nathorst, Commander K. Grant and Dr C. Vittadini. In recent years he has trained two very good fillies in Exchange (Musidora Stakes and Yorkshire Oaks) and Bringley (Park Hill Stakes). In his younger days he was a great supporter of hunting and polo at Newmarket, while his friendly, modest personality has made him one of racing's most popular characters. His brothers Tom, Colledge and Fred were all trainers, too.

LEADER, Thomas Edward (b 1903)

Ted Leader was born in 1903 and is a son of the late Tom Leader and a nephew of Harvey Leader. He was originally apprenticed to Harvey Leader but it was as a rider under National Hunt rules that he established his reputation, in particular riding many winners for his father, a very successful jumping trainer. In his prime there was no better rider round Aintree than Ted Leader, and apart from winning the 1927 Grand National on Sprig, trained by his father, he won the Grand Sefton Chase and the Champion Chase twice. He also won the Imperial Cup twice, the Cheltenham Gold Cup twice and the Champion Hurdle. One season he was champion jockey under National Hunt rules.

He took out a licence to train in 1934 and has trained at Newmarket ever since apart from a period of war-time service with the RAF. Before the war the best horse he trained was the late Mr O. V. Watney's Wychwood Abbot, who won the Champion Stakes twice, the Kempton Jubilee and the Cambridgeshire. After the war he had a long association with Mr H. J. Joel, winning the Middle Park Stakes, Nunthorpe Stakes, St James's Palace Stakes twice, Goodwood Stakes three times, Goodwood Cup and National Stakes. Among his present owners are Mrs D. Crossman, Mrs S. S. Hayward, Maj M. G. Wyatt, Mr J. W. Rogers, Mr J. D. Rogers, Mr C. B. Stewardson, Mrs P. Arnold and Mr George Brown.

LEADING JOCKEY, ETC

See under Jockey.

LEASE

The lease of a horse has to be registered with Messrs Weatherby and the terms are agreed upon by the two parties concerned.

LEE, Brian (b 1941)

Brian Lee was apprenticed to E. Davey. A very useful light-weight, he has won the Lincolnshire Handicap, the Liverpool Autumn Cup, the Kempton Jubilee, the Rosebery Memorial Handicap, and the Usher-Vaux Brewery Gold Tankard twice.

LEG

To state that a horse 'has a leg' means that the horse in question is lame or at any rate is suffering from some sort of leg trouble.

LEGERDEMAIN

In 1849 Legerdemain slipped a foal the day after winning the Cesarewitch.

LE HAAR

Le Haar, by Vieux Manoir out of Mince Pie, by Teleferique, was bred in France by Baron de Zuylen de Nyevelt and won three races worth over 3,000,000 francs (old). He stands at Haras des Sablonnets, Le Lude, Sarthe, France, and his best winners in England have been Niksar (Two Thousand Guineas) and Exbury (Coronation Cup). In France Exbury won the Grand Prix de Saint Cloud and the Prix de l'Arc de Triomphe.

LEICESTER

Leicester, which can hardly claim to be numbered among England's lovelier racecourses, provides modest sport for midland enthusiasts. It is only 25 miles from Nottingham and less than 50 from Birmingham. It is a right-handed, undulating track which is very nearly two miles round. The straight mile, which joins the round course 5f from home, is mainly downhill for the first 4f, then up hill for the next 2f, gradually levelling off to the winning post. The bends into the straight and after the winning post have been cambered. Despite the undulations, it enjoys the reputation of being a fair, galloping course. The draw is unimportant.

Clerk of the Course: Mr John Hughes, Windrush, Black Bourton, Oxon. Tel: Carterton 397.

Best Times:

Distance	*Horse-Age-Weight*	*Date*	*Time*
5f	Papido 3-8-2	25-9-51	59.2
5f	Whimsical Walker 2-8-10	21-9-53	59
6f	Carlyle 3-7-8	28-8-65	1min 10.8
6f	Master Knock 2-7-2	6-11-61	1min 11.4
7f	Indian Beam 3-8-7	19-9-61	1min 24.8
7f	Identical 2-8-2	21-9-53	1min 24.4
8f	Mariapolis 3-8-3	19-9-61	1min 34.4
8f	Coonbeam 2-8-11	25-9-67	1min 38.2
10f	Jago 4-7-5	27-7-69	2min 4.7
12f	Gyroscope 4-7-11	21-9-64	2min 28.5

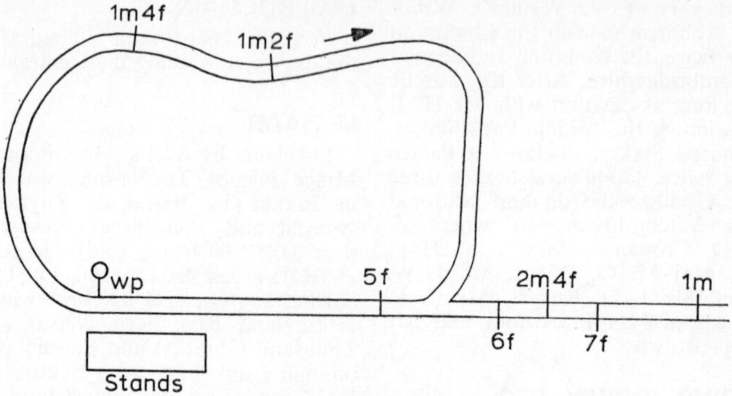

LEICESTER

LE KSAR

Le Ksar, owned by M. de Saint-Alary and trained in France by F. Carter, won the Two Thousand Guineas in 1937. He was second in the French Two Thousand. He retired to the stud in France and then stood for a few seasons in England before being exported to Argentina. He was by Ksar out of Queen Iseult, by Teddy.

LE LEVANSTELL

Le Levanstell, foaled in 1957, was bred in Ireland by the McGrath Trust Company and is a bay by Le Lavandou out of Stella's Sister, by Ballyogan. He won six races worth over £11,000, including the Sussex Stakes and Queen Elizabeth II Stakes. He is syndicated and stands at the Trimblestown Stud, Co Meath. The best of his offspring so far is Levmoss (q.v.). In 1970 he was sire of the French Oaks winner Sweet Mimosa.

LEMBERG

Lemberg, owned and bred by 'Mr Fairie', the 'nom de course' of Mr A. W. Cox, was foaled in 1907 and was a half-brother by Cyllene to that great horse Bayardo, being out of Galicia, by Galopin, one of the most famous mares in the Stud Book. Lemberg won the Derby, was second in the Two Thousand Guineas and third in the St Leger. He also dead-heated for the Eclipse Stakes and won the Coronation Cup. He was trained by Alec Taylor at Manton. He was champion sire in 1922. Among his good winners were Lemonora (Grand Prix de Paris), Ellangowan (Two Thousand Guineas) and Taj Mah (One Thousand Guineas).

LEMONORA

Lemonora, by Lemberg out of Honora, by Gallinule, was foaled in 1918. Trained by Alec Taylor at Manton, he won the 1921 Grand Prix de Paris, being one of the very few English horses to win that race this century. He also won the Newmarket Stakes. As a sire he proved extremely disappointing.

LENGTH

A length represents the length of a horse from nose to tail, approximately 8ft.

LETHERBY, Dennis (b 1947)

Dennis Letherby was apprenticed firstly to A. M. Smyth and then to W. Stephenson. His most important success so far was to win the Totalisator Spring Handicap on Barwin. In 1966 he rode 47 winners. He now rides for M. H. Easterby and R. Hollinshead.

LEVERHULME, third Viscount

Lord Leverhulme was born in 1915 and served in the Cheshire Yeomanry. He is a member of the Jockey Club and steward at Chester, Haydock Park and Aintree. His flat-race horses are trained by Fulke Johnson Houghton. Colours: green and yellow hoops, yellow sleeves and quartered cap.

LEVMOSS

Levmoss was bred in 1965 by the McGrath Trust Company and was owned and trained not far from Dublin by Seamus McGrath. By the miler Le Levanstell out of a mare by Ballymoss, he was a good staying three-year-old, winning the Oxfordshire Stakes, in which he beat Canterbury and Park Top, and finishing third in the French St Leger.

In 1969 he proved himself an outstanding stayer by winning the Ascot Gold Cup and its French equivalent, the Prix du Cadran. Better still, though, was to come. In October he brought off one of the biggest surprises for a long time when, brilliantly ridden by Bill Williamson, he won the 1½m Prix de l'Arc de Triomphe, beating four European Derby winners and the winners of the Grand Prix, French Oaks and the King George VI and Queen Elizabeth Stakes. This victory earned him £89,000 and concluded a great racing career. He now stands at the Brownstown Stud, Co Kildare, at a fee of 3,000 guineas.

LEWIS, Geoffrey (b 1935)

Geoff Lewis, a Welshman, was apprenticed to Staff Ingham. Short and stocky, he has few weight problems and can go to scale at 8st. Up to 1969 his best season was in 1965 when he rode 93 winners. In 1969 he topped the hundred for the first time, gave Lester Piggott a tough fight for the championship and rode his first classic

winner, Right Tack, in the Two Thousand Guineas. He also won the Irish Derby on Prince Regent. His many successes include the Royal Hunt Cup, Stewards' Cup, William Hill Gold Cup, Coronation Stakes, Victoria Cup, St James's Palace Stakes, Lockinge Stakes and Champion Stakes. Prior to 1969 he had a lengthy association with the Kingsclere stable, first with Capt Peter Hastings-Bass and then with Ian Balding. He has the reputation of being the best golfer among modern jockeys. In 1970 he rode Precipice Wood to victory in the Gold Cup.

LEWIS, Ifor Morel (b 1937)

Ifor Lewis has been training since 1959. He conducts a 'mixed' stable at Berkeley House, Lambourn.

LICENCES

See OFFICIALS, LICENCES FOR.

LIGHT BROCADE

By Galloper Light out of Trilogy, Light Brocade, trained by Frank Butters and ridden by Bernard Carslake, won the 1934 Oaks for the late Lord Durham. She also won the Cheveley Park Stakes and was second in the One Thousand Guineas. She was a disappointing brood mare.

LILY AGNES

Lily Agnes, by Macaroni, was a famous mare that bred the mighty Ormonde, winner of the 'Triple Crown' (1886); Farewell, winner of the One Thousand Guineas; and Ornament, dam of the great filly Sceptre who won every classic bar the Derby.

LIMELIGHT

One of the best horses bred and owned by King George V, Limelight was by Pharos out of Vervaine, by Louviers, and won the Hardwicke Stakes, Newbury Spring Cup and Jersey Stakes. His record as a sire was mediocre.

LINACRE

Foaled in 1960, Linacre was bred by the late Lord Ennisdale and is a black by Rockefella out of True Picture, by Panorama. Trained by Paddy Prendagast, he won six races in England, Ireland and France, including the Irish Two Thousand Guineas and the Queen Elizabeth II Stakes. He now stands at the Irish National Stud at a fee of 400 gn. In 1970 he was sire of the Irish One Thousand Guineas winner Black Satin.

LINCOLN HANDICAP

See under DONCASTER.

LINDLEY, Jimmy Frederick (b 1935)

Jimmy Lindley, one of the strongest and most stylish of modern jockeys, from 1949-54 was apprenticed to Tom Masson. He does not have an easy time of it with his weight—he has ridden under National Hunt rules—but he can go to scale at 8st 7lb. Among the good races he has won are the Two Thousand Guineas (twice), the King George VI and Queen Elizabeth Stakes, the Middle Park Stakes (twice), the Queen Mary Stakes (three times), the Italian Oaks, the Irish Oaks and the Coronation Cup. His Two Thousand Guineas victories were gained on Only for Life and Kashmir II. His best season so far was in 1963 when he rode 71 winners. His lengthy association with Jeremy Tree's stable ended in 1969. He was retained in 1970 to ride the French-trained horses of Mr and Mrs Howell Jackson.

LINGFIELD

Twenty-seven miles from London and 30 from Brighton, Lingfield is a pretty and deservedly popular course. It is a left-handed circuit of roughly 10f with pronounced gradients. The steep descent to the final bend makes it a particularly appropriate track for testing candidates for the Derby and the Oaks and the most important race of the season there is the Lingfield Derby Trial in May. On several occasions the winner of that event has gone on to win the Derby.

The straight course of 7f 140yd is downhill the entire way. It joins the round course half a mile from the winning post. Speed and a good action are the main requisites for a horse at Lingfield. On the straight course the draw favours high numbers except in heavy going when the reverse is the case. A lot of work has been done to improve the drainage as at one time the track was liable to become waterlogged in wet weather.

Clerk of the Course: Major P. Beckwith-Smith, Carewell Lodge, Lingfield, Surrey. Tel: Lingfield 399.

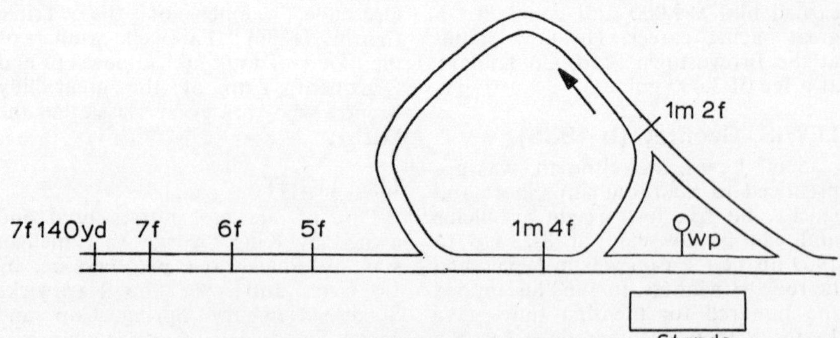

LINGFIELD

Best Times:

Distance	*Horse-Age-Weight*	*Date*	*Time*
5f	Marguerite 3-8-9	7-10-64	56.8
5f	Woodcote Inn 2-8-4	26-8-50	57.5
6f	Royal Yacht 4-7-4	11-6-65	1min 8.4
6f	The Ritz 2-9-3	11-6-65	1min 8.6
7f	Polar Jest 8-7-10	19-8-55	1min 20.2
7f	Fritillary II 2-8-11	7-10-64	1min 22.2
7f 140yd	Persian Empire 4-8-3	9-9-67	1min 27.6
7f 140yd	Spree 2-8-12	2-11-62	1min 38.8
10f	Picture Palace 3-6-13	8-10-64	2min 5.9
12f	General Wolfe 4-8-10	8-10-69	3min 33.9
16f	Frontin 4-7-7	7-10-69	3min 24.7

LISTED RACE

Listed races are important races, nominated by the Stewards of the Jockey Club, and run in countries outside Great Britain. The winning of one of these races automatically puts a horse in a certain category from the penalty point of view, no matter what the value of the prize money may be.

LIVERPOOL

The future of racing at Liverpool remains uncertain. It has been reduced to a single meeting a year at which flat-racing comes a poor second to racing under National Hunt rules. The flat-race course is an oval one just over 1m 3f in circumference. Five-furlong races are run on a separate straight course.

Managing Director and Secretary: Mrs M. D. Topham, Racecourse Office, Aintree, Liverpool. Tel: Aintree 3500.

Clerk of the Course: Mr J. C. Bidwell-Topham, Racecourse Office, Aintree, Liverpool. Tel: Aintree 3500.

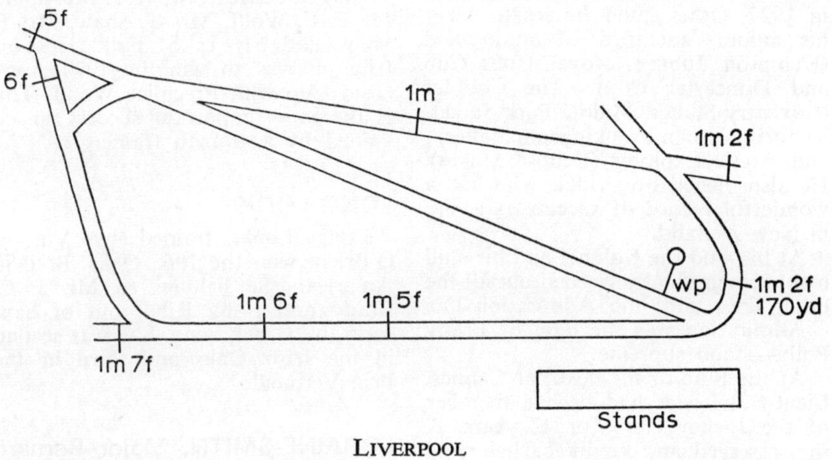

LIVERPOOL

Best Times:

Distance	*Horse-Age-Weight*	*Date*	*Time*
5f	Sutherland 2-8-12	5-6-63	60.4
6f	Miladdo 5-8-1	23-5-64	1min 10.9
6f	Sharuk 2-9-2	5-7-62	1min 14
8f	Printer 4-9-7	5-6-63	1min 39.2

10f	Celtic King 3-8-12	24-6-64	2min 5
10f 170yd	Dairialatan 5-8-8	29-6-60	2min 12.6
13f	Migoli 3-8-10	5-11-47	2min 47.2
14f	Gallant Scot 4-9-4	7-11-47	3min 4.5
15f	Auralia 4-9-5	4-8-47	3min 19.4

LOANINGDALE

Bred by Lady Nunburnholme, Loaningdale was by Colorado out of Perfection, by Orby. He won over £12,000 in stakes when trained by Sir Cecil Boyd-Rochfort, his main success being in the Eclipse Stakes in 1933. He was exported to Uruguay.

LODER, Lieut-Col Giles Hubert, MC (1885-1966)

Lieut-Col Giles Loder inherited the famous Eyrefield Stud in Co Kildare in 1914 from his uncle, Major Eustace Loder (see below). He was still serving in the Scots Guards in 1920 when he won the Derby with Spion Kop. It now seems long odds against a serving soldier ever owning a Derby winner again. Col Loder's only other classic winner in England was Cresta Run, who won the One Thousand Guineas in 1927. Other good horses to carry his colours included Colorado Kid (Kempton Jubilee, Royal Hunt Cup and Doncaster Cup); The Cobbler (Coventry Stakes, Middle Park Stakes, Victoria Cup and Wokingham Stakes); and Arctic Explorer (Eclipse Stakes). He also owned Foxbridge, who had a wonderful record of success as a sire in New Zealand.

At his stud the Colonel and his stud managers gradually weeded out all the other lines until the Admiration line—Admiration was the dam of Pretty Polly—stood supreme.

At the time of his death at Cannes, Lieut-Col Loder had been a member of the Jockey Club for 42 years. A shy, reserved and kindly bachelor, he was noted for his skill as a gardener and for his loyalty to those who served him.

LODER, Major Eustace (b 1867)

Major Eustace Loder served in the 12th Lancers for 15 years. Not for nothing was he known as 'Lucky Loder'. For 300 gn he bought Spearmint who won both the Derby and the Grand Prix. In addition Major Loder owned and bred Pretty Polly, one of the outstanding fillies of this century.

LOMAX, Mrs Rosemary Ann (b 1928)

Mrs Lomax was born in 1928 and rode over 40 point-to-point winners. She has actually held a licence since 1966, the stable till then being conducted in the name of her husband, Mr Ian Lomax, a well-known cricketer who has played for Somerset. The stable at Baydon is a 'mixed' one and the owners include Mr C. A. Cyzer, Mrs C. W. Emmett, Mr J. N. Peatt, Mr G. C. F. Hurt, Mr R. J. McAlpine, Mr F. F. Wolff, Mrs T. Shaw, Mrs P. Shaw and Mr L. S. Falk. Her big triumph was to win the 1970 Ascot Gold Cup with Precipice Wood. This is the most important success so far gained by a woman trainer.

LONG LOOK

Long Look, trained by Vincent O'Brien, won the 1965 Oaks. Bred in America, she belongs to Mr J. C. Brady and is by Ribot out of Santorin, by Greek Song. She was second in the Irish Oaks and third in the Prix Vermeille.

LORAINE-SMITH, Major Bernard Lawson, MC (b 1913)

Major Loraine-Smith served firstly in Probyn's Horse and then in the 7th Hussars. He was appointed a Stewards' Secretary under Rules of Racing and National Hunt rules in 1963.

LORD LYON

Mr R. Sutton's Lord Lyon, by Stockwell, won the Two Thousand Guineas, the Derby and the St Leger in 1866. In all he won 17 races and over £26,000 in stakes, a very big sum in those days.

LOUVIERS

Louviers, owned by Mr W. Raphael, was by Isinglass out of St Louvaine and thus a brother of Louvois, second in the Derby in 1913 and winner of the Two Thousand Guineas. Louviers himself was beaten by a very short head by King Edward VII's Minoru in the 1909 Derby. He was not a success as a sire in England and was exported to Russia.

LOUVOIS

Winner of the Two Thousand Guineas and second in the Derby in 1913, Mr W. Raphael's Louvois, by Isinglass, was a brother of Louviers who was beaten by inches in the 1909 Derby by Minoru. He sired St Louis, winner of the 1922 Two Thousand Guineas.

LOVE IN IDLENESS

Bred by Sir Gilbert Greenall, Love in Idleness was by Bachelor's Double out of Cornfield, by Isinglass. Trained by Alec Taylor and owned by Mr J. Watson, she won the Oaks and Park Hill Stakes in 1921. Altogether she won nine races worth over £12,000. She bred six winners of which the best were Violator and Lo Zingaro.

LOVELY ROSA

By Tolgus out of Napoule, by Bachelor's Double, Sir Abe Bailey's Lovely Rosa won the Oaks in 1936, trained by Harry Cottrill and ridden by Tommy Weston. At the stud she bred Saracen, dam of Wilwyn, winner of 21 races and the only English horse to have won the Laurel Park International up to the time of the victory of Karabas in 1969.

LOWE, Professor Bruce

A well-known and influential theorist on bloodstock breeding was the Australian, Bruce Lowe. He traced the pedigrees of all the mares in the Stud Book of his own era back through the female line to their original foundation mares in the earlier volumes. He found there were about 50 of these original mares with living progeny in the direct female line. The descendants of each of these original mares comprised a family which he then classified according to the number of Derby, Oaks and St Leger winners it had produced. The first five families were designated 'Running Families' and were rated superior in racing merit to the remainder. Another group included those that were strong in the sire element and these he called 'Sire Families'. From these classifications certain rather complex deductions were made on how to breed a good horse or a successful stallion.

Bruce Lowe's laborious research revealed many hitherto unrecognised details about the manner in which the thoroughbred had developed, and through his work knowledge of the subject was substantially increased.

Although modern breeders tend to ignore Bruce Lowe's family numbers, these family numbers are frequently used in private stud books, stallion registers and so forth. Running Family numbers are always printed in italics, sire families in bold type.

LOWE, John

A smart light-weight rider apprenticed to Jack Watts. He rode 13 winners in 1969 and can go to scale at 7st 2.

LOYD, Christopher Lewis, MC (b 1923)

Mr C. L. Loyd, a well-known Berkshire landowner, served in the Coldstream Guards during World War II. For a time he rode under National Hunt rules. He is a member of the Jockey Club, steward at Bath, Salisbury and Newbury, and owner of the

Lockinge and Kitford Stud. His trainer is Fulke Johnson Houghton. Colours: black, grey sleeves.

LUCERO

Lucero, by Solonaway, won three races including the Irish Two Thousand Guineas and the Sussex Stakes. Before being exported to Panama, he sired that fine sprinter Lucasland.

LUCKY BRIEF

Lucky Brief was foaled in 1959 and was bred by the late Mr W. H. Cockerline, being a bay by Counsel out of Welsh Rose, by Owen Tudor. He won seven races worth over £7,000, his victories including the Dante Stakes at York. He retired to the Limestone Stud, Gainsborough, Lincolnshire, at a fee of 300 gn and is sire of the speedy Cheb's Lad, winner of the Champagne Stakes.

LUCYROWE

Lucyrowe is owned by Mr Louis Freedman who paid 9,000 gn for her as a yearling. A daughter of Crepello, she was originally trained by Walter Nightingall and on his death she joined Peter Walwyn's stable. In 1969 she proved herself a brilliant filly up to 1¼m and would in all probability have won the One Thousand Guineas had she not been badly knocked about in the early stages of a distinctly rough race. Her victories included the Kempton One Thousand Guineas Trial, Ebbisham Stakes, Coronation Stakes, Nassau Stakes and Sun Chariot Stakes. She was second to Habitat in the Wills Mile. Her first mate at the stud was to be Sir Ivor.

LYNCHRIS

Lynchris, who unfortunately died all too young, was a really good stayer that won the Irish Oaks, Yorkshire Oaks and Irish St Leger as well as three other races. Bred by the Baroda Stud, she was by Sayajirao out of Scollata, by Niccola dell'Arca.

M

McALPINE, Sir Robin, CBE (b 1906)

Sir Robin McAlpine is a partner in Sir Robert McAlpine and Sons. He is a member of the Jockey Club, a former President of the the Racehorse Owners' Association, a member of the Council of the Thoroughbred Breeders Association and a steward at Ascot and Alexandra Park. His trainer is John Waugh. Colours: McAlpine tartan, gold hoop on sleeves, gold cap.

McCASKILL, William

A thoroughly competent apprentice attached to Denys Smith's stable. He rode 18 winners in 1969.

MACDONALD-BUCHANAN, Capt John, MC (b 1925)

Capt Macdonald-Buchanan served in the Scots Guards. He is a member of the Jockey Club and a steward at Warwick and Wolverhampton. His trainers are N. Murless and J. A. Waugh. Colours: white, black seams, red cap with gold tassel.

MACDONALD-BUCHANAN, Hon Lady

Lady Macdonald-Buchanan is the daughter of the late Lord Woolavington and wife of Major Sir Reginald Macdonald-Buchanan (see below). She inherited and has maintained the wide bloodstock-breeding interests of her father and owns the Lavington, Egerton and Lordship Studs. She bred and owned the war-time Derby and Gold Cup winner, Owen Tudor, and she bred the brilliant sprinter Abernant who carried her husband's colours. Her trainer is J. A. J. Waugh. Colours: white, black hoop and armlets, red cap with gold tassel.

MACDONALD-BUCHANAN, Major Sir Reginald Narcissus, KCVO, MBE, MC (b 1896)

Major Sir Reginald Macdonald-Buchanan served in the Scots Guards. He is a member of the Jockey Club and was Senior Steward in 1952. For 10 years he was a member of the Racecourse Betting Control Board. The best horse to have carried his colours of black, white hoop and armlets, is Abernant who won 14 races worth over £26,000. His trainers are N. Murless, H. Cecil and J. A. J. Waugh.

McGRATH, Joseph (1895-1966)

Mr Joseph McGrath played a leading part in the history of the Irish Turf in modern times. A patriotic Irishman, he fought for the freedom of his country during 'the troubles', was a member of the first Dail and subsequently Minister of Labour and Minister of Commerce. He founded the famous and highly successful 'Irish Hospitals Sweep', was a leading owner and breeder in Ireland, and was largely responsible for the modernising of the Curragh racecourse.

In 1941 he bought the Brownstown Stud which now covers 500 acres and contains 135 boxes. In 1944 he bought Nasrullah, reputedly for some 19,000 gn, and sold him to an American syndicate for £130,000 in 1950. Both in Great Britain and America Nasrullah proved one of the greatest stallions of modern times. Mr McGrath won the 1951 Derby with Arctic Prince whom he exported to America six years later. He also owned Windsor Slipper, the unbeaten winner of six races including the Irish 'Triple Crown'; Solar Slipper (Champion Stakes and third in the St Leger); Panaslipper (Irish Derby and second in the Epsom Derby); and Silken Glider (Irish Oaks and second in the Epsom Oaks).

McGRATH, Seamus (b 1923)

Seamus McGrath trains at Sandyford, Co Dublin. Among the big races he has won are the Irish Derby, Irish Oaks, Queen's Vase, St James's Palace Stakes, Royal Hunt Cup, Chesterfield Cup and Cambridgeshire, but his big triumph came in 1969 when he won the Gold Cup, Prix du Cadran and Prix de l'Arc de Triomphe with Levmoss (q.v.). He is a son of the late Mr Joseph McGrath (see above). In 1970 he won the French Oaks with Sweet Mimosa.

McHARG, Col William Wilson, OBE, MC, TD (b 1918)

Clerk of the Course at Edinburgh and Ayr.

McINTOSH, Norman (b 1931)

Norman McIntosh enjoyed a long association with George Boyd, to whom he was apprenticed from 1948 to 1953. He rode his first winner in 1949 at Hamilton Park. His riding weight is still 7st and his best season so far was 1960 when he rode 37 winners. Big races he has won include the Lincolnshire Handicap, Ayr Gold Cup, Magnet Cup and Northumberland Cup.

McKAY, D. J.

A very promising young rider, Dennis McKay is apprenticed to J. Walsh. He had a very good season in 1969, riding 30 winners, and won the Cesarewitch on Floridian.

MADDEN, Otto (1870-1941)

Otto Madden was born in Germany of English parents. His father had ridden the famous Hungarian mare Kincsem in many of her races. His own career had its ups and downs—at one point he forfeited his licence for a season for "consorting with persons of known bad character"—but he was four times champion jockey. He won the Derby on Jeddah, the Two Thousand Guineas on Norman III, the Oaks on Musa and Sunny Jane, and the St Leger on Challacombe. He retired to take up training in 1909 but returned to the saddle in World War I. In his closing years he was a popular and respected figure at Newmarket, being churchwarden at St Agnes. He left over £50,000 when he died.

MADDEN, Peter

A promising rider apprenticed to Doug Marks. He can go to scale at 7st 2 and rode 14 winners in 1969.

MADDOCK, Harold Russell (b 1921)

'Russ' Maddock was born in Australia and rode his first winner there in 1936. He rode with much success in Queensland before trying his luck in England. His most important English successes so far have been his victories in the Nunthorpe Stakes on Althrey Don, in the Princess Elizabeth Stakes on Pytchley Princess, and the Vaux Gold Tankard on Quartette.

MAHER, Danny

Danny Maher was an American jockey who came to England in 1900 with a big reputation which he certainly justified. He swiftly adapted his style to suit English courses and proved himself an artist of a very high order. Occasionally he overdid his favourite waiting tactics but at his best he was second to none. He rode three Derby winners—Rock Sand (1903), Cicero (1905) and Spearmint (1906). A man of outstanding charm and intelligence, he was greatly liked by men such as the late Lord Rosebery and the late Lord Derby, but there was a strain of weakness in his character and some of his racing friends did him little credit. He was inclined to burn the candle at both ends and in addition he was tubercular. His health had gone by 1914 and he died not long afterwards.

MAHMOUD

Mahmoud, foaled in 1933, was bred and owned by the Aga Khan and trained by Frank Butters. He was by Blenheim out of Mah Mahal, a daughter of the famous Mumtaz Mahal. A smallish, light grey colt with an Arab-like head, he was a high-class two-year-old. The following season, after being beaten by inches in the Two Thousand Guineas, he won the Derby on very firm going in the record time of 2 min 33 4/5ths sec. He never won again; he was beaten in the St James's Palace Stakes and the St Leger and was then hustled off to the stud. In 1940 he was exported to America for £20,000. He did extremely well there and one year was champion sire.

MAIDEN

A 'maiden' is a horse that has never won a race other than a match or private sweepstake or the Newmarket Challenge Cup or Whip.

MAID OF THE MIST

Maid of the Mist, by Cyllene out of the immortal Sceptre, was one of the late Lord Astor's most successful brood mares. She bred Craig An Eran (Two Thousand Guineas and Eclipse); Sunny Jane (Oaks); and Hamoaze, who won £1,355 herself and bred Buchan (Eclipse Stakes and placed in all three classics; subsequently champion sire); Tamar (second in the Derby); Saltash (Eclipse Stakes); and St Germans (second in the Derby and a highly successful sire in America). Other descendants in tail female of Maid of the Mist are Tiberius (Gold Cup); Creme Brulée, a gelding that won over £9,000; and Betty, winner of over £7,000.

MAITLAND, David (b 1947)

David Maitland was apprenticed to Gordon Smyth. He rode his first winner in 1965 and rode 30 winners in 1966, including the Cambridgeshire on Dites. He can go to scale at 7st 4 and in 1970 is riding for Mr David Robinson.

MAJORITY BLUE

Foaled in 1961, Majority Blue was bred by the Irish National Stud and is by Major Portion out of Gorm Abu, by My Babu. He won nine races including the Cory and Orrery Stakes (carrying 9st 11lb) and the Diadem Stakes. He stands at the Lismacue Stud, Co Tipperary, at a fee of £198.

MAJOR PORTION

Owned and bred by Mr H. J. Joel and trained by Ted Leader, Major Portion was foaled in 1955 and is a chestnut by Court Martial out of Better Half, by Mieuxcé. A high-class miler, he won six races worth over £24,000, including the St James's Palace Stakes, Sussex Stakes, Queen Elizabeth II Stakes, Chesham Stakes and Middle Park Stakes. He was second in the Two Thousand Guineas and third in the Champion Stakes. He stands at the Egerton Stud, Newmarket, at a fee of 700 gn. His son Soleil won the French Two Thousand Guineas, Prix Morny and Grand Criterium.

MAKIN, Peter James (b 1944)

Peter Makin worked with the late Tom Yates, and with Toby Balding before assisting Arthur Budgett for 2½ years. He took out a licence himself in 1967 and trains at East Hendred, near Wantage. His owners include Mr R. Colville, Mrs A. P. D. Smyth, Mr F. G. Rowe, Mr L. C. Armstrong, Mr R. C. Bush, Mrs R. M. Bushnell, Mr R. W. S. Dilley and Mr D. Strauss.

MALVA

Malva, by Charles O'Malley, belonged to Lord Carnarvon and bred the Derby winner Blenheim; King Salmon, winner of the Coronation Cup and Eclipse Stakes; and His Grace, winner of over £6,000.

MANACLE

Manacle is syndicated and stands at King Edward's Place Stud, Wiltshire. Foaled in 1964, he won 11 races and over £8,000 when trained for Mr Charles Engelhard by Jack Watts, proving himself a good and genuine sprinter. He is by Sing Sing out of Hard and Fast, by Hard Sauce.

MANCHESTER

Manchester racecourse ceased to exist in 1964. For Manchester Handicap, see under Doncaster.

MANDAMUS

Mandamus, by Petition out of Great Fun, by Big Game, was bred by Mr W. Hill and foaled in 1960. As a yearling he was bought for 5,400 gn and for Mr I. E. Kornberg, whose horses are trained by B. van Cutsem, he won eight races and over £24,000. His main success was to win the William Hill Gold Cup. He stands at the Side Hill Stud, Newmarket, at a fee of £300.

MANNA

Manna, by Phalaris out of Waffles, was bought as a yearling in 1923 by Mr H. E. Morriss, a Shanghai bullion broker, for 6,300 gn. Trained by Fred Darling, Manna won the Two Thousand Guineas and the Derby. He broke down in the St Leger and never ran again. The best horse he sired was Colombo, winner of the Two Thousand Guineas and over £26,000 in stakes.

MANNING, James Frederick Charles (b 1900)

Mr J. F. C. Manning's first racing appointment was in 1920 and he has been Jockey Club Clerk of the Scales since 1934.

MARCHETTA

Marchetta, foaled in 1907 by Marco out of Hettie Sorrel, founded one of the most famous families in modern racing. It has divided into two main branches descended from Marchetta's daughters Rose Red and Sweet Lavender. The Rose Red branch has produced Larkspur, Aurora, Alycidon, Borealis, Acropolis, Festoon and Celtic Ash. From the Sweet Lavender branch come My Babu, Sayani, Ambiorix, Cagire II, Turn-To and Klairon.

MARCH PAST

March Past, bred by the late Capt E. A. Ingram and owned by Mrs Trimmer-Thompson, was foaled in 1950 and is a brown horse by Petition out of Marcelette, by William of Valence. Trained by Ken Cundell, he won 10 races worth over £10,000, including the Solario, Greenham and Wokingham Stakes. Standing at the Southcourt Stud, Leighton Buzzard, at a fee of £350, he has proved a versatile and successful stallion, his winners including Major Rose, who won the Cesarewitch with 9st 4lb; Queen's Hussar, a fine miler that won the Sussex Stakes; Christmas Review, winner of over £12,000; Smartie, winner of the Royal Hunt Cup and over £12,000; and Scots Fusilier, winner of over £10,000. He has also sired numerous winners under National Hunt rules.

MARE

A mare is a female thoroughbred aged five years or upwards.

MARGADALE, Lord, TD, DL (b 1906)

Lord Margadale served in the Wiltshire Yeomanry. For 12 years he was Conservative MP for Salisbury. He is a member of the Jockey Club and was Senior Steward in 1968. His trainers are J. Tree and G. Balding. Colours: dark green, white cap.

MARGUERITE VERNAUT

Marguerite Vernaut, a very good Italian filly by Toulouse Lautrec, came to England and won the Champion Stakes in 1960.

MARKS, Douglas (b 1922)

Douglas Marks was apprenticed to W. R. Jarvis. It was as a little-known apprentice that he won the 1940 One Thousand Guineas and Oaks on that temperamental filly Godiva. He rode under National Hunt rules from 1946-51 and took out a licence to train in 1949. At one time his stable was essentially a 'mixed' one but now he chiefly concentrates on the flat. With Golden Fire he won the Chester Cup, Goodwood Stakes (twice) and Cesarewitch. His stable is at Upper Lambourn and his owners include Mr L. Charteris, Mr Clive Graham, Mr Frankie Vaughan, Lady Craddock, Mr C. Berlin and Mr and Mrs C. Grainger.

MARSH, Alec (b 1908)

Alec Marsh was born in 1908 and before the war was one of the leading amateur riders. For three years in succession in fact he was top amateur under National Hunt rules. At Aintree he won the Grand Sefton and the Foxhunters Chase. Altogether he rode in 960 races under National Hunt rules and on the flat, winning 163. In the war he served in the RAF and from 1946 to 1947 was starter to the Royal Calcutta Turf Club. He became a starter under Jockey Club Rules in 1947 and was appointed Jockey Club Starter in 1953.

MARSH, Marcus (b 1904)

Marcus Marsh, son of Richard Marsh (see below) learnt the art of training from his father, Capt R. F. K. Gooch and Fred Darling before setting up on his own in 1929. In 1934 he enjoyed his first major success when he won the Derby and St Leger with Windsor Lad. In World War II he served in the RAF, was shot down and was a prisoner of war in Germany for nearly five years. After the war he was soon in his stride again and trained an outstanding sprinter in The Bug. On the retirement of Frank Butters he took over the Aga Khan's horses and among the good winners he trained for him were Tulyar (1952 Derby, St Leger, Eclipse Stakes and King George VI and Queen Elizabeth Stakes) and Palestine (Two Thousand Guineas). He retired in 1966.

MARSH, Richard (b 1851)

Richard Marsh was the son of a Kentish hop-farmer. He joined a Newmarket stable as a small boy but soon got too heavy to ride on the flat. However, he did well over fences and hurdles. He first made his name as a trainer with jumpers belonging to the Duke of Hamilton, but he won the 1883 St Leger with Ossian and the One Thousand Guineas and the Oaks in 1886 with Miss Jummy. He became trainer to the Prince of Wales, later King Edward VII, in 1893 and for him he won the Derby with Persimmon (1896), Diamond Jubilee (1900) and Minoru (1909). Persimmon also won the St Leger, Eclipse Stakes and Gold Cup; Diamond Jubilee the Two Thousand Guineas and St Leger; and Minoru the Two Thousand Guineas. Marsh also won the Derby in 1898 for Mr J. W. Larnach with the 100-1 chance Jeddah.

Tall, hospitable and beautifully dressed, Marsh was never a man to spend much time in counting the pennies. He married a daughter of the famous Beckhampton trainer, Sam Darling. Their son Marcus (see above) trained two Derby winners.

MARSHALL, William Cyril, DFC (b 1918)

Bill Marshall served as a fighter pilot in the RAF during World War II, being awarded the DFC. After the war he rode as an amateur under National Hunt rules till 1950, and from 1950 till 1957 as a professional. He took out a licence to train in 1950 and since then he has conducted a successful 'mixed' stable. Among the races he has won are the Brown Jack Stakes, Goodwood Stakes and City and Suburban. In 1969 he enjoyed his best ever season on the flat thanks to the exploits of My Swanee and Raffingora, who won 13 good races between them. He is skilled at placing indifferent horses at minor meetings and is reputed to be a very shrewd judge of a bet. His stables are at Ogbourne Maisey, near Marlborough.

MARSHAM, A. J. B. (b 1919)

James Marsham, brother of Cloudesley Marsham, the commentator, was born in 1919. He was educated at Eton and at Oxford where he obtained 'blues' for cricket and golf. In the war he served in the 60th Rifles and was captured in Greece. He was appointed a stewards' secretary under the Rules of Racing and under National Hunt rules in 1966.

MARSHAM, C. G. B. (b 1917)

Cloudesley Marsham is the elder brother of James Marsham, a stewards' secretary. Born in 1917, he was educated at Eton and served in the East Kent Yeomanry. Like his brother he was for several years a prisoner of war in Germany. He is a highly competent racecourse commentator.

MARSYAS II

M. M. Boussac's Marsyas II, by the Gold Cup winner Trimdon, was an outstanding stayer in the immediate post-war era. In France he won the Prix du Cadran four times; in England he won the Queen Alexandra Stakes, Goodwood Cup and Doncaster Cup. He was not a stud success.

MARTIAL

Martial, a big, powerful chestnut by Hill Gail out of Discipliner, by Court Martial, and thus a half-brother to Skymaster and El Gallo, was bred by Capt A. D. Rogers and foaled in 1957. Owned by Mr R. N. Webster and trained by Paddy Prendergast, he won three races, including the Coventry Stakes and the Two Thousand Guineas. He was syndicated for the stud, but in 1967 was exported to Argentina.

MARTIN, John Henry (1875-1944)

Born in New York, he was usually known as 'Skeets' Martin and was one of the first American jockeys to ride with success in England. He won the Derby on Ard Patrick in 1902. The following year he won the Two Thousand Guineas on Rock Sand. He was well enough off when he retired from racing but lost his money in property speculation, and died penniless in Switzerland.

MASAKA

Masaka, owned and bred by the Aga Khan, was foaled in 1947 and was by Nearco out of Majideh, by Mahmoud. Trained by Frank Butters she was a good but temperamental filly, winning six races worth over £21,000. As a two-year-old she won the Queen Mary Stakes and the July Stakes. The following season, ridden by K. Gethin, she was favourite for the One Thousand Guineas but was in wayward mood, stuck her toes in at the start and declined to race. However, ridden by Nevett she duly won the Oaks and she won the Irish Oaks, too. Her daughter Bara Bibi won the Park Hill Stakes at Doncaster.

MASON, R. E. G. (b 1916)

Ron Mason served in World War II in the RAF. A man of some versatility, he was at one time a speedway rider and has interests in a haulage contracting business. He has been remarkably successful since he took out a licence to train in 1959, having won the Lincolnshire Handicap, Queen Elizabeth II Stakes, Royal Hunt Cup, Totalisator Spring Handicap, Northumberland Plate, Middle Park Stakes, St James's Palace Stakes and Ayr Gold Cup. His stables are at Guilsborough,

Northamptonshire, and among his owners are Mr C. Chambers, Mrs W. Kendrick, Lord Kilmany, Hon Mr G. A. Weir, Mr G. B. Turnbull and Mrs J. D. Mitchell.

MASSINE

The French horse Massine, who won the Ascot Gold Cup in 1924, was one of the best winners of that event between the two World Wars. By Consols out of Mauri, by Ajax, he won 11 races in France including the Prix de l'Arc de Triomphe. He proved a high-class sire, among his winners being Mieuxcé (French Derby and Grand Prix); Strip The Willow (French Derby and Grand Prix); Laeken (French St Leger and sire of the great hurdler Sir Ken); Maravedis, sire of Souverain who won the Ascot Gold Cup, Grand Prix and French St Leger; Chaudière (Prix du Cadran); and Feerie (French One Thousand Guineas and Oaks). Massine died in 1939.

MASSON, Thomas (d 1969)

Tom Masson at one time rode show-horses and point-to-pointers for the late Mr Bertram Mills of circus fame. He took out a licence to train in 1939 and then ran a small 'mixed' stable at Lewes, during which period he earned the reputation of being particularly good with 'difficult' and temperamental horses. He was a successful tutor of young riders and Jimmy Lindley and Bobby Elliott were among his apprentices. He won the Ascot Stakes with Shatter and the Lingfield Derby Trial with Pindaric. The Queen was a patron of the stable. He died from injuries received in a car crash in 1969 and his son Michael took over the stable.

MATADOR

Matador was bred by Lieut-Col D. F. G. Darley and was foaled in 1953, being by Golden Cloud out of Spanish Galantry, by Mazarin. He was owned firstly by the late Mr J. E. Ferguson and subsequently by Mr Stanhope Joel, and it was in the colours of the latter that he won the Stewards Cup as a three-year-old with 9st 2lb. He also won the July Cup and the Cork and Orrery Stakes. As a stallion he did well in 1962 (£21,001) and in 1963 (£25,203), but he was not consistent and was exported to Japan in 1967.

MATCH

A 'match' is a race between horses, the property of two different owners, on terms agreed by them.

MATCH III

Owned and bred by M. F. Dupré, Match III, foaled in 1958, was by Tantième out of the famous Relic mare Relance, dam of the Derby winner Relko and the French Derby winner Reliance. Match won the Prix Juigné, Prix Noailles, the French St Leger, the Grand Prix de St Cloud, the King George VI and Queen Elizabeth Stakes and the Washington International Stakes. When his racing career was over he was purchased to stand in England but unfortunately died all too young. There is every indication from the stock he did produce that he would also have made a great sire.

MAXWELL, William Farnham (b 1905)

This successful Lambourn trainer at the age of 18 went to work in the Hon Aubrey Hasting's jumping stable at Wroughton. He became a thoroughly competent steeplechase rider although he never had the good fortune to win any of the main events. Before World War II, in which he served in the RAF, he held a trainer's licence in Ireland, but from 1940 to 1953 he acted as assistant trainer to Capt Evan Williams at Kingsclere. On the latter's retirement, he set up on his own. His main achievement has been to win the Ascot Gold Cup three times, with Pandofell in 1961 and with Fighting Charlie in 1965 and 1966. Other good races he has won include the Doncaster Cup, Yorkshire Cup, July Cup, Queen's Prize, Portland Handicap and Northumberland Plate. Among his owners are Mr V. Barclay, Maj E. T. Baring, Dame Gladys Cooper, Sir Brian Fairfax Lucy, Mr Robin Fox, Mr Robert Morley, Mr C. A. S. Palmer, Maj P. Dennis, Mrs H. O. H. Frelinghuysen, Lieut-Cmdr Lennox Cotton, Mr J. McShane, Mr John Sutton, Lord Vestey and Sir Ian Walker-Okeover. His best season was 1965 when he won over £29,000 in stakes. In 1970 he trained the very fast filly Cawston's Pride, winner of the Queen Mary Stakes at Ascot.

MEACOCK, John

John Meacock trains about a score of moderate horses, mostly his own, at Alresford, Hampshire.

MEADOW COURT

Foaled in 1962, Meadow Court was bred by Mrs Parker Poe and is a chestnut horse by Court Harwell out of Meadow Music, by Tom Fool. Bought by Paddy Prendergast for 3,000 gn as a yearling and trained by him for a partnership of three American owners that included Mr Bing Crosby, he won three races and over £100,000 in prize money, his victories including the Irish Derby and the King George VI and Queen Elizabeth Stakes, while he was second in the Derby and the St Leger. He was syndicated for stud but his career as a stallion has not been altogether satisfactory.

MELD

Meld, bred and owned by Lady Zia Wernher and trained by Sir Cecil Boyd-Rochfort, was one of the outstanding fillies of the century. Foaled in 1952 she is by Alycidon out of Daily Double, a Fair Trial mare whose grandam was Double Life, the famous foundation mare of the Someries Stud. A bay combining superb quality with immense power, Meld's only defeat was in her initial race when she was second to her better-fancied stable companion Corporal in a 5f event at Newmarket. On her only other appearance as a two-year-old she won the Quy Maiden Stakes at Newmarket.

As a three-year-old she ran four times, winning the One Thousand Guineas, the Oaks, the Coronation Stakes at Ascot and the St Leger. She was not at her best for the St Leger and in fact ran a temperature and started to cough a few hours later. In all she won five races worth £43,049. At the stud she proved disappointing until her son Charlottown won the 1966 Derby.

MERCER, Emmanuel Lionel (1930-1959)

To the sincere sorrow of the racing world, 'Manny' Mercer was killed at Ascot on 16th September 1959. He was only 29 years of age. His mount, Priddy Fair, reared, slipped and fell on the way to the post. Mercer's head came into contact with a concrete support of the rails and in addition he was kicked in the face by Priddy Fair as she struggled to regain her feet.

The elder brother of Joe Mercer, 'Manny' Mercer was born in Stockport and apprenticed to Jim Russell at Mablethorpe. When Russell's licence was withdrawn in 1947, Mercer's indentures were transferred to George Colling. His first big success came in 1948 when he won the Lincoln on the 100-1 outsider Jockey Treble. At the time his riding weight was 5st 8lb. He rode 21 winners that season, 16 in 1949 and lost his apprentice allowance early the following year. He had 37 winners in 1950. At this period E. C. Elliott was first-jockey to George Colling and Mercer owed a great deal to Elliott's advice and encouragement. To his death Mercer loyally continued to ride for George Colling's stable, despite several offers of far bigger retainers for his services.

He rode a good deal for owners for whom Jack Jarvis and Harry Wragg trained. In 1953 he won the One Thousand Guineas on Happy Laughter trained by Jarvis, and in 1954 the Two Thousand Guineas on Darius trained by Wragg. Two years later he won the Irish Derby on Talgo and the Irish Oaks on Garden State, partnering the former into second place in the Prix de l'Arc de Triomphe behind Ribot. From the beginning of Wilwyn's three-year-old career that colt was always ridden by Mercer. The most notable of their 19 victories together was that in the first Washington International at Laurel Park.

In eight seasons from 1951 to 1958 inclusive, Mercer rode more than 100 winners four times and finished in the top four jockeys every year bar 1957, when he was fifth, and in 1955. He was second in 1954 and three times third. In 1958, his last full season, he had 125 winning rides. At the time of his death in 1959 he had ridden 100 winners.

A simple, loyal and friendly person, 'Manny' Mercer never pretended to have an eye for a horse or any particular interest in pedigrees, but he rode horses not only with style, but with sympathy and understanding, too. His judgement was as sound in a race as when driving one of the fast cars that gave him so much pleasure. He married Susan Wragg, the daughter of Harry Wragg.

MERCER, Joseph (b 1934)

A younger brother of the late 'Manny' Mercer (see above), Joe Mercer is married to Harry Carr's daughter. He served his apprenticeship with the late Major F. B. Sneyd who at one time had both Eph and Doug Smith under his care. Joe rode his first winner at Bath in 1950. He was top apprentice in 1952 and 1953 and rapidly established a reputation as one of the most competent and consistent of modern riders. His best seasons so far were 1964 and 1965, in both of which he rode 106 winners. For a good many years now he has been associated with the Astor horses, firstly when they were trained by Jack Colling and subsequently by Dick Hern. He rode his first classic winner in 1953 on Lord Astor's Ambiguity, in the Oaks, his second on Mr J. J. Astor's Provoke in the 1965 St Leger. It was on Lord Astor's Grey of Falloden that he won the Cesarewitch, Grey of Falloden carrying the record weight of 9st 6lb. He has also won the Irish Derby, Gold Cup, Coronation Stakes (three times), Jubilee Handicap (twice), Northumberland Plate (twice), Newbury Spring Cup (four times), Doncaster Cup, Jockey Club Cup, Queen Elizabeth II Stakes and Queen's Prize.

MEREDITH, John Hills (b 1912)

John Meredith was educated at Eton. He was appointed a handicapper in 1946.

MESA

M. Pierre Wertheimer's Mesa, ridden by W. Johnstone and trained by P. Corbière, won the One Thousand Guineas and was third in the Oaks in 1935. In the Oaks she had a very bad run and was desperately unlucky not to win. She was by Kircubbin out of Mackwiller, by Verwood.

MID-DAY SUN

Mid-day Sun was the first horse to carry a lady's colours to victory in the Epsom Derby. Foaled in 1934, he was by Solario out of Bridge of Allan, and after failing to make his reserve at the Doncaster sales was bought privately for 2,000 gn on behalf of Miss L. M. Talbot, who shortly afterwards married Mr G. B. Miller, and her mother, Mrs J. A. W. Talbot.

Trained by Fred Butters, Mid-day Sun was a moderate two-year-old and won only once in eight races. In the Free Handicap he was rated at 7st 1lb, 34lb below the top-weight, Foray. However, he improved immensely during the winter. He won the Free

Handicap from Exhibitionnist, who later won the One Thousand Guineas, and the Oaks, and he was then third in the Two Thousand Guineas. He won the Lingfield Derby Trial, and beautifully ridden by Michael Beary, he won the Derby from the rank outsider Sandsprite. He then won the Hardwicke Stakes at Royal Ascot and was desperately unlucky not to win the St Leger, in which he was third behind Chulmleigh after being very badly hampered. That was his final race. The start of his stud career coincided with the war and he never got a full quota of mares sent to him. Largely through lack of opportunity, he failed to make the grade and was eventually exported to New Zealand, where he died in 1954. His best winner was Sterope who twice won the Cambridgeshire.

MIDDLE PARK STAKES

See under NEWMARKET.

MIDGET II

M. Pierre Wertheimers' Midget II, a fine big grey by Djebe out of Mimi, by Black Devil, won the Cheveley Park Stakes, Coronation Stakes and the Queen Elizabeth II Stakes in England, while she was second in the One Thousand Guineas and the Royal Hunt Cup. In France she won three races, including the Prix de la Foret. Her daughter Mige won the Cheveley Park Stakes in 1968.

MIDSUMMER NIGHT II

Midsummer Night II, bred in America, was foaled in 1957 and is by Djeddah out of Night Sound, by Mahmoud. He was trained in England for his owner-breeder Mr P. Mellon, by the late Capt Peter Hastings-Bass and won five races worth over £7,000 including the Cambridgeshire. He was syndicated for the stud and stands at the Derisley Wood Stud, Newmarket. He is sire of that good miler Jimmy Reppin.

MIEUXCE

Mieuxcé, by Massine, won five races in France including the French Derby and Grand Prix. He went to the stud in England and sired the Oaks winner Commotion. His daughters have done well as brood mares and one of them. Crepuscule, produced the dual classic winner Crepello; Honeylight (One Thousand Guineas); and Twilight Alley (Gold Cup).

MIGOLI

The Aga Khan's grey colt Migoli, by Bois Roussel, was a game and consistent horse that was second in the Derby in 1947 and then trounced Tudor Minstrel in the Eclipse Stakes. As a four-year-old he won the Prix de l'Arc de Triomphe, but that event did not then hold the immense prestige that it undoubtedly possesses today. As a sire Migoli proved disappointing.

MILESIAN

Milesian was foaled in 1953 and is by My Babu out of Oatflake, by Coup de Lyon. He won four races worth over £8,000, including the Imperial Produce Stakes. He has done well as a sire and stands at the Palmerston Stud, Co Kildare, at a fee of 1,000 gn. He is the property of Meath Thoroughbred Breeders Ltd.

MILLER, Mrs G. B.

The owner, in partnership with her mother Mrs J. A. W. Talbot, of the 1937 Derby winner Mid-day Sun, the first Epsom Derby winner to carry the colours of a lady-owner.

MINORU

Minoru was the third and final Derby winner of King Edward VII. He won that race, and also the Two Thousand Guineas, in 1909. He was in fact not the property of the King, being leased to him for racing by Col Hall-Walker, later Lord Wavertree. At the end of his racing career Minoru was returned to his owner, who exported him to Russia where he disappeared during the Revolution.

MIRACLE

Miracle, by Manna, was bred by the late Lord Beaverbrook and bought by Lord Rosebery as a yearling for the trifling sum of 170 gn. His four victories included the Gimcrack, Newmarket and Eclipse Stakes and he was third in the 1932 Derby won by April the Fifth. He failed as a sire.

MIRALGO

Miralgo, by Aureole, won four races and over £28,000 for Mr G. Oldham, including the Timeform Gold Cup and the Hardwicke Stakes. He stood for a time at the Irish National Stud before being exported to Japan.

MITCHELL, Cyril

Cyril Mitchell was apprenticed to the late W. Payne and rode firstly on the flat and later under National Hunt rules. Since training at Epsom his outstanding winner has been that fine sprinter Be Friendly, whose victories include the Kempton Two Thousand Guineas Trial, the Kings Stand Stakes, the Ayr Gold Cup, Vernons November Sprint Cup (twice), the Sceptre Stakes, the Palace House Stakes and the Prix de l'Abbaye. Mitchell has also won the Queen's Prize with Ulster Prince. Among his owners are Mr P. J. O'Sullevan, Mr S. Raphael, Mr M. E. Eversfield, Mr M. Phillips, Mrs R. Castello, Mrs M. Mead, Mrs C. M. Elliot and Mrs S. Drooglever. His best season so far was 1967 when he won over £16,000 in stakes.

MITCHELL, Victor J. (b 1921)

Vic Mitchell was apprenticed to George Digby at Exning. In 1939 he won the Lincoln on Squadron Castle. He served in the RAF during World War II, was shot down over Germany and was for three years a prisoner of war. He conducts a small stable at Malton and among his patrons are Mr J. Ismay, Mr A. Crogan, Mrs E.

Knowles, Mrs O. Steele, Mrs K. Lewis, Mr D. Curtis and Mr G. Holmes.

MOLONY, Tim (b 1919)

Tim Molony, five times champion jockey under National Hunt rules, now runs a 'mixed' stable at Wymondham, near Melton Mowbray, having taken out a licence to train in 1960.

MONADE

Foaled in 1959, Monade is by Klairon out of Mormyre, by Atys. In the colours of Mr G. Goulandris and trained by J. Lieux, she won eight races in France including the Prix Vermeille. In England she won the Oaks.

MONOLULU, PRINCE (d 1965)

Peter McKay, far better known as Prince Ras Monolulu, was a big powerful coloured man who came to England—from where is unknown—at the turn of the century. With his baggy trousers, umbrella and ostrich feathers, combined with his raucous and familiar cry of "I gotta horse", he became by far the best-known racecourse tipster in the country. In fact he had become an accepted part of the English racing scene long before his death in 1965. He was believed to be well over 80 when he died.

MONSIEUR L'AMIRAL

Monsieur L'Amiral, foaled in 1941, was a typical, tough French-bred stayer by Admiral Drake. He won two races in France and in England the Cesarewitch, Goodwood Cup and Queen Alexandra Stakes.

MONTAVAL

Bred and owned by Mr R. B. Strassburger, Montaval, foaled in 1953, is a bay horse by Norseman out of Ballynash, by Nasrullah. He won four races worth over 3,000,000 (old) francs in France while in England he was second in the Derby and the Eclipse Stakes and won the King George VI and Queen Elizabeth Stakes. He was exported to Japan in 1961.

MOORE, Capt Charles, MVO, MC (1881-1965)

Capt Charles Moore was appointed racing manager to King George VI in 1937, and on the King's death he held office as racing manager to the Queen till his retirement in 1963, when he was succeeded by Major Richard Shelly. One of his most important acts in his position was to advise the King to appoint Capt (later Sir) Cecil Boyd-Rochfort as his trainer. Under Capt Moore's shrewd guidance the royal studs emerged from a long era of decline and it was greatly to his credit that the Queen's horses enjoyed a wonderful period of success between 1954 and 1960, the Queen heading the list of winning owners in 1954 and 1960. He bought Malapert, dam of the Queen's Two Thousand Guineas winner Pall Mall for only 120 gn. He conducted his duties with efficiency, charm and wit, but could be brusque, even formidable, if he thought the occasion demanded it.

MOORE, George (b 1923)

This brilliant Australian jockey rode for Noel Murless's stable in 1967, winning the Two Thousand Guineas and the Derby on Royal Palace and the One Thousand Guineas on Fleet. He also won the King George VI and Queen Elizabeth Stakes on Busted. Altogether he rode 72 winners that season, at the conclusion of which he decided to return to Australia.

Moore, who combines power with gentle persuasion in his riding, and is a superb judge of pace, had gone to France in 1959 to ride for Prince Aly Khan and his victory on Taboun in the Two Thousand Guineas that year was his first ride in an English classic race. He also won the French Derby and the Grand Prix on Charlottesville; the Prix de l'Arc de Triomphe and the Eclipse on Saint Crespin III; the Grand Prix de St Cloud and the Ascot Gold Cup on Sheshoon; the French One Thousand on Ginetta; the Irish One Thousand on Florentina; and the Gimcrack and Champagne Stakes on Paddy's Sister.

MOORE, Reginald Patrick John (b 1921)

Pat Moore took out a licence to train in 1952 and at Newmarket successfully combines racing with farming. The best horse he has so far trained on the flat is Passenger, who won the William Hill Gold Cup and the Bunbury Cup.

His best season so far was 1963 when he won over £13,000 in stakes.

MORGANETTE

Morganette, by Springfield, was a selling plater that had gone in the wind. At the stud, though, she bred Galtee More and Ard Patrick, who both won the Derby (1897 and 1902), and Blairfinde, winner of the Irish Derby.

MORRIS, Derek William (b 1923)

This useful light-weight rider was apprenticed firstly to Reg Day and then to Bobby Jones. He rode his first winner in 1947 and his best season so far was 1956 when he rode 34 winners. His most important successes have been the Lincolnshire Handicap, the Queen's Prize and the Rosebery Stakes.

MORRISS, Henry E. (d 1951)

A bullion broker with extensive business interests in the Far East, Mr Morriss won the Two Thousand Guineas and the Derby with Manna in 1925. He also bred the 1940 Derby winner Pont l'Eveque, whom he sold at the end of the colt's two-year-old season to his trainer Fred Darling. With Pasch he won the Two Thousand Guineas and Eclipse Stakes in 1938.

MORTON, Charles (d 1936)

Charles Morton, who was over 80 when he died at Brighton in 1936, learnt the business from Tom Parr who had trained for Admiral Rous and who in Morton's view was the finest trainer and best judge of a horse he ever met. He himself was neat in dress, quiet in speech and manner and extremely conscientious. His greatest period of success was when he was training at Wantage for Mr J. B. Joel. Undoubtedly his most remarkable feat was to win the 1911 Derby with Sunstar who had really broken down the previous week and was so lame after the race that he could hardly hobble into the unsaddling enclosure.

Morton's classic successes were as follows:

Two Thousand Guineas: Sunstar (1911)
One Thousand Guineas: Jest (1913); Princess Dorrie (1914)
Derby: Sunstar (1911); Humorist (1921)
Oaks: Our Lassie (1902); Jest (1913); Glass Doll (1907); Princess Dorrie (1914)
St Leger: Your Majesty (1908); Black Jester (1914).

MOSSBOROUGH

Foaled in 1947, Mossborough was bred by the late Lord Derby and is by Nearco out of All Moonshine, by Bobsleigh. He was by no means an outstanding racehorse, winning five races worth £4,600, his main successes being in the Churchill Stakes at Ascot and the Liverpool Autumn Cup. He was also second in the Eclipse. As a sire, though, he has exceeded all expectations, his outstanding winners in England being Ballymoss and Noblesse. He was champion sire in 1958. In the United States his son Cavan won the Belmont Stakes and over $135,000. Mossborough was syndicated and stands at the New England Stud, Newmarket.

MOURNE

Mourne was foaled in 1954 and is a half-brother by Vieux Manoir to Montaval. In France he won three races worth over 5,000,000 (old) francs. He is now owned by a syndicate and stands at the Fort Union Stud, Co Limerick.

MOWERINA

Mowerina (1876) is the most famous thoroughbred to have been foaled in Denmark. By Scottish Chief, she ran for four seasons in England and won 16 of her 34 races. A foundation mare of the Duke of Portland's stud, she bred Donovan (Derby and St Leger), Semolina (One Thousand Guineas) and Raeburn (a good winner and third in the Derby).

MR JINKS

Bred and owned by Major D. McCalmont and trained by 'Atty' Persse, Mr Jinks was foaled in 1926 and was a grey by Tetratema out of False Piety, by Lemberg. A very good horse up to a mile, he won nine races worth over £25,000, including the New Stakes, July Stakes, Two Thousand Guineas and St James's Palace Stakes. He made a promising start as a sire but later on his record was disappointing.

MRS BUTTERWICK

One of the smallest of classic winners, Mrs Butterwick, by St Simon, stood just 15 hands when she won the 1893 Oaks. From her the St Leger winner Singapore and that good sprinter Portlaw were descended.

MULHALL, J.

He has a stable of over 30 horses at York and won 10 races in 1969.

MULLION, Mr and Mrs J. R.

This Scottish-born shipowner and his wife, who own the Ardenode Stud, Co Kildare, have been very successful with their horses, most of which are trained in Ireland by P. J. Prendergast. Mr Mullion's best winner so far is Ragusa who won the Irish Derby, the St Leger, the Eclipse Stakes and the King George VI and Queen Elizabeth Stakes. Other good winners in the Mullion colours include Paddy's Sister (Queen Mary Stakes, Gimcrack Stakes and Champagne Stakes); Court Harwell (second in St Leger); Floribunda (New Stakes, Nunthorpe Stakes and King George Stakes); and Hardicanute (Timeform Gold Cup and Champagne Stakes).

Mr Mullion's racing colours are white, Robertson tartan, sash and cap; those of his wife are white, red collar and cuffs, tartan cap.

MUMTAZ MAHAL

Mumtaz Mahal, foaled in 1921, was a filly whose tremendous speed as a two-year-old captured the imagination of the racing public. Commonly known as "the flying filly", she was bred at the Sledmere Stud and was a grey by The Tetrarch out of Lady Josephine, by Sundridge. As a yearling she was sent up to Doncaster sales and bought for 9,100 gn by George Lambton, acting on behalf of the Aga Khan.

She went to R. C. Dawson's stable at Whatcombe to be trained and in 1923 she won successively and in brilliant style the Spring Stakes at Newmarket, the Queen Mary Stakes at Ascot, the National Breeders Produce Stakes at Sandown, the Molecomb Stakes at Goodwood and the Champagne Stakes at Doncaster. Unwisely, as it turned out, she was started for the Imperial Produce Stakes at Kempton in the autumn when she was not at her best, and in heavy going she was beaten half a length by Arcade, who received 7lb, to the astonishment and dismay of her many admirers.

Despite her obvious stamina limitations, she ran in the One Thousand Guineas and the Coronation Stakes as a three-year-old and failed in both those events. However, she ended her career in appropriate style by decisive victories in the 6f King George Stakes at Goodwood and the 5f Nunthorpe Stakes at York. Altogether she won seven races worth over £13,000.

Considering her own excellence, her offspring, particularly her fillies, were disappointing on the racecourse, but it was a different story when her daughters were at the stud and through them she has exercised immense influence on bloodstock breeding throughout the world. There is only space here to mention Mah Mahal, dam of the Derby winner Mahmoud, and Mumtaz Begum, dam of Nasrullah who was champion sire both in England and in the United States.

MURLESS, Charles Francis Noel (b 1910)

Noel Murless was born in Cheshire. He was always interested in horses, and hunted and rode in point-to-points in his teens. He was first of all attached to Frank Hartigan's stable and rode with meagre success under National Hunt rules. Later on he assisted Hubert Hartigan, first at Penrith and later in Ireland. From those two shrewd and experienced Irish brothers he learnt a great deal.

He took out a licence to train in 1935 and his stable at Hambleton in Yorkshire was so successful after World War II that he was invited to succeed the great Fred Darling at Beckhampton. He accepted, but he was never really happy there and a few years later moved to Newmarket. Since then he has never looked back and he is now generally accepted as the foremost English trainer of the day. He trained the horses leased by the National Stud to the Queen—this arrangement has ceased because the National Stud no longer keeps mares —and his main patrons at present are Mr H. J. Joel, Lady Sassoon, Col John Hornung, Mr S. Joel, Mr J. E. Oppenheimer, Mr J. R. Hindley, Lord Howard de Walden, Mrs V. Hue-Williams, Mr George A. Pope junior and Mrs Murless. In 1967 he won £256,899 in stakes for his owners, easily a record for an English trainer.

His main successes have been as follows:

Two Thousand Guineas: Crepello (1957); Royal Palace (1967)

One Thousand Guineas: Queenpot (1948); Petite Etoile (1959); Fleet (1967); Caergwrle (1968)
Derby: Crepello (1957); St Paddy (1960); Royal Palace (1967)
Oaks: Carozza (1967); Petite Etoile (1959); Lupe (1970)
Coronate Cup: Caliban (1970)
St Leger: Ridge Wood (1949); St Paddy (1960); Aurelius (1961)
King George VI and Queen Elizabeth Stakes: Aunt Edith (1966); Busted (1967); Royal Palace (1968)
Eclipse Stakes: St Paddy (1961); Busted (1967); Royal Palace (1968)
Gold Cup: Twilight Alley (1963)
Champion Stakes: Petite Etoile (1959)
Coronation Cup: Petite Etoile (1960-61); Royal Palace (1968)
Prix Vermeille: Aunt Edith (1965)
Grand Prix de St Cloud: Hopeful Venture (1968).

A tall, thin, anxious-looking man who takes his responsibilities very seriously, Murless is devoted to his horses and is a great stableman with a flair for understanding the characteristics and capabilities of each individual horse under his care. He is very patient, and the interests of his horses come first, even when it involves making an unpopular decision.

MURRAY, Anthony

Tony Murray is a son of Paddy Murray who rode a lot of winners under National Hunt rules for Reg Hobbs just after World War II. Tony had a good grounding in the hunting field and the show-ring while in the school holidays he used to ride gallops for Capt Tim Forster at Letcombe Bassett. On leaving school he was apprenticed to 'Frenchie' Nicholson and in May 1966 he rode his first winner. In 1967 he made fine progress and rode 37 winners, his successes including the Victoria Cup and Great Metropolitan. He had won 31 races in 1968, including the Ascot Stakes, when he had a very severe fall at Windsor, receiving extensive facial injuries. Happily he made a complete recovery and was able to ride for Doug Smith's stable in 1969, riding 44 winners.

MURRAY, W. F.

Bill Murray was head lad to Sam Hall for twenty years before taking out a licence himself three years ago. He trains at Middleham and his main success so far has been to win the 1970 Chester Cup with Altogether.

MUSIDORA

Musidora was bred by Mr F. F. Tuthill and is by Nasrullah out of Painted Vale, by Gainsborough. Owned by Mr N. P. Donaldson and trained by Capt Charles Elsey, she won the One Thousand Guineas and the Oaks in 1949. As a brood mare she has proved disappointing.

MY BABU

My Babu, originally named Lerins, was foaled in 1945. Bred in France by Mr Peter Beatty, he is by Djebel out of Perfume II, by Badruddin. He was trained by 'Sam' Armstrong and in the colours of HH the Maharaja of Baroda, he won 10½ races worth over £29,000, including the Woodcote Stakes, New Stakes, Craven Stakes, Two Thousand Guineas and Victoria Cup. He went to the stud in Ireland in 1950 but in 1956 was sold to go to the United States for £214,000. He sired the 1955 Two Thousand Guineas winner Our Babu.

MY DEAR

Owned and bred by Mr A. W. Cox and trained by Alec Taylor, My Dear was foaled in 1915 and was by Beppo out of Silesia, by Spearmint. She won eight races including the Oaks, Champion Stakes and Liverpool Autumn Cup. At the stud she bred three winners of over £6,000 in stakes.

MY LOVE

My Love, owned in partnership by

the Aga Khan and M. L. Volterra, was trained in France by Richard Carver. A bay colt by Vatellor, he brought off a great double in 1948 when he won both the Derby and the Grand Prix. He was not a success as a sire in France and was exported to Argentina.

MYROBELLA

Myrobella was 30 years of age when she died at the National Stud in 1960. A beautiful grey filly by Tetratema out of Dolabella, she was leased for racing to Lord Lonsdale and trained by Fred Darling. She did not stay beyond 6f but nevertheless won 11 races and over £13,000 in stakes. As a two-year-old she headed the Free Handicap, being rated 7lb superior to Hyperion. Among her victories were the National Breeders Produce Stakes, the Champagne Stakes and the July Cup. At the stud her winners included Big Game, who won the Two Thousand Guineas and became a successful sire; and Snowberry, who won the Queen Mary Stakes and was dam of the St Leger winner Chamossaire.

N

NAGAMI

Nagami, a chestnut by Nimbus out of Jennifer, by Hyperion, was foaled in 1955. Trained by Harry Wragg he won the Coronation Cup and was placed in the Two Thousand Guineas, Derby and St Leger. In Italy he won the Gran Premio de Jockey Club and in France the Grand Prix du Printemps at St Cloud.

NAGLE, Mrs Florence (b 1894)

Mrs Nagle has been in the racing game for a good many years. In 1937 she was second in the Derby with Sandsprite. It was largely through her courage and indomitable persistence that the racing authorities were finally persuaded to yield and to grant women licences to train in 1966. Since then Mrs Nagle has held a licence herself, training at Petworth her own horses and those of Miss Newton Deakin. Among the races she has won as an owner are the Liverpool St Leger and the Midland Cambridgeshire.

NAMING OF HORSES

A name cannot be registered for a horse unless it is at least a yearling, except in the case of horses foaled elsewhere than in Great Britain, Ireland or the Channel Islands, or if the horse is outside these countries at the date of registration.

A name or, by permission of the Stewards of the Jockey Club, a change of name, can only be registered for a horse at the Registry Office in London, with the following description—age, colour, whether a horse, mare or gelding, and the registered or Stud Book names or descriptions of its sire and dam. If the dam was covered by more than one stallion, the names of all must be stated. In all cases such pedigree and description must be given as will clearly distinguish the horse from all other horses, and if the pedigree of the sire or dam is unknown, such further particulars must be given as to where, when, and from whom it was purchased or obtained, as will identify it, and a Certificate of Markings signed by a veterinary surgeon who is neither the owner nor the trainer of the horse. If there is no other horse of the same name, and provided the name is not that of a celebrated horse or mare, the name will be registered and will from the Monday after registration be the horse's name under the Rules of Racing. A list of names registered is published in the *Racing Calendar*.

If the same name is simultaneously claimed for two horses, the order of priority is determined by lot in the Registry Office.

A name may be reserved for a living foal on payment of a fee of 10s. Application to reserve a name has to be made in writing to the Registry Office. A name cannot be reserved for more than 12 months.

See Rules of Racing (31).

NARRATOR

Foaled in 1951, Narrator was a bay horse by Nearco out of Phase, by Windsor Lad. He won four races for his owner-breeder, the late Major L. B. Holliday, including the Champion Stakes and Coronation Cup. Syndicated for the stud, he sired many good winners including Night Off (One Thousand Guineas and Cheveley Park Stakes); Nortia (Lingfield Oaks Trial, Nassau Stakes and Magnet Cup) and Narratus (Great Metropolitan and Chester Cup). He died in 1969.

NASRAM II

Nasram II, by Nasrullah, was foaled in 1960. He won a couple of races in France, trained by E. Fellows, and created a sensation in England by defeating Santa Claus in the King George VI and Queen Elizabeth Stakes. Now syndicated, he stands at Haras de la Verrerie, La Cochère (Orne), France.

NASRULLAH

Bred by the late Aga Khan in 1940, Nasrullah was by Nearco out of Mumtaz Begum, by Blenheim out of the famous Mumtaz Mahal. Trained by Frank Butters, Nasrullah won the Coventry Stakes as a two-year-old, beating the future Derby winner Straight Deal, but in a gruelling race for the Middle Park Stakes he went under by a neck to Lord Rosebery's game filly Ribbon. That race left a permanent mark on him and subsequently his temperament was unreliable. As a three-year-old he wore blinkers and was reluctant to go down to the start. It was perhaps unfortunate that owing to war-time restrictions he raced only at Newmarket, a course he had come to dislike. He was fourth in the Two Thousand Guineas, third in the Derby and won the Champion Stakes. On his day and in the right mood he was undoubtedly a high-class colt. In all he won £3,348 in stakes.

In August 1944 he was bought by the British Bloodstock Agency on behalf of the 'Nasrullah Syndicate' which in fact consisted solely of Messrs G. McElligott and Bert Kerr. For 19,000 gn they passed him on to Mr Joseph McGrath.

As a sire Nasrullah was outstandingly and consistently successful. He headed the list in 1951 and was twice second and twice third. He sired Musidora (One Thousand Guineas and Oaks); Nearula (Two Thousand Guineas); Belle of All (One Thousand Guineas); and Never Say Die (Derby and St Leger). One of his first crop of runners was Noor who went to America and won $346,940, on three occasions beating the allegedly unbeatable Citation.

It was a great loss to the British breeding industry when in 1950 Mr A. B. Hancock bought Nasrullah on behalf of an American syndicate for $370,000. In the United States Nasrullah was just as successful as he had been in England. Twice he was champion sire and three times he was second. Among his best American winners were Nashua, 'Horse of the Year' for 1955; Leallah, champion two-year-old filly of 1956; Bold Ruler, 'Horse of the Year' for 1957; Nadir, champion two-year-old for 1957; and Bald Eagle, twice winner of the Washington International at Laurel Park.

Nasrullah died in 1959. His sons Grey Sovereign and Princely Gift have done well as sires in England, while Never Say Die sired the Derby winner Larkspur and the dual classic winner Never Too Late. Bold Ruler has done outstandingly well as a sire in the United States and Orgoglio proved a great success in Australia.

NATHOO

Owned and bred by the late Aga Khan, Nathoo was foaled in 1945 and was by Nasrullah out of Taj Shirin, by Gainsborough. He won five races, including the Irish Derby, and over £11,000 in prize money. He went to the stud in America.

NATIONAL STAKES

Formerly the National Breeders Produce Stakes. See under SANDOWN PARK.

NATIONAL STUD

In 1915 Col W. Hall Walker, later Lord Wavertree, presented his stud at Tully, Co Kildare, to the British nation for the purpose of forming the National Stud. As well as the stud, the gift comprised four stallions; 45 top-grade mares; some foals, yearlings and hunters; 600 head of cattle; carthorses; forage: in fact everything which was on the land, including the famous Japanese garden, or in the buildings, including furniture and pictures. The difference between bloodstock values at the period and those existing today is shown by the fact that the total value of all livestock there was estimated to be £74,000. The first Director of the National Stud was the late Sir Henry Greer, a former army officer with long experience both as owner and breeder.

During World War II the disadvantages of having the English National Stud located in Eire became increasingly apparent and in 1944 all the land at Tully became vested in Ireland while the livestock were transferred to the stud at Gillingham in Dorset that had originally been established by the late Lord Furness.

From its inception until 1963 the National Stud was under the authority of the Ministry of Agriculture, but in that year responsibility for the stud was taken over by the Levy Board. It was then decided that the National Stud should not go on breeding in opposition to commercial studs and that the future function of the stud should be to concentrate on the standing of stallions and the holding of shares in top-class syndicated stallions. Accordingly the brood mares, yearling fillies and filly-foals were dispersed, the yearling colts and colt-foals being permitted to continue through their racing career on lease to the Queen in the normal manner. Before the war the National Stud used to lease colts and fillies for racing purposes to the late Lord Lonsdale; on his death they were leased to King George VI, and following his death, to the Queen.

At the same time as this fundamental change in policy was made, it was decided to build a new National Stud at Newmarket on land taken on a long lease from the Jockey Club. By private treaty the National Stud at Gillingham was sold to Mr Simon Wingfield Digby, MP. In 1964 nine of the National Stud's yearling fillies were sold for an average price of 7,433 gn; later in the year 30 mares and foals from the National Stud realised a total of 271,920 gn.

Since its inception there have been only three Directors of the National Stud; Sir Henry Greer, KCVO (1916-33); Mr Noble Johnson (1934-37); and Mr Peter Burrell, CBE (1937 to date).

Stallions standing at the National Stud are Never Say Die, Tudor Melody, Stupendous and Hopeful Venture.

Among the good horses bred at the National Stud are Blandford (sire of four Derby winners); Royal Lancer (St Leger); Big Game (Two Thousand Guineas); Chamossaire (St Leger and champion sire); Sun Chariot (One Thousand Guineas, Oaks and St Leger); Myrobella (11 races worth over £16,000 and dam of Big Game); Anneta (Irish One Thousand); Carrozza (Oaks); Hopeful Venture (Grand Prix de Saint Cloud and Hardwicke Stakes); and The Panther (Two Thousand Guineas).

NATIONAL TRAINERS' ASSOCIATION

The National Trainers Association was formed in 1964 but has no formal constitution. The objects of the Association are to study and promote the interests of flat-race horse-trainers; to consider all questions affecting them and their rights and liabilities; to make suggestions and improvements in relation to all matters affecting such trainers and racing generally, and to this end to consult with, and work in concert with the Jockey Club, Weatherby and Sons, the Levy Board and all such persons and bodies as may seem to be in the interests of the Association.

NATIVE PRINCE

Foaled in 1964, Native Prince was bred in America and is by Native Dancer out of Sungari, by Eight Thirty. He won five races in the United States and now stands at a fee of £450 at the Mount Coote Stud, Co Limerick.

NEARCO

Nearco was one of the best of the many great horses bred in Italy by Signor Federico Tesio at his Dormello Stud. By Pharos out of Nogara, Nearco was a horse of perfect size and great quality. He was the unbeaten winner of 14 races including the Grand Prix de Paris, in which he trounced the Derby winner Bois Roussel. Thought not really a true stayer, his superb class and brilliant speed enabled him to win over nearly two miles.

Bought as a stallion for £60,000 by the bookmaker Mr M. H. Benson, he proved an outstanding sire in England. He was twice champion sire and between 1942 and 1956 was never lower than eighth on the list. Among the good horses he got were Dante (Derby), Nimbus (Two Thousand Guineas and Derby), Sayajirao (St Leger), Masaka (Oaks) and Neasham Belle (Oaks). The Derby winners Tulyar and Arctic Prince were out of Nearco mares.

Nearco had immense influence on bloodstock breeding not only in England, but also in America where his son Nasrullah was twice leading sire. He is great-grandsire of Nijinsky.

NEARULA

Nearula was foaled in 1950 and was a bay horse by Nasrullah out of Respite, by Flag of Truce. Bred by Messrs R. More O'Ferrall and C. Sweeney, he was bought for 3,000 gn as a yearling by Capt Charles Elsey acting on behalf of Mr W. Humble. He was a very good two-year-old and won the Middle Park Stakes by four lengths. The following season he won the Two Thousand Guineas by four lengths but unfortunately his Derby preparation was interrupted by an injury to his foot and he was unplaced at Epsom behind Pinza. However, he won the St James's Palace Stakes and the Champion Stakes. Altogether he won seven races and over £27,000 in stakes. Unfortunately his stud career was of brief duration as he died of a ruptured blood vessel in 1960.

NEASHAM BELLE

Owned and bred by the late Major L. B. Holliday, Neasham Belle was by Nearco out of Phase, by Windsor Lad, and thus a sister of the Champion and Eclipse Stakes winner Narrator. She won the Oaks in 1951. As a brood mare she has proved disappointing.

NEIL GOW

Foaled in 1907, Neil Gow was owned and bred by the late Lord Rosebery and was by Marco out of Chelandry. A beautiful chestnut horse, difficult to fault except for rather weak hocks, he was by nature high-mettled, inclined to be troublesome at the start and gave his trainer many anxious moments. He was a brilliant two-year-old, his wins including the Champagne Stakes, and the following year he won the Two Thousand Guineas, Danny Maher riding a superb race to beat Lemberg by a short head. Before the Derby, Neil Gow sprung a curb, missed his final gallop and was fourth to Lemberg. He met Lemberg again in the Eclipse Stakes and after a wonderful race they ran a dead-heat. In his St Leger preparation Neil Gow broke down and never ran again. He died after eight seasons at the stud but nevertheless made a name for himself as a successful sire of brood mares. Of his sons, the Cambridgeshire winner Re-echo did extremely well as a sire in the Argentine.

NELCIUS

Nelcius was foaled in 1963 and is by Teneraze out of Namagua, by Fontenay. He won the French Derby and now stands at the Meddler Stud, Kentford, near Newmarket, at a fee of 700 gn.

NELSON, Major Peter Maurice (b 1913)

From Marlborough and the RMC, where he had distinguished himself at cricket and racquets, Major Nelson joined the Royal Berkshire Regiment and was a regular soldier for 14 years. He took out a trainer's licence in 1947 and once established, he has been consistently successful although he has yet to win a classic event. Good races he has won include the Stewards Cup, Coventry Stakes, Bessborough Stakes, Queen Mary Stakes, Brighton Cup, City and Suburban, Esher Cup and Liverpool St Leger. His stables are at Upper Lambourn and his owners include Hon A. Berry, Lord Carnarvon, Mr L. H. Chen, Mr R. Clifford-Turner, Mr P. A. V. Cooper, Mrs R. Grosvenor, Mr J. H. Hawes, Mr C. F. Hughesdon, Major and Mrs V. McCalmont, M. H. L. Middleton, Sir Brian and Lady Mountain, HH the Prince of Baroda, Mr B. Samuel, Lord and Lady Tryon, Mr R. F. Scully and Mr J. Sacher.

NEOCRACY

By Nearco out of Harina, by Blandford, Neocracy was dam of two high-class horses in Tulyar (Derby, St Leger, Eclipse and King George VI and Queen Elizabeth Stakes); and Saint Crespin III (Imperial Produce Stakes, Eclipse Stakes and Prix de l'Arc de Triomphe).

NESBITT, Stephen (b 1930)

Stephen Nesbitt was apprenticed to H. Lowe. He took out a trainer's licence in 1966 and runs a small stable at Diggle, near Oldham, Lancashire.

NEVER SAY DIE

Bred in the United States by Mr Robert Sterling Clark, Never Say Die is a chestnut by Nasrullah out of Singing Grass. He was sent to England to be trained by Joe Lawson at Newmarket and though a useful two-year-old, he appeared to be well below classic standard. However, he made immense improvement as a three-year-old and ridden by Lester Piggott, then 18 years of age, he won the Derby at 33-1 by two lengths. In the King Edward VII Stakes at Ascot he was beaten in a rough race, after which Piggott was suspended for the rest of the season. With Charlie Smirke in the saddle, he won the St Leger, his final race, by 12 lengths. As a token of his regard for the English Turf, Mr Clark presented Never Say Die to the National Stud. Though not consistently successful at the stud, Never Say Die was champion sire in 1962. He has so far sired a Derby winner in Larkspur, and a winner of the One Thousand Guineas and the Oaks in Never Too Late.

NEVER TOO LATE II

Bred in America and trained in France by E. Pollet for Mrs Howell E. Jackson, Never Too Late II won the One Thousand Guineas and the Oaks in 1960. She was also second in the Champion Stakes and won three races in France. She is by the Derby and St Leger winner Never Say Die out of the English-bred mare Gloria Nicky, by Alycidon.

NEVETT, William

When he rode Owen Tudor to victory in the Derby in 1941, William Nevett was a private in the Royal Army Ordnance Corps. Born in Lancashire, he was apprenticed to the late Dobson Peacock at Middleham in 1916 and in due course became the outstanding rider in the north. He rode his thousandth winner in 1940. He won the Derby again on Ocean Swell in 1944 and for the third time on Dante in 1945. All his three Derby winners were gained in war-substitute races at Newmarket. His other classic success was on the Aga Khan's Masaka in the 1948 Oaks. On retirement he trained for a time at Ripon, but soon found it considerably less profitable than riding and wisely gave it up.

NEWBURY

Newbury racecourse was primarily the inspiration, during his retirement, of the famous John Porter who had trained for many years at neighbouring Kingsclere. When travelling to

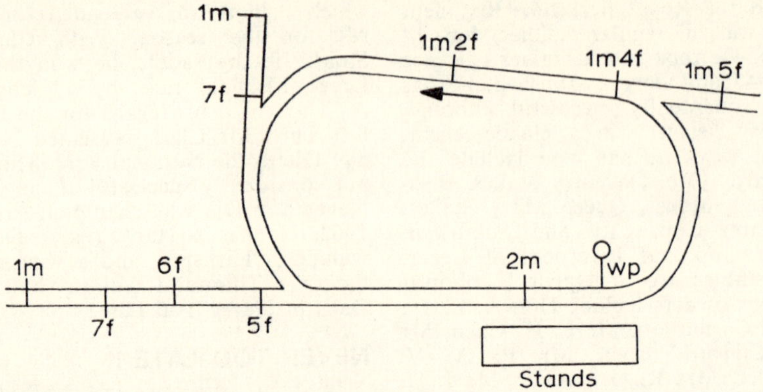

NEWBURY

London by rail he often noticed a level stretch of land just south of the railway that seemed ideal for a racecourse. Mr L. H. Baxendale of Greenham was prepared to sell the land, but when Porter approached the Jockey Club with his plan, that eminent body proved coldly discouraging. In fact but for strong support from King Edward VII, once a patron of Porter's stable, the project would very likely have been dropped.

Fifty-six miles from London, Newbury owed much in the past at any rate to the excellence of the railway service, while the proximity of so many Berkshire and Wiltshire stables has always ensured a plentiful supply of runners. There are no great races run at Newbury, but the general level of the sport there is high and the programmes carefully thought out. The executive gives the impression of making every endeavour to please racegoers and improvements, not least in the cheap enclosures, are constantly being made. It is not surprising that Newbury enjoys considerable popularity with the racegoing public.

It is arguable that Newbury's most popular race is a steeplechase, the Hennessy Gold Cup. On the flat the Spring, Summer and Autumn Cups are well-established handicaps over 1m, 1½m and 2m respectively. The Greenham Stakes is rated a significant trial for the Two Thousand Guineas, while the Lockinge Stakes is one of the more important mile races of the season.

During World War II Newbury became an important depot for military stores and the whole racecourse was covered with roads, railway lines and vast stretches of concrete. It seemed improbable at the time that racing could ever take place there again, but as soon as hostilities were over, the task of clearing up was tackled with such commendable energy and determination that racing was resumed in 1949. Newbury's post-war recovery, its many improvements and the quality of the sport provided owed, and still owes, much to that shrewd and experienced racing official, Mr Geoffrey Freer, for many years Clerk of the Course.

Clerk of the Course: Capt C. B. Toller, The Racecourse, Newbury. Tel: Newbury 15.

Best Times:

Distance	*Horse-Age-Weight*	*Date*	*Time*
5f	Minstrel's Gallery 3-8-12	18/6/55	59.8
5f	Zuccherene 2-8-7	25/6/59	60.6

Distance	*Horse-Age-Weight*	*Date*	*Time*
6f	Rolled Gold 4-8-1	3/10/59	1min 11.2
6f	Coronation Scot 2-8-3	3/10/53	1min 12.6
7f st	Firestreak 3-9-7	29/5/59	1min 24.4
7f st	Sweet Moss 2-8-6	27/7/63	1min 26.4
7f 6yd rnd	Bucktail 4-7-1	25/6/59	1min 26.8
7f 6yd rnd	H.V.C. 2-8-6	26/10/51	1min 29.6
8f rnd	Candid Picture 3-8-12	26/7/63	1min 37
8f rnd	Nightman 2-8-9	27/10/51	1min 39
8f st	Great Uncle Fred 4-9-7	15/6/67	1min 37
10f	Bacchus 3-7-5	22/6/49	2min 5.5
11f	Right Wheel 3-9-0	11/5/67	2min 21.2
12f	Vidi Vici 4-8-9	21/6/51	2min 29.2
13f 60yd	Poaching 5-8-1	4/5/57	2min 47.5
16f	Flighty Frances 5-8-10	3/10/53	3min 26.6

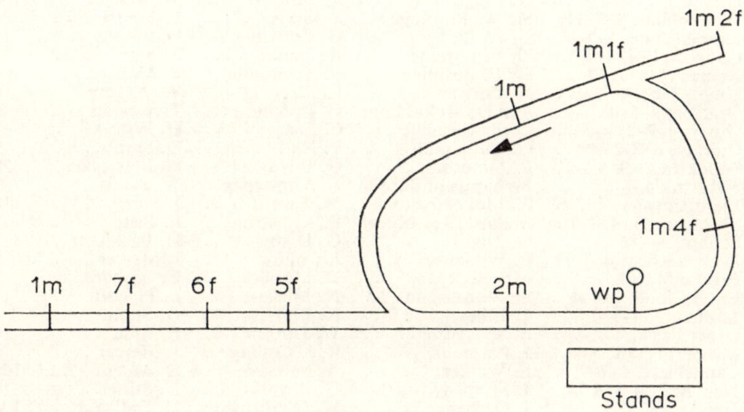

NEWCASTLE

NEWCASTLE

The Newcastle course is attractively laid out in Gosforth Park. The amenities are modern and excellent. The track itself has the reputation of being a stiff one, particularly when the going is heavy. It is a left-handed circuit of 1m 6f with a run-in of just about 4f. The turns are well-banked and can be taken at speed, thereby offering no respite for a tiring horse. The last 4f, except for the final 200yd which are level, is uphill. Stamina and resolution are the qualities a horse needs here.

The big race of the year is the Northumberland Plate, a 2m handicap which draws a very big crowd. London journalists are apt to refer to it as the 'Pitmen's Derby', but up north it is just called 'The Plate'. Another popular event is the Scottish and Newcastle Breweries Stakes, a 10f sponsored handicap for three-year-olds run in May.

Clerk of the Course: Mr A. C. Newton, High Gosforth Park Co, Ltd, High Gosforth Park, Newcastle-upon-Tyne. Tel: Wideopen 2020.

Distance	*Horse-Age-Weight*	*Date*	*Time*
5f	Weensland 4-9-0	21/6/51	58.6
5f	Dunce Cap 2-8-2	6/8/62	59.2
6f	Comobeau 3-9-3	23/6/60	1min 11.6
6f	Kursaal 2-8-7	1/7/67	1min 14
7f	Arion 5-10-0	30/6/62	1min 25.2
7f	Petros 2-8-8	27/8/66	1min 28.6
8f rnd	Brink 4-6-12	4/10/47	1min 39.8
8f rnd	Tudor Royal 2-7-12	6/9/58	1min 46.2
9f	Ferniehurst 3-6-3	23/6/36	1min 52
10f 30yd	Heckley 8-7-5	14/10/59	2min 10.6
12f 6yd	Kesrullah 4-8-13	25/6/53	2min 38.4
16f	Nectar II 4-7-12	23/6/37	3min 22

Northumberland Plate, 2m

Handicap. First run 1833. *Run at Liverpool* 1946. *No race* 1940 *to* 1945.

		OWNER	TRAINER	JOCKEY	SP
1930	Show Girl, 4–8–4	Lady Ludlow	J. Watts	C. Elliott	100–8
1931	Blue Vision, 4–7–4	M. Evans	I. Anthony	K. Gethin	11–4
1932	Pomarrel, 5–7–5	J. Thompson	M. Peacock	J. Dines	8–1
1933	Leonard, 7–7–9	H. Clayton	C. Elsey	W. Bullock	100–7
1934	Whiteplains, 4–7–11	Sir W. Burbidge	J. Jarvis	E. Smith	25–1
1935	Doreen Jane, 5–7–8	Sir A. Bailey	H. Cottrill	D. Smith	15–8
1936	Coup de Roi, 4–7–13	Sir P. Loraine	R. Dawson	E. Smith	5–2
1937	Nectar II, 4–7–12	Sir E. Bushby	F. Armstrong	P. Maher	100–8
1938	Union Jack, 4–8–0	N. Christey	C. Elsey	W. Nevett	10–1
1939	Oracion, 4–8–0	Maj D. McCalmont	G. Lambton	T. Weston	9–1
1946	Gusty, 4–9–2	Lord Allendale	C. Elsey	H. Wragg	7–4
1947	Culrain, 6–7–2	G. Cullington	T. Hall	D. Smith	9–2
1948	Pappatea, 5–9–5	R. Simpson	G. Boyd	H. Blackshaw	20–1
1949	Fol Ami, 4–7–1	Maharaja of Baroda	F. Armstrong	W. Snaith	9–2
1950	Light Cavalry, 4–7–6	A. McLeod	M. Everitt	J. Sime	10–1
1951	Sycomore II, 4–8–3	Maharaja of Morvi	F. Armstrong	E. Britt	9–4
1952	Souepi, 4–7–6	G. Digby	G. Digby	H. Packham	5–4
1953	Nick la Rocca, 4–8–11	F. Williams	J. Colling	J. Mercer	9–4
1954	Friseur, 4–8–2	Mrs R. Ryan	N. Murless	G. Richards	7–1
1955	Little Cloud, 4–8–4	Sir V. Sassoon	N. Murless	L. Piggott	13–2
1956	Jardiniere, 4–8–0	T. Lilley	N. Murless	D. Smith	2–1
1957	Great Rock, 4–7–8	Mrs A. Straker	W. Dutton	E. Hide	10–1
1958	Master of Arts, 5–8–4	J. Astor	R. J. Colling	J. Mercer	7–2
1959	Cannebiere, 6–7–9	E. Walker	A. Barclay	D. Morris	100–7
1960	New Brig, 4–8–8	J. Kennedy	G. Boyd	N. Stirk	10–1
1961	Utrillo, 4–7–1	J. Gerber	W. O'Gorman	D. Cullen	100–7
1962	Bordone, 4–8–5	A. Grant	G. Fenningworth	G. Littlewood	100–7
1963	Horse Radish, 4–7–8	N. Wachman	F. Maxwell	P. Robinson	8–1
1964	Peter Piper, 4–7–9	Mrs V. Phillips	R. Mason	J. Wilson	28–1
1965	Cagirama, 6–7–5	Mrs S. Carson	G. Boyd	N. McIntosh	9–1
1966	Sweet Story, 4–8–4	Dule of Roxburghe	R. Peacock	J. Etherington	100–7
1967	Piaco, 4–9–1	Mrs O. V. Watney	G. Barling	M. Thomas	100–30
1968	Amateur, 4–7–9	Lord Derby	B. van Cutsem	W. Carson	100–9
1969	Even Say, 4–7–11	S. Terry	R. Jarvis	F. Durr	6–1
1970	Philoctetes, 6–7–12	P. Bull	S. Ingham	P. Eddery	20–1

NEWMARKET

Newmarket is the headquarters of English flat-racing. Racing has been conducted there since the days of the Stuarts. In the time of James I hunting and hawking took pride of place over racing, but Charles II was a racing enthusiast and is the only King of England to have won a race on the flat with himself as rider. He founded the Newmarket Town Plate and won it on two occasions. The famous Rowley Mile is named after him, as 'Old Rowley' was his nickname, derived from his favourite hack who bore that name.

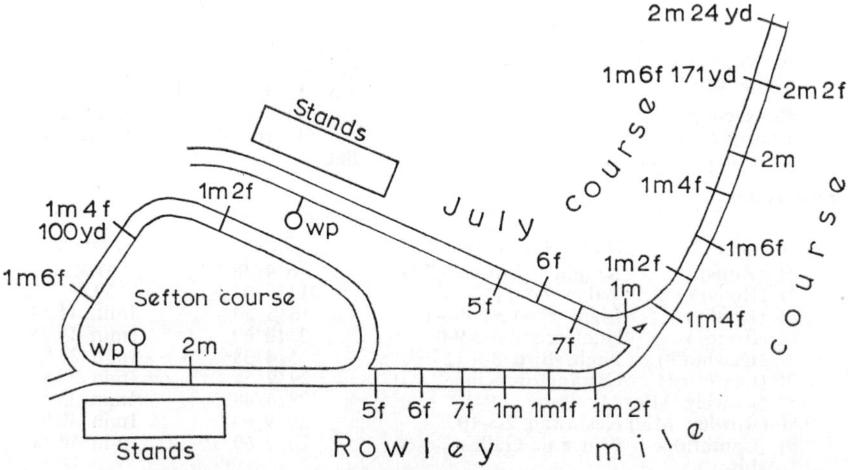

NEWMARKET

Not only is Newmarket the main training centre, but it is also the home of racing's governing body, the Jockey Club, whose premises are in the High Street. The Jockey Club owns Newmarket Heath and the two racecourses, thanks largely to the foresight and generosity of the fourth Duke of Portland, who was a member of the club for over 50 years and died at an advanced age in 1854. The main races run at Newmarket are the Two Thousand Guineas and the One Thousand Guineas at the Spring Meeting; the Middle Park Stakes, the Cheveley Park Stakes and the Cesarewitch at the October Meeting; and the Dewhurst Stakes, Champion Stakes and the Cambridgeshire at the Houghton Meeting, also held in October. These races are all run on the Rowley Mile course. The July course was kept going during World War II and all the classic races were run there bar the St Leger in 1940, 1941 and 1945.

Newmarket racecourse as a whole is shaped roughly like the letter Y with straight arms and the tail bent to the right. The tail is represented by the Beacon course which turns right at the junction into the July course on the right and the Rowley Mile course on the left.

The Rowley Mile course is one of the best, fairest and most testing in the country and is used for all except the summer meetings. All races up to 1m 2f inclusive (except on the Sefton course) are perfectly straight with little rise or fall as far as 'the Bushes', about 2f from the finish. From that point the course runs downhill for a furlong to 'the Dip', the final furlong being uphill. Races exceeding 1m 2f start on the Beacon course and have a right-hand turn into the straight. The two-mile Sefton course is circular in shape; starting in front of the stands, it turns right-handed and rejoins the Rowley Mile course 4f from the winning post. The course runs downhill from 11f to 7½f out.

The surroundings at Newmarket tend to be severe and until recently amenities verged on the spartan; hence the money recently spent to try a give a 'cosier' atmosphere. Both the Rowley Mile course and the July course were laid out before the days when spectators came into the reckoning. Because of this much of the running in the Cesarewitch, for example, cannot be seen from the stands; in fact watching that event has been described as "hanging about in Suffolk to see a race that is run in Cambridgeshire". As a palliative, the Sefton course was opened in 1958.

The lengths of the various courses are as follows:

Rous course: 5f
Bretby course: 6f
Dewhurst Stakes course: 7f
Rowley Mile: 1m
Cambridgeshire course: 1m 1f
Across the flat: 1m 2f
Sefton course: 2m, 1m 6f, 1m 4f, 1m 2f, right hand
Cesarewitch course: 2m 2f, 2m, 1m 6f, 1m 4f, finishing across the flat

Best Times:

Note. Electric times introduced in 1952.

Distance	*Horse-Age-Weight*	*Date*	*Time*
5f (Rous)	Knight's Armour 3-8-9	6/4/38	57.4
5f (Rous)	Wilna 2-8-11	31/10/52	59.6
6f (Bretby)	Light Harvest 4-8-1	16/5/50	1min 11.14
6f (Bretby)	Huntercombe 2-9-0	2/10/69	1min 11.35
7f (Dewhurst)	Night Bird 3-8-11	5/4/38	1min 24.8
7f (Dewhurst)	Cardington King 2-9-0	29/9/54	1min 25.85
8f (Rowley Mle)	My Babu 3-9-0	28/4/48	1min 35.8
8f (Rowley Mle)	Kesrawan 2-8-10	20/9/69	1min 39.65
9f (Cambridge-shire)	Prince de Galles 3-8-10	20/9/69	1min 50.38
10f (Across the flat)	Barrowby Gem 3-8-5	27/10/36	2min 3.4
10f (Sefton)	Henry VII 3-9-3	14/10/61	2min 4.81
12f (Cesarewitch)	High Stakes 6-9-3	28/4/48	2min 29.8
12f 100yd (Sefton)	Astrapi 3-7-12	6/10/69	2min 56.74
14f (Sefton)	Bravi 6-7-12	26/4/61	2min 56.89
16f (Cesarewitch)	Chantry 4-8-12	29/9/53	3min 27.27
18f (Cesarewitch)	Whiteway 3-7-12	15/10/47	3min 47.5

Note. Electric times introduced in 1952.

July Course

The meetings in June, July and August are held on this charming course, which has a pleasant paddock with plenty of trees for shade. All races up to 1m inclusive are straight with a steadily increasing downhill gradient after 2f, the final furlong being uphill. Races of 1m 2f or over start on the Beacon course, turning right into the straight mile. The lengths of the courses are shown below:

Chesterfield course: 5f
Bunbury Mile: 1m, 7f, 6f
Suffolk Stakes course: 1m 4f, 1m 2f
Summer course: 2m 24yd, 1m 6f 171yd

Clerk of the Course (both courses) is Mr P. B. Firth, Jockey Club Office, Newmarket. Tel. Newmarket 2437.

Best Times:

Distance	*Horse-Age-Weight*	*Date*	*Time*
5f (Chesterfield)	Light Grey 3-8-6	3/7/62	58.68
5f (Chesterfield)	Dante 2-9-0	17/6/44	58.8
6f (Bunbury)	Lucasland 4-8-11	14/7/66	1min 11.33
6f (Bunbury)	Tzigane 2-9-0	3/7/62	1min 12.14
7f (Bunbury)	Ti-Chin 5-7-8	17/6/44	1min 23.6
7f (Bunbury)	Auskerry 2-9-0	8/7/65	1min 26.6
8f (Bunbury)	Pink Flower 4-9-7	6/6/44	1min 36.8
10f (Suffolk)	Borealis 3-9-7	2/5/44	2min 2.8
12f (Suffolk)	Dante 3-9-0	9/6/45	2min 26.6
14f 171yd (Summer)	Anglo-Iranian 9-7-12	3/7/59	3min 9.18
16f 24yd (Summer)	Luncheon Hour 4-8-0	21/11/40	3min 18

Two Thousand Guineas, 1m

First run in 1809. *Three-year-olds, colts* 9*st, fillies* 8*st* 11*lb.*

		OWNER	TRAINER	JOCKEY	SP
1900	Diamond Jubilee	Prince of Wales	R. Marsh	H. Jones	11–4
1901	Handicapper	Sir E. Cassel	F. Day	W. Halsey	33–1
1902	Sceptre	R. Sievier	R. Sievier	H. Randall	4–1
1903	Rock Sand	Sir J. Miller	G. Blackwell	J. Martin	6–4
1904	St. Amant	L. de Rothschild	A. Hayhoe	K. Cannon	11–4
1905	Vedas	W. de W-Fenton	W. Robinson	H. Jones	11–2
1906	Gorgos	A. James	R. Marsh	H. Jones	20–1
1907	Slieve Gallion	Capt J. Greer	S. Darling	W. Higgs	4–11
1908	Norman III	A. Belmont	J. Watson	O. Madden	25–1
1909	Minoru	King Edward VII	R. Marsh	H. Jones	4–1
1910	Neil Gow	Lord Rosebery	P. Peck	D. Maher	2–1
1911	Sunstar	J. Joel	C. Morton	G. Stern	5–1
1912	Sweeper II	H. Duryea	H. Persse	D. Maher	6–1
1913	Louvois	W. Raphael	D. Waugh	J. Reiff	25–1
1914	Kennymore	Sir J. Thursby	A. Taylor	G. Stern	2–1
1915	Pommern	S. Joel	C. Peck	S. Donoghue	2–1
1916	Clarissimus	Lord Falmouth	W. Waugh	J. Clark	100–7
1917	Gay Crusader	'Mr Fairie'	A. Taylor	S. Donoghue	9–4
1918	Gainsborough	Lady J. Douglas	A. Taylor	J. Childs	4–1
1919	The Panther	Sir A. Black	G. Manser	R. Cooper	10–1
1920	Tetratema	Maj D. McCalmont	H. Persse	B. Carslake	2–1
1921	Craig an Eran	Lord Astor	A. Taylor	J. Brennan	100–6
1922	St. Louis	Lord Queensborough	P. Gilpin	G. Archibald	6–1
1923	Ellangowan	Lord Rosebery	J. Jarvis	C. Elliott	5–1
1924	Diophon	Aga Khan	R. Dawson	G. Hulme	11–2
1925	Manna	H. Morriss	F. Darling	S. Donoghue	100–8
1926	Colorado	Lord Derby	G. Lambton	T. Weston	100–8
1927	Adam's Apple	C. Whitburn	H. Cottrill	J. Leach	20–1
1928	Flamingo	Sir L. Philipps	J. Jarvis	C. Elliott	5–1
1929	Mr. Jinks	Maj D. McCalmont	H. Persse	H. Beasley	5–2
1930	Diolite	Sir H. Hirst	F. Templeman	F. Fox	10–1
1931	Cameronian	J. Dewar	F. Darling	J. Childs	100–8
1932	Orwell	W. Singer	J. Lawson	R. Jones	evens
1933	Rodosto	Princesse de Lucinge	H. Count	R. Brethes	9–1
1934	Colombo	Lord Glanely	T. Hogg	W. Johnstone	2–7
1935	Bahram	Aga Khan	Fk. Butters	F. Fox	7–2
1936	Pay Up	Lord Astor	J. Lawson	R. Dick	11–2
1937	Le Ksar	E. de St. Alary	F. Carter	C. Semblat	20–1
1938	Pasch	H. Morriss	F. Darling	G. Richards	5–2
1939	Blue Peter	Lord Rosebery	J. Jarvis	E. Smith	5–1
1940	Djébel	M. Boussac	A. Swann	C. Elliott	9–4
1941	Lambert Simnel	Duke of Westminster	F. Templeman	C. Elliott	10–1
1942	Big Game	King George VI	F. Darling	G. Richards	8–11
1943	Kingsway	A. Saunders	J. Lawson	S. Wragg	18–1
1944	Garden Path	Lord Derby	W. Earl	H. Wragg	5–1
1945	Court Martial	Lord Astor	J. Lawson	C. Richards	13–2
1946	Happy Knight	Sir W. Cooke	H. Jelliss	T. Weston	28–1
1947	Tudor Minstrel	J. Dewar	F. Darling	G. Richards	11–8
1948	My Babu	Maharaja of Baroda	F. Armstrong	C. Smirke	2–1
1949	Nimbus	Mrs M. Glenister	G. Colling	C. Elliott	10–1
1950	Palestine	Aga Khan	M. Marsh	C. Smirke	4–1
1951	Ki Ming	Ley On	M. Beary	A. Breasley	100–8
1952	Thunderhead II	E. Constant	E. Pollet	R. Poincelet	100–7
1953	Nearula	W. Humble	C. Elsey	E. Britt	2–1
1954	Darius	Sir P. Loraine	H. Wragg	E. Mercer	8–1
1955	Our Babu	D. Robinson	G. Brooke	D. Smith	13–2
1956	Gilles de Retz	A. Samuel	C. Jerdein	F. Barlow	50–1
1957	Crepello	Sir V. Sassoon	N. Murless	L. Piggott	7–2
1958	Pall Mall	The Queen	C. B-Rochfort	D. Smith	20–1
1959	Taboun	Aly Khan	A. Head	G. Moore	5–2
1960	Martial	R. Webster	P. Prendergast	R. Hutchinson	18–1
1961	Rockavon	T. Yuill	G.Boyd	N. Stirk	66–1
1962	Privy Councillor	Maj G. Glover	T. Waugh	W. Rickaby	100–6

Two Thousand Guineas (contd)	OWNER	TRAINER	JOCKEY	SP
1963 Only for Life	Miss M. Sheriffe	J. Tree	J. Lindley	33–1
1964 Baldric II	Mrs H. Jackson	E. Fellows	W. Pyers	20–1
1965 Niksar	W. Harvey	W. Nightingall.	D. Keith	100–8
1966 Kashmir II	P. Butler	C. Bartholomew	J. Lindley	7–1
1967 Royal Palace	H. Joel	N. Murless	G. Moore	100–30
1968 Sir Ivor	R. Guest	V. O'Brien	L. Piggott	11–8
1969 Right Tack	J. R. Brown	J. Sutcliffe, Jn.	G. Lewis	15–2
1970 Nijinsky	C. Engelhard	V. O'Brien	L. Piggott	4–7

One Thousand Guineas, 1m

Three-year-old fillies, 9st.

	OWNER	TRAINER	JOCKEY	SP
1900 Winifreda	L. Brassey	T. Jennings	S. Loates	11–2
1901 Aida	Sir J. Miller	G. Blackwell	D. Maher	13–8
1902 Sceptre	R. Sievier	R. Sievier	H. Randall	1–2
1903 Quintessence	Lord Falmouth	J. Chandler	H. Randall	4–1
1904 Pretty Polly	Maj E. Loder	P. Gilpin	W. Lane	1–4
1905 Cherry Lass	W. H. Walker	W. Robinson	G. McCall	5–4
1906 Flair	Sir D. Cooper	P. Gilpin	B. Dillon	10–11
1907 Witch Elm	W. H. Walker	W. Robinson	B. Lynham	4–1
1908 Rhodora	R. Crocker	G. Allen	L. Lyne	100–8
1909 Electra	L. Neumann	P. Gilpin	B. Dillon	9–1
1910 Winkipop	W. Astor	W. Waugh	B. Lynham	5–2
1911 Atmah	J. de Rothschild	F. Pratt	F. Fox	7–1
1912 Tagalie	W. Raphael	D. Waugh	L. Hewitt	20–1
1913 Jest	J. Joel	C. Morton	F. Rickaby	9–1
1914 Princess Dorrie	J. Joel	C. Morton	W. Huxley	9–1
1915 Vaucluse	Lord Rosebery	F. Hartigan	F. Rickaby	5–2
1916 Canyon	Lord Derby	G. Lambton	F. Rickaby	9–4
1917 Diadem	Lord d'Abernon	G. Lambton	F. Rickaby	6–4
1918 Ferry	Lord Derby	G. Lambton	B. Carslake	50–1
1919 Roseway	Sir E. Hulton	F. Hartigan	A. Whalley	2–1
1920 Cinna	Sir R. Jardine	T. Waugh	W. Griggs	4–1
1921 Bettina	W. Raphael	P. Linton	G. Bellhouse	33–1
1922 Silver Urn	B. Parr	H. Persse	B. Carslake	10–1
1923 Tranquil	Lord Derby	G. Lambton	E. Gardner	5–2
1924 Plack	Lord Rosebery	J. Jarvis	C. Elliott	8–1
1925 Saucy Sue	Lord Astor	A. Taylor	F. Bullock	1–4
1926 Pillion	A. de Rothschild	J. Watson	R. Perryman	25–1
1927 Cresta Run	Lieut-Col G. Loder	P. Gilpin	A. Balding	10–1
1928 Scuttle	King George V	W. Jarvis	J. Childs	15–8
1929 Taj Mah	S. Guthmann	J. Torterolo	W. Sibbritt	33–1
1930 Fair Isle	Lord Derby	Fk. Butters	T. Weston	7–4
1931 Four Course	Lord Ellesmere	F. Darling	C. Elliott	100–9
1932 Kandy	M. de St. Alary	V. Gilpin	C. Elliott	33–1
1933 Brown Betty	W. Woodward	C. B-Rochfort	J. Childs	8–1
1934 Campanula	Sir G. Bullough	J. Jarvis	H. Wragg	2–5
1935 Mesa	P. Wertheimer	M. P. Corbiere	W. Johnstone	8–1
1936 Tide-way	Lord Derby	C. Leader	R. Perryman	100–30
1937 Exhibitionnist	Sir V. Sassoon	J. Lawson	S. Donoghue	10–1
1938 Rockfel	Sir H. C-Owen	O. Bell	S. Wragg	8–1
1939 Galatea II	R. Clark	J. Lawson	R. Jones	6–1
1940 Godiva	Lord Rothermere	W. Jarvis	D. Marks	10–1
1941 Dancing Time	Lord Glanely	J. Lawson	R. Perryman	100–8
1942 Sun Chariot	King George VI	F. Darling	G. Richards	evens
1943 Herringbone	Lord Derby	W. Earl	H. Wragg	15–2
1944 Picture Play	H. Joel	J. Watts	C. Elliott	15–2
1945 Sun Stream	Lord Derby	W. Earl	H. Wragg	5–2
1946 Hypericum	King George VI	C. B-Rochfort	D. Smith	100–6
1947 Imprudence	Mme P. Corbiere	J. Lieux	W. Johnstone	4–1
1948 Queenpot	Sir P. Loraine	N. Murless	G. Richards	6–1
1949 Musidora	N. Donaldson	C. Elsey	E. Britt	100–8
1950 Camaree	J. Ternynck	A. Lieux	W. Johnstone	10–1
1951 Belle of All	H. Tufton	N. Bertie	G. Richards	4–1
1952 Zabara	Sir M. McAlpine	V. Smyth	K. Gethin	7–1
1953 Happy Laughter	H. Wills	J. Jarvis	E. Mercer	10–1
1954 Festoon	J. Dewar	N. Cannon	A. Breasley	9–2

	OWNER	TRAINER	JOCKEY	SP
1955 Meld	Lady Wernher ..	C. B-Rochfort .	W. Carr	11–2
1956 Honeylight	Sir V. Sassoon ..	C. Elsey	E. Britt	100–6
1957 Rose Royale II ..	Aga Khan	A. Head	C. Smirke ..	6–1
1958 Bella Paola	F. Dupré	F. Mathet ..	S. Boullenger .	8–11
1959 Petite Etoile	Aly Khan	N. Murless ..	D. Smith.. ..	8–1
1960 Never Too Late II ..	Mrs H. Jackson ..	E. Pollet	R. Poincelet ..	8–11
1961 Sweet Solera	Mrs S. Castello ..	R. Day	W. Rickaby ..	4–1
1962 Abermaid..	R. M. O'Ferrall ..	H. Wragg ..	W. Williamson	100–6
1963 Hula Dancer	Mrs P. Widener ..	E. Pollet	J. Deforge ..	1–2
1964 Pourparler	Lady Granard ..	P. Prendergast .	G. Bougoure ..	11–2
1965 Night Off	Maj L. Holliday ..	W. Wharton ..	W. Williamson	9–2
1966 Glad Rags	Mrs J. P. Mills ..	V. O'Brien ..	P. Cook	100–6
1967 Fleet	R. C. Boucher ..	N. Murless ..	G. Moore ..	11–2
1968 Caergwrle	Mrs N. Murless ..	N. Murless ..	A. Barclay ..	4–1
1969 Full Dress II	R. B. Moller . ..	H. Wragg ..	R. Hutchinson	7–1
1970 Humble Duty	Jean, Lady Ashcombe	P. Walwyn ..	L. Piggott ..	7–2

Cheveley Park Stakes, 6f

First run 1814. *Two-year-old fillies*, 8*st* 11*lb*. *First run* 1870. *No race* 1939. *Run at Nottingham* 1940.

	OWNER	TRAINER	JOCKEY	SP
1930 The Leopard, 8–7 ..	Sir C. Hyde	N. Scobie . ..	B. Carslake ..	15–8
1931 Concordia, 8–7 ..	A. Cox	J. Lawson ..	R. Jones	evens
1932 Brown Betty	W. Woodward ..	C. B-Rochfort .	J. Childs . ..	2–1
1933 Light Brocade, 9–7..	Lord Durham ..	Fk. Butters ..	B. Carslake ..	11–8
1934 Lady Gabrial, 8–7 ..	D. Sullivan	H. Persse . ..	B. Carslake ..	13–8
1935 Ferrybridge, 8–7 ..	R. Watson	M. Hartigan ..	M. Beary . ..	5–1
1936 Celestial Way, 8–7 ..	H. Cecil	G. Lambton ..	B. Carslake ..	3–1
1937 Stafaralla, 8–12 ..	Aly Khan	Fk. Butters ..	H. Wragg ..	4–9
1938 Seaway, 8–12	Maj J. Courtauld .	B. Jarvis	T. Lowrey ..	20–1
1940 Keystone, 8–12 ..	P. Beatty	F. Darling ..	G. Richards ..	8–13
1941 Perfect Peace, 8–12 .	Lord Glanely ..	J. Lawson ..	H. Wragg ..	2–1
1942 Lady Sybil, 8–12 ..	M. Benson	W. Pratt	G. Richards ..	11–10
1943 Fair Fame, 8–12 ..	Mrs B. Lavington	H. Leader ..	F. Lane	5–4
1944 Sweet Cygnet, 8–12 .	H. Leven	T. Rimell . ..	C. Elliott . ..	100–6
1945 Neolight, 8–12 ..	J. Dewar	F. Darling ..	G. Richards ..	13–8
1946 Djerba, 8–12	M. Boussac	C. Semblat ..	C. Elliott . ..	9–2
1947 Ash Blonde, 8–12 ..	Lord Astor	R. J. Colling ..	P. Evans . ..	100–8
1948 Pambidian, 8–12 ..	C. Harper	W. Nightingall.	G. Richards ..	100–6
1949 Corejada, 8–12 . ..	M. Boussac	C. Semblat ..	C. Elliott . ..	9–4
1950 Belle of All, 8–12 ..	H. Tufton	N. Bertie.. ..	G. Richards ..	5–4
1951 Zabara, 8–12	Sir M. McAlpine..	V. Smyth . ..	G. Richards ..	10–11
1952 Bebe Grande, 8–12..	J. Gerber	F. Armstrong..	G. Richards ..	1–2
1953 Sixpence, 8–12 . ..	A. Hawkins	P. Prendergast .	G. Richards ..	4–1
1954 Gloria Nicky, 8–12 .	Mrs R. Digby ..	N. Bertie.. ..	A. Breasley ..	10–1
1955 Midget II, 8–12 ..	P. Wertheimer ..	A. Head	R. Poincelet ..	evens
1956 Sarcelle, 8–12	K. Mason	N. Cannon ..	A. Breasley ..	4–6
1957 Rich and Rare, 8–12	T. Blackwell . ..	J. Jarvis	E. Mercer ..	5–1
1958 Lindsay, 8–12	F. Ellison	R. Peacock ..	E. Mercer ..	100–8
1959 Queensberry, 8–12 ..	Col B. Hornung ..	J. A. Waugh ..	E. Smith . ..	2–5
1960 Opaline II, 8–12 ..	Aly Khan	A. Head	G. Moore ..	11–10
1961 Display, 8–11	Lady Granard ..	P. Prendergast .	R. Hutchinson	8–11
1962 My Goodness Me, 8–11	D. Robinson . ..	G. Brooke ..	E. Smith . ..	100–8
1963 Crimea II, 8–11 ..	Mrs J. Hanes ..	C. B-Rochfort .	W. Carr	9–1
1964 Night Off, 8–11 ..	Maj L. Holliday ..	W. Wharton ..	J. Mercer . ..	20–1
1965 Berkeley Springs, 8–11	P. Mellon	I. Balding ..	G. Lewis . ..	100–8
1966 Fleet, 8–11	R. C. Boucher ..	N. Murless ..	L. Piggott ..	5–2
1967 Lalibela, 8–11	J. P. Philipps . ..	V. O'Brien ..	L. Piggott ..	5–1
1968 Mige, 8–11	Mme P. Wertheimer	A. Head	J. Taillard ..	5–2
1969 Humble Duty, 8–11	Jean, Lady Ashcombe . ..	P. Walwyn ..	D. Keith . ..	11–4

Middle Park Stakes, 6f

Two-year-olds. First run 1866. *Run at Nottingham* 1940.

		OWNER	TRAINER	JOCKEY	SP
1930	Portlaw, 9–3	Sir A. Bailey	H. Persse	H. Beasley	evens
1931	Orwell, 9–3	W. Singer	J. Lawson	R. Jones	4–11
1932	Felicitation, 9–0	Aga Khan	Fk. Butters	M. Beary	3–1
1933	Medieval Knight, 9–0	J. Dewar	F. Darling	G. Richards	100–30
1934	Bahram, 9–0	Aga Khan	Fk. Butters	F. Fox	2–7
1935	Abjer, 9–0	M. Boussac	G. Lambton	C. Elliott	8–1
1936	Fair Copy, 9–0	Lord Derby	C. Leader	R. Perryman	13–8
1937	Scottish Union, 9–0	J. Rank	N. Cannon	G. Richards	10–1
1938	Foxbrough II, 9–0	W. Woodward	C. B-Rochfort	P. Beasley	13–8
1939	Djebel, 9–0	M. Boussac	C. Semblat	C. Elliott	9–1
1940	Hyacinthus, 9–0	A. Bassett	H. Persse	P. Beasley	10–1
1941	Sun Chariot, 8–11	King George VI	F. Darling	H. Wragg	11–4
1942	Ribbon, 8–11	Lord Rosebery	J. Jarvis	E. Smith	9–2
1943	Orestes, 9–0	Miss D. Paget	W. Nightingall	T. Carey	7–4
1944	Dante, 9–0	Sir E. Ohlson	M. Peacock	W. Nevett	2–5
1945	Khaled, 9–0	Aga Khan	Fk. Butters	G. Richards	2–5
1946	Saravan, 9–0	Princess Aly Khan	Fk. Butters	C. Elliott	100–8
1947	The Cobbler, 9–0	Lieut-Col G. Loder	F. Darling	G. Richards	8–11
1948	Abernant, 9–0	Maj R. M-Buchanan	N. Murless	G. Richards	1–7
1949	Masked Light, 9–0	E. Wanless	N. Scobie	D. Smith	7–2
1950	Big Dipper, 9–0	Mrs J. Bryce	C. B-Rochfort	W. Carr	2–5
1951	King's Bench, 9–0	A. Tompsett	M. Feakes	C. Elliott	7–2
1952	Nearula, 9–0	W. Humble	C. Elsey	E. Britt	13–2
1953	Royal Challenger, 9–0	A. Gordon	P. Beasley	G. Richards	4–1
1954	Our Babu, 9–0	D. Robinson	G. Brooke	D. Smith	6–1
1955	Buisson Ardent, 9–0	Aga Khan	A. Head	D. Smith	9–2
1956	Pipe of Peace, 9–0	S. Niarchos	Sir G. Richards	A. Breasley	8–1
1957	Major Portion, 9–0	H. Joel	T. Leader	E. Smith	11–2
1958	Masham, 9–0	A. Ellis	G. Brooke	D. Smith	2–1
1959	Venture VII, 9–0	Aly Khan	A. Head	G. Moore	1–4
1960	Skymaster, 9–0	Duke of Norfolk	W. Smyth	A. Breasley	100–30
1961	Gustav, 9–0	J. Whitney	J. Tree	J. Lindley	100–6
1962	Crocket, 9–0	D. van Clief	G. Brooke	E. Smith	5–4
1963	Showdown, 9–0	Mrs D. Prenn	F. Winter	D. Smith	100–30
1964	Spanish Express, 9–0	Mrs G. Marcow	L. Hall	J. Mercer	9–1
1965	Track Spare, 9–0	R. Mason	R. Mason	J. Lindley	10–1
1966	Bold Lad, 9–0	Lady Granard	P. Prendergast	D. Lake	2–7
1967	Petingo, 9–0	Capt M. Lemos	F. Armstrong	L. Piggott	1–4
1968	Right Tack, 9–0	J. R. Brown	J. Sutcliffe, Jn.	G. Lewis	11–2
1969	Huntercombe, 9–0	H. H. Renshaw	A. Budgett	E. Johnson	3–1

Cambridgeshire Stakes, 1m 1f

Handicap. Not run 1942 *to* 1944. *First run* 1839.

		OWNER	TRAINER	JOCKEY	SP
1930	The Pen, 3–7–4	Mrs M. Hartigan	M. Hartigan	C. Richards	50–1
1931	Disarmament, 3–7–11	H. Clayton	C. Elsey	W. Nevett	18–1
1932	Pullover, 3–6–11	Mrs C. Robinson	M. Peacock	A. Richardson	100–1
1933	Raymond, 3–8–4	Sir A. Bailey	J. Lawson	G. Nicoll	33–1
1934	Wychwood Abbot, 3–8–6	O. Watney	T. Leader	R. Perryman	9–1
1935	Commander III, 5–7–11	G. Foster	A. B. Briscoe	T. Hawcroft	28–1
1936	Dan Bulger, 3–7–13	Sir A. Bailey	H. Cottrill	T. Weston	7–1
1937	Artist's Prince, 4–6–12	Maj R. Glover	J. Dines	A. Richardson	13–1
1938	Helleniqua, 5–6–12	J. Meller	W. Webb	B. Guimard	50–1
1939	Class I: Gyroscope, 3–7–7	Mrs H. Leader	H. Leader	R. Lacey	100–6
	Class II: Orichalque, 6–8–10	Lord Dufferin	W. Beatty	J. Simpson	25–1
1940	Caxton, 4–7–9	Maj T. Rigg	F. Armstrong	P. Evans	100–7

	OWNER	TRAINER	JOCKEY	SP
1941 Rue de la Paix, 5–8–13	L. Abelson	G. Beeby	T. Carey	18–1
1945 Esquire, 3–6–3	J. Bueno	R. Colling	G. Packer	40–1
1946 Sayani, 3–9–4	Mme J. Lieux	J. Lieux	W. Johnstone	25–1
1947 Fairey Fulmer, 4–8–12	G. Tachmindji	O. Bell	T. Gosling	28–1
1948 Sterope, 3–7–4	J. Townley	P. Beasley	D. Schofield	25–1
1949 Sterope, 4–9–4	J. Townley	P. Beasley	C. Elliott	25–1
1950 Kelling, 3–7–10	C. Jarvis	A. Waugh	D. Smith	100–7
1951 Fleeting Moment, 5–7–13	Mrs M. Johnson	T. Bartlam	A. Breasley	28–1
1952 Richer, 3–8–0	G. Baylis	S. Ingham	K. Gethin	100–6
1953 Jupiter	Lord Lambton	P. Beasley	G. Richards	100–6
1954 Minstrel, 3–7–0	Lord Rosebery	J. Jarvis	C. Gaston	66–1
1955 Retrial, 3–7–1	Lady Z. Wernher	C. B-Rochfort	P. Robinson	18–1
1956 Loppylugs, 4–7–8	J. Beary	J. Beary	E. Smith	100–7
1957 Stephanotis, 4–8–5	A. Plesch	J. Rogers	W. Carr	100–6
1958 London Cry, 4–9–5	M. Sobell	G. Richards	A. Breasley	22–1
1959 Rexequus, 3–8–7	J. Adam	G. Boyd	N. Stirk	25–1
1960 Midsummer Night II, 3–7–12	P. Mellon	P. H-Bass	D. Keith	40–1
1961 { Violetta III, 3–7–8	R. Moller	H. Wragg	C. Parkes	33–1
1961 { Henry the Seventh, 3–8–4	H. Joel	W. Elsey	E. Hide	100–8
1962 Hidden Meaning, 3–9–0	Cmdr K. Grant	H. Leader	A. Breasley	7–1
1963 Commander-in-Chief, 4–8–0	H. Whitehouse	E. Cousins	F. Durr	100–7
1964 Hasty Cloud, 6–7–10	G. Walters	H. Wallington	J. Wilson	100–8
1965 Tarqogan, 5–9–3	J. McGrath	S. McGrath	W. Williamson	100–8
1966 Dites, 4–7–4	R. Midwood	H. Leader	D. Maitland	33–1
1967 Lacquer, 3–8–6	R. Moller	H. Wragg	R. Hutchinson	20–1
1968 Emerilo, 4–7–9	D. Green	P. Allden	M. Thomas	20–1
1969 Prince de Galles, 3–7–12	A. Swift	P. Robinson	F. Durr	5–2

Cesarewitch Stakes, 2m 2f

Handicap. First run 1839. *Run over Summer Course* 2m 24yd 1939 *to* 1941. *No race* 1942 *to* 1944.

	OWNER	TRAINER	JOCKEY	SP
1930 Ut Majeur, 3–8–3	Aga Khan	R. Dawson	M. Beary	100–8
1931 Noble Star, 4–8–12	F. Cundell	L. Cundell	F. Fox	100–6
1932 Nitsichin, 4–8–9	D. Kennedy	P. Thrale	M. Beary	10–1
1933 Seminole, 4–8–0	J. Widener	C. B-Rochfort	F. Fox	100–6
1934 Enfield, 3–7–10	M. Field	C. B-Rochfort	J. Sirett	7–1
1935 Near Relation, 3–7–9	Sir A. Butt	Fk. Butters	E. Smith	22–1
1936 Fet, 5–6–12	S. Freeman	H. Hedges	A. Richardson	10–1
1937 Punch, 4–7–11	T. Westhead	C. Tabor	S. Wragg	17–1
1938 Contrevent, 3–6–10	Princess de F. Lucinge	H. Count	A. Tucker	100–7
1939 Cantatrice II, 4–7–5	Sir A. Butt	Fk. Butters	D. Smith	7–2
1940 Hunter's Moon IV, 4–9–5	E. Esmond	F. Darling	G. Richards	100–8
1941 Filator, 3–7–12	Lady C-Owen	O. Bell	S. Wragg	100–9
1945 Kerry Piper, 4–8–1	Sir H. Bruce	F. Armstrong	E. Britt	25–1
1946 Monsieur l'Amiral, 5–8–5	H. B-Hankey	E. Charlier	H. Wragg	33–1
1947 Whiteway, 3–7–12	Capt D. FitzGerald	W. Pratt	W. Evans	100–8
1948 Woodburn, 3–7–13	Lord Allendale	C. Elsey	E. Britt	100–9
1949 Strathspey, 4–7–11	J. Rank	N. Cannon	E. Smith	25–1
1950 Above Board, 3–7–10	King George VI	C. B-Rochfort	E. Smith	18–1
1951 Three Cheers, 3–7–8	C. Crofts	P. Thrale	E. Mercer	17–2
1952 Flush Royal, 7–8–13	G. MacLean	J. Fawcus	W. Nevett	33–1
1953 Chantry, 4–8–4	S. Ingham	S. Ingham	K. Gethin	4–1

Cesarewitch Stakes (contd)

Year	Winner	OWNER	TRAINER	JOCKEY	SP
1954	French Design, 7–8–3	S. Banks	G. Todd	D. Smith	100–6
1955	Curry, 4–7–6	F. Honour	F. Armstrong	P. Tulk	100–6
1956	Prelone, 3–7–3	A. Allen	W. Hide	E. Hide	20–1
1957	Sandiacre, 5–7–8	T. Farr	W. Dutton	D. Smith	100–8
1958	Morecambe, 5–9–1	J. Bullock	S. Hall	J. Sime	15–2
1959	Come to Daddy, 4–7–8	T. Farr	W. Lyde	D. Smith	6–1
1960	Alcove, 3–7–8	Lord Derby	J. Watts	D. Smith	100–30
1961	Avon's Pride, 4–7–11	Maj L. Holliday	W. Hern	E. Smith	100–8
1962	Golden Fire, 4–7–11	G. Ridley	D. Marks	D. Yates	25–1
1963	Utrillo, 6–8–0	J. Gerber	H. Price	J. Sime	100–8
1964	Grey of Falloden, 5–9–6	Lord Astor	W. Hern	J. Mercer	20–1
1965	Mintmaster, 4–7–9	E. Collington	A. Cooper	J. Sime	13–2
1966	Persian Lancer, 8–7–8	Lord Belper	H. Price	D. Smith	100–7
1967	Boismoss, 3–7–1	J. G. Spriggs	M. W. Easterby	E. Johnson	100–9
1968	Major Rose, 5–9–4	R. L. Heaton	H. Price	L. Piggott	9–1
1969	Floridian, 5–7–4	A. Patchett	L. Shedden	D. Mckay	20–1

Dewhurst Stakes, 7f

Two-year-olds. First run in 1875. *Not run in* 1940.

Year	Winner	OWNER	TRAINER	JOCKEY	SP
1930	Sangre, 8–9		H. Persse	H. Beasley	11–10
1931	Firdaussi, 8–13	Aga Khan	F. Butters	M. Beary	11–10
1932	Hyperion, 9–5	G. Lambton	G. Lambton	T. Weston	100–7
1933	Mrs Rustom, 9–3	Aga Khan	F. Butters	M. Beary	5–4
1934	Hairan, 9–5	Aga Khan	F. Butters	F. Fox	8–13
1935	Bala Hissar, 8–9	Aga Khan	F. Butters	C. Smirke	5–2
1936	Sultan Mohamed, 8–9	Aga Khan	F. Butters	G. Richards	20–1
1937	Manorite, 8–9	D. Kennedy	P. Thrale	E. Smith	20–1
1938	Casanova, 8–9	Lady Z. Wernher	C. B-Rochfort	P. Beasley	8–11
1940	Fettes, 8–9	Mrs R. M-Buchanan	F. Darling	G. Richards	3–1
1941	Canyonero, 9–2	F. Bezner	W. Nightingall	T. Carey	13–8
1942	Umiddad, 8–9	Aga Khan	F. Butters	D. Smith	6–4
1943	Effervescence, 9–2	Mrs M. Hartigan	R. J. Colling	G. Richards	6–1
1944	Paper Weight, 9–2	Sir A. Butt	F. Butters	A. Wragg	11–8
1945	Hypericum, 8–11	King George VI	C. B-Rochfort	D. Smith	4–7
1946	Migoli, 9–0	Aga Khan	F. Butters	G. Richards	5–1
1947	Pride of India, 8–13	H. Joel	J. Watts	J. Sime	5–2
1948	Royal Forest, 9–3	Mrs R. M-Buchanan	N. Murless	G. Richards	5–4
1949	Emperor II, 8–13	M. Boussac	C. Semblat	C. Elliott	7–2
1950	Turco II, 8–13	W. Woodward	C. B-Rochfort	W. Carr	11–8
1951	Marsyad, 8–9	M. Boussac	C. Semblat	W. Johnstone	7–1
1952	Pinza, 8–13	Sir V. Sassoon	N. Bertie	G. Richards	evens
1953	Infatuation, 9–3	Sir M. McAlpine	V. Smyth	K. Gethin	11–8
1954	My Smokey, 8–9	Mrs D. Robinson	J. Watts	D. Smith	7–2
1955	Dacian, 8–9	Maj L. Holliday	H. Cottrill	W. Snaith	7–1
1956	Crepello, 8–9	Sir V. Sassoon	N. Murless	L. Piggott	1–2
1957	Torbella III, 8–6	Comte de Chambure	W. Clout	A. Breasley	9–4
1958	Billum, 8–13	W. Humble	C. Elsey	E. Hide	6–1
1959	Ancient Lights, 8–9	H. Joel	T. Leader	E. Smith	100–7
1960	Bounteous, 8–13	Mrs H. Leggatt	P. Beasley	J. Sime	2–1
1961	River Chanter, 9–2	R. Sigtia	G. Todd	J. Mercer	100–30
1962	Follow Suit, 8–12	Lieut-Col G. Loder	N. Murless	L. Piggott	10–1
1963	Kings Lane, 8–12	L. Chamberlain	S. Hall	J. Sime	10–1
1964	Silly Season, 9–2	P. Mellon	I. Balding	G. Lewis	13–2
1965	Pretendre, 8–12	J. Lilley	J. Jarvis	R. Hutchinson	11–2
1966	Dart Board, 8–12	M. Sobell	Sir G. Richards	D. Smith	10–1
1967	Hametus, 8–12	Lady Beaverbrook	W. Nightingall	F. Durr	100–9
1968	Ribofilio, 8–12	C. Engelhard	R. Houghton	L. Piggott	8–11
1969	Nijinsky	C. Engelhard	V. O'Brien	L. Piggott	1–3

Champion Stakes, 1m 2f

Colts and fillies. First run in 1877. *No race* 1939.

		OWNER	TRAINER	JOCKEY	SP
1930	Rustom Pasha, 3–8–7	Aga Khan	R. Dawson	H. Wragg	6–1
1931	Goyescas, 3–8–7	M. Boussac	B. Jarvis	C. Elliott	5–1
1932	Cameronian, 4–9–0	J. A. Dewar	F. Darling	G. Richards	11–10
1933	Dastur, 4–9–0	Aga Khan	F. Butters	M. Beary	2–5
1933	Chatelaine, 3–8–4	E. T-Smith	F. Templeman	G. Richards	9–2
1934	Umidwar, 3–8–7	Aga Khan	F. Butters	F. Fox	5–4
1935	Wychwood Abbot, 4–9–0	O. Watney	T. Leader	R. Perryman	4–6
1936	Wychwood Abbot, 5–9–0	O. Watney	T. Leader	R. Perryman	10–11
1937	Flares, 4–9–0	W. Woodward	C. B-Rochfort	P. Beasley	evens
1938	Rockfel, 3–8–5	Sir H. C-Owen	O. Bell	H. Wragg	2–1
1940	Hippius, 3–8–8–	Lord Rosebery	J. Jarvis	E. Smith	100–8
1941	Hippius, 4–9–0	Lord Rosebery	J. Jarvis	E. Smith	6–4
1942	Big Game, 3–8–3	King George VI	F. Darling	G. Richards	11–10
1943	Nasrullah, 3–8–6	Aga Khan	F. Butters	G. Richards	100–30
1944	Hycilla, 3–8–2	W. Woodward	C. B-Rochfort	W. Nevett	10–1
1945	Court Martial, 3–8–7	Lord Astor	J. Lawson	C. Richards	4–11
1946	Honeyway, 5–9–0	Lord Milford	J. Jarvis	E. Smith	8–1
1947	Migoli, 3–8–8	Aga Khan	F. Butters	G. Richards	evens
1948	Solar Slipper, 3–8–8	J. McGrath	H. Smyth	E. Smith	6–1
1949	Djeddah, 4–9–0	M. Boussac	C. Semblat	C. Elliott	4–6
1950	Peter Flower, 4–9–0	Lord Rosebery	J. Jarvis	W. Rickaby	3–1
1951	Dynamiter, 3–8–7	M. Boussac	C. Semblat	C. Elliott	100–8
1952	Dynamiter, 4–9–0	M. Boussac	J. Glynn	C. Elliott	4–5
1953	Nearula, 3–8–7	W. Humble	C. Elsey	E. Britt	4–1
1954	Narrator, 3–8–7	Maj L. Holliday	H. Cottrill	F. Barlow	20–1
1955	Hafiz, II, 3–8–7	Aga Khan	A. Head	R. Poincelet	100–30
1956	Hugh Lupus, 4–9–0	Lady S. Vernon	N. Murless	W. Johnstone	3–1
1957	Rose Royale II, 3–8–4	Aly Khan	A. Head	J. Massard	5–2
1958	Bella Paola, 3–8–4	F. Dupré	F. Mathet	G. Lequeux	4–1
1959	Petite Etoile, 3–8–5	Aly Khan	N. Murless	L. Piggott	2–11
1960	Marguerite Vernaut, 3–8–4	Marchese della Rochetta	U. Penco	E. Camici	9–4
1961	Bobar II, 3–8–7	Mme G. Courtois	R. Corme	M. Garcia	100–8
1962	Arctic Storm, 3–8–7	Mrs E. Carroll	J. Oxx	W. Williamson	6–1
1963	Hula Dancer, 3–8–4	Mrs P. Widener	E. Pollet	J. Deforge	9–2
1964	Baldric II, 3–8–7	Mrs H. Jackson	E. Fellows	W. Pyers	7–2
1965	Silly Season, 3–8–7	P. Mellon	I. Balding	G. Lewis	100–8
1966	Pieces of Eight, 3–8–7	Contesse de la Valdene	V. O'Brien	L. Piggott	5–4
1967	Reform, 3–8–7	M. Sobell	Sir G. Richards	A. Breasley	100–30
1968	Sir Ivor, 3–8–7	R. Guest	V. O'Brien	L. Piggott	8–1
1969	Flossy, 3–8–4	H. Berlin	F. Boutin	J. Deforge	100–7
1970	Connaught, 5–9–5	H. J. Joel	N. Murless	A. Barclay	5–4

NEWS OF THE WORLD STAKES

See under Goodwood.

NEWTON, A. C.

Clerk of the Course at Newcastle and Ripon.

NICHOLSON, Herbert Charles Denton (b 1913)

'Frenchie' Nicholson was born in France where his father was huntsman to a French pack. He was apprenticed firstly to Charles Clout in France for three years and then he came to England, where he was six years with Stanley Wootton's stable at Epsom. Broad and strongly built, he was too heavy for the flat but became a leading rider under National Hunt rules, winning the Gold Cup and Champion Hurdle and twice riding four winners in a day at Cheltenham.

He began training at Cheltenham in

1946 and has conducted a 'mixed' stable there ever since. He has deservedly earned a reputation as a fine trainer of young riders; his son David is a leading performer under National Hunt rules, while Paul Cook and Tony Murray were among his apprentices. His patrons include the Earl of Sefton, Lord Vestey, Mr J. Preston-Jones, Mrs H. V. Bearman, Mrs J. E. Gardner and Mrs K. Pope.

NICK

Certain lines of blood appear to have an affinity for, and to produce particularly good results, when mated to other specific lines. This phenomenon is usually termed a 'nick'.

NIGHT HAWK

Night Hawk, by Gallinule, won the 1913 St Leger for Lord Wavertree. He was exported to Australia.

NIGHTINGALL, Walter (1895-1968)

Walter Nightingall came of a famous Epsom racing famiy. His father, whom he succeeded at the South Hatch stable at Epsom, was a successful trainer and two Nightingalls rode winners of the Grand National. Walter Nightingall himself was apprenticed to his father. He took out a trainer's licence in 1926 when his father died, and his career until his death was one of consistent success. Altogether he trained over 1,800 winners, having many victories under National Hunt rules between the wars. He won the Derby in 1943 with Miss Dorothy Paget's Straight Deal and the Two Thousand Guineas in 1965 with Mr W. Harvey's Niksar. After World War II he was appointed trainer to Sir Winston Churchill, for whom he won good races with Colonist II, High Hat, Vienna, Welsh Abbot and Tudor Monarch. He was a modest, friendly man of considerable charm; his horses were always out to win and throughout his career he served the Turf with distinction.

NIGHT OFF

Bred and owned by the late Major L. B. Holliday, Night Off is by Narrator out of Persuader, by Petition. Trained by W. Wharton she won the Cheveley Park Stakes in 1964 and the following year the One Thousand Guineas.

NIJINSKY

By Northern Dancer out of Flaming Page, Nijinsky was bred in Canada in 1967 and is trained by Vincent O'Brien for Mr Engelhard. He won all his five races as a two-year-old, including the Railway Stakes, Angelsey Stakes and Beresford Stakes in Ireland and the Dewhurst Stakes in England. He was placed top of the Free Handicap and justified that position in 1970 by a fluent victory when hot favourite for the Two Thousand Guineas. He followed up that success by winning the Derby, ridden by Lester Piggott, and the Irish Derby, ridden by Liam Ward.

NIKSAR

Niksar, foaled in 1962, was bred in France by the Marquis de Nicolay and is by Le Haar, a member of the Blandford male line, out of Niskampe, by Shikampur. He was bought for £4,650 at the Deauville Yearling Sales by the late Walter Nightingall, acting on behalf of Mr Wilfred Harvey, well known in the printing and publishing world. Niksar won the Kempton Two Thousand Guineas Trial and the Two Thousand Guineas, while he was fourth in the Derby and third in the Champion Stakes. At the close of his three-year-old career, he was sold for export to Australia.

NIMBUS

Nimbus, by Nearco, was bred by Mr William Hill and sold for 5,000 gn as a yearling to George Colling who was acting on behalf of Mr H. A. Glenister, an official of the Midland Bank. Mr Glenister gave Nimbus as a birthday present to his wife. As a two-year-old Nimbus showed high promise, and the following season he won the Two Thousand Guineas and the Derby, both by very narrow margins. It was the first time that the racecourse camera decided the Derby result. Nimbus, apart from a walk-over, never ran again after Epsom. He hardly came up to expectations as a sire and was eventually exported to Japan.

NOBLESSE

A brilliant filly at her best, Noblesse, foaled in 1960, is by Mossborough out of Duke's Delight, by His Grace. She was bred by Mrs P. G. Margetts and as a yearling was bought on behalf of the American owner Mrs J. M. Olin for 4,200 gn. Trained by Paddy Prendergast she won four races and over £46,000 in prize money, her victories being the Blue Seal Stakes, Timeform Gold Cup, Musidora Stakes and the Oaks. Her win in the 1963 Oaks was one of the easiest ever recorded in that event as she won in a canter by ten lengths.

NOBLE STAR

Foaled in 1927, Noble Star was hardly bred in the height of fashion, being by Hapsburg out of Hesper, by Herodote, but he proved a really good stayer and his 11 victories included the Ascot Stakes, Goodwood Stakes, Cesarewitch and Jockey Club Cup. He also did quite well as a sire.

NOMINATIONS, VOID

For many years the Jockey Club were worried by the question of nominations rendered void by the death of an owner. Backed by legal opinion, the Jockey Club had always acted on the principle that fees and forfeits incurred for horses entered under Jockey Club rules could not be recovered under process of law, because if they were contracts, they were contracts by way of gambling and wagering, and thus without legal sanction. If a living owner evaded his forfeit liabilities, his name was published in the forfeit list in the *Racing Calendar*. As that deterrent could hardly be inflicted with decency on a dead man or on his executors, the 'Void Nomination' rule came into existence, the rule stipulating that when an owner died, all entries for his horses ceased to exist.

The matter was under discussion in 1927 when Mr Edgar Wallace, the well-known author and journalist and a very keen racing man, suggested a 'friendly' action between the Jockey Club and himself. It was agreed that Mr Wallace should be sued in the High Court for the recovery of £4 in respect of a horse of his entered at Newmarket. In the Chancery Court the verdict was in favour of Mr Wallace, much to his disappointment, as when the action was pending he could not run any of his horses, since if he by chance won a race, the £4 in dispute would have been automatically appropriated. The case then was taken to the Court of Appeal where the Master of the Rolls and Lords Justice Lawrence and Russell found in favour of the Jockey Club. All expenses incurred by Mr Wallace were paid by the Jockey Club.

NOMINATOR

The 'nominator' is the person in whose name a horse is entered for a race.

NOOR

Owned and bred by the late Aga Khan and foaled in 1945, Noor won four races worth over £4,000 in England and was placed in the Derby and the Eclipse Stakes. In America, where he eventually retired to the stud, he won eight races worth $339,000, including the Hollywood Gold Cup.

NORFOLK, Duchess of (b 1916)

The Duchess of Norfolk is one of the best-known personalities in English racing. A successful point-to-point rider before her marriage and a fine rider to hounds, she knows every aspect of the racing game and is reputed to be an extremely shrewd judge both of a yearling and of the form-book. She takes a keen personal interest in the running of the Arundel stable. Colours: sky blue and scarlet check, sky blue sleeves and scarlet cap.

NORFOLK, sixteenth Duke of, KG, PC, KCVO (b 1908)

The Duke of Norfolk served firstly in the Royal Horse Guards and later in the Royal Sussex Regiment. For many years a member of the Jockey Club, he has earned the reputation of being a thoroughly sound and extremely conscientious administrator. Apart from serving as a Steward of the Jockey Club and as Vice-Chairman of the Turf Board, he headed the Norfolk Committee on the future pattern of racing and also a committee appointed to inquire into the problem of doping. He is Her Majesty's representative at Ascot and is responsible for the organisation and the quality of the racing there. Considering his many public duties, not least in the county of Sussex, it is remarkable how much valuable work he has been able to do for racing. There are few more enthusiastic owner-breeders but so far he has hardly had the luck he deserves, and he has yet to win a classic. His trainer at Arundel is John Dunlop. Colours: sky blue, sky blue and scarlet quartered cap.

NOTTINGHAM

No race of more than a passing significance is run at this long-established Midland course, but sport there is usually quite brisk. The track is a left-handed circuit of about 1½m, which joins the straight mile about 4½f from the winning post. The turns

Best Times:

Distance	*Horse-Age-Weight*	*Date*	*Time*
5f	Minstrel King 5-8-8	29/3/60	58.4
5f	Belgrave Square 2-9-2	7/8/67	59.7
6f	Janeat 3-8-2	10/7/62	1min 10.8
6f	Chartered Accountant 2-9-7	14/8/62	1min 12.8
7f 50yd	Conifer 3-7-2	29/7/68	1min 30.2
8f 50yd	March Blue 7-7-4	16/4/68	1min 42.2
10f	Fleet Street 3-9-0	20/8/46	2min 2.8
11f	Hurry de Savoie 3-9-3	5/7/37	2min 20
13f	Alignment 3-7-11	12/8/68	2min 44.8
16f	Fet 5-7-7	5/10/36	3min 24

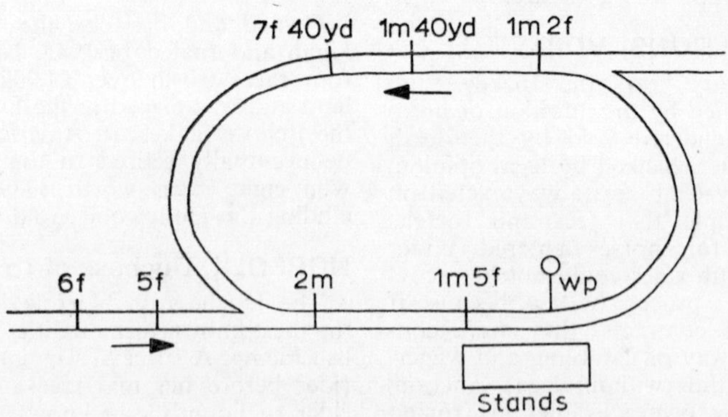

NOTTINGHAM

are reasonably easy, but in general the course is better suited to a sharp, well-balanced horse than to a long-striding one. The few gradients are of a minor nature.

Clerk of the Course: Mr D. Heyman, Woollerton House, Wendover, Bucks. Tel: Wendover 3194.

NUCLEUS

Foaled in 1952, Nucleus was owned and bred by Miss Dorothy Paget and was by Nimbus out of Angelus, by Blandford. He proved himself a high-class horse, winning eight races worth over £14,000, including the King Edward VII Stakes, Jockey Club Stakes and Winston Churchill Stakes. He was second to that great filly Meld in the St Leger. Piggott, rider of Nucleus, lodged an objection after the race but it was quickly overruled. At times Nucleus appeared to have a wayward temperament and to be 'difficult', and the reason of this only became apparent when he died suddenly of an acute brain disease.

NUMBER CLOTH

Every horse running in a race carries a saddlecloth bearing a number corresponding with his number on the race-card. The cloth is given to the jockey when he weighs out and must be worn so that the number is clearly visible. The jockey must put the cloth in the scale and include it in his weight. Immediately he has weighed in after the race, he gives the number cloth to the official appointed to receive it.

NUNTHORPE STAKES

See under York.

NURSERY HANDICAP

A nursery handicap is a handicap confined to two-year-olds.

O

OAKS, THE

See under Epsom.

O'BRIEN, Michael Victor (b 1917)

'Vincent' O'Brien's career has not been without its dramas and reverses, but it is probably true to say that he is the greatest trainer in Irish racing history.

He rode a few winners as an amateur and took out a licence to train in 1944. At first his stable was concerned with National Hunt racing and he proved wonderfully skilful with steeplechasers and hurdlers, winning the Grand National three times, the Cheltenham Gold Cup four times and the Champion Hurdle three times. In the 1950s he turned his attention to the flat with conspicuously successful results and the main English races he has so far won are as follows:

Two Thousand Guineas: Sir Ivor (1968); Nijinsky (1970)
One Thousand Guineas: Glad Rags (1966)
Derby: Larkspur (1962); Sir Ivor (1968); Nijinsky (1970)
Oaks: Long Look (1965); Valoris (1966)
St Leger: Ballymoss (1957)
Coronation Cup: Ballymoss (1958)
Ascot Gold Cup: Gladness (1958)
Eclipse Stakes: Ballymoss (1958); Pieces of Eight (1966)
King George VI and Queen Elizabeth Stakes: Ballymoss
Champion Stakes: Pieces of Eight (1966).

In France he has won the Prix de l'Arc de Triomphe with Ballymoss and the Grand Criterium with Sir Ivor. He has won the Irish Derby three times, the Irish Oaks three times, the Irish St Leger three times, the Irish Two Thousand Guineas once and the Irish One Thousand Guineas once.

Small, trim and self-possessed, O'Brien is first and foremost a perfectionist and no trouble is too great as far as the well-being of his horses is concerned. Patrons of his Tipperary stable include Mr Raymond Guest, Mr C. Clore, Mr Charles Engelhard, Mr J. Cox Brady, the Countess de la Valdene, and Mr J. P. Philipps.

OCEAN SWELL

Bred and owned by Lord Rosebery, Ocean Swell, by Blue Peter out of Jiffy, by Hurry On, is the only horse this century to have won the Derby and the Ascot Gold Cup. Trained by Jack Jarvis, he won a war-substitute Derby at Newmarket in 1944 and the Gold Cup the following year. He had not proved a stud success when he died in 1954.

OFFICIALS, Licences for

The following officials require a licence granted annually by the Stewards of the Jockey Club: clerk of the course, handicapper, clerk of the scales, judge, starters, veterinary officer, stewards' secretary, inspector of courses.

The Clerk of the Course shall be appointed for every meeting by the executive of that meeting, subject to the approval of the stewards, and shall be paid by the executive. All other officials shall be appointed for every meeting of the Joint Administrative Authority as required by the terms of their employment.

No two offices shall be held by one person, unless by special permission.

Jockeys' valets, starters' assistants and advance flagmen require an annual licence.

Ring inspectors and gatekeepers employed at more than one meeting also require an annual licence from the Stewards of the Jockey Club.

The Jockey Club Stakeholders are stakeholders for all meetings and are paid in accordance with Rule 179.

Complaints against an official have to be made to the stewards in writing, signed by the complainant.

See RULES OF RACING (20).

O'GORMAN, William Gerard (1913-1969)

W. G. O'Gorman trained at Graham Place, Newmarket. His successes included the King's Stand Stakes (twice), the Gimcrack Stakes, the Stewards' Cup, the Northumberland Plate, the Britannia Stakes and the Newbury Spring Cup. He died very suddenly in 1969 and the stable was taken over by his son W. A. O'Gorman who shortly afterwards won the Stewards' Cup with Royal Smoke.

OLDHAM, Gerald Anthony (b 1925)

Mr Oldham, now an international financier living in Switzerland, was born in 1925 and served four years in the Coldstream Guards. He has enjoyed many successes as an owner and among the good horses he has had are Lucero (Irish Two Thousand Guineas); Talgo (Irish Derby); Fidalgo (Irish Derby and Chester Vase); Cynara (Queen Mary Stakes); Miralgo (Timeform Gold Cup and Hardwicke Stakes); Sovrango (Ormonde Stakes twice and Chester Vase); Espresso (Manchester Cup, Grosser Preis von Baden twice and Vaux Gold Tankard); Corinto (William Hill Gold Cup); Salvo (Vaux Gold Tankard, Hardwicke Stakes, Yorkshire Cup, Grosser Preis von Baden and second in the Prix de l'Arc de Triomphe); Chicago (Cumberland Lodge Stakes and Gran Premio del Jockey Club, Milan); and Intermezzo (St Leger). His trainer is Harry Wragg and his colours chocolate and white hoops, white cap. In 1970 he won the £48,000 Prix Lupin with Stintino, who was subsequently third to Nijinsky in the Derby.

OLDROYD, Geoffrey (b 1946)

Geoffrey Oldroyd was apprenticed to H. P. Rohan from 1961 to 1968. He rode his first winner in 1963 at Stockton. He rode 20 winners in 1966.

ONCIDIUM

Oncidium was bred and owned by Lord Howard de Walden and is by Alcide out of Malcolmia, by Sayani. He won five races and over £29,000 in stakes, his successes including the Royal Stakes, Lingfield Derby Trial, Jockey Club Cup and Coronation Cup. He was much fancied for the 1964 Derby but finished unplaced behind Santa Claus. He was trained firstly by Jack Waugh and later in his career by George Todd. He was ultimately exported to Japan.

O'NEILL, Frank

Frank O'Neill, who died in New York aged 74, was one of the most successful of the many American jockeys who came to find fame and fortune in Europe before World War I. He settled in France and between 1910 and 1922 was champion jockey there in every year bar one. In 1910 he rode 156 winners, in 1911 163, and in 1913 162. He gained his first English classic success in 1911 when he won the St Leger on Prince Palatine, on whom he won the Ascot Gold Cup the following season. After the war he won the 1920 Derby on Spion Kop, a lucky mount as the stable jockey Arthur Smith elected to ride Sarchedon. In 1924 he won the Oaks on Straitlace. That year he won the Lincoln on Sir Gallahad III, the Kempton Jubilee on Parth and the Queen Alexandra Stakes on Rose Prince.

He was not a stylist, but a tough, determined rider who rode a strong finish and was inclined to be hard on his horses. On retirement he opened a bar in Paris that became a rendezvous for the Parisian racing world.

ONE THOUSAND GUINEAS

See under NEWMARKET.

ONLY FOR LIFE

By Chanteur II out of Life Sentence, by Court Martial, Only For Life was foaled in 1960 and was bought as a yearling for 1,600 gn by Miss Monica Sheriffe. Trained by Jeremy Tree he won the Two Thousand Guineas and the King Edward VII Stakes. Before export to Japan in 1966, he sired The Elk, winner of the £19,000 *Observer* Gold Cup in 1968.

ORBY

Mr R. B. Croker's Orby, trained by Col F. McCabe at Glencairn, Co Dublin, was the first Irish-trained horse to win the Derby, a feat he accomplished in 1907. Col McCabe was a doctor who suspended his medical interests to become private trainer to Mr Croker. Orby sired a Derby winner in Grand Parade, but most of his descendants were noted for their speed rather than for stamina.

ORLASS FAMILY

Orlass, foaled in 1914, was by the Derby winner Orby and won five races, all in Ireland and all over 5f. Though a sprinter herself, many of her descendants were top-class middle distance performers and she had immense influence on the late Major L. B. Holliday's stud. Among her descendants are Hethersett, Neasham Belle, Narrator, None Nicer, Netherton Maid and Crisper, who all carried the Holliday colours. Other notable descendants are Gay Time, Elopement, Nucleus and Derring-Do.

ORME

The Duke of Westminster's Orme, by Ormonde, was a high-class horse that was unable to run in the Two Thousand Guineas or the Derby owing to poisoning. It has never been proved beyond doubt whether he was deliberately poisoned through malice or as a result of severe dental infection. The former is the more probable. In the St Leger he was unplaced behind La Fleche, but beat her in the Eclipse the following year. He sired the 1899 'Triple Crown' winner Flying Fox who was exported to France and exercised great influence on bloodstock breeding there. He also sired the 1907 Derby winner Orby, and Witch Elm who won the One Thousand Guineas the same year. He was champion sire in 1899.

ORMONDE

Owned and bred by the first Duke of Westminster, Ormonde was a bay colt by Bend Or out of Lily Agnes and was trained by John Porter. He was unquestionably one of the greatest horses in English racing history and at two, three and four years of age he was never beaten. Besides winning the Two Thousand Guineas, 1886 Derby and St Leger, his victories included the Hardwicke Stakes (twice), the Champion Stakes, the Dewhurst Plate, the Free Handicap, the Champion Stakes and the Imperial Gold Cup. His success was all the more remarkable in that for much of his career he suffered from respiratory trouble. His stud career unfortunately proved an anti-climax. He was 21 when he died in America in 1904. His skeleton was set up in the Natural History Museum, South Kensington.

ORMSTON, John Glaholme (b 1909)

Jack Ormston, once a speedway rider, before World War I rode in steeplechases as an amateur and in point-to-points. He took out a licence to train in 1946 and his stables are at Richmond, Yorkshire. His most important success so far has been to win the Portland Handicap. Among his owners are Mr T. H. Bennett, Mr H. C. Hutchinson, Lord Kilmany, Mr

R. O. Manners, Mr E. Holland-Martin, Mr J. Monk, Capt R. Ramsden, Mr G. Rickman, Mr J. F. Simpson, Capt E. Ramsden, Hon G. Weir, and Mrs A. D. Fife.

ORPEN

Foaled in 1928, Orpen belonged to Sir John Rutherford and was trained by Joe Lawson at Manton. By Solario out of Harpy, by Swynford, he was a good but unlucky horse, finishing second in the Derby, St Leger and Ascot Gold Cup. In addition he was third in the Two Thousand Guineas. His five victories included the Hardwicke Stakes, Churchill Stakes and Yorkshire Cup. He proved a stud failure.

ORPHEUS

Sir Hugo Cunliffe-Owen's Orpheus, by Orby, was third to Spion Kop in the Derby and won the Champion Stakes. He became extremely bad-tempered and was an indifferent sire although he did get one very good sprinted in Concerto.

ORWELL

Orwell, foaled in 1929, was bred by Lord Furness and owned by Mr W. M. G. Singer. By Gainsborough out of Golden Hair, by Golden Sun, he was trained by Joe Lawson at Manton and proved a brilliant two-year-old, his victories including the National Breeders Produce Stakes. He was a hot favourite for the two Thousand Guineas, which he won, but he failed in the Derby and the St Leger. He was not a success as a sire.

OSBORNE, John

John Osborne was a member of a Suffolk family that migrated to Yorkshire. He had his first ride in 1846 and his last one in 1892. Completely incorruptible, quite a rare quality in north-country jockeys at that time, he was for years the idol of Yorkshire. He rode very short for those days and because of his style was known as 'the old pusher'. He won the Derby in 1869 on Pretender. He trained successfully for a number of years and lived to a great age.

OUR BABU

Our Babu was foaled in 1952 and is by My Babu out of Glen Line, by Blue Peter, being thus a half-brother to King of the Tudors. Owned by Mr David Robinson and trained by Geoffrey Brooke, he won the Champagne Stakes, Middle Park Stakes and Two Thousand Guineas. He was exported to America in 1956, returned to England in 1963 and was sent to Japan in 1967.

OWEN TUDOR

Fred Darling's seventh and last Derby winner was in 1941 when Owen Tudor won, bred and owned by Mrs (now the Hon Lady)) Macdonald-Buchanan and ridden by W. Nevett. By Hyperion out of Mary Tudor II, Owen Tudor was not consistent but he was a good horse on his day and won a war-substitute Gold Cup the following season. As a sire he got two exceptionally fast horses in Tudor Minstrel and Abernant; a high-class middle distance horse in Right Royal V who slammed St Paddy in the King George VI and Queen Elizabeth Stakes; and a fine stayer in Elpenor who won the Ascot Gold Cup for M. M. Boussac.

OVERNIGHT DECLARATION OFFICE

The present Overnight Declarations Office is at Weatherby and Sons, Denington House, Wellingborough, Northants.

OWNER

The 'owner' of a horse includes 'part-owner' and 'lessee' but not 'lessor', and the lessor of a horse shall be deemed to have no interest in the horse for the purposes of Rule 94, unless he receives a share of the prize money won by the horse and contributes to the expense of running it.

Owner's Contributions

Statistics published in 1968 showed that owners themselves contribute no less than 24 per cent of the prize money available on the flat. In France the figure is about 4 per cent, in America less than that.

OWNERS, LEADING

1900	Prince of Wales	£29,585
1901	Sir G. Blundell Maple	£21,370
1902	Mr R. S. Sievier	£23,686
1903	Sir James Miller	£24,768
1904	Sir James Miller	£28,923
1905	Col W. Hall Walker	£23,678
1906	Lord Derby	£32,926
1907	Col W. Hall Walker	£17,910
1908	Mr J. B. Joel	£26,246
1909	Mr Fairie*	£37,719
1910	Mr Fairie*	£35,352
1911	Lord Derby	£42,781
1912	Mr T. Pilkington	£20,822
1913	Mr J. B. Joel	£25,430
1914	Mr J. B. Joel	£30,724
1915	Mr L. Neumann	£13,546
1916	Mr E. Hulton	£13,764
1917	Mr Fairie*	£11,751
1918	Lady James Douglas	£14,735
1919	Lord Glanely	£30,514
1920	Sir R. Jardine	£19,385
1921	Mr S. B. Joel	£33,048
1922	Lord Woolavington	£32,090
1923	Lord Derby	£40,388
1924	HH Aga Khan	£44,367
1925	Lord Astor	£35,723
1926	Lord Woolavington	£47,256
1927	Lord Derby	£40,155
1928	Lord Derby	£65,603
1929	HH Aga Khan	£39,886
1930	HH Aga Khan	£46,259
1931	Mr J. A. Dewar	£39,034
1932	HH Aga Khan	£57,778
1933	Lord Derby	£27,559
1934	HH Aga Khan	£64,898
1935	HH Aga Khan	£49,201
1936	Lord Astor	£38,131
1937	HH Aga Khan	£30,655
1938	Lord Derby	£34,434
1939	Lord Rosebery	£38,465
1940	Lord Rothermere	£6,869
1941	Lord Glanely	£8,762
1942	King George VI	£10,536
1943	Miss D. Paget	£13,146
1944	HH Aga Khan	£13,985
1945	Lord Derby	£25,067
1946	HH Aga Khan	£24,118
1947	HH Aga Khan	£44,020
1948	HH Aga Khan	£46,393
1949	HH Aga Khan	£68,916
1950	M. M. Boussac	£57,044
1951	M. M. Boussac	£39,340
1952	HH Aga Khan	£92,519
1953	Sir V. Sassoon	£58,579
1954	The Queen	£40,994
1955	Lady Zia Wernher	£46,345
1956	Major L. B. Holliday	£39,327
1957	The Queen	£62,211
1958	Mr J. McShain	£63,264
1959	Prince Aly Khan	£100,668
1960	Sir V. Sassoon	£90,069
1961	Major L. B. Holliday	£39,227
1962	Major L. B. Holliday	£70,206
1963	Mrs J. R. Mullion	£68,882
1964	Mrs H. E. Jackson	£98,270
1965	M. J. Ternynck	£65,301
1966	Lady Zia Wernher	£78,075
1967	Mr H. J. Joel	£120,923
1968	Mr R. Guest	£97,076

* 'Mr Fairie' was the *nom de course* of Mr A. W. Cox.

OXLEY, John Elliott (b 1930)

John Oxley, after Eton and service in the King's Royal Rifle Corps, was assistant to Geoffrey Brooke from 1957 to 1958. He then went as assistant to George Colling and on the latter's death in 1959 took over the stable which he has conducted successfully at Hurworth House, Newmarket, ever since. In 1964 he won the Oaks with Sir Foster Robinson's Homeward Bound, who also won the Princess Elizabeth Stakes and Yorkshire Oaks. He has won the Dante Stakes with Merchant Venturer, who was second in the Derby, and with Hermes; the Yorkshire Cup with Cutter; the Ebbisham Stakes with Daisy Chain; the Coronation Stakes with Ocean; the King Edward VII Stakes with Mariner; the Falmouth Stakes with Alborada; the Great Voltigeur Stakes with Hermes; the Jockey Club Cup with Hermes; the Jockey Club Stakes with Torpid; and the Lincolnshire Handicap with Frankincense. Among his owners are Lord and Lady Halifax, Major-Gen Sir Randle Feilden, Lady Susan Watson, Major-Gen Sir George Burns, Lieut-Col John Chandos-Pole, Mr J. B. Fenwick, Mr R. D. Hollingsworth, Mr A. M. G. Kidson, Capt J. Macdonald-Buchanan, Mr S. Mercer, Brig J. E. Swetenham and Hon Mrs Brian Rootes.

OXX, John

A leading Irish trainer whose English successes include the Champion Stakes with Arctic Storm; the Diadem Stakes with Majority Blue; the Cork and Orrery Stakes with Majority Blue and Current Coin; the Queen Alexandra Stakes with Panic and the Gordon Stakes with Gay Challenger.

P

PADDOCK

The paddock is usually taken to mean the area of ground on a racecourse that includes the parade ring, weighing room and unsaddling enclosure. In most cases it is accessible only to those persons in the members' enclosure or in Tattersalls.

PAGET, Hon Dorothy (1906-1960)

The Hon Dorothy Paget was the second daughter of the first and last Baron Queenborough. A cousin of Mr John Hay Whitney, she inherited a huge fortune from her maternal grandfather and this enabled her to race on a vast scale, both on the flat and over jumps, for more than 30 years.

Extremely shy and retiring by nature, she was recognised as one of racing's eccentrics and for the last 20 years of her life she was a recluse, avoiding as far as possible human contact outside her own small and devoted female entourage. She was easily distinguished on the racecourse since she invariably wore a blue felt hat, that owed nothing to current fashion, and a shapeless grey coat that extended nearly to her ankles. Her face, round, heavy and pale, was framed in lank dark hair. Stories circulated of her curious mode of life; of the odd hours that she kept and the gargantuan meals she was alleged to consume. Possibly she was never a really popular figure with the racing public, but she was respected for her independence, admired for the firm manner in which she successfully kept the press at arms length, and appreciated for the lavish patronage she gave to the Turf.

Being forthright and demanding, she was liable to terminate at short notice the services of trainers and jockeys. She was generous though, and those who possessed the knack of handling her successfully, usually became genuinely fond of her. She betted on a very big scale indeed, many of her most audacious wagers being on second-rate jumpers at minor meetings under National Hunt rules. Before World War II, she was a staunch supporter of pony racing at Northolt.

Her most famous racehorse was the steeplechaser Golden Miller, winner of the Grand National in record time and of five Cheltenham Gold Cups. Considering the money spent on yearlings and the scope of her own stud, she was not particularly successful on the flat, but she did win the 1943 Derby with Straight Deal, trained by Walter Nightingall. Another good horse of hers was Aldborough, winner of the Queen Alexandra Stakes and the Doncaster Cup. A notorious performer to carry her colours was Tuppence, who in three days before the Derby, was backed from 125-1 to 10-1. He finished eighteenth. At the time of her death Miss Paget's flat-race horses were trained by Sir Gordon Richards.

PALAIS ROYAL II

M. Jacques Wittouck's Palais Royal II came from France in 1928 to win the Cambridgeshire. A son of Bruleur, he was a most versatile performer, being second in the St Leger, Coronation Cup and Jockey Club Cup; third in the Ascot Gold Cup and the Cambridgeshire. He won six races in France and the Grand International at Ostend. He sired the dams of Nikellora (French One Thousand Guineas, French Oaks and Prix de l'Arc de Triomphe); and of Souverain

(Grand Prix, French St Leger and Ascot Gold Cup).

PALESTINE

Bred by the late Aga Khan, Palestine was foaled in 1947 and is a grey horse by Fair Trial out of Una, by Tetratema. Trained by Marcus Marsh, he showed brilliant speed as a two-year-old, winning the Sandown Park Stud Produce Stakes, Coventry Stakes, National Breeders Produce Stakes, Richmond Stakes, Gimcrack Stakes and Champagne Stakes. He was probably a bit stale by October when he was beaten by Masked Light in the Middle Park Stakes.

As a three-year-old he was a really good horse up to 1m, winning the Henry VIII Stakes at Hurst Park, the Two Thousand Guineas, St James's Palace Stakes, Red Rose Stakes at Manchester and Sussex Stakes. He failed to stay in the Eclipse and finished fourth. Altogether he won 11 races and over £38,000.

At the stud he has perhaps not been quite the success generally anticipated, but his winners include Pall Mall (Two Thousand Guineas), Palariva (£12,488), Zeus Boy (£11,615), Green Banner (£11,597) and the Rabbi (£10,206). He is now owned by Mr W. J. McEnery and stands at the Portmarnock Stud, Malahide, Co Dublin, at a fee of 600 gn.

PALL MALL

Bred by the Queen, Pall Mall was foaled in 1955 and is a chestnut horse by Palestine out of Malapert, by Portlaw. The late Capt Charles Moore, racing manager to King George VI and later to the Queen, bought Malapert for the Royal Stud for 120 gn. Malapert carried two lines of The Tetrarch in her pedigree and Moore desired to inbreed further to this source of speed by sending her to Kingstone, then standing at Sandringham and virtually the last tail-male descendant of the Herod line in England.

For three years Malapert was covered by Kingstone but the produce were useless. Moore then sent her to Big Game, whose maternal grandsire is The Tetrarch's son Tetratema, and after Big Game to Palestine, whose maternal grandsire is likewise Tetratema. The result of this union with Palestine was Pall Mall.

Trained by Sir Cecil Boyd-Rochfort, Pall Mall was a good, fast two-year-old, winning the New Stakes at Royal Ascot and being placed in the July, Gimcrack and Champagne Stakes.

First time out as a three-year-old Pall Mall was unplaced in the Two Thousand Guineas Trial at Kempton but soon showed the form all wrong by winning firstly the Classic Trial Stakes at Thirsk and then the Two Thousand Guineas at 20-1. He also won the Lockinge Stakes at Newbury, while in the Sussex Stakes he was second to Major Portion, who had been second to him in the Guineas. As a four-year-old he won the Lockinge Stakes again and the Midsummer Stakes at Newmarket. He ran a great race in the Royal Hunt Cup to finish second under 9st 7lb.

He has produced a consistent flow of winners at the stud, the best of them so far being Reform, winner of the St James's Palace Stakes, Sussex Stakes, Queen Elizabeth II Stakes, Champion Stakes and over £44,000 in prize money. He is syndicated and stands at the Ballykisteen Stud, Tipperary.

PAMPERED KING

Bred and owned by the late Major L. B. Holliday, Pampered King was foaled in 1954 and is a bay horse by Prince Chevalier out of Netherton Maid, by Nearco. His racing record was nothing out of the ordinary; he was in training for four seasons and won four races worth £3,238, his main success being the Brighton Autumn Cup. However, he has done very well as a sire, and among his winners are David Jack (£14,173); Pugnacity (£11,800); Wrekin Rambler (Goodwood Cup and £9,523); Ludham (£8,191 in England and £53,000 in America); and Czar Alexander (£1,481 in England and over £150,000 in America). Pampered King was exported to America in 1669.

PAN II

Owned by M. E. Constant and trained in France by E. Pollet, Pan II, by Atys, won the Ascot Gold Cup and the Goodwood Cup in 1951. In France he won four races including the French St Leger.

PANASLIPPER

Owned and bred by the late Mr J. McGrath, Panaslipper was foaled in 1952 and is by Solar Slipper out of Panastrid, by Panorama. In 1955 he was second to Phil Drake in the Derby and won the Irish Derby. He won four races worth over £9,000 and was third in the Champion Stakes. In 1964 he was exported to Japan.

PANDOFELL

Bred by Mr H. J. Joel, who unfortunately sold him before he disclosed his great merits, Pandofell was foaled in 1957 and is by Solar Slipper out of Nadika, by Nosca. Trained by F. Maxwell he won the Queen's Prize, Yorkshire Cup, Ascot Gold Cup and Doncaster Cup. All told he won eight races worth over £20,000. Out and out stayers are rarely popular with breeders in this country and he had not been long at the stud in this country before he was sold for export to Russia. Before he left he sired that good but unpredictable stayer Piaco, whose many successes included the Doncaster Cup and Northumberland Plate; and Pandora Bay, winner of the Ribblesdale Stakes and third in the Oaks. For most of his racing career Pandofell was owned by Mr H. Warwick Daw, who bought him as a two-year-old for 600 gn at the December Sales.

PANORAMA

Panorama, by Sir Cosmo out of Happy Climax, was one of the most successful sprinting sires in English racing history. When he died in 1955 his stock had won 48½ races worth over £198,000. He has done very well, too, as a sire of brood mares.

PANTHER, THE

Bred at the National Stud, owned by Sir Alec Black and trained by G. Manser, The Panther was foaled in 1916 and was by Tracery out of the rather wayward Countess Zia, by Gallinule. He showed high promise as a two-year-old, but it was regarded as a rather silly joke when his owner, who knew little about racing, sent him up to the Newmarket Sales in 1918 with a reserve of 40,000 gn on him. "This will give a chance to all comers", Sir Alec Black observed. "If he passes out of the ring unsold, there will be no further opportunity to buy him".

The Panther won the Two Thousand Guineas and started at 6-5 favourite for the Derby. His temper that day was abominable and he ran badly. He also failed in the Irish Derby and the Champion Stakes. He was duly exported to the Argentine where he sired winners of over £60,000 in stakes. In 1929 he was repatriated to England but died two years after his return.

PAPPA FOURWAY

Bred by the Ballykisteen Stud and trained by the late W. P. Dutton, Pappa Fourway is by Pappageno II out of Oola Hills, by Denturius. Foaled in 1952, he proved a brilliant sprinter, among his successes being the July Cup, King's Stand Stakes, Diadem Stakes and the Tetrarch Stakes at Manchester. Altogether he won 12 races worth over £9,000, having cost less than £200 as a yearing. He was exported to the United States.

PAPYRUS

Owned by Mr Ben Irish, trained by Basil Jarvis and ridden by Stephen Donoghue, Papyrus won the 1923 Derby. In the autumn of that year he was sent to America to run in a match against the leading American three-year-old Zev. Papyrus was soundly beaten. He was not a success as a sire.

PARADE RING

Every racecourse must have a railed-off parade ring in the paddock where the horses parade after they have been saddled and where the jockeys assemble and mount.

PARDAL

Pardal, foaled in 1947, was bred and owned by M. M. Boussac and was by the unbeaten Pharis II out of Adargatis, by Asterus. As a three-year-old he was placed in the Prix Juigné, Prix Hocquart and Irish Derby but he did not in fact win a race until he was four. He then won two races in France and the Princess of Wales's Stakes, Great Yorkshire Stakes, Jockey Club Stakes and Lowther Stakes in England. He was not nearly such a good horse as his brother Ardan, but he proved a better sire.

Purchased as a stallion by Mr R. F. Watson and some associates, he was syndicated at £1,650 a share and sent to stand at the Lanwades Stud, Newmarket. In his old age the syndicate parted company with him, and he stood at the Rossenarra Stud, Co Kilkenny, at a fee of 300 gn. His best winner so far has of course been Psidium, winner of the 1961 Derby. Other good winners by him are Parbury and Pardallo II, both winners of the Ascot Gold Cup; Eudaemon (£13,049); London Cry (£11,999); Firestreak (£11,459); and Pardao (£10,922). He is also sire of Decies, who won the National Stakes in 1969, was sold at Newmarket for 110,000 guineas and as a three year old won the Blue Riband Trial Stakes and the Irish Two Thousand Guineas. Pardal died in 1969.

PARDAO

Foaled in 1958, Pardao was bred by the Sledmere Stud and bought as a yearling on behalf of Mrs C. O. Iselin for 7,000 gn. By Pardal out of Three Weeks, by Big Game, he was trained by Sir Cecil Boyd-Rochfort and as a two-year-old he won the Fenwolf Stakes at Ascot. At three he won the Lingfield Derby Trial and the Gordon Stakes at Goodwood; he was also third in the Derby and fourth in the St Leger. When he was four he won the Jockey Club Cup (then 1½m) and was later sent to America. When he was five he won two good handicaps there. He retired to the stud in England in 1964 and at once drew attention to himself by siring Sovereign, a very fast filly that won over £13,000 in stakes. He is now syndicated and stands at the Lanwades stud, Moulton, Newmarket.

PARK HILL STAKES

See under DONCASTER.

PARK TOP

Park Top was bred in 1964 by Mrs Scott at the Buttermilk Stud, Oxfordshire, and as a yearling was bought at Newmarket by Bernard van Cutsem on behalf of the Duke of Devonshire for 500 gn. By Kalydon out of Nellie Park, by Arctic Prince, she did not run as a two-year-old, but the following season won four of her five races, including the Ribblesdale Stakes at Royal Ascot.

In 1968 she again did well, winning the Brighton Challenge Cup for the second year running and the Prix d'Hedouville at Longchamp. She was also close up third to Levmoss and Canterbury in the Oxfordshire Stakes.

The Duke of Devonshire was persuaded by the Duchess to keep Park Top in training as a five-year-old and this fine big bay mare proved better than ever. Apart from winning a couple of nice races in France, she carried off the Coronation Cup, Hardwicke Stakes and King George VI and Queen Elizabeth Stakes. She certainly ought to have won the Eclipse Stakes, too, but Geoff Lewis was well below his best form on that occasion and she was most unluckily beaten by

Wolver Hollow. She was probably a shade unlucky, too, when second to Levmoss in the Prix de l'Arc de Triomphe, Piggott delivering his challenge just too late. She was clearly stale when subsequently runner-up in the Champion Stakes. In 1970 she won La Coupe at Longchamp, but in the Coronation Cup was beaten by Caliban, Piggott riding a somewhat indifferent race.

PARNELL, Ryan Farnham (b 1934)

Apprenticed to W. Stephenson from 1949 to 1953, R. F. Parnell has travelled much since then and has ridden the winner of the Kenya Derby twice. He has also won the Danish Oaks twice, the Danish One Thousand Guineas three times and the Danish Two Thousand Guineas twice. In Ireland, where he is now riding, he has won the Irish Two Thousand Guineas and the Gallinule Stakes.

PARSONS, John

John Parsons is believed to have been only 16 years old when he rode Caractacus to victory in the 1862 Derby. After this singular triumph he vanished into obscurity.

PARTH

Foaled in 1920, Parth was by Polymelus out of Willia, by William the Third. In England he won six races worth over £5,000, including the Churchill Stakes and Kempton Jubilee and was third in the Derby. In France he won the Prix de l'Arc de Triomphe. He did well as a sire in France without reaching the top rank.

PARTHIA

Owned and bred by Sir Humphrey de Trafford, Parthia, by Persian Gulf, won the Derby in 1959. He was the only Derby winner trained by Sir Cecil Boyd-Rochfort and the only one ridden by Harry Carr. He was not an outstanding horse and his subsequent career was disappointing. He sired a fair number of winners, the best of them being that good staying filly Parthian Glance and the 1969 Oaks winner Sleeping Partner. He was exported to Japan in 1968.

PASCH

Foaled in 1935, Pasch was bred by the Banstead Manor Stud and owned by Mr H. E. Morriss. Trained by Fred Darling, he did not run as a two-year-old but the following season won the Two Thousand Guineas and the Eclipse and was third to his stable companion Bois Roussel in the Derby. He died after one season at the stud. He was by Blandford out of Pasca, by Manna. Pasca was grandam of the 1953 Derby winner Pinza.

PASSPORT

A 'passport' under the Rules of Racing is the approved diagrammatic document of identity of a horse issued on the authority of the Stewards of the Jockey Club or that of any recognised Turf Authority.

PATTERN RACES

Pattern races are those which are necessary to provide a comprehensive system of tests for the best horses of various ages and over various distances in accordance with the officially accepted pattern of racing. These races set the standard of English racing.

Prize money and the pattern of racing have been deeply studied in recent years. In 1965 a committee was appointed under the Duke of Norfolk to study the pattern of racing, and in 1967 a committee under Lord Porchester, called the Race Planning Committee, was set up to continue the work of the Duke of Norfolk's committee.

PAVEH

Paveh was foaled in 1963 and is by Tropique out of Persian Shoe, by Tehran. Trained in Ireland by T. Ainsworth, he proved a high-class miler as a three-year-old, winning the

Irish Two Thousand Guineas and the Sussex Stakes. In the Irish Derby he was third to Sodium and Charlottown. All told he won six races and over £35,000. He is owned by Mr P. A. B. Widener and stands at the Ennistown Stud, Co Meath, at a fee of 400 gn.

PAYNE, William John (b 1910)

Bill Payne is the son of W. H. Payne, a noted National Hunt jockey and later a successful trainer under both rules. 'Young' Bill Payne became a highly competent rider over fences and hurdles early in life and would have won the 1928 Grand National on Great Span if the saddle had not slipped two fences from home. His first rides under National Hunt rules had been at the tender age of 14.

In World War II he served with the Yorkshire Dragoons, reaching the rank of Major, and afterwards he assisted his father till taking out a licence himself in 1955. His stable at Eastbury in Berkshire is a small one but the horses are cleverly placed and win at least their share of races. Patrons of the stable include Mr C. Birks, Lt-Col S. L. Green, Maj H. W. Hall and Mr F. F. Wolff.

PAYNE-GALLWEY, Col Peter, DSO (b 1906)

Col Payne-Gallwey joined the 11th Hussars after Eton and the RMC. In the 1930s he was one of the leading amateur riders, winning over 60 races including the Grand Military Gold Cup. He had a most distinguished war record, being awarded the DSO and two bars. He began training jumpers in 1949—he had trained a good many winners in Egypt before the war—but gradually he has turned to the flat. The stable at Upper Lambourn is a small one and it was a great achievement to win the Stewards' Cup two years running with Sky Diver. Patrons of the stable include Mrs P. Dawes, Mr J. Cole, Mrs G. Hunt, Mr J. Fane, Lady Phoebe Phipps, Mrs W. R. Kennion, Capt N. Conant and Col A. F. G. Renton.

PAY UP

Foaled in 1933, Pay Up was by Fairway out of Book Debt, by Buchan. Bred and owned by the late Lord Astor and trained by Joe Lawson, he won the Free Handicap and the Two Thousand Guineas. He proved a moderate sire.

PEACOCK, Matthew (1879-1951)

A famous and much-loved Yorkshire character, noted for his blunt outspokenness and his hatred of humbug and dishonesty, 'Matt' Peacock assisted his father, Dobson Peacock, for many years at Manor House, Middleham, before taking out a trainer's licence himself. The best horse he ever trained was Dante who won the Derby in 1945. The rumours and uncertainty that surrounded Dante's St Leger preparation—he was eventually withdrawn from the race—made Peacock a worried and unhappy man and he never quite regained his old buoyancy. A true Yorkshireman, his usual farewell after an Ascot or Newmarket meeting was "Goodbye; now I'm off back to England".

PEACOCK, Richard Dobson (b 1924)

Richard Peacock was born in 1924 and served in the Royal Scots Greys from 1942 to 1947. He assisted his father, the late M. J. Peacock (see above), before taking out a licence himself in 1951. Among the many good races he has won are the Cheveley Park Stakes, Gimcrack Stakes, Chesham Stakes, Seaton Delavel Plate, Free Handicap, Northumberland Plate, Usher Vaux Gold Tankard and Yorkshire Cup. The good horses he has trained include Tudor Melody, Precast, Guide, Lindsay, Border Legend, Sweet Story and Erudite. His stables are at Middleham, Yorkshire, and his owners include the Duke of Roxburghe, Lieut-Col J. Hornung, Lieut-Col R. Taylor, Mr J. Liley, Mr Cecil Moores, Sir Edward Hanmer, the Duke of Northumberland and Mr F. A. P. Tattersall.

PEARL DIVER

Baron G. de Waldner's Pearl Diver, by Vatellor, won the Derby in 1947, thereby opening a new phase in English racing, a phase in which the hitherto undisputed supremacy of the British thoroughbred was continually and successfully challenged, chiefly by horses bred in France. Pearl Diver failed to make his mark as a sire and in 1957 was exported to Japan.

PEARL MAIDEN FAMILY

Foaled in 1918, Pearl Maiden, by Phaleron, was a famous brood mare. Her offspring included Pearlweed (French Derby), Pearl Cap (French Oaks and Prix de l'Arc de Triomphe), Indus (French Two Thousand Guineas) and Bipearl (French One Thousand Guineas). Among her descendants are the Derby winner Pearl Diver and the Prix de l'Arc de Triomphe winner Molvedo.

PECK, Charles (1873-1941)

A member of a famous racing family, Charles Peck acted for a good many years as private trainer to Mr S. B. Joel. His best winners were Pommern who won the Two Thousand Guineas, Derby and St Leger in 1915; Bachelors Button, who beat Pretty Polly in the Ascot Gold Cup; and Polymelus who won the Cambridgeshire and became a most successful sire. After service with the Royal Horse Artillery in World War I, he trained for Mr S. B. Joel again in 1925 but in 1926 became private trainer to Mr Joel's brother Mr J. B. Joel. All told he trained 444 winners of £215,000 in stakes.

PENALTY

In some races penalties can be incurred by horses which win between the closing of entries, or the publication of weights in a handicap, and the running of the race concerned, in which they will then be compelled to carry additional weight. The scale of penalties varies considerably and conditions for allotting penalties differ according to different races. For the classics and many other races there are no penalties. See also Weights and Penalties.

PENCILLER

This is a very old-fashioned slang term for those bookmakers on the rails between Tattersalls and the Members' Enclosure. Most of their business is credit and the bets are pencilled in a book by the clerk.

PENNYCOMEQUICK

Owned and bred by the late Lord Astor and trained by Joe Lawson, Pennycomequick, by Hurry On out of Plymstock, by Polymelus, won three races, including the Oaks. She bred seven winners, including High Stakes, a gelding that won 32 races worth over £21,000.

PEPPIATT COMMITTEE

The Peppiatt Committee, under the chairmanship of Sir Leslie Peppiatt, a former President of the Law Society, was appointed in 1958 by the Home Secretary "to investigate whether it is desirable and practible that persons engaged in betting on horse races, otherwise than by means of the totalisator, should be required to make a contribution conducive to the improvement of breeds of horses or the sport of horse racing; and if so, to advise on the amount and on the means of securing it." In due course the committee replied that this was indeed both desirable and practicable, their findings forming a most significant milestone in the history of English racing, leading as they did to the levy on betting and the formation of the Betting Levy Board which now plays such a vital part in the sport.

PERDITA II

Bought on behalf of the Prince of Wales, later King Edward VII, by

John Porter for 900 gn, Perdita II bred two Derby winners, Persimmon and Diamond Jubilee.

PERRYMAN, Richard (b 1903)

Dick Perryman was apprenticed to Fred Leader. He became a leading jockey between the wars, winning the One Thousand Guineas three times and the Ascot Gold Cup twice. He started training in 1943 and his most successful phase came just after World War II when he won the St Leger with Chamossaire (1945) and the Derby and St Leger with Airborne (1946). He now lives in Australia.

PERSIAN GULF

A half-brother to Precipitation by Bahram, Persian Gulf won a war-time Coronation Cup and £2,123 in stakes. At the stud he sired Parthia (Derby), Zabara (One Thousand Guineas), Zarathustra (Irish Derby, Irish St Leger, Ascot Stakes, Ascot Gold Cup and Goodwood Cup) and Queen of Sheba (Irish One Thousand and Royal Hunt Cup). He had a more impressive record at the stud than on the racecourse, being third in the sires' list in 1959, fourth in 1952 and fifth in 1951 and 1954.

PERSIMMON

Persimmon was bred by the Prince of Wales, later King Edward VII. By St Simon out of that famous mare Perdita II, he was a full-brother to Diamond Jubilee, winner of the 'Triple Crown' in 1900. He won the Derby and the St Leger in 1896 and the following year the Eclipse Stakes and the Gold Cup. He is the last Epsom Derby winner to have won the Cup. He was a highly successful sire, the best of his offspring being the famous mare Sceptre.

PERSSE, Henry Seymour (1869-1960)

'Atty' Persse was 91 when he died. For roundabout 50 years he was somewhere near the peak of the training profession. When he retired, he remarked in an interview "For nearly 70 years I've had the life of an amateur rider and an owner-trainer and I've loved every minute of it". He once wrote "Good trainers are born, not made. Without natural flair it is far better to keep away from racing stables and run a garage". He himself possessed undoubted flair and could train trainers as well as horses ; among his pupils were his brother-in-law Geoffrey Brooke and Sir Cecil Boyd-Rochfort.

Educated at Cheltenham and Oxford, he was always mad about horses and avoided entry into the family business of whisky distilling by going to America where he rode a lot of winners. He returned to England in 1897 and won the National Hunt Chase on Marpessa. In 1906 he was third in the Grand National on Aunt May. A bad fall at Hurst Park eventually caused his retirement from raceriding and left him lame for life.

He started training in Ireland in 1902. In 1906 he moved to England and in 1908 he bought the Chattis Hill Stables at Stockbridge. Under his skilful direction they became one of the most famous of English racing establishments. As a trainer he was dedicated to his job and a severe disciplinarian. He was fully conscious of his responsibilities to his owners, avowed none to the public, and did not much care for the press. Above all he was a great trainer of two-year-olds and had the happy knack of preparing them so that they were rarely at a disadvantage first time out. "The great thing in training a two-year-old," he wrote, "is to keep its speed, and if it loses it, it must be rested at once". The most famous horse he trained was The Tetrarch, owned by his cousin Major Dermot McCalmont. A grey with curious white markings, hence his nickname of 'The Spotted Wonder', The Tetrarch was never beaten and was probably the fastest horse ever seen on the English Turf.

Persse won the Two Thousand Guineas with Sweeper II, Tetratema and Mr Jinks; and the One Thousand Guineas with Silver Urn. His lucky race was the Kempton Jubilee, which he won on six occasions. One of his Jubilee winners was Bachelor's Double, who also won the Irish Derby, the City and Suburban and the Royal Hunt Cup. Val d'Assa and Queen of Sheba also won the Hunt Cup for the Chattis Hill Stable. Among the many fast two-year-olds that Persse produced were Thyestes, The Satrap, Portlaw, Doctor Dolittle, Queen of the Nore and Lindos Ojos. He won the Stewards Cup with Tetrameter, the Victoria Cup with Sir Archibald and the Yellow Dwarf and the Coronation Cup with Apelle. He could train stayers, too, and landed a very big coup when Sanctum won the Cesarewitch. He also won the Chester Cup with St Mary's Kirk.

It was a great grief to Persse when his son John, whom he had hoped would carry on the stable, was killed in action in Italy. He decided to retire, but eventually gave way to the entreaties of his friends and started up again at Kingsdown, Lambourn. He eventually retired for good on his wife's death in 1953. As he grew older he mellowed considerably and his sense of fun and his skill as a raconteur were a constant delight to all who knew him well. He left £152,000.

PETCH, Major Leslie (b 1900)

Major Petch's first racing appointment was as judge in 1928. He is now Clerk of the Course at York, Redcar and Catterick, having taken up these appointments in 1955, 1946 and 1946 respectively. He has deservedly earned the reputation of being one of the most imaginative and go-ahead officials in the sport today and he certainly possesses a rare flair for publicity.

PETITE ETOILE

Bred by the late Aga Khan and the late Prince Aly Khan, Petite Etoile is a grey by Petition out of the Bois Roussel mare Star of Iran, a descendant of Mumtaz Mahal. Trained by Noel Murless, she proved herself one of the outstanding fillies of this century and between 1958 and 1961 she won 14 races over distances from 5f to 1½m, her victories including the One Thousand Guineas, Oaks, Free Handicap, Sussex Stakes, Yorkshire Oaks, Champion Stakes and the Coronation Cup (twice). She was second to Aggressor in the King George VI and Queen Elizabeth Stakes. Altogether she won over £72,000 in stakes. In training she was high-mettled and often difficult; at the stud she has so far failed to make her mark.

PETITION

Bred and owned by Sir Alfred Butt and trained by Frank Butters, Petition was foaled in 1944 and died 20 years later. By Fair Trial out of Art Paper, by Artist's Proof, he was a top-class two-year-old, winning among other races the New, Gimcrack and Champagne Stakes. The following season he was expected to give the brilliant Tudor Minstrel a hard race in the Two Thousand Guineas, but he slipped up just before the start, and, though it was not apparent at the time, injured himself. He never really recovered his form that season. As a four-year-old he was back to his best and won the Victoria Cup and Eclipse Stakes. A horse of delightful temperament, he made a very good sire, his best winners being the famous Petite Etoile (see above); Pushful, winner of over £27,000; and March Past, winner of over £10,000 and a successful sire. He also got Coronation Year, winner of the Victoria Cup and City and Suburban; and Ocean, winner of the Coronation Stakes.

PHALARIS

Phalaris, owned by the seventeenth Earl of Derby, was by Polymelus out of Bromus, and was foaled in 1913. A high-class middle-distance handicapper, he won 15 races worth over £5,000 during World War I. During his 12 years at the stud he achieved remarkable success and has exerted tremendous influence on modern pedigrees all over the world. His sons included Pharos and Fairway, who were full brothers. Distinguished members of the Phalaris male line include Pharis, Blue Peter, Nearco, Nasrullah, Nimbus, Dante, Royal Charger, Watling Street, Fair Trial, Court Martial, Palestine, Pall Mall, Sayajirao, Petition and many other good horses.

PHARAMOND

Foaled in 1925, Pharamond was owned and bred by the late Lord Derby and was by Phalaris out of Selene, and thus a half-brother to Hyperion. He was a good two-year-old, winning the Middle Park Stakes, but failed to train on. Exported to America, he became a leading sire there.

PHAROS

Owned and bred by the seventeenth Earl of Derby, Pharos was a very good but not a great racehorse. By Phalaris out of Scapa Flow, he was full-brother to Fairway (St Leger) and Fair Isle (One Thousand Guineas). Beaten a length in the Derby by Papyrus in 1923, he ran for four seasons, winning 14 of his 30 races, including the Champion Stakes. He never won beyond 1¼m.

As a sire he was an outstanding success, firstly in England, later in France where he died aged 17. In England his best winners were Cameronian (Two Thousand Guineas and Derby), Firdaussi (St Leger) and Rhodes Scholar (Eclipse Stakes). On the Continent he got Nearco in Italy and Pharis in France, both unbeaten and both winners of the Grand Prix. He was champion sire in England in 1931 and in France in 1935 and 1939.

PHIL DRAKE

Madame Leon Volterra's Phil Drake, by Admiral Drake, won the Derby and the Grand Prix in 1955, a double only previously achieved this century by Spearmint and My Love.

PHILIPPS, Hon James Perrott, TD

Mr Philipps was born in 1905 and served in the Leicestershire Yeomanry, Shropshire Yeomanry and the Royal Artillery. Among many business interests he is Chairman of Tote Investors Ltd. A member of the Jockey Club, he is a steward at Kempton and Ascot and is President of the Thoroughbred Breeders Association. He owns the Dalham Hall Stud, Newmarket, and among the good horses he has bred and owned are Great Nephew (second in the Two Thousand Guineas and a good winner in France); Running Blue (Free Handicap and Lingfield Oaks Trial); Pinzon (Sandringham Stakes, Paradise Stakes and Winston Churchill Stakes) and Lalibela (Cheveley Park Stakes). His horses are trained by Bruce Hobbs in England, Vincent O'Brien in Ireland and by Etienne Pollet in France. Colours: black, white sleeves and sash, halved cap.

PHOTOGRAPH

A 'photograph' under the Rules of Racing is the photograph taken when the horses pass the winning post by the camera installed under the authority of the Stewards of the Jockey Club.

The first finish ('photo-finish') to be decided by the camera was in the Great Metropolitan Stakes at Epsom in 1947.

PICAROON

Foaled in 1922, Picaroon was by Beppo out of Ciceronnetta. Unfortunately he was plagued by ill-health, but there is little doubt that he was a very good colt indeed. Trained by Alec Taylor he won eight races including the Middle Park and Champion Stakes. He died aged four.

PICTURE PLAY

Foaled in 1941, Picture Play was bred and owned by Mr H. J. Joel and was by Donatello II out of Amuse, by Phalaris. She won the One Thousand Guineas. She bred seven winners and is great-grandam of the Derby winner Royal Palace.

PIGGOTT, Lester (b 1935)

Lester Piggott is married to Susan, daughter of the Newmarket trainer F. Armstrong. Racing is in his blood as his father, Keith Piggott, was a capable jumping jockey and subsequently ran a small 'mixed' stable very shrewdly. Lester's grandfather, Ernest Piggott, rode two Grand National winners and married a Miss Cannon, sister of Mornington and Kempton Cannon who both rode Derby winners. As regards the bottom half of his pedigree, Lester's mother was before her marriage a Miss Rickaby, a member of a famous racing family, and sister of Fred and Bill Rickaby.

Lester was apprenticed to his father and rode his first winner at the age of 13. Precociously brilliant as a boy, he managed to survive a period of rather nauseating adulation by the popular press, but rather too frequently fearlessness, coupled with sheer determination to win, degenerated into recklessness and brought him into conflict with the authorities. He rode his first Derby winner, Never Say Die, at the age of 18 and a few weeks later, as the result of his riding of Never Say Die in the King Edward VII Stakes at Ascot, he was suspended for the rest of the meeting and reported to the Stewards of the Jockey Club.

In due course the Stewards of the Jockey Club informed him that "they had taken notice of his dangerous and erratic riding both this season and in previous seasons, and that in spite of continuous warnings, he continued to show complete disregard for the Rules of Racing and for the safety of other jockeys". A statement was then issued that before any application for a renewal of his licence could be entertained—he had been suspended for the rest of the season—he must be attached to some trainer other than his father for six months. The trainer selected was Jack Jarvis, an excellent choice.

Some people took the view that the stewards had been hard on Piggott, but the suspension proved a blessing in the long run and a turning point for the better in his career. It must be emphasised that numerous brushes with authority have never adversely affected his nerve or his confidence, nor have they ever diminished his immense popularity with the general public who readily forgive his indiscretions because his sins are due to a burning ambition to win whatever the cost. Small punters feel he is essentially on their side.

In the course of time he has learnt to temper boldness and dash with respect for the rules and for the necks of his fellow-riders. Furthermore he places far less reliance on the whip than was at one time the case. Tall for a jockey, he rides very short indeed—too short for control, some critics say—and with his behind stuck up in the air, he is easily recognisable even if not particularly elegant. Cool, unimaginative, and in consequence unmoved by the importance of the occasion, he is flexible in his methods and can ride a waiting race, as on Sir Ivor in the 1968 Derby, as effectively as he can force the pace if he considers the occasion is suitable. There is certainly no stronger finisher in the game.

Perhaps because he has always been slightly hard of hearing, he has never been a notable conversationalist but he has the knack of summing up a person or a situation in a few trenchant words. Having been pitchforked into a tough adult world at an early age, he gives the impression of being 'hard-boiled' and unsentimental. He is reputed to be knowledgeable about money and to study the financial columns of the newspapers with close attention. He is certainly a 'character' and stories of his deeds and comments form part of the lore and legend of modern racing. He had a long, successful, though not invariably smooth association with Noel Murless' stable which he elected to terminate in 1967 to ride 'free-lance'. He thus missed winning the Derby on Royal Palace. His best season was in 1966 when he rode 191 winners. He has been Champion Jockey on seven occasions. His classic winners are as follows:

One Thousand Guineas: Humble Duty (1970)

Two Thousand Guineas: Crepello (1957); Sir Ivor (1968); Nijinsky (1970)

Derby: Never Say Die (1954); Crepello (1957); St Paddy (1960); Sir Ivor (1968); Nijinsky (1970)

Oaks: Carozza (1957); Petite Etoile (1959); Valoris (1966)

St Leger: St Paddy (1960); Aurelius (1961); Ribocco (1967); Ribero (1968).

He has won the Irish Sweeps Derby on Meadow Court, Ribocco and Ribero. In 1970 he won the Grand Prix de Paris on Word of Honour.

PILGRIMAGE

This famous mare, by The Earl or The Palmer out of Lady Audley, had high racing ability and in 1878 won the Two Thousand Guineas. At the stud she bred Canterbury Pilgrim, who won the Oaks and was dam of Swynford (St Leger) and other good winners, including Chaucer who did extremely well as a sire. Pilgrimage was also dam of Jeddah (Derby) and Loved One, sire of the dams of the Derby winners Sunstar and Sansovino.

PILLION

Owned and bred by Mr A. de Rothschild, Pillion was foaled in 1923 and was by Chaucer out of Double Back, by Bachelor's Double. Trained by J. Watson, she won three races including the One Thousand Guineas. She was not a success as a brood mare.

PINTURISCHIO

Foaled in 1958, Pinturischio was bred at the Sassoon Studs and is a bay horse by Pinza out of Natalina Da Murano, by Orsenigo. Trained by Noel Murless, he made his first racecourse appearance in the Wood Ditton Stakes as a three-year-old. He won that event and was then fourth in the Two Thousand Guineas in which he started favourite. Shortly before the Derby, for which he was ante-post favourite, he was unfortunately 'got at'. Not only was he unable to run in the Derby, but he never saw a racecourse again. He now stands at the Eve Stud, Wood Ditton, Newmarket, at a fee of £98.

PINZA

Pinza, by Chanteur II, was a big, powerful, slightly coarse bay colt bred by Fred Darling. As a yearling he was bought for 1,500 gn on behalf of Sir Victor Sassoon and was sent to be trained by Norman Bertie at Newmarket. He proved himself a great racehorse at his best, though not perhaps an entirely sound one. He won the 1953 Derby by four lengths, defeating the Queen's colt Aureole and giving Sir Gordon Richards his one and only victory in the Derby. He then won the King George VI and Queen Elizabeth Stakes in equally decisive fashion. Unfortunately he broke down soon afterwards and never ran again. He has not been a success as a sire.

PIPE OF PEACE

Foaled in 1954, Pipe of Peace was bred by the late Major-Gen John Combe and is by Supreme Court out of Red Briar, by Owen Tudor. In the colours of Mr S. Niarchos, he won the Middle Park Stakes and the Greenham Stakes and was third in both the Two Thousand Guineas and the Derby. He was exported for stud purposes to Australia.

PIPER, Edwin (1888-1951)

Edwin Piper won the 1913 Derby on the 100-1 outsider Aboyeur following the disqualification of the favourite Craganour. Piper obtained little riding after World War I and gradually dropped out of the game.

PIRATE KING

Bred and owned by the late Major L. B. Holliday, Pirate King was foaled in 1953 and is by Prince Chevalier out of Netherton Maid by Nearco, being thus a full brother to Pampered King. He won four races worth £8,443, including the St James's Palace Stakes. He went to the stud in Australia in 1958 and his offspring won 242 races there. He returned to England in 1964 and is now the property of a syndicate, standing at the Hanstead Stud, Aylesbury, Buckinghamshire.

PLACK

Plack was foaled in 1921. Bred by the late Lord Rosebery, she was a chestnut by Hurry On and although an inveterate tail-swisher, she was a good, tough, game filly. She won nine races worth over £11,000, including the One Thousand Guineas, Newmarket Oaks and Jockey Club Cup. She was second in the Oaks. She bred four winners of which Afterthought, whom she produced when in her 20th year, won the Jockey Club Cup and was second in the Oaks, Champion Stakes and Gold Cup.

PLAISANTERIE

Foaled in 1882, Plaisanterie, by Wellingtonia, won 16 races and achieved the rare feat of winning the Cesarewitch and Cambridgeshire the same year. She was the grandam of the St Leger winner Tracery.

PLASSY

Plassy was foaled in 1932. Bred by the late Lord Derby, he was by Bosworth out of Pladda, by Phalaris, and proved himself a really good horse, winning six races worth over £9,000, including the Coronation Cup and Jockey Club Stakes. He went to the stud in France and looked like doing well, but unfortunately died young. He sired Nepenthe, winner of the French Gold Cup, and Vandale, who won over two million (old) francs and sired the French Derby winner Herbager, and the French Oaks winner Douave.

PLATE

1. A 'plate' is a race for which a prize or prizes of definite value are guaranteed by the Race-fund, the entrance fee, forfeit, subscription, or other contribution of owners going to the race-fund, subject to the provisions of Rule 159 as to the disposal of surplus. That rule states that any surplus over the advertised value of a plate shall be paid to the credit of the Joint Administrative Authority.

2. A plate is a light shoe worn by a horse for racing. The expression 'to spread a plate' means that the shoe has widened out and protruded from under the horse's foot. Obviously this can be a serious handicap in a race.

PLUCKY LIEGE

One of the greatest mares of this century, Plucky Liège was foaled in 1912 and was by Spearmint out of Concertina, by St Simon. Bred by Lord Michelham, for whom she won four two-year-old races worth £1,811, she was first called Lucky Liège but this was changed on account of her owner's admiration for the defence of Liège in 1914.

Plucky Liège went to the stud in France. The first of her offspring of any note was Sir Gallahad III, by Teddy. His successes included the French Two Thousand Guineas and the Lincolnshire Handicap. For two years he was at the stud in France and while there sired Galaday II, dam of the One Thousand Guineas and Oaks winner Galatea II, and great-grandam of the Derby and St Leger winner Never Say Die. Sir Gallahad III then went to America, where he was an outstanding success and was champion sire four times.

Bull Dog and Quatre Bras were full brothers of Sir Gallahad III and like him they both went to America. Bull Dog did almost as well as a sire there as his elder brother and Bull Lea, by

Bull Dog, was champion sire five times, the best of his offspring being Citation, who won over a million dollars. Quatre Bras, who won 10 races in America besides winning in France, did well as a sire, too, but his achievements were not on a par with those of his brothers.

Plucky Liège's son Bel Aethel, owned by the Duke of Norfolk, was of small account, but Admiral Drake, by Craig an Eran, won the Grand Prix de Paris and sired the Derby winner Phil Drake.

Plucky Liège also bred the winners Marguerite de Valois, Chivalry, Elsa de Brabant, Noble Lady and Noor Jahan, while at the advanced age of 23 she produced Bois Roussel, by Vatout, who won the Derby in 1938 and was champion sire in 1949.

It would be difficult to exaggerate the influence Plucky Liège has had on bloodstock breeding all over the world.

POGROM

Pogrom, foaled in 1919, was bred by the late Lord Astor and was by Lemberg out of Popingoal, by Dark Ronald. Trained by Alec Taylor, she won the Oaks, Newmarket Oaks and Coronation Stakes. Her half-sister, Book Law, was second in the Oaks and won the St Leger.

POLEMARCH

Foaled in 1918, Polemarch was bred and owned by Lord Londonderry and was by The Tetrarch out of Pomace, by Polymelus. Trained by Tom Green, he won five races including the St Leger. He was one of three St Leger winners sired by The Tetrarch. He was exported to the Argentine and did well as a sire there.

POLLET, Etienne

Etienne Pollet is one of the outstanding French trainers of the post-war era. His successes in England include the Derby (Sea Bird), Two Thousand Guineas (Thunderhead II), One Thousand Guineas and Oaks (Never Too Late II), King George VI and Queen Elizabeth Stakes (Right Royal V), Ascot Gold Cup (Pan II), One Thousand Guineas and Champion Stakes (Hula Dancer).

POLYMELUS

Polymelus, by Cyllene, was a very good middle-distance horse that was suspected of not being a genuine stayer. In 1906 Mr S. B. Joel bought Polymelus, then a four-year-old, at the Newmarket October Sales for 4,000 gn. Before that season was over Polymelus won the Duke of York Stakes at Kempton, and then, with a 10lb penalty, the Cambridgeshire. He was a hot favourite for the Cambridgeshire and Mr Joel and his friends won £100,000 in bets. As a sire Polymelus was an outstanding success. He was five times champion and got three Derby winners, Pommern, Fifinella and Humorist. However, his immense influence on thoroughbred breeding today comes through the handicapper Phalaris, sire of Fairway and Pharos.

POLYPHONTES

Foaled in 1921, Polyphontes was owned and bred by Mr S. B. Joel and was by Polymelus out of St Josephine, by St Denis. He won four races worth over £26,000, including the Eclipse Stakes twice and the Ascot Derby. He proved a moderate sire.

POMMERN

Pommern, by Polymelus, owned by Mr S. B. Joel and trained by C. Peck, won a war-substitute 'Triple Crown' in 1915. He was not a stud success.

PONTEFRACT

Set in country-side that has suffered greatly through industrialisation, Pontefract is one of the minor Yorkshire meetings. It has a long history, though, and racing is known to have taken place there during the Civil War. In fact in March 1644, a fortnight before the royalist stronghold of Pontefract Castle, "the key to the north", surrendered to the Roundheads, a race-

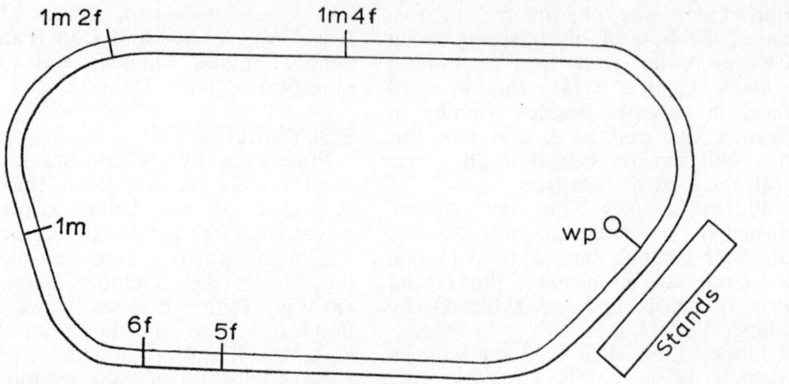

PONTEFRACT

meeting was held there. In 1649 Pontefract Castle, which for six hundred years had played its part in English history, was razed to the ground at the request of the prudent citizens of Pontefract who had conveniently changed from support of Charles I to support of Cromwell. Today Pontefract seems to be mainly noted for the manufacture of 'Liquorice Allsorts'

The track is left-handed, $1\frac{1}{2}$m round with a sharp bend into the 2f straight. It is noticeably undulating but the final 3f are uphill, rendering the course quite a test of stamina, particularly for two-year-olds. Low numbers are best in the draw, particularly in sprint races. With a good draw, though, a swift start is essential to avoid being cut off as the runners crowd over to the rails.

Clerk of the Course: Col C. Egerton MC, TD, Russell House, Russell St, Stockton-on-Tees. Tel: Stockton-on-Tees 67154

Best Times:

Distance	*Horse-Age-Weight*	*Date*	*Time*
5f	Young Vigorous 5-7-13	19/6/52	62
5f	High Table 2-8-13	28/5/65	62.8
6f	Burning Bow 3-8-12	5/7/41	1min 14.8
6f	Janie Dawnay 2-9-0	2/10/47	1min 15
8f	Nevison's Lad 5-8-12	14/5/65	1min 41.4
8f	Gulf of Happiness 2-8-5	2/10/53	1min 45.4
10f	Good Sport 4-7-12	7/8/44	2min 11.2
12f	Tehran Court 4-7-11	24/9/64	2min 36

PONT L'EVEQUE

Foaled in 1937, Pont l'Eveque was bred by Mr H. E. Morriss and was by the Grand Prix winner Barneveldt out of Ponteba, by Belfonds. Ponteba, carrying Pont l'Eveque, was imported from France by Mr Morriss in 1936. Trained by Fred Darling, Pont l'Eveque was a moderate two-year-old and at the end of the season Mr Morriss asked Darling to find a buyer. Darling decided to take a chance and bought the colt himself for £500.

Pont l'Eveque did well physically during the winter and won a race at Newbury in the spring with singular ease. Darling then cabled to Mr Morriss, who was in the Far East, offering him a half share in Pont l'Eveque for 2,500 gn. Perhaps not surprisingly under the circumstances, Mr Morriss did not reply. Pont l'Eveque was beaten in the Newmarket

Stakes, but starting at 10-1 and ridden by Sam Wragg, he won the Derby, run at Newmarket, by three lengths.

In his only other race Pont l'Eveque was third in the Champion Stakes. In 1942 he was exported to the Argentine but did only moderately as a sire there.

POPE, Major Michael Brownfield, MC (b 1917)

Major Michael Pope served in the Royal Horse Guards and the North Irish Horse during World War II. He began training in 1947 and his stables are at Streatley, Berkshire. He has won the Wokingham Stakes with Golden Leg, the Great Metropolitan with Luxury Hotel, and the Queen's Prize with Royal Ridge. He also trained that game and consistent handicapper Birdbrook. Among his owners are Lord Shrewsbury, Sir Edwin and Lady McAlpine, Mr A. B. Pope, Mr C. G. Glover, Mr Guy Smith and Mrs J. F. C. Bryce.

PORCHESTER, Lord (b 1924)

Lord Porchester served in the Royal Horse Guards. He is a member of the Jockey Club and a steward at Ascot and Windsor. The best horse he has so far owned is Tamerlane, whom he bought for 5,000 gn and whose victories included the New Stakes, July Stakes and St James's Palace Stakes. In the autumn of 1969 Lord Porchester was appointed Racing Manager to the Queen. His trainer is J. M. Clayton. Colours: Eton blue, black hooped cap.

PORTER, John (b 1938)

Born at Rugeley, John Porter was one of the greatest trainers of the Victorian era. He trained Blue Gown, Shotover, St Blaise, Ormonde, Sainfoin, Common and Flying Fox to win the Derby and he had 16 other classic successes as well. At one time he trained for the Prince of Wales, later King Edward VII. Honest, conscientious and hardly noted for his humour, he was largely instrumental in planning the construction of Newbury racecourse (q.v.).

R

PORTLAND, fourth Duke of (d 1854)

The fourth Duke of Portland won the 1819 Derby with Tiresias. When he died in 1854, he had been a member of the Jockey Club for over 50 years. In 1831 he advanced money to the Jockey Club for the purchase at Newmarket of the Coffee Room, New Rooms and adjuncts. He owned part of Newmarket Heath and did much work at his own expense to improve the Heath as a racing centre. Furthermore he bought land surrounding the Heath in case it should ever fall into the hands of persons hostile to racing.

In 1827 he was instrumental in establishing the Jockey Club's right to warn allegedly undesirable individuals off Newmarket Heath. There was a disputed bet, and the Jockey Club's decision on that matter greatly displeased a certain Mr Hawkins who showed his feelings in a somewhat uncouth manner by swearing horribly at Lord Wharncliffe. The Jockey Club thereupon warned him off the Heath. Mr Hawkins fought back gamely and brought an action against the Jockey Club. The case was defended by the Duke of Portland on behalf of the Club, and the Club's right to the action taken against Mr Hawkins was upheld by the judge.

Nowadays the Jockey Club takes no cognisance of betting disputes which are settled by Tattersalls' Committee.

PORTLAND, sixth Duke of (1856-1942)

The sixth Duke of Portland was an ensign in the Coldstream Guards when he succeeded to a title and a fortune in 1879. He at once decided to revive the glories of the Welbeck Stud and wisely chose Matt Dawson as his trainer. On Dawson's advice he bought St Simon at the sale of Prince Batthyany's horses for 1,600 gn. St Simon was undefeated on the racecourse but owing to the rule then existing he could not run in the classics owing to the death of his nominator, Prince Batthyany. There has never been a greater stallion than St Simon who was champion sire on nine occasions.

Nor did the Duke's luck end with St Simon, as between 1884 and 1902 he won 14 classics and two Ascot Gold Cups. He won the Two Thousand Guineas with Ayrshire (1888); the One Thousand Guineas with Semolina (1890) and Aimiable (1894); the Derby with Ayrshire (1888) and Donovan (1889); the Oaks with Memoir (1890), Mrs Butterwick (1893), Aimiable (1894) and La Roche (1900); and the St Leger with Donovan (1889) and Memoir (1890). His Gold Cup winners were St Simon (1884) and William the Third (1902).

With the turn of the century the Duke's luck began to run out. He lost his enthusiasm for the Turf and his colours were seldom seen in the last 27 years of his life. He was 86 when he died in 1942. A generous, friendly and straightforward man, he dispersed much of the prize money he won on the Turf in charity.

PORTLAND HANDICAP

See under Doncaster.

PORTLAW

Foaled in 1928, Portlaw was a grey by Beresford out of Portree, by Stefan the Great. Extremely fast, he won nine races worth over £10,000, including the Champagne and Middle Park Stakes. He did quite well as a sire, among his stock being the sprinter Portobello who won 14 races. Portlaw also sired the dams of Pall Mall and Sing Sing.

POST

'Post' is a slightly muddling term for newcomers to racing as it is used to denote both the start and the finish. "Going down to the post" means a horse is cantering down to the start; while "got his head in front on the post" denotes a horse taking the lead just as it passes the winning post.

POURPARLER

Bred by Cmdr Peter Fitzgerald, Pourparler was foaled in 1961 and is by Hugh Lupus out of Review, by Panorama, and she is thus a half-sister to Fleet (Cheveley Park Stakes, One Thousand Guineas and Coronation Stakes) and to Display (National Stakes and Coronation Stakes). Owned by Beatrice, Lady Granard and trained by Paddy Prendergast, Pourparler won the National Stakes, Lowther Stakes and One Thousand Guineas and in all over £38,000 in prize money.

POWELL, Patrick (b 1928)

Paddy Powell junior is the son of Paddy Powell who was a well-known Irish rider under National Hunt rules in the 1920s. Paddy Powell junior served his apprenticeship firstly with R. More O'Ferrall and then with R. Warden. He has been a leading rider in Ireland for many years both on the flat and over hurdles, among the races he has won being the Irish Derby, Irish St Leger and Galway Hurdle.

PRATT, William Archer (1877-1957)

Willie Pratt was the son of the Cheltenham trainer Francis Platt, whose wife was Fred Archer's sister. Willie was apprenticed to James Ryan at Newmarket and when he was 14 he dead-heated for the Cesarewitch on Red Eyes. Fifty years later he trained Whiteway to win the Cesarewitch.

When still a boy he was appointed jockey to the powerful Rothschild stable in France and between 1898 and 1903 he rode the winner of the Grand Prix on four occasions. In 1904 he was appointed trainer to M. Jean Stern and trained in France with success till 1940 when he returned to England and set up a small stable. During Walter Earl's serious illness in

1949, he took charge of the Stanley House stable and prepared that great stayer to win the Goodwood and Doncaster Cups.

PRATT & Co.

Pratt and Company, now managed by Mr B. E. Robinson, Mr H. C. Clifton and Mr D. Hubbard, run Alexandra Park, Cheltenham, Folkestone, Fontwell Park and Plumpton racecourses. Cheltenham, Fontwell and Plumpton only stage racing under National Hunt rules.

PRECIPITATION

Owned and bred by Lady Zia Wernher, Precipitation was by Hurry On out of that very successful brood mare Double Life, who had won the Cambridgeshire. Precipitation did not run as a two-year-old or compete in the classics, but he was a top-class racehorse, his successes including the King Edward VII Stakes at Ascot, the Jockey Club Stakes at Newmarket and the Ascot Gold Cup. He ensured the survival of the Hurry On male line by siring Chamossaire, who won the 1945 St Leger and sired the Derby winner Santa Claus. Besides Chamossaire, Precipitation sired Airborne (Derby and St Leger), Premonition (St Leger), Why Hurry (Oaks) and Sheshoon (Gold Cup). He died in 1957.

PREDOMINATE

Foaled in 1952, Predominate was bred by Mr J. McCutcheon and was by Preciptic out of Garryhinch, by Great Scot. As a yearling he was bought in Dublin for 1,150 gn by Ken Cundell acting for Mrs G. Trimmer-Thompson. For her he won five races worth £2,580 at two, three and four years of age. He then went hurdling, winning two races. The following year Mr H. J. Joel bought him as a hurdling prospect. But Predominate did not really like hurdling and eventually it was decided to keep him for the flat. Trained by Ted Leader, he was second in the Cesarewitch—he had been third in that race for his previous owner—and won the Queen Alexandra Stakes, the Goodwood Stakes three years running, and at nine years of age the coveted Goodwood Cup. He had thus won an important race at the big Goodwood meeting four years in succession. The Cup was his final race. In all, this gallant old gelding had won 14 races and over £17,000 in prize money.

PREMONITION

Foaled in 1950, Premonition was bred by the Dunchurch Lodge Stud and is by Precipitation out of Trial Ground, by Fair Trial. Owned by Brig W. P. Wyatt and trained by Capt C. Boyd-Rochfort he won eight races worth over £27,000, including the St Leger, Blue Riband Trial Stakes, Voltigeur Stakes, Winston Churchill Stakes and Yorkshire Cup. He also won the Irish Derby but was disqualified, unjustifiably so in the opinion of most of those who saw the race. He started joint favourite for the Epsom Derby with Pinza, but ran disappointingly. He has not been a success as a sire.

PRENDERGAST, P. J.

Paddy Prendergast was not born with a silver spoon in his mouth and this great Irish trainer certainly came up the hard way. Before World War II he was a minor steeplechase jockey riding for the most part mediocre horses at second class meetings. It would have been impossible at that stage to visualise his becoming one of the world's greatest trainers.

After the war he got his chance as a trainer and seized it with both hands. For the past 20 years his career has been one of almost unbroken success except for one rather sharp brush with the English racing authorities. One of the main reasons for this swift climb to fame is his skill in picking yearlings, and two very fast two-year-olds that helped to make his name, The Pie King and Windy City, were by no means fashionably bred. For some years now, however, he has had a number of wealthy American patrons who have been able to pay top prices at the sales. His owners include Lady Granard, Lord and Lady Elveden, Mr G. M. Bell, Mr B. Crosby, Mr C. Clore, Mr L. M. Gelb, Mr and Mrs J. R. Mullion, Mrs Parker Poe, Mr and Mrs J. M. Olin, Mr M. Rayne and Col W. Stirling.

His big winners in England so far are as follows:

Two Thousand Guineas: Martial (1960)
One Thousand Guineas: Pourparler (1964)
Oaks: Noblesse (1963)
St Leger: Ragusa (1963)
Chester Cup: Credo (1964)
Coventry Stakes: The Pie King (1953); Typhoon (1960); Young Emperor (1965); Bold Lad (1966); Prince Tenderfoot (1969)
Queen Mary Stakes: Paddy's Sister (1959); Grizel (1968)
National Breeders Produce Stakes (now the National Stakes): Display (1961); Whistling Wind (1962); Pourparler (1963)
Eclipse Stakes: Khalkis (1963); Ragusa (1964)
King George VI and Queen Elizabeth Stakes: Ragusa (1963); Meadow Court (1965)
Sussex Stakes: Carlemont (1965)
Gimcrack Stakes: Windy City (1951); The Pie King (1953); Paddy's Sister (1959); Young Emperor (1965)
Champagne Stakes: Paddy's Sister (1959); Hardicanute (1964); Bold Lad (1968)
Middle Park Stakes: Bold Lad (1966)
Cheveley Park Stakes: Sixpence (1963); Display (1961)
Observer Gold Cup: Noblesse (1962); Hardicanute (1964).

PRESS GANG

Foaled in 1927, Press Gang was bred by Lord Woolavington and was a superbly bred chestnut by Hurry On out of Fifinella, winner of the Derby and the Oaks. He was not entirely reliable but won over £10,000 in stakes, his successes including the Middle Park Stakes and the Princess of Wales's Stakes. He was a failure as a sire and was exported to Russia.

PRETENDER

Mr J. Johnstone's Pretender, trained by Tom Dawson at Tupgill, won the Derby in 1869. No north-country horse has won the Epsom Derby since, though Dante won a war-substitute Derby at Newmarket in 1945.

PRETENDRE

Bred by the late Princess Royal, Pretendre is by Doutelle out of Limicola, by Verso II, and was bought as a foal in 1964 for 3,600 gn by Mr J. A. C. Lilley, who sent him to be trained by Jack Jarvis. A big, impressive chestnut, Pretendre made immense improvement during the course of his two-year-old career. At first it was thought that he was nothing out of the ordinary but in the autumn it became apparent that he was a stayer of high promise and he won the Dewhurst Stakes and the *Observer* Gold Cup. The following year he started off in great style with an impressive win in the Blue Riband Trial at Epsom but in the Two Thousand Guineas he found the pace too fast over a distance rather too short for him and he finished unplaced. However, he ran the race of his life in the Derby in which, ridden by Paul Cook, he was only beaten a neck by Charlottown. He won the King Edward VII Stakes at Ascot, was third in the Eclipse Stakes but disappointed in the St Leger in which he was unplaced behind Sodium. At the end of the season he was sold for a big price through the British Bloodstock Agency to the American owner Mr Bunker Hunt, and stood in Lexington, USA. In 1969 he returned to this country for one season before being transferred to New Zealand.

PRETTY POLLY

Pretty Polly, one of the great fillies of English racing history, was foaled in 1901. Bred in Ireland by Major Eustace Loder, she was a big, powerful chestnut by Gallinule (who had gone wrong in his wind and was inclined to break bloodvessels), out of Admiration, by Saraband. Admiration was a very modest performer; she won two minor events on the flat in Ireland and was placed in a military steeplechase at Punchestown.

Pretty Polly went to Newmarket to be trained by Peter Gilpin. At first she gave out little promise and was very sluggish in her work but gradually she began to improve. Even so it came as a surprise to her trainer when she won her first race, the International Stakes at Sandown, by 10 lengths. Before the season was over she was the idol of the racing public, winning eight more races including the National Breeders Produce Stakes, the Champagne Stakes, the Cheveley Park Stakes and the Middle Park Stakes. Not once was she in danger of defeat.

The following season she won the One Thousand Guineas, the Oaks, the Coronation Stakes at Ascot, the Nassau Stakes at Goodwood, the St Leger and the Park Hill Stakes. At that point Major Loder decided he would like her to take on the best horses in France so she was sent over to Paris to run in the Prix du Conseil Municipal at Longchamp. She had a bad train journey and to the consternation of the racing world, she was beaten by the unconsidered Presto II. Danny Maher, who rode her, said that although she had won the St Leger in record time, she was not in fact a true stayer. The Paris race was over 1½m.

On her return to England, Pretty Polly won the Free Handicap, giving weight and a beating to the Derby winner St Amant.

As a four-year-old she was unbeaten, winning the Coronation Cup, Champion Stakes, Limekiln Stakes and Jockey Club Cup. As a five-year-old she won the Coronation Cup and the March Stakes but in the Ascot Gold Cup, her final race, she was beaten a length by Bachelor's Button. She was not quite at her best that day and in addition her rider, Bernard Dillon, lost his head and disobeyed orders. Possibly the distance was a shade too far for her, too. Altogether she won 22 of her 24 races and over £37,000 in stakes.

She was too highly strung and nervous to make an ideal brood mare and she was not a good mother with the result that her offspring were inclined to be delicate when young. She never produced anything half as good as herself, but one daughter, Molly Desmond, won the Cheveley Park Stakes, and another, Polly Flinders, the National Breeders Produce Stakes. However, her stud reputation has been ensured by the many glittering successes won by later descendants. She died in 1931.

PRICE, Capt H. Ryan (b 1912)

Ryan Price began training in 1937 but it was only after World War II, in which he served with the Commandos, that he became well known to the public. He made his reputation as a jumping trainer and he has won almost every big race under National Hunt rules, but in recent years his interests have veered more and more towards the flat. He has certainly had some big successes on the flat, winning the Cesarewitch with Utrillo, Persian Lancer and Major Rose, the Chester Cup with Major Rose, the Queen's Prize with Eborneezer, the Manchester November Handicap with Chief Barker, the Ascot Stakes with Lexicon and the National Stakes with Quarryknowe. In 1970 Price handed over all his jumpers to the care of Josh Gifford and announced his intention of concentrating in future on the flat.

PRIMERA

Foaled in 1954, Primera was bred by HH Maharaja Gaekwar of Baroda and is by My Babu out of Pirette, by Deiri. He raced until he was six and improved with age. Altogether he won eight races worth over £18,000, including the Churchill Stakes, Ormonde Stakes, Princess of Wales's Stakes (twice) and Ebor Handicap with 9st. In 1959 he was close up fifth in the Prix de l'Arc de Triomphe. As a sire he has not been consistent but he sired two very good fillies in Aunt Edith (Nassau Stakes, Prix Vermeille, Yorkshire Cup and King George VI and Queen Elizabeth Stakes), and Greengage (Coronation Stakes and over £18,000 in stakes). In 1969 he was exported to Japan. In 1970 his daughter Lupe won the Oaks.

PRINCE CHEVALIER

Foaled in France in 1943, Prince Chevalier was a handsome bay colt by Prince Rose out of Chevalerie, by Abbot's Speed. He was a top-class performer, winning the French Derby and finishing second in the Grand Prix, the French St Leger and the Prix de l'Arc de Triomphe. Brought to England as a sire, he got the 1951 Derby winner Arctic Prince. Other good winners he sired were Doutelle, whose early death was such a loss to breeders, and Court Harwell, sire of the Irish Sweeps Derby winner Meadow Court. His best winner in France was Charlottesville, who won the French Derby and the Grand Prix, and sired the 1966 Derby winner Charlottown.

PRINCELY GIFT

Foaled in 1951, Princely Gift was bred by Mr A. E. Allnat and is a bay horse by Nasrullah out of Blue Gem, by Blue Peter. Trained by Noel Murless and owned by Sir Victor Sassoon, he proved a high-class sprinter, winning nine races and over £6,000 in stakes. His best performance was to win the Portland Handicap with 9st 4lb. The property of a syndicate, he stands at Old Connell Stud, Newbridge, Co Kildare, and has done consistently well as a sire. Among his winners are Frankincense (£12,836), Tesco Boy (£10,090), Jadeite (£9,259), Berber (£8,959), Caterina (£8,117), Alcan (£7,715), Faberge II (£7,610), So Blessed (£7,589), Kings Troop (£6,690) and Floribunda (£6,668).

PRINCE PALATINE

Foaled in 1908, Prince Palatine was the best racing son of a great sire in Persimmon and one of the finest stayers seen on the English Turf this century. Bred by Lord Wavertree and owned for most of his racing career by Mr T. R. Pilkington, he was not an entirely taking horse in appearance, being a very bad walker—he suffered intermittently from foot trouble—and always had an untidy mane and tail. He sometimes ran unaccountably badly, probably on account of his feet, but on his day he was the best stayer in the world.

Trained by Beardsley at Whatcombe, he won 11 races worth over £36,000 including the St Leger, Eclipse Stakes, Ascot Gold Cup (twice), Coronation Cup, Jockey Club Stakes and Doncaster Cup. In 1913 Mr J. B. Joel created a sensation by buying Prince Palatine for £45,000 just before the big Goodwood meeting. Prince Palatine was started in the Goodwood Cup, but owing to foot trouble was quite unfit to run. Towards the finish, he was staggering from sheer exhaustion and the race undoubtedly broke his heart.

Perhaps because of his terrible Goodwood ordeal, Prince Palatine was not a success as a sire, his career being divided between England, France and the United States before he was burnt to death at the age of 16 in America. However, when in England he got Rose Prince (Cesarewitch and Alexandra Stakes) who carried on the sire line through Prince Rose, Prince Chevalier, Arctic Prince and Princequillo.

PRINCE REGENT

Bred in 1966 by the Comtesse de la Valdene and owned by her, Prince Regent is a dark brown colt by Right Royal V out of Noduleuse, by Nosca. Trained at Chantilly by E. Pollet, he won twice as a two-year-old, once over 9f, and as a three-year-old swiftly proved his merit by victories in the Prix Greffulhe and the Prix Lupin. His trainer confidently expected him to win the Derby and he certainly ought to have done so but Deforge unfortunately rode an ill-judged race and Prince Regent, despite making a remarkable late run from the rear of the field, could only finish third to Blakeney and Shoemaker. However, he earned a nice consolation prize in the Irish Sweeps Derby, which he won in great style, admirably ridden by Geoff Lewis and showing terrific acceleration in the final furlong to overhaul Ribofilio who had looked all over a winner. He finished fifth in the Prix de l'Arc de Triomphe, beating all the other three-year-olds in that race.

PRINCE SIMON

Owned and bred by Mr William Woodward, chairman for many years of the New York Jockey Club, Prince Simon was an exceptionally handsome colt trained at Newmarket by Capt Cecil Boyd-Rochfort. Favourite for the Two Thousand Guineas, Prince Simon failed by a short head to catch Palestine. A hot favourite for the Derby, he was beaten a head by a not particularly good French colt in Galcador. In the King Edward VII Stakes at Ascot he started at 8-1 on and got beaten. He never ran again. His stud career proved a fiasco.

PRINCESS DORRIE

Owned and bred by Mr J. B. Joel, Princess Dorrie was bred in 1911 and was by Your Majesty, not on the whole a success as a sire, out of Doris, by Loved One. She won two races, the One Thousand Guineas and the Oaks. She was not a success at the stud.

PRIVY COUNCILLOR

Owned and bred by Major Gerald Glover, Privy Councillor was foaled in 1959 and is a chestnut horse by Counsel out of High Number, by His Highness. Trained by Tom Waugh, he was nothing out of the ordinary as a two-year-old, winning races at Birmingham, Leicester and Warwick. He made immense improvement, though, and the following season after winning the Free Handicap with 8st 4lb, he won the Two Thousand Guineas by three lengths, starting at 100-6 and ridden by W. Rickaby. The rest of his career was an anti-climax and he did not win again. After some years at the stud in this country, he was exported to Japan.

PRIZE MONEY

At all levels, prize money is substantially higher in the USA and in France than it is in England. In other parts of the world, the level is much the same or not as high as in England, but in many cases the owners' expenses are less and the quality of the bloodstock much lower. It must be remembered, though, that in most overseas countries a Tote monopoly exists and in consequence a far higher proportion of the profits from betting are ploughed back into the sport. Where bookmakers do exist abroad they tend to be strictly controlled and sharply taxed. In America racecourse attendances are boosted by the fact that all off-course betting is illegal.

In Britain, racecourse executives are responsible for the provision of the prize money offered in the races they stage after taking into account the money provided by owners in the form of entry fees and forfeits. In recent years, increased wages, costs and taxation have imposed heavy burdens on racecourses and owners alike with the result that racecourses have been unable to raise prize money to an adequate level. On the other hand it is unrealistic to expect owners to face the heavy costs of maintaining horses in training without increased prize money. Although it is true that prize money has increased over the past 25 years, it has failed to keep pace with the increase in costs, let alone with the marked drop in the purchasing power of the pound.

PROVOKE

Bred and owned by Mr J. J. Astor, Provoke was a bay horse by Aureole out of Tantalizer, by Tantième. He took plenty of time to come to hand when sent to be trained by Dick Hern but he made rapid improvement as a three-year-old and at Doncaster, in torrential rain and on heavy going, he defeated the 11-4 on favourite Meadow Court by 10 lengths and won the 1965 St Leger at 28-1.

He did not run again that season. The following year he contracted a virus infection that afflicted his stable and was unable to run. He was then sold for export to Russia but died soon after his arrival there.

PSIDIUM

Mrs A. Plesch's Psidium, trained by Harry Wragg and ridden by R. Poincelet, won the Derby in 1961 at 66-1. As he never ran again, it is a moot point whether he was a very good horse or whether his victory was one of those curious flukes that sometimes happen in racing. The best horse he has so far sired is the rather inconsistent Sodium, who won the 1966 St Leger and the Irish Derby.

Psidium's Derby victory was an example of the international character of modern racing. Bred in Ireland, Psidium is by the French-bred sire Pardal out of Dinarella, who was bred in Italy. Mrs Plesch is the wife of a Hungarian-born financier, Harry Wragg is English and Poincelet French. Psidium is syndicated and stands at the Cheveley Park Stud, Newmarket.

PUNTER

A slang term for anyone foolish enough to bet on horse-racing.

Q

QUASHED

During the past hundred years only five fillies or mares have won the Gold Cup at Ascot. These are Brigantine (1869), Apology (1876), La Fleche (1894), Quashed (1936) and Gladness (1958). Quashed also won the Oaks and is the only winner of that race, bar the American-bred Cap and Bells, who is ineligible for inclusion in the Stud Book. Foaled in 1932, Quashed was bred by Lady Barbara Smith and was by Quashed out of that good mare Verdict, winner of the Cambridgeshire and the Coronation Cup. Verdict was doubly half-bred as both her sire and her dam were thus classified.

Quashed was leased for racing to Lord Stanley who sent her to be trained by Colledge Leader. Tall and leggy, she took a long time to come to hand and her first victory was in a modest event at Gatwick only three weeks before the Oaks, in which, ridden by H. Jellis, she was friendless in the market at 33-1. However, running on with immense determination, she got up in the final stride to beat Ankaret by a short head, with the hot favourite Mesa, indifferently ridden by Johnstone, close up third. Later in the season she won the Prince Edward Handicap at Manchester and the Jockey Club Cup.

She was kept in training as a four-year-old with the Gold Cup as her main objective. She dead-heated for the Great Metropolitan, won the Ormonde Stakes at Chester, and then crowned her career by winning a tremendous battle for the Gold Cup, defeating the American horse Omaha by inches. It was a gruelling contest and she thoroughly deserved the tribute paid to her by Mr Somerville Tattersall—"the gamest mare of all time". The race took a lot out of her though, tough as she was, and she was never the same again although she won the Jockey Club Cup for the second time in the autumn. She ran in the Gold Cup again the following year but could only finish third. Altogether she won over £18,000 in stakes. Unfortunately she was a stud failure and never bred a winner.

QUEEN ALEXANDRA STAKES

See under Ascot.

QUEEN ELIZABETH II STAKES

See under Ascot.

QUEEN MARY STAKES

See under Ascot.

QUEENPOT

Queenpot, foaled in 1945, was bred and owned by Sir Percy Loraine and trained by Noel Murless. By Big Game out of Poker Chip, by The Recorder, she won five races including the One Thousand Guineas. She bred six winners, but not one of any consequence.

QUEEN OF SHEBA

Foaled in 1948, Queen of Sheba was owned and bred by Major D. McCalmont and trained by H. S. Persse. By Persian Gulf out of Ojala, by Buen Ojo, she won the Irish One Thousand Guineas, the Cheshire Oaks and the Royal Hunt Cup. She bred nine winners, of which the best were Menelek and Jibuti.

QUEEN'S HUSSAR

Foaled in 1960, Queen's Hussar was bred and owned by Lord Carnarvon and trained by 'Atty' Corbett. By March Past out of Jojo, by Vilmorin, he won seven races, including the Sussex and Lockinge Stakes, and over £21,000 in prize money. He stands at his owner's Highclere Stud, Berkshire, at a fee of £250.

QUEEN'S VASE

See under ASCOT.

QUINTESSENCE

Foaled in 1900, Lord Falmouth's Quintessence, trained by Chandler, won the One Thousand Guineas and was never beaten. By St Frusquin out of Margarine, she was dam of Clarissimus who won the Two Thousand Guineas and did extremely well as a sire in France. He sired the dams of Donatello II and Pharis.

QUISLING

This smart Irish sprinter, foaled in 1961, raced until he was six and won ten races worth over £7,000. By High Treason out of Lake Lavandou, by Le Lavandou, he stands at the Athgarvan Stud, Co Kildare, at a fee of £98.

QUORUM

Foaled in 1954 Quorum was bred and owned by Mr T. H. Farr and trained by Col W. Lyde. A handsome grey by the sprinter Vilmorin out of Akimbo by the Derby winner Bois Roussel, he was a very good horse up to a mile, winning the Free Handicap, Jersey Stakes and Sussex Stakes and finishing second to Crepello in the Two Thousand Guineas. He is now owned by the Littleton Stud, Winchester, and stands there at a fee of £300. He has sired a lot of winners and many of them stay remarkably well, as for example Beddard (Queen's Vase), Quartette (Vaux Gold Tankard) and Casting Vote (Bass and Worthington Bowl and Lanark Silver Bell). He is also sire of the speedy Quarryknowe, winner of the National Stakes in 1969.

R

RABELAIS

Rabelais, by St Simon, was foaled in 1900 and was placed in the Two Thousand Guineas and the Derby, besides winning the Goodwood Cup. He was sold to France for £900 and though he was very much on the small side he proved a sire of the highest order. His influence is immense as the St Simon line, pre-eminent at the turn of the century, was on the point of extinction in England so swiftly had it declined, and it was sustained only by the Rabelais line in France. Rabelais, who lived till his thirtieth year, sired the Derby winner Durbar II. From Rabelais, too, the mighty Ribot is descended, while Rabelais is also the grandsire of Nogara, dam of Nearco.

RACECOURSE

All the racecourses in Great Britain on which flat racing takes place have individual entries. The complete list is as follows:

Alexandra Park
Ascot
Ayr
Bath
Beverley
Brighton
Carlisle
Catterick
Chepstow
Chester
Doncaster
Edinburgh
Epsom
Folkestone
Goodwood
Hamilton Park
Haydock
Kempton
Lanark
Leicester
Lingfield
Liverpool
Newbury
Newcastle
Newmarket
Nottingham
Pontefract
Redcar
Ripon
Salisbury
Sandown
Teesside Park
Thirsk
Warwick
Windsor
Wolverhampton
Yarmouth
York

RACECOURSE ASSOCIATION

The object of the Racecourse Association Ltd is to consider all questions affecting the welfare of racecourse owners and to watch over all matters affecting their rights. The Association is constituted in three areas, Northern, Midland and Southern, and its membership includes all racecourses conducted under the Rules of Racing.

RACECOURSE HOLDINGS TRUST

Racecourse Holdings Trust Ltd was formed in 1964 and was originally set up to take over Cheltenham racecourse. The trust is a non-profit making company, whose directors receive no fees, and it is supported by the Levy Board which services the loans required or provides the necessary capital at a lower rate of interest than is obtainable in the open market. The trust's object is to acquire at a fair and agreed price the shares in racecourse companies, the shareholders of which are prepared to sell their shares. The trust's latest acquisitions are Epsom and Sandown.

RACEGOERS CLUB

The Racegoers Club, though a very recent institution, can boast over 10,000 members. The club, whose main objective is to get more people to go racing more often, is in fact run by the Racing Information Bureau (q.v.).

A number of racecourses offer concessions to club members, and in addition numerous visits are organised to places of racing interest. There are also expeditions to France for the Prix de l'Arc de Triomphe and to the United States for the Washington International at Laurel Park. Special travel facilities are provided for big meetings at home. Owning horses and sponsoring races are two of the club's latest facets. It costs £1 to join the club. The secretary of the club is Mr Anthony Fairbairn.

RACEHORSE OWNERS' ASSOCIATION

The Racehorse Owners' Association Ltd exists to promote the interests of owners, both under Jockey Club and National Hunt Committee Rules.

President: Mr J. U. Baillie.

Secretary: Lieut-Col F. M. Beale.

Address: 26 Charing Cross Road, London WC2.
Tel: 01-836 0461.

RACECOURSE TECHNICAL SERVICES

Racecourse Technical Services Ltd was formed in 1967 as a strengthening and modification of the Race Finish Recording Company Ltd. All the shares of the company are owned by the Levy Board which meets the costs of the services provided, namely the photo-finish, the camera patrol and race timing services, the public address system and closed circuit television on racecourses. In 1968 Racecourse Technical Services took over from the Jockey Club the responsibility for starting stalls. The board of directors comprises seven persons and includes representatives from the Jockey Club and the Racecourse Association.

RACEFORM

A very popular weekly form book giving the results of past races and comments on the appearance and performance of the competitors.

RACE MEETINGS, REGULATIONS FOR

All racecourses have to be licensed, and all meetings have to be sanctioned by the Stewards of the Jockey Club. Applications for fixtures for the following year have to be made to the Secretary of the Jockey Club by 1st March of the current year. The application has to be accompanied by a statement of accounts for the preceding year made up to 1st December, on a form prescribed by the Stewards of the Jockey Club and obtainable at the Registry Office. This statement of accounts must be certified by a chartered accountant.

The conditions of every race before closing, and the full programme of every meeting, before it takes place, must be advertised in the *Racing Calendar*, and no alteration can be made in the conditions of any race after such publication.

The Stewards of the Jockey Club may, however, at their discretion, prohibit the advertisement of any race or of any meeting in the *Racing Calendar*, or call upon the Stewards to alter or expunge the conditions, even after advertisement.

At every meeting advertised in the *Racing Calendar*, one half at least of the total amount guaranteed for prize money must be for races of a mile or over for three-year-olds and upwards, and of this sum so apportioned not less than half shall be for races of 1¼m or upwards; but when more than one meeting is held at the same course during the current racing season, the apportionment may be calculated over each meeting or over all the meetings.

RACING CALENDAR

The *Racing Calendar* is the official publication of the Jockey Club. It is printed by Messrs Weatherby and Sons and issued every Thursday. It contains particulars of every race, that is to say the conditions, entries, handicaps, forfeit stages, final acceptances and results. It lists all race meetings; gives the registration of colours and names of horses, names of persons and horses on the Forfeit List, and reports all objections and disqualifications. Apprentice jockeys and their masters are listed and so are all licensed jockeys and trainers. The first public intimation of any 'warning off' is the official notice in the *Racing Calendar* on the Thursday after the ban has come into force.

RACING INFORMATION BUREAU

The Racing Information Bureau, now the Public Relations organisation which acts for the Jockey Club, the Racecourse Association and the 64 racecourses of Great Britain, was established in January 1964 with the object of supplying both national and provincial newspapers with news and feature stories, assisting race sponsors to obtain maximum publicity and co-operating with course executives in promoting race meetings.

The bureau's public relations officers attend race meetings where they liaise between the local stewards, racing officials and the press, radio and television. The bureau also provides a comprehensive central information service on a full range of racing subjects. One of the most successful promotions launched by the bureau has been the Racegoers Club (q.v.).

Director: Mr Anthony Fairbairn.

Deputy Director: Mr Geoffrey Webster.

Assistant Director: Miss Louise Gold.

Course Representatives:

Northern Area: Mr Tim Thompson

Midlands Area: Mr Laurie Brannan.

Southern Area: Mr Peter Squibb.

Features: Miss Dorothy Laird.

The bureau's address is 42 Portman Square, London W1.

RAGUSA

Ragusa was bred by Mr H. F. Guggenheim and is by the Italian horse Ribot out of Fantan II, by the French-bred Ambiorix II. Ragusa was rather small and unprepossessing in his younger days and as Sir Cecil Boyd-Rochfort, Mr Guggenheim's trainer, did not care much for him, he was sent up for sale as a yearling and bought by Paddy Prendergast on behalf of Mr J. R. Mullion for 3,800 gn.

He proved a wonderful bargain. He won his only race as a two-year-old and the following season he won the Irish Derby, the King George VI and Queen Elizabeth Stakes, the Great Voltigeur Stakes and the St Leger. In the Derby he was third behind Relko. As a four-year-old he won the Ardenode Stakes at Naas and the Eclipse Stakes and was unplaced in the Prix de l'Arc de Triomphe. All told he won seven races and £146,650.

He is the property of a syndicate and stands at the Ardenode Stud, Ballymore Eustace, Co Kildare.

RAILS

Barriers defining the limits of a race track.

RAISE YOU TEN

Owned by his breeder Mr P. A. B. Widener, Raise You Ten stands at the Loughton Stud at a fee of £98. By Tehran out of Visor, by Combat, he was trained by Sir Cecil Boyd-

Rochfort and proved himself a good stayer, winning the Royal Stakes, Doncaster Cup, Yorkshire Cup and Goodwood Cup.

RAJPIPLA, Maharaja of (1890-1951)

The Maharaja of Rajpipla won the Derby in 1934 with Windsor Lad, trained by Marcus Marsh and ridden by C. Smirke. Windsor Lad, whom he had bought for 1,300 gn as a yearling, was his first runner in that race. The following month Windsor Lad, again ridden by Smirke, was a singularly unlucky loser of the Eclipse Stakes and his owner was persuaded to sell him to Mr M. H. Benson, a bookmaker, for £50,000. Windsor Lad was never beaten again.

The present Maharaja is well-known on the racecourse and is rated a particularly shrewd punter.

RAMSHAW, G.

He is attached to S. Ingham's stable and can go to scale at 8st 2. He rode 10 winners in 1969.

RANAI

Ranai was one of the late Lord Derby's most successful mares. Bred in France in 1925, by Rabelais out of Dark Sedge, by Prestige, Lord Derby bought her at the Deauville Sales and she won two races for him in France. At the stud she bred ten winners including Watling Street (Derby) and Garden Path (Two Thousand Guineas). She is also grandam of Ruthless who never won a race but became champion sire in New Zealand.

RANDALL, Herbert (1877-1959)

The son of Sir Henry Randall, a Northampton shoe manufacturer, Herbert Randall rode firstly as an amateur, turning professional in 1902. He was associated with the famous mare Sceptre on whom he won the Two Thousand Guineas, the One Thousand Guineas and the Oaks. He was also on her when she was fourth in the Derby but he was not given the mount when she won the St Leger. The following season, 1903, he won the One Thousand Guineas on Quintessence. For several seasons he rode for Mr J. B. Joel, for whom he won the Oaks on Glass Doll in 1907. On that popular handicapper Dean Swift he won the City and Suburban in 1906 and 1908. He handed in his licence in 1914 and retired from the racing world.

RAYMOND, Bruce

Bruce Raymond was apprenticed to W. Stephenson, whose daughter he married. He rode his first winner in 1961 and was top apprentice in 1962. His best seasons so far were in 1965 and 1966 when he rode 25 winners in each year. Good races he has won include the City and Suburban, Newbury Autumn Cup and Liverpool Spring Cup. He has been associated for several seasons with Humphrey Cottrill's stable.

RAYSON, Denis (b 1913)

Denis Rayson was apprenticed to Joe Lawson. He was Arthur Budgett's head lad for 23 years before taking out a licence himself in 1963. He now conducts a 'mixed' stable at Exning, near Newmarket.

READ, Robert (b 1904)

Bob Read for 11 years rode under National Hunt rules, firstly as an amateur and later as a professional. He has held a trainer's licence for 46 years and though his Lambourn stable has never been a large one, the horses are placed with considerable skill and win at least their fair share of races. Read's owners include Mr B. Walsh, Mrs G. D. Mottram, Mrs M. Pountney, Mrs A. Elphinston, Mr P. E. Booth, Mr D. H. Pountney and Mr J. Simmons.

READER, Raymond (b 1928)

One of the most experienced lightweight jockeys in England, Ray

Reader was apprenticed to the late Walter Nightingall. His best season was 1950 when he rode 29 winners. Good races he has won include the Stewards' Cup, Britannia Stakes (twice), Rosebery Stakes (twice) and Esher Cup (twice).

REAVEY, Edward (b 1919)

Eddie Reavey served his apprenticeship firstly with E. Davey and then with Steve Donoghue. He rode his first winner on the flat in 1936 but he became too heavy and turned his attention to riding under National Hunt rules. He might well have ridden Zahia to victory in the 1948 Grand National but for Zahia taking the wrong course coming to the last fence. He took out a licence to train in 1956, and his stable at East Hendred, near Wantage, has done very well on the whole. The best horse he has so far trained is the sprinter Polyfoto who won the Nunthorpe Stakes and the Prix d'Arenberg. His eldest son Patrick shows promise as a rider. Patrons of Reavey's stable include Mr J. K. Dale, Mr K. Teagle, Mr A. W. Harding, Mr H. J. Hart, Mr. J. Nolan, Dr W. H. Tweddell and Mr J. McShane.

REAVEY, Patrick (b 1950)

This promising young rider is the eldest son of the East Hendred trainer E. Reavey. He is now attached to Fulke Johnson Houghton's stable.

RECOGNISED MEETING

A 'recognised meeting' is a meeting held under the sanction of a recognised Turf Authority.

REDCAR

In recent times racing at this popular seaside course has made a notable advance, thanks largely to Major Leslie Petch who has a commendable flair not only for publicity, but for knowing what his customers want. Sponsored handicaps are a feature of the Redcar programmes.

The track is a couple of miles round with a straight 9f that joins the round course 5f from the winning post. There are virtually no gradients, and though the bends are on the sharp side their influence is counterbalanced by the long back straight and the run-in. The draw is not considered to be of significance.

Clerk of the Course: Major L. Petch, Liverton Lodge, Loftus, Saltburn, Yorkshire. Tel: Loftus 318.

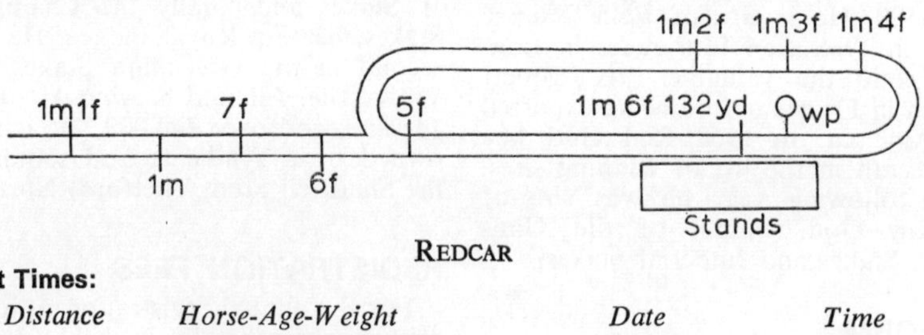

REDCAR

Best Times:

Distance	*Horse-Age-Weight*	*Date*	*Time*
5f	Shamrock Star 4-7-9	7/6/60	57.8
5f	Blackwell 2-8-12	27/7/49	59
6f	Flying William 6-8-4	2/5/58	1min 9
6f	Swashbuckler 2-9-0	8/8/52	1min 12.2
7f	Rub-a-Dub 6-7-8	25/5/53	1min 22.6
7f	Polly Gilles 2-7-8	16/9/61	1min 24.8
8f	Sanctum 5-8-2	12/8/61	1min 36.4
8f	Barden Beck 2-8-6	5/9/64	1min 39
9f	Le Texas 6-9-0	31/7/52	1min 49
10f	Tale of Two Cities 5-7-8	21/5/56	2min 2.4
11f	Tomdor 5-9-0	1/8/63	2min 19

Distance	*Horse-Age-Weight*	*Date*	*Time*
12f	Family Affair 4-7-5	2/5/58	2min 30.6
14f 132yd	Off Key 4-8-5	1/8/61	3min 4.6

Vaux Gold Tankard, 1m 6f 132yd

		OWNER	TRAINER	JOCKEY	SP
1959	Morecambe 6-9-3	J. Bullock	S. Hall	J. Sime	7-2
1960	Red Dragon 5-8-13	Princess Royal	N. Bertie	J. Sime	100-8
1961	Off Key 4-8-5	Sir V. Sassoon	N. Murless	L. Piggott	100-7
1962	Monterrico 3-7-9	H. Bousher	H. Wragg	R. Elliott	5-1
1963	Espresso 5-9-9	G. Oldham	H. Wragg	W. Williamson	7-1
1964	I Titan 3-8-3	Mrs. V. Hue-Williams	N. Murless	S. Clayton	3-1
1965	Atilla 4-7-13	A. Askew	H. Wragg	F. Durr	3-1
1966	Salvo 3-6-9	G. Oldham	H. Wragg	F. Johnson	15-1
1967	Farm Walk 5-7-11	W. G. Barker	P. Beasley	L. Brown	10-1
1968	Quartette 4-7-10	B. W. Hager	T. Gosling	R. Maddock	6-1
1969	Philoctetes 5-7-7	P. Bull	S. Ingham	P. Eddery	5-2

RED GOD

Bred in America in 1954 by Mr H. F. Guggenheim, Red God is a chestnut horse by Nasrullah out of Spring Run, by Menow. He came to England to be trained by Sir Cecil Boyd-Rochfort and as a two-year-old won the Richmond Stakes at Goodwood. At three and four years of age he raced in America, winning four races worth $29,000. He is now owned by Mr Guggenheim and stands at the Loughtown Stud, Co Kildare, at a fee of £500. He is sire of Folle Rousse who in 1968 won four races in England and the valuable Prix Robert Papin in France before being exported to America. In 1968 Red God was thirteenth in the list of winning sires. The following year he was sire of Yellow God, winner of the Gimcrack Stakes and Imperial Stakes.

REFORM

Reform was one of the best and most consistent middle distance horses seen on the English Turf in recent years. Bred in 1964 by the Ballymacoll Stud Farm Ltd, he was not a prepossessing yearling and in fact was not sent up for sale as it was reckoned he would do the Stud no credit. Accordingly Mr M. Sobell kept him for himself and sent him to be trained by Sir Gordon Richards. A bay by Pall Mall out of Country House, by Vieux Manoir, Reform was fourth in his first race as a two-year-old and won all the remaining six, including the Berkshire Stakes at Newbury, the Granville Stakes and Clarence House Stakes at Ascot, and the Rous Memorial Stakes at Goodwood.

The following season he won the St James's Stakes, St James's Palace Stakes, Sussex Stakes, Queen Elizabeth II Stakes and finally the Champion Stakes, beating Royal Palace. He was second in the Greenham Stakes and Wills Mile. All told he won 11 of his 14 races and over £44,000. He is now owned by a syndicate and stands at the Shadwell Stud, Thetford, Norfolk.

REGISTRATION FEES

For the annual registration of authority to act generally on behalf of an owner, £5.

For every registration of partnership in owning a horse, and on every change thereof, £5 for each horse.

For every annual registration of colours, £2.

For registration of foreign and veterinary certificates, 5s. for each certificate.

For registration of a horse's name, 10s. and for a change of name after the horse has run, £5.

For reservation of a horse's name (see Naming of Horses), 10s.

All fees and fines are paid to the credit of the Joint Administrative Authority.

REGISTRY OFFICE

The Registry Office is Messrs. Weatherby's office, 42 Portman Square, London W1.

REIFF, Johnny

Among the American jockeys who came over to Europe at the turn of the century were Johnny Reiff and his elder brother Lester. Johnny Reiff first appeared on English racecourses as an angel-faced little boy in knickerbockers and an Eton collar, but he soon proved that he was rather less innocent than he looked. In his youth he was a brilliant lightweight and subsequently he won the Derby on Orby in 1907 and on Tagalie in 1912. He also rode Craganour who was first past the post in the 1913 Derby but was subsequently disqualified. He went over to France when the American millionaires started racing there and seldom came to England except for a major event. His brother Lester, who won the 1901 Derby on Volodyovski, was a fine rider who had a lot of trouble over weight. There is no doubt that Lester was hand in glove with some big and disreputable American gamblers and it came as no surprise when the Jockey Club imposed a ban on him. Both the Reiff brothers had been brought over to England by an American trainer called Wishard, a confirmed doper of horses and the associate of some fairly desperate characters.

REIGH COUNT

Foaled in 1925, Reigh Count, by Sunreigh, was an American horse that won 11 races worth $168,000 in the United States and coming to England, won the Coronation Cup and was second in the Ascot Gold Cup.

RELANCE III

Relance III, by Relic out of Polaire II, by Le Volcan, is a famous French mare that produced Relko (French Two Thousand Guineas, Epsom Derby, French St Leger, Prix Ganay, Coronation Cup and Grand Prix de St Cloud); Match III (King George VI and Queen Elizabeth Stakes and Washington International); and Reliance II (French Derby, Grand Prix and French St Leger).

RELIANCE II

Reliance II is owned by a syndicate and stands at the Harwood Stud, Newbury, Berkshire. Bred in 1962 by the late M. F. Dupré, he is a bay horse by Tantième out of Relance III and thus a full brother to Match III and a three parts brother to the Derby winner Relko. He did not run as a two-year-old but at three he ran six times, his only defeat being when he finished second to the brilliant Sea Bird in the Prix de l'Arc de Triomphe. His victories included the Prix Hocquart, French Derby, Grand Prix and French St Leger.

RELIC

Relic was bred in America in 1945 and is a black horse by War Relic out of Bridal Colors, by Black Toney. In America he won five races (maximum distance 7f) worth $72,300. In 1950 he retired to the stud in the land of his birth and his stock there have won over 150 races and $1,113,000. In 1951 he was sent to France and there his offspring have so far won over 300 races and over 2,000,000 francs. His winners there include Buisson Ardent (French Two Thousand), Venture VII (Prix Djebel), Mincio (French Two Thousand), Victorian Order (Prix d'Arenberg) and Texanita (Prix d'Arenberg). He also sired the famous mare Relance III (q.v.). He came to England in 1957 and is the sire of the winners of over

170 races and over £190,000 in prize money. His winners here include Pieces of Eight (Eclipse and Champion Stakes), Venture VII (Imperial Produce Stakes and Middle Park Stakes), and Old Tom (Lincolnshire Handicap). He is owned by a syndicate and stands at the Longholes Stud, Newmarket.

RELKO

Relko is a brown horse by Tanerko out of Relance, by Relic. Bred and owned by the late M. F. Dupré and trained in France by F. Mathet, he won the 1963 Derby with Yves St Martin in the saddle. Other successes included the French Two Thousand Guineas, the Prix Ganay, the Prix Royal Oak, the Grand Prix de St Cloud and the Coronation Cup. He could only finish sixth in the Prix de l'Arc de Triomphe as a three-year-old.

After his Derby success Relko was to have run in the Irish Derby, but was found to be lame at the start and had to be withdrawn.

On 11th July, two weeks after the Irish Derby, an announcement was made by the Jockey Club concerning positive reactions to routine dope tests at Epsom. No names were given at that stage, but it soon became known that Relko was one of the horses concerned. The following statement appeared in the *Racing Calendar* on 29th August:

> The stewards of the Epsom Summer Meeting referred to the Stewards of the Jockey Club the reports which they have received from the club's analysts on the examination ordered to be made of Relko after winning the Derby Stakes on 29th May.
>
> The Stewards of the Jockey Club held their enquiry at the Registry Office on 28th August, when they heard evidence from the trainer, and other parties concerned including technical witnesses called on their behalf. They also took evidence from the Stewards' Advisory Committee.
>
> The Stewards were satisfied that a substance other than a normal nutrient was present in the horse.
>
> From the technical evidence they were not sure satisfied that it was administered with the intention of increasing its speed or improving its stamina, courage, or conduct in the race.
>
> They adjourned the case for further enquiry in conjunction with the police.

Finally, the following notice appeared in the *Racing Calendar* on 3rd October:

> The Stewards of the Jockey Club, having considered the report on their further enquiries, are satisfied that the trainer and his employees have no case to answer under Rule 102(11).
>
> They found no evidence which would justify a disqualification of Relko under Rule 66(c).

In 1964 Lord Sefton bought a half share in Relko who is three parts brother to those good horses Match III and Reliance. Relko is now at stud in England. He is sire of Breton, winner in 1969 of the Grand Criterium.

RHODES SCHOLAR

Bred by the late Lord Astor and foaled in 1933, Rhodes Scholar was by Pharos out of the Oaks winner Book Law. Trained by Joe Lawson, he won the St James's Palace Stakes, Ribblesdale Stakes and Eclipse Stakes. After two years at the stud in England he was exported to America where he did moderately well. The best horse he sired was the American-bred St Leger winner Black Tarquin.

RIBBLESDALE STAKES

See under Ascot.

RIBBON

Bred and owned by Lord Rosebery, Ribbon was a very game little filly by Fairway out of Bongrace, by Spion Kop. She won the Middle Park Stakes, beating Nasrullah, and in 1943 was second in the One Thousand Guineas, Oaks and St Leger. Everyone, bar the judge, thought that she had won the St Leger. She was beaten a neck in the Oaks, and a neck in the One

Thousand Guineas too. She was not a success as a brood mare.

RIBERO

Ribero was bred in America in 1965 by Mrs J. G. Rogers and as a yearling was bought by Mr Charles Engelhard for $50,000. "The last of the cheap Ribots", Mr Engelhard is alleged to have said. By Ribot out of Libra, by Hyperion, Ribero is a full brother to Mr Engelhard's Ribocco. Like Ribocco, he was trained by Fulke Johnson Houghton and like Ribocco he won the Irish Derby and the Doncaster St Leger. He did not retain his form as a four-year-old. He is now owned by a syndicate and stands at the Sandringham Stud.

RIBOCCO

Bred in America in 1964 by Mrs J. G. Rogers, Ribocco was bought for $35,000 as a yearling by Mr Charles Engelhard who sent him to England to be trained by Fulke Johnson Houghton. Among Ribocco's victories were the *Observer* Gold Cup, the Irish Derby and the Doncaster St Leger. He was second in the Derby to Royal Palace and close up third in the Prix de l'Arc de Triomphe. By Ribot out of Libra, by Hyperion, he was retired to the stud in America after finishing seventh in the Washington International at Laurel Park. He is a full brother to Ribero who won the Irish Derby and the Doncaster St Leger for Mr Engelhard the following year.

RIBOFILIO

Bred in America, this Ribot colt was bought by Mr Charles Engelhard for $100,000. Trained in England by Fulke Johnson Houghton, he was the outstanding two-year-old of 1968 and headed the Free Handicap. His career in 1969 proved an anti-climax. He was favourite for the Two Thousand Guineas, the Derby, the Irish Derby and the St Leger but lost the lot. In the Two Thousand Guineas he had to be pulled up and no satisfactory explanation exists for that lamentable display. At the end of the season he returned to America where he has won as a four year old.

RIBOT

Perhaps the greatest racehorse of this century, Ribot was foaled in 1952 and was bred in Italy by the Razza Dormello-Olgiata. By Tenerani out of Romanella, by El Greco, he was the undefeated winner of 16 races. In England he won the King George VI and Queen Elizabeth Stakes and in France he twice won the Prix de l'Arc de Triomphe. By no means outstanding in looks, he has spent most of his stud life in America but his European winners include Molvedo (Prix de l'Arc de Triomphe), Prince Royal II (Prix de l'Arc de Triomphe), Ragusa (St Leger, Irish Derby, King George VI and Queen Elizabeth Stakes, Eclipse Stakes), Ribocco (St Leger and Irish Derby), Ribero (St Leger and Irish Derby), Romulus (Sussex Stakes, Queen Elizabeth II Stakes) and Long Look (Oaks).

RICHARDS, Sir Gordon (b 1904)

One of the outstanding personalities in English racing, Sir Gordon Richards, who was born in Shropshire, was apprenticed to Martin Hartigan and rode his first winner in 1921. He swiftly established himself and was champion for the first time in 1925. In 1926 he suffered a grave illness demanding convalescence in Switzerland, but he made a complete recovery and was champion again in 1927. From that point his career never looked back and when he eventually retired following a bad fall at Sandown in 1954, he had been champion no fewer than 26 times. Altogether he rode 4,870 winners, a total unapproached by any other rider, while the 269 winners he rode in 1947 formed another record. At one Chepstow meeting he rode every winner except that of the last race on the second day.

His classic winners were as follows:

Two Thousand Guineas: Pasch (1938); Big Game (1942); Tudor Minstrel (1947)

One Thousand Guineas: Sun Chariot (1942); Queenpot (1948); Belle of All (1951)

Derby: Pinza (1953).

Oaks: Rose of England (1930); Sun Chariot (1942)

St Leger: Singapore (1930); Chulmleigh (1937); Turkhan (1940); Sun Chariot (1942); Tehran (1944).

Small, sturdy and short in the leg, he was hardly such a polished horseman as Steve Donoghue and his style tended to be unorthodox. In a really close finish he seemed to ride not only rather upright, but often sideways and with a completely loose rein. Yet he retained complete control and his mounts very rarely became unbalanced. He was uncannily good at the start, usually in just the right place at the right moment, and above all he possessed an overwhelming determination to win. He used his whip to encourage and not to chastise, and in fact he seldom hit a horse. Success, combined with adulation from the press and public, has never turned his head or altered his pleasing personality. His way of life has always been modest and his standard of integrity extremely high. Both as rider, and since then as a trainer, he has been a worthy representative of the best traditions of the Turf. He received his knighthood just before he rode Pinza to victory in the Derby.

As a trainer he is extremely patient and does not believe in hurrying his horses. His best winners have been Reform, Firestreak, Pipe of Peace, Court Harwell, Induna and Greengage. His stable at Whitsbury was considerably reduced at the end of 1969, and he now trains only for Lady Beaverbrook, Mr and Mrs M. Sobell and Mr A. Weinstock.

RICKABY, William (b 1917)

Bill Rickaby comes from a famous racing family. It was a Rickaby who trained the 1855 Derby winner, Wild Dayrell. Bill's grandfather was a well-known jockey and so was his father, who was killed in World War I. Bill's brother Fred rode with much success until he became too heavy and is now a trainer in South Africa; his sister is Lester Piggott's mother. Bill himself is married to Ryan Jarvis's sister.

He was apprenticed to Walter Griggs and then to George Lambton, riding his first winner in 1933. Except for war service in the Royal Artillery in which he held the rank of Major, he rode with success until he retired in 1968 to take up a racing appointment in Hong Kong. Few jockeys have been more popular or enjoyed such a high reputation for integrity. When he rode Silver Spray to victory at Newmarket on his last ride in public, he was given a memorable reception.

Big races he won include the Two Thousand Guineas on Privy Councillor, the One Thousand Guineas and Oaks on Sweet Solera and the Eclipse Stakes on Busted. He also won the Irish Derby, Irish Oaks, Yorkshire Cup (twice), Goodwood Cup, July Cup, Jockey Club Cup (twice), Manchester Cup, Champion Stakes, Jockey Club Stakes, Goodwood Stakes, Lincolnshire Handicap and Jubilee Handicap. In addition, he won important races in India and Scandinavia. His best season was 1953 when he rode 83 winners. The racing world was saddened recently to hear of his very severe car accident in Hong Kong. It is to be feared that recovery will prove a very slow progress.

RIDDEN FOR HIRE

The Rules of Racing state that professional hunt servants, grooms, apprentices, stable-lads, and persons who are or who have been employed as paid servants in any capacity in private, hunting, racing, livery, or horsedealers' stables, also persons who have ever received payment, directly or indirectly, for riding in a race are regarded as having 'ridden for hire', and are professional riders for the purposes of the rules.

RIDGE WOOD

Trained by Noel Murless for Mr G. R. Smith, Ridge Wood was bred by the Sledmere Stud and was by Bois Roussel out of Hanging Fall, by Solario. He won seven races, including the St Leger, and over £21,000. He had made little mark as a sire when he died in Ireland in 1956.

RIG

A rig is a horse whose testicles, or one of whose testicles, have not, or has not, descended.

RIGHT BOY

One of the outstanding sprinters of the past 25 years, Right Boy was bred in Ireland in 1954 by Mr W. J. Byrne and is a grey by Impeccable out of Happy Ogan, by Ballyogan. Trained by the late W. P. Dutton and by H. P. Rohan, he won 16 races and over £17,000, his victories including the King's Stand Stakes, Nunthorpe Stakes (twice), King George Stakes (twice), July Cup (twice) and Cork and Orrery Stakes (twice). The property of a syndicate, he stands at the Limestone Stud, Gainsborough, Lincolnshire, and has done quite well as a sire.

RIGHT ROYAL V

Bred in France in 1958 by Madame Jean Couturié, Right Royal V is a big brown horse by the Derby winner Owen Tudor out of Bastia, by Tornado. Trained by E. Pollet, he proved himself a great racehorse. In France he won the Grand Criterium, the French Two Thousand Guineas, the Prix Lupin and the French Derby. He was second to Molvedo in the Prix de l'Arc de Triomphe. In England he won the King George VI and Queen Elizabeth Stakes, completely outclassing the Derby and St Leger winner St Paddy.

Right Royal V is the property of a syndicate and retired to the Haras du Mesnil, Savigne-l'Eveque, France, in 1961. He is sire of Salvo who in England won the Vaux Gold Tankard, Newbury Autumn Cup, Yorkshire Cup and Hardwicke Stakes, while in Germany he was second in the Preis von Europa and won the Grosser Preis von Baden. In France he was just beaten in the Prix de l'Arc de Triomphe. Right Royal V is also sire of Ruysdael, winner of the Italian Derby, and of Prince Regent, winner of the Prix Greffulhe and the Prix Lupin and Irish Derby.

RIGHT TACK

Bred in Ireland in 1966 by Mr P. Larkin, Right Tack is a far from fashionably bred bay colt, albeit a very good-looking one, by Hard Tack out of Polly Macaw, by Polly's Jet. Both his sire and his dam were sprinters. Bought as a yearling for 3,200 gn by Mr J. R. Brown who sent him to be trained by John Sutcliffe junior, Right Tack went from strength to strength as a two-year-old, winning five of his six races and finishing the season with victories in the Imperial and Middle Park Stakes.

As a three-year-old, he was beaten by Tower Walk on firm going, which did not suit him, in the Greenham Stakes at Newbury, but then won in succession the Two Thousand Guineas, Irish Two Thousand Guineas and the St James's Palace Stakes. He then contracted the cough and on his reappearance failed to stay in the 10f Peter Hastings Stakes at Newbury, being trounced by Principal Boy. In his last race before retirement to the stud he was unplaced behind Habitat in the Prix du Moulin.

RINGER

A slang term for a horse which is dishonestly substituted for another.

RIPON

This Yorkshire course is within

handy distance of Harrogate and York and the standard of sport there is quite high. It is a right-handed track, 1m 5f round, with a straight 6f joining the round course 5f from the winning post. It is undulating and somewhat sharp in character. The run-in is uphill for the first half, followed by a slight decline to within a few yards of the winning post, where the ground rises again. Low numbers in the draw are favoured on the straight course and owing to the long bend soon after the start, high numbers are best in races over 1m.

Clerk of the Course: Mr A. C. Newton, High Gosforth Park Co Ltd, High Gosforth Park, Newcastle-upon-Tyne. Tel: Wideopen 2020.

RIVER CHANTER

River Chanter was bred in 1959, and racing for four seasons, won seven races and £15,055. He is now owned by Mr Bernard Myers and stands at the Walton Manor Stud, Bletchley, Buckinghamshire.

ROAN ROCKET

Roan Rocket was bred in 1961 by Lady Ainsworth and is a grey horse by Buisson Ardent out of Farandole II, by Deux Pour Cent. He was bought as a yearling by Mr T. F. C. Frost who sent him to be trained by George Todd. Up to 1¼m he was a high-class horse and won five races

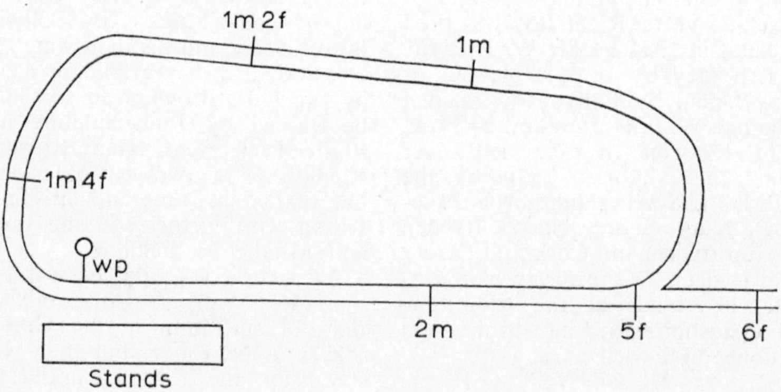

RIPON

Best Times:

Distance	*Horse-Age-Weight*	*Date*	*Time*
5f	Castle Mona 4-7-2	22/7/66	58
5f	Pisces 2-9-4	26/7/69	58.4
6f	Quoit 5-7-0	23/7/66	1min 9.8
6f	Demokratikos 2-8-12	27/7/63	1min 12.4
8f	Loose Cover 3-7-5	23/7/66	1min 37.4
8f	Con Brio 2-8-10	14/9/63	1min 42.4
9f	Tarqogan 6-9-6	20/8/66	1min 51.8
10f	Starpoint 4-8-5	7/8/50	2min 5
12f	Cholo 6-8-7	27/9/41	2min 32.2
14f 132yd	Grey of Falloden 5-9-13	25/7/64	3min 8
16f	Rising Dawn 5-8-13	2/5/62	3min 27.2
18f	Minute Gun 4-8-8	30/8/61	3min 51.4

and over £34,000. His victories included the St James's Palace Stakes and Sussex Stakes. As a four-year-old he was beaten a short head in the Eclipse and was also second in the Sussex Stakes. He is the property of a partnership and stands at the Dunchurch Lodge Stud, Newmarket. He had his first runners in 1969 and they did extremely well.

ROARER

A slang term for a horse that has gone in his wind.

ROBERTSON, James Bell (1860-1940)

Mr J. B. Robertson was usually granted the courtesy title of 'Professor'. He was in fact a veterinary surgeon who devoted his life to journalism. He was rightly regarded as the leading authority of his day on the breeding of the racehorse. A regular contributor to the *Sporting Chronicle*, *Sunday Times* and *Bloodstock Breeders Review*, he did work of great value in relating the discoveries of the science of genetics to the special case of the thoroughbred.

ROBINSON, Bryan

Clerk of the Course at Folkestone.

ROBINSON, George Noel (b 1918)

George Robinson was apprenticed to Fred Darling and began training in 1955. He runs a small 'mixed' stable at Beal, near Berwick-on-Tweed. In 1964 he won the Usher-Vaux Brewery Gold Tankard with Pluit.

ROBINSON, George William

Willy Robinson is a very distinguished rider under National Hunt rules, but was second in the 1959 Derby on Paddys Point.

ROBINSON, Jem (b 1794)

Born at Newmarket, Jem Robinson was a very fine rider, the equal of young Sam Chifney in technical skill and certainly his superior in respect of integrity. He rode six Derby winners, a number never exceeded and equalled only by Steve Donoghue. His winners were Azor (1817), Cedric (1824), Middleton (1825), Mameluke (1827), Cadland (1828) and Bay Middleton (1836). When getting on in years he broke his thigh and thereafter was handicapped by one leg being four inches shorter than the other. In 1824 he made a bet that in one week he would ride the winners of the Derby and the Oaks and get married. He won his money.

ROBINSON, Peter John (b 1936)

Peter Robinson was apprenticed for five years to Harry Wragg. He rode his first winner in 1953 and his best season was 1962 when he rode 60 winners. Good races he won include the Lincolnshire Handicap (three times), Newbury Spring Cup, Royal Hunt Cup, Ebor Handicap, Jubilee Handicap, Chester Cup, Chester Vase, Chesterfield Cup, Ayr Gold Cup, *News of the World* Handicap and Magnet Cup. He rode four winners at Warwick on 10th September 1962. In 1969 he took over Teddy Lambton's stable when the latter retired and landed a gamble when Prince de Galles won the Cambridgeshire at 5-2.

ROBSON, Albert George (b 1942)

'Brig' Robson was apprenticed for three years to H. D. Peacock and for three to G. Fenningworth. He was very badly hurt in the car crash in which Fenningworth was killed but happily made a complete recovery. He rode his first winner in 1962 and his best season so far was 1965 when he rode 44 winners.

ROBSON, Robert (d 1838)

Robson made a great name for himself as a trainer in the days when trainers held a comparatively low place in the social order and were in fact often referred to as 'training-grooms'. He was far less severe in his methods than most of his contemporaries and he trained seven Derby winners, a number never exceeded and equalled only by John Porter and Fred Darling. His winners were Waxy (1793), Tyrant (1802), Pope (1809), Whalebone (1810), Whisker (1815), Azor (1817), Emilius (1823). On his retirement in 1828, ten years before he died, he was presented by leading members of the Turf with a handsome piece of plate in recognition of his professional skill and his character.

ROBSON, Thomas William, MRCVS (b 1924)

T. W. Robson qualified at the Royal Veterinary College, Edinburgh, in 1950. A first-class amateur rider, he won the Scottish Grand National on two occasions. He took out a licence to train in 1954 and except for a brief interlude has been running a 'mixed' stable at Penrith, Cumberland, ever since. On the flat his main successes have been to win the Chester Cup and Ascot Stakes with Harvest Gold.

ROCKAVON

Bred by the Biddlesden Park Stud in 1958, Rockavon is a bay horse by Rockefella out of Cosmetic, by Sir Cosmo. As a foal he was bought for 420 gn by Mr R. J. Donworth, who re-sold him as a yearling to Mr T. C. Yuill for 2,300 gn. Trained by George Boyd, he won three modest events as a two-year-old, two at Hamilton Park and one at Stockton. As a three-year-old he bought off a very big surprise when he won the Two Thousand Guineas at 66-1, ridden by N. Stirk. He also won the Heddon Stakes at Newcastle. He was syndicated for the stud and stood in this country till he was sent to France in 1969.

ROCKEFELLA

Rockefella, foaled in 1941, was a beautifully bred horse by Hyperion out of the dual classic winner Rockfel. His racing record was modest but he did well as a sire, his winners including Rockavon (Two Thousand Guineas and £24,253), Outcrop (£12,738), Dalnamein (£11,589), Cash and Courage (£10,124) and Elopement (£9,675).

ROCKFEL

Owned and bred by Sir Hugo Cunliffe-Owen and trained by Capt O. M. Bell, Rockfel was one of the most brilliant fillies to race in England this century. A daughter of the Derby winner Felstead, she ran in a selling race as a two-year-old but rapidly improved and as a three-year-old in 1938 she won the One Thousand Guineas, the Oaks, the Champion Stakes and the Aintree Derby. Her form in the Champion Stakes and the Aintree Derby showed conclusively that she was far superior to the colts of her age. Unfortunately she died from a twisted gut in 1941. Rockefella (see above) was her son.

ROCK SAND

Bred and owned by Sir James Miller and trained by George Blackwell at Newmarket, Rock Sand, by Sainfoin out of Roquebrune, won the 'Triple Crown' in 1903. Soon after his racing career was over Sir James Miller died and Rock Sand was sold for £25,000 to Mr August Belmont, president of the New York Jockey Club. He did well as a sire in America but was ultimately exported to France where he died in 1914.

RODOSTO

In 1933 Princesse de Faucigny-Lucinge's Rodosto, trained by H. Count, won the Two Thousand Guineas and the French Two Thousand Guineas as well. Most of his stud career was spent in France but when an old horse he was exported to the Argentine. The best of his stock was Dogat, winner of the French Two Thousand Guineas.

ROE, John (b 1938)

This competent Irish jockey's English successes include the William Hill Gold Cup, Royal Hunt Cup, Cork and Orrery Stakes and Queen Alexandra Stakes.

ROGERS, John Michael (b 1925)

'Mick' Rogers comes of a well-known Anglo-Irish racing family. He has never had a big stable at the Curragh but he has won the Derby with Hard Ridden (1958) and with Santa Claus (1964). In the summer of 1970, he announced his intention to retire from training.

ROHAN, Hubert Patrick (b 1933)

From 1956 to 1958 Pat Rohan assisted his father-in-law the late W. P. Dutton (q.v.) and on Dutton's death he took over the stable at Malton. Among the good horses he has trained are Right Boy, Sandiacre, Althrey Don and Tin Whistle, while his successes in important races include the Cork and Orrery Stakes (twice), the July Cup (twice), the Nunthorpe Stakes (twice), the Brown Jack Stakes, the Seaton Delavel Stakes (twice) and the King George Stakes. The many patrons of his stable include Lord Grimthorpe, Mr A. J. Hornblower, Mr B. P. Jenks, Capt T. E. Langton, Lady Manton, Mr and Mrs R. J. McAlpine, Mr N. Nuttall, Mr W. A. Richardson, Major E. C. R. Sheffield, Mr G. N. Sutherland, Mrs L. H. Brown, Mr E. Bolam, Mr K. O. Boardman, Mr M. Clayton, Mr P. Duffy, Mr W. Gilbert, Mr Bert Kerr, Mr J. F. Morrison, Mrs P. Oppenheimer and Mrs K. M. Way.

ROI HERODE

Roi Hérode was bred in France in 1904 and was a grey horse by Le Samaritain. He was not top class and in fact was something of a plodder, but Mr E. Kennedy bought him for £2,000 with the object of reviving in Great Britain the Herod sire line. His first crop of runners included The Tetrarch, perhaps the fastest horse ever seen on the English Turf. Roi Hérode lived till he was 27 but never sired another horse of comparable ability.

ROMULUS

Bred in 1959 by Mr P. Bull, Romulus is a bay horse by Ribot out of Arietta, by Tudor Minstrel. Owned by Mr C. Engelhard and trained by Fulke Johnson Houghton, he ran five times as a two-year-old, winning the Virginia Water Stakes at Ascot and being beaten a neck in the Champagne Stakes. As a three-year-old he won the Greenham Stakes, Hungerford Stakes, Sussex Stakes, Queen Elizabeth II Stakes and the Prix du Moulin de Longchamp. He was second in the Two Thousand Guineas and fell in the Derby. In all he won £12,765 in England, 102,000 francs in France. He had yet to make his mark as a sire when he was exported to Japan in 1969.

ROSEBERY, fifth Earl of (1848-1929)

The fifth Earl of Rosebery is the only man to have won the Derby when holding office as Prime Minister. This he accomplished in 1894 when Ladas won the great race for him at Epsom.

Lord Rosebery was a patron of the Turf from early manhood, most of his many good winners being bred at his Mentmore Stud, near Leighton Buzzard. The full range of his classic successes is as follows:

Two Thousand Guineas: Ladas (1894); Neil Gow (1910); Ellangowan (1923)

One Thousand Guineas: Chelandry (1897); Vaucluse (1915); Plack (1924)

Derby: Ladas (1894); Sir Visto (1895); Cicero (1905)

Oaks: Bonnie Jean (1885)

St Leger: Sir Visto (1895).

Lord Rosebery retained his interest in racing till the end of his life.

ROSEBERY, sixth Earl of, KT, DSO, MC (b 1882)

The sixth Earl of Rosebery succeeded his father (see above) in 1929. In his youth he was a notable all-round sportsman; he captained Surrey at cricket, was just about the best heavyweight to hounds in the country, and was on the fringe of international standard at polo. For more than forty years he has been one of the most active members of the Jockey Club and his work as a racing administrator has been notable for shrewdness and determination, backed up by a remarkable memory and a formidable power of repartee. Like many other people who think quickly and resent wasting time, he has never been noted for his tolerance of fools and bores. At one time he was rated a somewhat formidable character, but he has undoubtedly mellowed with age.

His association with his trainer Sir Jack Jarvis was long, successful and harmonious. On Jarvis's death in 1968, Lord Rosebery's horses were taken over by Doug Smith. He has twice won the Derby with horses he bred at his Mentmore Stud—with Blue Peter in 1939 and with Ocean Swell in 1945. Blue Peter also won the Two Thousand Guineas and Eclipse Stakes, Ocean Swell the Ascot Gold Cup. Lord Rosebery won the St Leger in 1931 with Sandwich, who was very unlucky not to win the Derby, and he won the Eclipse Stakes in 1932 with Miracle, who only cost 175 gn as a yearling. In 1969 Lord Rosebery won the Oaks for the first time with Sleeping Partner, who also won the Ribblesdale Stakes. Colours: primrose and rose hoops, primrose cap.

ROSEDROP

Rosedrop, by St Frusquin, won the Oaks in 1910 and was dam of the 'Triple Crown' winner and outstanding sire Gainsborough.

ROSE OF ENGLAND

Bred by Lady James Douglas, Rose of England was by Teddy out of Perce Neige, by Neil Gow, and won the 1930 Oaks for Lord Glanely. At the stud she bred Chulmleigh, who won the St Leger and was exported to the Argentine; British Empire, who won over £5,000 in England and did very well as a sire in the Argentine; Coastal Traffic, who was at the stud successively in Ireland, France and America and then in France again; and Faerie Queen, grandam of Arabian Night, who was second in the Derby and was sold in Argentina in 1955 for £41,000.

ROSE ROYALE II

Rose Royale II was bred by the late Aga Khan and is by Prince Bio out of Rose of Yeroda, by Nearco. Trained in France by Alec Head, she won the One Thousand Guineas and the Champion Stakes in 1957.

ROSEWAY

By Stornaway out of Rose of Ayrshire, by Ayrshire, Roseway won the One Thousand Guineas in 1919 for her owner-breeder Sir Edward Hulton. She was also second in the Oaks. She made little mark as a brood mare.

ROSY LEGEND

Foaled in France in 1931, Rosy Legend, by Dark Legend, was a very successful mare whose progeny included Dante (Derby) and Sayajirao (St Leger).

ROTHSCHILD, Anthony de (d 1961)

Mr Anthony de Rothschild is one of the few English owners to have won the Grand Prix de Paris this century. This he did in 1919 with Galloper Light. In 1926 he won the One Thousand Guineas with Pillion. He disposed of all his bloodstock in 1944.

ROTHSCHILD, James A. de DCM (1878-1957)

Mr J. A. de Rothschild was in his heyday one of the biggest and boldest punters on the English Turf. When he won the Cambridgeshire in 1919 with Brigand he won £80,000; when he won that race again two years later with Milenko the odds were shorter and he won only £30,000. He won the Ascot Gold Cup with Bomba, the last three-year-old to win that event; the One Thousand Guineas with Atmah; and the Grand Prix de Paris with Reine Lumière. A fabulous character of highly distinctive appearance and a man of immense pride and courage, he is the only member of the Jockey Club to have been awarded the DCM, a decoration for valour restricted to NCOs and men.

ROUS, Admiral Henry John (1795-1877)

Admiral Rous dominated the English Turf from 1846 till his death. Vigorous, determined, utterly honest and extremely shrewd, he was a born leader with a single weakness—impetuosity. To his own detriment he had the unfortunate habit of writing hasty letters to the newspapers before he was fully conversant with the facts about which he was writing.

He served with credit in the Royal Navy, his outstanding feat being to bring the storm-battered frigate *Pique* safely home from Newfoundland to Spithead, a distance of some 1,500 miles, in 20 days, although *Pique* was rudderless and was leaking at the rate of two feet of water an hour.

He was elected to the Jockey Club in 1821 and in periods of unemployment during his naval service, he made a profound study of racing and in particular of the rules of the sport. He was first elected a Steward of the Jockey Club in 1838 and eventually became, just like Sir Charles Bunbury, "a sort of perpetual president". In 1850 he published *The Laws and Practice of Horse-Racing*, a publication that established his position as the leading Turf authority of the day. The four main sections of this book dealt with the development of the thoroughbred; the Newmarket Rules of Racing, with a clear and precise explanation of those rules; the duties of racing officials; and a list of difficult and complicated racing cases with the judgement pronounced in each case.

He was an expert handicapper who was not easily hoodwinked. "Every great handicap", he used to say, "is a premium to fraud". In 1855, when 60 years of age, he accepted the post of public handicapper but luckily he possessed the zest and industry required for this exacting post and he used to sit up half the night studying form. With apparently inexhaustible energy he not only attended all important race-meetings, but was out on Newmarket Heath most mornings as well, watching the horses work and jotting down what he had seen in his notebook.

At Newmarket he used to watch the races from the Bushes, a point two furlongs from the winning post, as he reckoned it the ideal pitch from which to spot non-triers. If he saw what he thought was a bad case, he would roar at the jockey as he went by. If there was trouble at the start, he used to go down himself and sort it out. All this time he was a Steward of the Jockey Club and it says much for his energy and integrity that he carried out his manifold tasks to the complete satisfaction of the majority. He certainly established a new high standard as regards handicapping.

Not the least of his services was to take in hand the Jockey Club financial position. This was anything but satisfactory when he began to devote his attention to it but he succeeded in raising the revenue derived from Newmarket from £3,000 a year to £18,000.

He detested heavy betting and strongly opposed lavish presents to jockeys, whom he felt should be kept in their place, and that place a fairly humble one. He retained his strength and vigour until he was over 80 and by and large racing has never had a truer friend. Though for 25 years his word was law, he was never arrogant or overbearing in his determination to achieve a high standard in all that mattered. Some of his sayings are certainly still applicable today, such as his advice to owners: "Keep yourself in the best company and your horses in the worst".

ROXBURGHE, ninth Duke of (b 1913)

The Duke of Roxburghe served in the Royal Horse Guards. He is a member of the Jockey Club, has held office as Steward and Senior Steward, and is a steward at Edinburgh, Hamilton Park, Lanark, Liverpool and Newcastle. The best horse he has so far owned is Sweet Story, whose successes included the Northumberland Plate and the Yorkshire Cup. His trainer is R. D. Peacock. Colours: silver, dark green sleeves.

ROYAL CHARGER

Foaled in 1942, Royal Charger was a handsome chestnut by Nearco out of Sun Princess, by Solario. Trained by Jack Jarvis for Sir John Jarvis, Royal Charger showed little promise early on and at one point it was proposed to send him up to the December Sales. However, he gradually improved and at three and four years of age he was a very good horse indeed. He was third in the Two Thousand Guineas and won the Ayr Gold Cup with 9st 7lb. At the conclusion of his racing career he was sold to the Irish National Stud for 50,000 gn. In 1953 he was sold for export to America. Among his winners were Happy Laughter (One Thousand Guineas and £26,908), Gilles de Retz (Two Thousand Guineas), Sea Charger (Irish Two Thousand and Irish St Leger), Royal Serenade (£10,791 in England and a good winner in America too), and Turn To (best American two-year-old of 1954 and grandsire of Sir Ivor).

ROYAL HUNT CUP

See under Ascot.

ROYAL LANCER

Royal Lancer was bred by the National Stud and was by Spearmint out of Royal Favour, by White Eagle. In the colours of the late Lord Lonsdale and trained by A. Sadler junior, he won the 1922 St Leger at 33-1. He also won the Irish St Leger. He failed as a sire and ended up in South Africa. He was ridden in the St Leger by the late Bobby Jones, then a young apprentice. Bobby was still waiting for his present when Lord Lonsdale died years later.

ROYAL LODGE STAKES

See under Ascot.

ROYAL MINSTREL

Bred in Ireland by Mr J. J. Maher, Royal Minstrel was foaled in 1925 and was an exceptionally handsome grey by Tetratema out of Harpsichord, by Louvois. Trained by Sir Cecil Boyd-Rochfort, firstly for Capt G. P. Gough and later for Mr J. H. Whitney, Royal Minstrel never ran as a two-year-old. The following season he was beaten by inches by Flamingo in the Two Thousand Guineas. Up to ten furlongs he was a really good horse, winning the Eclipse Stakes, in which he slammed Fairway, the St James's Palace Stakes, the Cork and Orrery Stakes and the Victoria Cup. In the Victoria Cup he was given only 8st 8lb and represented a handicap certainty at the weights. In a memorable duel for the July Cup he was just beaten by Lord Ellesmere's game little filly Tiffin who was never defeated.

Royal Minstrel retired to the stud in America where he sired First Fiddle, winner of $398,000 and a good many other winners. His mares did well, too. Eventually he came back to England but had not established himself there when he died.

ROYAL PALACE

Royal Palace was foaled in 1964 and is a bay by Ballymoss out of Crystal Palace, by Solar Slipper. Bred and owned by Mr H. J. Joel and trained by Noel Murless at Newmarket, he won two of his three races as a two-year-old, his most important success being in the Royal Lodge Stakes at Ascot. That season he was ridden by Lester Piggott. In 1967, ridden by George Moore, he won the Two Thousand Guineas and the Derby. Owing to a mishap he had to miss the St Leger and was not at his best when third behind Reform in the Champion Stakes. As a four-year-old, partnered by Sandy Barclay, he was undefeated, his victories including the Coronation Cup, Eclipse Stakes and King George VI and Queen Elizabeth Stakes. On his retirement to the stud his victories had earned him over £163,000, a record total for a horse trained in England. He is now the property of Mr H. J. Joel, Hon Lady Macdonald-Buchanan and Lord Howard de Walden and stands at the Egerton Stud, Newmarket.

ROYAL PALM

Bred at the Hilltown Stud in 1952, Royal Palm is a bay horse by Royal Charger out of Pasquinade, by Pasch, and is thus a full brother to Royal Serenade who won over £10,000 in England and $153,000 in America where he is now a leading sire. Royal Palm himself was a good, tough performer up to a mile. As a two-year-old he won the Woodcote Stakes and Horris Hill Stakes. The following season he ran 14 times, winning the St James's Stakes, Empire Handicap, Town Handicap at Newmarket, Nunthorpe Stakes and Challenge Stakes. Altogether he won eight races and over £10,000 in stakes. The property of a syndicate, he stands at the Limestone Stud, Gainsborough, Lincolnshire. Among his many winners are Young Christopher (£11,784), Royal Rubicon (£8,008) and Royal Avenue (£7,340 in England and Ireland and £15,621 in France).

RULES OF RACING

The Rules of Racing are the copyright of the Trustees of the Jockey Club by whose permission they are reprinted here. The Rules are subject to frequent amendment, addition or deletion and, in the 1970 version given here, include all modifications announced by the Stewards of the Jockey Club from January to May 1970.

The published Rules also contain a list of all office-holders, members and ex-officio members of the Jockey Club, a list of definitions of terms that appear in the Rules and a number of instructions by the Stewards of the Jockey Club. These are not included but appear in this Encyclopaedia in their appropriate alphabetical position.

Appendix B (scale of weight for age for steeple chases and hurdle races) has been omitted.

The Rules of Racing apply to all Meetings held under the sanction of the Jockey Club and to all races run at such Meetings.

Part 1

Stewards of the Jockey Club and Stewards of Meetings

Stewards of the Jockey Club

1. The Stewards of the Jockey Club have power, at their discretion.
   (i) To grant or to refuse to grant licences to Racecourses and to make it a condition of a licence being granted that
      (a) the Racecourse shall be a member of the association of Racecourses currently approved by the Jockey Club.
      (b) facilities shall be afforded on the Racecourse for the operation of the Totalisator.
   (ii) To withdraw licences to Racecourses.

(iii) To fix the dates on which all meetings shall be held and in the case of emergency or expediency to order the abandonment of any race or Race Meeting or to make any alteration in the date of any such Meeting and to supervise and make such alterations as they may think advisable in the programme of, or the conditions of any race at, any Meeting.

(iv) To sanction Point-to-Point fixtures, to authorise the publication of "Jockey Club Regulations for Point-to-Point Steeple Chases" and to make any alterations to them from time to time that they consider necessary.

(v) To prohibit the advertisement of any race or meeting in the *Racing Calendar*, or call upon the Stewards to alter or expunge any conditions, even after advertisement.

(vi) To grant or to refuse to grant and to renew or to refuse to renew licences to officials, jockeys, and trainers and permits to trainers and amateur riders. Every application for renewal of any licence or permit shall be treated and regarded in all respects and for all purposes as if it were the first application by the applicant for such a licence or permit.

(vii) To accept or to refuse to accept or to cancel any registration under these Rules, notwithstanding any implication to the contrary whether contained in Rules 31 or elsewhere.

(viii) To accept or to refuse to accept entries, and in the case of expediency to refuse to allow a horse duly entered to run in any race, in which event the Stewards may direct that the entrance money be remitted to the owner.

(ix) To allow or to refuse to allow any person to act or to continue to act as an authorised agent.

(x) To make enquiry into and deal with any matter relating to racing whether such matters arise in Great Britain or elsewhere.

(xi) To entertain and determine appeals from the Stewards of Meetings as provided for by Rules 176-179.

(xii) To entertain and decide objections lodged under Rule 170 (v).

(xiii) To authorise the publication in the *Racing Calendar* of their decisions respecting any matter and of the decisions and reports of Stewards of Meetings.

(xiv) To publish in the *Racing Calendar* from time to time instructions as they may think fit.

(xv) To exercise any other powers conferred upon them by these Rules and to take any such action as they consider necessary for the purpose of carrying out or putting into effect these Rules.

(xvi) In cases of emergency or expediency, to modify the Rules of Racing or Regulations or any part thereof, or to suspend any Rule or Regulation or any part thereof, for such period or periods as they think fit, without giving previous notice, but should they do so they shall report the fact in the two subsequent issues of the *Racing Calendar*.

2. (i) The Stewards of the Jockey Club have power if good cause is shown or when any person has committed any breach of the Rules of Racing to withdraw or suspend his licence or permit.

(ii) When any person has committed any breach of the

Rules of Racing the Stewards of the Jockey Club have power at their discretion to impose also upon such person any one or more of the following penalties namely—

(a) They may impose any fine not exceeding £500.

(b) They may declare him a disqualified person.

Save that where any Rule prescribes a maximum penalty they may not impose any greater penalty or any penalty of some other kind save that where any Rule prescribes a mandatory penalty they shall impose that penalty. Save as aforesaid the powers given by this Rule are not and are not to be construed as being in any way or in any instance limited or excluded by reason of the fact that some Rules do while others do not prescribe penalties for their breach.

3. The Stewards of the Jockey Club take no cognisance of any disputes or claims with respect to bets, but they will give effect to an official report made to them by the Committee or Tattersall's.

4. The Stewards of the Jockey Club have free access to all stands, rooms, enclosures, and other places used for the purposes of Racing under these Rules.

Stewards of Meetings

10. There must be at least three Stewards for every Meeting appointed by the Racecourse Executive and approved by the Stewards of the Jockey Club, and each Steward may appoint a deputy at any time.

11. Should there not be three Stewards or their deputies present, the Clerk of the Course shall, without delay, see that any vacancy or vacancies are filled, so that there shall be three persons to act, and shall notify conspicuously such appointment.

Powers of the Stewards of Meetings

12. The Stewards have control over, and have free access to, all stands, rooms, enclosures, and other places used for the purposes of the Meeting.

13. The Stewards shall exclude from all places under their control every disqualified person, and all such persons or description of persons as they may from time to time, be required by the Stewards of the Jockey Club to exclude.

14. The Stewards of a Meeting have full power—

(i) to make (and, if necessary, to vary) all such arrangements for the conduct of the meeting as they think fit, and to dispense with the Starting Gate or Starting Stalls, as provided in Rule 28.

(ii) Under exceptional circumstances or if the weather or ground be in an unfit state for running to abandon a day's racing or to abandon any races or to postpone any races to the following day or days within the original fixture, provided that all the races originally advertised for any day shall be included in that day's programme.

Should the Stewards abandon a day's racing on the grounds specified above a Certificate must be drawn up stating the day and the hour when the decision to abandon was arrived at. In the case of a day's racing advertised to take place on a Monday, the decision to abandon shall not be made earlier than 10 a.m. on the preceding Saturday and in all other cases the decision shall not be made before 10 a.m. on the day preceding that on which the day's racing has been advertised to take place. The Certificate must be signed by two of the Stewards or by one Steward and the Clerk of the Course and without delay despatched to the *Racing Calendar* Office.

(iii) To leave out or to alter any (but not more than two) fences or flights of hurdles in the circuit of the course if their retention would necessitate the abandonment of the day's racing, but the original advertised distance of a race must not be decreased.
Should the Stewards authorise the abandonment or postponement of any races, the deletion of any fences or flights of hurdles or vary in any way the programme as originally advertised they shall without delay report to the *Racing Calendar* Office their reasons for so doing.

(iv) To determine all questions arising in reference to racing at the meeting, except as otherwise provided in these Rules and sdbject to appeal under Rule 176.

(v) To call for proof (see Rule 170 (i)) that a horse is neither itself disqualified in any respect, nor nominated by, nor the property, wholly or in part, of a disqualified person; and in default of such proof being given to their satisfaction they may declare the horse disqualified. They have power to prevent from running any horse which cannot be shown to be qualified under these Rules or under the conditions of the race.

(vi) At any time to order an examination by such person or persons as they think fit, of any horse entered for a race, or which has run in a race.

(vii) To exclude at their discretion any person from all or any places under their control.

(viii) To enquire into, regulate, control, take cognisance of, and adjudicate upon, the conduct of all officials, and of all owners, nominators, trainers, riders, grooms, persons attendant upon horses, and of all persons frequenting the Stands or other places used for the purpose of the Meeting.

(ix) By notices exhibited on the Number Board or elsewhere and by any form of public address system at the Racecourse to state and announce that an objection has been lodged, the subject and nature thereof, and also their decision in respect of such objection, or of any other matter coming within their jurisdiction.

15. (i) When in the opinion of the Stewards any person has committed any breach of the Rules of Racing they have power at their discretion to impose upon such person a fine not exceeding £50.

(ii) When in the opinion of the Stewards there is a reasonable suspicion that any person has committed any breach of the Rules of Racing which in their opinion ought to be considered by the Stewards of the Jockey Club, or where in their opinion any person has committed any breach of the Rules of Racing and in their opinion some fine or punishment in excess of £50 ought to be imposed upon such person, they have power at their discretion to report the matter to the Stewards of the Jockey Club.

16. The Stewards, as such, shall not entertain any disputes relating to bets.

Suspension of Riders

17. (i) When in the opinion of the Stewards any rider has committed any breach of or been guilty of any offence under Rule 151 the Stewards in addition to their foregoing powers, have power to suspend him from riding at that racecourse for any period up to seven days beginning at the commencement of the second day after the day of their decision.

(ii) When any rider has been suspended under sub-Rule (i) of this Rule the Stewards of the Jockey Club shall automatically, subject only to the provisions of sub-Rule (iv), suspend the rider from riding in any race at any Meeting at any time on any day up to and including the last day of his suspension.

(iii) Stewards who have suspended a rider from riding shall, if there is a film of the race, forward the film forthwith to the Stewards of the Jockey Club or, if there is no film, shall at the request of the Stewards of the Jockey Club forward to them any transcript of evidence, or such notes of evidence, statements or other material as may be required by the Stewards of the Jockey Club.

(iv) The Stewards of the Jockey Club may at their discretion consider any such film, transcript, notes of evidence, statements or other material and may at their discretion cancel any such order of suspension or reduce the period of the suspension.

(v) On entertaining any appeal from the decision of the Stewards or on a full enquiry into the matters the Stewards of the Jockey Club may without prejudice to the powers contained in Rule 2 extend the period of suspension.

PART 2

GENERAL

General

20. The following officials and other persons require a licence granted annually by the Stewards of the Jockey Club; Clerk of the Course, Handicapper, Clerk of the Scales, Judge, Starter, Assistant Starter, Veterinary Officer, Stewards' Secretary, Inspector of Courses, Ring Inspectors and Jockeys' Valets.

(i) The Clerk of the Course shall be appointed for every Meeting by the Executive of that Meeting, subject to the approval of the Stewards of the Jockey Club, and shall be paid by the Executive.

(ii) All other officials shall be appointed for every Meeting by the Stewards of the Jockey Club. They shall receive such remuneration from the Jockey Club as is required by the terms of their employment. No two offices for the same fixture shall be held by one person, unless by special permission of the Stewards of the Jockey Club.

(iii) The Stakeholders appointed by the Jockey Club shall be Stakeholders for all Meetings.

21. In case of emergency, the Stewards may, during a Meeting, appoint a licensed or unlicensed substitute to fill any of the abovenamed offices for that Meeting only.

22. Every complaint against an official shall be made to the Stewards in writing, signed by the complainant.

Clerk of the Course

23. The Clerk of the Course, or his

authorised substitute, is the sole person responsible to the Stewards for the general arrangements of the Meeting, and the proper construction and maintenance of the Course and fences, he shall see that the Course is properly measured and marked and shall—

(i) arrange for the publication, under the sanction of the Stewards, of a daily official card of the races, containing the conditions of each race, as published in the *Racing Calendar,* the names of the horses engaged together with the saddle cloth number allotted to them by the *Racing Calendar* Office, their pedigrees or descriptions, and such other particulars as the Stewards of the Jockey Club may require. He shall send a copy of each day's card to the *Racing Calendar* Office.

A horse may appear on the card in the name of the owner instead of that of the nominator and the Stewards may, in special circumstances, grant permission for a horse to run in the name of the trainer or of some other person. The Clerk of the Course shall, in such latter case, make a report to the *Racing Calendar* Office, stating the grounds upon which the permission was granted.

(ii) see that a parade ring is provided in the paddock. All horses running at the meeting shall be saddled in the paddock and brought into the parade ring a reasonable time before the signal to mount is given. The attendants shall be provided with badges bearing numbers corresponding with those on the card. In the case of any horse not being brought into the parade ring, or a badge not being exhibited, the trainer shall be reported to the Stewards. No horse shall be admitted to the paddock unless he has been declared to run under Rule 120, or is advertised on the race card for sale. The parade ring shall be reserved strictly for those horses which are about to run. No person shall, without special leave from the Stewards, be allowed access to the parade ring except officials of the meeting and owners, trainers and riders of horses about to run in the next race. Any person refusing to leave shall be reported to the Stewards. For the purpose of this Rule, the Stewards shall determine whether or not the Race-course Stabling forms part of the paddock.

(iii) see that a clean number-cloth, of a pattern approved by the Stewards of the Jockey Club, is provided for every horse for which a rider presents himself to be weighed out.

(iv) have in his possession, for the information of the Stewards, a list of persons disqualified and of persons warned off, and of trainers and riders reported, also a copy of the latest Monthly Forfeit List, and he shall not allow any horse which, or the owner or nominator of which, is in the Forfeit List to start for any race.

(v) make a return to the *Racing Calendar* Office of any Deputy Steward or official appointed, of all complaints to and decisions of the Stewards, of any accident happening in a flat race between the time a jockey weighed out and weighed in, and the result of the enquiry into the accident, which must be held by the Stewards, of all fines inflicted, and of all horses sold or claimed, and these matters will be published in the next available *Racing Calendar*, unless otherwise ordered by the Stewards of the Jockey Club.

Clerk of the Scales

24. The Clerk of the Scales shall—
   (i) weigh the riders in accordance with the Rules (see Parts 14 and 16).
   (ii) exhibit the number (as shown on the official card) of each horse for which a rider has been declared, together with the names of the riders and, in the case of a flat race, the draw for places, and the numbers shall not be taken down until the horses are started. He shall also furnish the Starter with a list of runners.
   When the numbers have been exhibited no alteration or addition except as allowed for in Rules 27 and 28 can be made without leave of the Stewards whose reasons for such permission shall be reported to the *Racing Calendar* Office.
   Should permission have been given for a horse's number to be added after the numbers have been exhibited, the original draw for places shall stand, and the horse added shall be given the highest number.
   (iii) If extra weight or any variation from the weight appearing on the card be declared at scale, for any horse, exhibit such weight with the number, also any alteration of colours, and if a horse be wearing hood or blinkers.
   The following colours on the number board shall denote allowances claimed under Rule 109:—
      7lb allowance — RED number on a WHITE board.
      5lb allowance — BLACK number on an ORANGE board.
      3lb allowance — WHITE number on a BLUE board.
   (iv) at once order such alterations on the number board as the Stewards shall sanction under sub-Rule (ii) of this Rule.
   (v) Should a horse be withdrawn under Rule 28 (x) or 28 (xiii), at once withdraw the number, order a black and white flag to be hoisted, exhibit a notice on the number board stating whether such horse has come under Starter's orders or not, and immediately report to the Stewards that the number is withdrawn by order of the Starter.
   (vi) in all cases, except as provided in Rule 160 (iv), weigh in the riders of the horses placed by the Judge, and report to the Stewards any rider not presenting himself to be weighed in.
   (vii) Should an objection be lodged or an enquiry be called for under Rule 171 (iii), at once order the appropriate signal to be hoisted on the number board, together with the grounds for objection.
   The appropriate signal shall be:—
      All right, Blue flag.
      Objection and/or enquiry under Rule 171 (iii), Red flag with White E.
      Enquiry completed, placings unaltered, enquiry flag replaced by White flag.
      Enquiry completed, placings altered, enquiry flag replaced by Green flag.

(*The Stewards of the Jockey Club have modified Rule 24 (vii) to provide that if the Stewards call for an enquiry into matters contained in Rule 154 the appropriate signal to be hoisted on the Number Board shall be a Red flag with a White E.*)

   (viii) at the close of each day's racing send a return to the *Racing Calendar* Office of the weights carried in every race and the names of the riders, specifying overweight, if any, and of the horses which failed to complete the course, stating the reasons.

Handicapper

25. (i) The Handicapper in making a handicap, shall allot the weights to be carried in accordance with the definition of a handicap and the provisions of Rules 94 and 95. The weights for all handicaps shall be published in the *Racing Calendar* and no alteration shall be made to a weight allotted by the handicapper after publication, except that by express permission of the Stewards, a weight may be affixed for a horse duly entered, but whose name or weight has been omitted from the handicap.

(ii) The Handicapper, unless otherwise instructed, must attend the meeting to which he is appointed. The name of the Handicapper attending the meeting shall appear in the *Racing Calendar* containing the report of the meeting.

The Judge

26. (i) The Judge, or his authorised substitute, must occupy the judge's box at the time the horses pass the winning-post, or the race shall be void. He must announce his decision immediately, or after consulting the photograph, and shall base his decision exclusively on the position of the horses' noses at the time they pass the winning post. Such decision shall be final, unless an objection to the winner, or any placed horses, is made and sustained; provided that this Rule shall not prevent a Judge from correcting any mistake, such correction being subject to confirmation by the Stewards.

(ii) The Judge shall, at the close of each day's racing, sign and send a report of the result of each race to the *Racing Calendar* Office.

Stakeholder

27. (i) The Stakeholders, or their appointed agent, shall not allow a rider to be weighed out for any horse until such horse's stake for that race, and the forfeits for every horse belonging to the same owner, or standing in his name, the jockey's fee, and any arrears claimed under these Rules, have been paid, or the Stakeholders shall themselves be liable.

(ii) The Stakeholders shall at the expiration of fifteen days after the Meeting render an account and pay over all stakes and added money to the persons entitled.

Except that where in respect of any race a horse has been the subject of an examination under Rule 14 (vi), the Stakeholders shall not pay over any money to which any person would (but for this exception) be entitled in respect of the said horse by reason of the said race until authorised to do so by the Stewards of the Jockey Club.

(iii) The full amount of all added money advertised by any Meeting to be given in prizes must be paid to the Stakeholders within three days of the conclusion of the Meeting.

Starter and Starting

28. (i) The Starter shall obtain a list of runners for each race from the Clerk of the Scales in the Weighing Room.

(ii) Every horse shall be at the Post ready to start at the

appointed time. In races confined to apprentices horses shall not be led to the Start.

(iii) All riders who arrive at the Starting Post must immediately place themselves under the control of the Starter.

(iv) The horses must be started by the Official Starter, or his authorised substitute, and all races shall be started from Starting Stalls or by a Starting Gate approved by the Stewards of the Jockey Club but, by their special permission, or in the case of emergency by permission of the Stewards of the Meeting or the Starter, a race may be started with a flag.

(v) The Starter shall call over the names of the runners and for Flat races assign the horses to the places drawn by lot, all horses taking their place at the Start in the order drawn for them. The rider who has drawn No. 1 must always be placed on the left and other riders must take their places in consecutive numbers from the left.

(vi) The Starter shall give all orders necessary for securing a fair start. The horses must be started, as far as possible, in a line, but they may be started at such reasonable distance behind the Starting Post as the Starter thinks necessary.

(vii) In a start from a Starting Gate or with a Flag, the Starter has full power to remove an unruly horse and, should he do so, he must place it at such distance to one side of or behind the other runners that it cannot gain any advantage itself or cause danger to, or prejudice the chances of the other horses and riders engaged in the race. Permission may be given by the Starter for a horse to be held or the Starter may himself order an unruly horse to be held, but in all cases the horse must be held "at a stand" behind the other runners. Should an unruly horse cause undue delay it may be "left".

(viii) In a start from Starting Stalls, the Starter has full power to remove an unruly horse but no horse shall be permitted to start from outside the Stalls, nor is it permitted for a horse to be held in the Stalls. A horse which refuses to enter the Stalls shall be withdrawn by the Starter.

(ix) The Starter shall order the white flag denoting that the horses are under Starter's orders to be hoisted:

(a) for races started from Starting Stalls when all the horses are in the Stalls.

(b) for races started from a Starting Gate when he has mounted his rostrum.

(c) for races started by Flag when he has taken up his position to start the race.

(x) Should the Starter consider that through any cause a horse is unable to start he shall at once notify the Clerk of the Scales that the number must be withdrawn and shall inform him whether the horse came under Starter's orders or not. No horse which has come under Starter's orders shall be withdrawn except under the provisions of sub-Rules (x) or (xiii) of this Rule.

(xi) The Starter has power to inflict a fine not exceeding £10 on any rider who misconducts himself at the Post and should a rider be so fined the Starter shall report the fact at once to the Stewards. He shall also report to the Stewards any rider who misconducts himself at the start.

(xii) Should the Starter consider that through any faulty action of the Starting Gate or Starting Stall a fair Start has not been effected he shall declare it a false Start and order the riders, by means of a recall flag, to return to the Post. The Starter's decision on these points shall be final.

(xiii) A start in front of the Starting Post, or on a wrong course, or before the appointed time, is void.

(a) For Flat races the horses must be started again as soon as practicable but, in the event of any horse running the course from a false start, or from a void start, the owner may, with the consent of the Stewards, withdraw his horse from the race; the horse shall, nevertheless, be considered as having come under Starter's orders.

(b) In Steeple Chases or Hurdle races, unless at least one rider returns to the Starter after the recall flag has been raised for a false start, the race shall be void. Should only one rider return to the Starter and satisfy him as to his having obeyed the recall flag, his horse shall be considered as having walked over for the race. Should more than one return the race shall be started again as soon as the course is clear. Horses which complete a circuit of the course or fall shall not be considered as having obeyed the recall flag. All horses which were recalled by the Starter shall, nevertheless, be considered as having come under Starter's orders. The Starter's decision on all matters covered by this sub-Rule shall be final.

(xiv) The Starter shall report to the Stewards, for transmission to the *Racing Calendar* Office, all cases in which he has dispensed with the Starting Stalls or Starting Gate or made any notification under sub-Rule (x), and his reasons for doing so, the time at which the race was started, and by whom or by what cause any delay was occasioned.

PART 3

HORSES

Age

30. The age of a horse shall be reckoned as beginning on the 1st January in the year in which he is foaled.

Registration of Names

31. (i) A name cannot be registered for a horse before it is a yearling unless the horse is foaled elsewhere than in Great Britain, Ireland or the Channel Islands, or is outside these countries at the date of registration.

(ii) A name can only be registered for a horse by application to the *Racing Calendar* Office on the prescribed form, unless otherwise ordered by the Stewards of the Jockey Club.

(iii) The application must state the colour, sex and age together with the registered name of the sire and dam but if either the sire or dam is not registered such further particulars must be given as will clearly identify the horse from all other horses.

(iv) The application must be accompanied by a certificate of age and markings signed by a Veterinary Surgeon who is neither the owner nor the trainer nor a person for whom the trainer of the horse holds a current Identity Card, but a veterinary certificate of markings is not required for a horse which is outside Great Britain, Ireland or the Channel Islands at the date of registration.

(v) If the name is available the criteria laid down by the Stewards of the Jockey Club in "Registered Names of Horses" and has not been reserved under sub-Rule (vii) of this Rule, the name will be registered and will, from the Monday after registration, be the horse's name under these Rules.

(vi) A numeral may only be added, when a name is not available, if the horse was foaled in Great Britain, Ireland or the Channel Islands and is not in the General Stud Book.

(vii) When a name is registered for a horse foaled outside Great Britain, Ireland or the Channel Islands, a letter code will be added to denote the country of origin.

(viii) A name, if available, may be reserved for a living foal by application made in writing to the *Racing Calendar* Office stating the sire and dam of the foal. A name so reserved can only be registered in accordance with the preceding paragraphs of this Rule and the registration fee shall be incurred in addition to the reservation fee. A name cannot be reserved for more than twelve months. A reserved name does not identify a horse for the purposes of these Rules.

(ix) A name may not be changed for any horse:
(a) that is more than three years old, or
(b) whose name has been registered by another recognised Turf Authority except with the permission of that Turf Authority, or
(c) that has been entered under the Rules of any recognised Turf Authority.

(x) A change of name must be applied for in the same way as a registration of name.

(xi) If the same name be simultaneously claimed for two horses, the order of priority shall be determined by lot at the *Racing Calendar* Office.

(xii) Every provision contained in this Rule shall be subject to the power conferred upon the Stewards of the Jockey Club by Rule 1 (vii) to accept or to refuse to accept or to cancel any registration under these Rules, notwithstanding any contrary implication which may be contained in any such provision.

(xiii) A list of names registered and changes of names shall be published in the *Racing Calendar*.

(xiv) The following name registration fees are payable:
(a) for the reservation of a name . . 10s.
(b) for the registration of a name . . 10s.
(c) for a change of name 10s.

(*The Stewards of the Jockey Club have modified Rule 31* (*xiv*) *to provide that, on and after April 1st, 1970, the fees for the registration of Horses' Names shall be as follows:—*

Under 2 years old	*10s.*
2 years old	*£2*
3 and 4 years old	*£5*
5 years old and upwards	*£10*)

Passports for Horses

32. (i) Passports will be issued annually for named two years old horses in the care of licensed trainers and other horses as

authorised by the Stewards of the Jockey Club. They are returnable on demand and are issued subject to the instructions laid down by the Stewards of the Jockey Club for their use.

(ii) The Stewards of the Jockey Club may require such passports to be lodged with the Clerk of the Course for any race before the horses are declared under Rule 141 (i) so that the horse's identification may be verified by a Veterinary Surgeon before running.

Foreign Horses

33. A horse foaled elsewhere than in Great Britain, Ireland, or the Channel Islands shall not be declared a runner under Rule 141 (i) for any race until:

(i) A Passport has been lodged with the Clerk of the Course for verification by a Veterinary Surgeon, or

(ii) there have been deposited either at the *Racing Calendar* Office or with the Clerk of the Course of the Meeting, for transmission to the *Racing Calendar* Office, the following certificates, and a fee of 5s. paid on each of them:

(a) A certificate of pedigree, stating the name, pedigree, age, sex, and colour of the horse, and any mark by which it may be distinguished, signed by the official Stud Book authority of the country in which the horse was foaled. Should there not be an official Stud Book, the Stewards of the Jockey Club may approve of the certificate being signed by the Secretary of the recognised Turf Authority and

(b) A certificate of identification, which must also state the age, colour, and sex, and any marks by which the horse may be identified, and must be signed in Great Britain, Ireland, or the Channel Islands by a Veterinary Surgeon who is neither the owner nor the trainer nor a person for whom the trainer of the horse holds a current Identity Card.

34. A horse which has been out of Great Britain, Ireland, or the Channel Islands (but not from one to the other of any of those places) shall not be declared a runner under Rule 141 (i) for any race under these Rules unless:

(i) A Passport has been lodged with the Clerk of the Course for verification by a Veterinary Surgeon, or

(ii) There has been lodged either at the *Racing Calendar* Office or with the Clerk of the Course of the Meeting, for transmission to the *Racing Calendar* Office, the following certificates:—

(a) A certificate of his pedigree which was issued by the Stud Book Authority on his leaving the country (except under special circumstances and with the permission of the Stewards of the Jockey Club) and

(b) A Certificate of Identification as laid down in Rule 33 (ii) (b).

The Stewards of the Jockey Club may also require any further proof of identification in any particular case, and may declare any horse disqualified in default thereof.

Vaccination of Horses

35. A horse trained elsewhere than in Great Britain or which has

been out of Great Britain shall not enter any racecourse stables or be declared a runner under Rule 141 (i) unless it has a Veterinary Certificate showing that it has a primary Vaccination against Equine Influenza and that that Vaccination or a further one has been carried out during the previous twelve months.

Rule 35 will not apply to Steeple Chases and Hurdle Races until July 1st, 1970.

(INFLUENZA VACCINATION, 1970

As the result of discussions between the Turf Authorities of England, France and Ireland, it has been agreed that the vaccination requirements for horses going abroad to race in any of the three countries in 1970 should be modified as follows:—

The horse must have been vaccinated with a vaccine approved in its country of domicile. The vaccination to be either

(a) A primary vaccination (consisting of two injections) given within the previous 18 months and before November 1st, 1969, or

(b) A primary vaccination or booster given within the previous 12 months and since November 1st, 1969.

From January 1st, 1971, the full requirements of the Rules and Instructions of the three countries as already published will be in force.

MODIFICATION OF RULE

The Stewards of the Jockey Club have modified Rule 35 in accordance with above for 1970.)

PART 4

OWNERS, RECOGNISED CLUBS AND COMPANIES, SYNDICATES, PARTNERSHIPS, LEASES, COLOURS

Owners

40. No owner shall make use of an assumed name for the purpose of entering or running horses, and any horse entered under an assumed name shall, on objection, be disqualified. Nothing in these Rules shall prevent the personal representative of a deceased owner running a horse solely under the description "Executor(s) (or Administrator(s) or Personal Representative) of . . . deceased".

Recognised Clubs

41. A "recognised Club" is a Club, whether proprietary or members, which has been approved and registered as a "recognised Club" by the Stewards of the Jockey Club.

The Stewards of the Jockey Club shall have complete discretion whether to approve and register any Club as a recognised Club or not, save that they shall refuse to approve and register a Club as a recognised Club unless:

(i) they are satisfied that the Club was established before the 1st June, 1968 (or such other date as they may from time to time determine) for normal social and recreational pursuits and that those pursuits have not and have never had any connection direct or indirect with racehorse ownership anywhere in the world;

(ii) they have approved the Rules of the Club and any amendments or additions to or deletions from the Rules required by them have been duly made by the Club;

(iii) a list of members of the Club complete as at midnight on the day before lodgment has been lodged at the Registry Office if so required by the Stewards of the Jockey Club.

Any amendment or addition to or deletion from the Rules of the Club made after the Rules have been approved by the Stewards of the Jockey Club shall be notified to the Stewards of the Jockey Club and the Stewards may at any time require the Club to furnish an up-to-date list of members. Without prejudice to the foregoing, the Stewards of the Jockey Club may at their absolute discretion at any time and without assigning any reason therefor withdraw their approval of the Club which thereupon shall cease to be a recognised Club.

42. (i) A recognised Club may enter and run a horse under its own name provided that the legal ownership of the horse is vested in a body of not more than four trustees on behalf of the Club each of whom has been and is of whose names has been and is registered at the approved by the Stewards of the Jockey Club and each Registry Office. The Stewards of the Jockey Club shall not approve trustees and their names may not be registered unless the Stewards of the Jockey Club have approved any trust deed or other document appointing the trustees and establishing their powers and unless any amendment or addition to or deletion from the trust deed or other document required by the Stewards of the Jockey Club has been duly made by the Club. Without prejudice to the foregoing the Stewards may at their absolute discretion refuse to approve any trustee without assigning any reason therefor and they may at their absolute discretion at any time and without assigning any reason therefor withdraw the approval of any trustee and cancel the registration of his name.

(ii) The horse shall be entered in the name of one of the trustees, but there will be no objection to the horse running under the name of the Club.

(iii) The trustees shall for the purposes of these Rules be treated as though they are joint owners and are subject to all the liabilities, duties and privileges of joint ownership.

(iv) The Stewards of the Jockey Club take no cognisance of any disputes arising between the trustees and the members of the Club.

(v) Other than having the privilege of running the horse under the name of the Club no privilege of ownership shall attach to any member of the Club other than the trustees.

Recognised Companies

43. A "recognised Company" means a company incorporated under any statutory enactment and whether with limited or unlimited liability of which the principal object is to carry on the business of breeding bloodstock and which has been registered at the Registry Office as a "recognised Company".

The Stewards of the Jockey Club shall have complete discretion whether to register a Company as a recognised Company or not save that they shall refuse to register such a Company unless they are satisfied both as to its principal object and that the business of breeding bloodstock is being carried on as a main activity of the Company. The Stewards of the Jockey Club may at their absolute discretion at any time and without assigning any reason therefor cancel the registration of a Company as a recognised Company.

44. A recognised Company may enter and run a horse in its sole ownership through a nominee. Such nominee shall be approved

by the Stewards of the Jockey Club who may at their absolute discretion refuse their approval without assigning any reason therefor. They may at their absolute discretion at any time and without assigning any reason therefor withdraw their approval. The name of the nominee when and so long as he is approved by the Stewards of the Jockey Club shall be registered at the Registry Office together with the particulars of the horse concerned. The nominee when registered shall be subject to these Rules in all respects as if he were an absolute owner. A recognised Company may cancel a registration of its nominee only after lodging with the Stewards of the Jockey Club such sum as in the opinion of the Stewards (whose decision shall be final) is sufficient to cover all outstanding liabilities incurred by the nominee in respect of the horse. No horse belonging to a recognised Company may fulfil any engagement whilst there is no nominee in respect of it on the Register.

Syndicates

45. (i) A syndicate of not more than 12 persons may share an interest in a horse provided that the legal ownership of the horse is vested in not more than four members of the syndicate who shall be treated as joint owners and be subject to all the liabilities, duties and privileges of joint ownership.

(ii) The horse may not be entered or run in any race unless and until the names of the members of the syndicate and of the joint owners have been lodged at the Registry Office and approved by the Stewards of the Jockey Club who may at their absolute discretion grant or withhold their approval.

(iii) The Stewards may at their absolute discretion at any time and without assigning any reason therefor withdraw their approval of any member of the syndicate, in which event the horse shall cease to be eligible to enter or run in any race until fresh arrangements approved by the Stewards have been made.

(iv) The horse shall not be eligible to be entered or run in any race whilst any member of the syndicate is a disqualified person.

Partnerships, Sales With Contingencies, Leases etc.

46. The name of the horse must be registered before registration under this Rule can be made.

(i) Where a horse is owned by more than one person other than by syndicates to which the foregoing Rule applies, a document stating the name and address of every person, of whom there shall not be more than four, having an interest in such horse, and the relative proportions of such interest, must, except as allowed by Rule 112 (ii), be signed by all the parties, or their authorised agents and lodged at the *Racing Calendar* Office or with the Clerk of the Course for transmission to the *Racing Calendar* Office, whereupon the partnership shall be deemed to be registered unless thereafter the Stewards of the Jockey Club refuse to accept the registration. All partners shall be jointly and severally liable for every stake or forfeit, and no part owner shall assign his share, or any part thereof, in a horse without the consent of his partners.

(ii) Where a horse is sold with contingencies, leased, or is the subject of any other joint arrangement, a document stating the names and addresses of all the parties interested shall be signed and lodged as above, and shall state fully the terms of such sale with contingencies, lease, or other arrangement whereupon the sale with contingencies, lease, or other arrangement shall be deemed to be registered unless thereafter the Stewards of the Jockey Club refuse to accept the registration. No party to a lease shall assign his interest in the same without the consent of all other parties to it.

(iii) Where a horse is the property of a syndicate, or a partnership, or where it is the subject of any sale with contingencies, lease or arrangement requiring registration under this Rule, registration of the partnership, sale with contingencies, lease or arrangement must have been effected before the horse may be entered for any race or run in any race.

(iv) If any horse starts for any race without the particulars of such partnership, sale with contingencies, lease or arrangement having been lodged he shall, on an objection under Rule 170 (v) be disqualified, unless it be proved to the satisfaction of the Stewards of the Jockey Club that the omission to lodge the particulars thereof was accidental and unless the Stewards of the Jockey Club certify that they accept the registration thereof, in which case the person responsible for the omission to lodge the particulars shall be fined not less than £5.

(v) All partnerships, sales with contingencies, leases and other joint arrangements, shall be published in the next available *Racing Calendar* and any termination, or severance, must be notified at once to the *Racing Calendar* Office for publication.

(vi) A fee of £5 shall be paid for each horse for each registration under this Rule.

Racing Colours

47. (i) Racing colours shall be registered annually by application at the *Racing Calendar* Office and colours so registered shall not be taken by any other person.
All disputes as to the right to particular colours shall be settled by the Stewards of the Jockey Club.

(ii) Any person running a horse in colours other than those registered in his own name, without a special declaration to the Overnight Declarations Office by the time fixed for declaring runners under Rule 120 (i), shall be fined not less than £2 nor more than £10.

(iii) An annual fee of £2 shall be paid for each registration of colours.

PART 5

TRAINERS

50. Every trainer in Great Britain of a horse running under these Rules (except as provided in sub-Rule (ii) of this Rule), must obtain from the Stewards of the Jockey Club a licence or permit as follows, which may be granted subject to such restrictions as the Stewards consider necessary:—

(i) For Flat races, a Flat race trainer's licence to be applied for annually.

(ii) For Steeple Chases and Hurdle races, a Steeple Chase and Hurdle race trainer's licence, or, in the case of persons training only those horses which are the sole property of themselves, or of their spouses, sons or unmarried daughters, a Steeple Chase and Hurdle race trainer's permit, such licence or permit to be applied for each season; except that, for the sole purpose of Hunters' Steeple Chases, a horse may also be trained privately without licence or permit by the proprietor of the stable from whence the horse was regularly and fairly hunted, during the current season as required for a Hunters' Certificate, but in the event the owner shall be treated as trainer for all purposes under these Rules.

The fees to be paid in respect of each such licence or permit shall be such as the Stewards of the Jockey Club shall from time to time decide. The sum of £1 from each fee shall be allocated to the Bentinck or Rendlesham Benevolent Funds as directed by the Stewards of the Jockey Club.

51. Every trainer shall conduct his business properly and with due regard to the interest of his owners. Any negligent or improper conduct in respect of his business shall constitute an offence under these Rules punishable by the Stewards of the Jockey Club by virtue of the powers contained in Rule 2.

52. Where any horse has run in any race under these Rules and has been found, on examination under Rule 14 (vi), to have re ceived any substance (other than a normal nutrient) which could have altered its racing performance at the time of runing in the said race, the trainer of the horse in question shall be fined not less than £100 or, at the discretion of the Stewards of the Jockey Club, his licence or permit shall be withdrawn.

53. (i) No trainer shall employ any person to work in his stable who has previously been in a training stable without referring to his last employer, and receiving a satisfactory reply in writing. Any person prevented by this Rule from obtaining or retaining employment shall have the right of appeal to the Stewards of the Jockey Club.

(ii) No trainer shall engage or retain any person in respect of whom a current Identity Card has not been issued by or on behalf of the Stewards of the Jockey Club.

(iii) Identity Cards are issued only upon the application of the trainer concerned and must be accompanied by the written consent of the proposed employee to be bound by the Rules of Racing. Identity Cards are the property of the Stewards of the Jockey Club; they are returnable on demand and may be granted subject to conditions, refused or cancelled at any time at their absolute discretion.

Note: Application forms for Identity Cards and forms of consent to be signed by proposed employees must be obtained from the Registry Office.

(iv) Any trainer infringing sub-Rules (i) and (ii) of this Rule shall be reported to the Stewards of the Jockey Club.

N.B.—For the purposes of this Rule, trainer shall be understood to mean a person holding a licence or permit to train under Rule 50.

PART 6

RIDERS

Amateur Riders

60. No person shall ride as an amateur rider in any race until he

has obtained from the Stewards of the Jockey Club subject to such restrictions as the Stewards consider necessary:

(i) For Flat races a Flat race permit to ride as an amateur to be applied for annually. Holders of these permits may only ride in races confined to Amateur riders.

(ii) (a) For Steeple Chases and Hurdle races until he has ridden ten winners collectively under the Rules of any recognised Turf Authority, a Steeple Chase and Hurdle race "A" permit to ride as an amateur to be applied for each season.

(b) For Steeple Chases and Hurdle races after he has ridden ten winners collectively under the Rules of any recognised Turf Authority, a Steeple Chase and Hurdle race "B" permit to ride as an amateur to be applied for each season. The first application for this permit may be made after he has ridden seven winners.

61. An amateur rider who holds a trainer's licence under the Rules of any recognised Turf Authority shall only be qualified to ride horses the sole property of himself or his wife, but this restriction shall not apply to a person holding a Steeple Chase or Hurdle race trainer's permit under these Rules.

62. A fee of £2 shall be paid for each permit to ride.

Jockeys

63. No person who has ever ridden for hire shall ride in any race, except an apprentice as provided for below, until he has obtained from the Stewards of the Jockey Club subject to such restrictions as the Stewards consider necessary:

(i) For Flat races, a Flat race jockey's licence or an apprentice jockey's licence, each to be applied for annually.

Apprentice jockeys' licences must be applied for by the master and they are granted only in respect of lads who have, of their own free will, and with the consent of their parents or guardians, bound themselves for a period of not less than three years to a Flat race trainer licensed under these Rules, are over fifteen but under twenty-three years of age and have never, at the time of the first application for an apprentice licence, ridden as full jockeys under the Rules of any recognised Turf Authority.

On attaining the age of twenty-three no lad may ride as an apprentice.

An apprentice, provided he has never previously held a licence or ridden under the Rules of any recognised Turf Authority, may, if he fulfils the above conditions, ride for one week without a licence.

In the event of

(a) the apprenticeship agreement being cancelled by consent

(b) the apprentice leaving the master's establishment without the master's consent express or implied, or

(c) the master relinquishing his trainer's licence or having it suspended or withdrawn

(d) the apprenticeship terminating for any other reason

the apprentice's licence shall forthwith be automatically revoked, save that

In the event of the death of the master the apprentice jockey's licence shall remain in force for seven clear days from the date of death and thereafter shall be automatically revoked.

During the seven days period the apprentice shall be answerable to the Stewards of the Jockey Club in the same manner as he would otherwise have been answerable to the master and all fees earned by the apprentice during this period shall be paid to them. The Stewards of the Jockey Club shall during this period pay to the apprentice such remuneration as in the circumstances they think fair.

64. Licences are only granted on the condition that a jockey is not an owner or part-owner of any racehorse, and does not bet on horse racing or receive presents in connection with a race from persons other than the owner of the horse he rides in that race. Any jockey who may be proved, to the satisfaction of the Stewards of the Jockey Club, to have contravened any of the above conditions will have his licence withdrawn.

65. (i) Every jockey shall pay £1 and every apprentice 10s., for his licence to ride in Flat races, to be applied as his subscription to the Bentinck Benevolent Fund.
(ii) Every jockey shall pay £1 10s. for his licence to ride in Steeple Chases and Hurdle races, one half to be applied as his subscription to the Rendlesham Fund and one half to be applied for the purpose of the Horserace Betting Levy Board (Racing Industry) Accident Scheme.

General

66. Any horse ridden in a race in contravention of Rules 60 and 63 of these Rules shall, on objection, be liable to be disqualified by the Stewards of the Jockey Club.

67. (i) An amateur rider or a jockey whose permit or licence has been suspended by the Stewards of the Jockey Club or by any other recognised Turf Authority shall not ride in any race during the period of his suspension.
(ii) If an amateur rider or a jockey becomes a disqualified person his permit or licence is thereby revoked.

68. A list of the amateur riders and licensed jockeys shall be published in the *Racing Calendar*.

Part 7
Riders Fees, Expenses and Retainers

Fees and Expenses

70. In Flat races—
(i) the fee to a jockey riding on a temporary licence shall be £8 13s.
(ii) the fee to a jockey shall be £10 10s., from which shall be deducted:
(a) £1 15s. to be paid into an expense fund from which a jockey shall be entitled to £3 for each day of each meeting at which he rides (no other charge for expenses shall be made).
(b) 2s. to be applied for the purpose of the Horserace Betting Levy Board (Racing Industry) Accident Scheme.

71. In Steeple Chases and Hurdle races—
(i) the fee to a jockey riding on

a temporary licence shall be £12 15s.

(ii) the fee to a jockey shall be £13 10s., from which shall be deducted 15s. to be applied for the purpose of the Horserace Betting Levy Board (Racing Industry) Accident Scheme.

In addition when a jockey is requested to leave home for the purpose of riding, the cost of travelling expenses and £1 a day for living may be charged to the owner or divided between the owners at whose request he left home. Every jockey sending in a charge for expenses at a meeting shall state at the same time what charge has been made to other owners for attending the same meeting.

(The Stewards of the Jockey Club have modified Rules 70 and 71 to provide that a jockey's fee is payable when the jockey has weighed out for, and is fit to ride in, a race, and that race has not been abandoned by the time fixed for declaration under Rule 141.)

Jockeys' Retainers

72. Every jockey at the termination of his apprenticeship is free to form engagements for himself, irrespective of any which have been made for him during such apprenticeship.
The terms of all agreements must be registered and no agreement shall provide for a jockey to ride for a lower fee than that laid down in Rules 70 and 71.
In the absence of special agreement, a jockey's retainer terminates at the end of the relevant racing season. Half the agreed retaining fee must be paid in advance, and the remainder at the termination of the retainer.

73. Employers retaining the same jockey have precedence according to the priority of their retainers but the Stewards of the Jockey Club may adjudicate between persons claiming the services of any jockey, and on disputes between jockeys and their employers, and have power to cancel any agreement between them.

PART 8

REGULATIONS FOR RACE MEETINGS

Licenses and Fixtures

80. All Racecourses must be licensed, and all meetings sanctioned by the Stewards of the Jockey Club.

81. Racecourses requiring fixtures for the following year must send to the Registry Office by March 1st of the current year.
(i) A statement of accounts for the preceding year made up to December 31st on a form prescribed by the Stewards of the Jockey Club, and obtainable at the Registry Office. Such statement must be certified by a Chartered, or Certified Accountant.
(ii) Such other information as may be required by the Stewards of the Jockey Club.

Steeple Chase and Hurdle Race Courses

82. In all Steeple Chase courses—
(i) All fences, except those at water-jumps, must be not less than four feet six inches in height.
(ii) In the first two miles there shall be at least twelve fences, and in each succeeding mile at least six fences.
(iii) In the first two miles there shall be at least one ditch six feet wide and two feet deep on the take-off side of a fence, guarded by a bank and rail not exceeding two feet in height.

(iv) There shall be a water-jump at least twelve feet wide and two feet deep*, guarded by a fence not exceeding three feet in height and this water-jump may be regarded as one of the fences prescribed by section (ii).

* NOTE.—The shelve from the floor of the water on the landing side to begin six feet from the landing edge. A horizontal turfed shelf two inches below the surface of the water to extend inwards from the landing edge of the water for eighteen inches to meet the top of the shelve.

83. In all Hurdle race courses

(i) All hurdles must be not less than three feet six inches in height from the bottom bar to the top bar.

(ii) In the first two miles there shall be at least eight flights of hurdles with an additional flight of hurdles for every complete quarter of a mile beyond that distance.

PART 9

PROGRAMMES, HANDICAPS AND SELLING RACES

General Regulations for Programmes

90. The conditions of every race before closing and the full programme of every meeting before it takes place must be published in the *Racing Calendar* and no alterations can be made in the conditions of any race after such publication except as provided in sub-Rule (v) of this Rule, but a race may be declared void if the number of entries required by advertisement is not obtained. This Rule shall not preclude the addition of more money to a race before the time of closing.

(i) The advertisement before closing must state that the meeting is subject to the Rules of Racing, the dates on which it is to be held, the dates for closing the races and, where necessary, for the declaration of forfeit, when the weights for the handicaps will be published and the time from which penalties for winning will be incurred, the dates for declarations to run under Rule 120 (i) and for cancellations thereof, the name of the Handicapper and, for Flat races, the lowest permitted handicap weight and the times of the first and last races.

(ii) The full programme of every meeting must state the names of three or more persons as Stewards and the names of the Clerk of the Course, Clerk of the Scales, Handicapper, Judge and Starter.

(iii) Conditions of races shall provide

(a) the liability at any monetary stage and the total liability for runners shall be in accordance with the percentages laid down from time to time by the Stewards of the Jockey Club.

(b) the minimum advertised value of plates and minimum amounts to be added to sweepstakes shall be not less than that laid down from time to time by the Stewards of the Jockey Club.

(c) the value of prizes not in money must be advertised.

(iv) (a) In plates of the advertised value of £4,000 or more or sweepstakes with £4,000 or more added, there shall be a fourth prize, the second shall receive 20 per cent, the third 10 per cent and the fourth 3 per cent for Flat races and not less than 5 per cent in Steeple Chases and Hurdle races, of the advertised value of the plate or of the whole stakes, but excluding any prize given specifically to the trainer, rider or stable in the conditions of the race.

(b) in all other races there shall not be a fourth prize except by permission of the Stewards of the Jockey Club, the second shall receive 20 per cent and the third 10 per cent of the advertised value of the plate, or in the case of sweepstakes, of the amount added thereto or of the whole stakes, but excluding any prize given specifically to the trainer, rider or stable in the conditions of the race.

(c) no prize shall be given to any but the first four horses placed and any additional prizes to trainers, riders or the stable of the first four horses placed are subject to the approval of the Stewards of the Jockey Club.

(v) In the event of any part of the conditions of a race being omitted from the advertisement the Stewards of the Jockey Club shall give such directions as may seem to them in the circumstances to be just.

Regulations for Programmes for Flat Races

91. At every meeting at which Flat races are advertised the following Rules for programmes shall apply for Flat races.

Distribution of Prize Money

(i) One-half at least of the total amount guaranteed for prizes shall be apportioned to races of a mile or over for three yrs old or upwards, and of the sum so apportioned not less than a half shall be for races of a mile and a quarter or upwards; but where more than one meeting is held at the same place during the current racing season, the apportionment may be calculated over each meeting or over all the meetings.

Restrictions on Running

(ii) (a) Yearlings shall not run for any race.

(b) There shall be no race of less distance than five furlongs.

Two yrs old

(iii) Of the races confined to two yrs old there shall not be more than two races a day before September 1st, nor more than three a day at any time, and two-year-olds shall not run—

(a) more than five furlongs before the Epsom Summer Meeting.

(b) more than six furlongs before July 1st.

(c) more than seven furlongs before September 1st.

(d) for handicaps before August 1st, nor in handicaps with older horses.

(e) in any race with selling conditions, after having won such race.

(f) in any plate of the advertised value of more than £1,500, or in any sweepstakes with more than £1,000 added before the Epsom Summer Meeting, or after the commencement of that Meeting without the specific permission of the Stewards of the Jockey Club, in any plate of the advertised value of more than £5,000, or in any sweepstakes with more than £5,000 added.

General

(iv) (a) There shall not be more than one race per day with selling conditions at any race meeting.

(b) In each day's programme there shall be two races of a mile or upwards of the minimum aggregate distance of two miles and a half. These races must differ at least one furlong in distance, and they shall fill with five entries. Neither of these shall be open to two yrs old, and one of them shall be neither a handicap nor a race with selling conditions.

(c) In each day's programme there shall not be more than two races, to which three yrs old or upwards are admitted, of less than seven furlongs, and of these two races only one may be less than six furlongs.

(d) The programme for Saturdays and Bank Holidays shall consist solely of sweepstakes. The programmes for all other days shall not include more than three plates.

(e) Upon all Race-courses having four or more days' racing during the year (except those having only one fixture) there shall be at least two races during the season confined to apprentices.

(f) Matches and private sweepstakes may be sanctioned by the Stewards, independent of the above regulations. No prize can be added to private sweepstakes or matches.

Handicaps

(v) (a) There shall be not more than three handicaps, including nursery handicaps, per day in any programme of six races. In cases where a seventh race is included, it may be an additional handicap.

(b) There shall not be any handicap confined to maidens, or to horses which have not won at the time of closing, or to horses which have not won a race at closing below a minimum value. Such minimum value shall be laid down from time to time by the Stewards of the Jockey Club.

(c) Except by specific permission of the Stewards of the Jockey Club there shall be no handicap plate of the advertised value of more than £5,000, or handicap sweepstakes with more than £5,000 added.

(d) In handicaps there shall be no clause permitting an alteration of the weights after publication by the claim of a selling allowance.

Weights

(vi) No horse shall carry less than 7st in any race except in a nursery handicap where the lowest weight may be 6st 7lb unless in either case an apprentice allowance under Rule 109 is claimed. In any race confined to apprentices the lowest weight carried may be 6st 7lb.

Regulations for Programmes for Steeple Chases and Hurdle Races

92. At every meeting at which Steeple Chases or Hurdle races are advertised the following regulations for programmes shall apply to the Steeple Chases and Hurdle races.

Distribution of Prize Money

(i) One-half at least of the total amount guaranteed for prizes shall be apportioned to Steeple Chases; but where more than one meeting is held at the same place during the current year, the apportionment may be calculated over each meeting, or all the meetings.

Restrictions on Running

(ii) (a) No horse shall run for a Hurdle race until the 1st of July of the year in which he is three yrs old, for a Steeple Chase until the 1st July of the year in which he is four yrs old, nor for any race for which certificates from Masters of Hounds are required until the 1st of February of the year in which he is five yrs old.

(b) There shall be no race of less distance than two miles.

(iii) With respect to Hunters' Steeple Chases—

(a) No such race shall be run before February 1st of the current Steeple Chase and Hurdle race Season, and in all such races the qualification in respect of having been hunted shall be limited to that season.

(b) No horse shall be qualified to be entered or start in such races which has run in a race between November 1st and January 31st (inclusive) of the current Steeple Chase and Hurdle race Season.

(c) For all such races a Hunter's Certificate upon the form issued by the Stewards of the Jockey Club, in respect of every horse, must be deposited at the *Racing Calendar* Office with a fee of 10s. for registration, but such registration cannot be made unless the horse's name has also been registered. A certificate so registered by noon on a Wednesday shall qualify the horse concerned to run on and after the Monday following.

General

(iv) (a) There shall be in each day's programme at least two Steeple Chases, one of which must be of three miles or upwards.

(b) Not more than one selling race per day may be included in the programme.

(c) In the conditions of any race there shall be no restrictions with regard to training stables, nor shall there be any riders' allowances other than those provided by Rule 109 except in those races confined to riders who have not ridden twenty-five winners.

Handicaps

(v) No handicaps shall be permitted that are confined to horses which are maidens or which have not won a Steeple Chase and/or a Hurdle race at the time of entry.

Weights

(vi) No horse shall carry less than 10st except in a Handicap Steeple Chase of three miles and a half and upwards, when the lowest weight may be 9st 7lb, unless in either case a rider's allowance as provided in Rule 109 is claimed.

Mixed Meetings

93. At Meetings where both Flat races and Steeple Chases or Hurdle races are advertised to be run the regulations for Programmes contained in Rules 91 and 92 shall apply as far as possible, but the complete programme shall be subject to approval by the Stewards of the Jockey Club.

Special Rules Applicable to Handicaps

94. At every meeting at which Flat races are advertised the following

special conditions shall apply for Flat race handicaps:—

(i) No horse shall run in a handicap which has not run three times in Flat races or won a Flat race under these Rules before the Sunday previous to the publication of weights.

(ii) In handicaps confined to apprentices there shall be no minimum top weight and in handicaps not confined to apprentices the top weight to be allotted shall be:

(a) in handicaps confined to three yrs old taking place before August 1st, and in nursery handicaps not less than 9st 7lb.

(b) in all other handicaps, not less than 10st.

(iii) If in handicaps in which forfeit may be declared by a fixed time, the highest weight accepting in races listed under (a) above be less than 9st, or, in races listed under (b) above be less than 9st 7lb, it shall be raised to that weight and all other acceptances equally. Such raising of weights shall apply only at the first declaration of forfeit.

95. At every Meeting at which Steeple Chases and Hurdle races are advertised the following special conditions shall apply for Steeple Chase and Hurdle race handicaps:—

(i) In handicaps to which £2,000 or more is guaranteed by the Race Fund:

(a) in races of three and a half miles or upwards, the top weight shall be 12st and the lowest weight not less than 9st 7lb.

(b) in all other races, the top weight shall be 12st 7lb and the lowest weight not less than 10st.

(c) no penalty shall increase a horse's weight above 12st and 12st 7lb respectively.

(d) If, in the opinion of the handicapper, not more than two of the horses entered are a clear 14lb better than the rest of the entry, the handicapper shall frame his handicap down to 21lb below the permitted lowest weight. In these handicaps when the highest original handicap weight of horses declared to run under Rule 120 (i) is less than 12st in the Liverpool Grand National Steeple Chase and in races of under three and a half miles, or less than 11st 7lb in other races, it shall be raised to that weight and the other weights increased accordingly. The weights of any horses then still handicapped below the permitted lowest weight shall be raised to it. When the weights are raised under the provisions of this sub-Rule any penalties incurred since the date stated in the conditions of the race shall be added to the raised weights and not to the original handicap weights.

(ii) In handicaps to which less than £2,000 is guaranteed by the Race Fund:

(a) in Steeple Chases of three and a half miles or upwards the top weight shall be not less than 12st, and the lowest weight not less than 9st 7lb.

(b) in all other races the top weight shall be not less than 12st 7lb and the lowest weight not less than 10st.

(iii) A horse shall be allotted top weight in a handicap unless before the Sunday previous to the publication of the weights he has either

(a) run three times collectively in Steeple Chases or Hurdle races in Great Britain or in Steeple Chases or Hurdle races in Ireland value £400 or more to the winner, or

(b) has won a Steeple Chase or Hurdle race in Great Britain or won a Steeple Chase or Hurdle race in Ireland value £750 or more to the winner.

But in a handicap for all ages, three, four, and five yrs old may be given the weight-for-age allowance from the top weight of the handicap as provided by Appendix B.

96. The following Rules relating to Selling races apply to all Selling races but in optional Selling races they apply only to horses run as entered to be sold.

(i) In selling races, the selling price shall be not less than half of the advertised value of any plate of not more than £1,000, or half the amount of the added money of any sweepstakes, with not more than £1,000 added.

In plates of the advertised value of more than £1,000, and sweepstakes with more than £1,000 added, the selling price shall be not less than £500.

(ii) In all selling races the winner shall be offered for sale by auction immediately after the race, and the surplus over the selling price shall go to the Race Fund.

(iii) In the case of a dead-heat, each of the horses dividing is a winner for the purposes of the Rules relating to claiming and selling, and if a selling race, both shall be put up to auction, and any surplus shall go to the Race Fund.

(iv) If a horse walk over (or there be no second horse placed) for a selling race, the winner is still liable to be sold.

(v) No person shall prevent or seek to prevent any other person from bidding for the winner of a selling race, whether by offering any consideration or guarantee or by means of a threat or otherwise; and no person shall accept or offer to accept, any consideration or guarantee or other inducement to refrain from bidding. Any person so offending shall be fined £50 or reported to the Stewards of the Jockey Club.

(vi) If sold, or bought in, the horse shall not leave the place of sale without permission of the auctioneer, and a written order given for his delivery to the actual bidder who alone shall be responsible for the price; and if the horse be not paid for, or the price secured to the satisfaction of the auctioneer within a quarter of an hour, he may put the horse up a second time, and the purchaser at the first sale shall be responsible for any deficiency arising from the second, and shall be treated as a defaulter until it is paid. Whoever issues the delivery order for a horse sold, bought in, or claimed, is responsible for the money, and shall, if required, pay the same over to the person entitled, the day after the horse is delivered.

97. All other horses starting may be claimed for the selling price plus the value of the stakes or advertised value of the plate subject to the following conditions:—

(i) If two or more persons claim the same horse, the auctioneer shall hold an auction between the claimants in the Clerk of the Course's Office, or in any place appointed by him, any surplus above the claiming price shall be divided between the Race Fund and the Jockey Club; if no bid is made, the claim shall be determined by lot by the Clerk of the Scales.

(ii) No person can claim more than one horse.

(iii) Every claim, which must be accompanied by a fee of £10, must be made in writing to the Clerk of the Scales within ten minutes of the All Right signal being given.

(iv) The price of every horse claimed must be paid to, or secured to the satisfaction of, the Stakeholder, within a quarter of an hour of the conclusion of the time for making claims, and an order given by him for the delivery of the horse. If the price be not paid or secured as above, the claimant forfeits his right and shall be reported to the Stewards of the Jockey Club.

98. The foregoing Rules relating to selling races, are subject to the following provisions:—

(i) If an objection be made under Rule 170 (iv), and the winner is disqualified or his placing altered, the time for selling and claiming shall be fixed by the Stewards.

(ii) Where an objection is made on any other ground than those mentioned in Rule 170 (iv) and sustained, the sale of the winner, the disposal of the surplus, and any claims under Rule 97 of the horse originally placed second or of any beaten horse shall not be affected, and the horse to whom the race is awarded shall not be offered for sale, nor shall the original winner be liable to be claimed, but in cases where an objection has been lodged on the ground of fraud or substitution, or on the ground that the winner has run at an unrecognised Meeting, and sustained, the Stewards of the Jockey Club may order the sale to be annulled.

(iii) Where the winner has been the subject of an examination under Rule 14 (vi) and has been found to have received any substance (other than a normal nutrient) which could alter its racing performance at the time of racing, the Stewards of the Jockey Club may order the sale to be annulled.

Claiming Races

99. In claiming races all horses starting may be claimed for not less than their published claiming price subject to the following conditions: —

(i) Every claim must be made in writing in the name of one person and shall be in the form of a sealed claim, to the Clerk of the Scales within ten minutes of the All Right signal being given.

(ii) The horse shall go to the person submitting the highest claim but if there are two or more equal claims for the same horse the successful claim shall be determined by lot by the Clerk of the Scales.

(iii) No horse may be claimed by its owner or part owner nor may it be claimed to return to the stable from which it was trained for the race.

(iv) No person shall claim more than one horse.

(v) Any surplus above the published claiming price for the horse shall go to the Race Fund.

(vi) The price of every horse claimed must be paid to, or secured to the satisfaction of, the Stakeholder, within a quarter of an hour of the conclusion of the time for making claims, and an order given by him for the delivery of the horse. If the price be not paid or secured as above, the claimant forfeits his right and shall be reported to the Stewards of the Jockey Club.

PART 10

PENALTIES AND ALLOWANCES

Calculation

100. In calculating the amount a horse has won in any one or more races, account shall be taken of all cups or moneys whether derived from stakes, bonus, or any other source, gained by him for his owner or for any other person, but, on and after January 1st, 1970, excluding any prize given specifically to the trainer, rider or stable in the conditions of the race.
The value of a race to the winner after deduction of the entrance fee, but before deduction of the percentages payable under Rule 134, and, in the case of a dead-heat, after the prizes have been divided in accordance with Rule 157, shall be published in the *Racing Calendar* and this shall be used for the purpose of calculating penalties, allowances and qualifications.
(NOTE—For the purpose of calculating penalties, any surplus on the sale of the winners in the case of a dead-heat for first place in a selling race prior to March 2nd, 1967, and any sums assigned to the Bentinck Benevolent, Rous Memorial or Rendelsham Benevolent Funds, or surplus from entrance or subscription in the case of a dead-heat for first place prior to January 1st, 1968, are not taken into account.)

101. For the purpose of calculating the value of races run out of Great Britain, Ireland, and the Channel Islands, the following rates of exchange to the £ (sterling) will be used:

	Before 18/11/67	From 19/11/67	
U.S. Dollar	2.75	2.42	
Canadian Dollar	2.75	2.60	
Belgian Franc	140	120	
Danish Kroner	19.30	18.03	
Norwegian Kroner	19.90	17.25	
Swedish Kroner	14.40	12.50	
Italian Lira	1760	1510	
Spanish Peseta	105	170	
Argentine Peso	110	110	
	N.F.		From 11/8/69
French Franc	13.82	11.84	13.30
			From 27/10/69
German Mark	12	9.63	8.83

The above rates may be varied at any time at the discretion of the Stewards of the Jockey Club who may also fix a ratio of "points" to money in respect of races run in countries where points rather than money are used to indicate the importance of a race.
In assessing distances of races in kilometres, 200 metres shall be taken to equal one furlong.

Penalties

102. When any race is in dispute both the horse that came in first and any horse claiming the race shall be liable to all the penalties attaching to the winner of that race till the matter be decided.

103. (i) Penalties for winning a fixed sum shall be understood to mean for winning it in one race, unless specified to the contrary.
(ii) If in the conditions of a race a fixed penalty has to be carried for winning a race specified by name, horses running a dead-heat for such race shall carry the penalty fixed as if the race had been won outright.
(iii) In all cases where the conditions of Steeple Chases or Hurdle races impose penalties for having won one or more races, there shall be no exceptions in respect of selling races.

104. Penalties are not cumulative unless so declared by the conditions of the race.

105. (i) In all flat races, except races confined to apprentices, in which the conditions provide for a specific penalty for winners, such penalties shall not be applicable to winners of races confined to apprentices which take place after March 1st, 1966.
(ii) In all steeple chases and hurdle races, except Opportunity Jockeys' races, in which the conditions provide for a specific penalty for winners, such penalties shall not be applicable to winners of Opportunity Jockeys' races which take place after June 30th, 1970.

(*The Stewards of the Jockey Club have modified Rule 105* (*ii*) *to read as follows:—*

105. (*ii*) *In all steeple chases and hurdle races, except Opportunity races, in which the conditions provide for a specific penalty for winners, such penalties shall not be applicable to winners of Opportunity races which take place after June 30th, 1970.*)

106. (i) A Challenge Cup is not estimated in the value of a race until it is finally won, but when won outright the winner must carry a penalty in respect of the full value of the Cup and money prize.
(ii) Extra weights shall not be incurred in respect of matches or private sweepstakes, or of the Newmarket Challenge Cup or Whip.
(iii) No horse shall carry extra weight for having run second, or in any lower place in a race.

Allowances

107. (i) No horses shall receive allowance of weight, or be relieved from extra weight, for having been beaten in one or more races: provided that this Rule shall not prohibit maiden allowances or allowances to horses that have not won within a specified time, or races of a specified value or distance.
(ii) No allowance of weight shall be made to any horse:

(a) for being the produce of a stallion or mare whose produce never won a race.
(b) for being the first produce of a mare.
(c) for being the produce of a stallion covering at, or under, a particular fee.
(d) for being half-bred.

(iii) In Flat races no allowance of weight shall be made in respect of geldings, as such, in any plate of the advertised value of £3,000 or more or in any sweepstakes with £3,000 or more added.

108. Allowances are cumulative unless otherwise specified.

Riders Allowances

109. Riders' allowances may be claimed as follows:—

(i) All lads duly qualified to ride as apprentices under the provisions of Rule 63, are permitted, during their apprenticeship, to claim the following allowances in Flat races:
7lb until they have won 10 Flat races; thereafter
5lb until they have won 50 Flat races; thereafter
3lb until they have won 75 Flat races.
Apprentice races are to be excepted in all of the above cases.
These allowances can be claimed in the flat races set out below, with the exception of races confined to apprentices:
(a) All handicaps and all selling races.
(b) All sweepstakes for three yrs old or upwards to which not more than £1,000 is added.
(c) All plates of three yrs old or upwards of the advertised value of not more than £1,000.
(d) All sweepstakes in which two yrs old can run, to which not more than £1,000 is added.
(e) All plates in which two yrs old can run, of the advertised value of not more than £1,000.
Allowances can only be claimed under this Rule for lads duly apprenticed to a licensed trainer carrying on his business in Great Britain, Ireland, or the Channel Islands.

(ii) All riders who have not won twenty-five races collectively under the Rules of any recognised Turf Authority, shall be entitled to the following allowances in all Steeple Chases or Hurdle races in which the total amount of added money in a sweepstakes, or the advertised value of a plate, including the value of any Cups, but excluding the value of any Challenge Cup, does not exceed £2,000, except races confined to such riders.
7lb until they have won 10 races; thereafter
5lb until they have won 15 races; thereafter
3lb until they have won 25 races.

PART 11

ENTRIES, ACCEPTANCES, SUBSCRIPTIONS, DECLARATIONS OF RUNNERS AND CANCELLATIONS

Entries and Acceptances

110. (i) No race, with the exception of a sweepstake to which £4,000 or more is added, shall close earlier than thirty-one days before the first day of the Meeting.

(ii) No race shall close earlier than the February in the year in which the horses concerned are two yrs old, and no Flat race shall close after the last Wednesday in November.

111. (i) Every entry and every acceptance shall be fixed to close at 12 noon on Wednesdays only, such entry or acceptance must be lodged at the *Racing Calendar* Office and is subject to withdrawal or alteration up to the time of closing.

(ii) Entries may also close to any recognised Turf Authority, if special mention is made of this in the advertisement of the race in the *Racing Calendar*.

(iii) The list of entries shall be closed at the advertised time, and no entry shall be admitted on any ground after that time.

Form of Entry or Nomination

112. (i) Entries, and alterations or withdrawals of such entries before the time of closing shall be made in writing, signed by the owner of the horse, or his authorised agent. For the purpose of this Rule a telegram or telex message shall be deemed to be in writing.

(ii) Entries made under Rule 111 (ii) to other recognised Turf Authorities, shall be made in like manner. Such entries shall in all respects be subject to these Rules, except that Registrations under Rule 46, or of Authority to Act, need not be registered in this country provided that in these respects the entry would be valid under the Rules of the Turf Authority of the country where the entry is received.

113. (i) No horse shall be entered unnamed. The entry shall be in the name of one person, and shall state the name of the owner and the registered name of the horse except as provided for in sub-Rules (ii) and (iii) of this Rule.

(ii) A horse foaled outside Great Britain, Ireland, or the Channel Islands may be entered by stating its registered name in the country of origin together with such pedigree or description as will identify it.

(iii) In making an entry to any recognised Turf Authority outside Great Britain or the Channel Islands under Rule 111 (ii), the horse shall be considered as identified by giving the name registered for the horse in the country where the entry is made.

(iv) No horse shall be entered in the name of any person as his owner unless that person's interest or property in the horse is at least equal to that of any other one person except as provided for in Rule 44.

114. (i) An acceptance for a free handicap shall be considered as equivalent to an entry, but if the horse be wrongly described the acceptance shall be void.

(ii) Entries and subscriptions shall not become void (except as allowed for in Rule 118) on the death of the person in whose name they are made or taken, and all rights, privileges, and liabilities that could have attached to the deceased person had he or she been alive shall attach to his or her personal representative.

115. In cases hereinafter mentioned any accidental error, or violation of Rules affecting entries may be corrected on payment of a fine of not less than £5, provided always that the Stewards are satisfied that there had been no fraud.

(i) Incorrect description of the owner of the horse according to the Rules of Entry. Correction must be made by the time fixed for the declaration of runners under Rule 120 (i). Such declaration to run by his owner or duly authorised agent is deemed to be a correction of entry under this Rule.

(ii) Omission to lodge particulars of partnerships, &c., according to Rule 46, provided that the document is lodged and the fine paid before the rider weighs out for the race concerned.

If any horse runs without the prescribed correction having been made, the Stewards of the Jockey Club may inflict fines upon, or otherwise deal with, any persons responsible for such errors.

Declarations of Forfeit

116. Every declaration of forfeit shall be fixed to be made by 12 noon on Tuesdays only and must be lodged at the *Racing Calendar* Office by that time.

(i) For races closing within thirty-one days of the first day of a meeting there shall be no declaration of forfeit.

(ii) In all other races:—

(a) A declaration of forfeit shall be fixed for the Tuesday in the week two weeks before the first day of the meeting.

(b) An additional declaration of forfeit may be fixed for a handicap on any Tuesday after the publication of weights.

(iii) For Flat races other than handicaps:—

(a) Additional declarations of forfeit may be fixed, but only on the following days:—

the Tuesday after the Newmarket Craven Meeting,

the first Tuesday in July, and

the third Tuesday in November.

(b) In races closing before the year of running, no declaration of forfeit shall be fixed before the third Tuesday in November in the year of closing.

Form of Declaration of Forfeit and Striking Out of Engagement

117. (i) Declarations of forfeit and striking out of engagements shall be made in writing to the *Racing Calendar* Office by the owner of the engagement or his authorised agent, subject to the Rules relating to sales with engagements. For the purpose of this Rule a telegram or telex message shall be deemed to be in writing.

(ii) The document striking a horse out of engagements shall state the name of the horse and give details of the engagement, but such document does not constitute a cancellation under Rule 120 (iii).

(iii) The notification of the death of a horse to the *Racing Calendar* Office shall withdraw the horse from all engagements including those for which he has been declared to run under Rule 120 (i).

PART 12

SALE WITH ENGAGEMENTS

118. When a horse is sold with his engagements, or any part of them, the seller cannot strike the horse out of any of such engagements, and, on default of the purchaser, remains liable for the amount of the forfeits in each, but should the horse, or his owner, appear in the Forfeit List, the seller may, at any time before their names are removed from the list, strike

the horse out of any engagement, if he can by this means reduce his liability. An engagement in a Private Sweepstakes, or Match, cannot be transferred, and shall be rendered void on the death of the nominator.

119. (i) In all cases of changes of ownership when the engagements of the horse or any part of them are transferred, the written acknowledgement of both parties, or their authorised agents, that the horse was transferred with engagements together with details of the engagements transferred, must be lodged at the *Racing Calendar* Office or with the Clerk of the Course for transmission to the *Racing Calendar* Office before the horse starts for such engagements. If certain engagements only are specified, those only are sold with the horse.

(ii) If a horse start for any race without such transfer having been lodged, he shall, on objection, be disqualified, unless it be proved to the satisfaction of the Stewards of the Jockey Club that the omission was accidental, in which case the person responsible shall be fined not less than £5.

Declarations of Runners and Cancellations

120. (i) Every declaration of a runner must be lodged at the Overnight Declarations Office by 12 noon, or at such a place and at such a time as the Stewards of the Jockey Club shall from time to time direct, on the day fixed for declarations in the conditions of the race.
Such declarations shall be subject to withdrawal or alteration up to the time fixed for declaration.

(ii) All declarations, withdrawals and alterations made under this Rule shall state the name of the horse, the name of the Meeting and the name of the race, and shall be in writing signed by the owner or his authorised agent. They may also be made by telegram, telex or telephone, subject to such restrictions as the Stewards of the Jockey Club may from time to time impose.

(iii) Declarations not withdrawn under sub-Rule (i) of this Rule may be cancelled in like manner up to 11 a.m. on the day fixed in the conditions of the race.

121. If, in the opinion of the Stewards, there are at the time fixed for cancellations under sub-Rule (iii) of Rule 120 too many runners in a race to be started safely from the Starting Gate, they may divide the race or reduce the declared runners to a number that they consider safe, as follows:—

(a) Flat races other than handicaps being plates of the advertised value of not more than £1,000 or Sweepstakes to which not more than £1,000 is added shall be divided.

(b) Steeple Chases and Hurdle races other than handicaps being plates of the advertised value of not more than £800 or sweepstakes to which not more than £800 is added shall be divided.

(c) In all handicaps the runners shall be reduced by the elimination of the horses with the lowest weights at the time. When a decision has to be made between two or more horses with the same weight it shall be determined by ballot.

(d) In all other races the runners shall be reduced by the elimination of horses by ballot.

(*The Stewards of the Jockey Club have modified Rule 121 to provide that on and after 13th March, 1970, no horse shall be eliminated from more than one Flat race and one Steeple Chase or Hurdle Race during the current year.*)

122. For Flat races, subsequent to the operation of sub-Rule (iii) of Rule 120 and Rule 121, the draw allotting positions at the start shall then be made at the Overnight Declarations Office.

PART 13

ENTRANCE MONEY, PRIZE MONEY AND FORFEIT LIST

Liability for Entrances

130. (i) The nominator is liable as well as every owner of the horse at the time of nomination for the entrance money, stake or forfeit but if the entry is transferred to any other person he is liable only in case of default by the transferee.

(ii) A person making a wrong nomination is equally liable but where a horse has been accidentally entered for a race for which it is not qualified the entry may be deleted up to the time fixed for declaration of runners under Rule 120 on payment of a fine of £5.

(iii) Entrance money, stakes and arrears must be paid in cash if so required to the stakeholders and entrance money must if so required be paid at the time of entry.

(iv) If a race be never run or be void, stakes, forfeits and entrance money shall be returned.

(v) No entrance money, stake, forfeit or fine is payable in respect of horses eliminated under the provisions of Rule 121.

Distribution of Prizes

131. (i) In plates the entrance money, forfeits, &c., shall go to the Race Fund unless otherwise specified in the conditions of the race but should there be any surplus over the advertised value it shall be paid to the Jockey Club.

(ii) In sweepstakes the entrance, forfeits, &c., shall be distributed in accordance with the conditions of the race subject to the provisions of Rule 134.

132. If the winner has walked over, or no horse has been place second, or in any lower place, the money or prize provided by the conditions for the horse placed second, or in any lower place, shall be dealt with as follows, namely:

(i) If part of the stakes or plate, it shall go to the winner; or

(ii) If a separate donation from the race fund, or any other source, it shall not be given at all.

133. When a Cup (other than a Challenge Cup) or plate or any added money is advertised to be run for, it shall be given in the event of a walk-over.

134. The following deductions shall be made by the Stakeholder from the amount won by the winner of every race (calculated as in Part 10):

(i) for the trainer of the horse at the time of winning—10 per cent where the trainer holds a licence to train under these Rules.

(ii) for the jockey who rode the horse—7½ per cent.

(iii) for the stable from which the

horse has been trained—2½ per cent except when the horse is trained outside Great Britain or privately under Rule 50 (ii).

The Unpaid Forfeit List

135. (i) An Unpaid Forfeit List shall be kept at the Registry Office, and shall be published in the *Racing Calendar* in February and July. It shall include all arrears which have been notified by the Stakeholder of any Meeting held under these Rules, or as otherwise provided under these Rules, and shall state the name or names of the persons from whom, and the horses (if any) in respect of which the same are due. "Arrears" which have been so published must be paid direct to the Registry Office, and until so paid shall not be removed from the list.

(*The Stewards of the Jockey Club have modified Rule 153 (i) to provide that the unpaid Forfeit List shall not be published in July 1970.*)

(ii) A corrected alphabetical Index of horses and owners in the last Forfeit List and Irish Forfeit List shall be published in the first Calendar of every month. Such monthly list stall commence not less than three years before the time at which it is published, and shall be carried down to and include the latest Forfeit List which has been published in the *Racing Calendar*.

136. Where a person is prevented by these Rules from entering or starting a horse for any race without paying arrears, for which he would not otherwise be liable, he may, by paying the same, enter or start the horse and place the arrears on the Forfeit List as due to himself, and in like manner the seller of a horse with engagements may, if compelled to pay them by the purchaser's default, place the amount on the Forfeit List, as due from the purchaser to himself.

137. So long as the name of a person is in the Unpaid Forfeit List, even though the arrears arose or the Forfeit List was published under the previous Rules of Racing or National Hunt Rules, or so long as the name of a person is in the official Forfeit List published by the recognised Turf Authority of any country, he is a disqualified person.

138. If a horse which, or the owner of which, is in the Forfeit List be entered for any race, the nominator of such horse may be fined a sum not exceeding £50.

PART 14

WEIGHING-OUT, EXHIBITING NUMBERS, ETC.

The Weighing Room

140. No person shall, without special leave from the Stewards, be admitted to the Weighing Room, except an official of the Meeting, the owner, trainer, and rider, or other person having the care of a horse engaged in the race, or a licensed Jockey's Valet, and any person refusing to leave shall be reported to the Stewards.

No persons other than officials of Meetings, amateur riders engaged to ride, jockeys, licensed apprentices and jockeys' valets shall be permitted access to Riders' Dressing Rooms with the following exception:—For Steeple Chases and Hurdle races, trainers or their representatives shall be permitted such access when, in emergency, a rider has to be engaged at short notice.

Weighing-Out

141. (i) No rider shall be weighed out (except as provided below) for any race unless the name of

the race and of the horse and the rider have been given in writing by the owner, trainer, or their authorised agent, to the Clerk of the Course not less than three-quarters of an hour before the time fixed for the race. It must be stated in such declaration if the horse be running in hood or blinkers, and if a horse is to run in a hood which is fitted with blinkers, both must be declared.

(*The Stewards of the Jockey Club have modified Rule 141* (*i*) *to provide that on and after March 23rd, 1970, declaration may* only *be made by the owner, trainer, employee of the trainer on production of his Stable Employees' Identity Card, or other person on production of a written authorisation signed by the owner or trainer and available only for the day of the race.*)

(ii) The trainer is responsible that the horse carries the correct weight in accordance with the conditions of the race. The trainer is required to declare the weight his horse will carry if different from that appearing on the race-card to the Clerk of the Scales before the rider weighs out. Failure to make this declaration will render the trainer liable to a fine of not less than £5. Riders allowances will not be taken into consideration when declaring a weight under this sub-Rule.

(iii) Should a rider, who has been declared, not present himself to be weighed, another rider may, with the permission of the Stewards, be substituted provided always that he can be weighed within the time specified in section (iv) of this Rule, but unless they are satisfied, after enquiry, that the absence of the rider was due to unavoidable circumstances, they shall, after dealing with the case under their powers, make a report to the Stewards of the Jockey Club.

(iv) Every rider must be weighed for a specified horse by the Clerk of the Scales, at the appointed place, not less than a quarter of an hour before the time fixed for the race. In exceptional cases, the Stewards may extend the time allowed for declaring runners under this Rule, weighing, declaring weight, and for exhibiting the numbers.

142. If a rider intends to carry overweight, he must declare the amount thereof at the time of weighing out or, if in doubt as to his proper weight, he may declare the weight he intends to carry.
The number cloth and any hood, blinkers, martingale, breastplate, or clothing, must be put into the scale and included in the rider's weight.
No skull cap, whip, bridle, rings, plates, or anything worn on a horse's legs, shall be allowed in the scales, either in weighing out or weighing in.

143. If a rider after he has been weighed for a specified horse, and before he has come under Starter's Orders, is prevented by accident or illness from riding in the race, another jockey may be substituted provided there is no unreasonable delay.

Running and Walking Over Non Runners

144. (i) Every horse which has been declared a runner under Rule 120 and in respect of which the declaration has not been cancelled or the horse eliminated as allowed for in Rules 120 (iii) and 121 respectively, shall run in the race. If he fails to do so, either because

(*above*) NEVER SAY DIE. The 1954 Derby at Tattenham Corner. The winner, Never Say Die (L. Piggott up) is fifth behind Landau, Rowston Manor, Blue Sail and Darius. (*below*) NIJINSKY. Mr C. W. Engelhard's Nijinsky, Lester Piggott up. Top two year old of 1969, Nijinsky won the Two Thousand Guineas, the Derby and the Irish Sweeps Derby the following season

NIMBUS. The first Derby photo-finish. Nimbus (C. Elliott up) wins from Armour Drake and Swallow Tail

O'BRIEN, MICHAEL VICTOR. Vincent O'Brien with the Australian rider Pat Glennam at Epsom on the morning of the Derby

he is debarred by these Rules from so doing or for any other reason, the Stewards shall hold an enquiry. Unless they are satisfied that the horse was unfit to run or that circumstances acceptable to the Stewards prevented the horse from running, the Stewards shall fine the owner and/or his representative not less than £25 in the case of a Flat race, and £15 in the case of a Steeple Chase or Hurdle race, or refer the matter to the Stewards of the Jockey Club. A report shall in every case be made to the *Racing Calendar* Office.

(ii) If a veterinary certificate is submitted in connection with this Rule it must clearly state the time and date of the veterinary examination and the condition which renders the horse unfit and it must be signed by a Veterinary Surgeon who is neither the owner, nor the trainer, nor a person for whom the trainer of the horse holds a current Identity Card.

Equipment

145. The saddle comprises the saddle itself, the girth, the surcingle, the stirrup irons, and the leathers or webs, and the rider is responsible for the fit condition of the saddle which he uses, but in the case of an apprentice or where a stable employee rides for the trainer who employs him the responsibility rests with the trainer.

146. (i) No rider shall ride in any race unless he is wearing a skull cap of a pattern approved by the Stewards of the Jockey Club. The rider or, in the case of an apprentice, his master, is responsible for the serviceable condition of the skull cap.

(ii) Spurs are not permitted in races confined to apprentices.

(iii) The use of blinding hoods or any form of shutter hood is prohibited.

(iv) No substitute for a whip shall be carried in any race.

147. (i) Every horse running a race shall carry a number cloth which must be worn so that the number is clearly visible.

(ii) When a rider is weighed out with a hood or blinkers they must be worn by the horse on the way to the start and during the race and if it is not possible for the horse to wear them he shall not run.

Part 15

Running Void Races, Walking Over and Dead Heats

Before the Race

150. (i) Every horse must be ridden in front of the Stand before going to the post, and the Stewards shall decide the distance to be traversed. If a horse is not ridden in front of the Stand the Stewards shall hold an enquiry as to whether the rider made reasonable endeavour to comply with this Rule.

(ii) There shall be no preliminary jump allowed before any race.

The Race

151. (i) Every horse which runs in a race shall be run on its merits, whether its owner runs another horse in the race or not.

(ii) The rider of every horse shall take all reasonable and permissible measures throughout the race to ensure that his horse is given a full opportunity to win or of obtaining the best possible placing.

(iii) No owner, trainer, rider or other person shall prevent or try to prevent any horse from winning a race or of obtaining the best possible placing.

(iv) The rider of any horse who, in the opinion of the Stewards of the Meeting or the Stewards of the Jockey Club, has been guilty of dangerous, careless, improper or foul riding shall be guilty of an offence.

152. (i) Any horse getting away from its rider in a Steeple Chase or Hurdle race, may be remounted, but should it have run out of the course or continued in the race before being caught it shall be brought back to the part of the course where it parted from its rider, and shall continue by jumping all fences or hurdles from that point. Any rider so losing his horse may be assisted in catching it and remounting it without risk of disqualification.

(ii) If a horse having refused any fence, or hurdle, in a Steeple Chase or Hurdle race, has been led over it by any of the by-standers, or has been given a lead over by any horseman not riding in the race, the horse shall, on an objection under Rule 170 (iv), be disqualified.

(iii) If a horse run the wrong side of a direction post or flag, or miss a fence or hurdle, his rider shall turn back and ride the course correctly from such point, or he shall pull up. He shall not otherwise continue in the race, or his horse shall, on an objection under Rule 170 (iv) be disqualified.

153. (i) A horse shall, on an objection under Rule 170 (iv), be disqualified if his rider, by foul riding, jeopardised the chance of success of any other horse in a race.

(ii) A horse is liable, on an objection under Rule 170 (iv), to be disqualified or his placing in the race altered—

(a) if he or his rider jostle another horse or rider;

(b) if in a steeple chase or hurdle race he cross another horse at, or in the run home from, the last fence or hurdle, so as to interfere with that or any other horse's chance.

(c) if in a flat race he crosses another horse in any part of the race so as to interfere with that or any other horse's chance.

Void Races

154. (i) If a race has been run by all the horses at wrong weights, or over a wrong course, or distance, or before the appointed time, or if the Judge is not in the box at the time the horses pass the winning post, the Stewards shall order a flat race to be run again the same day if practicable, but if otherwise, or in the case of a Steeple Chase or Hurdle race, it shall be void.

(ii) If no qualified horse cover the course in accordance with these Rules the race may be declared void.

Walking Over

155. In walking over for a race, in no case shall it be necessary for a horse to "walk over" the entire course, but if only one horse shall have been declared a runner under Rule 141, that horse shall be ridden past the Judge's box, and shall then be deemed the winner.

Dead-Heats

156. When horses run a dead-heat, for first or any lower place, the owners shall divide, and the dead-heat shall not be run off, but on

a dead-heat for a match, the match is off.

157. When two horses run a dead-heat for first place, all prizes to which the first and second horses would have been entitled shall be divided equally between them and this principle shall be observed in dividing the prizes whatever the number of dead-heaters and whatever the place for which the dead-heat is run. Each horse that divides a prize for first place shall be deemed a winner (for penalties, see Rules 100 and 103).

158. When a dead-heat is run for second place, and an objection is made to the winner of the race, and sustained, the horses which ran the dead-heat shall be deemed to have run a dead-heat for first place.

159. If the dividing owners cannot agree as to which of them is to have a cup or other prize which cannot be divided, the question shall be determined by lot by the Stewards, who shall decide what sum of money shall be paid by the owner who takes such cup or other indivisible prize, to the other owners or owner.

PART 16

WEIGHING-IN

160. (i) Immediately after pulling up, the riders of the horses placed first, second, and third in each race must ride their horses to the place appointed for unsaddling, and the horses shall remain there until ordered to be taken away by the Clerk of the Scales. The other riders may dismount within a reasonable distance. Every rider must present himself to be weighed by the Clerk of the Scales at once, and, if he fail to complete the course, report the reason. If a rider be prevented from riding back to weigh in by reason of accident or illness, by which he or his horse is disabled, he may walk or be carried to the scales.

(ii) In cases where the Judge, in consulting the photograph, has not announced his decision before the jockeys return to weigh in, they may dismount either inside or within a reasonable distance of the place appointed for unsaddling the winner. In such cases the Clerk of the Scales shall weigh in all jockeys until such time as the Judge's decision is announced.

(iii) If a rider does not present himself to be weighed in, or dismount before reaching the place appointed for that purpose, or touch (except accidentally) any person or thing other than his own equipment before weighing in, his horse shall, on an objection under Rule 170 (iv), be disqualified, unless he can satisfy the Stewards that he was justified by extraordinary circumstances.

(iv) If a jockey be too ill to weigh in, his horse shall not be disqualified provided that the jockey weighed out at not less than his proper weight.

161. (i) In weighing in, a jockey shall include in his weight everything that the horse has carried in the race, except as provided in Rule 142.

(ii) If a rider weighs in at more than 4lb over his proper weight or over the weight at which he weighed out in a Steeple Chase or Hurdle race, or more than 2lb in a Flat race, he shall be reported to the Stewards. The horse shall not be disqualified under this Rule.

(iii) If a rider cannot draw the weight at which he weighed out, the Clerk of the Scales shall allow him 2lb in a Steeple Chase or Hurdle race, or 1lb in a Flat race. If he cannot then draw the weight, his horse shall, on an objection under Rule 170 (iv), be disqualified.

(iv) If a horse carry less than the weight he should carry in accordance with the conditions of the race and these Rules, he shall, on an objection under Rule 170 (v) be disqualified.

162. When the riders have weighed in to the satisfaction of the Clerk of the Scales, at not less than the weight at which they weighed out, except as under Rule 161 (iii), the Stewards shall authorise the All Right signal to be hoisted over the number board: Provided they shall not authorise this until—

(i) The period allowed for objecting under section (iv) of Rule 170 has elapsed.

(ii) Any objection which may have been lodged on grounds mentioned in section (iv) of Rule 170 has been decided.

(iii) A decision in any enquiry under Rule 171 (iii) has been made.

No objection on any grounds other than those mentioned in Rule 170 (iv) shall be entertained prior to the hoisting of the signal. After the signal has been hoisted no alteration shall be made to the numbers of the winner or placed horses on the board.

PART 17

DISPUTES, OBJECTIONS AND APPEALS

Disputes and Objections

170. (i) If an objection to a horse engaged not later than half-past ten in the morning of the day of the race, the Stewards may require his qualification to be proved before the race; and in default of such proof being given to their satisfaction they may declare him disqualified.

(ii) An objection to the distance of a course officially designated must be made before a race.

(iii) An objection to any decision of the Clerk of the Scales must be made at once.

(iv) An objection to a horse on the grounds of a cross, jostle, or any act on the part of his rider, or of his not having run the proper course, or of the race having been run on a wrong course, or of any other matter occurring in the race, or before weighing in, or on the ground that the rider did not present himself to weigh in, or that he could not draw the weight at which he weighed out, must be made within five minutes after the winner has been weighed in, or, within five minutes of the time the Judge has announced his decision on all placings, whichever be later (see also Rule 171 (iii)). The Stewards may extend the above period if they are satisfied that it could not have been made within that time. No objection on any other ground than these shall be heard within this time.

(v) An objection on any other ground than those laid down in Rule 170 (iv) shall be received within fourteen days of the conclusion of a Meeting. No objection under this paragraph may be heard until the signal has been hoisted in accordance with Rule 162.

(vi) In cases of fraud, or wilful misstatement, there shall be no limit to the time for objecting, provided the Stewards are satisfied there has been no unnecessary delay on the part of the objector. Such objection shall not be heard until the signal has been hoisted in accordance with Rule 162.

(vii) Nothing in this Rule shall restrict the operation at any time of Rules 1, 2, and 15.

171. (i) Every objection shall be in writing, and must be signed by the owner of some horse engaged in the race, or by his authorised agent, trainer, or rider.

(a) In cases coming under sub-Rule (iv) of Rule 170 it must be made to the Clerk of the Scales.

(b) In cases coming under sub-Rule (v) of Rule 170 it must be made to the Stewards of the Jockey Club at the Registry Office.

(c) In other cases it must be made to the Clerk of the Course.

The objector shall, at the time he makes the objection, deposit the sum of £5, which, if the case be decided against him, shall be forfeited to the Jockey Club, unless there was good and reasonable ground for the objection; and in the event of the objection being decided to be frivolous or vexatious, it shall be in the power of the Stewards to fine the objector any additional sum not exceeding £20.

(ii) An objection may also be made without deposit by a Steward or licensed official of a Meeting in his official capacity. Such objection shall be in writing and signed by the Steward or licensed official.

(iii) An enquiry called for by the Stewards on any matter contained in Rule 170 (iv) within the time prescribed by Rule 170 (iv), shall have the force and consequences of an objection and all relevant Rules shall operate as if an objection had been lodged.

(iv) An objection cannot be withdrawn without leave of the Stewards.

172. (i) Every objection in cases coming under sub-Rule (v) of Rule 170 shall be decided by the Stewards of the Jockey Club.

(ii) Every other objection shall be decided by at least three Stewards and their consideration of an objection under Rule 170 (iv) shall constitute an enquiry under Rule 171 (iii). Should no decision be given by the Stewards within seven days of the objection being lodged, the Clerk of the Course shall report the case to the Stewards of the Jockey Club who may at their discretion decide the matter and if they consider there has been any negligence, order any additional expense arising therefrom to be defrayed out of the funds of the Meeting at which the case occurred.

(iii) All costs and expenses in relation to determining an objection or conducting an enquiry, and any reasonable compensation for outlay incurred, shall be paid by such person or persons, and in such proportions, as in cases coming under sub-Rule (v) of Rule 170 the Stewards of the Jockey Club, or in cases under sub-Rule (iv) of that Rule, as the Stewards shall direct.

173. (ii) No horse shall be disqualified on account of any error or violation of Rule in its entry, which might have been corrected on payment of a fine, but the Stewards of the Jockey Club may inflict fines upon, or otherwise deal with,

any persons responsible for such errors.

174. Pending the determination of an objection, any prize which the horse objected to may have won or may win in the race, shall be withheld until the objection is determined, and any forfeit payable by the owner of any other horse shall be paid to and held by the Stakeholder for the person who may be entitled to it.

175. If an objection to a horse which has won, or been placed in a race, be declared valid, the horse shall be regarded as having been last in the race, and shall not be entitled to any prize; the other horses shall take positions accordingly.
Provided always that where the ground for objection is an offence arising under Rule 153 (ii) and the Stewards are satisfied that the interference was accidental they may in their discretion, and in lieu of disqualification, alter the placing of the first four horses.

Appeals

176. Any party to an objection or any person brought before the Stewards who is aggrieved by their decision shall be entitled to appeal to the Stewards of the Jockey Club except that where grounds of appeal consist solely of allegations that the Stewards have reached a wrong decision on fact the leave of the Stewards or of the Stewards of the Jockey Club must first be obtained.

177. The Appellant shall lodge a notice of appeal with the Registry Office within 7 days, or in the case of an appeal by a rider against a suspension under Rule 17 (i) within 24 hours, of the decision of the Stewards being announced, or, when the decision on suspension under Rule 17 (i) is announced on a Saturday, within 48 hours, together with a deposit of £20 which shall be forfeit unless the Stewards of the Jockey Club shall decide there were good and reasonable grounds for the appeal.

178. (i) The Notice of Appeal must state in general terms the grounds of appeal and be signed by the appellant. The Appeal shall be heard by three Stewards of the Jockey Club. If three Stewards are not available the places of the absent Stewards shall be taken by other members of the Jockey Club specifically appointed by the Stewards of the Jockey Club to hear that particular appeal.
(ii) The Stewards of the Jockey Club may confirm or reverse the decision of the Stewards or may exercise any of the powers given to them by Rule 2.

179. All costs and expenses in relation to the hearing of an appeal, and any reasonable compensation for outlay incurred, shall be paid by such person or persons, and in such proportions, as the Stewards of the Jockey Club shall direct.

PART 18

DISQUALIFICATION OF HORSES

180. (i) Any horse which has been the subject of fraudulent practice may, at the discretion of the Stewards of the Jockey Club, be disqualified for such time and for such races as they shall determine.
(ii) Where a horse has been the subject of an examination under Rule 14 (vi) and has been found to have received any substance (other than a normal nutrient) which could alter its racing performance

at the time of racing, the horse shall be disqualified for the race in question and may, at the discretion of the Stewards of the Jockey Club, be disqualified for such time and for such races as they shall determine.

181. A horse is not qualified to be entered or start for any race:—
(i) If he has run at any unrecognised meeting.
(ii) If and so long as he is in the ownership or part ownership of a disqualified person, or so long as any disqualified person has any interest in such horse's winnings in such race.
(iii) If and so long as he is in the stable of, or under the care and management of, a disqualified person, but when such person, other than the owner or part owner, incurs disqualification under Rule 137 or Rule 193 the horse shall be qualified to be entered or run until 14 days have elapsed from the date of publication in the Forfeit List, see Rule 137, or from the date of the disqualification under Rule 193.
(iv) If and so long as he is in the Forfeit List.
(v) In any case in which he is by these Rules or by the conditions of the race declared to be disqualified.
(vi) If he has been declared disqualified by the Stewards of the Jockey Club.

182. A horse is not qualified to start for any race:—
(i) Unless he is duly entered for the same.
(ii) Unless he has been declared a runner under Rule 120.
(iii) Unless it is trained by
(a) a licence or permit holder or other person qualified under Rule 50 to train for the race in question, or
(b) a duly qualified trainer in the country where the horse is trained if it is trained abroad.
(iv) If he has been tubed on the day of the race.

183. If a horse which is not qualified according to Rules 180, 181, or 182, be entered or run for any race, he shall on objection under Rule 170 (v) be disqualified by the Stewards of the Jockey Club.
The following Rule will come into force on February 1st, 1970.

184. A horse trained under Rule 182 (iii) (a) is not qualified to start for any race unless for the 28 days immediately prior to the race it has been in the care of and trained by persons holding licences or unrestricted permits under these Rules or by persons who are duly qualified trainers in the country where the horse has been trained; except that in steeple chases and hurdle races confined to amateur riders the horse may also have been in the care of a person qualified under Rule 50 to train the horse for the race in question.
The following Rule will come into force on February 1st, 1970.

185. If a horse which is not qualified according to Rule 184 run for any race he shall on objection under Rule 170 (v) be liable to be disqualified by the Stewards of the Jockey Club.

PART 19

CORRUPT PRACTICES AND DISQUALIFICATIONS OF PERSONS

190. Any person found guilty of a corrupt or fraudulent practice whether or not his conduct constitutes a breach of any other of these Rules may be declared a disqualified person or otherwise penalised by the Stewards of the

Jockey Club in accordance with their powers under Rule 2 of these Rules.

191. Without prejudice to the generality of Rule 190 every person is guilty of a corrupt practice within the meaning of these Rules who:—

(i) Administers or allows to be administered or connives at the administration to a horse of a substance (other than a normal nutrient) which could alter its racing performance at the time of racing; or

(ii) Gives or offers, or promises directly or indirectly, any bribe in any form to any person having official duties in relation to a race or racehorse, or to any trainer, rider, agent or other person having charge of, or access to, any racehorse; or

(iii) Being a person having official duties in relation to a race, or being a trainer, rider, agent or other person having charge of, or access to, any racehorse, accept or offers to accept any bribe in any form; or

(iv) Wilfully enters or causes to be entered for any race, or causes to start in any race, a horse which he knows or believes to be disqualified; or

(v) Surreptitiously obtains information respecting a trial from any person or persons engaged in it, or in the service of the owner or trainer of the horses tried, or respecting any horse in training from any person in such service; or

(vi) Deliberately misleads the Stewards of a Meeting or the Stewards of the Jockey Club at any enquiry; or

(vii) Is guilty of, or conspires with any other person for the commission of, or connives at any other person being guilty of, any corrupt (or fraudulent) practice in relation to racing in this or any other country, or is convicted of any criminal offence in relation to racing in this or any other country.

Every person so offending shall be warned off all places where these Rules are in force.

192. When a person is warned off, and so long as his exclusion continues, he is a disqualified person.

193. If any person be reported by the Committee of Tattersall's he shall be declared a disqualified person. On receiving a notification that such report is withdrawn, the Stewards of the Jockey Club shall withdraw their notice of disqualification and notify the defaulter to that effect by sending a notice to his last known address.

174. (i) Any person on whom disqualifications have been imposed by any recognised Turf Authority, is a disqualified person under these Rules so long as the disqualification continues.

(ii) Any person who owns, trains, or rides a horse at an unrecognised meeting in Great Britain or Ireland, or any person who acts in any official capacity in connection with such a meeting, is a disqualified person for twelve months from the date of such offence, or for such lesser time as the Stewards of the Jockey Club shall think fit, but this Rule shall not apply to pony or galloway races at meetings confined to pony or galloway racing.

(iii) Any person who offers or promises any reward, either by way of fee, present, expenses, or any considerations whatsoever to an Amateur Rider for riding in a race is liable to be made a disqualified person by the Stewards of the Jockey Club.

(iv) Any person, being an owner of horses, who by advertisement, circular, letter, or other means offers to give information concerning his own or other horses in return for monetary considerations, or any owner of horses who connives at such practice, is liable to be made a disqualified person by the Stewards of the Jockey Club.

195. A disqualified person, so long as his disqualification lasts, shall not:—

(i) Act as Steward or Official at any recognised Meeting.

(ii) Act as authorised agent under these Rules.

(iii) Enter, run, train, or ride a horse in any race at any recognised Meeting, or ride in trials.

(iv) Enter any Racecourse, Stand, or Enclosure.

(v) Except with permission of the Stewards of the Jockey Club be employed in any Racing Stable.

PART 20

FEES

General

200. All fees, fines, and deposits forfeited shall be paid to the credit of the Jockey Club unless otherwise stated in these Rules.

Authority To Act Fees

201. For the annual registration of authority to act generally on behalf of an owner, a fee of £5 is payable.

Fixture Fees

202. On fixtures being granted to a Meeting, fees, the amount of which the Stewards of the Jockey Club shall from time to time decide, will be payable to the Jockey Club, when the Fixture takes place. Should the Fixture, or any part of it, be abandoned, the fees shall nevertheless be paid, unless otherwise ordered by the Stewards of the Jockey Club.

PART 21

MISCELLANEOUS

General

210. (i) No person shall aid or abet the commission of any breach of these Rules.

(ii) No person shall be guilty of any violent or improper conduct on any land or premises owned, used, licensed or controlled by the Stewards of any meeting or by the Stewards of the Jockey Club, and no person shall do any act likely to cause serious damage to the interests of horseracing in Great Britain whether or not such act shall constitute a breach of any of the foregoing Rules of Racing.

(iii) No person shall without permission of the Stewards of the Jockey Club associate in connection with horseracing in Great Britain with any person known to be warned off or disqualified or known to have done any act likely to cause serious damage to the interests of horseracing in Great Britain, whether or not constituting a breach of the Rules of Racing.

Instructions

211. Every person shall comply with every instruction of the Stewards of the Jockey Club published in the *Racing Calendar* from time to time.

New Rules

212. Notice of any proposed new Rule (in which term is included the

repeal or alteration of an existing Rule) shall be sent by the Keeper of the Match Book to the Members of the Jockey Club at least fourteen days before the Meeting at which such Rule is to be proposed. The draft Rule shall also be advertised in the *Racing Calendar* with the date of the Meeting of the Jockey Club at which it is to be proposed. To be passed the Rule must be approved by a simple majority of the Members of the Jockey Club present at the Meeting, who must decide the date upon which the new or altered Rule is to come into operation, but the Rule as passed must be published in the *Racing Calendar* again before that date.

Point-To-Point Steeple Chases

213. Point-to-Point Steeple Chases are held under the sanction of the Jockey Club and under Regulations entitled "Jockey Club Regulations for Point to Point Steeple Chases" published from time to time by the Stewards of the Jockey Club and every person taking part in these races shall comply with these Regulations.

Registration of Stallion Fees

214. To qualify for entry in any race the conditions of which require the horse to have been sired by a stallion covering at, or under, a particular fee, the following statements of the stallion's covering must have been lodged at the *Racing Calendar* Office:

(i) A statement of the fee at which the stallion will cover public mares. This to be lodged for publication in the *Racing Calendar* by February 1st of the year of covering (an advertisement in the *Racing Calendar* by that date to be considered equivalent).

(ii) A statement, to be lodged by September 1st, that the stallion has covered at a sum not greater than the published fee, unqualified by financial contingencies of any kind, not less than five public mares the property of persons other than the owner or owners of the stallion; but if the Stewards of the Jockey Club are satisfied that every reasonable effort, including six advertisements in the *Racing Calendar* prior to May 1st, has been made to fulfil this condition, they may, notwithstanding failure to do so, order a stallion to be registered in accordance with this Rule.

All stallions for which the above statements have been duly lodged to the satisfaction of the Stewards will then be registered, and a list published in the first *Racing Calendar* in October, and with the Index of Races Past for the Year. For the purpose of reckoning the fee the groom's fee must be added to the fee of the stallion.

Sentences Imposed by the Stewards of the Jockey Club and Stewards of the National Hunt Commitee

216. The Stewards of the Jockey Club confirm all current sentences imposed prior to the 1st January, 1969, by the Stewards of the Jockey Club or by the Stewards of the National Hunt Committee and all persons warned off prior to the 1st January, 1969, remain disqualified persons so long as their exclusion continues.

APPENDIX A

SCALE OF WEIGHT FOR AGE FOR FLAT RACES

NOTE.—Attention is drawn to the provisions of Rule 91 (VI).

Distance	Age	Mar. & April st lb	May st lb	June st lb	July st lb	Aug. st lb	Sept. st lb	Oct. st lb	Nov. st lb
Five furlongs.	Two yrs	6 0	6 2	6 7	6 10	7 2	7 7	7 9	7 12
	Three yrs	8 4	8 3	8 5	8 7	8 9	8 12	8 12	8 13
	Four yrs	9 4	9 0	9 0	9 0	9 0	9 0	9 0	9 0
	Five, six, aged	9 5	9 0	9 0	9 0	9 0	9 0	9 0	9 0
Six furlongs.	Two yrs	—	6 4	6 7	6 11	7 0	7 6	7 9	7 13
	Three yrs	8 5	8 6	8 8	8 10	8 12	9 0	9 2	9 3
	Four yrs	9 7	9 7	9 7	9 7	9 7	9 7	9 7	9 7
	Five, six, aged	9 9	9 8	9 7	9 7	9 7	9 7	9 7	9 7
One mile.	Two yrs	—	—	—	—	—	6 7	6 9	6 12
	Three yrs	7 8	7 11	7 13	8 2	8 4	8 6	8 7	8 8
	Four yrs	9 0	9 0	9 0	9 0	9 0	9 0	9 0	9 0
	Five, six, aged	9 4	9 3	9 2	9 0	9 0	9 0	9 0	9 0
One mile and half.	Two yrs	—	—	—	—	—	6 0	6 4	6 7
	Three yrs	7 7	7 9	7 11	7 13	8 1	8 3	8 5	8 7
	Four yrs	9 0	9 0	9 0	9 0	9 0	9 0	9 0	9 0
	Five, six, aged	9 5	9 4	9 3	9 2	9 1	9 0	9 0	9 0
Two miles.	Two yrs	—	—	—	—	—	6 0	6 2	6 2
	Three yrs	7 8	7 11	7 12	8 0	8 3	8 4	8 5	8 5
	Four yrs	9 4	9 4	9 4	9 4	9 4	9 4	9 4	9 4
	Five, six, aged	9 10	9 9	9 8	9 7	9 6	9 5	9 4	9 4
Three miles.	Three yrs	7 1	7 4	7 5	7 7	7 9	7 11	7 13	7 13
	Four yrs	9 0	9 0	9 0	9 0	9 0	9 0	9 0	9 0
	Five yrs	9 8	9 7	9 6	9 5	9 5	9 4	9 3	9 3
	Six & aged	9 10	9 8	9 7	9 6	9 5	9 4	9 3	9 3

THE SCALE OF WEIGHT FOR AGE as given above, is published under the sanction of the Stewards of the Jockey Club as a guide to Managers of Race Meetings, but is not intended to be imperative, especially as regards the weights of two and three years old relatively to the older horses in selling races early in the year.

It is founded on the scale published by Admiral Rous, and revised by him in 1873, but has been modified in accordance with suggestions from the principal trainers and practical authorities, and has been further revised since.

RUNNER

All horses which come under the starter's orders are designated 'runners'.

A runner is also the term used for employees of bookmakers whose job is to lay off excess commissions by transferring them to other bookmakers.

RUNNING REIN

Running Rein, belonging to Mr A. Wood, was first past the post in the 1844 Derby. He was in actual fact a four-year-old called Maccabaeus. Thanks chiefly to the energy of Lord George Bentinck (q.v.), the fraud was disclosed. Running Rein was disqualified and the race awarded to Colonel Peel's Orlando. The villain behind the plot was a disreputable gambler called Goodman Levy who fled the country when it was clear that the fraud had failed.

RUSSELL, Alexander John (b 1918)

A. J. Russell was apprenticed to J. Tortorello in France and rode his first winner in 1935 at Le Tremblay. He has been riding successfully for many years now in the north, his best season being in 1957 when he rode 60 winners. That year he rode all six winners in one afternoon at Bogside. Good races he has won include the Zetland Gold Cup, Free Handicap, Lanark Silver Bell, Jersey Stakes and Sussex Stakes.

RUSSELL, James (d 1961)

Born in Australia, James Russell trained with considerable success in South Africa before settling in England in 1928. In England he won the Lincoln in 1934 with Play On and in 1936 with Over Coat.

In April 1947 his licence was withdrawn when tests in respect of a horse of his, a winner at Lincoln, showed a positive reaction to dope. The following year he sued the Stewards of the Jockey Club, alleging that his licence had been wrongfully withdrawn and claiming damages for alleged breach of contract. He also claimed damages for alleged libel in the *Racing Calendar*. The Lord Chief Justice, Lord Goddard, ruled there was no cause of action in libel, but left to the jury the question of whether Russell received a fair hearing from the Stewards. On that point the jury failed to agree. Lord Goddard then said that in his opinion the defence submission was right and there was no case to go before the jury at all. Accordingly he dismissed the action with costs. Russell's appeal was dismissed in December by the Court of Appeal.

RUSTOM PASHA

Bred by the late Aga Khan in 1927, Rustom Pasha was by the great stayer Son-in-Law out of that extremely fast mare Cos. He himself proved a high-class middle distance horse, his victories including the Eclipse Stakes and Champion Stakes. He was at the stud firstly in France and then in the Argentine. His daughter Rustom Mahal, out of Mumtaz Mahal, was the dam of Abernant. In the 1930 Derby Rustom Pasha started at 9-2 and was shouted home by his happy owner who was blissfully unaware that it was not Rustom Pasha winning but his 18-1 second string Blenheim.

RYAN, D.

He is attached to W. Stephenson's stable and can go to scale at 8st 2. On four occasions he has ridden more than 20 winners in a season.

S

SADDLE CLOTHS

Saddle cloths were first used in 1923.

SAGACITY

One of the many good stayers trained by Sir Cecil Boyd-Rochfort, Sagacity was foaled in 1958 and is by Le Sage out of Double Charm, by Epigram. He won the Yorkshire and Goodwood Cups and was second in the Ascot Gold Cup and the Doncaster Cup.

ST AMANT

Mr Leopold de Rothschild's St Amant, by St Frusquin, was a horse of uncertain temperament that led from start to finish to win the 1904 Derby which was run during a terrible thunderstorm. The rest of his career, bar a win in the Jockey Club Stakes, was disappointing. He made little mark as a sire.

SAINT CRESPIN III

Bred in 1956 by the late Aga Khan and the late Prince Aly Khan, Saint Crespin III is a half-brother to the Derby and St Leger winner Tulyar by Aureole. Trained in France by Alec Head, he won four races including the Imperial Produce Stakes, Eclipse Stakes and Prix de l'Arc de Triomphe. He is now owned by a syndicate and stands at the Gilltown Stud, Co Kildare. Among his winners are Dolina (Italian Oaks), Casaque Grise (Prix Vermeille), Le Cordonnier (*News of the World* Stakes), Mige (Cheveley Park Stakes), and Shoemaker (runner-up in the 1969 Derby).

ST FRUSQUIN

Mr Leopold de Rothschild's St Frusquin was one of the best sons of St Simon. He won 11 races, including the Two Thousand Guineas, worth over £33,000. In the 1896 Derby he was beaten a neck by another son of St Simon, Persimmon. He was twice champion sire.

ST GERMANS

St Germans was bred in 1921 by the late Lord Astor and was a half-brother by Swynford to Buchan and other good winners. Trained by Alec Taylor, he was second in the Derby and won nine races including the Doncaster and Coronation Cups. He was exported to America where he was a great success as a sire, among his offspring being that very good horse Twenty Grand.

ST JAMES'S PALACE STAKES

See under Ascot.

ST LEGER

See under Doncaster.

ST LOUIS

St Louis, by Louvois, won the Two Thousand Guineas in 1922. He made little mark as a sire.

ST PADDY

St Paddy was foaled in 1957 and was Sir Victor Sassoon's fourth and last Derby winner. Bred by his owner, he is by Aureole out of Edie Kelly. Besides the Derby, he won the Two Thousand Guineas, the Hardwicke Stakes and the Eclipse Stakes. In the King George VI and Queen Elizabeth Stakes in 1961 he was slammed by the French horse Right Royal V. He was widely regarded as a high-class horse but not a great battler when it came to a struggle. He stands at the Beech House Stud, Newmarket, and is the sire of Connaught, second in the Derby, and of St Pauli Girl, second in the One Thousand Guineas and the Oaks.

ST SIMON

St Simon, perhaps the greatest of English thoroughbreds, was a bay horse by Galopin out of St Angela. He was bred by Prince Batthyany, a Hungarian who had made England his home. The Prince was the owner of Galopin, who won the Derby for him in 1875. In 1883 the Prince dropped dead from a heart attack just outside the Jockey Club Luncheon Room at Newmarket, half an hour before Galliard, a son of Galopin, won the Two Thousand Guineas. Because of his owner's death, St Simon came up for sale when he was a two-year-old at Newmarket in July. He had no classic engagements, these being rendered void on account of the death of his nominator according to the rule existing at that time. For 1,600 gn he was bought by the young Duke of Portland, whose trainer was the famous Mat Dawson.

St Simon had not run at the time of his purchase and he was at once entered for suitable races that had not closed. He won twice at Goodwood and then carried off the Devonshire Nursery at Derby under top weight. At Doncaster he won the Prince of Wales Nursery by eight lengths from 20 opponents, to some of which he was conceding 44lb. He finished the season by defeating the Duke of Westminster's good two-year-old, Duke of Richmond, in a match.

The following year he received a walk-over in the Epsom Gold Cup and then won the Ascot Gold Cup by 20 lengths. He next won a gold cup over a mile at Gosforth Park and concluded his racing career by winning the Goodwood Cup by 20 lengths. Not once had he ever been extended, or anything like it. Mat Dawson rated him as good over a furlong as over a mile. Mat, who had trained six Derby winners, once observed "I have only trained one real smasher in my life—St Simon".

St Simon was rested in 1885, commencing stud duties the following year. His fee to start with was 50 gn but rose to 500 gn, a very big sum for those days. His stud record remains unsurpassed. He was champion sire nine times and finished in the first three on five other occasions. Six times he was leading sire of winning brood mares. He sired 17 classic winners and altogether sired the winners of 571 races worth over £553,000. He dropped down dead at the advanced age of 27.

He stood just on 16 hands and was so perfectly proportioned that he looked smaller than in fact he was. He possessed outstanding quality, shoulders so sloped that he seemed to be short in the back, and great length from hip to hock. He was higher at the croup than at the withers. His constitution was exceptionally robust and to the day of his death he was very rarely off colour. He possessed quite exceptional vitality, sweated freely, was highly-strung and quick-tempered. Many of these characteristics he transmitted to his stock, the outstanding member of which was Persimmon (q.v.).

SALISBURY

Salisbury is one of the oldest racecourses in England and it is recorded that Queen Elizabeth went to the races there not long before Drake sailed from Plymouth to defeat the Spanish Armada. The big prize at Salisbury on that occasion was a golden bell valued at £50. It was won by a horse owned by the third Lord Cumberland.

Situated on a hill a few miles outside the city, the track consists of fine old turf that provides admirable going and it is rare indeed for the ground to get really hard. The standard of racing is quite good and fields are nearly always strong because of the proximity of so many Berkshire and

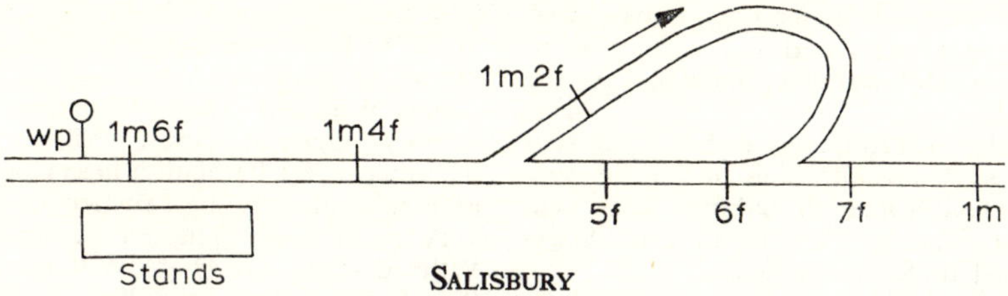

SALISBURY

Wiltshire stables. Many a good two-year-old has had its first introduction to racing at Salisbury, particularly in the days when Fred Darling trained at Beckhampton, Alec Taylor at Manton, and Noel Cannon at Druids Lodge. In the heyday of the Bibury Club, which until quite recently used to stage a three-day meeting in July, there were too many races for amateur riders to suit the public taste but that is a thing of the past.

The course consists of a mile track which is straight except for a slight right-hand elbow about 5f from the winning post, and a right-handed loop which leaves the mile course at the elbow and rejoins it 7f from home. The 1m 6f start is opposite the club enclosure, the horses running down the straight away from the stands, round the loop, and then back up the straight. The final 4f is uphill and calls for stamina, but the undulations and a sharp turn on the loop call for good balance and adaptability. High numbers in the draw have an advantage in races of 5f and 6f owing to the bend soon after the start, but a quick break is needed to avoid being cut off.

Clerk of the Course: Capt R. C. G. Vivian, Charlton House, Tetbury, Glos. Tel: Tetbury 310. Captain Vivian is due to retire in 1970 and his place will be taken by Major H. W. Hibbert.

Best Times:

Distance	*Horse-Age-Weight*	*Date*	*Time*
5f	Willies Kuda 5-9-1	30/6/65	61.36
5f	Fortunate Lady C 2-8-3	6/6/42	61.2
6f	Ujiji 3-9-2	25/4/42	1min 13.4
6f	Rosambre 2-8-9	30/6/65	1min 14.62
7f	Big Game 3-9-6	2/5/42	1min 28.2
7f	Black Satin 2-8-11	14/8/69	1min 29.44
8f	Reversion 3-9-6	4/10/41	1min 41.4
10f	Gratin 3-8-3	11/8/65	2min 9.12
12f	Forum 4-9-1	19/4/54	2min 36
14f	Shahpoor 5-9-7	20/5/44	3min 0.8

SALIVA TEST

A laboratory test to see if a horse has been doped.

SALMON LEAP

Bred and owned by Mrs Arthur James, Salmon Leap was foaled in 1927 and was by Salmon Trout out of Stony Ford, by Swynford. His victories included the Coronation Cup, Goodwood Cup and Newbury Summer Cup, while he was second in the Gold Cup at Ascot. He made little mark at the stud over here and was exported to South Africa in 1941.

SALMON TROUT

Bred in 1921 by Lord Furness, Salmon Trout was by The Tetrarch out of Salamandra, by St Frusquin. Bought by the Aga Khan as a yearling and trained by R. C. Dawson, he won five races, including a sensational St Leger concerning which there were lurid stories linking the name of Salmon Trout's jockey, Bernard Carslake, with that of a leading bookmaker. The bookmaker had laid Salmon Trout heavily and was very hard hit by the result.

Salmon Trout was not a great success as a sire although he did get two top-class horses in Salmon Leap and King Salmon. He was eventually exported to South Africa.

SALTASH

Bred in 1920 by the late Lord Astor, Saltash was by Sunstar out of Hamoaze and thus a full-brother to Buchan and a half-brother to St Germans. He won the Eclipse Stakes and subsequently did well as a sire in Australia.

SALVO

Salvo was bred in America in 1963 and is a chestnut by Right Royal V out of Maenza, by Macherio. Owned by Mr G. A. Oldham and trained by Harry Wragg, he only ran once as a two-year-old, finishing second in the Houghton Stakes. The following season he won the Craven Stakes, Vaux Gold Tankard and Newbury Autumn Cup and was just beaten in Germany in the Preis von Europa. He reached his peak as a four-year-old, winning the Yorkshire Cup, Hardwicke Stakes and Grosser Preis von Baden. He was second in the John Porter Stakes, King George VI and Queen Elizabeth Stakes and the Prix de l'Arc de Triomphe. He is now owned by a syndicate and stands at the Sandwich Stud, Newmarket.

SAMMY DAVIS

Sammy Davis, by Whistler, was a very smart sprinter that won five races worth over £7,000, including the Diadem Stakes. He was syndicated for the stud and stood until 1968 at the National Stud, West Grinstead, Sussex, when he was exported to Japan.

SANDOWN PARK

Sandown Park, Esher, is only 15 miles from London. By English standards it is a modern racecourse, the first meeting having been held there in 1875. The three men who instituted racing at Sandown and laid out the course were Mr Hwfa Williams; his brother General Owen Williams, a Member of Parliament, a heavy bettor, and subsequently part-owner of that very good horse The Bard; and Sir Wilfred Brett. Mr Hwfa Williams was the dominating personality and held office as Chairman and as Clerk of the Course for nearly 50 years.

The charm of Sandown, deservedly one of the most popular courses in the country, particularly in respect of racing under National Hunt rules, is based on the fact that the stands and enclosures are sited on a hill. It is possible to see nearly all the running just standing on the lawns in front of the stands, and on no other major course is viewing rendered so easy for the onlooker.

From the start Sandown proved a success and with the support and encouragement of Mr Leopold de Rothschild, Mr Hwfa Williams decided to stage the first £10,000-race in England, the 1m 2f Eclipse Stakes. It was first run in 1886 and was won by Major H. T. Barclay's good horse Bendigo, who defeated the 1884 Derby winner St Gatien. Perhaps the greatest race for the Eclipse was in 1903 when Ard Patrick, who had won the Derby the year before, defeated the famous filly Sceptre, winner of four classic races in 1902, and Rock Sand who won the 'Triple Crown' in 1903. Another memorable race came in 1910 when the Derby winner Lemberg ran a dead-heat with Neil Gow, winner of the Two Thousand Guineas. In recent years the Eclipse has tended to be overshadowed by the King George VI and Queen Elizabeth Stakes at Ascot run later in the month. However, Ballymoss and Busted have both won the two races the same year.

Another celebrated Sandown race is the 5f National Stakes for two-year-olds, previously the National Breeders Produce Stakes. The Tetrarch won this race after being virtually left at

(*left*) PIGGOTT, LESTER. Lester Piggott, who has so far ridden five Derby winners

(*right*) PORTER, JOHN. Trainer of seven Derby winners, John Porter of Kingsclere

(*left*) RICHARDS, SIR GORDON. Sir Gordon Richards in his riding days, wearing the royal colours

ROSEBERY, FIFTH EARL OF. Lord Rosebery, who won the Derby while holding office as Prime Minister, arriving at a Jockey Club meeting in 1915 to decide whether racing should continue during the war

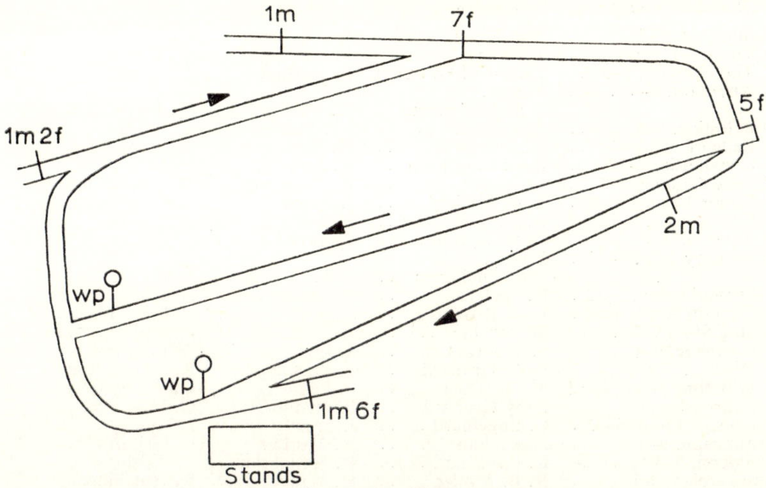

SANDOWN PARK

the post and another famous winner was the Aga Khan's Bahram who was never defeated.

Sandown is a right-handed track of 1m 5f. The 4f run-in is uphill almost the entire way and so is the straight 5f course. Sandown is a stiff course but a fair one, demanding the qualities of stamina and resolution. Because of the lay-out of the course, it is not possible to run 6f races there.

Clerk of the Course: Major P. Beckwith-Smith. Sandown Park Club, Esher, Surrey. Tel: Esher 63072.

Best Times:

Distance	*Horse-Weight-Age*	*Date*	*Time*
5f	No Fear 3-7-8	26/4/57	60.2
5f	Vivacious 2-8-7	25/10/47	60.8
7f	Nero's Love 4-8-8	13/6/59	1min 28
7f	Happy Omen 2-9-3	7/9/62	1min 29.6
8f	Adrasto 4-9-0	16/6/62	1min 39.6
8f	Stansfield 2-8-13	2/9/67	1min 43
10f	St Paddy 5-9-5	4/7/70	2min 6
13f 110yds	His Story 4-9-0	19/5/61	2min 56.5
2m	Barley Bree 5-7-3	9/9/61	3min 52

National Stakes, 5f

Two-year-olds. Formerly the National Breeders Produce Stakes. First run 1889. *Run at Ascot* 1946. *No race* 1940 *to* 1945.

	OWNER	TRAINER	JOCKEY	SP
1930 Thyestes, 0–0	Maj D. McCalmont	H. Persse	H. Beasley	9–2
1931 Orwell, 9–5	W. Singer	J. Lawson	R. Jones	5–4
1932 Myrobella, 8–7	Lord Lonsdale	F. Darling	G. Richards	21–20
1933 Colombo, 9–5	Lord Glanely	T. Hogg	G. Richards	85–40
1934 Bahram, 8–10	Aga Khan	Fk. Butters	R. Perryman	20–1
1935 Wyndham, 9–5	Miss D. Paget	D. Snow	C. Smirke	4–1
1936 Full Sail, 8–10	Lord Rosebery	J. Jarvis	R. Jones	20–1
1937 Portmarnock, 8–10	Sir H. de Trafford	C. B-Rochfort	P. Beasley	10–1
1938 Rogerstone Castle, 8–10	Mrs D. Thomas	S. Donoghue	C. Elliott	100–6

National Stakes (contd)

	OWNER	TRAINER	JOCKEY	SP
1939 Stardust, 9–5	Aga Khan	Fk. Butters ..	C. Smirke ..	7–1
1946 Tudor Minstrel, 9–5.	J. Dewar	F. Darling ..	G. Richards ..	4–9
1947 The Cobbler, 9–5 ..	Lieut-Col G. Loder	F. Darling ..	G. Richards ..	1–3
1948 Abernant, 9–5 . ..	Maj R. M-Buchanan ..	N. Murless ..	G. Richards ..	1–2
1949 Palestine, 9–5	Aga Khan	Fk. Butters ..	C. Smirke ..	4–6
1950 Belle of All, 8–7 ..	H. Tufton	N. Bertie.. ..	G. Younger ..	20–1
1951 Constantia, 8–12 ..	Lord Fairhaven ..	R. Jarvis . ..	P. Maher . ..	5–2
1952 Bebe Grande, 8–7 ..	J. Gerber	F. Armstrong..	W. Snaith ..	9–2
1953 Tudor Honey, 8–10 .	Lord Milford ..	J. Jarvis	E. Mercer ..	10–1
1954 Courageous, 8–10 ..	Maj L. Holliday ..	H. Cottrill ..	F. Barlow ..	20–1
1955 Rustam, 9–5	Lady Wyfold . ..	G. Brooke ..	D. Smith.. ..	100–30
1956 Military Law, 8–12 .	Mrs R. M-Buchanan ..	J. A. Waugh ..	J. Mercer . ..	100–30
1957 Promulgation, 8–12 .	H. Joel	T. Leader . ..	E. Smith . ..	8–1
1958 Captain Kidd, 8–12 .	Lord Rosebery ..	J. Jarvis	E. Mercer ..	7–1
1959 Sing Sing, 9–2 . ..	W. Stirling	J. Watts	D. Smith.. ..	11–4
1960 Kerrabee, 9–4	S. Wootton	S. Ingham. ..	A. Breasley ..	6–1
1961 Display, 8–9	Lady Granard ..	P. Prendergast .	R. Hutchinson	6–5
1962 Whistling Wind, 8–12	M. Sheehan	P. Prendergast .	G. Bougoure ..	8–13
1963 Pourparler, 8–9 ..	Lady Granard ..	P. Prendergast .	G. Bougoure ..	3–1
1964 Double Jump, 8–12 .	C. Engelhard . ..	J. Tree	J. Lindley ..	evens
1965 Zahedan, 9–0	Aga Khan	N. Murless ..	L. Piggott ..	11–8
1966 Falcon, 9–4	C. Engelhard . ..	R. Houghton .	L. Piggott ..	8–13
1967 Sovereign, 9–1.. ..	R. B. Moller . ..	H. Wragg ..	R. Hutchinson	8–11
1968 Tower Walk, 9–0 ..	V. Hardy	G. Barling ..	M. Thomas ..	7–4
1969 Quarryknowe, 9–0 ..	Lord Weir	H. Price	A. Murray ..	3–1

Eclipse Stakes, 1m 2f

First run 1886. *Run at Ascot* 1946. *No race* 1940 *to* 1945.

	OWNER	TRAINER	JOCKEY	SP
1930 Rustom Pasha, 3–8–9	Aga Khan	R. Dawson ..	H. Wragg ..	4–1
1931 Caerleon, 4–9–4 ..	Lord Derby	G. Lambton ..	T. Weston ..	25–1
1932 Miracle, 3–8–9 . ..	Lord Rosebery ..	J. Jarvis	H. Wragg ..	10–1
1933 Loaningdale, 4–9–7 .	Col G. Wilson ..	C. B-Rochfort .	J. Childs . ..	9–2
1934 King Salmon, 4–9–7	Sir R. Brooke ..	O. Bell	H. Wragg ..	4–1
1935 Windsor Lad, 4–9–10	M. Benson	M. Marsh ..	C. Smirke ..	4–7
1936 Rhodes Scholar, 3–8–9	Lord Astor	J. Lawson ..	R. Dick	11–8
1937 Boswell, 4–9–10 ..	W. Woodward ..	C. B-Rochfort .	P. Beasley ..	20–1
1938 Pasch, 3–8–12	H. Morriss	F. Darling ..	G. Richards ..	13–8
1939 Blue Peter, 3–8–12 ..	Lord Rosebery ..	J. Jarvis	E. Smith . ..	2–7
1946 Gulf Stream, 3–8–6 .	Lord Derby	W. Earl	H. Wragg ..	8–13
1947 Migoli, 3–8–9	Aga Khan	Fk. Butters ..	C. Smirke ..	7–2
1948 Petition, 4–9–7 . ..	Sir A. Butt	Fk. Butters ..	K. Gethin ..	8–1
1949 Djeddah, 4–9–4 ..	M. Boussac	C. Semblat ..	C. Elliott . ..	6–4
1950 Flocon, 4–9–4 . ..	Baron de Waldner	P. Carter.. ..	F. Palmer ..	100–9
1951 Mystery IX, 3–8–2 .	Mrs E. Esmond ..	P. Carter.. ..	L. Piggott ..	100–8
1952 Tulyar, 3–8–2	Aga Khan	M. Marsh ..	C. Smirke ..	1–3
1953 Argur, 4–9–0	M. Boussac	J. Glynn	C. Elliott . ..	100–9
1954 King of the Tudors, 4–9–7	F. Dennis	W. Stephenson	K. Gethin ..	9–2
1955 Darius, 4–9–7	Sir P. Loraine ..	H. Wragg ..	L. Piggott ..	11–10
1956 Tropique, 4–9–7 ..	Baron de Rothschild	G. Watson ..	P. Blanc	3–1
1957 Arctic Explorer, 3–8–9	Lieut-Col G. Loder	N. Murless ..	L. Piggott ..	100–30
1958 Ballymoss, 4–9–7 ..	J. McShain	V. O'Brien ..	A. Breasley ..	8–11
1959 Saint Crespin III, 3–8–9	Aly Khan	A. Head	G. Moore ..	5–2
1960 Javelot, 4–9–0 . ..	Baron de Waldner	P. Carter.. ..	F. Palmer ..	4–1
1961 St Paddy, 4–9–7 ..	Sir V. Sassoon ..	N. Murless ..	L. Piggott ..	2–13
1962 Henry the Seventh, 4–9–0	H. Joel	W. Elsey . ..	E. Hide	8–11
1963 Khalkis, 3–8–2 . ..	Lord Elveden ..	P. Prendergast .	G. Bougoure ..	7–4
1964 Ragusa, 4–9–0.. ..	J. Mullion	P. Prendergast .	G. Bougoure ..	4–6

	OWNER	TRAINER	JOCKEY	SP
1965 Canisbay, 4–9–5 ..	The Queen	C. B-Rochfort .	S Clayton ..	20–1
1966 Pieces of Eight,3–8–7	Contesse de la Valdene	V. O'Brien ..	L. Piggott ..	11–10
1967 Busted, 4–9–5	S. Joel	N. Murless ..	W. Rickaby ..	8–1
1968 Royal Palace, 4–9–5.	H. Joel	N. Murless ..	A. Barclay ..	9–4
1969 Wolver Hollow, 5–9–5	Mrs C. Iselin . ..	H. Cecil	L. Piggott ..	8–1
1970 Connaught 5–9–5 .	H. J. Joel	N. Murless ..	A. Barclay ..	5–4

SANDWICH

Sandwich was bred in 1928 by Mr J. J. Maher and was a half-brother to the Derby winner Manna by Sansovino. Bought as a yearling by Lord Rosebery and trained by Jack Jarvis, he won the Chester Vase, King Edward VII Stakes and St Leger. He was a terribly unlucky loser of the Derby, Harry Wragg riding one of his less successful races and getting badly shut in in the straight. Sandwich did not add to his reputation as a four-year-old and he failed as a sire.

SANSOVINO

Bred in 1921 by the late Lord Derby, Sansovino was by Swynford out of that famous mare Gondolette, by Loved One. He was trained by the Hon George Lambton and as a two-year-old won both his races, the Ham Stakes at Goodwood and the Gimcrack Stakes. The following season he ran with promise when close up third in the Newmarket Stakes and shortly afterwards did a very impressive gallop at Newmarket. Immediately after the gallop one of the jockeys who had taken part in it grabbed his wife's jewellery, pawned it, and put every penny of the money he had raised on Sansovino for the Derby.

The going at Epsom was terribly heavy that year and rain fell in torrents throughout Derby day. Many of the cars and buses got stuck and did not get out till the following morning. The conditions, though, suited Sansovino, who loved the mud, and ridden by Tommy Weston he won by six lengths. It was the first time for 137 years that the race had been won by an Earl of Derby.

Sansovino ran twice at Ascot, winning the Prince of Wales's Stakes and finishing unplaced in the Hardwicke Stakes. He was unplaced in the St Leger but he had been coughing not long before the race and was not at his best by a long way.

As a four-year-old he had leg trouble and was never really right, but proved his speed by beating Diophon, winner of the Two Thousand Guineas, over a mile at Lingfield. He was unplaced in the City and Suburban and is the last Derby winner to have competed in that event. As a sire he was a shade disappointing but got Sandwich (St Leger); Jacopo (a top-class two-year-old and a successful sire in America); Monument (Coronation Cup); Buckleigh (Jockey Club Cup); Sans Peine (Goodwood Cup); and Sansonnet (dam of Tudor Minstrel).

Sansovino died in 1940.

SANTA CLAUS

Santa Claus was a bay by Chamossaire out of Aunt Clara, by Arctic Prince. He was bred in Warwickshire by Dr F. A. Smorfitt and bought as a yearling for 1,200 gn on behalf of Mr J. Ismay. In 1964, trained at the Curragh by J. M. Rogers and ridden by A. Breasley, he won the Derby. Other successes included the Irish Two Thousand Guineas and the Irish Derby. He was second in the King George VI and Queen Elizabeth Stakes and also in the Prix de l'Arc de Triomphe. He stood at the Airlie Stud, Lucan, Co Dublin till his sudden death in 1970. He sired Reindeer, winner of the Irish St Leger in 1969.

SANTORB

Bred in 1921 by Capt Charles

Moore, Santorb, by Santoi, was a very good stayer, winning the Ascot Gold Cup, Doncaster Cup and Newbury Summer Cup. He was only at the stud in England for four years before being exported to Hungary but left his mark by siring Rockliffe, dam of the brilliant Rockfel (q.v.).

SASSOON, Sir Victor, Bart (1882-1961)

Sir Victor Sassoon was educated at Harrow and Cambridge and succeeded to the baronetcy in 1924. In World War I, he served in the RFC. A member of a famous Jewish family that emigrated from Baghdad to India early in the nineteenth century, his business interests were mainly concerned with E. D. Sassoon and Co, bankers, merchants and mill owners.

For over 30 years Sir Victor was in truth a pillar of the Turf. He came into the sport almost by accident. In India he got to know Jimmy Crawford, the son of an Ayrshire blacksmith and a successful amateur rider on the Indian Turf. In 1922 Crawford went to England to train for Mr M. Goculdas, a Bombay cotton magnate. Goculdas got into financial difficulties and Sassoon took over his racing interests, consisting of over a hundred horses in India and a number in England. In India he raced as 'Mr Eve' and when he established a stud at Newmarket he named it the Eve Stud.

In 1925 he really began to launch out on the English Turf and spent what was then considered a fortune on yearlings. He bought the Fitzroy House stables at Newmarket and installed Jimmy Crawford as his trainer. The 1925 yearlings included the highly-strung Gay Crusader colt Hot Night who ran second to Call Boy in the Derby. When Crawford died, Sir Victor divided his horses between Basil Jarvis, Joe Lawson and Matt Peacock, while he also sent some to Jack Rogers in Ireland.

In 1937 Sir Victor enjoyed his first English classic successes when he won the One Thousand Guineas and the Oaks with Exhibitionnist, trained by Joe Lawson. She was by Solario out of Lady Wembley, a mare bought by Crawford for only 750 gn. The same year Sir Victor won the Irish Two Thousand Guineas and the Irish Derby with Phideas. He had won the Irish 'Triple Crown' two years previously with Museum. In 1936 he purchased the French horse Mieuxcé, who, although disappointing as a sire of winners, did well as a sire of brood mares.

Sir Victor's peak period of success in racing came between 1953 and 1960 when he won the Derby on four occasions. Considering his many expensive purchases, it is ironical that two of his Derby winners, Pinza (1953) and Hard Ridden (1958) cost only 1,500 gn and 270 gn respectively. Pinza, trained by Norman Bertie, also won the King George VI and Queen Elizabeth Stakes. Hard Ridden, trained by Mick Rogers, won the Irish Two Thousand Guineas before his Epsom triumph. Noel Murless trained Sir Victor's two other Derby winners, Crepello (1957) and St Paddy (1960). Crepello also won the Two Thousand Guineas, St Paddy the St Leger and Eclipse Stakes. Sir Victor won the One Thousand Guineas in 1956 with Honeylight trained by Capt Charles Elsey. She was a half-sister to Crepello and to the 1963 Gold Cup winner Twilight Alley.

Like a good many other rich men, Sir Victor was not always easy to get on with, but considering his contribution to racing and the invaluable financial advice he could surely have given, it seems odd that he was never elected to the Jockey Club.

SASSOON, Lady (b 1920)

Lady Sassoon has carried on the breeding and racing interests of her late husband, Sir Victor Sassoon, including the Sassoon Studs which incorporate the Beech House Stud and the Eve Stud at Newmarket, the Thornton Stud in Yorkshire and the Killeen Stud in Co Meath. Good horses owned by Lady Sassoon include Twilight Alley (Gold Cup); The Creditor (Jersey Stakes, Lockinge Stakes and Queen Elizabeth II Stakes); Sweet Moss (Dee Stakes, Dante Stakes, Gordon Stakes and Rous Memorial Stakes); Soft Angels (Royal Lodge Stakes); and Sucaryl (*News of the World* Stakes and David Robinson Stakes). Lady Sassoon's trainers are Noel Murless and J. M. Rogers. Colours: peacock blue and old gold hoops, gold sleeves.

SAUCY SUE

Foaled in 1922, Saucy Sue was one of the late Lord Astor's best fillies. By Swynford out of Good and Gay, she won eight races including the One Thousand Guineas, Oaks and Coronation Stakes. She only bred one winner, Truculent, at the stud.

SAYAJIRAO

Foaled in 1944, Sayajirao was by Nearco out of Rosy Legend and thus a brother of the Derby winner Dante. As a yearling he was purchased by the Maharaja of Baroda for the then record sum of 28,000 gn. Trained by 'Sam' Armstrong, he was backward as a two-year-old but the following season he won the Lingfield Derby Trial, the Irish Derby, the Warren Stakes at Goodwood and the St Leger. In addition he was third in both the Two Thousand Guineas and the Derby. As a four-year-old he won the Hardwicke Stakes at Ascot and was only just beaten by Petition in the Eclipse Stakes. In all he won £19,342 in stakes.

At the stud Sayajirao was rather slow to make his mark and the fact that a good many of his stock needed time and were out-and-out stayers did not increase his popularity with commercial breeders. His best winners were Indiana (Chester Vase, Great Voltigeur Stakes and St Leger); Gladness (Ascot Gold Cup, Goodwood Cup, Ebor Handicap); Lynchris (Irish Oaks, Yorkshire Oaks, Irish St Leger); and I Say (Coronation Cup). He died in 1966.

SAYANI

Sayani, by Fair Copy, was a very good French horse that won four races in France and four in England. His best performance was to win the Cambridgeshire in 1946 as a three-year-old with 9st 4lb on his back. He was champion sire in France in 1953 and shortly afterwards was exported to Brazil.

SCAPA FLOW

Scapa Flow, by Chaucer out of Anchora, was a famous mare belonging to the seventeenth Earl of Derby. Her sons and daughters won 63 races worth £85,649. She herself had competed in selling races. Two of her offspring, Fairway and Fair Isle, were classic winners, while Pharos was champion sire both in England and in France.

SCEPTRE

Sceptre, by Persimmon out of Ornament, by Bend Or, was one of the best and bravest fillies ever to race in England. Foaled in 1899, she was bred by the first Duke of Westminster who died later that year. She came up for sale as a yearling and was bought for 10,000 gn, a huge sum in those days, by Mr Robert Sievier, a journalist and adventurer who was a bold and occasionally unscrupulous gambler.

As a two-year-old, trained by Charles Morton, she won the Woodcote Stakes at Epsom and the July Stakes at Newmarket but had trained off when she was beaten in the Champagne Stakes at Doncaster.

The following year Sievier trained her himself. Despite a very hard race—she was narrowly beaten—in the Lincolnshire Handicap when she was far below her best, she won both the Two Thousand Guineas and the One Thousand Guineas. Her preparation for the Derby suffered interruption for a day or two at a critical stage and as she was a thick-winded filly this may have cost her the race, in which she finished fourth to Ard Patrick.

However, she won the Oaks two days later. Sievier, hard up despite the filly's successes, at once packed her off to Paris for the Grand Prix in which, indifferently ridden, she was unplaced. On her return from France she was sent to Royal Ascot where she was fourth in the Coronation Stakes and won the St James's Palace Stakes. Thus she had five races against top-class opposition in under a month.

She was then afforded a brief rest, but returned to the fray at Goodwood where she was beaten in the Sussex Stakes and won the Nassau Stakes. She duly won the St Leger but her greedy owner pulled her out again two days later for the Park Hill Stakes and she was beaten.

Next year a gamble in the Lincoln with her failed and Sievier then sold her for 25,000 gn to Mr (later Sir) William Bass, who sent her to Alec Taylor to be trained. She was in very poor condition when she arrived at Manton but Taylor gradually built her up and she won the Hardwicke Stakes at Ascot. She was just beaten by Ard Patrick, who had won the Derby the year before, in a wonderful race for the Eclipse and then won in succession the Jockey Club Stakes, the Duke of York Stakes, the Champion Stakes and the Limekiln Stakes. As a five-year-old she was past her best, but in her three outings was third in the Hardwicke Stakes and the Gold Cup, and second in the Coronation Cup. Altogether she won 13 races worth over £38,000. The real tragedy of her career was the death of her breeder, the Duke of Westminster. If she had carried his colours and had been trained by John Porter, she would have been treated with far greater consideration and would probably have never been beaten.

Sceptre lived till she was 28. At the stud her own offspring were disappointing in respect of racing ability, but her descendants, in particular through her daughter Maid of the Mist, who was bought by Lord Astor, have played a notable part in Turf history, not only in this country, but in France, America and Australia as well.

SCOTT, A. C. (1904-1965)

The bookmaking profession suffered a heavy loss when Mr Archie Scott died in 1965 at the comparatively early age of 61. A very tall, spare man of infinite charm, humour and kindness, he was educated at Eton and Cambridge and began his career in bookmaking as clerk to Mr Sidney Fry, famous as a golfer and billiards player. Soon afterwards he set up on his own, but in 1933 he joined forces with Mr Dick Fry, no relation of Sidney. During the war he served overseas with the Green Howards and in 1945 he returned to the rails, making a book under the title of A. C. Scott Ltd. He had a large and distinguished clientele, but in the late 1950s he faced difficult times and in 1961 the business was taken over by Alfred Cope, who subsequently merged with William Hill.

Archie Scott's great contribution to his profession lay in his tireless and dedicated work as an administrator. His charm, tact, and the respect in which he was held were invaluable in his various posts as chairman of the National Bookmakers and Associated Bodies Joint Protection Association; chairman of the National B.P.A.; member of Tattersall's Committee on Betting; chairman of the Association of Rails Bookmakers; chairman of the Bookmakers Betting Levy Committee and their member on the Horserace Betting Levy Board. In addition he served as a member of the Peppiatt Committee, the preamble of the 1961 Betting Levy Act.

His death was hastened by two tragic blows in his closing years. His wife was killed in a car crash in 1962, and in 1965 his second son was killed on active service in Aden.

SCOTT, Bill (d 1848)

Born at Chippenham, near Newmarket, Bill Scott was one of the greatest riders of his time. He won the Derby four times—St Giles (1832), Mundig (1835), Attila (1842) and Cotherstone (1843). He rode nine winners of the St Leger, four of them in succession, and he also had three victories in the Oaks. His brother John (q.v.) won equal fame as a trainer and for many years they proved a formidable combination. Drink was Bill Scott's weakness and in the latter part of his career he was frequently unfit to ride. If he had not been blind drunk he would have won the 1846 Derby on his own horse Sir Tatton Sykes. (Jockeys could own horses in those days.)

SCOTT, John

The outstanding trainer of the mid-Victorian era, John Scott was born at Chippenham, near Newmarket, and was the brother of Bill Scott, the jockey. He trained at Malton in Yorkshire and between 1827 and 1863 he won the St Leger 16 times, a record that is unlikely ever to be broken. He also trained five Derby winners, nine Oaks winners, six winners of the Two Thousand Guineas and four of the One Thousand Guineas. His Derby winners were Mundig (1835), Attila (1842), Cotherstone (1833), Daniel O'Rourke (1852) and West Australian (1853). In many ways a likeable and entertaining man, he was inclined to be just a bit too crafty at times.

SCOTTISH UNION

Scottish Union was bred in 1935 by the Sledmere Stud and was by Cameronian out of Trustful, by Bachelor's Double. Bought as a yearling by Mr J. V. Rank and trained by Noel Cannon, he won six races including the Middle Park Stakes, St James's Palace Stakes, St Leger and Coronation Cup. He was second in the Two Thousand Guineas and the Derby and third in the Gold Cup. At the stud he got that gallant stayer Strathspey, whose victories included the Cesarewitch and Goodwood Stakes.

SCRATCH

To scratch a horse means to take it out of a race for which it has been entered.

SCRATCH II

Bred in 1947 by M. M. Boussac, Scratch II by Pharis II, won the Solario Stakes and St Leger in England; in France the Prix Greffulhe, French Derby and Prix Jean Prat. After a few seasons at the stud in France he was exported to the Argentine.

SCUTTLE

Bred in 1925 by King George V, Scuttle was by Captain Cuttle out of Stained Glass, by Tracery. She was the King's only classic winner, carrying off the One Thousand Guineas in 1928. She was second in the Oaks. She made little mark at the stud.

SEA BIRD II

Sea Bird II is a chestnut by the American-bred Dan Cupid out of Sicalade, by Sicambre. Bred and owned by M. J. Ternynck and trained by Etienne Pollet at Chantilly, he proved himself one of the best horses of this century, his victories in 1965 including the Derby, the Prix Greffulhe, the Prix Lupin, the Grand Prix de St Cloud and the Prix de l'Arc de Triomphe. He won both the Derby and the Prix de l'Arc de Triomphe with contemptuous ease. Altogether he won the equivalent of £225,000 in stakes. His solitary defeat was as a two-year-old when second to his stable-companion Grey Dawn in the Grand Criterium. He did not run as a four-year-old and was leased for five years to Mr John Galbreath of the Derby Dan Farm, Kentucky, USA.

SEAGRAVE, John (b 1933)

This well-known north-country jockey was born in 1933 and served his apprenticeship with W. Smallwood and E. Davey. He rode his first winner in 1948 and the biggest number of winners he has ridden in a season is 76. He ended his association with W. Elsey at the end of 1969 and arranged to ride for H. P. Rohan in 1970.

SEA HAWK

Sea Hawk was bred in 1963 in France where he won the Criterium de St Cloud and the Grand Prix de St Cloud. By Herbager out of Sea Nymph, by Free Man, he is now owned by Mr A. D. D. Rogers and stands at a fee of 1,000 gn at the Grangewilliam Stud, Maynooth, Co Kildare.

SECOND DAM

Grandmother.

SEFTON, seventh Earl of (b 1898)

Lord Sefton served in the Royal Horse Guards from 1917-30 and from 1939-45. Interested in most forms of sport, he has long been a prominent figure in the coursing world and up till World War II he was rated one of the best heavy-weights across Leicestershire. He has played a leading part in public life in Lancashire, his home county, and was lord mayor of Liverpool in 1944-45. He has for many years been one of the most active members of the Jockey Club and has held office as Senior Steward. He has been in no small degree responsible for the gradual modernisation of racing at Newmarket and the Sefton Course is in fact named after him. The best horses he has owned so far are Bob Cherry (Nottingham Stewards Cup, Festival Stakes and Cork and Orrery Stakes); Titian (New Ham Foal Stakes, Kempton Two Thousand Guineas Trial and Red Rose Stakes); Kipling (Gordon Stakes); and Gaul (King Edward VII Stakes and Jockey Club Stakes).

Lord Sefton's flat-race horses are trained by Ian Balding and Doug Smith. Colours: white, primrose sleeves, black cap.

SELENE

Selene, by Chaucer out of Serenissima, by Minoru, was bred in 1919 by the late Lord Derby. She was a tough, game mare, winning 15½ races, worth over £14,000, including the Park Hill Stakes and Liverpool Autumn Cup. As a brood-mare she was outstanding, among her offspring being Hyperion (Derby, St Leger and six times champion sire); Sickle (a leading two-year-old, placed in the Two Thousand Guineas and a highly influential sire in America); Pharamond (Middle Park Stakes and a leading sire in America); Hunters Moon (Newmarket Stakes and a leading sire in the Argentine); and All Moonshine (dam of the very successful sire Mossborough).

SELLING RACE

A selling race is one in which the conditions demand that every horse running, if a loser, may be claimed, and if a winner, must be offered for sale by auction. The lowest price at which the winner can be sold is laid down in the Rules of Racing and varies according to the value of the race. If at the auction the winner is sold for more than the stipulated selling price, the surplus goes not to the owner of the winner, but to the race-fund. A loser in a selling race can be claimed for the stipulated selling price plus the value of the stakes or advertised value of the plate. No person can claim more than one horse and each claim must be accompanied by a fee of £10. The claim has to be made in writing to the Clerk of the Course within fifteen minutes of the winner passing the scale or the judge announcing the decision on all placings, whichever be later. If two or more persons claim the same horse, the auctioneer holds an auction between the claimants in the office of the Clerk of the Course. Any surplus above the claiming price is divided between the race-fund and the Joint Administrative Authority.

SEMBLAT, C. H.

At one period a leading jockey in France, Semblat was for a time trainer to the French industrialist, M. M. Boussac. In 1950, the year M. Boussac's Galcador won the Derby, Semblat headed the trainers' list in England without once setting foot in this country.

SERENISSIMA

Serenissima, foaled in 1913, was one of the late Lord Derby's most famous mares. By Minoru out of Gondolette, she was a half-sister to the Derby winner Sansovino. She bred eight winners of 40 races worth over £47,000, including Selene (£14,000 and dam of Hyperion), Tranquil (One Thousand Guineas, St Leger and Jockey Club Cup) and Bosworth (Ascot Gold Cup).

SEXTON, Graham (b 1948)

Graham Sexton is apprenticed to Harry Wragg. In 1967 he rode 29 winners. He can go to scale still at 7st 5lb and among the good races he has won are the Royal Hunt Cup on Regal Light and the Newbury Autumn Cup on Salvo.

SHANTUNG

Bred in 1956 in France by Baron Guy de Rothschild, Shantung is by Sicambre out of Barley Corn, by Hyperion. He won three races in France and was third in the Derby. He started favourite for the Derby and was desperately unlucky not to win. Coming down the hill he collided with another runner and his rider, thinking the colt had broken a leg, pulled him back to last preparatory to pulling him up. In fact Shantung was not injured and ran on to such purpose in the straight that he finished only two lengths behind Parthia, the winner.

Shantung is owned by a syndicate and stands at the Banstead Manor Stud, Newmarket. He is sire of Silk Hat (Santa Ysabel Stakes, Santa Anita, USA); Felicio (Grand Prix de St Cloud in France); Cilena (Criterium Nazionale in Italy); Full Dress II (One Thousand Guineas); Saracena (Criterium de St Cloud and Prix St Alary); Lacquer (Irish One Thousand Guineas and Cambridgeshire); and Saraca (Prix Vermeille).

SHARMAN, John (b 1942)

John Sharman served his apprenticeship with Ron Smyth. His best season was 1965 when he rode 22 winners. In that year he won the Kempton Jubilee on Antiquarian.

SHEDDEN, L. H. (b 1902)

'Tommy' Shedden was assistant trainer to his father for five years and then from 1925 to 1935 he was head lad to R. Renton. He took out a licence to train in 1935 and his stable is at Wetherby, Yorkshire. His patrons include Mr A. Patchett, Mrs L. Brotherton, Mr G. Jarvis, Mr H. A. Whitfield, Mr S. Webster, Mr F. B. Dyson, Mr J. A. Simpson, Mrs R. Fell, Lord Mostyn, Mrs A. Poskitt and Mr P. Askwith. His big triumph was to win the 1969 Cesarewitch with Floridian.

SHEPPARD, Daniel Gurney

Born in 1908 and educated at Eton, Mr Dan Sheppard became a handicapper in 1936 and is now Jockey Club Handicapper.

SHESHOON

Bred in 1956 by the late Aga Khan and Prince Aly Khan, Sheshoon is a chestnut horse by Precipitation out of Noorani, by Nearco, and is thus a half-brother to Charlottesville. His successes included the Ascot Gold Cup, Grand Prix de St Cloud and Grosser Preis von Baden. He was just beaten in the Prix du Cadran. The property of a syndicate, he stands at the Limestone Stud, Gainsborough, Lincolnshire. His winners include

Samos III (French St Leger), Stintino (Prix Lupin and third in the Derby) and Sassafras (French Derby).

SHORT STORY

Bred in 1923 by the late Lord Astor, Short Story, by Buchan, won the 1926 Oaks. Of her progeny, Birthday Book won over £6,000 in stakes.

SHOTOVER

The Duke of Westminster's Shotover, by Hermit, is one of the six fillies that have won the Derby, a feat she accomplished in 1882.

SHOW

A list of betting odds is often described as a 'show'.

SICARELLE

Bred in France by Mme L. Volterra in 1953, Sicarelle, by Sicambre, won the 1956 Oaks.

SICKLE

Bred in 1924 by the late Lord Derby, Sickle was a half-brother by Phalaris to Hyperion. A good two-year-old and third in the Two Thousand Guineas, he was exported to America and became a leading sire there. Among his descendants are Native Dancer and Sea Bird.

SIEVIER, R. S.

Bob Sievier was born in a cab and led a stormy life. A big gambler who landed many successful coups but was almost always short of money, he bought the famous filly Sceptre (q.v.) for 10,000 guineas at the dispersal of the first Duke of Westminster's bloodstock. This was a record price for a yearling at the time. Trained by Sievier, Sceptre won every classic bar the Derby, in which she was fourth, in 1902. Her owner, though, was broke at the end of the season and had to sell her.

Sievier ran his horses honestly enough, but in other aspects of his life he seldom appeared hampered in his conduct by the possession of moral scruples. A libel action that exposed him in a singularly unflattering light terminated his active career on the Turf. He died hard up in 1939.

SIGNORINETTA

Bred, owned and trained at Newmarket by the Chevalier Ginistrelli, an Italian, Signorinetta brought off one of the surprises of the century when she won the 1908 Derby at 100-1. Two days later she won the Oaks. She never won another race and made little lasting mark as a brood mare. In both her Epsom triumphs she was ridden by W. Bullock.

SILLY SEASON

Bred in America in 1962 by his owner Mr P. Mellon, Silly Season is by Tom Fool out of Double Deal II, by Straight Deal. He was trained at Kingsclere by Ian Balding and won over £61,000 in prize money, his successes including the Coventry Stakes, Dewhurst Stakes, St James's Palace Stakes, Champion Stakes and Lockinge Stakes. In the Two Thousand Guineas he was beaten a length by Niksar. He was very narrowly beaten in the Sussex Stakes, Rous Memorial Stakes at Ascot and Queen Elizabeth II Stakes. He stands at the New England Stud, Newmarket, at a fee of 700 gn.

SILVER CLOUD

Silver Cloud was bred in 1959 by his owner, Mr T. F. Blackwell, and was trained by Sir Jack Jarvis. By Aureole out of Brolly, by Precipitation, he won five races worth over £7,000 including the Chester Vase and Princess of Wales's Stakes. He is now the property of a syndicate and stands at Dobson's Stud, Fawley, near Henley-on-Thames.

SILVER RING

This is the ring below Tattersall's on a racecourse. It was originally so called because the price of admission was less than a pound.

SILVER SHARK

Silver Shark was bred in France in 1963 by the Aga Khan and is a grey by Buisson Ardent out of Palsaka, by Palestine. He won ten races worth over 1,000,000 francs, including the Prix des Foals, Prix La Rochette, Prix de l'Abbaye de Longchamp, Prix Daphnis, Prix Jean Prat, Prix d'Ispahan and Prix du Moulin de Longchamp. He is owned by a syndicate and stands at the Sallymount Stud. Naas, Co Kildare.

SILVER URN

Owned and bred by Mr B. W. Parr and trained by 'Atty' Persse, Silver Urn, a daughter of Juggernaut, won the One Thousand Guineas in 1922. She bred five winners but they were not of great account.

SIME, Joseph (b 1923)

Joe Sime, for many years a successful northern jockey, served his apprenticeship with the late Dawson Waugh and rode his first winner in 1941. He was never troubled by his weight and up to his retirement in 1969 could go to scale at 7st 8. His best season was in 1960 when he rode 108 winners. He was leading apprentice in 1943, 1944 and 1946. Few jockeys have boasted a better record in big handicaps and he won the Lincoln Handicap three times, the Wokingham Stakes three times, the Northumberland Plate, the Ebor Handicap four times, the Cesarewitch three times, the Vaux Gold Tankard, the Manchester November Handicap, the Ayr Gold Cup, the William Hill Gold Cup, the Portland Handicap and the Royal Hunt Cup.

SINCLAIR, Miss Auriol (b 1918)

Miss Sinclair has for some years conducted most efficiently a 'mixed' stable at Lewes. She has actually held a licence only since 1966 when women were first permitted to train, but before that she controlled the stable though the licence was held by M. Bolton. The stable won the Rosebery Stakes in 1963 and the Wokingham Stakes in 1958. Patrons include Lieut-Cmdr Dawson Miller, Mr P. G. Goulandris, Hon Keith Mason, Hon David Montagu, Mrs S. Joseph, Mrs V. M. Payne, Mr I. Buchanan, Maj-Gen Sir F. de Guingand, Air Marshal Sir H. Edwardes Jones, Mr K. Kleinwort, Mrs E. H. Wickins, Mr E. L. Windsor and Mr E. W. Cripps.

SINGAPORE

Bred in 1927, Singapore was by Gainsborough out of Tetrabbazia, by The Tetrarch. For Lord Glanely he won the St Leger and was narrowly beaten in the Ascot Gold Cup. Before being exported to Brazil he sired the St Leger winner Chulmleigh and Indian Call, the dam of Ballymoss.

SING SING

Sing Sing was bred by his owner Col W. J. Stirling in 1957 and is a bay horse by Tudor Minstrel out of Agin the Law, by Portlaw. As a two-year-old he was the unbeaten winner of six races worth over £12,000, including the National Breeders Produce Stakes and Cornwallis Stakes. As a three-year-old he did not win, but was very narrowly beaten in the King's Stand Stakes and King George Stakes. Syndicated for the stud, he stands at the Lavington Stud, Petworth, Sussex. He has sired many winners, including the brilliant sprinter Song.

SIRES, LEADING

1901	St Simon	£28,672
1902	Persimmon	£36,810
1903	St Frusquin	£26,526
1904	Gallinule	£23,383
1905	Isinglass	£24,642
1906	Persimmon	£21,737
1907	Gallinule	£23,383
1908	Persimmon	£24,485
1909	Cyllene	£35,550
1910	Cyllene	£38,001
1911	Sundridge	£33,284
1912	Persimmon	£21,993
1913	Desmond	£30,973
1914	Polymelus	£29,607

1915	Polymelus	£17,738
1916	Polymelus	£16,081
1917	Bayardo	£12,337
1918	Bayardo	£16,560
1919	The Tetrarch	£27,976
1920	Polymelus	£39,704
1921	Polymelus	£34,307
1922	Lemberg	£32,988
1923	Swynford	£37,897
1924	Son-in-Law	£32,476
1925	Phalaris	£41,475
1926	Hurry On	£59,109
1927	Buchan	£45,918
1928	Phalaris	£46,393
1929	Tetratema	£53,026
1930	Son-in-Law	£44,755
1931	Pharos	£34,922
1932	Gainsborough	£34,790
1933	Gainsborough	£38,139
1934	Blandford	£75,706
1935	Blandford	£57,538
1936	Fairway	£57,931
1937	Solario	£52,889
1938	Blandford	£31,840
1939	Fairway	£53,441
1940	Hyperion	£13,407
1941	Hyperion	£22,700
1942	Hyperion	£13,801
1943	Fairway	£12,134
1944	Fairway	£15,704
1945	Hyperion	£39,727
1946	Hyperion	£52,961
1947	Nearco	£42,554
1948	Big Game	£40,690
1949	Nearco	£52,546
1950	Fair Trial	£37,887
1951	Nasrullah	£44,664
1952	Tehran	£83,177
1953	Chanteur II	£57,164
1954	Hyperion	£46,895
1955	Alycidon	£54,954
1956	Court Martial	£49,238
1957	Court Martial	£58,174
1958	Mossborough	£65,966
1959	Petition	£75,444
1960	Aureole	£89,076
1961	Aureole	£90,532
1962	King of the Tudors	£61,480
1963	Ribot	£121,288
1964	Chamossaire	£136,507
1965	Court Harwell	£112,708
1966	Psidium	£101,376
1967	Ballymoss	£113,601
1968	Ribot	£112,736
1969	Crepello	£88,538

SIRETT, Jack (b 1905)

Jack Sirett served his apprenticeship with Stanley Wootton. He was a highly successful light-weight jockey and between 1924 and 1953 rode over a thousand winners. He took out a licence to train in 1954 and his small Epsom stable invariably includes a high proportion of winners. Among his owners are Major Sir Reginald Macdonald-Buchanan, Mr G. R. Rickman, Mr E. Rickman, Mr S. Wootton, Brig A. B. Beauman, Mr W. Sherman, Col A. C. R. Waite, Mr K. C. Dodson, Mr B. W. Hager and and Capt A. D. D. Rogers.

SIR GALLAHAD III

Bred in France in 1920 by Capt J. D. Cohn, Sir Gallahad III won the French Two Thousand Guineas and nine other races in France, while in England he won the Lincolnshire Handicap. Exported to America, he became an outstandingly successful sire there. He was by Teddy out of that famous mare Plucky Liège (q.v.).

SIR IVOR

Sir Ivor was bred in the United States by his owner, Mr Raymond Guest, and is an exceptionally handsome bay by Sir Gaylord out of Attica, by Mr Trouble. Trained in Ireland by Vincent O'Brien, he was a top-class two-year-old, winning the National Stakes at the Curragh and the Grand Criterium at Longchamp. In 1968 he won the Ascot Two Thousand Guineas Trial, the Two Thousand Guineas, the Derby, the Champion Stakes and the Washington International Stakes at Laurel Park. He was second in the Irish Derby, the Prix Henry Delamarre, and the Prix de l'Arc de Triomphe. A courageous horse with great power of acceleration, he never ran a bad race and achieved the rare feat of winning in Ireland, France, England and America. His stud services are of course in great demand and a nomination to him costs £8,000, the highest fee ever demanded from British breeders.

SIR PETER TEAZLE

Sir Peter Teazle, by Highflyer, won the 1787 Derby for the twelfth Earl of Derby, who had named him in compliment to his second wife as she had made a great reputation on the stage in the part of Lady Teazle, in *The School for Scandal*. Sir Peter Teazle had never run before the Derby. He proved a highly successful sire, getting four Derby winners, four St Leger winners, and two winners of the Oaks.

SKILLING, J.

He rode 15 winners in 1969 and can go to scale at 7st 10. He is attached to J. Etherington's stable.

SKULL CAP

No jockey is permitted to ride in a race unless he is wearing a skull cap of the pattern approved by the Stewards of the Jockey Club.

SKY GIPSY

Sky Gipsy was bred by Mr L. Ryan in 1963 and is a chestnut horse by Skymaster out of Tudor Gipsy, by King of the Tudors. As a yearling he was bought on behalf of Lady Sarah FitzAlan Howard for 2,000 gn and was sent to be trained by Gordon Smyth at Arundel. He ran 14 times as a two-year-old, winning 10 races, including the Windsor Castle Stakes, July Stakes and Richmond Stakes. During the season he was sold to Mr R. E. Hibbert, a Texas oilman, and was exported to America. He raced there for three seasons, winning seven races and over $82,000 in prize money. He has now returned to this country and, owned by a syndicate, stands at the Upend Stud, Kirtling, Newmarket.

SKYMASTER

Skymaster was bred in 1958 by Capt A. A. D. Rogers and is a chestnut by Golden Cloud, out of the Court Martial mare Discipliner, dam of the Two Thousand Guineas winner Martial. Trained by Gordon Smyth, Skymaster won seven races worth over £10,000, including the Windsor Castle Stakes, Middle Park Stakes and Stewards' Cup. He now stands at Dolly's Grove Stud, Dunboyne, Co Meath, at a fee of £500. Among his winners are Sky Gipsy, winner of 17 races, that fine sprinter Be Friendly, and Sky Diver who won the Stewards' Cup two years running before being exported to Australia.

SLEEPING PARTNER

Sleeping Partner was bred in 1966 by her owner Lord Rosebery and is a grey filly by Parthia out of Old Dutch, by Fastnet Rock. As a two-year-old her form was not particularly distinguished but she made great strides the following season, winning the Lingfield Oaks Trial and the Oaks, ridden on both occasions by John Gorton. She followed up those victories by a most impressive success in the Ribblesdale Stakes at York. Unfortunately she got the cough badly and never found her form afterwards. She failed in her one race in 1970 and was then retired to the stud.

SLIEVE GALLION

Bred and owned by Capt Greer, later Sir Henry Greer, Director of the National Stud, Slieve Gallion was a black colt by Gallinule. He won the Two Thousand Guineas in 1907 and was third to Orby in the Derby. He only ran once after the Derby, winning the St James's Palace Stakes. He was then exported to Austria for £15,000.

SLOAN, Tod

Tod Sloan was a brilliant American jockey who came to England at the turn of the century and was largely instrumental in revolutionising race-riding over here. His style—short leathers and a pronounced, streamlined crouch—was ridiculed to start with and critics referred to him as a "monkey up a stick", but before very long he proved that his methods were far more effective than the traditional

English ones embodying long leathers and an upright seat.

Sloan had a wonderful understanding with horses and was a superb judge of pace. Unfortunately he mixed habitually with some of the least desirable characters in the racing world. It was no surprise when in 1900 the authorities told him it would be pointless to apply for a licence the following season.

SMALLEY, Capt R. B.

A former Royal Marine, Capt Smalley at one time owned and rode the famous chaser Halloween. He was appointed a starter in 1965.

SMIRKE, Charles

Charles Smirke, like many another fine rider, was originally apprenticed to Stanley Wootton. At his best—and he was always at his best on big occasions—he was the equal of any jockey riding. His long career in the saddle certainly had its ups and downs and from 1928 till 1933 he was banned by the Jockey Club after an incident at the start of a race at Gatwick. He rode in his first Derby in 1924, in his last one 35 years later, winning on Windsor Lad (1934); Mahmoud (1936); Tulyar (1952) and Hard Ridden (1958). He also won the One Thousand Guineas on Rose Royale II (1957); the St Leger on Windsor Lad (1934); Bahram (1935) and Tulyar (1952).

In temperament he was almost aggressively self-confident and never displayed the slightest sign of nerves. Possibly he was a bit too brash and cocky to win the affection of the racing community as a whole, but many admired him for his superb skill, his cheerfulness in bad times, and for an impudent sense of humour that could never be entirely subdued. Since he retired from riding, he is rarely seen on a racecourse.

SMITH, Lieut-Col Archibald William Anthony, DSO

Lieut-Col Smith served for 21 years in the Coldstream Guards. He rode in point-to-points and under National Hunt rules. He was appointed a starter in 1950.

SMITH, Denys (b 1924)

Denys Smith began training in 1961. Most of the 70 horses in his Bishop Auckland, Co Durham, stable are jumpers but he has a number of flat-racing performers as well. In 1969 he won the Lincoln and the William Hill Gold Cup with Mr J. Forrester's Foggy Bell, and altogether he won over £34,000 in stakes for his owners.

SMITH, Lieut-Col D. F. G., OBE MRCVS

Appointed veterinary officer under the Rules of Racing in 1962.

SMITH, Douglas (b 1917)

Doug Smith is the younger brother of Eph Smith (see below) and was born in 1917. After a long, honourable and successful career in the saddle he retired in 1967. His record in 1968 and 1969 suggests he has a bright future ahead of him as a trainer. In fact in 1969 he won over £94,000 in stakes for his owners.

As a small boy he was apprenticed to Major F. B. Sneyd and rode his first winner in 1931. Like his brother, he has never been beset by problems of weight and season after season he rode with consistent success. In particular he excelled at Newmarket and there has probably never been a better rider over the Rowley Mile. On five occasions—1954, 1955, 1956, 1958 and 1959—he was champion jockey. One year when he was champion, his brother-in-law, Fred Winter, was champion under National Hunt rules. He rode over 3,000 winners in all, his best season being 1947 when his winners totalled 173. He survived some serious accidents towards the close of his career, but his nerve and his dash remained unaffected.

He never won an Epsom classic but he won the Two Thousand Guineas on Our Babu and Pall Mall, the One Thousand Guineas on Hypericum and Petite Etoile. A wonderfully sound judge of pace, he was usually at his best in long distance races and he won the Ascot Gold Cup (twice), the Ascot Stakes (twice), the Doncaster cup (six times), the Goodwood Cup (three times), the Cesarewitch (six times), the Jockey Club Stakes (six times) and the Northumberland Plate (three times). Probably the best horse he ever rode was that great stayer Alycidon, winner of the Ascot, Goodwood and Doncaster Cups.

Quiet, modest and level-headed, Doug Smith is noted for his loyalty to his patrons and his association with Lord Derby must be one of the longest in modern racing history.

In 1969 he trained his first classic winner when he won the Oaks with Lord Rosebery's Sleeping Partner. His patrons, besides Lord Rosebery, include Mr R. C. Boucher, Mr R. L. Basset, Lieut-Col D. S. Cripps, Lady Cohen, Lord Derby, Mr Jocelyn Hambro, Mr Rupert Hambro, Hon Lady Hardy, Mrs C. B. Harvey, Lord Sefton, Mr W. Stirling, Lady Zia Wernher, Lady Wyfold, Mr A. Lilingston, Major V. McCalmont, Mr S. Mercer, Hon D. Montagu, Mr J. L. Pearce, Hon A. G. Samuel, Mr B. Schmidt-Bodner and Mr D. Van Clief.

SMITH, Eric Ephraim (b 1915)

Eph Smith, elder brother of Doug Smith (see above), is the son of a sporting Berkshire farmer. He showed riding ability at a precociously early age and in due course was apprenticed to Major F. B. Sneyd, who gave him his first opportunities to display his skill. He made the most of his early chances and untroubled by problems of weight, enjoyed a successful career in the saddle for more than thirty years.

He won the Two Thousand Guineas and the Derby on Blue Peter and the St Leger on Premonition. He won the Gold Cup (twice), the Eclipse Stakes, the King George VI and Queen Elizabeth Stakes, the Cesarewitch (three times), the Cambridgeshire, the Ascot Stakes (five times), the Goodwood Stakes (four times), the Lincolnshire Handicap (three times) and the Manchester November Handicap (twice). His best season was in 1947 when he rode 144 winners. Quiet and unflamboyant, he never permitted success to go to his head or the fact that he was always hard of hearing to affect his career. Now that he has retired, his main interests are shooting and the breeding and training of gun dogs.

SMITH, Stanley (b 1913)

Stan Smith served his apprenticeship with George Batchelor in France, his first winner being at Le Tremblay in 1927. He has had a lot of riding experience in India and won the Derby there in two successive years. His best season in England was in 1963 when he was retained by Lord Rosebery and won 41 races, including the Blue Riband Trial Stakes and the Stewards' Cup. The following year he won the City and Suburban.

SMYTH, Gordon (b 1926)

Gordon Smyth for 15 years assisted his father Bill Smyth and eventually succeeded him as trainer at the Duke of Norfolk's Arundel stable. At the end of 1965 he left Arundel and took over J. M. Gosden's stable at Lewes and in the following year he won the Derby with Charlottown. Big races he has won include the Coronation Cup, Gimcrack Stakes, Stewards' Cup, New Stakes, Rosebery Stakes, Richmond Stakes (twice) and Oxfordshire Stakes. Among his owners are Mr H. Allen, Mr W. Carter, Sir Rex and Lady Cohen, Mrs M. P. Dennis, Mrs A. Finney, Mrs G. Janson, Mr R. N. Richmond-Watson, Lieut-Col J. Samuelson, Mr C. Sweeny, Sir Harold and Lady Zia Wernher, Mr J. W. T. Wood and Mr A. Ross.

SMYTH, Herbert Edwin (b 1911)

Ted Smyth for 12 years assisted his father, the late Herbert Smyth who was one of racing's most notable characters and a peerless raconteur. Ted Smyth served in the RAF during World War II and began training in 1951. Good races he has won include the Wokingham Handicap, Lowther Stakes, Newbury Spring Cup, Brighton Cup and Acorn Stakes. Among his owners are Lady Galway, Lady Ilchester, Lord Wigg, Mr J. J. Astor, Mr S. Le Marchant, Mr and Mrs R. Crutchley, Lord Galway, Mr M. Lane, Mr T. E. S. Egerton, Mr M. Lane, Mrs C. Y. Bennett, Miss P. Major and Mrs V. Wallis.

SMYTH, Paul (b 1936)

Paul Smyth assisted his father Victor Smyth (q.v.) before taking over the stable at Epsom himself in 1965. Patrons include Mrs D. Chandler, Mr V. Brunt, Mr P. Arnsby-Wilson, Lieut-Col P. E. Hesse, Mr T. E. Morel and Mr M. Cunningham-Reid.

SMYTH, Ronald Victor (b 1915)

Ron Smyth was born in 1915. For many years he was a successful rider under National Hunt rules, and was champion jockey in 1941-42. He rode the winner of the Champion Hurdle on three occasions. Since 1947 he has been running a 'mixed' stable at Epsom and among the good races he has won are the Stewards' Cup and the King Edward VII Stakes. His owners include Mr and Mrs F. A. Laker, Mr W. R. Gibson, Mr E. R. and Lady Elizabeth More O'Ferrall, Lord Blakenham, Miss P. Wallis, Mrs R. Clifford Turner, Mr C. Sweeny, Capt Ian Bullen, Mrs O. Negus-Fancey, Mrs W. R. Gibson, Sir Robert Dean, Miss S. Rampton, Mr S. Lay, Mr R. E. Parkes and Hon Anthony Berry.

SMYTH, Victor

A successful and respected jockey (he won the Oaks on Brownhylda in 1923), he subsequently trained for many years at Epsom and won the 1952 One Thousand Guineas with Zabara. His son Paul (q.v.) took over his stable in 1965.

SNAITH, William (b 1928)

Willie Snaith is married to the late Bobby Jones's daughter. From 1943 to 1950 he was apprenticed to Sam Armstrong and was leading apprentice in 1949. Comparatively little is seen of him nowadays, but he was very successful in the 1950s, riding 73 winners in his best season. He has won the Stewards' Cup twice and the Royal Hunt Cup, while in India he has won the Oaks and the Eclipse Stakes.

SOBELL, Michael (b 1922)

Mr Sobell is well-known in the business and financial world. His first interest in racing was with jumpers but before very long he veered towards the flat. His first horse on the flat was London Cry whom he bought at the December Sales for 3,500 gn and whose subsequent successes included the Chesterfield Cup and the Cambridgeshire. In 1960 Mr Sobell bought the Ballymacoll Stud, Co Meath, from the executors of the late Miss Dorothy Paget and there he bred that very good horse Reform who won 11 of his 14 races, including the St James's Palace Stakes, Sussex Stakes, Queen Elizabeth II Stakes and the Champion Stakes. He also bred Dart Board who carried his colours into third place in the 1967 Derby. Mr Sobell's trainer is Sir Gordon Richards. Colours: pale blue, yellow and white checked cap.

SOCIETE d'ENCOURAGEMENT POUR L'AMELIORATION DES RACES DE CHEVAUX EN FRANCE

This is the governing body of French racing.

SODIUM

Sodium was bred in 1963 and is a bay horse by Psidium out of Gambade, by Big Game. As a yearling he was bought for 3,500 gn by George Todd on behalf of Mr R. J. Sigtia. He did not win a race during his first season but showed promise in both the Royal Lodge Stakes and the *Observer* Gold Cup. As a three-year-old he was not consistent, but a really good horse on his day, winning the Brighton Derby Trial, Irish Sweeps Derby and the St Leger. He was second in the King George VI and Queen Elizabeth Stakes and fourth in the Derby. He was disappointing as a four-year-old, his best effort being to finish second to Salvo in the Hardwicke Stakes. He is now owned by M. Daniel Wildenstein and stands at the Haras de Victot, Calvados, France.

SOLARIO

Solario, by Gainsborough out of Sun Worship, was owned by Sir John Rutherford and trained by Reg Day. He might have won the Derby but for losing lengths at the start when he got caught in a loose tape. He won the St Leger and the following year the Gold Cup. His owner died in 1932 and he was sent up for sale at Newmarket in December, fetching 47,000 gn, a very big price in those days. He got two Derby winners—Mid-day Sun (1937) and Straight Deal (1943)—as well as Dastur (second in the Two Thousand Guineas, Derby and St Leger) and Exhibitionnist (One Thousand Guineas and Oaks). He was champion sire in 1937.

SOLAR SLIPPER

Bred in 1945 by Mr Joseph McGrath, Solar Slipper was by Windsor Slipper out of that good mare Solar Flower, winner of over £10,000 in stakes. Solar Slipper himself won five races, including the Champion Stakes, and was third in the St Leger. Before being exported to America in 1956 he sired the Gold Cup winner Pandofell.

SOLEIL

Soleil, by Major Portion, was bred in 1963 by Baron Guy de Rothschild in France where he won, among other races, the Prix Morny, Grand Criterium and French Two Thousand Guineas. He was bought by an English syndicate and has been standing at the

King Edward Place Stud, near Swindon. Unfortunately his fertility record has been causing grave concern.

SOLONAWAY

Bred in 1946 by the Hilltown Stud, Solonaway won six races including the Irish Two Thousand Guineas and the Cork and Orrery Stakes. Before being exported to Japan in 1957, he sired Sweet Solera, winner of the One Thousand Guineas and the Oaks. He is by Solferino out of Anyway, by Grand Glacier.

SON-IN-LAW

A handsome brown horse by Dark Ronald, Son-in-Law was foaled in 1911 and was bred and owned by Sir Abe Bailey. His racing career was hampered by World War II but he proved himself a fine stayer winning the Goodwood Cup, the Cesarewitch and the Jockey Club Cup twice. As a sire of stayers he was outstanding and he sired the Gold Cup winners Foxlaw, Bosworth and Trimdon, the last-named winning that race twice. Foxlaw carried on the tradition by siring two Gold Cup winners, Foxhunter and Tiberius. Son-in-Law also sired Rustom Pasha, winner of the Eclipse Stakes and Champion Stakes, and Straitlace, winner of the Oaks. Before his death at the age of 30 he had twice been leading sire.

SOUEPI

Bred by Mr G. R. Digby and Mohammed Bey Sultan in 1948, Souepi is by Epigram out of Sousse, by Bala Hissar. A great stayer, he won the Gold Vase, Gold Cup and Goodwood Cup and dead-heated for the Doncaster Cup. Unfortunately there is little demand for staying sires in England and he was sold in 1954 for the trifling sum of 2,100 gn to go to Chile.

SOUVERAIN

Bred in France in 1943, Souverain was by Maravedis out of Jolie Reine, by Palais Royal. A stayer of the highest class, he won the Grand Prix, French St Leger and Prix Jean Prat in France, while in England he won the King George VI Stakes, trouncing the Derby and St Leger winner Airborne, and the Ascot Gold Cup. He was not a success as a sire.

SOVEREIGN LORD

Sovereign Lord was foaled in 1959 and is by Grey Sovereign out of Ardue, by Admiral's Walk. He was bought as a yearling for 12,500 gn by the Duke of Norfolk for whom he won the Richmond Stakes and Gimcrack Stakes. He did not win as a three-year-old but was second in the St James's Palace Stakes. After some years at the Southcourt Stud, Leighton Buzzard, he was exported to Japan in 1969.

SOVEREIGN PATH

Sovereign Path, foaled in 1956, is a grey horse by Grey Sovereign out of Mountain Path, by Bobsleigh. He was a game, consistent horse in training, winning eight races worth over £10,000, including the Newbury Autumn Foal Stakes, the Tetrarch Stakes at the Curragh, the Lockinge Stakes and Queen Elizabeth II Stakes. He is now owned by a syndicate and stands at the Burgage Stud, Co Carlow. He has done consistently well as a sire and among his many good winners are: Spanish Express (Middle Park Stakes), Petite Path (Queen Mary Stakes and Ayr Gold Cup), Regal Light (Royal Hunt Cup), King of Peace (Ascot Stakes), Supreme Sovereign (Free Handicap and Lockinge Stakes), Wolver Hollow (Eclipse Stakes) and Humble Duty (Cheveley Park Stakes and One Thousand Guineas).

SPEARMINT

Spearmint was bred by Sir Tatton Sykes at Sledmere and sold as a yearling for 300 gn to Major Eustace Loder. In 1906 he won the Derby, trained by Peter Gilpin and ridden by Danny Maher, and 11 days later the Grand Prix de Paris. He sired the 1920 Derby winner Spion Kop, also trained by Gilpin, and died in 1924.

SPEER, Robert George Templeman

Appointed a judge in 1955.

SPION KOP

Owned and bred by Col Giles Loder, Spion Kop was by Spearmint out of Hammerkop, by Gallinule. Trained by Peter Gilpin, he lacked pace as a two-year-old in 1919 and failed to win any of his six races though he was always placed.

The following season he was second in the Free Handicap carrying only 7st 4lb. However, early in May he won very easily over 1½m at Kempton and it was clear that staying was his game. In the Derby he was less fancied than his stable companion Sarchedon, but in a race run at a terrific pace under exceptionally fast conditions he outstayed his rivals and ridden by F. O'Neill, won by two lengths from Archaic.

In the Grand Prix Spion Kop was unplaced behind his stable companion Comrade and in fact he never won another race. As a sire he was inconsistent but among his offspring were Felstead, winner of the 1928 Derby; Kopi, winner of the Irish Derby and quite a successful sire in France; Bongrace, a really good staying mare; and The Bastard, who, under the more refined name of The Buzzard, made a great reputation as a sire in Australia.

SPLIT PASTERN

A split pastern represents a fracture of the largest digital bone. Recovery depends on the extent and severity of the injury.

SPORTING SILK

This is old-fashioned journalese for 'running'. For example, "Lord Crooksby's promising juvenile is due to sport silk for the first time in the Plodders Plate at Pontefract". The 'silk' refers to the jacket and cap worn by the jockey.

SPRINTER

A horse whose best distance is from five to seven furlongs is commonly described as a sprinter.

STAKEHOLDERS

The Jockey Club Stakeholders, Messrs Weatherby, are stakeholders for all meetings and are paid on the scale laid down in Rule 179, that is to say £15 a day at all meetings having four days or more consecutively, or six days at any time; at all other meetings £10 a day.

The stakeholders shall not allow a jockey to be weighed out for any horse till such a horse's stake for that race, and the forfeits for every horse belonging to that owner, or standing in his name, the jockey's fee, and any arrears claimed under the Rules of Racing, have been paid, or the stakeholders shall themselves be liable.

At the expiration of 15 days after the meeting, the stakeholders must render an account and pay out all stakes and added money to the persons entitled to receive them.

STANDISH, Sir Frank

Sir Frank Standish owned three Derby winners, Spread Eagle (1795), Didelot (1796) and Archduke (1799). It was for poisoning Sir Frank's Eagle colt by placing arsenic in a drinking trough at Newmarket that Daniel Dawson, the agent of two bookmakers called Bland, was hanged at Cambridge in 1812.

STANLEY, Hon Richard (b 1920)

Mr Richard Stanley served in the Grenadier Guards during World War II. From 1950 to 1966 he was Member of Parliament (Conservative) for Lancashire (North Fylde Division). He is a member of the Jockey Club, a steward at Ascot and Newbury, and owner of the New England Stud, Newmarket. His trainer is J. F. Watts. Colours: scarlet, blue hooped sleeves, quartered cap.

STANSFIELD, Derek (b 1929)

Derek Stansfield was apprenticed to the late Capt Charles Elsey. In 1945, at the age of 15, he rode the winner of the Lincolnshire Handicap. For a period he rode with considerable success in East Africa. He unfortunately died in 1969 as the result of a bad fall in a race.

STARKEY, Greville (b 1939)

Greville Starkey was apprenticed to Tom Jones at Newmarket and was leading apprentice in 1957 with 45 winners. For several years he was associated with John Oxley's stable but that association ended in 1969 and in 1970 he began riding for Henry Cecil. His best season so far was in 1961 when he rode 60 winners. His successes include the Oaks, Gold Cup, Lincolnshire Handicap, Jockey Club Stakes, Zetland Gold Cup, Imperial Stakes, Dante Stakes, Princess Elizabeth Stakes, Great Voltigeur Stakes, King Edward VII Stakes and Coronation Stakes.

STAR MOSS

Star Moss was bred in 1960 by his owner, Lord Fairhaven, and is a chestnut horse by Mossborough out of Star of France, by William of Valence. He won the Royal Lodge Stakes and the Ripon St Leger Trial and was second in the St Leger. He now stands at the Eve Stud, Wood Ditton, Newmarket, at a fee of £248.

STARTER

A starter is licensed annually by the Stewards of the Jockey Club. He is appointed to act at meetings by the Joint Administrative Authority and paid by that body in accordance with the terms of his employment.

The starter obtains a list of the runners and the draw from the Clerk of the Scales in the weighing room. He gives all orders necessary for securing a fair start. When using the starting gate as opposed to the stalls, he must start the horses as far as possible in a line; he is permitted to start them a reasonable distance behind the starting post if he deems it necessary.

After the starter has called over the names of the runners and the draw, he gives orders for a white flag to be raised, but except when the starting gate has been dispensed with, that order must not be given until he has mounted the starter's platform.

If the starter reckons that for some reason or other a horse is unable to start, he must at once notify the Clerk of the Scales that the number must be withdrawn and must tell him whether the horse has come under starter's orders or not.

A starter has power to remove an unruly horse from the place allotted in the draw, and if he does so he must place it at such a distance to one side that it cannot gain an advantage itself or prejudice the chances of the other horses and jockeys engaged in the race. Permission may be given by a starter for a horse to be held, or he may himself order an unruly horse to be held, but in all such cases the horse must be held 'at a stand' behind the other runners. Should an unruly horse cause delay, it may be 'left'.

If a starter thinks that through a faulty action of the starting gate a fair start has not been effected, he declares it 'no start' and by means of a re-call flag order the jockeys to return to the post. The starter's decision on these points is final.

A start in front of the starting post or on a wrong course or before the appointed time is void and the horses must be started again as soon as practicable. In the event of a horse running the course from a false start or from a void start, the owner may, with the consent of the stewards, withdraw his horse from the race; the horse, though, will be considered as having come under starter's orders.

A starter can fine up to £10 any jockey who misconducts himself at the start; if he does, he must report the fact to the stewards. He must also report to the stewards any case of a jockey misconducting himself at the start.

A starter must report to the stewards, for transmission to the *Racing Calendar* Office, all cases in which he has dispensed with the starting gate, or made any modification, and his reasons for doing it. He must also report the time at which each race was started, and by whom and by what means any delay was caused.

When starting stalls are used the team will include, in addition to the starter's assistant, the appropriate number of handlers.

The handlers are divided into permanent teams of two men who are accustomed to working together. These teams under the starter's assistant or foreman will always take up their position of the rails in the same order to await the arrival of the horses at the start. Each group is equipped with a leading rein and a blinding hood. Before beginning the starting operations, the starter's assistant or foreman points out to each team those horses whose entry into the stalls they are to control.

Entry into the stalls must be made in silence. The jockeys line their horses up in one row facing the stalls. On the starter's instructions, the jockeys move their horses forward into the stalls together and the handlers close the gates behind those horses that have gone in. The handlers then take charge of those horses that have declined to go in. They deal with these horses either simultaneously, or, if the horses in question are in neighbouring stalls, then normally in the order of the draw.

Two attempts are made to get the horses into the stalls with a rein, and one attempt with a blinding hood, unless a request not to do so has previously been made by the trainer to the starter, in which case an attempt with the hood is replaceable by a third attempt with the rein. If these attempts fail, the horse will be withdrawn from the race by the starter.

Difficult horses may be accompanied by someone from their stables, who, with the permission of the starter, is allowed to lead the horse into, but not remain, in the stalls.

Horses that have proved themselves reluctant to enter the stalls, may, at the starter's discretion, be put in first.

A starter must report to the stewards for publication in the *Racing Calendar* all cases in which he withdraws a horse that refuses to enter the stalls. Upon a third such report, the case is referred to the Stewards of the Jockey Club. Jockeys whose behaviour causes difficulty or delay can be dealt with in the same manner as in cases of misconduct at the starting gate. Trainers whose horses are not properly trained to stalls can be reported by the starter to the stewards.

STARTER (HORSE)

A horse is considered a starter if it is under the starter's orders when the white flag is raised.

STARTING GATE

The starting gate was used for the first time at Lincoln in 1900.

STARTING PRICE

See Bookmaker.

STARTING STALLS

Compartments with mechanically operated doors used to start most flat races. They were used for the first time in England in the Chesterfield Stakes at Newmarket on 8th July 1965.

STAYER

A horse is commonly described as a stayer if it needs a mile and a half or more to show its best form.

STEADY AIM

Steady Aim, by Felstead, won the 1948 Oaks for her owner-breeder, Sir Alfred Butt. She bred five winners but they were of no particular distinction.

STEDFAST

Foaled in 1908, Stedfast, by Chaucer, was one of the best winners owned by the late Lord Derby. He won 20 races worth over £26,000, including the Coronation Cup, Hardwicke Stakes and Jockey Club Stakes. He was second in the Two Thousand Guineas and the Derby. He sired the Oaks winner Brownhylda but otherwise his stud record was very disappointing.

STEPHENSON, William (b 1911)

Willy Stephenson was apprenticed to Major W. V. Beatty at Newmarket and rode many winners between 1925 and 1945. Since 1950 he has conducted a most successful 'mixed' stable at Royston. He won the Derby in 1951 with Arctic Prince and the Grand National in 1959 with Oxo. He also trained the great hurdler Sir Ken, winner of the Champion Hurdle three years running.

STEPHENSON, William Arthur (b 1920)

Arthur Stephenson began training at Bishop Auckland, Co Durham, in 1959. His stable comprises over 70 horses of which the great majority are jumpers.

STERN, George

George Stern was born in France of English parents and was bi-lingual. In his prime he was fully the equal of any jockey in France or in England and was a particularly strong finisher. He could look after himself under any circumstances and any rough stuff in a race was liable to be repaid with considerable interest. He rode for the most part in France but he won the 1914 Two Thousand Guineas on Kennymore; the 1911

Derby on Sunstar; and the 1906 St Leger on Troutbeck. He rode a terribly rough race in the 1907 Gold Cup on Eider, who dead-heated with The White Knight, and inevitably Eider was disqualified. A good many people had thought that Stern's riding on Troutbeck in the St Leger had merited stern official action.

STEROPE

Sterope, by Mid-day Sun, was a good handicapper trained by P. Beasley. He won the Cambridgeshire with 7st 4lb in 1948 and with 9st 4lb the following year.

STEWARDS' CUP

See under Goodwood.

STEWARDS OF MEETINGS

There must be at least three stewards for every meeting. Each steward may appoint a deputy at any time.

Should there not be three stewards or their deputies present, the Clerk of the Course shall, without delay, see that any vacancy or vacancies are filled, so that there shall be three persons to act.

The stewards of a meeting have full power to make (and if necessary, to vary) all such arrangements for the conduct of the meeting as they think fit, and to dispense with the starting gate as provided in Rule 134.

They have power, under exceptional circumstances, to abandon the meeting, or to abandon any races, or to postpone any races to the following day or days in the current week: provided always that all the races originally advertised for any day shall be included in that day's programme on the official card, and that the meeting is not extended further than one day beyond the days originally allotted to that fixture.

Should the stewards authorise the abandonment or postponement of any races, or vary in any way the programme as originally advertised, they shall, without delay, report to the *Racing Calendar* Office their reasons for so doing.

The stewards have control over, and they and the Stewards of the Jockey Club have free access to, all stands, rooms, enclosures, and other places used for the purposes of the meeting.

They shall exclude from all places under their control:

(i) Every person who is disqualified or who is warned off Newmarket Heath.

(ii) Every person whose name has been published in the Unpaid Forfeit List, until the default is cleared.

(iii) Every person who has been reported by the Committee of Tattersall's under Part XXIV.

(iv) Every person who has been declared by the Turf authorities of, or by the Stewards of, any recognised meeting in this or any other country to have been guilty of any corrupt or fraudulent practice on the Turf.

(v) All such persons or description of persons as they may from time to time be required to exclude by the Stewards of the Jockey Club.

They have power to exclude at their discretion any person from all or any places under their control.

The stewards have power to enquire into, regulate, control, take cognisance of, and adjudicate upon, the conduct of all officials, and of all owners, nominators, trainers, jockeys, grooms, persons attendant upon horses, and of all persons frequenting the stands or other places used for the purpose of the meeting.

When in the opinion of the stewards any person has committed any breach of the Rules of Racing they have power at their discretion to impose upon such person a fine not exceeding £50.

When in the opinion of the stewards there is a reasonable suspicion that any person has committed any breach of the Rules of Racing which in their opinion ought to be considered by the Stewards of the Jockey Club, or where in their opinion any person has committed any breach of the Rules of

Racing and in their opinion some fine or punishment in excess of £50 ought to be imposed upon such person, they have power at their discretion to report the matter to the Stewards of the Jockey Club.

When in the opinion of the stewards any jockey has committed any breach of the Rules of Racing the stewards, in addition to their foregoing powers, have power to suspend him from riding again at the meeting.

Any jockey suspended under the foregoing sub-rule of this rule shall not ride in any race at any meeting at any time on any day up to and including the last day of the meeting at which he was suspended.

The stewards have power by notices exhibited on the number board or elsewhere and by any form of public address system at the racecourse to state and announce that an objection has been lodged, the subject and nature thereof, and also their decision in respect of such objection, or of any other matter coming within their jurisdiction.

The stewards have power to determine all questions arising in reference to racing at the meeting, subject to appeal under Part XXIII, and should no decision have been arrived at by the stewards, within seven days of an objection being lodged, the Clerk of the Course shall then report the case to the Stewards of the Jockey Club who may at their discretion decide the matter, and, if they consider there has been any negligence, may order any additional expense arising therefrom to be defrayed out of the funds of the meeting at which the case occurred.

The stewards have power to call for proof (see Rule 168 (i)) that a horse is neither itself disqualified in any respect, nor nominated by, nor the property, wholly or in part, of a disqualified person; and in default of such proof being given to their satisfaction they may declare the horse disqualified. They have power to prevent from running any horse which cannot be shown to be qualified under these rules or under the conditions of the race.

The stewards have power at any time to order an examination by such person or persons as they think fit, of any horse entered for a race, or which has run in a race.

The stewards, as such, shall not entertain any dispute relating to bets.

STEWARDS OF THE JOCKEY CLUB

See JOCKEY CLUB.

STILL, Raymond

An apprentice of much promise attached to F. Armstrong's stable. He rode 19 winners in 1969.

STIRK, Norman

A North-country jockey whose main success was to win the Two Thousand Guineas on Rockavon. He also rode the winners of the Cambridgeshire and the Northumberland Plate.

STOCKTON

Now renamed Teesside Park (q.v.).

STOCKWELL

One of the great stallions of the nineteenth century, Stockwell, by The Baron, was bought by Lord Exeter as a yearling for £180. He won the Two Thousand Guineas and the St Leger in 1852 but was a sick horse when he failed in the Derby. He was a magnificent stamp of weight-carrying thoroughbred and at the stud he fully earned his title of 'Emperor of Stallions', transmitting to his stock the stoutness for which he was famous. On seven occasions he was champion sire and four times he was runner-up. He sired three Derby winners—Blair Athol, Lord Lyon and Doncaster—and in 1866 the first three horses in the Derby were all sired by him. Stockwell is the ancestor of the Phalaris male line, the most powerful one in England today. To him also traces the line of The Boss, a dominating sprinting influence in modern breeding, and that of Teddy, to whom French and American bloodstock owe so much.

STRAIGHT DEAL

Bred in 1940 by Miss Dorothy Paget, Straight Deal was by Solario out of Good Deal, by Apelle. Trained by Walter Nightingall, he won twice as a two-year-old and was second in the Coventry Stakes and Dewhurst Stakes. The following year he won a race at Windsor, was sixth in the Two Thousand Guineas and then, ridden by Tommy Carey, won the Derby by a head from Umiddad with Nasrullah close up third.

After the Derby he won a mile and a half race at Ascot. He started favourite for the St Leger, but finished third behind two good fillies, Herringbone and Ribbon. That was his last race. Possibly because he had a lot of unfashionable blood on his dam's side, he was always rather neglected by breeders but he got three good staying fillies in Ark Royal (£12,400), Kerkeb (£7,373) and Above Board (£5,110). He also got Aldborough, winner of the Doncaster Cup and Queen Alexandra Stakes, and Sicilian Prince, winner of the French St Leger. His daughters have done well as brood mares. He died in 1969.

STRAITLACE

Bred in 1921 by Lady Sykes and owned by Sir Edward Hulton, Straitlace was by Son-in-Law out of Stolen Kiss, by Best Man. She was a very high-class performer and trained by Dawson Waugh she won 11 races, including the Oaks and Coronation Stakes, and over £24,000. On her owner's death she was bought by Mr E. Esmond for 17,000 gn, at that time a record price for a brood mare. The best of her offspring was Lovelace, who won seven races in France.

STUD BOOK

The *General Stud Book* and the annual volumes of *Races Past* have been described as "the twin pillars that support the evolution of the thoroughbred". The former provides the pedigrees of brood mares and their foaling records; the latter provides evidence of the racecourse tests upon which the selection of the most suitable animals for breeding purposes must be based.

STUPENDOUS

Foaled in 1963, Stupendous is a bay or brown horse by Bold Ruler out of Magneto, by Ambiorix II. He was bred and raced in America where he proved himself a good horse up to nine furlongs, winning 11 races and more than $250,000. He is now owned by a syndicate in England and since 1968 has stood at the National Stud, Newmarket.

STURDY, Richmond Chartres (b 1912)

Richmond Sturdy first took out a licence in 1936. His stables are at Shrewton, Wiltshire, and among his owners are Dr C. D. Desai, Mr W. E. Mowlem, Mr S. Cohen, Mr A. R. Tenty, Mr R. G. Morcom, Mrs S. D. West and Mr G. W. Parish, Mr H. Grainger.

STURROCK, Terence (b 1946)

Apprenticed to D. Marks, his most important success so far was the 1968 Stewards' Cup on Sky Diver. He is now attached to P. Walwyn's stable.

SUN CAP

The French filly Sun Cap, owned by Mme R. Forget and trained by R. Carver, won the Oaks in 1954. A grey by Sunny Boy III out of Cappellina, by Le Capucin, she was subsequently purchased on behalf of Lady Macdonald-Buchanan. Unfortunately she has not been noticeably successful as a brood mare.

SUN CASTLE

Sun Castle, by Hyperion, won a war-time St Leger in 1941. He died before he could take up stud duties.

SUN CHARIOT

One of the greatest fillies of this century, Sun Chariot was bred by the National Stud, then in Ireland, in 1939 and was by Hyperion out of Clarence, by Diligence. Leased to King George VI for her racing career, she was sent to be trained by Fred Darling. At first she gave little sign of ability and it was proposed to send her back to Ireland, but luckily there was delay in securing an export licence and in the meantime she began to reveal her true merit.

Standing 15.2 hands, she was a robust, well-balanced, long, low filly with a faultess action. By nature she was unpredictable, quick-tempered and self-willed, giving grey hairs to all who were closely connected with her, particularly to Sir Gordon Richards who rode her.

As a two-year-old she was unbeaten, her successes including the Queen Mary Stakes and Middle Park Stakes. At Salisbury, in her first race the following season, she was in waspish, unco-operative mood and sustained the one defeat of her career. Early in May she won a small race at Salisbury, but again her behaviour was anything but attractive. However, she started an even money favourite for the One Thousand Guineas and won impressively.

In the Oaks she was in a thoroughly difficult mood. She spoiled three starts, and when at length the starter got them off, she darted away to the left. When the others had gone a furlong, she had covered about fifty yards, but she won in the end all the same. She gave her finest display in the St Leger, winning with contemptuous ease from the colts that had occupied the first three places in the Derby.

At the stud she bred Blue Train, a very good horse who was never beaten but whose career was curtailed by leg trouble; Gigantic, winner of the Imperial Produce Stakes and a successful sire in New Zealand; Landau, who won the Rous Memorial Stakes at Ascot and the Sussex Stakes and has done quite well as a sire in Australia; and Pindari, winner of the Solario Stakes, King Edward VII Stakes and Great Voltigeur Stakes.

Sun Chariot died in 1963.

SUNDRIDGE

Foaled in 1898, Sundridge, by Amphion, was unsound in his wind and began his career in selling races. However, he stayed in training for five years and won 16 short-distance races worth over £6,000. He went to the stud at a 9-gn fee but was champion sire in 1911 and top sire of winning brood mares in 1923. He sired the Derby winner Sunstar, whose dam also ran in sellers, while he also sired Jest, who won the One Thousand Guineas and the Oaks and was dam of the Derby winner Humorist. His sons Sun Briar and Sunreigh, full-brothers, exercised great influence on American blood lines.

SUNNY JANE

The late Lord Astor's Sunny Jane, by Sunstar out of Maid of the Mist, won the Oaks and was second in the One Thousand Guineas in 1917. She was exported to America.

SUNSTAR

Sunstar was by the sprinter Sundridge, that had gone in his wind, out of a mare that had run in selling races. Owned by Mr J. B. Joel and trained by Charles Morton, he proved a good, game horse. He won the 1911 Two Thousand Guineas and then, despite having really broken down in a gallop the week before Epsom, the Derby. He was so lame after the Derby that he could hardly hobble to the unsaddling enclosure and of course he never ran again. He was a successful sire and though never champion, got the winners of 440 races worth over £229,000. At one stage of his stud career there was a rumpus among breeders about the very large number of mares he was allowed to cover, but he was an exceptionally virile horse and thrived on his exertions.

SUN STREAM

Bred in 1942 by her owner the late Lord Derby, Sun Stream was a chestnut by Hyperion out of Drift, by Swynford. Trained by Walter Earl, she won five races including the One Thousand Guineas and the Oaks. At the stud she bred four winners of no particular distinction.

SUPER SAM

Super Sam was bred in 1962 by Mrs A. Levins Moore and is by Above Suspicion out of the Migoli mare Samaria, dam of Sammy Davis. Bought for 6,400 gn as a yearling, he won seven races and over £20,000 while he also won the Prix de Chantilly in France. His victories in England included the *News of the World* Stakes, Kenneth Robertson Stakes and John Collier Stakes. A stouthearted front-runner when in training, he now stands at the Balreask Stud, Navan, Co Meath, at a fee of 250 gn.

SUPREME COURT

Foaled in 1948, Supreme Court was by Persian Gulf or Precipitation out of Forecourt, by Fair Trial. Trained by Evan Williams, he won five races and over £36,000 in stakes. He was unbeaten as a three-year-old when his victories included the King George VI and Queen Elizabeth Festival of Britain Stakes, the King Edward VII Stakes and the Chester Vase. The best horse he sired was Pipe of Peace, winner of the Middle Park Stakes and third in the Two Thousand Guineas and the Derby.

SUSSEX STAKES

See under Goodwood.

SUTCLIFFE, John, Junior (b 1940)

John Sutcliffe rode as an amateur and later as a professional under National Hunt rules. He began training in 1962 and rapidly made a name for himself. In 1969 he won the Two Thousand Guineas and the Irish Two Thousand Guineas with Right Tack, who the previous year had won the Imperial Stakes and Middle Park Stakes. In 1968 he also won the Wills Mile with Jimmy Reppin, who had been third in the Two Thousand Guineas. In that year he won over £42,000 in prize money for his owners.

In 1969 he did even better as Right Tack, besides his other successes, won the St James's Palace Stakes, while Jimmy Reppin won the Sussex Stakes, Queen Elizabeth II Stakes and the £7,000 Prix Perth in France. His stables are at Epsom and among his owners are Mrs S. H. J. Bates, Mr R. Chinn, Mr D. Fisher, Mr C. Freud, Mr H. C. Hart, Mrs A. Harrison, Col P. E. Hesse, Mr A. D. R. Holland, Mr T. L. R. Holland, Mr W. Maskell, Sir W. Pigott-Brown, Sir Graham and Lady Rowlandson, Mr B. Schmidt-Bodner, Mr W. Sherman, Mrs D. M. Solomon and Mr J. B. Sunley.

SUTHERLAND, sixth Duke of (b 1915)

The Duke of Sutherland served in the Lothians and Border Yeomanry. He is a member of the Jockey Club and a steward at Ayr and Edinburgh. So far he has been less successful as an owner than his father, the late Lord Ellesmere, but he won the 1969 Dante Stakes with Activator. His trainer is G. Barling.

His colours are red, white sleeves, black cap.

SWALLOW TAIL

Bred and owned by Lord Derby, Swallow Tail was foaled in 1946 and is by Bois Roussel out of Schiaparelli, by Schiavoni. His six victories included the Royal Lodge Stakes, Chester Vase and King Edward VII Stakes. In a finish of heads he was third to Nimbus and Amour Drake in the Derby. When his racing career was over he was exported to Brazil.

SWANNELL, Major David William Ashburnham, MBE (b 1918)

Major Swannell served in the Durham Light Infantry for 18 years. Besides being an official handicapper, he is Clerk of the Course at Beverley and also county stand secretary at York.

SWEEPER II

An American-bred horse by Broomstick, Sweeper II, trained by 'Atty' Persse, won the Two Thousand Guineas in 1912 for Mr H. B. Duryea. He started a hot favourite for the Derby but finished down the course.

SWEEPSTAKE

A sweepstake is any race in which the entrance fees, forfeits, subscriptions and other contributions go to the winner or placed horses.

A private sweepstake denotes a race which is not advertised prior to closing and for which only owners with certain qualifications may enter horses. An example is the Arundel Castle Private Sweepstake—known to the vulgar as 'The Castle Carve-Up'—which until recently was run at Goodwood.

SWEET SOLERA

Bred in 1958 by Mrs D. M. Walker, Sweet Solera is by Solonaway out of Miss Gammon, by Grandmaster. She was bought as a yearling for 1,850 gn by Reg Day for one of his patrons, Mrs Castello, and proved an outstanding bargain. She won six races and over £40,000 in stakes, her victories including the Cherry Hinton Stakes, One Thousand Guineas and Oaks. She was slow to make a mark at the stud but is dam of Bon Appétit, a useful winner in France.

SWIFT, Brian (b 1937)

Brian Swift, son of the well-known bookmaker Jack Swift, is married to 'Scobie' Breasley's daughter. He served his apprenticeship with Jack Reardon and rode with fair success from 1961 till 1965. Among races he won were the Prix d'Arenberg, New Stakes and King's Stand Stakes. For 18 months he assisted the Epsom trainer S. Ingham before setting up on his own in 1967. His stables are at Headley, near Epsom, and among his owners are Mr and Mrs J. Astaire, Mr E. Hammond, Mr J. Levy, Mr R. J. Pritchard, Mr D. Quastel, Mr B. Shine, Mr J. L. Swift, Ruler of Bahrain, Sir Lionel Luckhoo, Mr S. Harris, Miss S. Groves and Mr E. Covell.

SWINBURN, Walter Robert (b 1937)

Wally Swinburn was apprenticed to 'Sam' Armstrong from 1951 to 1958, riding his first winner in 1953. His best season so far was 1961 when he rode 39 winners. His successes incude the Ebor Handicap, Queen's Prize, Winston Churchill Stakes, Sussex Stakes and the Prix de Moulin de Longchamp. He has made numerous winter visits to India and has ridden over 140 winners there. In 1969 he began to ride regularly in France, meeting with a fair measure of success.

SWYNFORD

Foaled in 1907, Swynford was bred and owned by Lord Derby and was a big, powerful brown colt by John O'Gaunt out of the Oaks winner Canterbury Pilgrim. He was trained by George Lambton and took a long time to come to hand; in fact his first victory was in the Hardwicke Stakes at Ascot as a three-year-old. From that point he began to improve rapidly and after an easy win in the Liverpool Cup, he won a controversial St Leger, beating the Derby winner Lemberg.

As a four-year-old his successes included the Hardwicke Stakes, Princess of Wales's Stakes and the Eclipse Stakes. He was a long-striding, freegoing horse that did best when permitted to force the pace, and his defeat by Lemberg in the Coronation Cup was due to the fact that Frank Wootton for some unexplained reason abandoned his usual tactics and rode a waiting race on him.

In September 1911 Swynford smashed a fetlock in a half-speed gallop. Fortunately skilled veterinary treatment saved him for the stud, as he was champion sire in 1923, second in 1924 and 1925, and third in 1921. He sired the Derby winner Sansovino and four other classic winners, all fillies. He also sired the famous stallion Blandford who got four Derby winners and one year was champion sire in England and in France as well.

SYKES, Sir Richard, Bart (b 1905)

Sir Richard Sykes served in the Green Howards during World War II. He is a member of the Jockey Club and a steward at York. He inherited the famous Sledmere Stud in Yorkshire where so many famous horses have been bred. During his ownership Chatelaine (Oaks), Scottish Union (St Leger) and Ridge Wood (St Leger) were bred there. Sir Richard now has horses with C. Bartholomew in France. Colours: orange, purple sleeves and cap.

SYNDICATION of STALLIONS

The practice of syndicating stallions has become common in the past 25 years, and in fact has become so widespread that it has largely superseded the old system, as far as top-class stallions are concerned, of standing stallions at a fixed covering fee. The syndication of a stallion involves its capitalisation in forty shares—most stallions cover forty mares each season—and the offer of some or all of the shares for sale. A breeder who buys a share has the right to send a mare to the stallion each season or to dispose of the nomination for a particular year to another breeder. If he wishes he can sell his share or shares all together. Most syndicates lay down rules for shareholders.

T

TABOUN

Taboun was bred in 1956 by the Aga Khan and Prince Aly Khan and was by Tabriz out of Queen of Basra, by Fair Trial. In the colours of Prince Aly Khan he won the Two Thousand Guineas in 1959, trained by Alec Head and ridden by George Moore. In France his successes included the Prix Robert Papin. His stud career was a brief one as he died young.

TACITUS

Tacitus is owned by Mr D. W. Molins who bought him as a yearling for 1,650 gn and sent him to be trained by the late Walter Nightingall. By Talgo out of Activate, by Pappageno II, Tacitus was a stouthearted and genuine performer, winning seven races and over £12,000. His victories included the Ladbroke Gold Cup, the Coronation Stakes (twice), the Lyons Maid Stakes and the Westbury Stakes. He stands at the Fawley Stud, Wantage, Berkshire, at a fee of £198.

TAGALIE

Owned by Mr W. Raphael, a rich London financier, and trained at Newmarket by Dawson Waugh, Tagalie is the only grey filly to have won the Derby, a feat she accomplished in 1912. She also won the One Thousand Guineas. She made no lasting impression as a brood mare.

TAJ MAH

Bred by the Aga Khan in 1926, Taj Mah was a bay filly by Lemberg out of Taj Mahal, by The Tetrarch. Owned by Mr S. Guthmann, ridden by W. Sibbritt and trained in France by J. Torterolo, she won the 1929 One Thousand Guineas at 33-1.

TAKAWALK II

Takawalk II was bred in America and trained in France where he won four races and over 170,000 francs. He is now owned by a syndicate and stands at the Ennistown Stud, Co Meath. He is by Native Dancer out of Ampola, by Pavot.

TALAHASSE

Talahasse, owned by Mr H. Loebstein and trained by 'Atty' Corbett, headed the Free Handicap in 1963. By Rustam out of Mary Ellard, by Tudor Minstrel, he won six races including the Hyperion Stakes, Gimcrack Stakes and Champagne Stakes.

TALGO

Talgo was bred by Brig C. M. Stewart in 1953 and is by Krakatao out of Miss France, by Jock II. Owned by Mr G. A. Oldham and trained by Harry Wragg, he won the Irish Derby and was second in the Prix de l'Arc de Triomphe. He was exported to Mexico in 1963.

TALMA II

Talma II was bred in 1948 by M. M. Boussac and is by Pharis II out of Thaouka, by Asterus. He came over for the St Leger in 1951 and despite deplorable behaviour in the paddock he was the best backed horse on the day. He won in truly remarkable style by what the judge estimated to be 10 lengths, but what appeared to most of those present to be more like 20. Neither before that race or after it did he ever show comparable form.

TAMBOURINE II

Bred in America and trained in France by E. Pollet, Tambourine II, by Princequillo, won the first race for the Irish Sweeps Derby in 1962.

TAMERLANE

Tamerlane was bred by the Worksop Manor Stud in 1952 and is a brown horse by Persian Gulf out of Eastern Empress by Nearco. Owned by Lord Porchester and trained by Jack Clayton, he won six races worth over £12,000, his victories including the New Stakes, July Stakes, Midland Breeders Foal Stakes and St James's Palace Stakes. He was beaten a neck by Our Babu in the Two Thousand Guineas. The property of a syndicate, he stands at the Woodpark Stud, Co Meath. His winners include Tamerlo (£10,681), Tiger (£7,491), Cassim (£6,609) and Bobsbest (£6,395).

TANAVAR

Tanavar was bred in France in 1960 and sold as a yearling to Mr H. J. Joel for 3,000 gn. By Tantième out of Navarra II, by Orsenigo, he won five races, including the Prince Edward Handicap at Manchester by 11 lengths with top weight. He is now owned by the Mitchelstown Stud where he stands at a fee of £98. He is sire of Tantivy, winner of the Queens Vase in 1969.

TARQOGAN

Tarqogan, bred by the McGrath Trust Company in 1960, stands at the Brownstown Stud, Co Kildare, at a fee of 198 gn. By Black Tarquin out of Rosyogan, by Ballyogan, he won six races and over £17,000. His victories included the Cambridgeshire with 9st 3lb, the Chesterfield Cup with 9st 1lb, and the Piccadilly Northern Cup. As a six-year-old he was third in the Cambridgeshire, with 9st 6lb.

TATTERSALLS

The firm of Tattersalls is famous all over the world for the sale of bloodstock. The founder of the firm was a Yorkshireman, Richard Tattersall, who was born in 1724. When he was 21 he journeyed south to seek his fortune and by 1766 had amassed sufficient capital to construct premises of his own that he hoped would become the acknowledged centre suitable for the sale of horses.

The land he had set his eyes on was at Hyde Park Corner and he secured a 99-year lease from Earl Grosvenor, a leading figure on the Turf of that period. The project prospered and 'The Corner', where sales were held twice weekly, soon became a rendezvous for fashionable London. Apart from the stables, kennels were built for the sale of hounds and dogs, and stands for the sale of carriages. A special room was set aside for members of the Jockey Club.

In 1865 the firm moved rather less than a mile westwards to a new site at Knightsbridge Green where sales were carried out on Mondays and occasional Thursdays up till 1939. The scene at these Monday Sales has been immortalised by H. M. Bateman in his cartoon "The man who bid half a guinea at Tattersalls".

After World War II the site was sold, the famous Rotunda with the statue of the fox removed to Newmarket, the sale yard and boxes demolished. In its place arose an office block in which Tattersalls have their London office today.

Towards the close of the eighteenth century, Tattersalls were conducting sales in the High Street at Newmarket outside the Jockey Club rooms. This practice continued until about 1860 when land behind Queensbury House, about two hundred yards from the present sales paddock, was rented. In 1870 the sales were transferred to Park Paddocks, the existing site, and have been held there without interruption since that date. In recent years land adjacent to Park Paddocks has been acquired and many improvements have been made, in particular the construction of the covered sales ring that was first used in the autumn of 1965.

The present Senior Partner of Tattersalls is Capt Kenneth Watt. The principal sales are the October Yearling Sales, the Houghton Yearling Sales (later in October), the Autumn Horses in Training and Mixed Sales, and the December Sales which are mixed and last a week. In 1969 an additional two-day yearling sale was held at the end of October.

It goes without saying that hundreds of famous horses have been sold at these sales. In 1967 Vaguely Noble, then a two-year-old, was sold for a new world record public auction price of 136,000 gn. As he won the Prix de l'Arc de Triomphe the following year, he proved a bargain. In 1969 a yearling colt by Ribot realised 37,000 gn, but that figure was surpassed the same year when a filly by Immortality, out of Review, was sold for 51,000 gn. Sixty-nine years previously Sceptre, one of the most famous mares in English racing history, had been sold as a yearling for 10,000 gn, rated a fantastic price at that period. At the other end of the scale Comrade, winner of the Grand Prix de Paris and the Prix de l'Arc de Triomphe, was sold as a yearling for 25 gn. The Hulton dispersal sale realised 288,380 gn, the Dewar dispersal sale 398,595 gn. In 1964, when the National Stud mares and foals were sold, the aggregate at the December Sales passed the two million guineas mark for the first time.

TATTERSALLS

Tattersalls enclosure on a racecourse is situated next to the club or members' stand and it is there that the main volume of on-course betting takes place. The public who pay to go into Tattersalls have access to the paddock.

TATTERSALLS COMMITTEE

This is a tribunal for settling all major betting disputes. The chairman is Major W. D. Gibson.

TAYLOR, Alec (1862-1943)

Alec Taylor, nicknamed 'The Wizard of Manton', was beyond argument one of the greatest trainers of this century. His grandfather had trained at Manton and so had his father 'Old Alec', who won the 1878 Derby with Sefton. When 'Old Alec' died in 1894, he left Manton to 'Young Alec' and his half-brother Tom. The two worked in partnership for some years but in 1902 'Young Alec' assumed control of the entire Manton property.

'Old Alec' had been hard on his horses and was reputed to give his yearlings a two-mile gallop before Christmas! His son was the most patient of men, regarding horses as mere babies till they were three. Most of his patrons were rich men who could afford to wait, and frequently a policy of patience and restraint earned handsome dividends. The list of famous races that Alec Taylor won is notable both for its length and for the small proportion of two-year-old events included.

Altogether Taylor trained the winners in England of 1,003 races worth over £839,000. He also trained Lemonora, who won the Grand Prix de Paris. His classic winners were Challacombe (1905 St Leger); Bayardo (1909 St Leger); Lemberg (1910 Derby); Rosedrop (1910 Oaks); Kennymore (1914 Two Thousand Guineas); Gay Crusader (1917 Two Thousand Guineas, Derby and St Leger); Sunny Jane (1917 Oaks); Gainsborough (1918 Two Thousand Guineas, Derby and St Leger); My Dear (1918 Oaks); Bayuda (1919 Oaks); Craig An Eran (1921 Two Thousand Guineas); Live In Idleness (1921 Oaks); Pogrom (1922 Oaks); Saucy Sue (1925 One Thousand Guineas and Oaks); Short Story (1926 Oaks); Book Law (1927 St Leger).

Among the owners Taylor trained for were Lady James Douglas, Lord Astor, Sir William Bass, Mr W. M. Cazalet, Mr A. R. Cox, Mr W. M. G. Singer, and Mr Somerville Tattersall. He was leading trainer on 12 occasions, seven of them in succession. After his retirement in 1927, he used to say that the best horse he ever trained was Picaroon, the cause of whose untimely death when in training was never cleared up.

A bachelor, dignified, frugal and reserved, Alec Taylor looked more like a country banker of the old school than the popular conception of a trainer of racehorses. He always preferred to carry his own bag than take a taxi and when he died he left close on £600,000.

TAYLOR, Arthur, CB.

Mr Taylor came from the Customs and Excise Department to succeed Sir Alexander Sim as Chairman of the Horserace Totalisator Board in April 1970.

TAYLOR, Brian

Brian Taylor was born in 1939 and had no family connection with racing. He was apprenticed to H. Leader from 1953 to 1962 and is his stable jockey today. He can go to scale at 8st 3lb and is a thoroughly sound and competent rider. He rode his first winner in 1956 at Yarmouth and his best season so far was 1966 when he rode 66 winners. Among the good races he has won are the Yorkshire Oaks (twice), the Park Hill Stakes, the Lingfield Derby Trial, the Musidora Stakes, the Two Thousand Guineas Trial and the One Thousand Guineas Trial at Kempton, and the Goodwood Stakes.

TAYLOR, Lieut-Col John Harvey (b 1915)

Served in the Durham Light Infantry from 1935 to 1959. Appointed a stewards' secretary under the Rules of Racing and National Hunt rules in 1967.

TEASER

The teaser is a humble member, but quite an important one, of every stud where a stallion holds court. An entire horse, his job is to tell the stud groom whether the mares are in use or not and he therefore bears much responsibility for the incidence of fertility.

TEESSIDE PARK

Teesside Park is 11 miles from Darlington and 34 from Newcastle. For years known as Stockton, it recently blossomed out as Teesside Park and at a cost of some £40,000 a course for National Hunt racing has been added.

It is a left-handed, oval-shaped track with a straight run-in of half a mile. The 5f and 6f courses both start on separate spurs. Neither is straight. The 5f course bends left to join the round course 4f from the winning post. The 6f course has a straight run of 2f before joining the round course on the home turn. It is generally reckoned a fast track with easy turns and it is no place for the plodder. Low numbers are strongly favoured in races over 5f and 6f; to a lesser degree over 7f and 1m.

Clerk of the Course: Col C. Egerton, MC, TD, Russell House, Russell Street, Stockton-on-Tees. Tel: Stockton 67154.

Best Times:

Distance	*Horse-Age-Weight*	*Date*	*Time*
5f	Majestic Scholar 4-8-0	1/6/63	57.6
5f	Queen Tanner 2-9-0	8/7/68	58.4
6f	Vilswitch 5-7-8	4/7/66	1min 11.2
6f	Hejaz 2-8-2	7/7/62	1min 12
7f	Minho 4-9-6	1/6/68	1min 23
7f	Frieze 2-8-11	13/10/51	1min 25.4
8f	Diredawa 4-9-8	23/6/45	1min 37.6
8f	Billy Boy 2-8-4	17/10/64	1min 39.8
9f	Straight King 5-9-10	1/6/68	1min 49
10f	Red Pixie 3-8-13	1/6/68	2min 3.2
12f	Danger 3-8-8	14/5/48	2min 31.2
15f	Guide 5-9-7	17/4/54	3min 12
18f 60yds	Miller's Neuk 5-8-10	27/7/64	4min 5.8

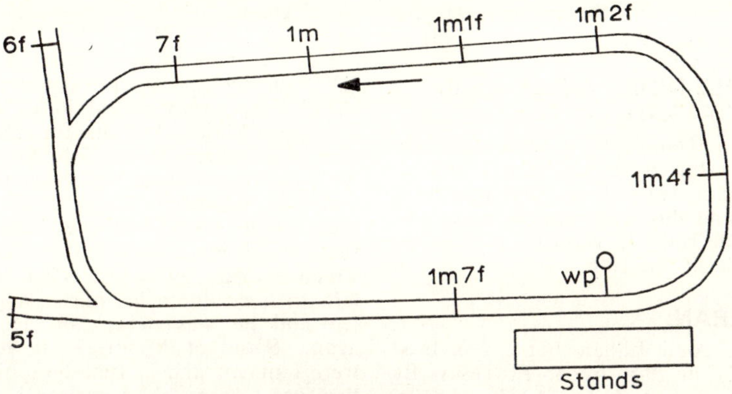

TEESSIDE PARK

TEHRAN

Tehran was bred in 1941 by Prince Aly Khan and was a bay horse by Bois Roussel out of Stafaralla, by Solario. For the Aga Khan he won six races including the St Leger, while he was second in the Derby and the Gold Cup and third in the Two Thousand Guineas. By far the best horse he sired was Tulyar (q.v.), winner of the Derby and St Leger and unbeaten as a three-year-old. Tehran also sired Amante (Irish Oaks), Mystery IX (Eclipse Stakes), Tabriz (sire of the Two Thousand Guineas winner Taboun) and Raise You Ten (Yorkshire, Goodwood and Doncaster Cups). Thanks to Tulyar, he was champion sire in 1952. He died in 1966.

TELEVISION

Direct televised coverage of races started in 1946 and has been gradually increasing over the years. There is no doubt that television does, in some degree, reduce attendances at race-meetings, particularly in inclement weather, but this disadvantage is off-set by the interest in racing which television stimulates among the public and by the volume of off-course betting that it creates.

In May 1964 a television committee set up by the Racecourse Association

2A

recommended that in relation to television, the object of the Association was to negotiate block contracts with the BBC and with independent television authorities. This object has not yet been achieved. Its purpose was not merely to benefit those courses whose meetings were being televised, but to form a fund in which those courses whose meetings were not televised would share. In the meantime, racecourses continue to negotiate their own contracts, many of which are of a long-term character. The existing arrangements with regard to fees expire at the end of 1970 but no agreement has been reached as to the contract period and scale of fees after that date. The report by Sir Henry Benson's Committee of Inquiry into the Racing Industry suggested that racing is not receiving as much income from television contracts as it could.

Finally, it is worth bearing in mind that without TV coverage, there would be very few sponsored races.

TELEVISION OF THE DERBY

The Derby was televised for the first time in 1932.

TEMPLEMAN, Sim

A north-country jockey who won

the Derby on Bloomsbury (1839), Cossack (1847) and Surplice (1848).

TEMPLE-NIDD, Adrian Keith (b 1934)

Keith Temple-Nidd served his apprenticeship with A. Budgett and R. Perryman. He rode his first winner in 1953 and his best season was 1962 when he rode 25 winners. He can go to scale at 7st 10lb.

TENERANI

This good Italian horse was bred in Italy in 1944 by Sr F. Tesio. By Bellini out of Tofanella, by Apelle, he won 14 races in Italy, including the Italian Derby, while in England he won the Queen Elizabeth Stakes at Ascot and the Goodwood Cup. His place in racing history is assured as sire of that great racehorse and outstanding sire, Ribot. He also sired Fighting Charlie, twice winner of the Ascot Gold Cup, and Tenterhooks (Gold Vase and Goodwood Cup).

TERESINA

Bred by Lady Sykes in 1920, Teresina, by Tracery, was bought as a yearling on behalf of the Aga Khan. She was a good and genuine racemare, winning the Jockey Club Stakes and Goodwood Cup, besides being placed in the Oaks, St Leger, Eclipse Stakes and Cesarewitch. She bred eight winners of 24 races, while one of her sons, Alibhai, who never ran, was a great success as a sire in America.

THE TETRARCH

The Tetrarch may well have been the fastest horse seen on an English racecourse this century. Bred in Ireland in 1911 by Mr Edward Kennedy, he was by a far from outstanding French stayer, Roi Herode, out of Vahren. His sire was a grey and he himself when in training was iron-grey with a number of curious white marks as if some joker had thrown a bucket of whitewash at him. Hence his nicknames of 'The Rocking Horse' and 'The Spotted Wonder'.

He was bought as a yearling for 1,300 gn by the Stockbridge trainer 'Atty' Persse who passed him on to his cousin Major Dermot McCalmont, then a subaltern in the 7th Hussars. As a two-year-old he ran seven times and was unbeaten. He won all his races very easily bar the National Breeders Produce Stakes at Sandown which he won by a neck after being left. In the autumn he injured a foreleg and he was never able to run again. Some of his trials at home were fantastic and in June he took on two very smart older sprinters over 5f and beat them pulling up by 10 lengths on 45lb worse terms than weight for age!

The Tetrarch hated restraint and his rider Steve Donoghue was convinced he would never have been a stayer. Nevertheless, the fact remains that The Tetrarch sired three St Leger winners in five years. Unfortunately, The Tetrarch, champion sire in 1919, was far from keen on stud duties. He only got 130 foals, of which 80 were winners, and from 1926 till his death in 1935 he was sterile. His best son was the very fast Tetratema (see below); his best daughter was the brilliant Mumtaz Mahal.

TETRATEMA

Owned and bred by Major Dermot McCalmont, Tetratema was a very fast grey horse by The Tetrarch. As a two-year-old he was unbeaten. He won the Two Thousand Guineas but failed to stay in the Derby and again in the Eclipse. After the Eclipse he was kept to sprinting and was never beaten again. Altogether he won 13 races worth over £21,000. He was leading sire in 1929. His best colts were Mr Jinks, Royal Minstrel and Theft; his best fillies, Tiffin, Myrobella and Four Course.

THIN, Major Peter Gordon, MC (b 1912)

Major Thin served in the Royals.

He was appointed a judge under National Hunt rules in 1959 and became a starter under the Rules of Racing and under National Hunt rules three years later.

THIRSK

Twenty-four miles from York, this agreeable and well-run course is particularly popular with northern trainers. It is a left-handed track of just over 1m 2f, with a straight 6f course which joins the round course 4f from the winning post. The 6f straight is mildly undulating throughout, so that although the rest of the track is flat and the turns are easy, it is not ideal for the long-striding or awkward galloper. In sprint races high numbers are slightly favoured.

Clerk of the Course: Mr W. G. C. Frith, Tabley Brook Farm, Over Tabley, Knutsford, Cheshire.

THOM, David Trenchard (b 1925)

David Thom served as a Royal Marine Commando in World War II and took out a trainer's licence in 1959. His stables are at Exning, near Newmarket, and his owners include Mr P. G. Finlinson, Mr W. Clarke, Mr C. Craze, Mrs A. Ellis, Mrs P. Hamilton, Mr B. Rutland, Mr J. Flaherty, Miss A. Benskin and Mr J. S. Edwards. Among the races he has won are the Doncaster Cup, Chester Cup, Bessborough Stakes, Acorn Stakes, Great Metropolitan and the Moet and Chandon Siver Magnum.

THOMAS, Arthur J. (b 1902)

Arthur Thomas runs a small 'mixed' stable at Warwick. He trains chiefly for himself, his other owners being Mrs L. Brotherton, Mrs B. Davis,

Best Times:

Distance	*Horse-Age-Weight*	*Date*	*Time*
5f	Sovereign Help 3-7-9	29/7/67	57.2
5f	Grey Steel 2-8-9	13/5/65	58.4
6f	Border Cruise 7-7-1	7/6/68	1min 10.6
6f	Spritely Star 2-8-2	2/10/36	1min 10.8
7f	Ardgay 3-8-7	30/5/64	1min 24.2
7f	Without Reproach 2-8-9	1/8/64	1min 26.4
8f	Silent Spring 5-8-1	7/6/68	1min 36.6
8f	St Mark 2-8-3	26/9/59	1min 40.2
12f	Casting Vote 4-8-2	1/8/64	2min 30
16f	Royal Pact 4-8-1	10/6/50	3min 23.8
17f	Fortune's Hope 3-7-4	6/9/69	3min 37.9

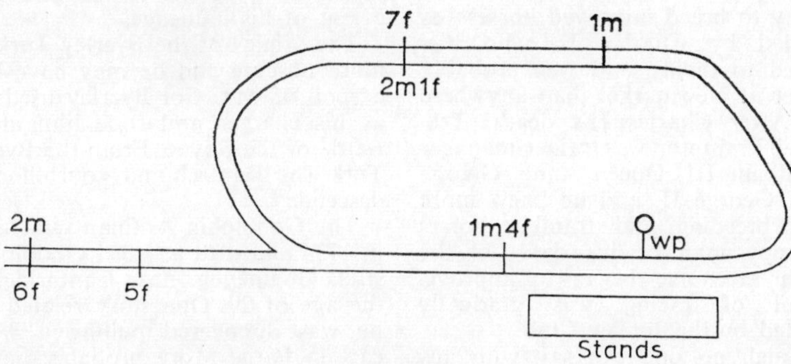

THIRSK

Mr A. Chatalos and Mr A. Crowther. He first took out a licence in 1956 and among the races he has won are the City and Suburban (twice), the Victoria Cup and the Challenge Stakes.

THOMAS, Myrddin Lloyd (b 1945)

Born in Wales, 'Taffy' Thomas was apprenticed to Geoffrey Barling for five years, eventually becoming Barling's stable jockey. His long association with the stable was terminated by mutual consent in 1969. Among the good races he has won are the Cambridgeshire, Doncaster Cup, Northumberland Plate, Dante Stakes, National Stakes, Greenham Stakes and Seaton Delaval Stakes. He rode 43 winners in 1964 and can go to scale at 7st 8lb.

THOROUGHBRED, ORIGINS OF THE

The origin of the thoroughbred is veiled in mystery. It is, however, safe to say that a period of intensive and remarkably rapid evolution took place between the middle of the seventeenth century and the first quarter of the nineteenth. During this era, the average height of a racehorse increased by six inches and there were corresponding increases in strength, length of stride and speed.

It was that uncouth, ramshackle monarch, James I, who established Newmarket as the racing centre of England, while the incentive to the nobility to breed improved horses was provided by Charles II, who was devoted to racing and was probably happier at Newmarket than anywhere else. After Charles II's death, Tregonwell Frampton was trainer-manager to William III, Queen Anne, George I and George II, and he knew more about breeding and training horses than any man of his day. As the British racehorse began to improve, control of racing was gradually assumed by the Jockey Club.

Though no one can say with any degree of certainty how the British thoroughbred was evolved, it is safe to assume that the faster and lighter native breeds were mated with horses imported from the East, from Italy and from Spain. Arabian blood was particularly favoured and this Arabian strain could be clearly seen in the great French horse Djebel (q.v.) and also in many of Djebel's descendants. Several leading seventeenth-century breeders were confident that Arabian stallions got the best racehorses, but a good many breeders used Barbs since the best Arabians were extremely expensive. Barbs came from Barbary, that part of North Africa that comprises modern Tunisia.

The General Stud Book listed 103 stallions which were imported or of wholly foreign pedigree. About half of these were Arabians, the rest Turks or Barbs. Three of them founded dynasties that have survived to modern times—the Darley Arabian (q.v.), the Byerley Turk and the Godolphin Arabian.

Of the three the Darley Arabian has easily surpassed the other two in point of numbers and from him stem the male lines of Blandford, St Simon, Phalaris, Teddy, The Boss, Son-in-Law, and Gainsborough (q.v.).

The Darley Arabian, a bay with a white blaze and four white feet, was foaled in 1700 and exported to England in 1704 by the British Consul in Aleppo, Mr Richard Darley, who sent him to his brother in Yorkshire. The Darley Arabian lived till he was 30 and it is impossible to exaggerate the extent of his influence.

The origins of the Byerley Turk are more obscure and he may have been a spoil of war. Col Byerley used him as his charger and rode him at the Battle of the Boyne. From the Byerley Turk The Tetrarch and Tourbillon are descended.

The Godolphin Arabian was foaled in 1734 and died at Lord Godolphin's stud, Gogmagog, near Cambridge, at the age of 29. One story related that he was discovered pulling a water-cart in Paris. More probably he was one of four Arabian horses given to the King of France by the Bey of Tunis. Three were turned loose in the Brittany forests, while the fourth was acquired by Mr Edward Coke, who passed him on to Lord Godolphin. The Godolphin Arabian's influence has been great and in 1891 the Editors of the General Stud Book wrote that there "is not a superior horse now on the Turf without a cross of the Godolphin Arabian, nor has there been for many years past". He is represented today by the Hurry On—Precipitation line.

Much uncertainty covers the identity of the mares who were the foundation stock of the thoroughbred. Seventy-eight mares were listed in Volume I of the General Stud Book but in fact this list contained a number of duplications. In any case it is impossible to state with any certainty the origins and pedigrees of these mares.

THOROUGHBRED BREEDERS ASSOCIATION

The principal object of the Thoroughbred Breeders Association is to encourage by means of the provision of educational or research facilities the science of producing and improving the thoroughbred horse. The association has its own organisation and staff through which breeders, Government departments and other bodies can obtain information and to which members can go for information and advice.

President: The Hon J. P. Philipps
Chairman of the Council: Mr C. L. Loyd
Secretary: Mr F. E. Birch
Address: 26 Bloomsbury Way, London, W.C.1
Tel: 01-405 4777

THUNDERHEAD II

Thunderhead II, by Merry Boy, was bred in France in 1949. In 1952, trained by E. Pollet and ridden by R. Poincelet, he won the Two Thousand Guineas by five lengths at 100-7. He won two races in France and was second in the French Two Thousand Guineas. When his racing days were over, he was exported to South Africa.

THURSBY, Sir George, Bart (1870-1941)

An extremely good rider by any standard, he was second in the Derby in 1904 on John O'Gaunt and second again on Picton two years later. In those days amateurs were permitted to ride on the flat against professionals.

TIBERIUS

Sir Abe Bailey's Tiberius, by Foxlaw, was foaled in 1928. He was a fine stayer, winning the Ascot Gold Cup and the Goodwood Cup, while he was placed in the Derby and the St Leger. He made little mark as a sire.

TIC TAC

'Tic-Tac' men are employed by bookmakers to signal the amount of money being wagered on horses in the various enclosures, or off the course. They usually wear white gloves and signal a pre-arranged code with hands and arms.

TIDEWAY

Bred by the late Lord Derby in 1933, Tideway was by Fairway out of Drift, by Swynford. She won three races worth over £10,000, including the One Thousand Guineas. She was dam of Gulf Stream, winner of the Gimcrack Stakes and the Eclipse Stakes and second in the Derby.

TIFFIN

Lord Ellesmere's Tiffin, by Tetratema, was foaled in 1926 and was an exceptionally fast and game little filly. She was the unbeaten winner of five races worth over £13,000 as a two-year-old and headed the Free Handicap. The following season her career was curtailed by a mishap but she won all the three races in which she competed, showing superb courage in beating Royal Minstrel in a memorable race for the July Cup. Unfortunately she died after producing her first foal, Merenda, who was a Royal Ascot winner as a two-year-old.

TIGER

Tiger, by Tamerlane, was foaled in 1960 and won three races worth over £7,000, including the Gordon Stakes at Goodwood. He is now standing at the Wyld Court Stud, near Newbury. His fee is £198; or £300, no foal no fee.

TINMAN

The nickname of the great Fred Archer.

TOBOGGAN

Bred in 1925 by the late Lord Derby, Toboggan was by Hurry On out of Glacier, by St Simon. She won seven races worth over £25,000, including the Oaks, Coronation Stakes and Jockey Club Stakes. At the stud Bobsleigh was the only winner she produced.

TODD, George

George Todd is in his mid-seventies, though as erect as a guardsman and remarkably unchanged in appearance during the past forty years. He was wounded on the Somme in World War I and has never greatly relished travelling to the Continent ever since. He worked with H. Lines for five years and was then for two years with the famous Tom Coulthwaite. Since 1921 he has conducted a highly successful 'mixed' stable and over the years a high proportion of his fancied runners have 'collected'. He seems to specialise in elderly handicappers that more often than not are ridden by boys rather than leading jockeys. In recent years, though, he has trained some high-class horses and in 1966 he won the St Leger and the Irish Derby with Sodium. Other good winners include Oncidium (Coronation Cup), Roan Rocket (St James's Palace Stakes and Sussex Stakes), Parthian Glance (Yorkshire Oaks, Park Hill Stakes and Ribblesdale Stakes), Trelawny (Chester Cup, Ascot Stakes twice, Queen Alexandra Stakes twice, Goodwood Cup), Dramatic (Stewards' Cup and Lincoln) and River Chanter (Dewhurst Stakes). He trains at Manton, near Marlborough, where Alec Taylor and Joe Lawson both trained so successfully, and his owners include Mr S. C. Banks, Mr R. L. Capon, Mr T. F. C. Frost, Mr P. J. King, Mr K. C. B. Mackenzie, Mr G. Strakosch, Mr R. J. Sigtia, Mrs D. C. N. Baring, Miss I. Bennett, Mrs A. F. Hurlstone, Miss I. Bennett and Lady Dempsey.

Besides being a very high-class professional trainer who knows every aspect of the game, he is a notable raconteur and one of racing's most entertaining characters.

TOLLER, Capt Charles Bolton (b 1922)

Capt Toller was a regular soldier in the 10th Hussars till 1953. In that year he was appointed a handicapper. He has also been Clerk of the Course at Bath since 1966 and at Newbury since 1967.

TOTE, THE

The Tote in Great Britain is operated under the title of the Horserace Totalisator Board and consists of three integrated units.

(i) The Horserace Totalisator Board is the parent organisation, and is also responsible for all planning and the operation of cash betting on racecourses.

(ii) Tote Investors is the credit betting organisation for the Tote with 60 branches throughout the country.

(iii) Tote Offices controls the Tote's chain of cash betting shops which at 1st March, 1969, numbered 39.

The Tote has two main objectives: to provide a pool betting service for backers as an alternative to betting with bookmakers; to make money for the general benefit and improvement of the racing industry.

History

The Tote came into being in August 1928, following the passing of the Racecourse Betting Act, 1928. It first operated on 2nd July 1929 at Newmarket and Carlisle.

The Act provided for a statutory body, the Racecourse Betting Control Board, which governed the operation of the racecourse totalisator. This Board consisted of 12 members, nominated either by Ministers (the Home Secretary, Chancellor of the Exchequer, Secretary for Scotland and Minister of Agriculture) or by racing bodies (the Jockey Club, National Hunt Committee, Racecourse Owners Association and Tattersalls Committee).

Tote turnover in the very early days was meagre, and operating expenses were high. The Tote was not sharing the vast off-course betting, and the organisation did not begin to thrive until a private company, Tote Investors Ltd, was formed in 1931 by a few knowledgeable racing men and leading owners who backed the project. Tote Investors Ltd's objective was to channel off-course bets to the Tote on the racecourse on a commission basis.

By 1934 all racecourses had been equipped with Tote buildings and Tote Investors Ltd was expanding. Tote turnover began to increase steadily each year until by 1939 it reached a total of over £9,000,000. After World War II, turnover in 1945 was only £7,000,000 but then came a steep rise in the number of days racing. By 1948 turnover was more than £26,000,000, the £30,000,000 mark was passed in 1960, and the record figure of £40,359,618 was achieved in the year 1966-67. Of that total, £18,428,660 was bet on-course and £21,930,957 off-course.

The racecourse Betting Control Board made contributions to the racing industry totalling £9,725,470 in the period 1929-61, though only £892,166 of this was passed on in the years 1929-45. Grants were applied to the improvement of accommodation and amenities, increases in prize money, subsidies towards the cost of transporting horses to meetings, and payments for each horse running.

In 1961 the whole financial structure of the racing industry was altered by the passing of the Betting Levy Act. This created the Horserace Betting Levy Board, with powers to levy both the Tote and bookmakers and to distribute the money for the improvement of the racing industry. The Racecourse Betting Control Board became the Horserace Totalisator Board—a much smaller board consisting of a Chairman and three other members, all of whom were appointed by the Secretary of State.

In 1962, it was agreed by the directors of Tote Investors Ltd that the Horserace Totalisator Board should acquire the capital of this company which hitherto had been operating as a separate commercial business. At the same time, a subsidiary of Tote Investors Ltd was formed with the title of Tote Offices Ltd with the aim of developing a chain of the off-course cash betting offices which were legalised under the Betting and Gaming Act of 1960. Changes were made in the board of Tote Investors Ltd so that all the members of the Horserace Totalisator Board were also directors of Tote Investors Ltd.

The Tote finally became an integrated unit on 1st October 1968. Employees of both Tote Investors Ltd and Tote Offices Ltd became employees of the parent body, the Horseracing Totalisator Board, and the three integrated organisations established their headquarters and planning staff at TIL House near Ludgate Circus, London E.C.4. The word 'Limited' was dropped from the title of Tote Investors and Tote Offices.

Services

Horserace Totalisator Board

HTB, besides being the parent organisation of the group, operates cash betting on racecourses. This involves the provision of staff for some 800 days racing, plus additional point-to-point fixtures.

The Tote in Great Britain provides a service under conditions which are more challenging than those in any other country in the world. It has to move its staff and the bulk of its equipment around the country giving a service at 64 different racecourses for meetings which last from only one to five days, in contrast to places such as America where meetings last up to 75 days. It is in competition with bookmakers and has to accept bets off-course up to the last minute from punters throughout the whole country.

In the course of a year, HTB staff travel more than 13 million miles to race meetings, which gives an illustration of the high overheads incurred in providing a Tote service in a country where racing is always likely to remain decentralised.

Under agreements entered into with racecourses, the Tote pays rent for the sites occupied by its buildings, which are erected by the Board. In addition the Board has to pay local rates as well as admission charges for its staff.

In order to maintain its service on racecourses, HTB has developed a headquarters operation, that includes an architects and engineers department, responsible for maintaining the huge range of Tote buildings on racecourses; an audit department, which keeps a constant eye on internal and external security; a stores department, which sends out to racecourses the millions of tickets needed every year, plus all the other equipment; and a staff department, which circulates the 3,800 temporary staff asking if they will be available to cover certain meetings, and then gives them detailed travelling instructions, tickets and racecourse passes.

HTB has to keep on its books neary 4,000 Tote operators to meet the demands of the peak days such as Easter Monday, when the Tote is required to give a service at 16 flat and jumping meetings and point-to-points.

Tote Investors

Tote Investors is responsible for the Tote's credit betting. It has 60 branches throughout the country and some 800 telephones. Clients may bet race by race right up to the 'off' and their money is transmitted to the racecourse for inclusion in the official pools.

Application for a Tote Investors credit account means provision of a bank reference, and a fairly stringent check is made on a potential client's credit-worthiness before an account is opened for him or her. Because the Tote has to return the bulk of the money it handles to successful backers and the remainder is earmarked for the Horserace Betting Levy Board or the Chancellor of the Exchequer's betting tax, every effort has to be made to keep bad debts to the minimum.

Departments within the Tote Investors organisation include enrolments, branch administration, a computer which carries out research programmes and produces clients' statements at the end of each week, a large filing and index department, where complete records of all clients' transactions may be found, a busy transmission department which passes on all off-course bets to the HTB control room on the racecourse, and a racecourse department, responsible for operating the Tote Investors credit counters to be found on every racecourse.

Tote Offices

Formed in 1961, Tote Offices had its headquarters at Hemel Hempstead but has now moved in to join the central Tote organisation at Ludgate Circus.

Tote Offices is responsible for the Tote's 55 cash betting offices. Unlike bookmakers' betting offices, which usually operate as independent units, Tote Offices and Tote Investors branches must be linked to the transmission system so that bets may be channelled through to the central pool.

Like all betting shops, however, Tote Offices are governed by the Betting, Gaming and Lotteries Act, 1963, and must make application to local magistrates for a licence to operate, thereafter being subject to fairly stringent regulations, including severe restrictions on the advertising of shops or the facilities that they offer.

Tote Offices had betting shops in only Blackpool, Bournemouth, Leicester, Liverpool and Sheffield by March 1963. By March 1966 the total had grown to 24 and by the middle of the following year it was 39.

Transmitting the Bets

The three sections of the Tote—HTB, Tote Investors and Tote Offices—are linked on race days by one of the largest private telephone systems in the country, geared to ensure that a bet placed just before the start of a race by a punter who may be 500 miles from the racecourse is included in the official pool.

To illustrate the path of a bet: a client of the Tote's credit office in Ayr, may telephone just before 2 pm with a 10s. place only bet on a horse in the 2 o'clock race at Bath. The bet is accepted by a telephonist and immediately handed to another operator who transmits it to the main office in Scotland, Glasgow. There it is amalgamated with other bets on the same horse, transmitted to the key office at Leeds and thence to the transmission room at Tote Investors, London.

Here rows of operators wearing headsets sit, each identified by signs showing the key office from which he is accepting bets—Leeds, Liverpool, Nottingham, Brighton, etc. Opposite each operator sits a collator who enters amalgamated bets on a collation sheet as they are called out. These lump sums are passed to other operators who are in continuous contact with the control room of the Tote on the racecourse.

In control, a team of operators make a final amalgamation of all the money bet off-course and all that taken on the racecourse, and as soon as the result of the race is known the dividends are calculated and cross checked. This operation is done at great speed so that the information can be passed to the pay-out windows, and back down the line to transmission and cash and credit offices.

Transmission in the Future

The Tote has now approached leading computer manufacturers with a specification for a much more advanced machine which would eventually handle bets placed throughout the country, on and off the course, and would also calculate dividends.

Stage One in this new deveopment will probably involve the installation of computer equipment which would accept collated horse reads from off-course points of sale—Tote Investors and Tote Offices—and would then, on the race result being made available to the computer, transmit the total off-course pool and the number of units on placed horses, to a teleprinter in the Control Room on the racecourse.

In *Stage Two* the racecourse cash sales would be brought into the system and the procedure reversed, with equipment on the racecourse transmitting the on-course pool and winning units to the central computer for calculation of the dividend.

Stage Three would involve the purchase of ticket issuing machines for both racecourse and cash offices which would automatically transmit details of each sale to the computer for dividend calculation. In the case of Tote Investors, telephonists would be equipped with keyboards linked to the computer which would transmit details of the bets accepted over the telephone.

This final stage is probably some years off, as the whole operation is geared to the amount of capital which can be found.

As a first step, Sir Alexander Sim, Chairman of the HTB, announced in September 1968, that the Minnesota-based firm Control Data Corporation had been asked to join with Tote computer experts in the formation of a team to study all the problems and to develop keyboard equipment suitable for Tote betting in this country. Control Data had previously produced the computer system used in Australia by the Totalisator Agencies Board.

Pools Operated by the Tote

The Tote in Great Britain offers a wider range of bets than totalisators in any other country in the world. These pools are:

Win: On all races. 4s. unit.

Place: First or second in races of 6 or 7 runners. First, second or third in races of 8 or more runners. 4s. unit.

Forecast: Selecting the first two placed horses. 3 to 6 runners, first two in correct order, 7 to 9 runners, first two in either order. 4s. unit.

Daily Double: Winners of the third and fifth races. 10s. unit.

Daily Treble: Winners of the second, fourth and sixth races. 5s. unit.

Jackpot: Naming the winners of the first six races on specified days. If the pool is not won, i.e. if no backer nominates six winners, 80 per cent of the pool is carried forward to the next day and 20 per cent retained for a consolation dividend. A consolation dividend will be paid to those backers with the highest number of consecutive winners starting with the first Jackpot race of the day, but with a minimum of four winners. If there is no bet on the last day nominating all six winners, a winning bet is one that nominates the highest number of winning horses in consecutive racecard order, beginning with the first race on which a winning selection has been received. 5s. unit.

In addition to these bets, clients of the Tote's credit and cash offices can indulge in a wide range of bets such as doubles, trebles, accumulators, 'Yankees', 'Canadians', forecast doubles, and many others. A proviso is that there must be an interval of 15 minutes between the races in which a client has his selections running, in order to allow time for any profit there may be from the first transaction to be re-invested on the next selection.

Off-course credit clients may telephone 4s. bets up to 2 pm. Thereafter the minimum investment is 10s., and this is also the minimum stake for all on-course credit bets.

The following deductions are made from Tote pools in order to cover the Government's 5 per cent betting duty, the Tote's contribution to the Horserace Betting Levy Board ($1\frac{1}{2}$ per cent of turnover in the year ending 31st March 1969).

Win and Place: $23\frac{1}{2}$ per cent of losing stakes.

Forecasts, Daily Double, Daily Treble and Jackpot: 25 per cent of losing stakes.

Tote Jackpot

While the mainstay of totalisator betting has always been the win and place pools, representing some 80 per cent of Tote turnover, a healthy contribution has been made by the Tote Jackpot, which was an immediate success from its inception at Royal Ascot in June 1966.

The Tote has been experimenting with a number of pools such as the Double Double (two Tote doubles on the same day) and the Quadpool (nominating four winners), but none had caught the public's imagination. The Jackpot, with its build up from day to day when it is not won, paid out £63,114 to a lady who scooped the pool on the third day of the first Ascot meeting at which it operated. By March 1969, some mammoth pools had accumulated, such as £203,000 at Ascot in June 1967 and £380,000 in July the same year.

An ever increasing number of bookmakers accept Jackpot bets and pass them on for inclusion in the official pool, and while the record pay-out of over £63,000 established in the first week has yet to be beaten, there were two dividends of more than £55,000 at Cheltenham in March 1968 and it must be only a matter of time before a six-figure dividend is achieved.

Sponsored Races

In addition to passing on the benefit of its operation to the Horserace Betting Levy Board for the improvement of racing, the Tote gives direct sponsorship to races at individual courses.

Two major races are staged:

The Totalisator Champion Novices' Chase, Cheltenham, March, £5,000

The Totalisator Free Handicap, Newmarket, April, £5,000

In addition, Tote Investors, who were one of the first companies to sponsor races, endow five or six smaller races annually. These are staged at a variety of courses and since July 1956 Tote Investors have sponsored races worth £131,000 on 35 different racecourses.

RECORD POOLS (up to Jan., 1970)

Total Pools	£	
Turnover on one day (all meetings)	602,336	Easter Monday 1969
Turnover on one day (one meeting)	476,233	Ascot (Gold Cup Day), 1966
Turnover for one meeting	1,907,157	Ascot, 14-18th June, 1966
Win and Place Pools	126,487	Epsom (Derby), 1967
Win Pool	63,469	Epsom (Derby), 1965
Place Pool	65,315	Epsom (Derby), 1967
Straight Forecast Pool	15,683	Ascot (Coronation Stakes), 1964
Dual Forecast Pool	17,187	Ascot (Gold Cup), 1966
Daily Double Pool	36,770	Ascot (Royal Hunt Cup and Bessborough Stakes), 1961
Daily Treble Pool	15,930	Ascot (Queen Mary Stakes, Coronation Stakes and Ribblesdale Stakes), 1963
Quadpool	10,572	Ascot (Gold Cup Day), 1965
Jackpot (Daily Turnover)	253,741	Goodwood, 28th July 1967
Jackpot (Total Pool)	380,898	Goodwood, 25-28th July 1967
Jackpot (Consolation Pool)	18,076	Goodwood, 27th July 1967
Big Race Special Double or Forecast	47,503	Derby Forecast Pool, 1936
Cash Pools (where different from above)		
Turnover on one day (one meeting)	263,967	Ascot (Royal Hunt Cup Day), 1966
Win and Place Pools	58,960	Ascot (Royal Hunt Cup), 1961
Win Pool	28,220	Ascot (Royal Hunt Cup), 1961
Place Pool	30,740	Ascot (Royal Hunt Cup), 1961

Record Dividends (up to January 1970)

	£	
Win	341 (2s. stake)	Haydock Park, 30th November 1929
Place	30 (2s. stake)	Nottingham, 25th October 1949
Straight Forecast	97 (2s. stake)	Towcester, 23rd October 1954
Dual Forecast	294 (4s. stake)	Kelso, 21st October 1967
Daily Double	5,062 (10s. stake)	Liverpool, 25th March 1938

Daily Treble	4,307 (5s. stake)	Ascot, 19th June 1952
Quadpool	2,510 (5s. stake)	Ascot, 18th June 1965
Jackpot	63,114 (5s. stake)	Ascot, 18th June 1966
Jackpot (Consolation Dividend)	8,331 (5s. stake)	Ascot, 23rd June 1967
Big Race Special Double or Forecast	8,899	Lincolnshire Handicap and Grand National Double, 1947

TOTE INVESTORS LIMITED

See TOTE, THE

TRACERY

Tracery was bred in America in 1909 by Mr August Belmont and was by Rock Sand out of Topiary, by Orme. Brought to this country, he proved a top-class racehorse, winning the St Leger, Eclipse Stakes, Champion Stakes and St James's Palace Stakes, besides finishing third in the Derby. In the Gold Cup he was brought down by a lunatic who ran out onto the course. He retired to the stud in England in 1914 and sired Papyrus (Derby), The Panther (Two Thousand Guineas) and Transvaal (Grand Prix de Paris). In 1920 he was sold for 53,000 gn to the Argentine. After his son Papyrus had won the Derby in 1923, he was brought back to this country by an English syndicate but died the following year.

TRACK SPARE

Track Spare was bred by Major and Mrs S. Johnson and was bought by Mr R. Mason for 1,600 gn as a yearling. Foaled in 1963, he is a bay by Sound Track out of Rosy Myth, by Nearco. Trained by his owner he won five races and over £28,000 in England, his victories including the Middle Park Stakes and St James's Palace Stakes. He stands at Old Connell Stud, Newbridge, Co Kildare, at a fee of £250.

TRADE UNIONISM

The Transport and General Workers Union represents many persons employed in racing establishments. The Union has had a relationship agreement with the Newmarket Trainers Federation since 1937, and in addition to Newmarket it has membership from stablemen in the Lambourn, Middleham, Epsom and Malton training areas. It also represents persons employed by bookmakers and the Tote. With regard to the Industrial Training Act 1964, the Union has a keen interest in the promotion of a proper apprenticeship scheme in the racing industry.

TRAINERS

Every trainer in Great Britain of a horse running under the Rules of Racing must obtain an annual licence from the Stewards of the Jockey Club, and pay a yearly sum, the amount of which the Stewards of the Jockey Club decide from time to time, and of which £1 shall be allocated to the Bentinck Benevolent Fund.

Every trainer shall conduct his business properly and with due regard to the interests of his owners. Any negligent or improper conduct in respect of his business constitutes an offence under the Rules of Racing punishable by the Stewards of the Jockey Club by virtue of their powers.

When any horse has run in any race under the Rules of Racing and has been found on examination to have received any substance (other than a normal nutrient) which could have altered its racing performance at the time of running in the race in question, the trainer of the horse in question shall be fined not less than £100, or, at the discretion of the Stewards of the Jockey Club, his licence may be withdrawn.

No trainer is permitted to engage or retain any stable servant in respect of whom a current Registration Card has not been issued by, or on behalf of, the Stewards of the Jockey Club and of the National Hunt Committee.

No trainer is permitted to engage any stable servant who has previously been in a training stable without referring to his last employer, and receiving a satisfactory reply in writing. A servant prevented by this particular Rule from obtaining or retaining employment has the right of appeal to the Stewards of the Jockey Club. Any trainer infringing this Rule is liable to be reported to the Stewards of the Jockey Club.

Registration Cards for stable servants are issued only on the application of the trainer concerned and every application must be made in writing and accompanied by the written consent of the stable servant to be bound by the Rules of Racing. Registration Cards are the property of the Stewards of the Jockey Club and of the National Hunt Committee; they are returnable on demand and may be granted subject to conditions, refused or cancelled at any time by the Stewards at their absolute discretion.

Application forms for Registration Cards and forms of consent to be signed by stable servants are obtainable only from the Registry Office.

Leading Trainers

1900	R. Marsh	£43,321
1901	J. Huggins	£29,142
1902	R. S. Sievier	£23,686
1903	G. Blackwell	£34,135
1904	P. P. Gilpin	£35,694
1905	W. T. Robinson	£34,466
1906	Hon George Lambton	£34,069
1907	A. Taylor	£24,708
1908	C. Morton	£26,431
1909	A. Taylor	£47,825
1910	A. Taylor	£52,364
1911	Hon George Lambton	£49,769
1912	Hon George Lambton	£22,884
1913	R. Wootton	£28,284
1914	A. Taylor	£52,052
1915	P. Gilpin	£15,324
1916	R. Dawson	£16,386
1917	A. Taylor	£17,924
1918	A. Taylor	£36,629
1919	A. Taylor	£33,208
1920	A. Taylor	£35,907
1921	A. Taylor	£48,280
1922	A. Taylor	£52,059
1923	A. Taylor	£49,190
1924	R. Dawson	£48,857
1925	A. Taylor	£56,570
1926	F. Darling	£63,408
1927	F. Butters	£57,468
1928	F. Butters	£57,539
1929	R. Dawson	£74,574
1930	H. S. Persse	£49,487
1931	J. Lawson	£93,899
1932	F. Butters	£72,436
1933	F. Darling	£44,277
1934	F. Butters	£88,844
1935	F. Butters	£59,688
1936	J. Lawson	£61,773
1937	C. Boyd-Rochfort	£61,213
1938	C. Boyd-Rochfort	£51,350
1939	J. L. Jarvis	£56,219
1940	F. Darling	£16,166
1941	F. Darling	£19,026
1942	F. Darling	£12,843
1943	W. Nightingall	£13,834
1944	F. Butters	£17,585
1945	W. Earl	£29,557
1946	F. Butters	£56,140
1947	F. Darling	£65,313
1948	N. Murless	£66,542
1949	F. Butters	£71,721
1950	C. H. Semblat	£57,044
1951	J. L. Jarvis	£56,397
1952	M. Marsh	£92,093
1953	J. L. Jarvis	£71,547
1954	C. Boyd-Rochfort	£63,326
1955	C. Boyd-Rochfort	£74,424
1956	C. F. Elsey	£61,621
1957	N. Murless	£116,898
1958	C. Boyd-Rochfort	£84,186
1959	N. Murless	£145,730
1960	N. Murless	£118,298
1961	N. Murless	£95,972
1962	W. Hern	£70,206
1963	P. Prendergast	£125,294
1964	P. Prendergast	£128,103
1965	P. Prendergast	£75,324
1966	M. V. O'Brien	£123,849
1967	N. Murless	£256,699
1968	N. Murless	£141,509
1969	A. M. Budgett	£105,349

Trainers of both Derby and Grand National Winners

Trainers that have had winners of

both the Derby and the Grand National are J. Jewitt, G. Blackwell, R. C. Dawson, W. Stephenson and M. V. O'Brien. The last-named has so far trained three Grand National winners and three Derby winners.

TRAINING CENTRES

Training tends to become a more centralised affair than it used to be. The maintenance of private gallops has become increasingly expensive and trainers find it cheaper and more convenient to have their stable at a recognised centre such as Newmarket, Epsom, Malton or the Lambourn district of Berkshire. There the gallops are maintained and used on a communal basis, trainers probably paying a fee in respect of each horse under their care. In addition, at these centres the best veterinary and transport services are readily available, while trainers and jockeys going to a distant meeting can share the cost of hiring an aircraft.

In the old days some of the craftier trainers with owners who liked to bet favoured secluded stables in the remoter parts of Salisbury plain. Secrets could be kept there, particularly as the discipline among employees used to be very strict indeed. Nowadays it is almost impossible to obtain stable labour at any place remote from a town of reasonable size. The lads will not stand it; nor will their wives.

TRANQUIL

Bred in 1920 by the late Lord Derby, Tranquil was a bay by Swynford out of Serenissima, by Minoru. She was a very fine performer, winning the One Thousand Guineas, St Leger and Jockey Club Cup. She was not a great success as a brood mare but produced three winners of seven races.

TRAVELLING ALLOWANCES

In Great Britain the cost of transporting horses to race-meetings is partially borne by the Levy Board.

TREE, Arthur Jeremy (b 1925)

Jeremy Tree served in the Life Guards for four years and began training in 1952. His stables are at Beckhampton, near Marlborough, where the great Fred Darling used to train, and among his owners are Mr G. Dudley Jun, Mr C. W. Engelhard, Mrs M. Sheriffe, Mr J. H. Whitney, Mrs D. Fitzgerald, Mr M. Longman, Lady Elizabeth Longman, Lord Margadale, Hon J. Morrison, Hon P. Morrison and Hon Mary Morrison. Among the good horses he has trained are Only For Life (Two Thousand Guineas), The Elk (*Observer* Gold Cup and Lingfield Derby Trial), Persian Road (Ebor Handicap), Double Bore (Goodwood Cup), Monet (Stewards' Cup), Gustav (Middle Park Stakes), Double Jump (National Stakes, Prix Pobert Papin and Gimcrack Stakes), Ros Rock (Free Handicap), Minor Portion (City and Suburban) and D'Urberville (King's Strand Stakes).

TRELAWNY

This famous stayer, a brown gelding by Black Tarquin out of Indian Night, by Umidwar, was bred by the Astor Studs in 1956. Mr J. J. Astor parted with him cheaply as a three-year-old and trained by George Todd, Trelawny then won the Chester Cup, the Brown Jack Stakes, the Ascot Stakes twice (with 9st 8lb and 10st), the Queen Alexandra Stakes twice and the Goodwood Cup. Altogether he won 11 races on the flat worth over £19,000. He was probably the most popular horse since Brown Jack.

TRIGO

Trigo, owned by Mr W. Barnett and trained at Whatcombe by R. C. Dawson, was by Blandford out of Athasi and won the Derby, St Leger and the Irish St Leger in 1929. He was a stud failure.

TRIMDON

Trimdon, by Son-in-Law, was bred

by Lord Durham in 1926 and proved an outstanding stayer, winning the Ascot Gold Cup twice, the Gold Vase, the Queen's Prize and the Yorkshire Cup. A three parts brother to the Gold Cup winner Foxhunter, he was not a stud success, but sired the great French stayer Marsyas II whose record of four victories in the Prix du Cadran (French Gold Cup) is unlikely ever to be equalled. Trimdon also sired Trimbush, who won 14 races, including the Doncaster Cup.

TRIPLE CROWN

To earn the mythical 'Triple Crown' a three-year-old must win the Two Thousand Guineas, the Derby and the St Leger.

The following horses have won the 'Triple Crown' (not counting the war years when substitute races were run): West Australian (1853), Gladiateur (1865), Lord Lyon (1866), Ormonde (1886), Common (1891), Isinglass (1893), Galtee More (1897), Flying Fox (1899), Diamond Jubilee (1900), Rock Sand (1903) and Bahram (1935).

Pommern (1915), Gay Crusader (1917) and Gainsborough (1918) won war-substitute races and are usually awarded 'Triple Crown' status.

TRISTAN

Tristan, by Hermit, was foaled in 1878. He was an extremely good horse and a very tough one indeed, but remarkably bad-tempered. All courses and all distances came alike to him and he won 25 races, including the Gold Cup. At one Royal Ascot meeting he won three long-distance races; shortly after that he won the 6f July Cup. In the nineteenth century horses were frequently more robust and certainly more versatile than they are today. Tristan sired Canterbury Pilgrim, winner of the Oaks and an influential brood-mare.

TROPIQUE

Bred in France by Baron Guy de Rothschild, Tropique was foaled in 1952 and is by Fontenay out of Aurore Boreale, by Brantôme. He won the Prix d'Harcourt and four other races in France while in England he won the Eclipse Stakes and Coronation Cup. He retired to the stud in England but went back to France in 1962. He is sire of Paveh, winner of the Irish Two Thousand Guineas and the Sussex Stakes.

TROUTBECK

The second Duke of Westminster's Troutbeck, by Ladas, won the St Leger in 1906. He failed as a sire both in England and America.

TRYON, Lord, KCVO, DSO (b 1906)

Lord Tryon served in the Grenadier Guards, commanding an armoured brigade in North-west Europe. He is keeper of Her Majesty's Privy Purse. He is a member of the Jockey Club and a steward at Ascot, Epsom and Salisbury. His trainer is P. Nelson. Colours: dark blue.

TUBING

'Tubing' is an operation to assist a horse with respiratory trouble. It consists of an operation on the animal's throat, a metal tube being inserted through which it breathes instead of through the normal nasal route. It is a process rarely resorted to nowadays.

TUDOR MELODY

Tudor Melody was bred in 1956 by Mrs A. Levins Moore and was sold for 610 gn as a yearling. By Tudor Minstrel out of Matelda, by Dante, he won five races as a two-year-old, including the Chesham Stakes and Prince of Wales's Stakes, and was placed top of the Free Handicap. He was then exported to America, where he raced for two seasons, winning twice. He returned to England and went to the stud in 1961. He has done extremely well and is now owned by a syndicate, standing at the National

Stud, Newmarket. His best winner so far is the French-trained Kashmir II, who won the Two Thousand Guineas in 1966.

TUDOR MINSTREL

Tudor Minstrel was bred and owned by Mr J. A. Dewar and was the last of the many great horses trained by Fred Darling. Foaled in 1944, he was by the Derby and Gold Cup winner Owen Tudor out of Sansonnet, by the Derby winner Sansovino out of Lady Juror, a staying mare by the great stayer Son-in-Law. On paper Tudor Minstrel had a stayer's pedigree, but the dominating influence in fact was the tremendous speed inherited through Lady Juror's dam, Lady Josephine, who also bred Mumtaz Mahal.

An immensely powerful bay, Tudor Minstrel was unbeaten as a two-year-old, his victories including the Coventry Stakes and the National Breeders Produce Stakes. The following season he won a small race at Bath and then carried off the Two Thousand Guineas by eight lengths. Prematurely hailed by the racing press as 'the horse of the century', he started at 7-4 on in the Derby, but failed to stay and finished a moderate fourth behind Pearl Diver. Some people criticised Gordon Richards's riding, saying that if he had permitted the hard-pulling Tudor Minstrel to stride along in front instead of endeavouring to restrain him, a process that the favourite clearly resented and fought against, Tudor Minstrel might well have won. That criticism, however, was soon proved invalid as after winning the St James's Palace Stakes at Ascot, Tudor Minstrel was beaten in the Eclipse Stakes by Migoli. No attempt on this occasion was made to restrain Tudor Minstrel who turned for home six lengths clear but was in trouble two furlongs from home.

Tudor Minstrel ended his career by winning the one mile Knights Royal Stakes at Ascot. Up to that distance he was brilliant, and had he been kept to it he might never have been beaten. As a sire he failed to come up to expectations and he was never higher in the list than seventh. He was exported to America in 1959.

TULK, Paul (b 1938)

Paul Tulk was apprenticed to 'Sam' Armstrong from 1953 to 1959. He rode his first winner in 1955 and his best season was 1967 when he rode 3[illegible] winners. He can go to scale at 7st 10lb. Among the good races he has won are the Cesarewitch, Free Handicap, Great Metropolitan and the Nunthorpe Stakes.

TULYAR

Tulyar was the fifth and last of the Aga Khan's five Derby winners. Bred by his owner, he was by the St Leger winner Tehran, who was otherwise not greatly distinguished as a sire, out of Neocracy, by Nearco. Trained by Marcus Marsh, he was no more than a useful stayer as a two-year-old, his main success being in the Buggins Farm Nursery at Haydock Park. In the Free Handicap he was rated 19lb inferior to Windy City.

As a three-year-old he was a very different proposition and was never beaten, winning in succession the 7f Henry VIII Stakes at Hurst Park, the 1m 6f Ormonde Stakes at Chester, the Lingfield Derby Trial, the Derby, the Eclipse Stakes, the King George VI and Queen Elizabeth Stakes and finally the St Leger. He may rarely have been spectacular, but as a three-year-old no rival ever got to the bottom of him. He won £76,417 in stakes, beating the record so long held by Isinglass who raced till he was five.

The Aga Khan sold Tulyar to the Irish National Stud for approximately £250,000. In 1955 he was sold again, this time to an American syndicate. He left Ireland in 1956 and became gravely ill soon afterwards. At one time his life was despaired of but he eventually recovered. He has never really established himself as a sire. He

(*above*) ROUS, ADMIRAL HENRY JOHN. Admiral Rous, a famous racing administrator of the mid-Victorian era. (*below*) ST SIMON. St Simon, a great racehorse and sire

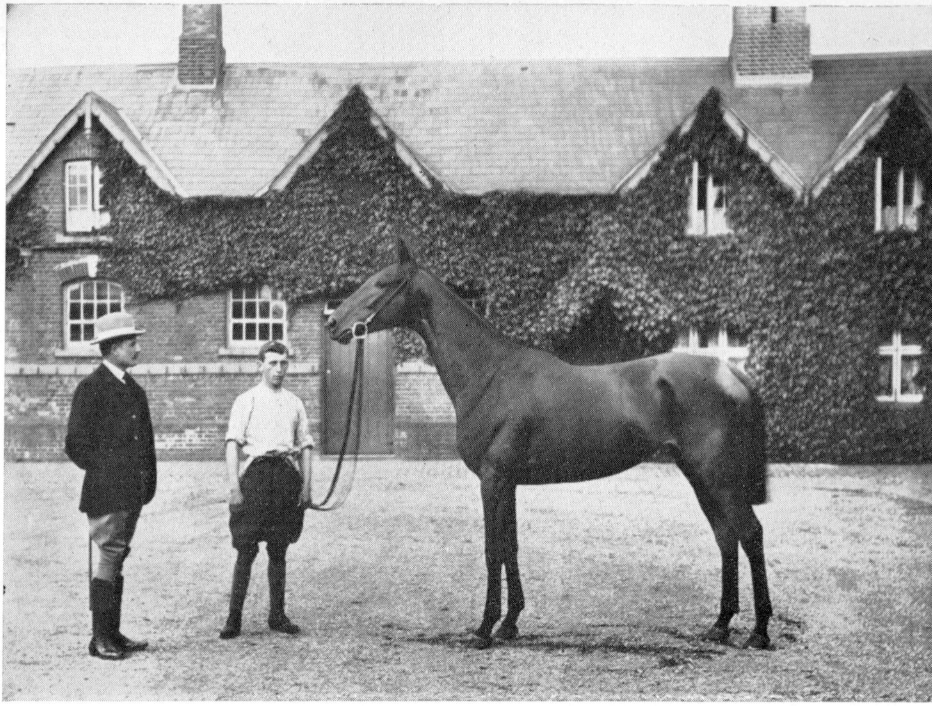

SCEPTRE. With Alec Taylor, Sceptre, winner of every classic except the Derby

SLOAN, TOD. The American jockey Tod Sloan, who did much to revolutionise the style of race-riding in this country

is half-brother to Saint Crespin III (q.v.).

TURF BOARD

In 1963 a joint committee formed of representatives of the Jockey Club and the National Hunt Committee and under the chairmanship of Lord Howard de Walden began to analyse the various categories of stewards' work with a view to recommending a method which would enable it to be handled more easily and suggesting any necessary reorganisation.

They completed their work early the following year, reporting to the Jockey Club and the National Hunt Committee in March. The report was accepted in principle, and a working party to give effect to the Report was at once formed. The final plan was announced to the press in July.

The really significant step was the formation of a Turf Board which would be concerned with matters of policy, its rulings and decisions being implemented through the existing executive machinery of the Jockey Club and the National Hunt Committee. In the briefest terms, the Turf Board now lays down the general policy, while the Jockey Club and the National Hunt Committee are responsible for the day-to-day running of the sport on the lines laid down by the Board.

The power of the Turf Board derives from the fact that it consists of the Stewards of the Jockey Club and the National Hunt Committee with the Senior Steward of the Jockey Club as chairman. One steward from each body is a vice-chairman. To provide the members of the Turf Board, it became necessary to increase the Jockey Club Stewards to five and the National Hunt Committee to four. To ensure seasonable measure of continuity, it was agreed that the Senior Steward of the Jockey Club should hold office, not for a single year as had been the practice until then, but for five. The first chairman of the Turf Board was Major-Gen Sir Randle Feilden. The vice-chairmen serve for two years.

With the approval of the Home Secretary, the chairman of the Levy Board and one of the other Government-appointed members of the Levy Board attend the meetings of the Turf Board by standing invitation and participate in the work and discussions of the Turf Board. This ensures that all questions of policy affecting the economics of racing are fully discussed by the Turf Board and the Levy Board from the outset.

The chairman of the Turf Board is also chairman of the joint Turf Authorities and the Joint Associations Liaison Committee. The joint Turf Authorities is the body comprising the five Stewards of the Jockey Club and the four Stewards of the National Hunt Committee. The Joint Associations Liaison Committee is the body consisting of the five Stewards of the Jockey Club, the four Stewards of the National Hunt Committee, together with representatives of the Racecourse Association, the Racecourse Owners Association, the Thoroughbred Breeders Association and the National Hunt Trainers Association (North and South Sections). (A modification to the last paragraph of course took place on the amalgamation of the Jockey Club with the National Hunt Committee in 1969).

Secretary of the Turf Board is Brig S. H. Kent.

TURKHAN

Bred by the Aga Khan in 1937, Turkhan was by Bahram out of Theresina, by Diophon. He won the St Leger and the Irish Derby and was second in the Derby. He was not a great success as a sire but his mares have done quite well. He was exported to France in 1952.

TWILIGHT ALLEY

Bred by the Sassoon Studs in 1959, Twilight Alley is a big chestnut horse, standing well over 17 hands, by Alycidon out of Crepuscule, by Mieuxcé.

He is thus three parts brother to the dual classic winner Crepello. He took a long time to come to hand and he never ran as a two-year-old. At the age of three he ran once, winning the Cranbourn Chase Stakes at Ascot. He ran three times the following season, finishing second in the Henry II Stakes, winning the Ascot Gold Cup and breaking down in the King George VI and Queen Elizabeth Stakes in which he had to be pulled up. He stands at the Beech House Stud, Newmarket, at a fee of 400 gn.

TWO THOUSAND GUINEAS

See under NEWMARKET.

TYPHOON

Typhoon was bred in 1958 by Mrs M. Clarke and sold as a yearling for 3,600 gn. By Honeyway out of Kingsworthy, by Kingstone, he was trained by Paddy Prendergast and won the Coventry Stakes and Richmond Stakes. As a three-year-old he was exported to America where he won 10 races and was placed 12 times, earning over $69,000. He returned to Ireland and went to the stud there in 1965. He now stands at the Balreask Stud, Navan, Co Meath, at a fee of 250 gn.

TYRONE

Tyrone was bred in France in 1954 by Mme J. Couturié. He won the Grand Criterium, the French Two Thousand Guineas and two other races. In the English Two Thousand Guineas he was fourth behind Crepello. Now owned by a syndicate, he stands at the Limestone Stud, Willoughton, Lincolnshire.

U

UDAIPUR

Bred by the Aga Khan in 1929, Udaipur was by Blandford out of Uganda, by Bridaine. She won four races including the Oaks and Coronation Stakes. She bred seven winners including Umiddad, who won the Gold Cup and was second in the Derby; and Dust Devil, winner of the Jockey Club Stakes.

UJIJI

Bred by the Aga Khan in 1939, Ujiji was by Umidwar out of Teresina, by Diophon. He won eight races, including the Gold Cup, and was third in the Derby. An undistinguished sire, he was exported to Sweden.

UMIDDAD

Umiddad was bred by the Aga Khan in 1940 and was by Dastur out of the Oaks winner Udaipur. He won seven races including the Dewhurst Stakes and the Gold Cup, and was second in the Derby. He did little good as a sire either in England or later in France.

UMIDWAR

Umidwar was bred in 1931 by the Aga Khan and was a full brother to the Oaks winner Udaipur, being by Blandford out of Uganda, by Bridaine. He won four races including the Jockey Club Stakes and the Champion Stakes. He did quite well as a sire, his brood mares being particularly successful.

UNDER STARTERS ORDERS

The horses are ready to run and the white flag goes up. From this point, all bets stand.

UNSADDLING ENCLOSURE

Where winners and placed horses are unsaddled after a race.

V

VAGUELY NOBLE

Vaguely Noble was bred in 1965 by the late Major L. B. Holliday and is a bay horse by Vienna out of Noble Lassie, by Nearco. As a two-year-old, trained by W. Wharton, his successes included the *Observer* Gold Cup which he won by seven lengths. Less than two months afterwards he came up for sale at Newmarket, and although he held no classic engagements, he was bought for the record public auction price for a thoroughbred of 136,000 gn. The purchaser was an American plastic surgeon, Dr Robert Franklyn, who the following spring sold a half-share in Vaguely Noble to another American, Mr N. Bunker Hunt.

After the sale Vaguely Noble went for a time to P. J. Prendergast in Ireland, but was soon transferred to Etienne Pollet in France. The main objective for 1968 was Europe's richest racing prize, the Prix de l'Arc de Triomphe and Vaguely Noble duly won it in the manner of a truly great racehorse. That was the end of his racing career and he is now at the stud in America.

VALETS

Jockeys' valets form an indispensable section of the racing community. They travel from meeting to meeting, look after the jockeys, keep their equipment in order and provide any that is required.

VALORIS

Mr Charles Clore's Valoris, by Tiziano, won the Irish One Thousand Guineas and the Epsom Oaks in 1966, trained by Vincent O'Brien and ridden by Lester Piggott.

VAN CLIEF, Daniel (b 1925)

Mr Van Clief was born in 1925 and served with the US 4th Infantry Division in five major campaigns. He is a patron of the Turf in America, where he is a member of the Jockey Club and a past President of the Virginia Thoroughbred Association, and also in England. The best horse he has owned in England is Crocket, who won the Coventry Stakes, Gimcrack Stakes, Middle Park Stakes and St James's Palace Stakes. His trainers are Doug Smith and Peter Walwyn. Colours: emerald green, sapphire sleeves and sash, quartered cap.

VAN CUTSEM, Bernard Henry (b 1916)

Bernard van Cutsem was prominent in sporting circles at Cambridge and shortly after leaving the university he took out a licence to train. His career, though, was interrupted by the war, during which he served in the Life Guards. On the conclusion of hostilities he resumed training again and gradually established his reputation. He is now regarded as one of the shrewdest and most competent men in the game. He holds strong views on the structure of racing in England and on more than one occasion comments by him have irked the bookmaking profession considerably.

A few years ago he succeeded Jack Watts as Lord Derby's trainer and he now has nearly 70 horses under his care at the Stanley Stables. Besides Lord Derby his patrons include the Duke of Devonshire, Mr F. W. Burmann, Sir Bryan Bonsor Bt, Mr I. Kornberg, Lord Scarborough, Hon K. Mason, Hon David Montagu, Lord Iveagh, Hon R. Stanley, Mr J. R. Thouron, Lady Delamere, Mr Nelson

Bunker Hunt, Mr E. More O'Ferrall, Mr R. More O'Ferrall, Lord Blandford, Dr C. Labreciossa, Lady Rotherwick and Capt M. Lemos.

The best winner he has so far trained is that gallant mare Park Top, whose victories include the Ribblesdale Stakes, Coronation Cup, Hardwicke Stakes and King George VI and Queen Elizabeth Stakes. He also trained Park Top's sire Kalydon; Mandamus, winner of eight races and over £24,000; that fine sprinter Mountain Call; and Karabas, winner of the City and Suburban, Prix du Consul Municipal and the Washington International at Laurel Park. In 1970 he added to his successes by training Decies to win the Irish Two Thousand Guineas.

VASEY, Melton Avril (b 1906)

M. A. Vasey, who trains at Kingsley House, Middleham, rode under National Hunt rules from 1923 till 1932. For a time he assisted his father, the late F. M. Vasey, and although he held a jumping trainer's licence as far back as 1925, it was not until 1952 that he began to train on the flat. His successes include the Ayr Gold Cup and the Free Handicap, while among his patrons are Mr L. Bentley, Mr T. H. Degg, Mr G. B. Turnbull, Mr H. D. Hill, Mr A. Soulsby and Mr A. Watson.

VATELLOR

Vatellor was an exceptionally tough and courageous horse, winning six times and being placed on 11 occasions in France. By Vatout out of Lady Elinor, by Teddy, he was a very successful sire and got two Derby winners, Pearl Diver and My Love.

VAUCLUSE

Owned and bred by the late Lord Rosebery, Vaucluse, by Dark Ronald, won the One Thousand Guineas in 1915. She bred five winners including that very good staying mare Bongrace.

VEDAS

Mr W. F. de Wend Fenton's Vedas, trained by W. Robinson, won the Two Thousand Guineas in 1905. Because of an injury he was unable to compete in the Derby.

VENTURE VII

Venture VII was bred in 1957 by the late Aga Khan and the late Prince Aly Khan and is by Relic out of Rose O'Lynn, by Pherozshah. He is thus a full brother to Buisson Ardent. Trained in France by Alec Head, he won the Imperial Produce Stakes, Middle Park Stakes, Prix Djebel, St James's Palace Stakes and the Sussex Stakes. He was beaten a head by Martial in the Two Thousand Guineas. He is now owned jointly by the Aga Khan and the Comtesse de la Valdene and stands at the Marly-la-Ville Stud, Marly-la-Ville (Seine-et-Oise), France, at a fee of 10,000 francs.

VERDICT

Lord Coventry's Verdict, foaled in 1920, was doubly half-bred, both her sire Shogun and her dame Finale being so classified. She was a good game mare and won eight races, including the Cambridgeshire, in which she beat the French horse Epinard in a memorable race, and the Coronation Cup. At the stud she bred Quashed, one of the gamest mares ever seen on the English Turf and winner of the Oaks and Ascot Gold Cup.

VERNEUIL

At Royal Ascot in 1878 the French horse Verneuil, trained by Tom Jennings, won the Gold Vase, Gold Cup and Alexandra Plate, all run over two miles or more, without being headed for a single stride in any of those races. Horses had to be tough in those days!

VETERINARY OFFICER and VETERINARY SURGEON

A Veterinary Officer at a race-meeting is a licensed official of the

Jockey Club who, for example, acts on their behalf in the collection of samples for forensic analysis. The Veterinary Surgeon, on the other hand, is engaged by the executive of the racecourse concerned and is responsible for the treatment of sick or injured horses.

VICTORIA CLUB

A London club, the members of which are chiefly bookmakers and professional backers.

VIDEO TAPE

A type of film that can be projected immediately and thus invaluable for inquiries and objections.

VIENNA

Vienna, who was sent to France in 1967, was bred and owned by Sir Winston Churchill. A chestnut horse by Aureole out of Turkish Blood, by Turkhan, he won six races and over £14,000 in England and the valuable Prix d'Harcourt in France. His English victories included the Blue Riband Trial Stakes, the Jack Olding Stakes and the Lyons Maid Stakes (twice). He was second in the Coronation Cup and third in the St Leger. As a sire his reputation rests largely on the triumphs of Vaguely Noble (q.v.).

VILMORAY

Vilmoray, bred in 1950 by Lieut-Col H. E. St George, is a chestnut by Vilmorin out of Iverley Way, by Apron. He was a good game sprinter, winning 13 races including the Severals Stakes (twice), July Cup and Portland Handicap. At the stud he has sired a fair number of winners, none, however, of any significance.

VIMY

Bred in France in 1952 by M. P. Wertheimer, Vimy, by Wild Risk, won the King George VI and Queen Elizabeth Stakes in 1955. He was bought by the Irish National Stud but was not a great success and was exported to Japan in 1964. He sired the Eclipse winner Khalkis, and Sans Le Sou, dam of Busted.

VIRAGO

A famous filly that as a three-year-old won those two popular handicaps at Epsom, the 10f City and Suburban and the 2¼m Great Metropolitan, on the same afternoon in 1854.

VIVIAN, Capt Robert Crespigny Gwynedd (b 1898)

Capt Bobby Vivian served in the Life Guards and was a successful amateur rider from 1920 to 1932. From 1932 till the outbreak of World War II he held a licence to train under National Hunt rules. After the war he became a racing official and he is now Clerk of the Course at Salisbury and Chester. Until recently he held a similar position at Chepstow.

VOLODYOVSKI

Known by the bookmakers as 'Bottle of Whisky', Volodyovski, by Florizel II, won the 1901 Derby for the American owner Mr W. C. Whitney, trained by an American trainer, J. Huggins, and ridden by an American jockey, Lester Reiff. He was narrowly and unluckily beaten in a very rough race for the St Leger. He failed completely as a sire.

VOLTIGEUR

One of the best horses ever to be trained in the North, Lord Zetland's Voltigeur, by Voltaire, won the Derby and the St Leger in 1850. In the St Leger he dead-heated with Russborough but then won the run-off. He had two famous races against the 1849 Derby and St Leger winner, The Flying Dutchman, winning one and being beaten in the other. From him the mighty St Simon is descended in tail-male.

VUILLER, Col

Col Vuiller, a French expert on bloodstock breeding, carried out intensive research in the early years of this century. He closely examined the pedigrees of 650 leading racehorses from the early days of the sport of racing down to his own time and from his observations made certain conclusions.

The pedigree of each horse under his scrutiny was examined down to the twelfth generation. There are 4,096 individuals in the twelfth generation and to each of these Col Vuiller allowed a value of one. Two points were allowed to each of the 2,048 individuals in the eleventh generation, and so on down to the two parents, who each had a value of 2,048. By applying this method to the 650 horses selected, he obtained an aggregate value for each ancestor and calculated not merely the individuals that ought to appear in the pedigree of 'a standard good horse', but also their proportions or 'dosages'. Put in the briefest and simplest terms, he reckoned that when a stallion or mare was lacking in any of the constituents of 'a standard good pedigree' a mate ought to be selected that would correct the 'dosage' in the expected offspring. Col Vuiller died in 1931 soon after the publication of his last book, *Les Croisements Rationnels dans la Race Pure*.

W

WAFFLES

Owned by Mr J. J. Maher, Waffles was foaled in 1917. She stood barely 15 hands and was never even broken. Her sire was the handicapper Buckwheat, while both her dam and her sire's dam were by St Simon.

Her first foal, Bunworry, won four races and was then sent to India. She ended up, though, in Senatore Tesio's famous Italian stud where she bred Bernina (Italian Two Thousand Guineas, One Thousand Guineas and Oaks and grandam of the Gold Cup winner Botticelli); Bozzetto (three times champion sire in Italy); Brueghel (leading sire in Australia); and Saucy Silver, dam of an American Grand National winner.

Waffles bred two English classic winners, Manna (Two Thousand Guineas and Derby) and Sandwich (St Leger). She also bred Parwiz, winner of over £3,000, and the notorious Tuppence who was the top-price yearling of 1931, was heavily backed to win Hyperion's Derby, never won a race and ended up in Russia.

WAINWRIGHT, Stanley (b 1928)

Stanley Wainwright trains at Norton, near Malton, in Yorkshire. He took out a licence to train in 1966, having served his apprenticeship with Capt C. F. Elsey and acted as travelling head lad to P. T. Beasley.

WALKER, I. S.

Ian Walker trains at Exning, near Newmarket. Among his patrons are Mr Wilfred Hyde White, Mrs E. Ostrer, Mr J. N. Sutton, Mr T. G. Warner, Mr A. Ball, Mr G. Rosen, Mrs M. C. Walker, Mr George Best, Major J. Rubin, Miss H. Monteith, Mr J. Long, and Mr J. Penfold. Before setting up on his own he was assistant to George Colling.

WALK-OVER

A walk-over is a race in which only a single runner takes part. The jockey of the horse in question must weigh out, mount at the appointed time, canter past the stands and then return to the unsaddling enclosure where he must unsaddle the horse and then be weighed in. The owner of the horse takes the prize money allotted to the second and third horses.

WALLABY II

Bred in France in 1955 by Baron G. de Waldner, Wallaby II, by Fast Fox, won the Ascot Gold Cup as a four-year-old, just beating Alcide. In France his successes included the French St Leger and Prix Jean Prat.

WALLER, Brig H. J. de W., MBE, MC (b 1917)

Brig 'Sam' Waller was a regular soldier in the Royal Artillery. He was appointed Secretary of the Horserace Betting Levy Board in 1965. His post was abolished in 1968 and he became Director-General of the Racecourse Association.

WALLINGTON, Harold, sen (b 1893)

Harold Wallington rode many winners under National Hunt rules before taking out a licence to train in 1937. He had considerable successes in important handicaps, winning the Cambridgeshire, Royal Hunt Cup, Victoria Cup (twice), William Hill Gold Cup, Esher Cup, Zetland Gold Cup and

Crocker Buteel Cup. He retired in 1969 and the control of his Epsom stable passed to his son, Harold Wallington junior.

WALLS, Tom (1883-1949)

The son of a builder and for a short time a constable in the Metropolitan Police, Tom Walls went on the stage in 1905 and became a highly successful light comedian, earning immense popularity in the series of Aldwych farces in which he appeared with Ralph Lynn and Robertson Hare. His first managerial venture was a farce aptly named *Tons of Money* which ran for two years.

He was always devoted to sport, to racing in particular, and trained a small string of horses at Epsom. His big triumph was to own and train the 1932 Derby winner April the Fifth. It gave him almost equal pleasure to train Crafty Alice, on whom his son, then an officer in the 5th Inniskilling Dragoon Guards, won the Grand Military Gold Cup at Sandown.

WALSH, James

James Walsh conducts a small stable at Winkfield, Berkshire. He served his apprenticeship with Harvey Leader, rode both on the flat and under National Hunt rules and took out a licence to train in 1948. His owners include Sir Thomas Pilkington, Col A. C. R. Waite and Mr G. E. Hill.

WALWYN, Fulke (b 1910)

Fulke Walwyn was for a brief period a regular soldier in the 9th Lancers. He was a top-class rider under National Hunt rules, first as an amateur and later as a professional, winning the Grand National in 1936 on Reynoldstown. He has proved an outstanding trainer of chasers and hurdlers, and at one period he trained flat-racers for Miss Dorothy Paget, for whom he won the Doncaster Cup and Queen Alexandra Stakes with Aldborough.

WALWYN, Peter (b 1933)

Peter Walwyn was educated at Charterhouse, and is married to a sister of Nick Gaselee, the well-known amateur rider. He was assistant for three years to Geoffrey Brooke before setting up on his own in 1957. A great enthusiast and a tremendously hard worker, he has risen to a leading position in his profession in a comparatively short time and at the beginning of 1970 he had nearly 80 horses in his stable at Seven Barrows, Lambourn. In 1969 his horses won 66 races in this country worth over £86,000 and he also enjoyed successes in France as well. Moreover, this record might have been even better with a bit of luck as he was runner-up in the Derby, Oaks and King George VI and Queen Elizabeth Stakes. He started off well in 1970 by winning the One Thousand Guineas with Humble Duty and the valuable Prix Jean de Chaudenay at Saint Cloud with Shoemaker.

Among other races he has won are the Coronation Stakes, Nassau Stakes, Yorkshire Oaks (twice), Doncaster Cup, Victoria Cup, Lowther Stakes, Duke of Edinburgh Stakes, Jockey Club Stakes, Sun Chariot Stakes and Cheveley Park Stakes. His owners include Jean, Lady Ashcombe, Major and Mrs E. Barker, Mr and Mrs I. Cameron, Lord Clinton, Mr and Mrs D. G. Van Clief, Mr and Mrs L. Freedman, Viscount Galway, Mr P. G. Goulandris, Mr J. R. Henderson, Colonel and Mrs F. Hue-Williams, Sir Herbert Ingram, Hon H. Lumley-Saville, Mrs A. Levins Moore, Mrs D. Mackinnon, Mr D. W. Molins, Mrs D. McCalmont, Mr A. D. G. Oldrey, Major J. H. Paine, Major P. Bengough, Colonel R. Poole, Mr E. de Rothschild, Mr C. Spence, Major and Mrs A. Smith-Bingham, Hon Mrs W. E. Wallace and Mr and Mrs G. P. Williams.

WARNING-OFF

See PORTLAND, FOURTH DUKE OF.

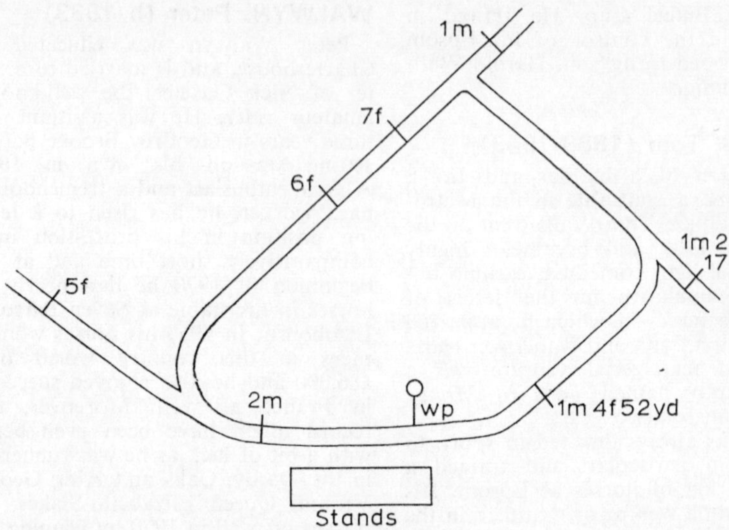

WARWICK

WARWICK

This long-established Midland course provides opportunities for moderate horses to make some contribution towards their keep. It is a left-handed circuit of 1m 6f with a run-in of 2½f. The 5f course has a pronounced left-handed elbow where it links up with the round course on the home turn. The elbow naturally confers an advantage on horses drawn with low numbers.

It was at a steeplechase meeting at Warwick in 1847 that Chandler is alleged to have made a record jump of 37 feet from take-off to landing, clearing a brook and two fallen horses.

Clerk of the Course: Mr D. Heyman, Woollerton House, Wendover, Bucks. Tel: Wendover 3194.

WATLING STREET

Watling Street, by Fairway, was the third and last Derby winner owned by the seventeenth Earl of Derby. He won a war-substitute Derby at Newmarket in 1942. He was not a success as a sire in England. In 1951 he was exported to the United States but died within a year of his arrival.

Best Times:

Distance	*Horse-Age-Weight*	*Date*	*Time*
5f	Shush Shush 4-7-4	3/6/57	58
5f	Tircelyn 2-9-0	8/6/57	58.6
6f	Pride of Kilmlick 4-9-5	1/7/60	1min 11.8
6f	High Flown 2-8-12	9/6/52	1min 13.8
7f	Blackshore 6-7-12	19/5/56	1min 23.8
7f	Chitra 2-6-11	12/10/53	1min 26.8
8f	No Worry 5-7-5	29/6/56	1min 37.4
8f	Clarification 2-8-10	8/10/55	1min 40
10f 170yd	Lullaby 3-9-0	13/10/69	2min 16.4
12f 52yd	Noirmont Buoy 5-8-12	19/6/67	2min 37.2
16f	Flighty Eyes 4-8-11	15/8/55	3min 26.8

WATTS, Jack

Jack Watts was one of the best riders in the late Victorian era. He won the Derby on Merry Hampton (1887), Sainfoin (1890), Ladas (1894), and Persimmon (1896). He received his early schooling from Tom Cannon and his style, quiet, cool-headed and unspectacular, reflected the methods of his tutor. He was extremely reserved in manner and even after winning the Derby on Persimmon in the royal colours, he barely permitted himself the luxury of a transitory smile. His son, grandson and great-grandson (qq.v.) were or are all trainers at Newmarket.

WATTS, John Evelyn (1887-1959)

Jack Watts died at Newmarket aged 72. He was the son of the famous jockey John Watts (see above), also known as Jack, and the father of the present Newmarket trainer Jack Watts (see below). He himself started training at Newmarket in 1907. In 1911 he went to Germany to manage a stable associated with the German Government's stud, but returned to England just before the outbreak of war, in which he served overseas with the Suffolk Yeomanry.

In 1922 he moved to Primrose Cottage, Newmarket, to train for Mr Frank Curzon, who controlled numerous London theatres, and for him he won the 1927 Derby with Call Boy. Mr Curzon was literally a dying man when he led Call Boy in at Epsom and in fact he died very soon afterwards.

In 1935 Watts moved to France to train for M. Boussac. With M. Boussac's famous mare Corrida, who was destined to be stolen by the Germans and was never recovered, he won the Prix de l'Arc de Triomphe (twice), the Grand Prix de Marseille (twice), the Berlin Grosser Preis, the Ostend Grand International, the Prix du Président de la République, and the Hardwicke Stakes at Ascot.

For a second time war interrupted Watts's career in Europe. He returned to England and from 1942 till he retired 10 years later he trained for Mr H. J. Joel, for whom he won the One Thousand Guineas with Picture Play.

WATTS, John Frederick (b 1911)

A member of a famous Newmarket family, Jack Watts was born in 1911. His father trained Call Boy to win the Derby; his grandfather rode four Derby winners; his son now runs his own stable at Newmarket.

Jack, who served for five years in the RAF Regiment during the war, took out a licence to train in 1950, having at times assisted his father, Colledge Leader and Willie Pratt. He succeeded George Colling as Lord Derby's trainer but the arrangement terminated in 1963, the year before he won the St Leger with Mr Charles Engelhard's Indiana, who had given Santa Claus such a hard race in the Derby.

Among the good races he has won are the Churchill Stakes; Dewhurst Stakes; Princess of Wales's Stakes; National Breeders Produce Stakes; St James's Palace Stakes; Cesarewitch; Goodwood Stakes; Manchester Cup; Chester Vase; Great Voltigeur Stakes; Queen Mary Stakes; and *News of the World* Stakes. His owners include Lady Aubrey-Fletcher, Sir Kenneth Butt Bt, Mr C. W. Engelhard, Mrs C. Brudenell-Bruce, Mr G. Cooper, Mr R. N. Richmond-Watson, Hon Richard Stanley, Mrs M. A. Farr, Mrs A. M. Hill and Mr P. Winstone.

WATTS, J. W.

Son of J. F. Watts, he began training at Newmarket in 1968. In 1970 he won the Royal Hunt Cup with Calpurnius.

WAUGH, Charles (1870-1949)

Charles Waugh trained before World War I in Germany and won two German Derbys for Kaiser Wilhelm.

WAUGH, Dawson (1872-1955)

Dawson Waugh, named after his god-father, the famous Matthew Dawson, was a member of a much-respected Newmarket family. His father, James Waugh, had trained at Russley for Mr Merry. His brother Willie succeeded John Porter at Kingsclere, and two other brothers trained at Newmarket. A sister was mother of that fine trainer Frank Butters.

Dawson Waugh assisted John Porter for some years and then trained in Hungary for a spell. In 1903 he became private trainer to Mr W. Raphael for whom he won the One Thousand Guineas and the Derby in 1912 with the grey filly Tagalie, and the Two Thousand Guineas in 1913 with Louvois. Louviers had been beaten a short head in the Derby in 1909 by Minoru. Waugh eventually parted company with Mr Raphael and after World War I his chief patrons were Sir Edward Hulton, for whom he won the Oaks with Straitlace, and Lord Howard de Walden. Little interested in betting, he was a man of great kindliness and the utmost integrity. There was no stable where apprentices were better cared for and among his protégés were Harry Blackshaw and Joe Sime.

WAUGH, Jack Alfred James (b 1911)

Jack Waugh was born in 1911 and is a son of the late R. T. Waugh and a brother of Tom Waugh (see below). From 1927 to 1932 he assisted his father, who was then training at Newmarket, while from 1932-39 he was with Basil Jarvis. After three years' service in the Royal Artillery during the war, he took out a licence to train himself and by and large has been very successful. He follows the family tradition by being unspectacular, highly conscientious and an excellent stableman. Among the scores of good races he has won are the July Cup (twice), Cheveley Park Stakes, Ribblesdale Stakes (twice), Wokingham Stakes, Coventry Stakes, National Breeders Produce Stakes, Ladbroke Gold Cup, Crocker Bulteel Cup, Queen Mary Stakes, Royal Lodge Stakes, Park Hill Stakes, Senior Service Gold Cup and the *News of the World* Stakes. Patrons of his Newmarket stable include Hon Lady Macdonald-Buchanan, Major Sir R. Macdonald-Buchanan, Mr A. J. Macdonald-Buchanan, Lord Fairhaven, Lord Howard de Walden, Major R. W. Bourne, Mr G. C. Gibson, Mrs R. Humphreys, Mr A. W. Parkinson, Mrs R. A. Raphael and Mrs M. G. Wyatt.

WAUGH, John Alexander (b 1931)

John Waugh was born in 1931 and is the son of the late Alec Waugh, who trained in Germany prior to World War I, and in Austria and Germany from 1920 to 1933 when he returned to England. John Waugh assisted his father for a time when his father was training at Newmarket and was then assistant to George Colling from 1951 to 1957 and to Reg Day from 1958 to 1960. Since 1960 he has been training at Fitzroy House, Newmarket, for Sir Robin McAlpine and family, and has done very well considering his limited opportunities.

WAUGH, Thomas Alexander (b 1915)

Tom Waugh, younger brother of Jack Waugh, was born in 1915. Before World War II, in which he served in the Royal Artillery, he assisted Fred Butters. From 1946 to 1949 he was with Frank Butters and from 1946 to 1955 with Harvey Leader. In 1956 he set up on his own at Newmarket. By far the best horse he has so far trained is Privy Councillor, winner in 1962 of the Free Handicap and Two Thousand Guineas. Patrons of the stable include Major Gerald Glover, Mr H. J. Joel, Brig H. R. Harris, Mrs W. J. Armstrong, Mrs James Barttelot, Commander Campbell-Johnstone and Mrs R. Newton.

WAVERTREE, Lord

Lord Wavertree, formerly Col W. Hall-Walker, was an eccentric, somewhat peppery individual who was rarely satisfied for long with his jockey or his trainer. A fervent student of the stars, he observed their course with the closest attention and all his important decisions were based on what the stars appeared to foretell. Unfortunately the stars advised him to sell Prince Palatine, who proceeded to win the St Leger and two Ascot Gold Cups. He bred the Two Thousand Guineas and Derby winner Minoru, who was leased for racing to King Edward VII. He presented Tully—now the Irish National Stud—to the British Government as a National Stud, while it was his flow of eloquent persuasiveness that induced the Aga Khan to take up racing on a princely scale.

WEATHERBY, David (b 1926)

Mr David Weatherby was educated at Winchester and did his National Service in the Coldstream Guards. He is Secretary to the Jockey Club and Keeper of the Match Book. His responsibilities include the day-to-day conduct of racing; administration and finance; fixtures and prize money; Jockey Club meetings; general purposes committee meetings; liaison for services provided for the Jockey Club; liaison with foreign Turf authorities.

WEATHERBY, E. W. (d 1967)

Mr Bill Weatherby, a member of the famous family that since 1771 has played such a distinguished part in the administration of the English Turf, became secretary to the Jockey Club in 1953. The previous occupant of that onerous post had been Sir Francis Weatherby, who in turn had succeeded Bill Weatherby's father.

In the 1960s Bill Weatherby was at the centre of the many changes that were taking place in English racing. All the reforms—in particular the overnight declaration of runners—threw more and more work on the firm of Weatherbys and called for an ever-increasing degree of modernisation and mechanisation. Bill Weatherby, the most loyal and conscientious of men, was under a considerable strain and his health began to suffer. In 1967 he collapsed and died at London Airport on his way to see the Irish Derby. He was in his sixty-third year.

WEATHERBY, Sir Francis, MC, (b 1885)

Sir Francis Weatherby, who died in 1969, served with the Oxfordshire Yeomanry in World War I. A distinguished cricketer in his youth, he was secretary to the Jockey Club, of which body he eventually became a member, from 1930 to 1952. He did much to keep racing ticking over during World War II.

WEATHERBY, Peter (b 1907)

Mr P. M. Weatherby was educated at Winchester. As chief executive of the Jockey Club secretariat, his responsibilities include all licensing; disciplinary cases and appeals; reports from inspectors of courses, incuding point-to-point inspectors; reviewing existing rules and examining suggestions for changes; and the integration of National Hunt interests with those of the Jockey Club.

WEATHERBY & SONS

Messrs Weatherby and Sons, 42 Portman Square, London W1, act as agents to the Jockey Club and a member of the Weatherby family has held office as Secretary to the Jockey Club continuously since 1770. They are publishers, on behalf of the Jockey Club, of the *Racing Calendar* and proprietors and compilers of the *General Stud Book*, the authoritative register of all British and Irish Thoroughbred bloodstock.

Over the years the continuity of government with regard to racing has been supplied by members of the Weatherby family, whose role in Turf affairs has been compared to that of those invaluable civil servants who serve and advise the successive members of the Cabinet. As a family, the Weatherbys possess the admirable qualities of the best type of civil servant, too; experience, discretion, loyalty, a dislike of publicity, and in most cases a Winchester education. Like civil servants, they are frequently subjected to criticism and at any rate until quite recently, it was often alleged that they conducted their immensely profitable business in a somewhat rigid and old-fashioned manner. They were also said to be allergic to change or innovation in the conduct of the sport.

Whatever the justice of these complaints, the Weatherby family has played an important and estimable part in the development and control of racing in this country and they can justly claim to be, in the words of a modern racing historian, "the very machinery of the Turf".

WEBSTER, Geoffrey

Son of Tom E. Webster, Geoffrey Webster worked for the *Sporting Life* and the *Daily Herald* before joining the Racing Information Bureau. He is Racecourse Public Relations Officer for the Southern Area.

WEEDEN, Derek (b 1931)

Derek Weeden served his apprenticeship with Sir Cecil Boyd-Rochfort and R. A. Jones. He rode under National Hunt rules for 14 years and for 12 years assisted Major M. Pope. He took out a licence to train on the flat in 1966 and his stable is at Worlington, near Bury St Edmunds.

WEEPER'S BOY

Foaled in 1961, Weepers Boy was bred by Major L. B. Holliday and is a chestnut by Whistler out of Fire Song, by The Phoenix. He won four races, including the Senior Service Gold Cup at York, and over £12,000 in prize money. He is now owned by Mr S. W. Everitt and stands at the Spa Stud, Droitwich, at a fee of £98.

WEIGHING ROOM, ADMITTANCE TO

No person shall, without special permission from the stewards, be admitted to the weighing-room except the owner, trainer, jockey, jockey's licensed valet, or other person having the care of a horse engaged in the race, and any person refusing to leave shall be reported to the stewards.

WEIGHT, HEAVIEST RECORDED

At York in 1788 Mr Maynard's mare beat Mr Baker's horse in a one mile match for 100 gn, both competitors carrying 30 stone.

WEIGHTS and PENALTIES

No horse must carry less than 7st in any race, except in nursery handicaps for which no horse may carry less than 6st 7lb, in both cases unless an apprentice allowance has been claimed. In raçes confined to apprentices, the lowest weight carried may be 6st 7lb.

In estimating the amount a horse has won in one or more races, account shall be taken of all cups or moneys whether derived from stakes, bonus, or any other source, gained by him for his owner or for any other person. In the case of a dead-heat for first place, account is taken only of the amount which the horse has gained for his owner or any other person after the prize has been divided.

In all cases the horse's own stake or entrance shall be deducted from the amount.

For the purpose of calculating penalties, any surplus on the sale of the winners in the case of a dead-heat in a selling race prior to 2nd January 1967, and any sums assigned to the Bentinck Benevolent Fund or Rous Memorial Fund or surplus from entrance or subscription in the case of a dead-heat for first place prior to 1st January 1968, shall not be taken into account.

If, in the conditions of a race a fixed penalty has to be carried for winning a race specified by name, horses running a dead-heat for that race must carry the full penalty fixed as if the race had been won outright.

The rates of exchange to be used in calculating the value of races won outside Great Britain, Ireland and the Channel Islands are laid down in the Rules of Racing. Those rates, though, are subject to variation at any time at the discretion of the Stewards of the Jockey Club.

In assessing distances of races in kilometres, 200 metres shall be taken to equal one furlong.

Winnings during the year must include all prizes to the time appointed for the start, and apply to all races except private sweepstakes or matches, in any country, and include dividing, walking-over or receiving forfeit.

No horse shall carry extra weight for having run second, or in any lower place in a race.

Extra weight is not incurred in respect of matches or private sweepstakes, or of the Newmarket Challenge Cup or Whip.

In all races, except races confined to apprentices, in which the conditions provide for a specific penalty for winners, those penalties are not applicable to winners of apprentice races which take place after 1st March, 1966. Penalties are not cumulative unless so declared by the conditions of the race.

When a race is in dispute, both the horse that came in first and any horse claiming the race is liable to all the penalties attaching to the winner of that race till the matter is decided. All penalties and allowances are calculated according to the amount of the value of each race as reported in the *Racing Calendar*.

The trainer is responsible that the horse carries the correct weight in accordance with the conditions of the race. The trainer is required to declare the weight his horse will carry if different from that appearing in the race-card. Such a declaration must be made to the Clerk of the Scales before the jockey weighs out. Failure to make the declaration renders the trainer liable to a fine of not less than £5. Riders' allowances are not taken into consideration when declaring a weight under this rule.

THE FOLLOWING SCALE OF WEIGHT FOR AGE is published under the sanction of the Stewards of the Jockey Club as a guide to managers of Race Meetings but is not intended to be imperative especially as regards the weights of two and three year olds relatively to the older horses in selling races early in the year.

It is founded on the scale published by Admiral Rous, and revised by him in 1873 but has been modified in accordance with suggestions from the principal trainers and practical authorities, and has been further revised since. See also Rule 116, RULES OF RACING.

A 'weight-for-age race' is any race which is not a handicap or a selling race.

		March & April st lb	May st lb	June st lb	July st lb	Aug. st lb	Sept. st lb	Oct. st lb	Nov. st lb
5f	Two yr.	6 0	6 2	6 7	6 10	7 2	7 7	7 9	7 12
	Three yr.	8 4	8 3	8 5	8 7	8 9	8 12	8 12	8 13
	Four yr.	9 4	9 0	9 0	9 0	9 0	9 0	9 0	9 0
	Five, six, and aged	9 5	9 0	9 0	9 0	9 0	9 0	9 0	9 0
6f	Two yr.	—	6 4	6 7	6 11	7 0	7 6	7 9	7 13
	Three yr.	8 5	8 6	8 8	8 10	8 12	9 0	9 2	9 3
	Four yr.	9 7	9 7	9 7	9 7	9 7	9 7	9 7	9 7
	Five, six, and aged	9 9	9 8	9 7	9 7	9 7	9 7	9 7	9 7
1m	Two yr.	—	—	—	—	—	6 7	6 9	6 12
	Three yr.	7 8	7 11	7 13	8 2	8 4	8 6	8 7	8 8
	Four yr.	9 0	9 0	9 0	9 0	9 0	9 0	9 0	9 0
	Five, six, and aged	9 4	9 3	9 2	9 0	9 0	9 0	9 0	9 0
1½m	Two yr.	—	—	—	—	—	6 0	6 4	6 7
	Three yr.	7 7	7 9	7 11	7 13	8 1	8 3	8 5	8 7
	Four yr.	9 0	9 0	9 0	9 0	9 0	9 0	9 0	9 0
	Five, six, and aged	9 5	9 4	9 3	9 2	9 1	9 0	9 0	9 0

2m	Two yr.	—	—	—	—	—	6 0	6 2	6 2
	Three yr.	7 8	7 11	7 12	8 0	8 3	8 4	8 5	8 5
	Four yr.	9 4	9 4	9 4	9 4	9 4	9 4	9 4	9 4
	Five, six, and aged	9 10	9 9	9 8	9 7	9 6	9 5	9 4	9 4
3m	Three yr.	7 1	7 4	7 5	7 7	7 9	7 11	7 13	7 13
	Four yr.	9 0	9 0	9 0	9 0	9 0	9 0	9 0	9 0
	Five yr.	9 8	9 7	9 6	9 5	9 5	9 4	9 3	9 3
	Six and aged	9 10	9 8	9 7	9 6	9 5	9 4	9 3	9 3

WELLS, John

John Wells was closely associated with Sir Joseph Hawley for whom he rode the Derby winners Beadsman (1858), Musjid (1859) and Blue Gown (1868). Tall for a jockey and in later life distinctly portly, he was nicknamed 'Tiny'. No stylist, he was capable, obedient and honest. His retainer was only £100 but he was generously rewarded when he won a good race.

WELSH ABBOT

Foaled in 1955, Welsh Abbot was bred and raced by Sir Winston Churchill. By Abernant out of Sister Sarah, by Abbot's Trace, he won five races and over £6,000, his best performance being his victory in the Portland Handicap as a three-year-old with 9st 2lb. After some seasons at the stud in this country, he was exported to Denmark.

WERNHER, Major-Gen Sir Harold, Bart, GCVO (b 1892)

Sir Harold Wernher served in the 12th Lancers in World War I and was re-employed in World War II, reaching the rank of major-general. Between the wars he was Master of the Fernie for 12 years. He is a member of the Jockey Club. The best horses he has owned are the famous stayer Brown Jack, who won the Queen Alexandra Stakes at Ascot six years running; and Aggressor, who won the Chesterfield Cup, Hardwicke Stakes and King George VI and Queen Elizabeth Stakes. His trainer is Gordon Smyth. Colours: green and yellow halved.

WERNHER, Lady Zia, CBE (b 1892)

Lady Zia Wernher is the wife of Major-Gen Sir Harold Wernher. She owns the Someries Stud, Newmarket, in conjunction with her daughters Mrs H. P. Philipps and Mrs D. Butters. The foundation mare of the stud was Double Life who was bought for £650 on behalf of Lady Zia by Sir Cecil Boyd-Rochfort, for many years her trainer. Double Life won the Chesterfield Cup and the Cambridgeshire and is directly responsible for 32 descendants who have won races worth over £200,000.

Lady Zia won the 1966 Derby with Charlottown, trained by Gordon Smyth, and she owned that great filly Meld who won the One Thousand Guineas, Oaks and St Leger. Other fine winners bred at the Someries Stud include Precipitation (Gold Cup and Jockey Club Stakes), Persian Gulf (Coronation Cup); Aggressor (Chesterfield Cup, Hardwicke Stakes and King George VI and Queen Elizabeth Stakes); Judicate (Irish St Leger); Retrial (Royal Hunt Cup and Cambridgeshire); Dickens (Goodwood Cup); and Double Eclipse (Jersey Stakes and Princess of Wales's Stakes). Lady Zia's trainers are Gordon Smyth and Doug Smith. Colours: green and yellow halved, yellow cap.

WEST AUSTRALIAN

Foaled in 1850, West Australian was bred and owned by Mr John Bowes. He won the Two Thousand Guines, the Derby and the St Leger, while as a four-year-old he won the Ascot Gold Cup. He was not a success

(*above*) STARTING GATE. The starting gate at Kempton. The starter is the late Major Robertson. (*below*) STARTING STALLS. The Chesterfield Stakes, Newmarket 1965. This was the first time starting stalls were used in this country

(*above*) THE TETRARCH. The Tetrarch, perhaps the fastest two year old ever seen on the English Turf and sire of three St Leger winners. (*below*) VAGUELY NOBLE. Vaguely Noble is sold by Tattersalls before a capacity crowd for 136,000 guineas

as a sire but Hurry On was descended from him in tail-male and Hurry On sired three Derby winners.

WESTMINSTER, first Duke of (1825-1899)

Hugh Lupus Grosvenor, first Duke of Westminster, was reputedly the richest man in England. He was one of the foremost owner-breeders in the last 20 years of the nineteenth century, and before his death he had won the Two Thousand Guineas with Shotover, Ormonde and Flying Fox; the One Thousand Guineas with Farewell; the Derby with Bend Or, Shotover, Ormonde and Flying Fox; and the St Leger with Ormonde and Flying Fox. Thus he owned two 'Triple Crown' winners in Ormonde, one of the best horses of the century, and Flying Fox. He also bred the famous filly Sceptre, winner of every classic bar the Derby, who was sold as a yearling after his death. A tall, upright man of patrician appearance, dignified, reserved and self-contained, he was an exceptional horseman and knew as much as any man about the breeding, training and riding of thoroughbreds.

WESTON, Tommy (b 1901)

Tommy Weston was brought up in a hard school; he served his apprenticeship in a Yorkshire stable controlled by a bookmaker. He became one of the outstanding riders of the inter-war era, combining great dash and courage with the best of hands. Even in his prime, though, he was liable to be somewhat erratic. He rode for Lord Derby for 11 years, a tribute to his character and ability, and his 11 victories in classic races included the Derby on Sansovino and Hyperion and the St Leger on Hyperion and Fairway. A distinct personality, he was always popular with the racing community, not least on account of his lively sense of humour. He served with credit in the Royal Navy during World War II and it is sad to know that he has not prospered since his retirement from riding.

WEYMES, Ernest

Ernest Weymes served in the RAF and assisted his father for seven years before taking out a licence in 1958. His stables are at Middleham, Yorkshire, and his owners include Lord Howard de Walden, Mrs G. S. Johnston, Mr G. Wilkinson, Mr E. B. C. Driffield, Mr L. Brook, Mrs M. G. Wyatt, Major M. G. Wyatt, Mr V. Capstick and Mr Ian McLaren.

WHALEBONE

Whalebone won the 1810 Derby for the Duke of Grafton. That famous writer 'The Druid' described him in the following somewhat unflattering terms: "Whalebone was as shabby to the eye as old Prunella herself. He had rather a Turkish pony look, and was broad and strong, with a shortish neck. His own feet grew very pumiced and his mares lost their speed early". Whalebone, who stood just over 15 hands, may not have been handsome but he exercised a profound influence on bloodstock breeding and a high proportion of the great horses in racing history include his name in their pedigree.

WHARTON, Walter (b 1924)

Walter Wharton for some years worked with his father who was well known in Yorkshire fox-hunting and horse-dealing circles. He started to train in 1951 and in 1964 was appointed trainer to Major Lionel Holliday, becoming a public trainer again in 1968. He won the One Thousand Guineas with Night Off and trained Vaguely Noble as a two-year-old, winning the *Observer* Gold Cup with him. Both in 1964 and in 1965 horses trained by him won over £50,000 in stakes. He has trained many winners under National Hunt rules, too, among his successes being the Topham Trophy at Aintree. He now trains over 50 horses at Richmond, Yorkshire, and his owners include the Earl of Rosebery, Mr Jabez Barker, Mr and Mrs J. E. Bigg, Lady Butt, Mr W. Cockburn, Mr T. Corrie, Sir

Hugh Fraser Bt, Mr S. R. Hebeler, Mrs J. R. Hindley, Sir Alistair Murray, Lady Sassoon, Mrs A. Stafford-Smith, Hon Mrs S. Taylor, Mr C. D. Sutherland, the Marquis of Zetland and Mr J. Wood.

WHELAN, Dermot (b 1920)

Dermot Whelan, nicknamed 'Boggy', was apprenticed to Martin Hartigan and later was for 10 years with R. V. Smyth's stable and for five with W. Payne. He served in the Royal Armoured Corps during World War II and took out a licence to train in 1955. A wit and a notable raconteur, he has won the Cheshire Oaks twice, the Wokingham Stakes, the Chesterfield Cup and the Kempton Jubilee. His best season so far was 1962 when he won over £12,000 in stakes for the patrons of his Epsom stable who include Lord and Lady Fermoy, Mr L. G. Albertini, Mr C. Henchley, Mrs D. B. Thompson, Mr. H. V. Tyler, Sir Raymond Brown, Mrs P. Bell, Mr E. Harrison, Mr C. Jarvis and Mr Emile Littler.

WHISTLER

Whistler was bred in 1950 by the Overbury Stud and is a chestnut horse by Panorama out of Farthing Damages, by Fair Trial. Sold as a yearling for 1,450 gn to the Maharaja Gaekwar of Baroda, he won six races, all as a two-year-old, including the Coventry Stakes. He has proved a most successful sire of fast horses and among his winners are Weeper's Boy (£12,449), Sound Track (£9,564). Miladdo (£8,911), Gentle Art (£8,697), Kerrabee (£8,072), Tin Whistle (£8,108) and Sammy Davis (£7,199). He is also sire of Mountain Call, a fine sprinter that won a dozen races. Whistler is now owned by a syndicate and stands at the Cloghran Stud, near Dublin (see below).

WHISTLING WIND

Whistling Wind was foaled in 1960 and is by Whistler out of Good as Gold, by Nimbus. He only ran as a two-year-old, winning all his three races, including the National Stakes at Sandown. He is owned by the Irish National Stud, where he stands at a fee of 400 gn.

THE WHITE KNIGHT

The White Knight, by Desmond, won the Gold Cup at Ascot in 1907 and again in 1908. In the former year he dead-heated with the French horse Eider, but George Stern on Eider rode a disgracefully rough race and Eider was disqualified. The White Knight was a sad failure as a sire.

WHITEMAN, Harry Edward (b 1896)

Harry Whiteman was apprenticed to his father. He rode from 1911 to 1932 and was then associated with the famous Fairlawne jumping stable where in fact he held the licence up to World War II. In 1945 Peter Cazalet assumed command at Fairlawne and Whiteman turned his attention to the flat, sending out many winners from his stable at Ayr. Among the good races he won were the Ayr Gold Cup, Nunthorpe Stakes and Vaux Gold Tankard. He retired in 1968.

WHITNEY, John Hay (b 1904)

Mr J. H. Whitney was United States Ambassador to Great Britain from 1957 to 1961. For 40 years a patron of English racing, he is an honorary member of the Jockey Club. The most famous horse to carry his colours in England was the brilliant steeplechaser Easter Hero, but he won the Eclipse Stakes in 1929 with Royal Minstrel. His trainers are A. J. Tree and H. Cecil. Colours: pink, black and white striped sleeves, white cap.

WHY HURRY

Bred in 1940 by the late Mr J. V. Rank and trained by Noel Cannon,

Why Hurry, by Precipitation, won the Oaks in 1943. At the stud she produced four somewhat moderate winners.

WIGG, Rt Hon Lord, PC (b 1900)

Lord Wigg served as a NCO in the Royal Tank Regiment from 1919 to 1937. In 1940 he re-joined the Army, retiring in 1946 as a colonel in the Royal Army Educational Corps.

From 1945 until 1967 he was Labour MP for Dudley, earning the reputation of being an expert on defence questions and also on all matters connected with betting and racing. He played a notable part in the passage of the Betting and Gaming Act, 1960. A strong and outspoken personality, he has always aroused feelings of either admiring loyalty or intense dislike among those who know him; nor are his enemies by any means confined to his political opponents. One of his closest parliamentary friends is that left-wing warrior Mr Emmanuel (now Lord) Shinwell, for whom he acted as Parliamentary Private Secretary when Mr Shinwell was Minister of Fuel and Power, Secretary of State for War, and finally, Minister of Defence. A friend from the opposite side of the House is Mr J. J. Astor, from whom he has sometimes leased horses.

In November 1967 Col Wigg, as he then was, was serving as Paymaster General in Mr Harold Wilson's Government and was commonly believed to occupy a position of considerable power behind the throne. However, he was then appointed to succeed Field Marshal Lord Harding as chairman of the Betting Levy Board and at the same time was created a life peer. He has always been a racing enthusiast—he is an owner in a small way—and he gained experience of racing administration during his term of service with the Racecourse Betting Control Board (1958-61) and the Horserace Totalisator Board (1961-64).

As chairman of the Levy Board, he has shown immense energy and drive, being determined to make English racing once again the best in the world. There are occasions when it would have been to his own benefit, and to the benefit of the sport, too, if he had numbered urbanity and tact among his virtues, but he has always been combative by nature and he has trodden, without any necessity at times, on a good many toes. All sections of the racing world, though, while not always approving of his views or his methods, agree that he has the good of the Turf at heart.

Not the least of his achievements has been the introduction of measures to improve the safety and security of all who work in racing. With the bookmakers he conducts a curious love-hate relationship. If it ever comes to a showdown with the bookmakers, Lord Wigg, with years of experience in the toughest parliamentary in-fighting behind him, will be an odds-on favourite to win.

WIGHTMAN, William Gilbert Rowell (b 1914)

Bill Wightman, when playing cricket as a boy for Dulwich, met the racing journalist Geoffrey Gilbey and as a result of that meeting he went to work for two years in Laing Ward's stable near Winchester. Later, again due to Gilbey, he trained ponies before taking out a licence to train on the flat and under National Hunt rules in 1937. Appropriately his first winner was Gilbey's chaser Sunny Peace.

Wightman served in the Royal Artillery in World War II and had the ill-luck to be captured by the Japanese, returning to England weighing less than eight stone. He started up again and quickly established his reputation through the exploits of that fine chaser Halloween. Nowadays his stable at Upham, near Southampton, is devoted chiefly to the flat and season after season it turns out at least its fair share of winners. Among the good horses that have been trained there are Fraxinus, who won the £10,000 *News of the World* Stakes, and Kingsfold, second to Tulyar in the St Leger. Patrons of the stable include Major H. S. Cayzer, Brig H. R. Harris, Mr W. Tufnell, Capt F. G. Barker, Lady Chesham, Major and Mrs W. D. Gibson, Mr D. E. Colebrook, Mrs P. Drury Lowe, Mr W. G. Lowndes, Mr G. R. Rickman, Captain and Mrs M. N. Tufnell, Miss L. Poyser, Mr E. B. Benjamin, Mrs G. B. Hunt, Mr D. M. McKellar, Mrs N. Parr, Hon William Douglas-Home, Mr J. W. Rothwell and Miss D. Terry.

WILLIAMS, D. H.

He conducts a 'mixed' stable of over 30 horses at Ferryhill, Co Durham. He had 14 winners on the flat in 1969.

WILLIAMSON, Bill (b 1922)

Bill Williamson is probably the best of the Australians riding in England today, although because of his modesty and apparent dislike of self-advertisement, his ability has not invariably received full recognition.

He rode his first winner in Australia in 1937 and in due course established a big reputation there. He came to England in 1960 and has won many important European events, his big triumphs of course being his victories on Levmoss and Vaguely Noble in the Prix de l'Arc de Triomphe. He has also won the One Thousand Guineas on Abermaid and Night Off; the *Observer* Gold Cup on Miralgo, Hardicanute and Vaguely Noble; and the Champion Stakes on Arctic Storm. In Ireland he has won the Irish Two Thousand Guineas, the Irish Oaks (three times) and the Irish St Leger (twice). In 1969 he achieved a notable double in winning the Ascot Gold Cup and its French equivalent, the Prix du Cadran, on Levmoss.

Like most Australians, he is a fine judge of pace, while his quiet, undemonstrative methods give little clue to observers as to the real and very effective strength of his finish.

WILLOUGHBY de BROKE, twentieth Baron, MC, AFC (b 1896)

Lord Willoughby de Broke served with the 17th/21st Lancers in World War I and in World War II with the Auxiliary Air Force. In his younger days he rode as an amateur. He was elected to the Jockey Club in 1941 and since then has been one of its most active and outspoken members. He was a Steward of the Jockey Club from 1944-46 and again from 1954-56. He has also served three terms of office as a Steward of the National Hunt Committee. From 1948 to 1954 he was chairman of Tattersalls Committee, and he is chairman of Cheltenham and Wolverhampton Racecourses and also of the Race-Finish Recording Co Ltd. He has bred and owned numerous winners, but none of outstanding merit. His trainer is H. Leader. Colours: yellow, chocolate hooped sleeves and cap.

WILL SOMERS

Will Somers, foaled in 1955, is by Tudor Minstrel out of Queen's Jest, by Nearco. His racing career was modest, as he only won two races worth just over £900, but he has done well as a sire, among his offspring being that successful handicapper Kamundu; Willipeg, a consistent sprinter; and Irish Minstrel, one of the best milers in France. He stands at the Ballykisteen Stud, Tipperary, where his fee in 1969 was £98.

WILMOT, Miss Norah (b 1889)

Miss Norah Wilmot has been a familiar and greatly-liked racing personality for many years. Always devoted to horses and racing, she assisted her father, the late Sir Robert Wilmot, from 1911 to 1931. Since his death she has gallantly carried on the stable at Binfield, Berkshire, though of course it was not until 1966 that the Jockey Club, thanks to the efforts of Miss Wilmot herself and even more so to those of Mrs Nagle, finally gave way and women were permitted to hold a licence. Till then Miss Wilmot, who has numbered the Queen among her patrons, had to run the stable in the name of her assistant or head lad. Among the good races she has won are the Goodwood Cup, Doncaster Cup, Newbury Spring Cup, Newbury Autumn Cup, Brown Jack Stakes and Blue Riband Trial Stakes.

WILMOT-SMITH, John Patrick, MRCVS

Appointed a veterinary officer under the Rules of Racing and National Hunt rules in 1966.

WILSON, John Murrin (b 1933)

'Jock' Wilson was apprenticed to Jack Reardon from 1948 to 1953. A sound and competent rider who can go to scale at 7st 10lb, he has won the Cambridgeshire, Northumberland Plate, Nunthorpe Stakes, Chester Vase and Newbury Spring Cup. The biggest number of winners he has had in one season is 39. He is attached to B. Swift's stable.

WILWYN

Bred by his owner Mr R. C. Boucher in 1948, Wilwyn is a bay horse by Pink Flower out of Saracen, by Donatello II. Trained by George Colling, he won 20 races, including the Free Handicap, Great Yorkshire Stakes, Rous Memorial Stakes and the International Stakes at Laurel Park, USA. He was exported to South Africa in 1959.

WINDMILL GIRL

Bred in 1961 by Major L. B. Holliday, Windmill Girl is by Hornbeam out of Chorus Beauty, by Chanteur II. She won the Ribblesdale Stakes, was second in the Oaks and is the dam of the Derby winner Blakeney.

WINDSOR

With the advent of the M4 motorway, Windsor has become more accessible than ever for metropolitan racegoers. The course, bounded on the north, east and south by the Thames and the Mill Stream, is a pretty one, but the stands can hardly be described as up-to-date and it is not easy to follow the running down the far end of the course. Nevertheless, Windsor undoubtedly possesses a charm of its own.

The course is a figure-of-eight one. It is just over 1m 6f round and is virtually level. The bends are on the sharp side, but there is a long run-in of 6f with only a slight elbow. High numbers are favoured in the draw on the sprint course, but they must be well away to avoid being cut off at the elbow.

Clerk of the Course: Mr D. W. Bushby, The Racecourse, Windsor, Berkshire. Tel: Windsor 65234.

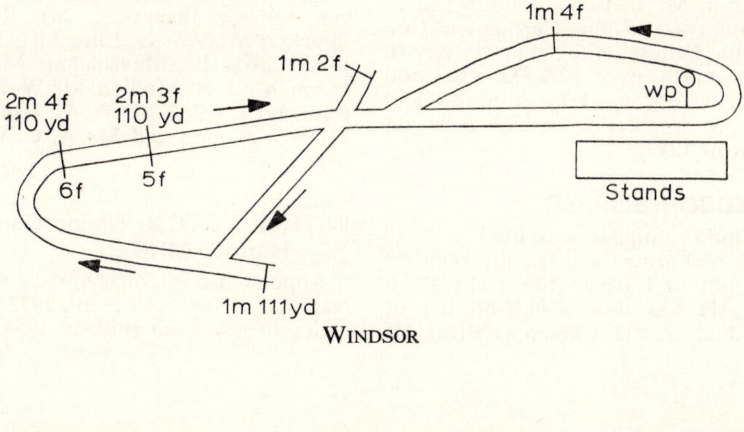

WINDSOR

Best Times:

Distance	*Horse-Age-Weight*	*Date*	*Time*
5f	Spanish Moon 2-9-0	27/6/64	59
6f	Free Style 3-8-12	27/6/64	1min 10.1
6f	Alpine Bloom 2-8-0	31/8/57	1min 12.2
6f	Winding River 2-8-4	29/8/69	1min 12
8f 70yd	Charlies Pal 4-6-10	30/8/69	1min 44.8
10f 25yd	Anopheles 5-7-5	8/9/69	2min 6.9
11f 150yd	Flying Shot 4-8-2	30/8/69	2min 25

WINDSOR LAD

Windsor Lad was one of the best Derby winners of the inter-war period. Foaled in 1931, he was bred by Mr Dan Sullivan and was by Blandford out of Resplendent. He was bought as a yearling for 1,300 gn by Marcus Marsh acting on behalf of the Maharajah of Rajpipla.

As a two-year-old Windsor Lad was no more than promising and was rated 18lb below Colombo in the Free Handicap. He improved out of all knowledge during the winter and the following season won the Chester Vase, the Newmarket Stakes and then the Derby. He ought to have won the Eclipse Stakes, too, but ridden by Smirke, who had won the Derby on him, he got hopelessly boxed in in the straight and was most unluckily beaten by King Salmon. He was never beaten again afterwards.

Soon after the Eclipse, as the result of some rather complicated negotiations, he became the property of a bookmaker, Mr M. H. Benson, who is said to have written out a cheque for £50,000. Windsor Lad won the St Leger in Mr Benson's colours and as a four-year-old the Coronation Cup and the Eclipse. Altogether he won 10 races worth over £36,000. His stud career was dogged by ill-health and after much suffering he had to be put down in 1943.

WINDSOR SLIPPER

Windsor Slipper was bred in 1939 by Lord Furness and was by Windsor Lad out of Carpet Slipper, by Phalaris. He was thus a half-brother of the dual classic winner Godiva. He was trained in Ireland and owing to the war never competed against top-class English horses, but he gave the impression of being very good indeed. He was the best of his age as a two-year-old and the following season won the Irish 'Triple Crown'. He sired The Cobbler, who won the Coventry Stakes, Middle Park Stakes, Victoria Cup and Wokingham Stakes; and Solar Slipper, winner of the Champion Stakes and third in the St Leger.

WINLAW, Anthony (b 1938)

Anthony Winlaw was appointed handicapper in 1966. He has written on cricket and rackets for the *Daily Telegraph*.

WINTER, John Rous (b 1929)

John Winter is the younger brother of Fred Winter, the famous rider and successful National Hunt trainer. He himself was apprenticed to his father and later was his assistant, finally taking over the stable in 1965. Among the patrons of his Newmarket stable are Mr C. Blackwell, Mr R. C. Boucher, Mr Warren Ellis, Miss B. A. Finn, Mrs B. Mavroleon, Mr D. Prenn, Mr J. R. Mullion, Mr W. Bryan Case, Mr I. Allen, Mr W. M. Jennings, Mr H. Solomon and Mr A. C. Walkling.

WITHERINGTON, Major Douglas Harold, MRCVS

Appointed a veterinary officer under National Hunt rules in 1952 and under Jockey Club rules in 1954.

WOLVERHAMPTON

It is not great racing at Wolverhampton, but every effort is made to give patrons good value for money. The amenities are first-rate and include a parade-ring in front of the stands, accessible to all enclosures, saddling boxes in view of all enclosures, a children's playground, and refreshment rooms where the racing can be fo- lowed from behind glass.

It is a left-handed, level course with separate tracks for flat-racing, hurdle-racing and steeplechasing. The flat course is nearly 1m 5f round, with easy turns and a run-in of 5f. The 5f 190yd straight course joins the round course at the home turn. High numbers in the draw are thought to hold a slight advantage on the straight course.

Clerk of the Course: Mr David Heyman, Woollerton House, Wendover, Buckinghamshire. Tel: Wendover 3914.

Best Times:

Distance	*Horse-Age-Weight*	*Date*	*Time*
5f	Rovira 3-8-11	3/8/59	57.8
5f	Soverena 2-9-0	3/7/67	57.1
5f 190yd*	Arizona 5-6-13	27/6/60	1min 6.5
5f 190yd*	Look Away 2-7-11	11/9/61	1min 9.4
7f	Vivid 3-7-13	1/8/60	1min 27.4
7f	Maria Helena 2-8-11	3/7/67	1min 29.6
8f	Contango 3-7-3	1/8/39	1min 38
8f	Alyba 2-7-9	14/9/64	1min 42.6
9f	Vigorous Action 7-8-6	22/7/67	1min 54.8
11f 25yd	Dashing 4-9-0	4/7/66	2min 22
12f 25yd	Kracadour 3-9-0	28/6/65	2min 37
16f 192yd	My Swan 3-7-7	6/10/69	3min 40

* All times taken from the flag at this distance

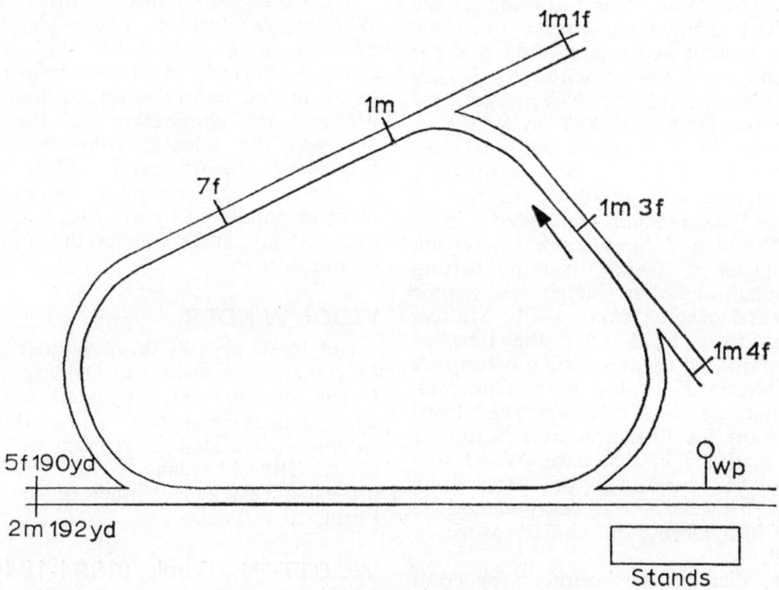

WOLVERHAMPTON

WOLVER HOLLOW

Bred in 1964 by the Gaybrook Stud and formerly owned by Mrs C. O. Iselin who died in 1970 at the age of 102, Wolver Hollow is a grey by Sovereign Path out of Cygnet, by that great stayer Caracalla II. For his first three seasons in training he was under the care of Sir Cecil Boyd-Rochfort, and on Sir Cecil's retirement he was trained by Henry Cecil. A big, tall colt that took a long time to come to hand, Wolver Hollow gained his main success as a five-year-old when, ridden by Piggott, he won the Eclipse Stakes. Whether he would have won if Lewis had not ridden a poor race on Park Top is open to question. The previous autumn Wolver Hollow had run a great race to finish second in the Cambridgeshire with 9st 8lb on his back. Before that he had won the Prix Ridgway at Deauville. As a three-year-old he was third in the Cambridgeshire with 8st 1lb.

WOOD, Charles (1854-1946)

Charles Wood was a leading jockey in the late Victorian era. Born in 1854, he left home at the age of 11 and for seven years was attached to Joseph Dawson's stable at Newmarket. He won the Derby in 1883 on St Blaise. During the first phase of his riding career his integrity was frequently questioned. Sherrard's Newmarket stable was in fact controlled jointly by Wood and Sir George Chetwynd, the latter of whom lived by betting although he had acted as Senior Steward of the Jockey Club. Matters came to a head after the Earl of Durham had made scathing comments on Sherrard's stable in a Gimcrack Dinner speech. Sir George sued Lord Durham for libel and as a result of the evidence in that case, Wood forfeited his licence to ride. After some years his licence was restored and he won the Derby on Galtee More in 1897.

He died at Eastbourne, very comfortably off.

WOODLAND, Percy (1884-1958)

Percy Woodland had an incomparable record as a rider, winning two French Derbys and two Grand Nationals, while he also won the Grand Steeplechase de Paris twice. After World War I he became a leading trainer under National Hunt rules.

WOOLAVINGTON, Lord

James Buchanan, first and last Lord Woolavington, was a shrewd, industrious Scot who amassed a huge fortune as a distiller of whisky. He left over £7,000,000 when he died in 1935. He won the Derby with Captain Cuttle in 1922 and with Coronach in 1926. Both were sired by Hurry On whom he had bought for 500 gn and was certainly the best horse he ever owned. His racing interests have been carried on by his daughter, Hon Lady Macdonald-Buchanan.

WOOLDRIDGE, Dr William Reginald, CBE, MSc, FRCVS, FRIC (d 1966)

The breeding industry owes Dr William Wooldridge a considerable debt as he dedicated his skill and energies towards work of immense value in the conservation of animal life and the elimination of disease. He was the scientific director and founder of the Animal Health Trust. In 1960 he was one of a committee of three appointed by the Jockey Club to investigate and report on the doping of racehorses.

WOOL WINDER

Col E. W. Baird's Wool Winder, by Martagon, was second to Orby in the Derby of 1907. He appeared somewhat unlucky to lose and unkind rumours circulated in respect of his rider, Otto Madden. Wool Winder proved a very easy winner of the St Leger.

WOOTTON, Frank (1894-1940)

Frank Wootton is the only man to

have been leading jockey on the flat and over the jumps as well.

His father Richard Wootton was an Australian who trained with success in Australia, South Africa and England. Frank Wootton came to England with his father and was only 13 when at Folkestone in 1906 he rode his first winner. He rode 15 other winners that season and the following year won the Cesarewitch on Demure, thereby landing a big gamble for Demure's Australian owner and his friends.

His progress to the top of his profession was swift and he captured the imagination of the public in a manner only equalled this century by Steve Donoghue, Sir Gordon Richards and Lester Piggott. Extremely intelligent, he was not only a brilliant horseman but had an almost uncanny ability in summing up the form and characteristics, not only of the horse he was riding, but of the other horses in the race. Like most Australian jockeys, he liked to stick to the rails. In a riding career on the flat that because of increasing weight only lasted seven years, he rode 882 winners from 3,866 mounts, showing the remarkable figure of 23 per cent of winning rides. He was champion jockey in 1909-10-11-12. He never won the Derby, but he won the Oaks, the St Leger and the Grand Prix de Paris. He rode seven winners at Royal Ascot in 1912.

In World War I he served in Mesopotamia and rode the winner of the Baghdad Grand National. In the early 1920s he rode under National Hunt rules, chiefly over hurdles, and was champion jockey in 1921 with over 60 winners. He rode in one Grand National but came to grief. For a few years he trained at Epsom, turning out over 100 winners. He returned to Australia in 1933 and it was there that he died. Stanley Wootton (see below) is his brother.

WOOTTON, Stanley, MC

Stanley Wootton, Australian by birth, is a son of the late Richard Wootton, a shrewd trainer of horses and a wonderful tutor of jockeys. He is a brother of the late Frank Wootton (see above).

Stanley Wootton was a fine jockey himself until he became too heavy. He served with distinction in World War I and afterwards trained with much success for many years at Treadwell House, Epsom. Few of his horses were of great distinction and indeed many of them were selling platers, but they were cleverly placed and won more often than not when the money—and sometimes it was big money—was down. He himself has always been far-sighted, a great organiser, a disciplinarian and above all completely unflappable, his cool comments on any situation being made with a somewhat old-fashioned precision of speech. Like his father, he possessed the art of producing fine jockeys, sometimes from unpromising material. Perhaps the most famous of his pupils was the great Charlie Smirke, while Staff Ingham achieved distinction first on the flat, later over hurdles, and has for many years been a successful trainer with something of the Wootton touch about his methods.

In 1925 Wootton bought the greater part of Walton Downs, Epsom, for £35,000. Recently he agreed to assign to the Levy Board the Walton Downs gallop so that there is now every prospect that Epsom will be preserved for all time for racing.

WORDEN II

Bred in France by the late Mr R. B. Strassburger, Worden II, who died in 1969, was by Wild Risk out of Sans Tares, by Sind. He won six races, his most notable achievement being his victory in the International Stakes at Laurel Park. He retired to the stud in France in 1954, coming to England in 1960. The best of his winners were Bon Mot (Prix de Arc Triomphe) and Karabas (Prix du Conseil Municipal and Washington International Stakes at Laurel Park). He also sired Golden Fire, winner of the Cesarewitch,

Chester Cup and Goodwood Stakes (twice).

WRAGG, Harry (b 1902)

The eldest and most accomplished of three brothers, Harry Wragg was the coolest and most calculating rider of his time. Intelligent, thoughtful and with unusual power of concentration, he was a superb judge of pace and excelled in waiting tactics, hence his nickname of 'The Head Waiter'. His classic victories were as follows:

One Thousand Guineas: Campanula (1934); Herringbone (1943); Sun Stream (1945)
Two Thousand Guineas: Garden Path (1944)
Derby: Felstead (1928); Blenheim (1930); Watling Street (1942)
Oaks: Rockfel (1938); Commotion (1941); Sun Stream (1945); Steady Aim (1946)
St Leger: Sandwich (1931); Herringbone (1943)

He also rode the winners of the Eclipse Stakes on five occasions.

As a trainer he has been consistently successful. He has so far won the Two Thousand Guineas with Darius (1954), the One Thousand Guineas with Abermaid (1962) and Full Dress II (1969); the Derby with Psidium (1961), and the St Leger with Intermezzo (1969). He has also won the Irish Derby (three times), the Irish Oaks (twice), the Irish Two Thousand Guineas, the Grosser Preis von Baden (twice), the Gran Premio del Jockey Club (twice) and the Eclipse Stakes.

His stables are at Newmarket and among his owners are Mr J. S. Cosgrove, Mr J. A. C. Lilley, Mr E. Turner, Mr D. P. D'Ambrumeuil, Lieut-Col N. E. Frieze, Mr R. B. Moller, Mr H. H. Morriss, Mr R. More O'Ferrall, Mr G. A. Oldham and Mr P. J. Oppenheimer.

WRAGG, Sam

Sam Wragg, younger brother of Harry Wragg (see above), won the 1940 Derby on Pont l'Evêque. He also won the Oaks on Chatelaine and the One Thousand Guineas on Rockfel.

WYCHWOOD ABBOT

Foaled in 1931, Wychwood Abbot, by The Black Abbot, was a high-class middle-distance performer. Owned by Mr O. V. Watney and trained by Ted Leader, he twice won the Champion Stakes. He also won the Cambridgeshire and dead-heated for the Jubilee.

Y

YANKEE

Yankee is a popular form of bet in which four horses are backed in doubles, trebles and an accumulator.

YARMOUTH

This well-run course, where the stands face the sea, has always been a popular one, particularly with East Coast holidaymakers. A high proportion of the runners come from Newmarket, just over 70 miles distant.

It is a left-handed track of 1m 4f with a run-in of 5f. The straight mile, level all the way, joins the round course at the home turn. There is a slight rise round the turn into the back straight and a corresponding decline into the finishing straight. High numbers are favoured in the draw on the straight course. The soil is sandy and quick-draining so the going is rarely heavy.

Clerk of the Course: Mr D. W. Bushby, 2 The Meadows, Portsmouth Road, Guildford, Surrey.

Best Times:

Distance	*Horse-Age-Weight*	*Date*	Time
5f 25yd	Field of Gold 3-9-0	1/6/39	61
5f 25yd	Aberbevine 2-8-8	14/6/67	60.9
6f	Denikin 4-8-4	4/7/51	1min 10.4
6f	Sinless 2-9-0	7/7/49	1min 11.6
7f	Brother Victor 5-7-7	9/7/59	1min 22.4
7f	Born Free 2-8-4	12/7/62	1min 24.6
8f	Laureat II 6-9-5	14/9/38	1min 35
8f	Foretelling 2-8-4	18/9/63	1min 38.2
10f	Sunlight Serenade 3-7-10	7/7/54	2min 5.2
14f	Sunflash 4-9-0	5/8/59	2min 59.4

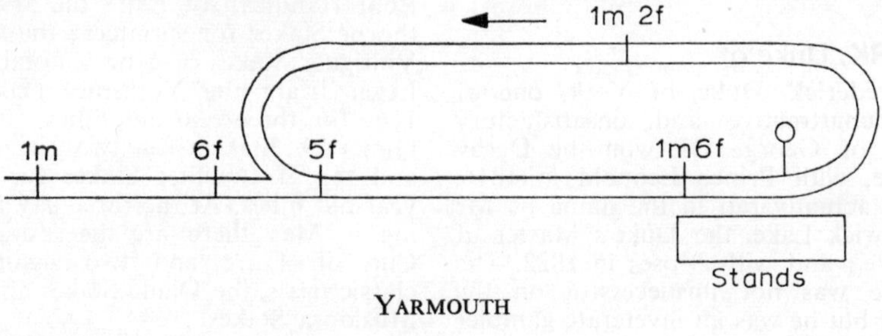

YARMOUTH

YATES, David

A useful jockey now attached to the stables of G. Beeby and of Mrs Lomax. He won the Cesarwitch, Goodwood Stakes (twice) and Chester Cup on Golden Fire; and the Chester Cup on Narratus. In 1964, his best season, he rode 26 winners. He was top apprentice in 1963.

YEARLING

A horse is a yearling during the twelve months from 1st January after it is born.

A Jockey Club Rule barring the racing of yearlings was instituted in 1859.

YELLOW GOD

Yellow God, by Red God, was bred by the Milford Stud, Co Carlow, and bought on behalf of Mr David Robinson for 5,600 gn. He was one of the best two-year-olds of 1969, winning the Gimcrack Stakes and Imperial Stakes and being beaten by inches in the Middle Park Stakes on going that was clearly too firm for him. Trained by Paul Davey, he is a full brother to the sprinter St Alphage. In 1970 he won the Kempton Two Thousand Guineas Trial, was runner-up to Nijinsky in the Two Thousand and won the Prix Palais Royal at Longchamp.

YELLOW JACK

Yellow Jack was a good horse of the mid-Victorian era with the unfortunate propensity of always finding one competitor just better than himself in every race in which he ran, including the Two Thousand Guineas and the Derby. To this day a horse that habitually runs second is sometimes referred to as 'a regular Yellow Jack'.

YEOMAN, Dennis (b 1932)

Dennis Yeoman was apprenticed to the late M. J. Peacock. For a couple of years he was head lad to W. Newton and then in 1959 he took out a licence himself. He now conducts a small stable at Catterick.

YORK, Duke of

Frederick, Duke of York, one of the unattractive and unsatisfactory sons of George III, won the Derby twice, with Prince Leopold in 1816, who actually ran in the name of Mr Warwick Lake, the Duke's Master of Horse; and with Moses in 1822. The Duke was not unsuccessful on the Turf but he was an inveterate gambler and left a mountain of debts behind him when he died. To discharge these, the Government is said to have ceded Cape Breton to his creditors.

YORK

As Newmarket was the main racing centre in the south in the eighteenth century, so was York the meeting where the best horses in the north used to run. York races were first run on Knavesmire in 1731 and they are still held on that famous expanse of common land twenty minutes' walk from the centre of the city.

In 1767 the men who ran York races decided to call themselves the Gimcrack Club to perpetuate the memory of a famous and popular grey horse named Gimcrack that won 27 races. The Gimcrack Stakes, founded in 1841, is run at the August meeting and the owner of the winner is traditionally the guest of honour at the Gimcrack Club Dinner in December when he makes the main speech of the evening, usually dealing with certain aspect of the state of the English Turf. It was at York in 1851 that one of the most famous matches in English racing history was run, that between The Flying Dutchman and Voltigeur.

Not for nothing is York called the 'Ascot of the North'. It is managed in a most enterprising and go-ahead fashion, the amenities are excellent and the standard of racing first-class. The big meeting is the three-day one in August when every event is worth over £1,000 to the winner. Among the main events at that fixture are the Ebor Handicap of $1\frac{3}{4}$m; the 5f Nunthorpe Stakes for sprinters; the Great Voltiguer Stakes of $1\frac{1}{2}$m, a notable St Leger trial; the Yorkshire Oaks of $1\frac{1}{2}$m for three-year-old fillies; the 6f Gimcrack Stakes for two-year-olds; and the 5f Lowther Stakes for two-year-old fillies. At the three-day meeting in May there are the Yorkshire Cup of $1\frac{3}{4}$m; and two significant classic trials, the Dante Stakes and the Musidora Stakes.

The 2m course is left-handed, wide, flat and with easy, sweeping turns. The 6f track which is being extended to provide a straight 7f, joins the round course just under 5f from home. All in all, the track provides an essentially fair test of the thoroughbred.

Manager, Secretary and Clerk of the Course: Major L. Petch, The Racecourse, York. Tel: York 22260.

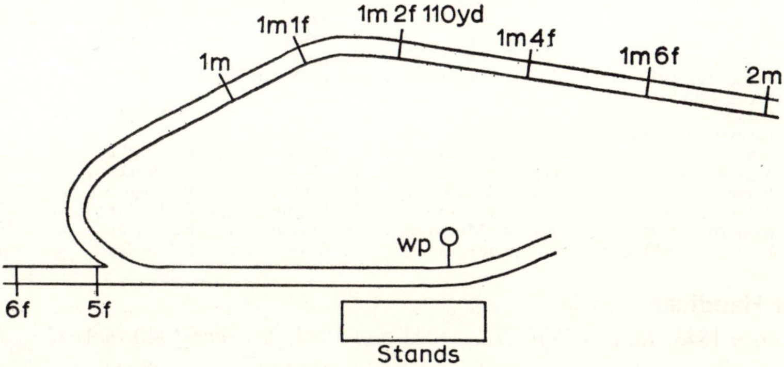

YORK

Best Times

Distance	Horse–age–weight	Date	Time
5f	Birkwood, 4–8–3	5 10 49	57.8
5f	Easy Going, 2–9–0	24 8 38	58.6
6f	Screech, 9–8–7	21 5 47	1min10.2
6f	Windy City, 2–9–0	23 8 51	1min11
7f	Fair Samela, 3–7–3	2 7 66	1min23.8
8f	High Stakes, 3–8–8	5 9 45	1min36.6
8f	Mount Rosa, 2–8–1	7 10 59	1min39.2
9f	Sailing Light, 4–8–4	19 8 53	1min51
10f 110yd	Chino, 4–7–6	26 5 59	2min 9
12f	Cap of Gold, 4–8–8	18 8 53	2min29.2
14f	Miraculous Atom, 5–8–11	24 8 49	2min55.4
16f	Blue Pennant, 4–7–6	23 5 46	3min21.6

Yorkshire Oaks, 1m 4f

Three-year-old fillies. First run 1849. *No race* 1940 *to* 1945.

		OWNER	TRAINER	JOCKEY	SP
1930	Glorious Devon, 7–12	Lord Glanely	T. Hogg	G. Richards	9–4
1931	Rackety Lassie, 7–12	S. Vlasto	C. B-Rochfort	J. Dines	100–6
1932	Will o' the Wisp, 8–5	Lord Woolavington	F. Darling	G. Richards	13–8
1932	Nash Light, 8–5	Lord Glanely	T. Hogg	F. Rickaby	6–1
1933	Star of England, 7–12	Lord Glanely	T. Hogg	G. Nicholl	10–1
1934	Dalmary, 7–12	Maj H. Cayzer	C. B-Rochfort	F. Fox	11–8
1935	Trigo Verde, 7–12	J. Rank	N. Cannon	G. Richards	11–10
1936	Silversol, 9–1	M. Peacock	M. Peacock	W. Nevett	8–1
1937	Sculpture, 7–12	Lord Astor	J. Lawson	G. Richards	6–1
1938	Joyce W., 7–12	Sir V. Sassoon	J. Lawson	W. Nevett	11–2
1939	Night Shift, 7–12	Lord Derby	W. Earl	A. Richardson	20–1
1946	Live Letters, 8–10	J. Rank	N. Cannon	T. Weston	8–1
1947	Ladycross, 8–5	Sir R. Sykes	C. B-Rochfort	W. Carr	2–1
1948	Angelola, 8–10	King George VI	C. B-Rochfort	E. Britt	4–1
1949	Unknown Quantity, 8–5	H. Wills	J. Jarvis	W. Rickaby	3–1

Yorkshire Oaks (contd)		OWNER	TRAINER	JOCKEY	SP
1950	Above Board, 8–0 ..	King George VI ..	C. B-Rochfort .	E. Smith . ..	100–30
1951	Sea Parrot, 8–10 ..	Lieut-Col G. Loder	N. Murless ..	G. Richards ..	13–2
1952	Frieze, 9–3	Capt A. Keith ..	C. Elsey	E. Britt	5–4
1953	Kerkeb, 8–5	Aga Khan	M. Marsh ..	G. Richards ..	7–4
1954	Feevagh, 8–5	J. McGrath	W. Stephenson	K. Gethin ..	20–1
1955	Ark Royal, 9–3 ..	R. Hollingsworth .	G. Colling ..	E. Mercer ..	evens
1956	Indian Twilight, 8–5	J. Astor..	R. J. Colling ..	J. Mercer . ..	13–2
1957	Almeria, 9–0	The Queen	C. B-Rochfort .	W. Carr	11–10
1958	None Nicer, 9–0 ..	Maj L. Holliday ..	W. Hern . ..	S. Clayton ..	4–1
1959	Petite Etoile, 9–0 ..	Aly Khan	N. Murless ..	L. Piggott ..	2–15
1960	Lynchris, 9–0	Mrs E. Fawcett ..	J. Oxx	W. Williamson.	5–4
1961	Tenacity, 9–0	Mrs W. R-Smith .	Sir G. Richards	A. Breasley ..	7–1
1962	West Side Story, 9–0	H. Joel	T. Leader . ..	E. Smith . ..	2–1
1963	Outcrop, 9–0	Maj J. Priestman..	G. Barling ..	E. Smith . ..	9–1
1964	Homeward Bound, 9–0	Sir F. Robinson ..	J. Oxley	G. Starkey ..	2–1
1965	Mabel, 9–0	G. Williams	P. Walwyn ..	J. Mercer . ..	7–4
1966	Parthian Glance, 9–0	Mrs Riley-Smith ..	G. Todd	L. Piggott ..	3–1
1967	Palatch, 9–0	Dr C. Vittadini ..	H. Leader ..	B. Taylor . ..	7–1
1968	Exchange, 9–0 . ..	Mrs R. Midwood .	H. Leader ..	B. Taylor . ..	7–2
1969	Frontier Goddess, 9–0	C. Spence	P. Walwyn ..	D. Keith . ..	3–1

Ebor Handicap, 1m 6f

First run 1843. *Run at Pontefract* 1943 *and* 1944. *No race* 1940 *to* 1942.

		OWNER	TRAINER	JOCKEY	SP
1930	Gentlemen's Relish, 4–7–5	J. Arkwright . ..	H. Persse . ..	J. Dines	20–1
	Coaster, 4–8–0 ..	Sir H. Hirst	F. Templeman	F. Fox	100–8
1931	Brown Jack, 7–9–5 .	Sir H. Wernher ..	I. Anthony ..	S. Donoghue ..	10–1
1932	Cat o' Nine Tails, 5–7–8	Mrs J. Carruthers .	J. Colling . ..	G. Richards ..	9–1
1933	Dictum, 5–7–4 . ..	Lady B. Smith ..	T. Rimell . ..	J. Dines	8–1
1934	Alcazar, 3–8–5 . ..	W. Woodward ..	C. B-Rochfort .	J. Childs . ..	10–1
1935	Museum, 3–7–13 ..	Sir V. Sassoon ..	J. Rogers . ..	S. Donoghue ..	100–8
1936	Penny Royal, 3–7–9	E. T-Smith	F. Templeman	G. Richards ..	100–8
1937	Weathervane, 4–7–10	Sir A. Bailey . ..	J. Lawson ..	T. Weston ..	100–6
1938	Foxglove II, 3–8–1 .	P. Beatty.	F. Darling ..	G. Richards ..	8–1
1939	Owenstown, 5–8–8 .	Sir T. Dixon . ..	M. Peacock ..	J. Taylor . ..	11–2
1943	Yorkshire Hussar, 4–8–7	J. Hetherton.. ..	C. Elsey	G. Littlewood .	100–6
1944	The Kernel, 4–8–7 ..	G. Oxtoby	G. Oxtoby ..	P. Evans . ..	100–8
1945	Wayside Inn, 3–8–6 .	Lord Derby	W. Earl	H. Wragg ..	20–1
1946	Foxtrot, 3–7–13 ..	H. Morriss	E. Lambton ..	E. Britt	3–1
1947	Procne, 4–8–4	H. Joel	C. Elsey	J. Sime	8–1
1948	Donino, 4–8–12 ..	W. Cockerline ..	A. Cooper ..	J. Sime	100–7
1949	Miraculous Atom, 5–8–11	H. Halmshaw ..	S. Hall	W. Nevett ..	100–7
1950	Cadzow Oak, 4–7–12	Maj G. Renwick .	J. Thwaites ..	J. Thompson ..	100–8
1951	Bob, 4–6–12	J. Hetherton.. ..	C. Elsey	E. Carter . ..	8–1
1952	Signification, 3–7–12	A. Bird	J. Pearce ..	H. Jones . ..	10–1
1953	Norooz, 4–8–4 . ..	Aga Khan	M. Marsh ..	R. Fawdon ..	100–9
1954	By Thunder!, 3–6–12	J. Gerber	F. Armstrong..	W. Swinburn ..	7–1
1955	Hyperion Kid, 3–7–2	Miss R. Olivier ..	H. Wragg ..	P. Robinson ..	100–8
1956	Donald, 3–7–10 ..	Lord Rosebery ..	J. Jarvis	D. Smith.. ..	5–1
1957	Morecambe, 4–7–9 .	J. Bullock	S. Hall	J. Sime	100–8
1958	Gladness, 5–9–7 ..	J. McShain	V. O'Brien ..	L. Piggott ..	5–1
1959	Primera, 5–9–0 . ..	S. Joel	N. Murless ..	L. Piggott ..	6–1
1960	Persian Road, 5–8–4	J. Whitney	J. Tree	G. Moore ..	18–1
1961	Die Hard, 4–8–9 ..	Maj L. Gardner ..	V. O'Brien ..	L. Piggott ..	11–2
1962	Sostenuto, 4–8–10 ..	P. Bull	W. Elsey . ..	Don Morris ..	9–1
1963	Partholon, 3–7–8 ..	Mrs A. Biddle ..	T. Shaw	J. Sime	100–6
1964	Proper Pride, 5–7–11	Maj L. Holliday ..	W. Wharton ..	D. Smith.. ..	28–1
1965	Twelfth Man, 4–7–5.	R. Moller	H. Wragg ..	P. Cook	6–1
1966	Lomond, 6–9–2 ..	W. Ruane	R. Jarvis . ..	E. Eldin	100–8
1967	Ovaltine, 3–6–11 ..	G. Cooper	J. Watts	E. Johnson ..	100–8
1968	Alignment, 3–7–8 ..	Lord Allendale ..	W. Elsey . ..	E. Johnson ..	9–1
1969	Big Hat, 4–7–3 . ..	Mrs M. Tennant .	D. Hanley ..	R. Still	40–1

Great Voltigeur Stakes, 1m 4f

Three-year-olds. First run 1950.

		OWNER	TRAINER	JOCKEY	SP
1950	Castle Rock, 9–7 ..	Lord Rosebery ..	J. Jarvis	W. Rickaby ..	5–6
1951	Border Legend, 9–0 .	Duke of Northumberland	R. Peacock ..	W. Nevett ..	4–1
1952	Childe Harold, 9–3 .	T. Farr	W. Dutton ..	J. Brace	7–4
1953	Premonition, 9–7 ..	Brig W. Wyatt ..	C. B-Rochfort .	W. Carr	4–5
1954	Blue Sail, 9–0	G. Bell	P. Prendergast .	W. Rickaby ..	3–1
1955	Acropolis, 9–7.. ..	Lady Derby	G. Colling ..	D. Smith.. ..	2–7
1956	Hornbeam, 9–3 ..	Lord Astor	J. Colling . ..	J. Mercer . ..	6–4
1957	Brioche, 9–0	W. Humble	C. Elsey	E. Britt	100–6
1958	Alcide, 9–0	Sir H. de Trafford.	C. B-Rochfort .	W. Carr	3–1
1959	Pindari, 9–0	The Queen	N. Murless ..	L. Piggott ..	11–10
1960	St Paddy, 9–0	Sir V. Sassoon ..	N. Murless ..	L. Piggott ..	4–11
1961	Just Great, 9–0 ..	Mrs J. Allen.. ..	S. Ingham ..	A. Breasley ..	3–1
1962	Hethersett, 9–0 . ..	Maj L. Holliday ..	W. Hern . ..	F. Durr	15–2
1963	Ragusa, 9–0	J. Mullion	P. Prendergast .	G. Bougoure ..	2–5
1964	Indiana, 9–0	C. Engelhard . ..	J. Watts	J. Lindley ..	4–7
1965	Ragazzo, 9–0	E. M. O'Ferrall ..	P. Prendergast .	L. Piggott ..	13–8
1966	Hermes, 9–0	R. D. Hollingsworth	J. Oxley	G. Starkey ..	15–2
1967	Great Host, 9–0 ..	L. M. Gelb	P. Prendergast .	W. Williamson.	3–1
1968	Connaught, 9–0 ..	H. Joel	N. Murless ..	A. Barclay ..	1–3
1969	Harmony Hall, 9–0 .	Sit H. Wernher ..	G. Smyth . ..	W. Williamson.	4–6

Nunthorpe Stakes, 5f

First run 1903. *Run at Newmarket* 1943 *and* 1944. *No race* 1940 *to* 1942.

		OWNER	TRAINER	JOCKEY	SP
1930	Tag End, 6–8–9 ..	J. Joel	C. Peck	B. Carslake ..	11–4
1931	Portlaw, 3–8–7 . ..	Sir A. Bailey . ..	H. Persse ..	H. Beasley ..	5–1
1932	Greenore, 3–8–4 ..	Lady Ludlow ..	O. Bell	H. Wragg ..	8–1
1933	Concerto, 5–8–12 ..	Sir H. C-Owen ..	O. Bell	B. Carslake ..	6–1
1934	Gold Bridge, 5–8–12	Lord Beatty	W. Beatty ..	C. Elliott . ..	6–5
1935	Shalfleet, 4–8–9 ..	H. Leader	H. Leader ..	H. Jelliss . ..	9–4
1936	Bellacose, 4–8–12 ..	P. Dunne	J. Colling . ..	P. Beasley ..	evens
1937	Ipsden, 4–8–9	Lady Ludlow ..	O. Bell	S. Wragg . ..	7–1
1938	Mickey the Greek, 4–8–12	H. Leach	H. Leach . ..	H. Wragg ..	5–1
1939	Portobello, 3–8–11 .	P. Dunne	J. Colling . ..	G. Richards ..	15–8
1943	Linklater, 7–9–0 ..	A. Saunders . ..	W. Smyth . ..	E. Smith . ..	9–2
1944	Sugar Palm, 6–9–0 .	Maj A. Bonsor ..	F. Hartigan ..	C. Elliott . ..	8–1
1945	Golden Cloud, 4–9–5	Mrs G. Lambton .	E. Lambton ..	M. Beary . ..	100–8
1946	The Bug, 3–9–0 ..	N. Wachman ..	M. Marsh . ..	C. Smirke ..	4–6
1947	Como, 5–9–5	Capt J. Fielden ..	G. Armstrong .	W. Carr	3–1
1948	Careless Nora,3–8–11	G. Frampton ..	J. Dines	C. Elliott . ..	6–4
1949	Abernant, 3–9–0 ..	Maj R. M-Buchanan ..	N. Murless ..	G. Richards ..	2–11
1950	Abernant, 4–9–5 ..	Maj R. M-Buchanan ..	N. Murless ..	G. Richards ..	7–100
1951	Royal Serenade, 3–9–0	Mrs G. Kohn ..	H. Wragg ..	C. Elliott . ..	4–1
1952	Royal Serenade, 4–9–5	G. Bell	H. Wragg ..	G. Richards ..	4–6
1953	High Treason, 2–7–3	H. Joel	T. Leader . ..	D. Greening ..	9–4
1954	My Babu, 2–7–3 ..	A. Wimbush . ..	P. Prendergast .	T. Carter . ..	7–1
1955	Royal Palm, 3–9–0 .	J. Gerber	F. Armstrong..	W. Snaith ..	11–10
1956	Ennis, 2–7–3	C. Harper	W. Nightingall.	P. Tulk	11–2
1957	Gratitude, 4–9–5 ..	Maj L. Holliday ..	H. Cottrill ..	W. Snaith ..	7–2
1958	Right Boy, 4–9–5 ..	G. Gilbert	W. Dutton ..	L. Piggott ..	8–100
1959	Right Boy, 5–9–5 ..	H. Wills	H. Rohan ..	L. Piggott ..	4–9
1960	Bleep-Bleep, 4–9–5 .	Mrs M. Turner ..	H. Cottrill ..	W. Carr	9–2
1961	Floribunda, 3–9–0 ..	Mrs J. Mullion ..	P. Prendergast .	R. Hutchinson	4–1
1962	Gay Mairi, 3–8–11 .	A. Macdonald ..	H. Whiteman .	A. Breasley ..	100–8
1963	Matatina, 3–8–11 ..	Mrs R. Wilson ..	F. Armstrong..	L. Piggott ..	7–2

Nunthorpe Stakes (contd)	OWNER	TRAINER	JOCKEY	SP
1964 Althrey Don, 3–9–0	J. Done	P. Rohan	R. Maddock	3–1
1965 Polyfoto, 3–9–0.	Mrs C. Reavey	E. Reavey	J. Wilson	20–1
1966 Caterina, 3–8–11	R. Scully	F. Armstrong	L. Piggott	13–2
1967 Forlorn River, 5–9–5	Mrs W. A. Richardson	W.A.Stephenson	B. Raymond	6–1
1968 So Blessed, 3–9–2	D. Robinson	M. Jarvis	F. Durr	4–6
1969 Tower Walk, 3–9–2	V. W. Hardy	G. Barling	L. Piggott	7–1

Gimcrack Stakes, 6f

Two-year-olds. First run 1846. *No race* 1940 *to* 1944.

	OWNER	TRAINER	JOCKEY	SP
1930 Four Course, 8–9	Lord Ellesmere	F. Darling	F. Fox	8–15
1931 Miracle, 8–7	Lord Rosebery	J. Jarvis	H. Wragg	4–7
1932 Young Lover, 8–7	Sir A. Butt	Fk. Butters	R. Perryman	100–8
1933 Mrs Rustom, 8–9	Aga Khan	Fk. Butters	M. Beary	4–7
1934 Bahram, 8–12	Aga Khan	Fk. Butters	R. Perryman	2–7
1935 Paul Beg, 8–7	Lord Milton	W. Easterby	H. Gunn	20–1
1936 Goya II, 8–7	M. Boussac	G. Lambton	C. Eliottl	6–1
1937 Golden Sovereign, 8–7	Sir A. Bailey	H. Cottrill	T. Weston	6–1
1938 Cockpit, 8–12	Lord Derby	C. Leader	R. Perryman	7–4
1939 Tant Mieux, 8–12	Aly Khan	F. Darling	G. Richards	6–1
1945 Gulf Stream, 9–0	Lord Derby	W. Earl	H. Wragg	7–2
1946 Petition, 9–0	Sir A. Butt	Fk. Butters	H. Wragg	13–8
1947 Black Tarquin, 9–0	W. Woodward	C. B-Rochfort	W. Carr	3–1
1948 Star King, 9–0	W. Harvey	J. C. Waugh	S. Wragg	15–2
1949 Palestine, 9–0	Aga Khan	Fk. Butters	G. Richards	1–25
1950 Cortil, 8–7	M. Boussac	C. Semblat	W. Johnstone	11–2
1951 Windy City, 9–0	R. Bell	P. Prendergast	G. Richards	5–4
1952 Bebe Grande, 8–11	J. Gerber	F. Armstrong	W. Snaith	7–2
1953 The Pie King, 9–0	R. Bell	P. Prendergast	G. Richards	1–3
1954 Precast, 8–11	F. Ellison	R. Peacock	W. Nevett	25–1
1955 Idle Rocks, 9–0	D. Robinson	G. Brooke	D. Smith	8–1
1956 Eudaemon, 9–0	Mrs E. Foster	C. Elsey	E. Britt	8–1
1957 Pheidippides, 9–0	P. Bull	C. Elsey	D. Smith	100–8
1958 Be Careful, 8–11	W. Hill	C. Elsey	E. Hide	10–1
1959 Paddy's Sister, 8–11	Mrs J. Mullion	P. Prendergast	G. Moore	4–11
1960 Test Case, 9–0	Sir A. Jarvis	J. Jarvis	E. Larkin	100–7
1961 Sovereign Lord, 9–0	Duke of Norfolk	G. Smyth	A. Breasley	10–1
1962 Crocket, 9–0	D. van Clief	G. Brooke	D. Smith	2–5
1963 Talahasse, 9–0	H. Loebstein	T. Corbett	L. Piggott	11–8
1964 Double Jump, 9–0	C. Engelhard	J. Tree	J. Lindley	evens
1965 Young Emperor, 9–0	Mrs P. Poe	P. Prendergast	L. Piggott	5–1
1966 Golden Horus, 9–0	Mrs D. M. Solomon	W. O'Gorman	J. Mercer	7–14
1967 Petingo, 9–0	Capt M. D. Lemos	F. Armstrong	L. Piggott	1–6
1968 Tudor Music, 9–0	D. Robinson	M. Jarvis	F. Durr	10–1
1969 Yellow God, 9–0	D. Robinson	P. Davey	F. Durr	7–2

YORKSHIRE OAKS

See under York.

YOUR MAJESTY

Mr J. B. Joel's Your Majesty, by Persimmon, started favourite for the St Leger in 1908 and won by half a length from White Eagle. He made no mark as a sire in this country but after six years was exported to the Argentine where he did well.

Z

ZABARA

Bred by Lady Wyfold in 1949, Zabara is by Persian Gulf out of Samovar, by Caerleon. Trained by Victor Smyth and in the colours of Sir M. McAlpine, she won six races and over £28,000. Her victories including the One Thousand Guineas, Coronation Stakes, Imperial Stakes and Cheveley Park Stakes. She was second in the Oaks. As a brood mare she has proved disappointing.

ZARATHUSTRA

Bred and owned by Sir Harold Gray, Zarathustra is by Persian Gulf out of Salvia, by Sansovino. At two and three years of age he was trained in Ireland by Michael Hurley, at four and five by Sir Cecil Boyd-Rochfort at Newmarket. He won 13 races from 5f to 2m 5f, his victories including the Irish Derby, Irish St Leger, Ascot Stakes, Goodwood Cup and Ascot Gold Cup. Unfortunately he was slow to make his mark as a sire and this good and versatile horse was sold for export to Japan.

ZETLAND, second Earl of

The second Earl of Zetland owned an outstanding Derby winner in Voltigeur whom he bought for 1,000 gn with a 500 gn contingency if Voltigeur won the 1850 Derby. Shortly before the Derby Lord Zetland discovered that forfeits of £400 were due from Voltigeur's nominator and unless these were paid, Voltigeur would be unable to run. With aristocratic disdain for the feelings and pockets of the thousands who had backed his horse, Lord Zetland gave orders for Voltigeur to be scratched. Servants and tenants on the Zetland estates who had had their limit on the horse, were in despair and sent a deputation to Lord Zetland's brother-in-law, Mr Williamson, who agreed to see what he could do. Mr Williamson induced Lord Zetland to change his mind and Voltigeur duly won at 16-1. Lord Zetland's coachman won £200, a goodly sum in those days, and nearly as much as Lord Zetland, no betting man, won himself. Thousands of Freemasons punted on Voltigeur as Lord Zetland was then the head of English Freemasonry.

ZETLAND, third Marquess of (b 1908)

The Marquess of Zetland served in the Yorkshire Hussars. He is a member of the Jockey Club and a steward at Catterick, Redcar, and York. His trainer is W. Wharton. Colours: white, red spots and cap.

ZEUS BOY

Foaled in 1958, Zeus Boy, by Palestine, won eight races and over £11,000. He stood at the Fawley Stud, Wantage, from 1963 to 1969 when he was exported to Turkey.

ZEV

The American horse Zev, at one time the largest stake winner in the world, defeated the Derby winner Papyrus in a famous match in America in 1923.

ZINDFANDEL

Zinfandel, by Persimmon, was a horse of outstanding ability and might well have won the Derby in 1903 but for the rule then existing that prevented him from running on account of the death of his nominator Col McCalmont. He then passed into the possession of Lord Howard de Walden for whom he won the Coronation Cup, beating Rock Sand and Sceptre who had won seven classic races between them. He also won the Ascot Gold Cup. There is a racing legend that when he won the Gold Cup, his owner was seated under a tree in the paddock, perusing the score of an opera.

Index

C

D

H

I

J

M

N

O

P

Q

R

S

T

U

V